Women
Film Directors

Women Film Directors

AN INTERNATIONAL BIO-CRITICAL DICTIONARY

Gwendolyn Audrey Foster

Greenwood Press
Westport, Connecticut • London

Library of Congress Cataloging-in-Publication Data

Foster, Gwendolyn Audrey.
  Women film directors : an international bio-critical dictionary /
  Gwendolyn Audrey Foster.
    p. cm.
  Includes bibliographical references and index.
  ISBN 0–313–28972–7 (alk. paper)
  1. Women motion picture producers and directors—Biography—
Dictionaries. I. Title.
  PN1998.2.F67   1995
  791.43'0233'0922—dc20
  [B]   95–7395

British Library Cataloguing in Publication Data is available.

Library of Congress Catalog Card Number: 95–7395
ISBN: 0–313–28972–7

First published in 1995

Greenwood Press, 88 Post Road West, Westport, CT 06881
An imprint of Greenwood Publishing Group, Inc.

Printed in the United States of America

The paper used in this book complies with the
Permanent Paper Standard issued by the National
Information Standards Organization (Z39.48–1984).

10 9 8 7 6 5 4 3 2 1

For W.W.D., my muse in all things, and for my grandmother, Audrey Mills Jennings (1920–1994), who raised me and instilled in me a fierce sense of independence, and a strong sense of self.

Contents

Preface

Women Film Directors: An International Bio-Critical Dictionary is a reference book designed primarily for use by students, historians, film critics, and film enthusiasts. The entries are arranged alphabetically and include biographical information, critical essay, selected filmography, and selected bibliographic information. Filmmakers were chosen on the basis of availability of information. As an American-based film scholar, I have no doubt been limited, to some extent, to a Western, Eurocentric tradition and knowledge base. Therefore I expect that I have inadvertently been unable to include all international women film directors in this book. Because I limited this study to women who directed film, rather than video, I have not included many women directors, such as Michelle Parkerson, an influential African-American lesbian video director, or many other female videomakers. I have tried not to be influenced by those studies that privilege and emphasize commercial success as a basis for inclusion; however, commercial success tends to heighten availability of films, and availability tends to heighten critical reception. I have tried to present as much information as possible, including the English-language title (where available) in entries on foreign filmmakers. I cite those critics who have been useful in my own work. I have not cited non-English sources in general, although I have cited a few. Throughout the book I refer to films by their best-known titles. In some cases I have included both the English title and the foreign-language title. In cases in which films are codirected, I have indicated this clearly. I sincerely hope this book will open up new research in the field of women film directors.

In creating *Women Film Directors,* I wish to thank Maureen Honey of the University of Nebraska, Lincoln, Women's Studies Program, for her unstinting support in completing the long and arduous work of this project, and Dana Miller for her help in typing this manuscript. I also wish to thank Sharon Harris and Joy Ritchie for their kind and incisive comments on my work. Sincere thanks as well to Linda Ray Pratt, Susan Rosowski, Oyekan

Owomoyela, Helen Moore, Stephen C. Behrendt, Akira Lippit, and Katherine Ronald. I am also deeply indebted to the research work of Jane Klain and Steven Klain, who dug through files in the Museum of Television and Radio, the National Film Archive of the British Film Institute, the National Film Board of Canada, and elsewhere to secure hard-to-find birthdates and other information; I also owe a debt to Patricia Thompson, editor and publisher of *Film Canada Yearbook,* for her extra help with data on Canadian filmmakers. At the Museum of Modern Art (MOMA), Larry Kardish, curator of the Department of Film, provided valuable information for the filmographies included here, as did many staff members of MOMA's Film Studies Center; I am deeply grateful for their assistance. My sincere thanks to Gloria Gibson-Hudson, Laura Crain, and Monique Threatt of the Black Film Center Archive at Indiana University. My thanks as well to Brian Zillig and the staff of the Interlibrary Loan Service, Love Library, at the University of Nebraska, Lincoln, for their help in securing many rare and precious articles and reference materials, and to the staff of Women Make Movies, Inc., who made available research materials on many of the women discussed here, so that I might better discuss their lives and careers. I would also like to thank my husband, Wheeler Winston Dixon, for his love and support during the long work of compiling and writing this volume.

In addition, the reference staffs of numerous archives and libraries around the world were of enormous help in completing this volume, and I thank them for their interest in, and support of, my work. I would be pleased to hear from anyone who has additional information for a second edition of this work; since cinema is dynamic, not static, it is inevitable that some of the listings here will be slightly outdated by publication, as new works and artists appear on the scene. I look forward to hearing from readers of this book and hope that *Women Film Directors* will ultimately be of interest to scholars, students, and general readers who wish to expand their knowledge of one of the most fascinating and yet still-unexamined areas of feminist endeavor: the cinema.

Introduction

There is no "typical" woman filmmaker. In creating *Women Film Directors: An International Bio-Critical Dictionary,* I first wish to stress that the various directorial visions showcased within this volume are as diverse as the practitioners themselves. There are as many different kinds of women making films today and yesterday as there are approaches to the cinematic art. They work with various budgets, production values, and social and economic concerns, and they all have different visions of what it means to them to be a woman filmmaker in today's society. In this volume, I have tried to gather some of the most important and influential women practitioners of the craft of cinema throughout its long history and tell the stories of their triumphs, dreams, and struggles. Discovering the identities of these figures of feminist self-determinism has often been a difficult task. As I researched this book, I found that one way to uncover the work of women filmmakers was to scrutinize the female figures in the lives of male directors. Often, wives, sisters, or "leading ladies" of celebrated directors turned out to be uncredited or marginalized women filmmakers.

In *Women Film Directors,* I have not included directors who work primarily in video or whose work is initially shown on television. My concentration here is on women who direct fictional narrative films and documentaries. By limiting my sample to the area of film production, rather than video production, I have managed to keep this book within a reasonable length.

Within these self-imposed restrictions, I wanted to give the reader some idea of the broad spectrum of concerns addressed by women as filmmakers in the past and present and concerns to be addressed in the future. Some of the filmmakers here are primarily "genre" artists, who deal within the Hollywood mainstream; others practice their craft as independents, either in the business sense of the term ("Hollywood mavericks") or as practitioners working entirely outside cinema as a profession. The types of films they make vary widely in subject matter, budget, and intended audience.

Ida Lupino claimed that she did her work simply because there was no one else available, but the passion of her efforts belies such modesty. Mai Zetterling, too, began as an actor but soon tired of working within the confines of a male-dominated system and created her own visions of the world. Beth B. used Super 8mm film to make her movies, simply because it was the cheapest material available, and she had to make her statement immediately, without waiting for an opportunity (or funding) that might never come.

Alice Guy (Guy-Blaché) was one of the first persons of either sex to make a film with a plot, (*La Fée Aux Choux,* or *The Cabbage Fairy*), in 1896, yet her work often goes without notice. Alice Guy made hundreds of short films and several features and wrote a series of articles on film direction that are quoted here. Lois Weber tackled issues of birth control when no one wanted to discuss the matter. Alile Sharon Larkin creates films for black women, alternative narratives to those films that denarrate the African experience for both women and men. Maya Deren and Sara Kathryn Arledge (director of the experimental film *Introspection* in 1941), were two of the founders of the experimental 16mm film in America; without their efforts, none of what happened in New York in the 1960s might have occurred. Yvonne Rainer makes uncompromising experimental films that deal with issues of menopause, rape, and sexual and social marginalization within our society. Trinh T. Minh-ha is a critic and documentarist whose work stretches the boundaries of exactly what we consider a "documentary film." Barbara Kopple is engaged in much the same work.

Carolee Schneemann deals with issues of sexuality, power, and gender, as does Barbara Hammer, yet both women work from entirely different (and yet not mutually exclusive) perspectives. The multiplicity of visions within this volume is startling; it forces us to look at ourselves as women and as members of society in a series of entirely new and enlightening ways. In this book, then, we can read the stories of those women who have taken up the camera to instruct, enlighten, entertain, and speak their minds on issues that are of great consequence to them. To these women and their labors, this book is ultimately dedicated.

For all of these women, the need to make films is of imperative importance. Whether working in the industry or making films with the aid of grants and personal financial subsidies, the women covered here have helped to shape the world of film as we know it today. Some voices of feminist film practice see themselves as harbingers of change, instructional forces, barometers of social reintegration; other women see themselves as workers within a tradition that they attempt to subvert from within. The immense contribution made by these women is a legacy rich in personal insight, hard work, careful study, and, often, sacrifice to achieve the aims they held for their creative endeavors. This book is a testament to the work these women have accomplished, often in the face of adversity, and to the continuing voice of women as a force for change and enlightenment within the cinema today.

Women Film Directors evolved from a compelling urge I have had since I studied women's literature and film at Douglass College to reclaim the legacy of women film directors. As a student of film and literature, I saw a huge disparity between feminist scholarship in literature and that in film. In the field of literature, feminists were successfully and actively involved in reclaiming women writers, but in film scholarship, most feminists were involved in criticizing films directed by men. They had, as I had, accepted the assumption that women had not directed any films until the 1970s. Women filmmakers, through their exclusion from history books, had been denied a sisterhood. Only recently have film scholars begun to correct this situation. Only recently have women filmmakers been able to "think back through their mothers," to use Virginia Woolf's phrase.

It became obvious to me that remedying the paucity of scholarship on women directors was compounded by an unavailability of the films made by women in the early days of cinema, many of which had been lost, neglected, or destroyed. While women of the pen could reasonably hope that their manuscripts could survive the test of time, women filmmakers have had no such luxury. My next task, then, was to set about digging and finding what was left of the legacy of early film directors. I was surprised and astounded at the amount of material I was able to secure. Film scholars such as Ally Acker, Annette Kuhn, Susannah Radstone, Barbara Quart, Janet Todd, and Louise Heck-Rabi have produced a remarkably persuasive body of film criticism that begins the belated recognition process of women film directors and their achievements. Nevertheless, it is painfully obvious that women directors, apart from a select few, remain invisible to the public and film critics and maybe, equally important, to one another.

One of the insights that I have come to discover is that some women filmmakers have managed to be influenced by one another, even if they have been marginalized or excluded from film scholarship. Barbara Hammer and several women directors credit the work of Maya Deren, for example, whose experimental films were profoundly personal and expressed a female camera-eye. Diana Barrie claims she was most influenced by Deren's *Meshes of the Afternoon*. Alice Guy-Blaché was a mentor of, and influence on, Lois Weber, who followed in her footsteps to produce, write, and direct her own material. Lois Weber, in turn, had a profound effect on the career of Dorothy Arzner, who had a successful directorial career within the confines of the studio system of Hollywood in the 1930s.

Arzner was replaced as the sole remaining woman directing in the early days of Hollywood by Ida Lupino, who was also isolated, in a sense, as the only woman working as a director in the late 1940s and through the

1950s. The antifeminist statements of Lupino, Arzner, and others directly contradict the content of their films, which often betray a feminist understanding of women's struggles and gender stereotypes. This denial of feminism is, at times, quite problematic. It has often served to further marginalize the work of women directors, but we must keep in mind that women have not always had, nor do they now have, the freedom of expression that men enjoy as film directors and artists. Margery Wilson, an early film director and author, advised women who wished to succeed to "never let [men] suspect she has a good mind" (Wilson, 185).

Dorothy Arzner admits she stifled her criticism of studio projects. As the only woman director in the studio system, she felt she "ought not complain," and yet she carefully maintained that no obstacles were put in her way by men in the business. Elinor Glyn, the famous author and early filmmaker, seemingly did not recognize the clearly sexist critical lambasting she received for her adroit and sharply observed comedy, *Knowing Men*. Ida May Park, another woman among many who directed in the 1920s, refused her first job of directing, thinking it an unfeminine job. Even contemporary women directors find the notion of a feminist approach to filmmaking incompatible with their need for acceptance in the industry. Shirley Clarke, for instance, refuses invitations to women's film festivals, even if she agrees that women directors should be recognized. French filmmaker Diane Kurys finds the idea of women's cinema "negative, dangerous, and reductive," at the same time claiming, "I am a feminist because I am a woman, I can't help it" (Vincendeau, 70).

Other women directors, on the other hand, make absolutely no excuses for their feminism. Carolee Schneemann, Yvonne Rainer, and Barbara Hammer, for example, make films that deal directly and uncompromisingly with issues of sexuality, power, and gender. Donna Deitch was primarily motivated to make *Desert Hearts* because she saw a lack of films, especially commercial films, that center around a lesbian relationship. Barbara Hammer was drawn to experimental, formalist filmmaking precisely because it did not seem to be (yet) the exclusive domain of men. There is no question that lesbian filmmakers make up an essential component of the history and practice of cinema. Andrea Weiss explains that the problems of reclaiming lesbian cinema history are "mindboggling, since not only is evidence of lesbian presence in the historical record negligible, but even evidence of its absence, erasure, or representation is elusive" (2). It would be one matter to say that this problem applies only to the study of early women film directors, as indeed it does, but the problem of access and erasure continues with contemporary lesbian cinema as well. If a woman director in Hollywood is a lesbian, because of the rampant homophobia that plagues the industry, she may be unwilling and/or unable to "come out" in public.

Andrea Weiss's *Vampires and Violets: Lesbians in Film* is a recent study of lesbian imagery in the cinema. Weiss "outs" Germaine Dulac, a French cinema pioneer who has long been recognized as a key figure in the early

French avant-garde. As I studied the images offered by other early women film directors, I found myself angered by the possible erasure of lesbian film history in the early years of cinema. In view of the themes and topics many early women directors addressed in their films, the question of their sexual address to their chosen material seems to me a topic of genuine importance. Germaine Dulac is studied at length in Weiss's book and in Sandy Flitterman-Lewis's *To Desire Differently*. Leontine Sagan, the pioneering German lesbian film director who created *Mädchen in Uniform*, is another early figure of major significance in the lesbian cinema.

Dorothy Arzner is the most widely known lesbian director of the early Hollywood cinema; her feature film work stretches from the late 1920s to the early 1940s. Arzner managed to infuse her films with transgressive images of same-sex eroticism without losing the support of the largely patriarchal Hollywood production system. After Arzner retired in 1943 from directing features, there was no lesbian directorial presence within the dominant Hollywood cinema, although this may be another example of historical erasure. Regardless of their sexuality, it seems that few women were allowed to publicly direct feature films in Hollywood between 1943 (the year Arzner retired) and 1949 (when Ida Lupino directed *Not Wanted*).

By the 1970s, lesbian and feminist filmmaking was once again in vogue, as it had been in the 1920s at Universal and other Hollywood studios. This time, however, the filmmaking activity began anew at the margins of discourse, in the independent films of Jan Oxenberg, Barbara Hammer, Michelle Parkerson, Yvonne Rainer, Ulrike Ottinger, and Chantal Akerman, who freely expressed lesbian themes in their work. Ottinger's *Madame X* (1977) offered a dazzling view of a lesbian utopia. Barbara Hammer's *Dyketactics* (1974) and her many other erotic films catered to the pleasure of women who love women. The lesbian sex scenes near the conclusion of Chantal Akerman's *Je, tu, il, elle* (1974) were unprecedented and met with great critical acclaim and discussion. The radical feminist movement welcomed the new lesbian cinema as an answer to the compulsory heterosexuality of dominant cinema.

In the 1980s, lesbian cinema continued to challenge the absence of positive lesbian representation within the Hollywood cinema with a new burst of lesbian commercial films. The French filmmaker Diane Kurys released *Entre Nous (Coup de Foudre)* (1983) to considerable acclaim, and Donna Deitch's *Desert Hearts* (1985) was also well received. In 1987, Michelle Parkerson directed the first lesbian coming-out narrative by an African-American woman filmmaker, *Stormé: The Lady of the Jewel Box*. In the same year, lesbian audiences were treated to the powerful eroticism of Su Friedrich's *Damned If You Don't* (1987), a film about a young nun who falls in love with a woman. Abigail Child directly addressed issues surrounding lesbian sexuality in *Mayhem* (1987), another challenging film about lesbian eroticism. Perhaps the most provocative lesbian filmmaking from this period comes from Germany, in the films of Monika Treut. Treut's *Virgin Machine* (1988) is a delightful comedy with a lesbian coming-out plotline.

Lesbian filmmakers in the 1980s and 1990s have also taken to the new medium of video for their works, because it is relatively inexpensive to produce. Although the scope of this book is confined to artists working primarily in film, it would be remiss of me not to mention the work of artists such as Sadie Benning, a pioneering lesbian video artist. A contemporary lesbian artist working in film is Annette Apon, whose *Crocodiles in Amsterdam* (1989) has been described as a lesbian action/"buddy" movie. The steady rise in the number of gay and lesbian film festivals has also had a strong influence on the favorable commercial and artistic reception and increasingly effective distribution of current lesbian cinema.

In recent years, lesbian filmmakers have been increasingly political in their works, as the level of gay and lesbian activism increases. In 1991, Pratibha Parmar directed *A Place of Rage,* a film that links issues such as homophobia and racism and calls for direct political action. Parmar's *Khush* (1991) is an exposé of the repression of homosexuality within the Asian community. Other political documentaries that have recently emerged from the lesbian filmmaking community include *Thank God I'm a Lesbian* (1992), directed by Laurie Colbert and Dominique Cardona, and *Forbidden Love* (1992), directed by Aerlyn Weissman and Lynn Fernie. Both films are important contributions to the visual history of lesbian culture. The recent "crossover" success of *Go Fish* (1994), a lesbian comedy directed by Rose Troche, points the way for a new generation of lesbian films that will enjoy mainstream commercial and artistic acclaim.

Whether or not feminist or lesbian in their self-conception, female-centered subject matters seem to be common to the films of many women in this collection. Lizzie Borden's *Working Girls,* a modern examination of prostitution, was preceded by the early work of Dorothy Davenport Reid and Lois Weber. Ida Lupino's *Not Wanted* centered on the issue of unwanted pregnancies. Muriel Box's favorite projects were female-centered films, *The Truth about Women* and *Too Young to Love.* Márta Mészáros, in fact, feels it is her "duty" to make films about women.

Some women directors wish to make films that employ newly defined heroines or that reverse gender expectations. Michelle Citron's *Daughter Rite* consists of a narrative about two sisters and their mother and ignores the trappings of heroism. Doris Dörrie's film, *Men,* is an attempt to see men as comic gender reversals of the mythic Marilyn Monroe type. Social concerns are also prevalent in the films and voices of women directors. Barbara Kopple's recent *American Dream* covers union battles. Agnieszka Holland is a Polish film director who is unafraid of handling unpopular, socially significant subjects. Marguerite Duras, a French critic and writer, and Trinh T. Minh-ha, a Vietnamese deconstructionist critic and documentarian, are centrally concerned with deprivileging the screen from its power to distort social reality. Trinh T. Minh-ha questions the ability of the image itself as a historicist account of truth. Clearly, then, women directors are often compelled to redefine the boundaries of cinema.

Fund-raising and its hardships are also central issues raised by the voices in this book. Women directors face lack of support not only as a result of their gender but also because they have a remarkable tendency to choose "controversial" or "difficult" subject matter. Shirley Clarke had enormous difficulties funding *The Cool World,* an early 1960s experimental film (shot in 35mm) about racism and drug dependency. British feature director Muriel Box faced similar difficulties proving herself in a male-dominated industry. Jodie Foster and Penny Marshall stand as proof that some women manage to find funding and support from Hollywood executives, but both have had to use their acting as leverage in the decision-making process. Today, as in the past, women are generally denied access to the equipment needed to make films, ostensibly because they lack the mechanical expertise to operate cameras and sound recording equipment. Even today, film production equipment and funds remain largely in the hands of men.

Racism in Hollywood is compounded by sexism. Film scholarship also has been subject to racism. Only recently, Gloria Gibson-Hudson and other feminist critics such as Mary Dean have uncovered the legacy of Eloyce Gist, the first African-American woman director. Gist wrote, directed, and screened evangelical films in the 1920s and 1930s. The new African-American "wave" of feature-filmmaking is dominated by men such as Spike Lee and John Singleton. African-American women directors such as Julie Dash, Kathleen Collins, Alile Sharon Larkin, and Barbara McCullough have so far not been offered lucrative package deals by industry executives. Similarly, Asian-American women directors have had major difficulties finding funding and distribution. Christine Choy faced enormous interference and lack of support in the production of her film *Who Killed Vincent Chin?,* a film about violence and racism directed against Asian Americans. Kathleen Collins spent over a year trying to fund her film *Women, Sisters, and Friends.*

Julie Dash continues to search aggressively for funding, even after the critical success of her Afrocentric *Daughters of the Dust.* Claire Denis was forced to face humiliation and scorn when attempting to finance her independent feature *Chocolat,* a film that directly attacks African colonization. Similarly, Ann Hui's *Boat People,* a critically successful film that documents the harsh realities of Vietnamese refugees, clearly deserves wider distribution. Distribution and finance remain formidable barriers for independent filmmakers to surmount. However, the recent emergence of African-American women directors such as Darnell Martin (*I Like It Like That,* 1994) suggests that women of color may at last be getting a chance as commercial filmmakers.

Even though a great deal of hardship seems to have been suffered by women directors, an impressive degree of perseverance seems to be a common factor in many of their experiences. Early pioneering film director Dorothy Davenport Reid faced the resentment of her male colleagues as she struggled to create her own cinematic visions of the woman's plight in American society. Yet Reid went on to make a series of intensely personal films that argued against drug addiction, prostitution, and sexism. Yvonne Rainer recently managed to fund a film about menopause, *Privilege,* despite its supposedly taboo subject matter, because of an incredibly loyal following and a fierce determination to make the film. For all of these women, the need to make films is a compelling need they must fulfill, no matter what the cost.

In creating *Women Film Directors,* I owe a debt that I freely acknowledge to other scholars who have previously mapped out the terrain of women's cinema. They have had to work in an area where precious little documentation is available. In the mid-to-late 1960s, when film studies as a discipline was first codified at the university level, it was generally supposed that women had very little to do with film as a historical artifact, except as actors, set decorators, and designers, all ancillary, rather than central, functions of the cinematographic process. However, although it is still being resisted by many mainstream film history texts, it is now clear that women have been present in all areas of production in film since the inception of the medium, particularly as directors, scenarists, and producers. Yet, for the most part, this enormous outpouring of creative energy goes undocumented and unexamined.

One of the most useful texts available is *The Women's Companion to International Film* (1994), originally published as *Women in Film: An International Guide* (1990), edited by Annette Kuhn and Susannah Radstone. This book, more than any other single source, began to uncover the breadth of the "lost" canon of female auteurs. Anyone unconvinced of the fact that women, from the primitive days of filmmaking to the present, have been actively participating in the art form of the cinema both behind and in front of the camera will surely be convinced by the many biographical and/or critical entries written by a diverse and knowledgeable group of scholars and gathered in this book. Each essay on an individual filmmaker includes a bibliography, filmography, and biographical information on women directors from Alice Guy-Blaché and Elvira Notari to Barbara Hammer and Carolee Schneemann. In addition, short critical essays, such as "Lesbian Independent Cinema" and "Psychoanalytic Film Theory," provide cross-referenced information on film "movements" and differing schools of critical thought. Since Kuhn and Radstone first edited this text in 1990, many more women directors have been rediscovered, and many more women filmmakers have entered commercial filmmaking.

Ally Acker's *Reel Women: Pioneers of the Cinema, 1896 to the Present* is an important addition to recent revisionist film scholarship, highlighting women's often unsung contributions to motion picture history. *Reel Women* is a study of women at work behind the camera, as directors, writers, cinematographers, producers, stuntwomen, animators, editors, scenarists, and publicists. Acker not only is concerned with independent women filmmakers but also chronicles the efforts of those women who managed to thrive in the confines of the male-dominated industry in Hollywood. Acker has used publicity materials, in-house studio publications, and numerous unpublished manuscripts and interviews. The text includes entries on such little-known filmmakers as Marion E. Wong, president of the almost forgotten Mandarin Film Company, which was one of the first ethnic film companies in America. Contemporary directors such as Julie Dash, Lina Wertmuller, and Stephanie Rothman are also discussed.

Anthony Slide's *Early Women Directors* also goes a long way toward rectifying the erasure of female film directors in dominant film scholarship. In this early study, Slide gathers a multitude of facts and sources on the first woman director, Alice Guy-Blaché, and early women directors such as Lois Weber, Margery Wilson, Dorothy Davenport Reid, Frances Marion, Dorothy Arzner, and many others. *Early Women Directors* has been frequently cited and used as a bibliographic source for many researchers of women in film. Slide is most effective at uncovering sources on women filmmakers of the teens and 1920s in the United States. Women, Slide notes, not only were active in early American filmmaking but predominated in the industry in many areas until the mid-1920s, when sexism, industry professionalization, and monopolization pushed them out of the director's chair.

Louise Heck-Rabi was one of the first film scholars to rigorously document the critical reception of women directors. In her book *Women Filmmakers: A Critical Reception,* Heck-Rabi chose eleven women filmmakers whose films had been screened and reviewed and seemed popular enough to warrant further investigation. Heck-Rabi's book goes a long way toward establishing a discourse on women filmmakers. For her book, Heck-Rabi methodically located hundreds of reviews of filmmakers Alice Guy, Germaine Dulac, Lois Weber, Dorothy Arzner, Leni Riefenstahl, Muriel Box, Maya Deren, Ida Lupino, Mai Zetterling, Shirley Clarke, and Agnes Varda. Heck-Rabi's text has the advantage of presenting a wealth of documentary evidence on the filmmakers whose work has often been ignored by other film history texts, and, for the most part, Heck-Rabi presents the material without extensive commentary, letting these contemporaneous critical commentaries speak for themselves. For an overview of the careers of these talented artists and the ways in which their work was interpreted (and/or misinterpreted) by the public, *Women Filmmakers: A Critical Reception* is an essential volume for the feminist cinema scholar.

Giuliana Bruno's *Streetwalking on a Ruined Map: Cultural Theory and the City Films of Elvira Notari* succeeds at unearthing the fragmentary relics of the life and work of marginalized filmmaker Elvira Notari (1875–1940). Notari was Italy's first and most prolific woman filmmaker, as well as a forerunner of neorealism. Bruno rethinks and reclaims the cultural map of Italian silent cinema, placing it within the context of the cultural theories of a number of disciplines. Sewing together the discourses of art history, cultural anthropology, architecture, feminist film theory, psychoanalytic theory, and the history of medical discourse and the body, Bruno weaves a lively and intercontextual metahistory of intellectual discourse. *Streetwalking on a Ruined Map* is as much indebted to cultural anthropological models as it is to recent film criticism. Giuliana Bruno's complex yet engaging discussion leads us into a host of disciplines but emerges as a reasoned and impassioned examination of the female body in the films of Elvira Notari, as it was discursively allegorized into industrialized society with the onset of the cinema, the medical industry, and the arcade.

Laura Mulvey's "Visual Pleasure and Narrative Cinema" has probably been one of the most frequently cited feminist theory articles in film scholarship. This article introduced the popularly received theory of the (Lacanian) "male gaze" and the female body as object of fetishistic scopophilia in traditional cinema. Drawing heavily upon Jacques Lacan and Sigmund Freud, Mulvey locates the female body in the patriarchal discourse of the cinema. Though Mulvey's essay has been useful in its analysis of cinema as a producer of "ego ideals," she embraces Lacanian theory to an exclusion of other reception theories. As a result, cinematic theory has been dominated by an emphasis on the passivity of the (presumably male) scopophiliac viewer, who derives pleasure in using the gaze at an objectified female body for pleasure (through narcissism, misplaced fear of castration, and identification with the image on-screen). For Mulvey, woman "is sexual difference," and she "always threatens," even as she provides visual pleasure. Though Mulvey's analysis of male filmmakers' depiction of the female as a signifier of castration is fruitful, especially in the case of Alfred Hitchcock's *Vertigo,* Mulvey's theory and Lacanian approaches to cinema in general tend to decenter the possibility of the female gaze, on the part of both a female audience and/or a female director.

Must we apply Lacanian theory to women's cinema? Is there an essential women's cinema? These questions can be addressed only when one confronts the entire history of cinema practice, that is, the totality of film production created by women and men. Mulvey's chief critical work operates in the arena of "radical filmmakers" who, she says, "free the look of the camera into its materiality in time and space and the look of the audience into dialectics, [or] passionate detachment (17)." In this assessment, Mulvey was no doubt thinking of directors such as Varda and Rainer, whose films insistently deny passive spectatorship.

In contrast, Claire Johnston's landmark essay, "Women's Cinema as

Counter-Cinema," is largely concerned with mythmaking in the cinema. Drawing upon Roland Barthes, Johnston locates the female body as an iconic type in traditional cinema. Johnston challenges the "conventional" notion that women directors who worked in mainstream Hollywood "had little opportunity for real expression within the dominant sexist ideology" (25). Dorothy Arzner, Ida Lupino, Nelly Kaplan, and other women directors are treated in this essay. Johnston was one of the first to critically valorize women filmmakers' achievements. Arzner's *Dance, Girl, Dance* is a case in point. Johnston notes that the central "opposing poles of myths of femininity" in the film center around woman as object/spectacle. Johnston locates the dialogic "contradiction between the desire to please [men] and self-expression" (29) in the film. Similarly, Lupino's *Not Wanted* is viewed as a subversion of Hollywood mythmaking, because of the withdrawal of a happy ending. For Johnston, Agnes Varda's films "mark a retrograde step in women's cinema" (30), because they "appear totally innocent to the workings of myth" (30). Johnston dislikes Varda's portrayal of female bodies, particularly in *Le Bonheur,* proclaiming them "facile" and not unlike those of advertising. In response, Johnston urges the creation of a countercinema: "[A]t this point in time, a strategy should be developed which embraces both the notion of films as a political tool and film as entertainment" (31).

Sandy Flitterman-Lewis was one of the founders of *Camera Obscura: A Journal of Feminism and Film Theory.* Her book, *To Desire Differently: Feminism and the French Cinema,* was originally a dissertation for comparative literature for the University of California—Berkeley, which received the dissertation award given by the Society for Cinema Studies. Flitterman-Lewis is most interested in the question of *authorship* in women's cinema, particularly in the work of Germaine Dulac, Marie Epstein, and Agnes Varda. Flitterman-Lewis locates an alternative cinematic "counter-discourse" that opposes the model of male filmmaking. Drawing from Laura Mulvey's psychoanalytic model of spectatorship and image-gaze reception of the female body, Flitterman-Lewis reexamines French cinema, finding a "counter-discourse" that

either at the margins or from the center of the structure itself, transcends distinctions of period and genre; and characterizes the very earliest efforts of French filmmakers to conceive of challenges to dominant cinematic representations from abroad. (4)

Flitterman-Lewis notes that Mulvey's criticism reinforces a "repressive binarism, one which is locked into conventional associations of masculinity with activity, femininity with passivity" (6). Flitterman-Lewis also argues with Mulvey's estimation that the female viewer "necessarily involves identification with an alien masculine gaze" (6). Mary Ann Doane, according to Flitterman-Lewis, locates the female spectator as "not outside of subjective or signifying processes at all" (7). Instead, Doane posits two ways of female looking, narcissistic identification with female hero or "transvestite" identification with male hero. Flitterman-Lewis sees de Lauretis's critical approach as an even less limiting system which "emphasizes the heterogeneity implicit in the female spectator's position" (8). Teresa de Lauretis, Flitterman-Lewis explains, rejects Mulvey's "masculinization" and Doane's "masochism" theories in favor of "a process by which the woman might identify as both subject and object of the Oedipal scenario continually restaged by dominant cinema" (8). De Lauretis allows for feminine desire in her discourse. This overview of feminist criticism leads to a discussion of femininity and authorship. Flitterman-Lewis delineates the problems of applying the "enunciative model" of authorship to films directed by women, which, of course, again raises the question of female desire. Feminine authorship is, for Flitterman-Lewis, (1) a "historical phenomenon," (2) a "desiring position," and (3) a "textual moment" (21). Flitterman-Lewis's feminist dialectic recognizes a cinema in which women "attempt to reinsert the subject—a sexed-subject—into the process of meaning production" (23). This is a novel approach to women's cinema and women in the cinema.

Flitterman-Lewis reclaims three women filmmakers' contributions to a feminist dialectic: first, Germaine Dulac, who "attempts to both explore and convey female subjectivity" (27) and "explore nonreferentiality" and next, Marie Epstein, whose "poetic realism" was denied authorial credit, due to her attachment to Jean Benoît-Lévy (who received sole directorial credit for her/their work) and whose film *La Maternelle* (*The Nursery School*) (1933) excels in the "creation of an alternative feminist cinema" (29). Finally, Flitterman-Lewis addresses the *nouvelle vague* filmmaker, Agnes Varda, who is credited for the first New Wave film *La Pointe-Courte* (1954). Varda's exploration of the boundaries of narrativity, her preoccupation with the feminine, and her "deconstruction and examination of the production of woman's image" (32) in films such as *Cleo from 5 to 7* (1961) and *Vagabond* (1985) culminate in a feminist examination of the "sexual exploitation of the woman's image" (32). Flitterman-Lewis concludes that regardless of the complex questions of subject/object relations in spectatorial theories of cinema, she has located three important examples of feminist authorship. *To Desire Differently* is a richly rewarding study of French cinema. American women directors deserve a similar critical treatment. Flitterman-Lewis's use of a performative critical model, an enunciatory privileging of the process of theory, and a flexible notion of feminine authorship and spectatorship delivers a fine model of methodology.

Teresa de Lauretis's influential *Alice Doesn't: Feminism, Semiotics, Cinema* is a collection of revised essays published originally in such periodicals as *Screen, Discourse, Cine-tracts,* and *Yale Italian Studies.* De Lauretis draws from Bakhtin, Saussure, Claire Johnston, Eco, and other critical au-

thorities, but she ultimately positions herself as an authority in female looking and female-looked-at-ness. Desire, authorship, subjectivity, and
criticism are the central themes of this work, which is as frequently cited
as Laura Mulvey's essay on narrative pleasure and the female body. The
essay "Through the Looking Glass" marks de Lauretis's as a critical revisionist, in the best sense of that term. When semiology "disregards the
questions of sexual difference" (8) and finds subjectivity "nonpertinent,"
psychoanalysis assumes this as the primary focus, but "both theories deny
women the status of subjects and producers of culture" (8). De Lauretis
prefers Eco's "productivist" accommodation of semiotics and extends his
theories to the female as a sign producer. In the essay "Imaging," de Lauretis expounds upon Mulvey's "Visual Pleasure" essay but finds that "spectators are not, as it were, either in the film text or simply outside the film
text, rather, we might say, they intersect the film as they are intersected by
cinema" (44).

In "Semiotics and Experience," Teresa de Lauretis denies that semiotics
necessarily negates human experience. Grounding the chapter with a cita-
tion from Virginia Woolf's *A Room of One's Own,* in which Woolf's "I"
sits on the banks of the Oxbridge River ruminating on women and fiction
and experiences a splitting of gendered selves, as represented by the (male)
instinct and the (female) scholar, de Lauretis debates the paradoxes involved in feminist approaches to patriarchal binarisms. Women, as "the
sex which is not one," have been read as "the underside of masculinity"
(164), and, for Catharine Mackinnon, gender socialization makes women
"exist for men" (166), but semioticians such as Umberto Eco and Julia
Kristeva undermine even the notion of self, thus subverting the previous
gendered models. For de Lauretis, woman is a sign or signs of inner and
outer self, and self-analysis, such as Woolf's, can rearticulate and reframe
the experience of women.

In *The Woman at the Keyhole: Feminism and Women's Cinema,* Judith
Mayne reconsiders female authorship, narrativity, and reception, using
women's films to demonstrate female voyeuristic pleasure, as the title suggests. Mayne's reconsiderations of women directors such as Dorothy Arzner, Maya Deren, and Germaine Dulac draw upon a wide range of critical
theories. Mayne admirably lays a formidable groundwork in her psychoanalytic treatment of male "primitive" filmmakers, whose work, as she
demonstrates, is, more often than not, a metaphoric expression of infantile
spectatorship in its "re-visioning" of female and nonwhite subjects. Like
Sandy Flitterman-Lewis in *To Desire Differently,* Judith Mayne locates a
form of primitive female narration in such films as Germaine Dulac's *Smiling Madame Beudet* (1922), Agnes Varda's *Cleo From 5 to 7* (1961), and
Chantal Akerman's *Jeanne Dielman* (1975).

Mayne's comparison of Trinh T. Minh-ha's *Reassemblage* (1982) with
early Lumiére films is a successful argument for an opening of the question

of stages of historicity in the cinema. This dialectical struggle is centered about authorship, race, and gender. Minh-ha's voice-over narrator directly reshapes the cinematic experience by speaking directly to/at the audience, for example, about the manner in which white filmmakers and critics assign meaning to the experiences of Africans. *Reassemblage,* according to Mayne, privileges the female body, so much so that "the film attempts simultaneously to question and to assume the maternal and nourishing properties of the female body" (215). Mayne's further explorations of Third World women of color in the cinema, as well as her refiguring of French women's cinema, articulate a female fascination with "otherness." For Mayne,

the lure of the "primitive" in women's cinema is also the lure of cultural constructions of the "other," and there is no guarantee that the displacement of the male subject simultaneously displaces his white skin or his western assumptions. (222)

Mayne cautions, then, against oversimplification of women's cinematic narrative approaches. For Mayne, the gaze is neither male nor female, but oscillating and subject to racial otherness as much as, or more than, oedipal forces. Mayne is suspicious of binarisms or preconfigurations. The readings of lesbian films, for example, those of Akerman or Ottinger, are narrated in such a manner of mutability that they "pose lesbianism both as a projection of patriarchal—and feminist—fantasies, and as another register of desire together" (154).

E. Ann Kaplan's volume *Psychoanalysis and Cinema* collects a group of important essays by Laura Mulvey, Mary Ann Doane, Claire Johnston, Kaja Silverman, Yvonne Rainer, and others, many of which first appeared in *Screen* and other cinema journals. Laura Mulvey updates some of her thoughts in "Afterthoughts on 'Visual Pleasure and Narrative Cinema.'" Anne Friedberg's "A Denial of Difference: Theories of Cinematic Identification" questions the implicit notions of identification of the psychoanalytic model. Friedberg applies a Metzian model of signification to the usual model of spectatorship. "Wholeness is not offered here; the ego ideal represented is not unified or whole, but a synecdochal signifier" (41), because cinematic representation inherently cuts up the body into pieces. Friedberg examines Mulvey's "Visual Pleasure in the Narrative Cinema" next, noting that "the female spectator [in Mulvey's model] is placed in a masochistic position of identifying either, on the one hand, with the woman who is punished by the narrative or treated as a scopophilic fetish or, on the other hand, identifying with the man who is controller of events" (42).

Mary Ann Doane's essay, "Remembering Women: Psychical and Historical Constructions in Film Theory," again takes on the question of cinematic construction of woman. Doane uses cinema apparatus theory to refigure a new notion of woman. Doane is less interested in dissecting the experience of the spectator in the usual scopophiliac model than in elucidating Jean-Louis Baudry's theories of cinema as apparatus. Doane notes how "the insistently spatial logic of apparatus theory has rigidly restricted the way in which vision has been understood as a psychical process within film theory" (51). For Baudry, the gaze is the camera. But for Doane, the gaze "cannot be mapped, diagrammed, only suggested, in the impossible topological figures Lacan appeals to in his later work" (53). Doane concludes that feminists must resist "the process of troping" that makes woman "everybody's Lady" (61). Sally Potter's experimental feature film *Gold Diggers* (1984), starring Julie Christie, is cited as an illustration of current feminist filmmaking that draws upon critical notions of the "female look."

Of the essays in Kaplan's *Psychoanalysis and the Cinema,* Yvonne Rainer's reconsideration of feminist spectatorship theory is one of the most interesting because Rainer approaches the matter from her perspective as filmmaker *and* critic and is therefore privy to a more complex vantage point than many feminist critics who are not themselves auteurs. Rainer's "Some Ruminations around the Cinematic Antidotes to the Oedipal Net(les) while Playing with De Lauraedipus Mulvey, or, He May Be off Screen, but . . ." is a playful attempt to bring Teresa de Lauretis's "Desire in Narrative" and Laura Mulvey's "Afterthoughts in 'Visual Pleasure and Narrative Cinema' " into a contemplation of Rainer's film *The Man Who Envied Women* (1985). Rainer locates female spectatorship in her films as being subject to continual mutability, both masculine and feminine, supporting her argument with de Lauretis and Mulvey.

The introduction to Janet Todd's *Women and Film,* written by James Lynn of the University of Southhampton, posits that "feminists who have embraced Lacan's critique of patriarchy have thereby committed themselves to a fundamentally tragic account of sexual difference" (6). Lynn dubs the "tragic feminism" (7) of Lacanian disciples as essentially phallocentric, in that it "emphatically opposes the attempts of his renegade pupils and associates to fashion 'feminine' discourses, uncontaminated by patriarchal assumptions" (7). Judith Mayne sees the task of the film critic as a project of rereading film "against the grain" (24) of classical cinema. Mayne denies that classical cinema is a monolithic patriarchal construction of passive images of women by men. Not only have women directed, but the female presence on the screen of male-directed cinema can be read, according to Mayne, with more depth than in a simplistic model of male fantasy.

Susan H. Léger's essay on "Marguerite Duras's Cinematic Spaces" elucidates the problematics of a woman director, from both an economic and critical viewpoint. Duras defines men as absence, effectively turning the tables on Lacanian theory: "[A] woman inhabits a place completely, the presence of a woman fills a place. A man passes through it, he doesn't really live there" (246). Léger applauds Duras's use of interior spaces, arguing against Pauline Kael's objections to them in *Le Camion*. Léger notes Duras's tendency to see woman's "story, as being inextricably linked to the house" (252), reminding us that Virginia Woolf did the same in *A Room of One's Own*. Léger defends Duras, who has also been attacked for her heroine's passivity: "More sympathetic critics see the creation of these silent women as the outcome of the rejection of masculine language" (254).

Mary Ann Doane departs from a purely psychoanalytic discourse in her book *Femmes Fatales: Feminism, Film Theory, Psychoanalysis,* alerting the reader of her "attraction-repulsion" relationship with/in psychoanalytic theory. Doane readily admits that she has "never felt an obligation to be 'faithful' to the texts of Freud and Lacan" (8), and she is impatient with those scholars who align themselves with such orthodoxy. She is equally impatient with antitheorists who dismiss structuralist, semiotic, and post-structuralist methodologies. Doane's essays borrow freely from those methodologies but concentrate on the question of the female body, here, that of the femme fatale, whose "disruptiveness" demands both psychoanalytic and iconographic analysis. "Because she [the femme fatale] seems to confound power, subjectivity, and agency with the very lack of these attributes, her relevance to feminist discourse is critical" (3).

"Woman's Stake: Filming the Female Body" returns to Lacanian territory. Doane spends considerable time reformulating Lacan's "justification for the privilege accorded to the phallus as signifier [which] appears to guarantee its derivation from a certain representation of the bodily organ" (170). Reworking the "woman as absence" topos, Doane ultimately joins Luce Irigaray and Julia Kristeva in their call for the reclamation of the female body (and language). Maternal fantasies are more relevant to feminist film criticism, especially in terms of the femme fatale, according to Doane. "Dark Continents" is a fascinating consideration of the troping of the body of the African American in films such as *Birth of a Nation, Tarzan,* and *Imitation of Life.*

Doane relates feminism to racism with her discussion of Freud's trope of woman as dark continent. The essay concludes with a call for feminists to reexamine their aesthetic notions of sublimation. The disruptive femme fatale is "othered" in a fashion somewhat like that of the nonwhite body. *Femmes Fatales* locates feminist film theory as a disruptive critical force that refuses to embrace or reject diverse methodologies. While Doane is certainly "at home" with psychoanalytic method, she is rapidly redefining a new critical feminist aesthetic that offers disruption rather than closure.

Trinh T. Minh-ha's *The Framer Framed* is, in many senses, a distinctly unusual and challenging work. A filmmaker herself, Trinh T. Minh-ha has also emerged as an important and influential film theorist. Using an alluring combination of critical text, frame blowups, and quotations from her intensely personal and political films, Trinh T. Minh-ha treats the reader to an exploration of her "object-oriented" filmic process, which she views as a spiritual and self-critical act. Extensive interviews with Laura Mulvey, Judith Mayne, and Pratibha Parmar expand the boundaries of the discourse within the volume dialectically into a heteroglossic examination of the film-maker's ouevre and the informing structural intent. In the structure thus provided to the reader, Trinh T. Minh-ha allows the textual auditor to become an eavesdropper of sorts, as she playfully and subjectively reviews her life and her films.

Drawing heavily on the writings of Roland Barthes, Hélène Cixous, Jean Baudrillard, and others, *The Framer Framed* is critically sophisticated and also useful from a feminist, new-historicist viewpoint. Like her films, *The Framer Framed* demonstrates Trinh T. Minh-ha's commitment to a process of continual questioning and forces the reader to confront the difficult issues of race, gender, and cinematic representation within a dominant patriarchy. More than anything else, Trinh T. Minh-ha is interested in liberating the boundaries of the cinema frame so that other women may follow in her footsteps, both as filmmakers and as theorists; this "double voice" gives her work added resonance and depth.

Also of great value to students and scholars is *Women Directors: The Emergence of a New Cinema* by Barbara Koenig Quart. Quart examines the work of pioneering directors such as Alice Guy, Lois Weber, Ida Lupino, and others but also devotes lengthy and perceptive chapters to Eastern European and Third World feminist cinema. In her book, Quart provides shot-by-shot analyses of many of the films that she examines, notably in the case of director Márta Mészáros, whose *Adoption* receives detailed analytical consideration, enabling the reader to visualize the camera movement within the film. In her discussion of *Adoption,* Quart notes that when we see the film, we "watch with the awareness of a woman behind the camera looking at women" (197), and thus the issue of the power of the female gaze is never far from her consideration of the films she examines.

Quart effectively intercuts interviews with the directors of the films she considers with critical commentary, offering the auteurs in question a chance to speak directly for themselves, rather than being distanced from the reader by a completely critical approach. Mészáros, for example, states forthrightly, "I have the obstinacy of a mule . . . [in the creation of my films, I] pursued my attempt to study the characters of types of women [who possessed] a strong personality, and [who were] capable of forming decisions for themselves" (193). Patriarchal models of criticism often have the tendency to separate the artist from the works they create. Quart finds it an absolute necessity to include the filmmaker's views as an integral part of the critical process.

bell hooks's *Black Looks: Race and Representation* includes a chapter on black women filmmakers that ought not to be missed by anyone interested in the power relationship of the "oppositional gaze" between black women spectators and filmmakers. hooks draws Lacanian theory into the arena of gender and racial difference in "looking" at a fictive construct.

The gaze of black women filmmakers such as Julie Dash, Michelle Parkerson, Eloyce Gist, Kathleen Collins, Ayoka Chenzira, and Zeinabu irene Davis is a topic of great interest to hooks, and she deals with it extensively in this well-researched and inventively constructed volume. What is different in the way that an African-American woman views a specific scene within a cinematic construct, as opposed to the "camera gaze" that would be given to the same scene under the auspices of a white female or white male or African-American male director? For hooks, "critical black female spectatorship emerges as a site of resistance" (128) and is one of the dominant goals of African-American consciousness. hooks notes that *Illusions, Daughters of the Dust,* and other films directed by black women "employ a deconstructive filmic practice to undermine existing grand cinematic narratives. . . " (130). With these telling critical comments in mind, one eagerly awaits the time when African-American women enjoy at least as great an opportunity within the spectrum of commercial and independent filmmaking as such male African-American directors as Spike Lee, Kevin Hooks, John Singleton, and others.

E. Deidre Pribram's collection of essays on female spectatorship, *Female Spectators: Looking at Film and Television,* is an important volume because it includes several studies that locate African-American feminists as cultural spectators, critics, and filmmakers. Alile Sharon Larkin's "Black Women Filmmakers Defining Ourselves: Feminism in Our Own Voice" locates the problematics of feminist discourse that "succumbs to racism when it segregates Black women from Black men and dismisses our history" (158). Larkin identifies several negative black mythic types in Hollywood films and challenges television programs that depict poor black families as agents in their own oppression. Larkin insists that African-American women directors who enter the field should always remember a "commitment to deal with the totality of our Black female experience" (169). Larkin discusses the work of Ayoka Chenzira, Julie Dash, and Kathleen Collins, as well as her own films.

Diane Carson, Linda Dittmar, and Janice R. Welsch's anthology *Multiple Voices in Feminist Film Criticism* and Pam Cook and Philip Dodd's collection *Women and Film: A Sight and Sound Reader,* provide extensive surveys of current feminist cinema scholarship and include a varied range of analytical perspectives, from cultural studies to postcolonial discourses. The stress on diversity makes *Multiple Voices* a lively and challenging text. The book also includes a section of course files for those interested in teaching courses on feminist film theory, women filmmakers, women of color in film, African-American women in film, women in Latin American cinema, and sexual representation of women in film. This section of course files is particularly useful because it includes personal accounts from six professors who share their experiences in the classroom with the reader, and each course file includes a comprehensive reading list.

Janice Welsch's course file achieves an excellent balance between feminist film theory and the history of the women's movement as a whole. This strategy acknowledges feminist film theory's ties to the overall struggles of women in both personal and social terms, smoothly guiding the student through units designed around the study of "Feminism—1970 to the Present," "Film Theory," and "Feminism, Film Theory, and Feminist Film Criticism." Diane Carson's course file "Women Filmmakers" is more directly focused on the history of women in the medium of film, even though the readings suggested by Carson are designed to introduce the student to basic precepts of feminist film practice as a larger discipline. The readings include psychoanalytic, Althusserian, Bakhtinian, semiotic, and poststructuralist approaches to feminist film criticism, with an eye toward issues of race, class, age, and sexual orientation. In the readings, Carson deals with many women filmmakers, from Alice Guy to Julie Dash, Alile Sharon Larkin, Ayoka Chenzira, Zeinabu irene Davis, and Su Friedrich. The films under consideration range from straightforward narratives to more experimental formats, and, all in all, Carson has done an impressive job of gathering a great deal of disparate material within the confines of one course.

Elizabeth Hadley Freydberg's course file, "Women of Color," makes significant inroads into the area of films and filmmakers of nonhegemonic culture. Freydberg selects films and study materials for units on Caribbean and Latin American women, lesbians, African women, and Native American women and exposes interracial alliances and concerns that cut across the borders of race and class. Freydberg notes that the issues inevitably raised by these films and the accompanying readings are often "volatile." But this volatility is matched by the emotional and intellectual challenges of a course that is effectively designed to embrace diversity and social difference and that also manages to retain a rigorous critical attitude toward the films and texts it contains.

The course file on "Black Women in American Film," offered by Frances Stubbs and Elizabeth Hadley Freydberg, works in a similar manner, but it is perhaps more specific in its emphasis on familiar stereotypes of black women within the discourse of American film. The course argues for a rewriting of film history and the abolishment of outdated and outmoded stereotypes and includes a list of related reading materials for further discussion. Julia Lesage offers advice for the professor of "Latin American and Caribbean Women in Film and Video," in a course file designed to raise group consciousness of media-sustained xenophobia. Media reception is at the heart of the pedagogical concerns of this course, which encourages students to question their own passivity as viewers and step away from their position as members of the ideologically dominant culture to better understand the mechanics of sexism and racism.

Chris Straayer, who teaches Sexual Representations in Film and Video at New York University, offers a course file designed to promote understanding of the regulation of the body and gender in heterosexist society. Straayer uses a combination of mainstream cinema genre films and excerpts from "pornographic" cinema to promote discussion of constructions of gender as created by heterosexism and the commodification of the feminine corpus. This course may be better suited to more advanced students because of the emphasis on fairly difficult readings and films, yet Straayer's blue-print moves toward a fascinating theoretical merging of these various "ter-ritories of the body" through the juxtapositioning of these seemingly disparate (but, in fact, intimately related) source materials. Students in Straayer's course are urged to interpret the transgressiveness of sexuality in horror films, documentaries on pornography (such as *Rate It X,* 1986), camp films, and classic gay and lesbian films, including Monika Treut's *Virgin Machine* (1988). One unit of Straayer's class is devoted to on-screen female sexual pleasure, firmly embracing both historical and theoretical concerns.

Women and Film: A Sight and Sound Reader, a collection of essays from the influential British film journal *Sight and Sound,* scrutinizes the debates surrounding the representation of women in film, as well as the works of women filmmakers and their concerns with this area of cinema practice. A section on women directors includes articles on Mira Nair, Jane Campion, Sally Potter, Julie Dash, Dorris Dörrie, Chantal Akerman, and Leni Rie-fenstahl. The editors are primarily concerned with recent questions of filmic practice by women rather than questions of canonical creation. *Women and Film* includes several brilliant sections on recent film theory, including "Queer Alternatives" and "Deconstructing Masculinity," which are theo-retically based on rereadings of gender and the cinema, including persuasive and complex examinations of the deleterious effects of dominant cinema practice on mainstream cinema audiences. Other essays include Carol Clo-ver's discussion of art, culture, and gender in "High and Low: The Trans-formation of the Rape-Revenge Movie," an extension of her previous work in this area, and Stephen Bourne's examination of the work of African-American actress Hattie McDaniels in "Denying Her Place: Hattie Mc-Daniels' Surprising Acts," which moves film theory into the area of transgressive cultural criticism. Amy Taubin's essay, "Queer Male Cinema and Feminism," locates a female audience identification within the context of gay cinematic practice, as an alternative to the heterosexist conventions of Hollywood, in an attempt to find a cinema of alternative feminist sexual desire. *Women and Film* is an excellent book, although it functions within a somewhat narrower range than many of the other texts discussed here. As a supplementary text, this volume is highly recommended for medium- to advanced-level courses on recent developments in feminist cinema prac-tice.

A voluminous body of work is being published on women in film, in both critical and popular "trade" books, as well as in national and specialized periodicals. As one example, Indiana University Press is publishing a special series of new volumes on individual women directors. In all these volumes, we can see the work of feminist film criticism and theoretical research being carried forward. The important work done by new cinema historicists demonstrates that there is a vast body of work by women film-makers waiting to be considered; the critical work that has been accomplished since that time proves that the debate in the area of feminist cinema practice is a continuing and engaging discourse. What is needed now, beyond the work done in this volume, is a comprehensive film history text at the undergraduate university level that fully explores the work of women directors, a text that valorizes the accomplishments of women and men equally. Once this is accomplished, an even wider critical debate can begin, encompassing all filmic texts created in various historical periods. The work of Notari, Weber, Dulac, and others demonstrates that there is a compelling alternative to patriarchal cinema. Because of this, the work of new historicists and/or cinema theoreticians is just beginning.

What of African, African-American, and Third World cinema practice, both historically and as a function of the present day? Perhaps the question posed by Gayatri Spivak, "Can the subaltern speak?" (1988), might properly be resituated in the discourse of the subaltern filmmaker. When the subaltern speaks, are "we" listening, or are "we" unable to listen? In an age in which there has been a voluminous outpouring of "postcolonial," "emergent" feminist criticism, a specious lack of dialogue addresses the scanty discourse on Third World women filmmakers. The speaking, writing, and filmic creative "testimony" of non-Western women challenges the crossing borders of feminism and arguably transforms and problematizes academic pedagogy. In my research, I was particularly struck by the complex ramifications of the last sentence of a section from a lengthy interview with Brazilian filmmaker Ana Carolina:

[W]hen I went to Cannes the reaction to my work received was as if I was a complete sex maniac. I never thought it was, nor did the public [in Brazil]. Strangely, here they're considered intellectual . . . we're perhaps amongst those who use sex the least, and that's possibly why the censor thinks we are more immoral. Because I deal with the family, sex in the family, sex in institutions. So it's very aggressive. But for the market I'm not a director who works with sex. *I don't know if that's the answer you wanted.* (Hartog, 68–69) (Foster's emphasis).

Throughout many of the interviews with women filmmakers I have read, there are fairly consistent topoi—of markers or gaps among artist, academician, audience, or critic—but Carolina's question, "I don't know if that's the answer you wanted [?]" locates an inherent situational anxiety in representation (and self-representation) of the postcolonial non-Western woman filmmaker. This representational crisis extends beyond the language of the speaking subaltern and is embedded in emerging postcolonial criticism.

Often, non-Western women filmmakers suffer from an emerging colonialism of critical privilege. Aware that she may well be subject to being "eaten as the Other," to coin a phrase of bell hooks, Carolina, in one short quip, subverts the discourse of a Western interview, wherein subject/object relation often disguises a wish for "containment." "Containment," as described by Jonathan Dollimore, destroys difference through a coerced conformity masquerading as voluntary submission" (94).

I do not wish to further suppress the testimony of non-Western women filmmakers by devaluing the critical apparatus of the Western interview. On the contrary, even if I cannot agree with Spivak's premise that "there is no unrepresentable subaltern subject that can know and speak itself," I strongly agree that "the intellectual's solution is not to abstain from representation" (1988, 285). But even a decentered approach does not effectively answer Spivak's question of "how to keep the ethnocentric subject from establishing itself by selectively defining an Other" (1988, 292). In a raging debate, scholars who are working in the areas of non-Western cultures, subaltern studies, and gender studies are all too often aware of the dangers inherent in interdisciplinary work, frequently characterized as essentialist, historicist, colonialist, and so on. The language of such warnings conveys a representational crisis not unlike that which erupts in the Ana Carolina interview. Linda Gordon, for example, effectively warns us of the "dangers of perceiving a common ground where there is none," when invoking the "difference motif" (96).

Gordon reminds us of "what is being avoided" when Western critics speak of one category of (racial and gendered) difference: "[T]he denial of the possibility of human subjectivity . . . belittles the search for shared meanings of womanhood" (105). Difference study, Gordon concludes, can often result in an environment that is "constricting, even paralyzing" (106) and has a "chilling effect on the struggle to recognize others and hence to end the categorization 'other' " (107). Filmmaker/critic Trinh T. Minh-ha underscores the problematics of studies of difference and the "other" with the statement, "The idea that there is a hidden truth in the other's culture that needs the joint effort of the outsider and the insider to be fully unveiled is highly misleading" (238). Even if we call into practice a decentered position, we are frequently reminded that we must not "silence by a telescoping act of interpretation the multiple and specific voices of the autobiographical texts [of non-Western women]" (Smith and Watson, xxviii). Sara Suleri's recent criticism of the categorization of a postcolonial woman identifies the "simplicities that underlie unthinking celebrations of oppression, elevating the racially female voice into a metaphor for 'the good' " (758–59).

Critics such as Elizabeth Abel argue, "If we produce our readings cautiously and locate them in self-conscious and self-critical relation, [we are] thereby expanding the possibilities of dialogue across as well as about racial boundaries" (498). Gayatri Spivak recently moved the responsibility of voicing non-Western identity back to those who have been subject to Western scrutiny: "The national artist in the Third World has a responsibility not to speak for the nation in response to a demand made for this craving for intercultural exchange" (1992, 798). Spivak locates the need for a speaking "feminist internationalist," granting, however, the ironies involved: "When we mobilize that secret ontic intimate knowledge, we lose it, but I see no other way" (803). In Spivak's schema, the Western critic becomes an Other and is, in effect, problematized.

Decolonizing the subject positionality of the critical power relationship is by no means a simple or straightforward task. It is an area fraught with issues of power relationships that cut across disciplines and deconstruct our most basic notions of identity. Critical discourse seems to be treading its wheels, mired in a muddy impasse that is well characterized by Spivak, who recognized, in 1987, that "the radical intellectual in the West is either caught in a deliberate choice of subalternity, granting to the oppressed either that very expressive subjectivity which s/he criticizes or, instead, a total unrepresentability" (1987, 209). Unfortunately, many women filmmakers have found their work deemed unrepresentable, to some extent because of this critical crisis of representation. The Sankofa Film and Video Collective responded to the silencing of neocolonial British black culture with its film *Passion of Remembrance* (1988). Martina Attile, a member of the collective, told an interviewer, "We couldn't deny our history, our knowledge" (Jackson and Rasenberger, 23). Describing the film community of "apprehension" in England as a "crisis," Attile's remarks could easily be applied to the academic environment. The collective "decided to use fiction because it opened up a space to fantasize about possibilities, even though we don't have answers" (Jackson and Rasenberger, 23).

The feminist critical community can learn from the example of this collective group and perhaps learn to pose more questions than answers. In doing so, perhaps we can adopt Linda Gordon's suggested strategy of "transformation of the difference slogan into a more relational, power-conscious, and subversive set of analytical premises and questions" (107). The task of cultural critic is not only centrally consumed with questioning "the politics of identity as given, but to show how all representations are constructed, for what purpose, by whom, and with what compliments" (Said, 314). Listening to the "subaltern" speak should be one of the main tenets of such a task, for if the subaltern is silenced, criticism as an "oppositional program may be compromised before the pact, and there will be no purposeful intervention as such within the cultural matrix," as R. C. Davis has warned (40).

Unfortunately, listening to the subaltern, to the voice of the Third World woman filmmaker, is often nearly impossible because of the constraints of academe, the limited access and distribution of Third World cinema, and the lack of publications on, about, and authored by Third World women in cinema. In addition, the inherent hegemonic presumptions of reading texts from "Other" worlds have been based on the notions of fixed identity and fixed historicity. As Yuejin Wang demonstrates, when "historical flux is acknowledged, the notion of cultural identity loses its fixity," and "the very paradigm of the self versus Other has to be reversed" (32). For Homi K. Bhabha, the latter is by no means simple or even operational, for "the term 'critical theory,' often untheorized and unargued, was definitely the Other" (111). Bhabha's comments concerning an academic film conference and the Western logocentrism of criticism reiterate common problematics of film criticism:

What is at stake in the naming of critical theory as "Western"? It is obviously a designation of institutional power and ideological Eurocentricity. Critical theory often engages with Third World within the familiar traditions and conditions of colonial anthropology either to "universalize" their meaning within its own cultural and academic discourse, or to sharpen its internal critique of the Western logocentric sign, the idealist "subject," or indeed the illusion and delusion of civil society. (123)

Critical approaches to Third World women's cinema, if one can even speak of such a category, are then located on the grid of intelligibility that is mired in Eurocentric power struggles of meaning and sign ownership. Even poststructural and postmodern approaches have been recently characterized as "metanarratives" that "threaten to treat ex-colonial peoples as bounded units, cut off from their historical contexts" (Coronil, 103). If "the concept 'woman' effaces the difference between women in specific socio-historical contexts, between women defined precisely as historical subjects rather than a psychic subject" (hooks, 124), how can one speak of "women's" cinema, much less Third World cinema? I agree with Trinh T. Minh-ha's statement, "The claim of identity is often a strategic claim" (157), and I am drawn to her own claim that

I make a distinction between an alienating notion of Otherness (The Other of man, the Other of the West) and an empowering notion of difference. As long as Difference is not given to us, the coast is clear. (185)

Sri Lankan filmmaker Laleen Jayamanne speaks of filmmaking itself as an interventionist strategy against Western subjugation/signification:

This is where filmmakers can intervene, the conditions for the rapid transformation of the culture are there, *Adynata,* a kind of pastiche of images of Orientalism, [is] meant as a condemnation of a certain Western or colonial gaze. . . . In fact Edward Said's *Orientalism* helped trigger the project. (Trinh T. Minh-ha, 249–50)

The critical testimony and the films of women such as Laleen Jayamanne and Trinh T. Minh-ha exemplify a site in which one can locate the speaking subalternity of a deobjectified postcolonial tongue/camera. We may well be better serving the needs of the critical questions of postcolonialism by assuming the subject position of the listener, rather than the dominant position of the gazer/criticizer, when we are listening to the Third World woman filmmaker. As Fernando Coronil suggests, perhaps this "practice of listening may support practices of decolonialization outside and within academia" (106). Subaltern cinema is not unlike the Subaltern Studies collective, which Spivak locates as oppositionally involved in "bringing hegemonic historiography to crisis" (1987, 198).

Like the Subaltern Studies collective, Trinh T. Minh-ha has come under attack for her desire to articulate identity within a critical discursive practice, most recently by Sara Suleri, who disagrees with many of the presumptions of Trinh T. Minh-ha. Suleri deems Trinh's "radical subjectivity" as "low grade romanticism" (761). For Suleri, the critical repositioning of the "radical body in the absence of historical context" is a "hidden and unnecessary desire to resuscitate the 'self' " (762). Suleri cautions against the dangers of divisive binarisms within feminist discourse, maintaining that the "category" of the Third World woman is as nascent and politically charged as "woman" herself. This political tension is evident in Judith Mayne's study of Trinh T. Minh-ha and Laleen Jayamanne's films. Mayne notes a discomfort with the category of Third World women's cinema, as it lays a "burden of the demonstration of cultural difference" (1990, 222), on the filmmaker. Nevertheless, Mayne points out that it is perhaps equally problematic to categorize Minh-ha [Trinh] and Jayamanne's films in a tradition of women's cinema, as this risks "the flattening out of difference" (1990, 221). Ironically, the cinematic approach to the body of the Third World woman in films by Trinh T. Minh-ha is the hallmark of what many feminists consider to be opening up the discursive knowledge of selves in Third World cinema.

Feminist criticism must continue to allow for violently opposing viewpoints, because, as Chandra Talpade Mohanty stresses, "however sophisticated or problematical its use as an explanatory construct, colonization almost invariably implies a relation of structural domination, and a suppression—often violent—of the heterogeneity of the subject(s) in question" (336). It would hardly be useful or prescient to suppress postmodern approaches of Third World women's cinema, especially to position a monologic feminist Third World definition of self. That the debate has been so rigorous reflects a continuing interest in defining the self, which, as Sidonie Smith and Julia Watson note, is central to Western meaning: "The politics of this 'I' have been the politics of centripetal consolidation and centrifugal domination" (xvii). The outlaw subaltern cinema of Trinh T. Minh-ha, like the work of much Third World women's cinema, is involved in a struggle similar to that of the postcolonial woman writer; as " 'illegitimate' speakers [they] have a way of exposing the instability of forms" (Smith and Watson, xx).

Turning again to the interview with Ana Carolina, I can hear a voice breaking the stability intrinsic to the Western form of interview, a disruption of the subject/object relation the Western interviewer, as well as a pronounced renunciation of Western feminism in many of the statements made by Ana Carolina. While the reviewer states, "It does not seem that Ana Carolina knows exactly what she wants to express in the film" (Hartog, 73), Carolina states in another interview, "What I want to say is in my films, not in my interviews" (Hartog, 75). In the passage that I previously used, Carolina "explains" the sexuality of her film *Mar de rosas* (1985) to Western reviewers. She is obviously hampered by the Westerner's inability to grasp her explanation, and she underscores her frustration with the interview process with the statement, "I don't know if that's the answer you wanted."

Carolina explains that her fiction film *Mar de rosas* was originally intended as a documentary. She then expresses disgust for the fiction form: "I had been ashamed to produce fiction, to imagine lies. More than anything else, fiction is a big lie, or a great truth, but it was very difficult for me to go that way" (Hartog, 65). Ana Carolina's remarks seem designed to decenter Western expectations. The interviewer describes her camera work as "icy and deliberately distant, reflexive" (74). This visual style explores the realm of Western subject/object relations theory in a manner similar to her testimony. As a filmmaker and speaker, Ana Carolina resists assimilation as Other. Western feminists "have much to learn from postcolonial critics such as Spivak and Ngugi [and Carolina] who have had to struggle against their own subject positions in order to speak through the historical contradictions that constrain their discourses" (McGee, 171).

Feminists cannot, as McGee warns, simply resort to "speaking for others or insisting that others speak for themselves" (124). The subaltern speaker is challenged by the limits of subjectivity and inclusivity. Sarah Maldoror, an African filmmaker, delineates her mutable status as Other:

I feel at home wherever I am. I am from everywhere and from nowhere. My ancestors were slaves. In my case it may sometimes be difficult to define myself. The West Indians blame me for not having lived in the West Indies, the Africans say I was not born in Africa and the French blame me for not being like them. (Pfaff, 205)

Maldoror is placed in the subject position when asked about *Sambizanga* (1972), a film about the events that led up to an armed uprising in Angola against Portuguese authorities. Maldoror explains why the film has so little on-screen violence:

Sambizanga is by no means a war film as, for instance, American cinema would regard it. The film intends to describe a real story which occurred in the 1960s at the beginning of anti-colonial resistance in Angola. I show how people try to organize a resistance movement. (Pfaff, 211)

Hong-Kong-based filmmaker Ann Hui is treated to the same Western "grilling" by the critics at Cannes, after a screening of *Boat People* (1984), as reported by interviewer Karen Jaehne. Jaehne states that the Cannes critical discussions "revolved indecisively around [the film's] reception in America" (16), in a demonstration of the "theoretical truism that works by inspiring in the colonized subject the desire to assume the identity of his or her colonizers" (Silverman, 299). Amazingly, Hui found herself in the (subject) position of trying to defend the amount of on-screen violence in the film. Hui responds that, in her view, "the violence was in fact restrained," adding, "when I showed the film to some of the refugees I knew, they asked me just the opposite question—why I had not shown some of the dreadful violence" (Jaehne, 17). Hui's "grilling" demonstrates a case in point that Trinh T. Minh-ha has expounded upon: "[E]very time you hear similar reactions to your films, you are bound to realize how small the limits and the territory remain in which you are allowed to work" (164). Eurocentric critical attacks on non-Western works, as in the case of *Boat People*, typify cases of "subject deprivation of the female" as described by Spivak (1987, 218). Western interviewers and critics all too easily subject the subaltern filmmaker to questions based on Western pre(assumptions).

Aparna Sen and Prema Karanth, two Indian film directors, exemplify the struggle to speak from a subaltern position on themes such as sexuality and the sanctity of marriage. As Barbara Quart demonstrates, Aparna Sen's *36 Chowringhee Lane* (1981) "can be seen as quite daring in an Indian context, for taking on the plight of an Anglo-Indian as its central subject; for its sexuality in an Indian cinema" (250). Suspended between indigenous and postcolonialized culture, the main character in Sen's *36 Chowringhee Lane* explores the subaltern status of the "no-man's land" of the Anglo-Indian figure. Prema Karanth's *Phaniyamma* is perhaps more directly involved, as Quart suggests, in "all the ways women have been buried, have been turned into selfless helpers in their various captivities in different cultures" (252). Quart's analysis avoids speaking for the subaltern, yet, to some extent, Quart's study reminds us of the subaltern status of non-Western women in film. Quart's chapter on Third World women filmmakers is one of the only available sources on non-Western women directors. (Annette Kuhn and Susannah Radstone's *The Women's Companion to International Film* also provides a great deal of information on the subject.) Nevertheless, the non-Western woman filmmaker is more often than not able to transgress gender and class stratification.

Women in Third World cinema are subject to Western generalizations, and their enunciations often seem designed to circumvent Western subjugation. In looking back at the Westerner as subject, the subaltern disrupts feminist and postcolonial discourse. As Sarah Maldoror told Sylvia Harvey, "I'm no adherent to the concept of the 'Third World.' I make films so that people—no matter what race or color they are—can understand them. For me there are only exploiters and the exploited, that's all. To make a film means to take a position" (73). Maldoror's comments seek to deconstruct and transform liberational struggles across the global discourses of gender, race, and class through self-representation. Christine Choy, who filmed *Who Killed Vincent Chin?* (1989), seems equally eager to dismiss an Othered categorization:

I always get classified as either one category or another: It started with "immigrant," later on I became an "Asian," later on I became a "woman of color," or "minority" and [the list] goes on and on and on . . . so many labels. (Hanson, 17)

Who Killed Vincent Chin? concerned the lenient sentencing of the convicted white murderers of a Chinese man who was a victim of an infamous hate crime in New York City. Choy's film attacks Western ignorance and culturally sanctioned racism. "Sanctioned ignorance," according to Spivak, "is inseparable from colonial domination" (1987, 199). Choy sanctions neither ignorance of Eurocentric racism nor the discursive power relations involved in naming the Asian-American woman as Other.

The politics of self-definition extends beyond the discourse of the Third World woman filmmaker to the discourse of all women filmmakers. Barbara Hammer disrupts expectations with her complaint, for example, that "I was becoming known as a lesbian filmmaker. Although I thought of myself as a film artist, I wasn't being seen that way" (37, 38). Similarly, Agnieszka Holland feels herself in the grip of a political "blackmail," in which "the thing that is most annoying is that you [as a Polish woman director] are condemned to be political" (Brunette, 17). Sally Potter has felt constrained by the limits of a patriarchal and colonialist film industry in which "women are generally 'allowed' to make the smaller kind of women's issue documentary film," and she sees her goal as disrupting those limitations (Cook, 29). Potter, it should be noted, has succeeded admirably in abrogating these artificial constraints with her most recent film, the highly successful crossover hit *Orlando* (1993).

New Zealand-born Jane Campion, director of *Sweetie* (1989), *An Angel at My Table* (1991), and, most recently, *The Piano* (1993), told Maitland McDonagh, "Anything and everything interests me, especially what I'm told not to look at" (22). Boundaries set out in Western conventions and criticism continue to be crossed by women filmmakers. For example, in an interview with Scott MacDonald, Yvonne Rainer expresses amazement at an audience member's negative response to her experimental work (*Privilege*, 1991). The response concretizes the artistic limitations that permeate

Western culture. "Why are you so committed to depriving the audience of pleasure?" Rainer was asked. "I always thought I was introducing *new* pleasures," she responded (26).

African-American director Alile Sharon Larkin expresses anger at what she sees as a movement that compels black women artists to "speak in a voice that is not really our own" (158). Larkin, not only a self-described "Black woman filmmaker" but an academic as well, repositions herself as an individual within a larger postcolonial movement:

[M]y objective is to contribute to the development of our own definitions. My objectives are ultimately no different from that of many Black male film-makers. Yet I find that my "gender-consciousness" is being defined by feminists within Western culture in the same way that my Blackness has been defined by that dominant culture. (158)

Larkin demonstrates that the crisis of representation in academic discourse is a complex, politically charged agenda. Toni Morrison, however, discourages "totalizing approaches to African-American scholarship which has no drive other than the exchange of domination-dominant Eurocentric scholarship replaced by dominant Afrocentric scholarship" (8). More interesting to Morrison and perhaps more pertinent is the underlying question, "[W]hat makes intellectual domination possible, how knowledge is transformed from invasion and conquest to revelation and choice; what ignites and informs the literary imagination, and what forces help establish the parameters of criticism" (Morrison, 8). Juxtaposing Larkin and Morrison, we have, then, not critical polarities at opposite ends of a spectrum but a heterogeneity of feminist approaches to colonialist hegemonies.

Speaking for/about an/other will be, and should continue to be, fraught with difficulties, enigmas, crises in representation, and fractures, because, as R. C. Davis notes:

The power to control the positions of speech and of what can be said—as Edward W. Said has said about authority in general and as Cixous and Spivak demonstrate about patriarchal authority specifically—"must be analyzed" before any effective social critique can take place. (41)

Cross-cultural readings in film are, as E. Ann Kaplan notes, "fraught with dangers," not only for the preceding reasons, but because film studies are often particularly rooted in psychoanalytic methodology. As Kaplan notes, "[U]ntil we know more about the unconscious of different cultures as it might pertain to the level of the imaginary" (40), how is the film critic to "read" the gaze formed outside Western subject-object relation? How can a Western Other presume to know anything about the psychology of a non-Western individual? Kaja Silverman notes that in the field of "symbolic and imaginary identification" image production, "specific positions from which we live on desire have important extra-psychic ramifications, as do the images through which we acquire our fictive selves" (337).

White feminists have much to learn from the speaking subaltern; we must learn how to listen more than we postulate. We can take responsibility, like Diane Bell, by not speaking for the Other but instead by "provid[ing] a basis on which cross-cultural understanding may be built, to locate issues of gender and race within a wider perspective, to offer an analysis of social change" (23). In adapting ourselves to the task, we might well listen to the voices of outlaw women in cinema such as Trinh T. Minh-ha:

The precarious line we walk on is one that allows us to challenge the West as the authoritative subject of feminist knowledge, while also resisting the terms of binarist discourse that would concede feminism to the West all over again. (153)

To address these many critical, historical, and cultural concerns in creating *Women Film Directors,* I have spent the past five years combing through reference materials and screening films, many of them by Third World, Eastern European, lesbian, and Native American filmmakers, to create a reference book that will include as many women filmmakers as possible and stress the works of those whom conventional cinema history has previously marginalized. *Women Film Directors* will serve as a reference book that is the first of its kind, not a study of one aspect of women as filmmakers, but a dictionary of women filmmakers, working in film to create new feminist visions of beauty and transcendent power.

In researching this volume, I searched through many existing research materials and then went beyond them, to primary sources such as interviews with individual filmmakers, to lists of films by women from the early 1900s that have seemingly been forgotten, to microfilm records of old and obscure journals, as well as the current literature available on lesbian, Third World, and multiracial directors. To make certain that I achieved a certain balance in this study, I read a great deal of film criticism and theory, which has become an integral part of this volume, in addition to viewing and studying an enormous number of films by women from different countries, races, and eras. I sought out both mainstream and marginalized works and incorporated them into this study, making this volume as comprehensive as possible.

Thus, *Women Film Directors* emerges as a critical dictionary created on these important film artists that lists numerous important (and overlooked) women filmmakers, with birth and death dates, selected filmographies, bibliographies, and detailed critical commentary. In one volume, the researcher will be able to find a general entry on most women directors; a reference guide that will direct the researcher to other materials on the directors, and a biographical overview of the directors' lives and work. One of my guiding principles in this book has been to make all of this material available in one text, rather than remain scattered in numerous volumes. I have no doubt that many more women directors remain historically undiscovered and I sincerely hope that this book will further the recovery project.

The source materials were, in many cases, scattered in a variety of archives both in the United States and abroad, particularly in London and Paris, and I have made research trips over the past several years to look through various private and public collections, such as the Cinémathèque Française, the Gaumont Archive, and the British Film Institute, as well as the National Archives in Washington, D.C. I have corresponded with many private collectors, sought out reference materials through interlibrary loan, dealt with distributors, and obtained preview cassettes of works by women filmmakers that are usually ignored in most mainstream critical studies, in an effort to make my work as all-encompassing as possible. I have been doing this research since 1985, so this book has been a long time in the making.

Indeed, as a filmmaker myself, I have been interested in women in film for many years, and I feel that this book is the logical culmination of my long-held interest in this area, as evidenced by the production of my hour-long documentary on pioneer women filmmakers, *Women Who Made the Movies* (1991), distributed by Women Make Movies, New York. Whether working in the industry or making films with the aid of grants and personal financial subsidies, the women showcased here have helped to shape the world of film as we know it today. Some feminist film practitioners see themselves as harbingers of change, instructional forces, barometers of social reintegration; other women see themselves as workers within a tradition that they attempt to subvert from within. The immense contribution made by these women is a legacy rich in personal insight, hard work, careful study, and, often, sacrifice. This book, "a thinking back through our mothers," is a testament to the work women directors have accomplished, often in the face of adversity, and to the continuing voice of women as a force for change and enlightenment within the cinema today.

REFERENCES

Abel, Elizabeth. "Black Writing, White Reading: Race and the Politics of Feminist Interpretation." *Critical Inquiry* 19.3 (spring 1993): 470–98.

Acker, Ally. *Reel Women: Pioneers of the Cinema, 1896 to the Present.* New York: Continuum, 1993.

Bell, Diane. "Aboriginal Women, Separate Places, and Feminism." In *A Reader in Feminist Knowledge,* edited by Sneja Gunew, 13–26. New York: Routledge, 1991.

Bhabha, Homi K. "The Commitment to Theory." In *Questions of Third Cinema,* edited by Jim Pines and Paul Willemen, 111–32. London: BFI, 1989.

Brunette, Peter. "Lessons from the Past: An Interview with Agnieszka Holland." *Cineaste* 15.1 (1986): 15–18.

Bruno, Giuliana. *Streetwalking on a Ruined Map: Cultural Theory and the City Films of Elvira Notari.* Princeton: Princeton University Press, 1993.

Carson, Diane, Linda Dittmar, and Janice R. Welsch, eds. *Multiple Voices in Feminist Film Criticism.* Minneapolis: University of Minnesota Press, 1994.

Cook, Pam. "*The Gold Diggers:* Interview with Sally Potter." *Framework* 24 (spring 1984): 12–31.

———, and Philip Dodd, eds. *Women and Film: A Sight and Sound Reader.* Philadelphia: Temple University Press, 1993.

Coronil, Fernando. "Can Postcoloniality Be Decolonized? Imperial Banality and Postcolonial Power." *Public Culture* 5.1 (fall 1992): 89–108.

Davis, R. C. "Cixous, Spivak, and Oppositional Theory." *Literature Interpretation Theory* 4.1 (1992): 29–42.

Dean, Mary, and Theresa Leiniger, eds., *The Harlem Renaissance from A to Z.* New York: Facts on File, forthcoming.

De Lauretis, Teresa. *Alice Doesn't: Feminism, Semiotics, Cinema.* Bloomington: Indiana University Press, 1984.

Doane, Mary Ann. *The Desire to Desire.* Bloomington: Indiana University Press, 1987.

———. *Femmes Fatales: Feminism, Film Theory, Psychoanalysis.* New York: Routledge, 1991.

Dollimore, Jonathan. *Sexual Dissidence: Augustine to Wilde, Freud to Foucault.* Oxford: Oxford University Press, 1991.

Flitterman-Lewis, Sandy. *To Desire Differently: Feminism and the French Cinema.* Urbana: University of Illinois Press, 1990.

Gibson-Hudson, Gloria. "Aspects of Black Feminist Cultural Ideology in Films by Black Women Independent Artists." In *Multiple Voices in Feminist Film Criticism,* edited by Diane Carson, Linda Dittmar, and Janice Welsch, pp. 365–379. Minneapolis: University of Missouri Press, 1994.

Gordon, Linda. "On 'Difference.' " *Genders* 10 (spring 1991): 91–111.

Hammer, Barbara. "Barbara Hammer Interviewed by Yann Beauvais." *Spiral* 6 (January 1986): 33–38.

Hanson, Peter. "NYU Professor's Journey into Film." *Washington Square News,* March 29, 1989, 5, 10, 17, 18.

Hartog, Simon. "Ana Carolina Teixeira Soares." *Framework* 28 (1985): 64–77.

Harvey, Sylvia. "Third World Perspectives: Focus on Sarah Maldoror." *Women and Film* 1.5–6 (1974): 71–75.

Heck-Rabi, Louise. *Women Filmmakers: A Critical Reception.* Metuchen, NJ: Scarecrow Press, 1984.

hooks, bell. *Black Looks: Race and Representation.* Boston: South End Press, 1992.

Jackson, Lynne, and Jean Rasenberger. "The Passion of Remembrance: An Interview with Martina Attile and Isaac Julien." *Cineaste* 14.4 (1988): 23–37.

Jaehne, Karen. "Boat People: An Interview with Ann Hui." *Cineaste* 13.2 (1984): 16–19.

Johnston, Claire. "Women's Cinema as Counter-Cinema." *Notes on Women's Cinema: Screen Pamphlet No. 2* (1974): 24–31.

Kaplan, E. Ann. "Problematizing Cross-Cultural Analysis: The Case of Women in the Recent Chinese Cinema." *Wide Angle* 11.2 (May 1989): 40–50.

———, ed. *Psychoanalysis and Cinema.* New York: Routledge, 1990.

Kuhn, Annette, and Susannah Radstone, eds. *The Women's Companion to International Film*. Berkeley: University of California Press, 1994.

Larkin, Alile Sharon. "Black Women Film-Makers Defining Ourselves: Feminism in Our Own Voice." In *Female Spectators: Looking at Film and Television*, edited by E. Deidre Pribram, 157–73. London: Verso, 1988.

MacDonald, Scott. "Yvonne Rainer with Scott MacDonald." *Film Quarterly* 45.1 (fall 1991): 25–32.

Mayne, Judith. *Loving with a Vengeance: Mass-Produced Fantasies for Women*. New York: Methuen, 1982.

———. *The Woman at the Keyhole: Feminism and Women's Cinema*. Bloomington: Indiana University Press, 1990.

McDonagh, Maitland. "Jane Campion's 'Angel' Is Another Quirky Soul." *New York Times,* May 19, 1991, 22.

McGee, Patrick. *Telling the Other: The Question of Value in Modern and Postcolonial Writing*. Ithaca: Cornell University Press, 1992.

Mohanty, Chandra Talpade. "Under Western Eyes: Feminist Scholarship and Colonial Discourses." *Boundary* 2.12 (1984): 336.

Morrison, Toni. *Playing in the Dark: Whiteness and the Literary Imagination*. Cambridge: Harvard University Press, 1992.

Mulvey, Laura. "Visual Pleasure and Narrative Cinema." *Screen* 16.3 (autumn 1975): 6–18.

———. "Afterthoughts on 'Visual Pleasure and the Narrative Cinema' Inspired by *Duel in the Sun*." *Framework* 15–17 (1981): 12–15.

Pfaff, Francoise. *Twenty-Five Black African Filmmakers*. New York: Greenwood Press, 1988.

Pribram, E. Deidre, ed. *Female Spectators: Looking at Film and Television*. London: Verso, 1988.

Quart, Barbara Koenig. *Women Directors: The Emergence of a New Cinema*. New York: Praeger, 1988.

Said, Edward W. *Culture and Imperialism*. New York: Knopf, 1993.

Silverman, Kaja. *Male Subjectivity at the Margins*. New York: Routledge, 1992.

Slide, Anthony. *Early Women Directors*. New York: Da Capo, 1984.

Smith, Sidonie, and Julia Watson, eds. Introduction, "De/Colonization and the Politics of Discourse in Women's Autobiographical Practices. In *De/Colonizing the Subject: The Politics of Gender in Women's Autobiography,* xi–xxvii. Minneapolis: University of Minnesota Press, 1992.

Spivak, Gayatri Chakravorty. *In Other Worlds: Essays in Cultural Politics*. New York: Methuen, 1987.

———. "Can the Subaltern Speak? In *Marxism and the Interpretation of Culture,* edited by Cary Nelson and Lawrence Grossberg, 271–316. Chicago: University of Illinois Press, 1988.

———. "Acting Bits/Identity Talk." *Critical Inquiry* 18.4 (summer 1992): 770–803.

Suleri, Sara. "Woman Skin Deep: Feminism and the Postcolonial Condition." *Critical Inquiry* 18.4 (summer 1992): 756–69.

Thompson, Felix. "Metaphors of Space: Polarization, Dualism and Third World Cinema." *Screen* 34.1 (spring 1993): 38–53.

Todd, Janet, ed. *Women and Film*. New York: Holmes and Meier, 1988.

Trinh T. Minh-ha. *The Framer Framed*. New York: Routledge, 1992.

Vincendeau, Ginette. "Like Eating a Lot of Madeleines: An Interview with Diane Kurys." *Monthly Film Bulletin* 58.686 (March 1991): 69–70.

Weiss, Andrea. *Vampires and Violets: Lesbians in Film*. New York: Penguin, 1993.

Wilson, Margery. *I Found My Way: An Autobiography*. Philadelphia: Lippincott, 1956.

Yuejin Wang. "The Cinematic Other and the Cultural Self? De-centering the Cultural Identity on Cinema." *Wide Angle* 11.2 (May 1989): 32–39.

A

ABREU, GILDA DE (1904–79). Brazil. Gilda de Abreu is one of the few women filmmakers to receive credit for her work as director in the early Brazilian cinema. It is quite probable that many more women worked in the capacity of director in early cinema but went uncredited because their attributions were marginalized in Brazilian cinema, in much the same manner as they were in mainstream Hollywood filmmaking. Delineating women's presence in early film is complicated by the fact that early Brazilian cinema was a "domestic undertaking," as noted by historians Elice Munerato and Maria Elena Darcy de Oliveira (35). Often the husband was the director, the wife and children actors, but certainly the wife was often the uncredited codirector or even the primary director of the project.

Breaking the mold of the "domestic" hierarchy of filmmaking, Gilda de Abreu moved easily in and out of her role as actress to director and writer. Like Carmen Santos, another early Brazilian woman actress turned director, Gilda de Abreu met with difficulties earning respect from the technical crews. Both wore slacks in order to play down their femininity and mark their authority on the set. Both formed their own distribution companies and therefore wrested more control over their efforts as actors and directors. Carmen Santos, who made films as early as 1916, began Brasil Vita Filme in 1932 in Rio de Janeiro and continued to direct and produce through the 1940s. Gilda de Abreu, who sang operettas in addition to her other talents, formed the distribution company Pro Arte in 1951.

Gilda de Abreu and her husband, Vicente Celestino, were well known in theater, radio, and cinema. *O ébrio* (*The Drunkard*) marks the first directorial credit of Gilda de Abreu. Nissa Torrents deems the film "one of Brazil's most popular films ever" (2). *O ébrio* is adapted from a play written by Abreu's husband. A 1946 box-office success, *O ébrio* was an enormous achievement for Abreu. Despite the film's success, Gilda de Abreu remains unknown to most cinema historians. In 1951, Abreu directed *Coração de madre* (*A Mother's Heart*), a film in which she acted as well as directed. Though she abandoned filmmaking, perhaps because of the on-set difficulties, Gilda de Abreu continued to be active as a screenwriter and novelist. As late as 1973, Abreu adapted one of her plays, *Mestica,* for a woman director, Lenita Perroy.

Gilda de Abreu marks the beginning of a growing tradition of Brazilian women directors. Not until the 1970s, however, did the number of feature films directed by women rise remarkably. Women directors such as Ana Carolina and Maria do Rosário owe a debt to the early women directors such as Carmen Santos and Gilda de Abreu, who modeled themselves as actresses, turned producer/directors.

SELECTED FILMOGRAPHY

O ébrio (The Drunkard) (1946)
Coração de madre (A Mother's Heart) (1951)

SELECTED BIBLIOGRAPHY

Burton, Julianne, ed. *Cinema and Social Change in Latin America.* Pittsburgh: University of Pittsburgh Press, 1990.

Freydberg, Elizabeth Hadley. "Women of Color: No Joy in the Seduction of Images." In *Multiple Voices in Feminist Film Criticism,* edited by Diane Carson, Linda Dittmar, and Janice Welsch, 468–80. Minneapolis: University of Minnesota Press, 1994.

Fusco, Coco, ed. *Reviewing Histories: Selections from New Latin American Cinema.* New York: Hallwalls, 1987.

Lawrence, Amy. "Women's Voices in Third World Cinema." In *Multiple Voices in Feminist Film Criticism,* edited by Diane Carson, Linda Dittmar, and Janice Welsch, 406–20. Minneapolis: University of Minnesota Press, 1994.

Lesage, Julia. "Latin American Women in Film and Video." In *Multiple Voices in Feminist Film Criticism,* edited by Diane Carson, Linda Dittmar, and Janice Welsch, 499–502. Minneapolis: University of Minnesota Press, 1994.

Munerato, Elice, and Maria Elena Darcy de Oliveira. "When Women Film." In *Brazilian Cinema,* edited by Randal Johnson and Robert Stam, 34–44. Rutherford, NJ: Fairleigh Dickinson University Press, 1982.

Paranagua, Paulo Antonio. *Le Cinéma brésilien.* Paris: Centre Georges Pompidou, 1987.

Pick, Zazuna, ed. *Latin American Filmmakers and the Third Cinema.* Ottowa: Carleton University, 1978.

Torrents, Nissa. "Abreu, Gilda de." In *The Women's Companion to International Film,* edited by Annette Kuhn with Susannah Radstone, 2–3. Berkeley: University of California Press, 1994.

AHRNE, MARIANNE (1940–). Sweden. Born in Sweden in 1940, Marianne Ahrne earned her B.A. at the University of Lund in 1966 and entered the Stockholm Film School the following year. Ahrne was primarily interested in acting and devoted her studies to the art form. As an actress, Ahrne was involved in the Théâtre des Carmes in Avignon, France, as well as the Odinteatret experimental theater in Denmark. Like many Swedish women directors of the 1970s, Ahrne began her film directing career as a documentarist working for Swedish and Italian television.

The rise of women directors in Sweden is directly attributable to the foundation of the Swedish Film Institute in 1963. Until this time, Swedish film was largely a system of apprenticeship that encouraged a patriarchal dominance. The establishment of the film institute broke this pattern and allowed women an opportunity to break into documentary and feature film production. Marianne Ahrne was one of the first women to move into documentary production in Sweden.

Though Ahrne's oeuvre is diverse, some of her films are notable for their specific attention to women's issues. *Abortproblem i Frankrike (Abortion Problems in France)* (1971) is a case in point. Though Ahrne dislikes the tendency to "categorize all films made by women according to the gender of the director" (Soila), her films are remarkably feminist in agenda. In 1974, Ahrne collaborated with Simone de Beauvoir on *Promenad i de gamlas land (Promenade in the Land of the Aged)*.

In addition to her documentary films, Marianne Ahrne directed many fantasy films in narrative form. Her interest in legend is marked by her vampire films: *Den sista riddarvampyren (The Last Knight Vampire)* (1972) and *Storstadsvampyrer (Big-City Vampires)* (1972). A young woman's story is infused in the fantasy narrative of *Drakar, drümmar och en flicka från verkligheten (Dragons, Dreams—and a Girl from Reality)* (1974). Unfortunately, Marianne Ahrne's films have received little attention or distribution in the United States. Within Sweden, however, women filmmakers have had astounding success and leadership roles in the cinema.

SELECTED FILMOGRAPHY

Balladen om Therese (The Ballad of Therese) (1970)
Illusionernäs Natt (Palace of Illusions) (1970)
Ferai (1970)
Få mig att skratta (Make Me Laugh) (1971)
Abortproblem i Frankrike (Abortion Problems in France) (1971)
Skilsmässoproblem i italien (Divorce Problems in Italy) (1971)
Den sista riddarvampyren (The Last Knight Vampire) (1972)
Storstadsvampyer (Big-City Vampires) (1972)
Camargue, det forlorade landet (Camargue—The Lost Country) (1972)
Drakar, drümmar och en flicka från verkligheten (Dragons, Dreams—and a Girl from Reality (1974)
Promenad i de gamlas land (Promenade in the Land of the Aged) (1974)
Fem dagar in Falköping (Five Days in Falköping) (1975)
Långt borta och nära (Near and Far Away) (1976)

Frihetens murar (*Roots of Grief*) (1978)
På liv och död (*A Matter of Life and Death*) (1986)

SELECTED BIBLIOGRAPHY

McIlroy, Brian. *World Cinema 2: Sweden*. London: Flicks Books, 1986.
Soila, Tytti. "Ahrne, Marianne." In *The Women's Companion to International Film*, edited by Annette Kuhn, with Susannah Radstone, 8. Berkeley: University of California Press, 1994.

AKERMAN, CHANTAL (1950–   ). Belgium. Chantal Akerman came to the United States after quitting film school in Belgium. Her first job was as a cashier for a pornography exhibitor on 55th Street in New York City. Claiming that she was profoundly influenced by Jean-Luc Godard's *Pierrot le Fou* (1965), Akerman was so determined to make films that she claims to have stolen the money to finance her early short film, *Hotel Monterey* (1972). She established her style even in these early efforts. In *Hotel Monterey*, for example, people move in and out of the frame of a stationary camera. Already, Akerman expresses an interest in the transient nature of modern urban life, with an emphatic eye toward spaces that underscore the discord of mobility, hotels, train stations, and the people who move within these spaces.

Je, tu, il, elle (1974) is Akerman's breakthrough feature-length film. The camera follows a woman, played by Akerman herself, who seems lost in a modern industrial world. The scene of this woman, naked and alone, eating sugar desperately, is remarkable for its intensity. The woman next hitchhikes and sexually seduces a truck driver. Feminist critics have spent many pages scrutinizing this scene, sometimes missing the humor inherent in such a treatment of sexuality. Next, the woman makes love to another woman in a highly charged sequence which attracted a great deal of attention from feminist critics. Because the camera records the action in a scientific manner, the scene has often been noted for its self-conscious display of dehumanization and lack of visual pleasure.

But, as Andrea Weiss points out, in *Vampires and Violets: Lesbians in Film*, this "absolutely uneroticized lesbian lovemaking scene must be credited for its courage in 1974, especially given that it includes the filmmaker in the scene and rejects art cinema conventions governing lesbian sexuality" (114). The camera positioning is specifically meant to deaestheticize the on-screen lovemaking, by making us aware of our offscreen voyeurism. The naturalistic use of sound also underscores the scene's break from Hollywood and art-house depictions of sexuality. However, not all critics have found the scene to be without eroticism. I find the scene to be more erotic than conventionally constructed sex scenes because of Akerman's embrace of natural sound and image and because of the tension that develops in watching such a radically different approach to the sexual body, in much the same way I find pleasure in Andy Warhol films. As Judith Mayne notes, "[O]ne could hardly find a contemporary women's film more saturated with authorial signature than *Je, tu, il, elle*" (129). Perhaps the difficulty of the avant-garde representation of the female body makes this film so memorable. The fact that the main woman character is played by the film-maker herself tends to move the critic into a discussion of subjectivity beyond the realm of the cinema frame.

Female identity and subjectivity are at the center of the thematic core of *Jeanne Dielman* (1974), Akerman's film of routine daily activities of a Belgian housewife and prostitute. As Teresa de Lauretis argues, in *Jeanne Dielman*, "the narrative suspense is not built on the expectation of a 'significant event,' . . . but is produced by the real-time gestures as common and 'insignificant' as peeling potatoes, washing dishes, or making coffee . . . what the film constructs—formally and artfully, to be sure—is a picture of female experience" (131). The routine existence of Jeanne Dielman is punctuated by a scene in which the woman suddenly kills a client with a pair of scissors after having sex with him. The almost unendurable, long take of the woman sitting at a table for several minutes after the murder (doing absolutely nothing) discourages audience identification, even as it builds tension in the same way the sex scenes do in *Je, tu, il, elle*.

News from Home (1976) and *Les rendezvous d'Anna* (1978) exemplify Akerman's continual risk-taking anticinema. In *News from Home*, Akerman lets the camera stare at urban spaces while an offscreen narrator (Akerman) reads letters from a mother to an absent daughter. Akerman uses the monotony of the mother's voice to create discord and disharmony, rather than using narrative plots designed to artificially construct human dilemma. *News from Home* can be read as an astute commentary on the artificiality of mainstream cinematic narrative conventions. Similarly, *Les rendezvous d'Anna* uses sameness to create drama. In the film, the camera follows a woman filmmaker who travels through depeopled spaces—hotels, train stations, underground railways. The filmmaker meets a man desperate for companionship. Rather than conform to conventional narrative closure devices, the woman leaves the man.

Les rendezvous d'Anna can be identified for Akerman's signature long takes, avoidance of close-ups, naturalistic sound, lack of mainstream narrative, and self-inscription as woman director. Sexual encounters are unfulfilling, and the film encourages a cerebral audience identification, rather than a "pleasurable" passive audience experience. *Toute une Nuit* (1982) continues the theme of solitude as it follows the monotonous sexual encounters of one particular night, as is suggested in the film's title. Couples do *not* get together in *Toute une Nuit*. Marsha Kinder describes the challenges posed by *Toute une Nuit*:

By denying us a single unifying story, by frequently pitting word against visual image and non-verbal sound, by discouraging us from identifying with any of the anonymous characters, by denying us a single unified subject position, . . . *Toute une Nuit* makes us change the way we read a film. (16)

Akerman's more recent film, *Night and Day* (1991), departs significantly in style from these earlier films. The film is much more commercially oriented and narratively constructed. The film centers around the life of Julie, a young woman who lives in Paris and who makes love to one man by night and another man by day. At the end of the film, Julie walks away from both lovers. The film is stunning in terms of cinematography and the use of color and framing. Critics have noted the lack of anger and intensity of *Night and Day,* in comparison with Akerman's earlier work. Nevertheless, *Night and Day* can be read as a significant feminist statement. The central protagonist explores her sexuality and simply walks away from the men without suffering, without even choosing one of the men. Akerman here regenders the love-triangle film in which a male hero chooses between traditionally binary opposites of good and bad women. Chantal Akerman's films will continue to challenge us with both their technique and their complex feminist discourse.

SELECTED FILMOGRAPHY

Saute ma ville (Blow up My Town) (1968)
L'enfant aimé (The Beloved Child, or I Play at Being a Married Woman) (1971)
La chambre 1 (1972)
Hotel Monterey (1972)
La chambre 2 (1972)
Le 15/8 (1973)
Hanging out–Yonkers (1973)
Je, tu, il, elle (1974)
Jeanne Dielman, 23 Quai du Commerce, 1080 Bruxelles (1974)
News from Home (1976)
Les rendezvous d'Anna (1978)
Dis-moi (Tell Me) (1980)
Toute une nuit (1982)
Les années 80 (The Eighties) (1983)
Un jour Pina m'a demandé (1983)
J'ai faim, j'ai froid (1984)
L'homme à la valise (The Man with the Suitcase) (1984)
Family Business, Une lettre de cinéaste (1985)
The Golden Eighties aka *Window Shopping* (1986)
American Stories (1988)
Night and Day (1991)
D'Est (1993)
Portrait of a Young Girl at the End of the 1960s in Brussels (1995)
Bordering on Fiction (video installation including *D'Est*) (1995)

SELECTED BIBLIOGRAPHY

Acker, Ally. *Reel Women: Pioneers of the Cinema, 1896 to the Present.* New York: Continuum, 1993.

Akerman, Chantal. "Contributions to the 400th Issue of *Cahiers du Cinema*." *Cahiers du Cinema* 400 (October 1987): 8.

de Lauretis, Teresa. *Technologies of Gender*. Bloomington: Indiana University Press, 1987.

Erens, Patricia, ed. *Feminist Film Criticism*. Bloomington: Indiana University Press, 1990.

Fischer, Lucy. "Shall We Dance? Feminist Cinema Remakes the Musical." *Film Criticism* 13.2 (winter 1989): 7–17.

Forbes, Jill. "Conservatory Blues/*Golden Eighties*." *Sight and Sound* 56.2 (spring 1987): 145.

Freidberg, Anne. "*Les Flâneurs du Mal*: Cinema and the Postmodern Condition." *PLMA* 106.3 (May 1991): 419–29.

Hayward, Susan, and Ginette Vincendeau, eds. *French Film: Texts and Contexts*. London: Routledge, 1990.

Hoberman, J. "All You Need Is Love." *Village Voice* (December 15, 1992): 53.

Kinder, Marsha. "The Subversive Potential of the Pseudo-Iterative." *Film Quarterly* 43.2 (winter 1989–1990): 2–23.

Kuhn, Annette. *Women's Pictures: Feminism and Cinema*. London: Routledge, 1982.

Martin, Angela. "Chantal Akerman's Films: Notes on Issues Raised for Feminism." In *Films for Women*, edited by Charlotte Brunsdon, 62–71. London: BFI, 1987.

Mayne, Judith. *The Woman at the Keyhole: Feminism and Women's Cinema*. Bloomington: Indiana University Press, 1990.

McRobbie, Angela. "Chantal Akerman and Feminist Filmaking." In *Women and Film: A Sight and Sound Reader*, edited by Pam Cook and Phillip Dodd, 198–203. Philadelphia: Temple University Press, 1993.

Oumano, Ellen. *Film Forum: Thirty-Five Top Filmmakers Discuss Their Craft*. New York: St. Martin's, 1985.

Rich, B. Ruby. "In the Name of Feminist Film Criticism." In *Multiple Voices in Feminist Film Criticism*, edited by Diane Carson, Linda Dittmar, and Janice Welsch, 27–47. Minneapolis: University of Minnesota Press, 1994.

Weiss, Andrea. *Vampires and Violets: Lesbians in Film*. New York: Penguin, 1993.

ALEMANN, CLAUDIA VON (1943–   ). Germany. Born in 1943 in West Germany, Claudia von Alemann studied sociology, art history, and film at the Ulm Institute in the 1960s. In 1973, she organized, with Helke Sander, another German woman filmmaker, the seminar on women's films in Berlin, an important, politically motivated initiative dedicated to the screening and appreciation of feminist films. As Julia Knight explains, the festival was important in that it "offered the first opportunity in Germany for women filmmakers to meet each other and discuss their work" (103). The festival made great inroads, yet women's films continued to receive little or negative attention from most mainstream critics. This led to the funding (by Helke Sander) of a feminist film journal, *Frauen und Film (Women and Film)*, in 1974. Among the films reviewed was Alemann's *Es kommt drauf* *an, sie zu verändern (The Point Is to Change It)* (1972–73). Like many of the films directed by women in Germany in this period, *The Point Is to Change It* directly addresses the social problem of women's exploitation in workplaces.

Not content to simply make films of commercial value, German women directors such as Claudia von Alemann make films that question mainstream depictions of women, and their work is often purposefully difficult and demanding for the reviewer. This is the case with *The Point Is to Change It,* which painstakingly documents the patriarchal devaluation of women's work. Women's role in the workforce, as we see in the film, is all too often misdocumented or altogether ignored. *The Point Is to Change It* is a barrage of factual information and mind-boggling statistics on women's devalued status in the public sphere. Very little takes place in the film; it is therefore an admittedly difficult film, but it is also an important feminist counterrepresentation that seeks to disrupt traditional approaches to the history of women as workers. As the title suggests, *The Point Is to Change It* is a manifesto calling for change and action.

Claudia von Alemann's films are distinctly political tracts that call for direct action. *The Women's Room* (1981) continues in that tradition. As an important figure in the New German Cinema, Alemann, like other women directors of the 1970s, frequently met with a refusal to acknowledge her existence as a filmmaker. Sexism in history making continued this affront. Alemann and other women directors were omitted from the first collections of interviews of directors of the New German Cinema (43) in a typical historical suppression of the contemporary voice of women in film. German women directors were effectively invisible in the history of New German Cinema, while male filmmakers such as Rainer Werner Fassbinder, Wim Wenders, and others became more and more internationally well known as the pioneers of the New German Cinema.

The suppression of women's role in the rise of the New German Cinema results in a misperception that women made few contributions to the formation of the aesthetics of the New German Cinema. This pattern of nonattribution conforms to the model of suppression of women's writing, as it is put forth by Joanna Russ in *How to Suppress Women's Writing.* Julia Knight's recent rereading of German film history moves toward rescuing and resuscitating suppressed knowledge of women directors' achievements, yet we in the West have an extraordinary problem involving ourselves in this struggle, because often the films by these talented, neglected women directors are difficult, if not impossible, to locate and screen. *The Point Is to Change It* was screened at the Ann Arbor Women's Film Festival in 1974.

SELECTED FILMOGRAPHY

Einfach (Simple) (1966)
Lustgewinn (Pleasure) (1967)
Fundevogel (Found Bird) (1967)

Das ist nur der Anfang—der Kampf geht weiter (It's Only the Beginning, the Struggle Goes On) (1969)
Brigitte (1970)
Algier (Algiers) (1970)
Kathleen und Eldridge Cleaver (Kathleen and Eldridge Cleaver) (1970)
Tu luc van doan—Aus eigner Kraft (Through One's Own Strength) (1971)
Es kommt drauf an, sie zu verändern (The Point Is to Change It) (1972–73)
Namibia (1973)
Filme der Sonne und der Nacht: Ariane Mnouchkine (Films of Sun and Night: Ariane Mnouchkine) (1977)
Reise nach Lyon (Blind Spot) (1980)
Das Frauenzimmer (The Women's Room) (1981)
Nebelland (Fogland) (1981–82)
Die Tür in der Mauer (The Door in the Wall) (1984)

SELECTED BIBLIOGRAPHY

Frieden, Sandra, Richard W. McCormick, Vibeke R. Petersen, and Laurie Melissa Vogelsang, eds. *Gender and German Cinema: Feminist Interventions Vol. 2; German Film History/German History on Film.* Oxford: Berg, 1993.
Knight, Julia. *Women and the New German Cinema.* London: Verso, 1992.
Quart, Barbara Koenig. *Women Directors: The Emergence of a New Cinema.* New York: Praeger, 1988.
Russ, Joanna. *How to Suppress Women's Writing.* Austin: University of Texas Press, 1983.
Sanford, John. *The New German Cinema.* London: Oswald Wolff, 1980.

AMARAL, SUZANA (1933–   ). Brazil. Among the numerous Brazilian women directors to emerge in the 1970s, Suzana Amaral, like Ana Carolina, began in documentary filmmaking. The number of Brazilian feature films directed by women increased significantly in the 1970s. Some of the directors and their films include Rosa Lacreta, *Encarnacao (Incarnation)* (1974), Vera de Figueiredo, *Feminino Plural* and *Samba da Criacao (Samba of the Creation of the World)* (1979), Maria do Rosario, *Marcados para viver (Branded for Life)* (1976), and Ana Carolina, *Mar de Rosas (A Sea of Roses)* (1977).

Suzana Amaral began filmmaking at the age of thirty-eight, working on documentaries and short art films. Often, Amaral's films for television deal with the everyday problems a woman faces in society. *A hora dele estrela (The Hour of the Star)* (1985) is Amaral's first feature film. *The Hour of the Star* is based on a novel by famed writer Clarice Lispector. Nissa Torrents, a specialist on Latin American film, notes that *The Hour of the Star* "upsets many stereotypes in its presentation of the female protagonist, who is neither beautiful nor middle-class." This notable transgression from conventional Brazilian film narrativity is highlighted by Amaral's inclusion of an unstable narrative conclusion. The heroine of *The Hour of the Star* does not make choices that conform to the usual proscriptions of narrative cinema. Instead, she poses questions, which we, as audience members, are invited to answer. The film provides no easy answers on marriage relationships, lovers, children, or romance; thus, the director embraces uncertainty, rather than closure, in this distinctly modern film. Amaral's film garnered high praise and awards at international film festival screenings.

SELECTED FILMOGRAPHY

Semana de 22 (The Week of 1922) (1971)
Coleçao de marfil (Ivory Collection) (1972)
Projeto pensamiento e linguajen (A Project for Thought and Speech) (1980)
São Paolo de todos nos (Our São Paolo) (1981)
A hora dele estrela (The Hour of the Star) (1985)

SELECTED BIBLIOGRAPHY

Johnson, Randal, and Robert Stam, eds. *Brazilian Cinema*. Rutherford, NJ: Fairleigh Dickinson University Press, 1982.
Third World Newsreel. *Third World Newsreel Catalogue*. New York: Third World Newsreel, 1994.
Torrents, Nissa. "Amaral, Suzana." In *The Women's Companion to International Film*, edited by Annette Kuhn, with Susannah Radstone, 13. Berkeley: University of California Press, 1994.

ANDERS, ALISON (1955–   ). United States. Currently one of the most successful independent women filmmakers in the United States, Alison Anders (daughter of Launa Anders, who acted in many films for directors Roger Corman and Francis Ford Coppola in the early 1960s) promises to be one of the most influential feminist filmmakers of the next few years. *Gas Food Lodging* (1991) was a low-budget film that received praise from both critics and audiences. Adapted from a novel by Richard Peck *(Don't Look and It Won't Hurt)*, *Gas Food Lodging* is a representative example of the new American cinema that revels in realism as much as it does romantic narrative. Anders drew from her own personal experiences to create a film that effectively depicts not only the difficulties of single motherhood but also the pain of female adolescence in contemporary American society. The autobiographical spirit is apparent in *Gas Food Lodging* in the treatment of the points of view of two teenage daughters and their waitress/mother, who live in a lower-class trailer park but aspire to "make it," nonetheless. Anders was gang-raped at the age of twelve, and she found very little support from her community. Later in life, she experienced first-hand trying to raise two daughters (as she worked her way through film school as a single mother). Both experiences are infused in the narrative.

Ione Skye plays Trudi, a reckless, sexually adventurous, difficult teenager in whom Anders appears to have infused the pain of her own teenage life. Brooke Adams does a remarkable job in the part of Nora, a lonesome single mother who, as a waitress, has to put up with the sexist customers at the diner, in order to support her two daughters. Clearly, Anders is familiar with the guilt, pain, pleasure, and costs of single motherhood in her depiction of Nora. When Nora's daughter Trudi gets pregnant, Nora takes it as a personal failure. Though she has romantic needs of her own, she clearly has her eye on a future for her daughters that is better than her own.

Actress Fairuza Balk plays Shade, the younger daughter, who guides the viewer through the film by her voice-over narration. In this way, Anders infuses the narrative with the feminine voice, which, in turn, promotes subjectivity and feminist modes of spectatorship. The viewer is carried along into the youngster's romantic yearning for her mother to find a partner. Shade gets the idea from watching early romantic Mexican melodramas. These films within the film, artfully lensed in black and white to look almost exactly like early popular films, provide *Gas Food Lodging* with a context of women watching popular representations of other women. The women in the films that Shade spends all her time watching live, suffer, and die in beautifully lit, romantically scored glory. Anders makes a sly, intertextual commentary of popular culture's influence on gender expectations, but she does this with a dull wit and an elegant light touch.

Shade puts her romantic ideas into practice as she attempts to find the right man for her mother. She sets up a blind date, ironically, with a married man with whom her mother had had a clandestine affair. The two adults pretend to not know one another, merely for the benefit of the hopeful daughter. A cable installer becomes a sort of running gag in the film. He meets Nora just as she breaks down, crying in her car about the impossible relationship she has with her difficult teenager, Trudi. He is clearly smitten, but Nora tries to drive him away. When the pair finally do fall into bed together, Anders treats the sex scene with refreshing, irreverent humor, departing from the Hollywood perfect gloss of mainstream filmmaking. Anders's subversive approach to the narrative includes a plot twist that turns on feminist expectations.

A reviewer for *Variety* calls *Gas Food Lodging* "fresh and unfettered . . . an example of a new cinema made by women and expressive of their lives" (Elley). Ben Thompson, a *Sight and Sound* critic, was most impressed by two novelties of *Gas Food Lodging*: first, its "impressively" cut figure of a mother, who escapes the easily drawn category of the "cloyingly warm and heroic" (51) and second, the film's development of the theme of "inadequacy: the father recognising his inability to do what he should, the mother sometimes giving up her struggle to get her children to understand her" (51). In *Gas Food Lodging*, Alison Anders demonstrates that personal feminist filmmaking can be accomplished on a modest budget. (The film was shot for $1.3 million.)

Unfortunately, Anders's next film, *Mi Vida Loca (My Crazy Life)* (1994), shows that not all low-budget feature films by women are guaranteed successes. *Mi Vida Loca*, like *Gas Food Lodging*, springs from real-life inspiration. Alison Anders got the idea of a film about female gang members as she watched the lives of her neighbors in Echo Park in Los Angeles. The plot revolves around two girl gang members who were best friends but had children by the same boy. Anders took this plot directly from the lives of the girls around her. Anders asked the gang members for their ideas, plot suggestions, line readings, and hand gestures. In addition, Anders cast some real gang members (nonactors) to work with the actors. This makes it all the more surprising that the acting in the film is often overwrought and lacking in realism. If one can get past the acting, there is a genuinely new story told in *Mi Vida Loca,* that of the female gangster in Los Angeles, a melodramatic plot suffused with realism. Anders herself calls the film "Douglas Sirk in the barrio," alluding to her melodramatic flair.

Mi Vida Loca is as feminist in content as *Gas Food Lodging,* if perhaps a bit more implausible, in that the two young women who share a boyfriend are able to maintain a sense of female community that surpasses the mundane patriarchal ideology of Los Angeles gang youth culture. However, the film is muddled, especially in comparison with *Gas Food Lodging.* Perhaps it was the interference of HBO, which insisted that the film have one continuous plot, rather than the multiple plots and points of view that Anders planned. Later, the film was cut into three stories almost as Anders had originally planned, seemingly reversing HBO's decision. Anders is currently writing and plans to direct *Grace of My Heart,* a film about a singer-songwriter trying to make it on her own in the 1950s. She is the recipient of a MacArthur Foundation "Genius Award."

SELECTED FILMOGRAPHY

Gas Food Lodging (1991)
Mi Vida Loca (My Crazy Life) (1994)

SELECTED BIBLIOGRAPHY

Benson, Sheila. "Girl Gangs Get Their Colors." *Interview* (June 1994): 96–97, 110.
Elley, Derek, ed. "*Gas Food Lodging.*" Variety Movie Guide 1994, 284. London: Hamlyn, 1993.
Thompson, Ben. "Gas Food Lodging." *Sight and Sound* 2.6 (September 1992) 51–52.

APON, ANNETTE (1949–   ). Netherlands. Annette Apon's *Crocodiles in Amsterdam* (1989) (a lesbian, buddy road movie) is one of a number of films directed by women that belong to a movement toward a New Wave of Dutch filmmaking in the 1980s. These films break away from a tradition of documentary films (usually subsidized by the government) and find an audience that appreciates films that lie somewhere between commercial and avant-garde narrative. *Crocodiles in Amsterdam* joins a host of recent New Wave films directed by women, including *De Deur van het Huis (The House Door)* (1985), directed by Hedy Honigmann, *De Still Oceaan (The Quiet Ocean)* (1985), directed by Digna Sinke, *Dagbork van een oud Dwaas (The Diary of an Old Fool)* (1987), directed by Lili Rademakers, *Iris* (1985), directed by Mady Saks, and the best-known film of the group:

A Question of Silence (1981), directed by Marleen Gorris. This movement away from documentary is surprising, considering the long tradition of documentary realism and social commentary in the Netherlands. Economic factors, which marry subsidized film art with commercial distribution, have spurred an anti-narrative wave of Dutch cinema.

Crocodiles in Amsterdam is one of the lucky few films to receive distribution in the United States and abroad. Screened at the Berlin Film Festival, Films de Femmes in Créteil (France), the Montreal Women's Film Festival, and the New York and San Francisco International Lesbian and Gay Film Festival, *Crocodiles in Amsterdam* is available from Women Make Movies, New York. *Crocodiles in Amsterdam,* like *Thelma and Louise* (1991), re-genders the traditional male road movie, creating a utopic milieu of female friendship, a denial of the laws of patriarchal society, a reclaiming of the female body, and, most radically perhaps, a sense of mastery over the physical landscape.

In *Crocodiles in Amsterdam,* Annette Apon plays off the buddy movie and the screwball comedy in creating her principal characters. Nina and Gino, the protagonists in the film, are drawn together by their differences. They are a sort of hybrid of Thelma and Louise, Bonnie and Clyde, and Gable and Lombard. Meeting by chance in Amsterdam, Gino is an irresponsible blonde with expensive, whimsical tastes, while Nina is a serious, politically active pacifist, paradoxically involved in terrorist acts. The mismatched couple are drawn together by screwball narrative conventions. The comedy drawn out of their polar opposition is both a takeoff on, and an embrace of, the screwball tradition.

Apon brings out excellent performances from her actresses. She has a fine sense of mise-en-scène. The buddy movie takes off on a series of madcap escapades, much in the flavor of *Thelma and Louise,* with a similar penchant for the edge between comedy and danger. But Apon takes the next logical step in the buddy movie by allowing the two women to display their physical and emotional attachment to one another. They may act like Thelma and Louise, but they make love like Gable and Lombard. Annette Apon crafts a screen that sizzles with the tension of erotic desire by exploring what draws opposites together into a volatile relationship. Moreover, Apon draws humor from this precariously blossoming relationship of lesbian desire. For example, Gino's capricious obsessions with home ownership and vacations to Sri Lanka disrupt Nina's plans to attack a bomb factory. Nina and Gino are forced into lives of bandit outsiders and perform transgressive outlaw acts of criminality as they seize control of their lives. Their bandit identity allows them to develop their own identities outside the boundaries of societal gender restrictions. When Gino, who plays the femme, seizes the gun from butch Nina and begins pumping lead at the audience, Apon creates a scene that directly presages a similar one in *Thelma and Louise. Crocodiles in Amsterdam* takes place in a noirish, stylistically futuristic world of blue, which gives the film a distinctly allegorical setting. It is a mythic journey through a female perspective of humor and irony. Annette Apon's earlier films include *Golven (The Waves)* (1982) and *Giovanni* (1983).

SELECTED FILMOGRAPHY

Golven (The Waves) (1982)
Giovanni (1983)
Crocodiles in Amsterdam (1989)

SELECTED BIBLIOGRAPHY

Cowie, Peter. *Dutch Cinema: An Illustrated History*. London: Tantivy Press, 1979.
Doty, Alexander. *Making Things Perfectly Queer*. Minneapolis: University of Minnesota Press, 1993.
Gever, Martha, John Greyson, and Pratibha Parmar, eds. *Queer Looks: Perspectives on Lesbian and Gay Film and Video*. New York: Routledge, 1993.
Women Make Movies, Inc. *1994 Film and Video Catalogue*. New York: Women Make Movies, Inc., 1994.

ARMSTRONG, GILLIAN (1950–   ). Australia. "You have to be able to play the men's game, and be harder than them and tougher than them," Gillian Armstrong told Chris Chase, a *New York Times* critic. Perhaps this personal philosophy accounts, in part, for the success of Australian director Gillian Armstrong. A strong feminist bent and a somewhat mordant sense of humor ("Who isn't threatened by having a woman get a lot of attention?" she told Chase) are glaringly apparent in the life and cinema of Gillian Armstrong. Critics have noted the Gothic sensibilities common to a number of recent Australian directors, including Jane Campion, Peter Weir, and Bruce Beresford, but Armstrong's films, however dark, are infused with stylistic inventiveness and humor that supersede easy categorization. *High Tide* (1987) and *My Brilliant Career* (1979) are masterpieces of feminist filmmaking.

Gillian Armstrong has been as honest and forthcoming in interviews as she is in her films. She remembers being an awkward teenager who wished she was thinner and had straight hair. Armstrong translated her awkwardness into the cinematic treasures of her early days as a documentary filmmaker: *Smokes and Lollies* (1975), *14's Good, 18's Better* (1980), and *Bingo, Bridesmaids and Braces* (1988), a loose trilogy of films that trace the lives of three young women. Armstrong told critic Mark Mordue that she tried to capture the everyday paths of average young females, in which "the sorting out process begins—sexual attraction—stereotypes—you start working out what you are considered to be in society. I'm the pretty one; I'm ugly; If only I had this" (270). The gap between confining socially imposed gender identities and the wish to define ourselves as women is a consistent theme through Armstrong's films.

Armstrong herself was advised to seek a more "realistic" female ambition (than film direction) as she studied film at Swinburne College of Advanced Education in Melbourne. Armstrong managed to work as a "tea girl" on a commercial film and then "graduated" to waitressing for industry types. In 1972, she joined the assistantship program at the Australian Film and Television School. Working as an editor for commercial film houses, Armstrong managed to gain experience and eventually began to plan her own films. One of her earliest efforts, *One Hundred a Day* (1973), is from a Stuart Marshall story of a young woman who works in a boot factory in the 1930s. Armstrong's camera never flinches as she captures the pain of the young woman who is forced to abort her baby. *Satdee Night* (1973) is an educational film concerning female sexuality.

Next, Armstrong worked as an art director for such films as *The Removalist* (David Williamson, 1975) as she found funding for her documentary coming-of-age stories. *14's Good, 18's Better* (1980) won awards, including one from the Victorian Teacher's Federation. *Bingo, Bridesmaids and Braces* (1988) has been compared with the British documentary *28 Up* (1985), directed by Michael Apted, another procedural film in which the same working-class people are interviewed over a number of years. *Bingo, Bridesmaids and Braces* differs from *28 Up* in that the latter is interested in sex roles more than working-class ambition and the effects of societal conditioning.

At twenty-six, Gillian Armstrong directed her first feature film, the highly praised *My Brilliant Career* (1979). (Not surprisingly, the film emerges from the director's central feminist preoccupation with the limitations of sex roles over career choice.) Felicity Collins claims that the film is the first feature film directed by a woman in Australia in over forty-six years. Early in Australian film, women such as the McDonough sisters, Lottie Lyell and Kate Howarde had been active as film directors, but sexism had effectively pushed women out of the industry in Australia as it had in the United States and internationally. Armstrong was understandably a bit uncomfortable being designated the first woman director of Australia, but, as she told Mark Mordue, "there are things that are different about female perspectives" (271).

My Brilliant Career revels in such a different perspective. It is the story of an aspiring female writer, based on a Miles Franklin novel of the same title and written for the screen by Eleanor Witcombe. Armstrong replaces the male writer/hero with an inspired nineteenth-century heroine, played beautifully by Judy Davis. As Stella Bruzzi, a British film critic, notes, *My Brilliant Career* is a "feminist reworking" (234) of such male-centered films as Stanley Kramer's *Inherit the Wind* (1960) or Fred Zinnemann's *A Man for All Seasons* (1966). The central character, Sybylla Mervyn, must transcend incredible obstacles to become a writer; certainly these are more pervasive and difficult than the obstacles that aspiring male authors meet. Sybylla, a teenage Bush woman, wants to escape the life set out for her, "being a wife out in the bush, having a baby every year." Sybylla is a role model in that she chooses to pursue her own goals, rather than be a victim of societal codes. The turn-of-the-century novel was set against a period of suffragist movement in New South Wales, when women were working for the right to vote. Armstrong's handling of the material transcends the usual bloodless costume drama period film. Forced into a life of near slavery, the central heroine works for a family in a harsh landscape designed to drive out any personal aspirations. Armstrong resists the urge to revel in her heroine's plight, instead managing to point the narrative toward the possibility of flight and personal achievement. For instance, Judy Davis, seen alone in the frame after sending off her manuscript, presents a lingering vision of underplayed pathos. As Manohla Dargis remarks on Armstrong's characters, "[H]er women work the border between passion and reason."

My Brilliant Career was invited to the Cannes Film Festival, which resulted in various offers from Hollywood. Armstrong, however, wished to remain in Australia, where she directed *Starstruck* (1983), a pop feminist musical comedy scored with punk rock. *Starstruck* revolves around the career plans of a teenage girl who wishes to make it big in the music industry. Armstrong interweaves the plot theme of career versus family when a talent prize becomes all-important for saving the family business. After *Starstruck*, Armstrong succumbed to one of the offers from Hollywood and directed *Mrs. Soffel* (1985). The film has Hollywood production values, but less of the complexity of Armstrong's other films. *Mrs. Soffel* stars Diane Keaton and Mel Gibson in a glossy, yet flat story of two brothers sentenced to death who may be saved by a woman who is married to the prison warden. The film did well in the United States, but Armstrong returned to Australia to direct the most beautiful film of her career, *High Tide* (1987).

High Tide stars Judy Davis again as a drifter who happens upon her daughter (who does not know her) and has to sing as a backup singer for an Elvis look-alike in order to survive. Along with Jane Campion's *Sweetie* (1989), *High Tide* is one of my favorite films because it represents a completely female sensibility that is surpassed by few works of cinema. The film has a Gothic flavor that is infused with a grimy realism and a feel for landscape, particularly the tide of the sea, which seems to lull the viewer along the journey of the central female heroine. Set in a poor coastal town in New South Wales, ironically named Eden, *High Tide* captures the everydayness of trailer camp life in a seaside town. A remarkable blend of touching futility and graceful hope, the film portrays the life of Lilli, who becomes stuck in a trailer park while waiting for her car to be fixed. The fact that she meets her daughter, Ally, in this same trailer park seems unbelievable, yet, in the context of the film, it is left open whether she stumbled onto her accidentally or not.

The pain of abandonment is seen through the eyes of the child, who is drawn to her mother, and, perhaps more painfully, through the eyes of Lilli, the mother who was too young to be able to deal with a child. The open wound between Lilli and her own mother, who has taken care of Lilli's child, is not smoothed over by the director. Instead, Armstrong presents the women in a vicious, realistic fight scene. The grandmother's inability to deal with her ambivalence toward her own daughter stands in pointed contrast to her overprotectiveness toward the granddaughter. The transient lifestyles of these women are painted against a backdrop of a society that looks for easily read "family values." Nothing is obvious or easily read in *High Tide,* most especially the motivations of Lilli, who rejects suitors, family, success, and everything else she is expected to embrace. The end of the film is provocatively ambiguous: will Lilli leave town with her daughter? But this is no simple melodrama with an easy ending. Perhaps that explains the magic of the film. As Brian McFarlane and Geoff Mayer conclude, *High Tide* evokes "the desire for a certain level of moral ambiguity and loose narrative causality" (86).

Ambiguity is a central preoccupation in Armstrong's *The Last Days of Chez Nous* (1993). A twisted family drama, this film treats the modern family as if it is the setting of a Gothic horror saga. The conflicting desires of the men and women thrown together in a family situation end in the devastation of the family. Lisa Harrow plays a young woman who is hell-bent on her own desires. She is, in some ways, typical of the strong women characters created in Armstrong films. Armstrong exposes the dreadful power relations inherent in a household. *The Last Days of Chez Nous* did very well at the box office and is admired by many critics. More recently, Gillian Armstrong directed a new version of Louisa May Alcott's *Little Women* (1994).

SELECTED FILMOGRAPHY

The Roof Needs Mowing (1971)
One Hundred a Day (1973)
Satdee Night (1973)
Gretel (1973)
Smokes and Lollies (1975)
The Singer and the Dancer (1976)
My Brilliant Career (1979)
14's Good, 18's Better (1980)
Starstruck (1983)
Not Just a Pretty Face (1983)
Mrs. Soffel (1985)
High Tide (1987)
Bingo, Bridesmaids and Braces (1988)
The Last Days of Chez Nous (1993)
Little Women (1994)

SELECTED BIBLIOGRAPHY

Bruzzi, Stella. "Jane Campion: Costume Drama and Reclaiming Women's Past." In *Women and Film: A Sight and Sound Reader,* edited by Pam Cook and Philip Dodd, 232–43. Philadelphia: Temple University Press, 1993.

Chase, Chris. "At the Movies: All over Town, Work by Women." *New York Times,* March, 4, 1983, C8.

Collins, Felicity. "Armstrong, Gillian." In *The Women's Companion to International Film,* edited by Annette Kuhn, with Susannah Radstone, 21–22. Berkeley: University of California Press, 1994.

Dargis, Manohla. "Her Brilliant Career." *Village Voice* 37.9 (March 2, 1993): 58.

Hamilton, Peter, and Sue Mathews. *American Dreams: Australian Movies.* Sydney: Currency Press, 1986.

James, Caryn. "A Distinctive Shade of Darkness." *New York Times,* November 28, 1993, Sec. 2, pp. 13, 22–33.

McFarlane, Brian, and Geoff Mayer. *New Australian Cinema: Sources and Parallels in American and British Film.* Cambridge: Cambridge University Press, 1992.

Mordue, Mark. *"Homeward Bound." Sight and Sound* 58.4 (autumn 1989): 270–73.

Rattigan, Neil. *Images of Australia: 100 Films of the New Australian Cinema.* Dallas: Southern Methodist University Press, 1991.

Warrick, Steve. *"High Tide." Film Quarterly* 42.4 (summer 1989): 21–26.

Wright, Andree. *Brilliant Careers.* Sydney: Pan Books, 1986.

ARZNER, DOROTHY (1906–79). United States. Lesbian film director Dorothy Arzner is the only woman who managed to work within the Hollywood studio system in the 1930s through the 1940s. Her sexual orientation and sexual politics, however, come through in her choice of subject matter and treatment of the female figure. Before Arzner, many women had been active as directors in the early Hollywood scene, but women had been pushed out of the directorial chair almost entirely by the time Arzner found the opportunity to direct. When asked why she did not marry, she repeatedly stated that she wanted a career, not marriage, thus deflecting questions about her sexual orientation. Known as "one of the boys," it appears that most Hollywood insiders were well aware of her lesbian identity, but a code of silence was the proper etiquette within the business of filmmaking, at least in this case.

Arzner's entry into the motion picture business was like that of many male directors. She attended the University of Southern California and planned to be a doctor but dropped out to pursue a career in motion pictures. She made an appointment to meet William de Mille, a studio executive, when she heard that a flu epidemic was causing a labor shortage. Her first job was typing scripts. Later she moved up to an editing position as a "cutter" for Realart Studio, a subsidiary of Paramount. She edited fifty-two films in this position as chief editor. Among her more famous editing jobs is the Rudolph Valentino film *Blood and Sand* (directed by Fred Niblo in 1922). In addition, Arzner directed some of the grueling second-unit scenes for *Blood and Sand,* depicting the bullfights for the film.

Arzner bargained with Paramount for her first opportunity as director of *Fashions for Women* (1927). She then directed a handful of other films before hitting her stride with *The Wild Party* (1929). Of all the films Arzner directed for Paramount, *The Wild Party* displays the most overtly expressed lesbian consciousness. Set at an all-female college, the film is ostensibly a heterosexual romance, but Arzner allows female same-sex sexuality to develop between periphery women characters. Predating another lesbian film, *Mäedchen in Uniform* (Leontine Sagan, Germany, 1931), *The Wild Party* captures the female sense of community and its arising passions in an all-female environment.

In *The Wild Party,* Arzner carefully articulates what happens when women stray from the confines of the safe all-girl environment: they are subject to the sexist advances of drunk, aggressive men. Arzner juxtaposes the threatening public sphere with an all-female dormitory, where women dress casually and look provocatively at other women. Andrea Weiss notes the "covert lesbian[ism]" suggested when, for example, Clara Bow jumps into the lap of her roommate, Shirley O'Hara, and fervently embraces her. Jealousies arise when Bow becomes involved with a boy. In an amazing display, O'Hara bursts into tears and admits her jealousy: "I'm jealous, you see; I love Helen, too!" As Weiss correctly notes, a lesbian point of view is "conveyed primarily through the spatial relationships between the women within the frame" (17). Arzner uses playful camera work and a bit of cross-dressing to carefully encode a significant lesbian overtone to *The Wild Party.* The film also deals with female bonding. Though the film features a heterosexual love affair, the female friendships are clearly deeper, longer lasting, and artfully highlighted in the film. Women cover up for one another in the film, and in one touching scene, Clara Bow saves her girlfriend from a "bad reputation" by taking the blame for the other girl's actions. *The Wild Party* was also hailed for its technical achievements. It was the first sound picture made at Paramount in which, reportedly, Arzner suggested the use of a fishing pole as a microphone extension, thus inventing the industry's first "boom microphone."

Working Girls (1930) continued Arzner's penchant for the creation of all-women environments set against the backdrop of patriarchal societal convention. Many of the themes of *Working Girls* are revisited in Arzner's famous later film *Dance, Girl, Dance* (1940). Those themes are developed around the difficulties women face in the male-defined work environment and the manner in which women are so often pitted against one another in society. Arzner's female characters were often career-oriented, as in the case of *Christopher Strong* (1933). Katharine Hepburn stars in this classic female narrative woven around the choice between family and career. However, Arzner problematizes both choices by virtue of the fact that both are deadly: the career as aviator and the love of a married man. Arzner's choice to have Hepburn's character commit suicide, in perhaps one of the most compellingly cut sequences in Hollywood filmmaking, is tragic. But, like women authors of the period, Arzner recognized and forced women audiences to recognize the terrible dead-end decisions that women often faced in the early twentieth century.

The difficulties of heterosexual relations and the emphasis on female community are hallmarks of Arzner's films. They exist, as Judith Mayne asserts, "in tension with each other" (113) and problematize mainstream depictions of heterotopic love. *Craig's Wife* (1936), made for Columbia, is another brilliantly executed Arzner film. Rosalind Russell stars in this brutal examination of female domesticity in which a manipulative woman is so driven to become the perfect embodiment of the perfect housewife that she destroys everyone around her, including herself. The film is a scathingly feminist attack on societal restrictions of women in a time when women were being moved back into the domestic sphere.

In a very famous scene, Arzner again criticized patriarchal sexual politics in *Dance, Girl, Dance* (1940). Judy, a dancer played by Maureen O'Hara, turns directly to her male audience, who actively objectifies and fetishizes her body, and delivers an acid-etched lecture to the men, berating them for their acts of voyeurism. Judy furthermore resists the temptation to use a patriarchal figure as a stepping-stone to a ballet career. When she finally does fall for Ralph Bellamy's character, Steve, Arzner shows her face in close-up as a mask of horror, completely subverting the cultural norm of the happy (heterosexual coupling) ending.

Arzner's last film, *First Comes Courage* (1943), starred Merle Oberon as a woman who sacrifices love for the safety and independence of her country. Again, Arzner made a film with a distinctly feminist tone, a film that centers on a strong, courageous female protagonist. It is unclear why Arzner left feature film direction after *First Comes Courage*. Shortly after leaving Columbia, she developed one of the first filmmaking courses in the United States, working at the Pasadena Playhouse in California. During World War II, Arzner directed instructional films for the Women's Army Corps; Arzner's work during this era underscores the director's continued commitment to women's history and women's issues. Arzner remained a close friend with Joan Crawford, who was a member of the board of directors of the Pepsi-Cola company in the 1950s. Working with Crawford, Arzner directed more than fifty television ads for the soft drink firm. In the 1960s, Arzner taught filmmaking at the University of California—Los Angeles (UCLA) for several years. In 1974, Arzner was finally honored by the Directors Guild of America. "No chauvinism," read the headline of the *Daily Variety* story covering the event, as if wishful thinking would erase Hollywood's pervasive history of sexism in the profession. Arzner was honored along with King Vidor, William Wellman, Francis Ford Coppola, and Robert Wise. Arzner was well aware of the sexist practices of film history, particularly its omission of early women film directors. "Whenever they would print an article about her being the 'only woman director,' she used to call up Lois Weber and apologize," *Variety* reports. "That's the kind of person she was" (5).

Dorothy Arzner is the subject of numerous articles and at least two new books. She remains one of the most important and interesting women directors to work in the heyday of Hollywood film production. Many of her films, unlike those of other women directors of early Hollywood, are available for screening, and some make occasional appearances on television. How Arzner managed to survive and thrive in Hollywood as a lesbian feminist is a question that continues to intrigue. Ally Acker terms her achievement a "sisyphian feat" (28). Arzner's pictures more than stand alone as exemplifications of an indefatigable spirit.

SELECTED FILMOGRAPHY

Fashions for Women (1927)
Ten Modern Commandments (1927)
Get Your Man (1927)
Manhattan Cocktail (1928)
The Wild Party (1929)
Sarah and Son (1930)
Anybody's Woman (1930)
Paramount on Parade (1930)
Working Girls (1930)
Honor among Lovers (1931)
Merrily We Go to Hell (1932)
Christopher Strong (1933)
Nana (1934)
Craig's Wife (1936)
The Bride Wore Red (1937)
Dance, Girl, Dance (1940)
First Comes Courage (1943)

SELECTED BIBLIOGRAPHY

Acker, Ally. *Reel Women: Pioneers of the Cinema 1896 to the Present.* New York: Continuum, 1993.
de Lauretis, Teresa. "Rethinking Women's Cinema: Aesthetics and Feminist Theory." In *Multiple Voices in Feminist Film Criticism,* edited by Diane Carson, Linda Dittmar, and Janice Welsch, 140–61. Minneapolis: University of Minnesota Press, 1994.
Foster, Gwendolyn, and Wheeler Winston Dixon. *The Women Who Made the Movies.* Coproduced with Nebraska Educational Television, 1991. Women Make Movies, Inc., distributor.
Heck-Rabi, Louise. *Women Filmmakers: A Critical Reception.* Metuchen, NJ: Scarecrow Press, 1984.

Houston, Beverle. "Missing in Action: Notes on Dorothy Arzner." *Wide Angle* 6.3 (1984): 24–31.

Johnston, Claire, ed. *Dorothy Arzner: Towards a Feminist Cinema*. London: BFI, 1975.

Kaplan, E. Ann. *Women & Film: Both Sides of the Camera*. New York: Methuen, 1983.

Kuhn, Annette. *Women's Pictures: Feminism and Cinema*. London: Routledge, 1982.

Mayne, Judith. *The Woman at the Keyhole: Feminism and Women's Cinema*. Bloomington: Indiana University Press, 1990.

———. *Directed by Dorothy Arzner*. Bloomington: Indiana University Press, 1994.

Todd, Janet, ed. *Women and Film*. New York: Holmes and Meier, 1988.

Variety, ed. "No Chauvinism: DGA Guys & Dolls Honor Dorothy Arzner Jan. 25." *Variety* (December 30, 1974): 5.

Weiss, Andrea. *Vampires and Violets: Lesbians in Film*. New York: Penguin, 1993.

ASANOVA, DINARA (1942–85). USSR (Kirghizia). Because of the extended political conflicts between the United States and the USSR, only a handful of Soviet cinema's extensive number of films have been screened for Western audiences. Women have been extremely active in Soviet cinema from its earliest days. Some of the women directors who have, so far, been recognized include Dinara Asanova, Ol'ga Preobrazhenskaya, Esfir Shub, Elizaveta Svilova, Iuliia Solntseva, Vera Stroeva, Lana Gogoberidze, Kira Muratova, and Aida Manasarova. Some came from backgrounds in acting, including Preobrazhenskaya, Solntseva, and others. Some crossed over from editing positions, including Esfir Shub and Elizaveta Svilova. The careers of several women directors married to well-known male directors have often been obscured by interest in their husband's work. For example, film historians are familiar with the work of Dziga Vertov, but few credit Vertov's wife, Elizaveta Svilova, for her virtuoso skill as an editor and director. Similarly, few critics of the West mention the close partnership between Iuliia Solntseva and the famous director Aleksandr Dovzhenko, or Lev Kuleshov's partner, Aleksandra Khokhlova. The films made by women in the Soviet Union are diverse in theme, as well as style. The pioneering efforts of a large number of women directors act as forerunners to a newer generation of Soviet women directors, who include women such as Dinara Asanova.

It is difficult to assess the career of Dinara Asanova, but it has been documented that her films were successful and popular in her own country. In 1970, she directed her first solo effort, *Rudolfino*. By 1974, she began to work at the Lenfilm Studio, where she directed at least nine feature films. Asanova's films were well known for their incisive handling of contemporary issues and social problems. Her work met with tremendous success in the Soviet Union, though she remains completely unknown in the West.

Like many women directors, even in the United States, Asanova clearly has a penchant for realism, especially in her handling of personal issues. The difficulties of romance are at the center of *Ne bolit golova u diatla (Woodpeckers Don't Get Headaches)* (1975), and teen crime is dealt with in *Patsany (Young Toughs)* (1983). Asanova, like many great Soviet directors, mixes professional actors with nonactors for a realistic, gritty effect. Hopefully, as the political ties between the West and the redeveloping nations of Russia open up new avenues of distribution, film historians, feminist critics, and all those interested in the cinema will be able to view Asanova's films. Only then can a complete history of Soviet cinema, one that includes women, be written. Gogoberidze is featured in a documentary directed by Sally Potter, entitled *Soviet Women Filmmakers* (1990). The video is distributed by Women Make Movies, Inc.

SELECTED FILMOGRAPHY

Rudolfino (1970)
Ne bolit golova u diatla (Woodpeckers Don't Get Headaches) (1975)
Kliuch bez prava peredachi (The Restricted Key) (1977)
Beda (Misfortune) (1978)
Zhena ushla (My Wife Has Left) (1980)
Nikudyshnaia (Good-for-Nothing) (1980)
Chto ty vybral (Which Would You Choose?) (1981)
Patsany (Young Toughs) (1983)
Milyi, dorogoi, liubimyi, edinstvennyi (Dear, Dearest, Beloved, Only One) (1984)

SELECTED BIBLIOGRAPHY

Attwood, Lynn. *Red Women on the Silver Screen*. London: Pandora, 1993.
Cowie, Peter, ed. *International Film Guide*. New York: A. S. Barnes, 1964–72.
Leyda, Jay. *Kino: A History of Russian and Soviet Film*. New York: Collier, 1973.
Vronskaya, Jeanne. *Young Soviet Film Makers*. London: Allen and Unwin, 1972.
Youngblood, Denise J. "Asanova, Dinara." In *The Women's Companion to International Film*, edited by Annette Kuhn and Susannah Radstone, 24–25. Berkeley: University of California Press, 1994.

ATTILE, MARTINA (1959–). United Kingdom. An original member of the renowned independent black filmmaking collective Sankofa, Martina Attile is active as a filmmaker and critic in London. Attile told Lynne Jackson and Jean Rasenberger how the collective began, in an interview in 1988:

Each of us were the only black student studying communications theory in our respective colleges. We set ourselves up as a black group because there was very little space allowed in the institutions for us to become intimate with our own experience. We couldn't deny our history, our knowledge. (23)

The collective was made up of Nadine Marsh-Edwards, Isaac Julien, Martina Attile, and Maureen Blackwood. Attile produced *Passion of Remembrance* (1986), the first Sankofa production, which was directed by

Maureen Blackwood and Isaac Julien. *Passion of Remembrance* charts entirely new cinematic territory. It is hailed as a classic film that treats a black perspective from a black filmmakers' point of view. Critics have championed the film for its representation of the black experience and its decided emphasis on diversity. The film is a montage of different points of view of the black experience, and both real and imagined narratives are included in the film. A couple argues about their social and racial experiences in modern-day Britain in the film's main narrative, which is intercut with video images of recent black history in England. The resultant film documents both celebration and anger. Attile explains the film's difficult structure in the *Cineaste* interview with Lynne Jackson and Jean Rasenberger:

The structure comes from trying to make the ideas accessible. People can become very static and unwilling to change. They feel safe and don't understand the different strategies that have to be used, the different voices that have to be heard. For many it is frightening, even for those discovering their own voices. . . . We decided to use fiction because it opened up a space to fantasize about possibilities, even though we don't have the answers. We present an optimism that imagines possibilities. (23)

As bell hooks explains, *Passion of Remembrance* is a film that springs from a new goal to transcend dated notions of black female spectatorship. Films in this black movement "employ a deconstructive filmic practice to undermine grand cinematic devices even as the rhetoric subjectivity in the realm of the visual" (hooks, 130). Most important, the Sankofa films and other films directed by black women are opening up new avenues of black female spectatorship and identity formation. As hooks notes, they form an "oppositional gaze" that invites black women into a process of "counter-memory, using it as a way to know the present and invent the future" (131).

It is important to note that black women filmmakers are involving themselves as critics and "herstorians" because the history-making process is as important as the filmmaking itself. For too long, feminism, especially feminist film criticism, has been a white woman's venture. Only in the very recent past have women of color emerged as recognized filmmakers and film critics. Martina Attile, Michelle Parkerson, Maureen Blackwood, Trinh T. Minh-ha, Pratibha Parmar, Ngozi Onwurah, Zeinabu irene Davis, Christine Choy, Ayoka Chenzira, Tracey Moffatt, and Julie Dash are just some of the many women of color who are making enormous strides into critical film theory and film and video production.

In addition to her work with Sankofa, Martina Attile directed *Dreaming Rivers* (1988), which is distributed by Women Make Movies, Inc., in New York. The thirty-minute film is comparable to Julie Dash's epic *Daughters of the Dust* in that both tell the tale of Caribbean families that experience migration. Both films are connected by the theme of exile and the importance of community and the physical landscape. In *Dreaming Rivers,* however, the narrative revolves around an older woman, "Miss T," who has been left in her one-room apartment by her husband and children, who have been drawn away to pursue their dreams. The title refers to the fragmentary nature of the memories of the family, who gather together for Miss T's funeral. The film is richly metaphorical and allegorical and an important entry in the developing canon of new black filmmaking.

Attile continues to be active in workshops on black women and representation. In the spring of 1984, Black Women and Representation Workshops were formed in London and funded by the Greater London Arts Council. The film workshops are led by such filmmaker/critics as Martina Attile and Maureen Blackwood. The formal and informal workshops discuss such topics as black stereotypes, the control of images, and access to control of images and often include screenings. In the notes from the workshops of 1984, Attile and Blackwood explain that their goal is to "establish an ongoing forum for discussion around the social and political implications of the fragmentation of black women in film/video/television" (203). Among the activities of the workshop are screenings and discussions of the "mammy" figure in such Hollywood films as *Gone with the Wind* and *Imitation of Life* and popular cartoons from the 1930s and 1940s.

Sankofa workshop participants discuss the colonialist depiction of the black female body as a "dark continent" that is colonized by mainstream Hollywood cinema. The ability to re/look at painfully racist images is an important step toward defining ownership of black female identity. The efforts of Sankofa, the Black Women and Representation Workshops, Women in Sync, and the Black Audio Collective represent enormous steps toward a countercinema of black female ownership. The Sankofa style is a move away from linear narrative filmmaking toward a montagist approach of multilayeredness that embraces the multivalencies of everyday experience. Martina Attile is to be credited for her input into the development of the Sankofa collective, as well as her activism and filmmaking.

SELECTED FILMOGRAPHY

Territories (1985)
Passion of Remembrance (1986)
Dreaming Rivers (1988)

SELECTED BIBLIOGRAPHY

Alexander, Karen. "Julie Dash: *Daughters of the Dust,* and a Black Aesthetic." In *Women and Film: A Sight and Sound Reader,* edited by Pam Cook and Philip Dodd, 224–31. Philadelphia: Temple University Press, 1993.

Attile, Martina, and Maureen Blackwood. "Black Women and Representation, Notes from the Workshops Held in London, 1984." In *Films for Women,* edited by Charlotte Brunsdon, 202–8. London: BFI, 1987.

Bhabha, Homi K. "The Other Question—The Stereotype and Colonial Discourse." *Screen* 24.6 (November–December 1983): 18–36.

Cartwright, Lisa, and Nina Fonoroff. "Narrative Is Narrative: So What Is New?" In *Multiple Voices in Feminist Film Criticism,* edited by Diane Carson, Linda Dittmar, and Janice Welsch, 124–39. Minneapolis: University of Minnesota Press, 1994.

de Lauretis, Teresa. *Technologies of Gender: Essays on Theory, Film, and Fiction.* Bloomington: Indiana University Press, 1987.

Erens, Patricia, ed. *Issues in Feminist Film Criticism.* Bloomington: Indiana University Press, 1990.

Fusco, Coco. "Sankofa and Black Audio Film Collective." In *Discourses: Conversations in Post Modern Art and Culture,* edited by Russell Ferguson, William Olander, Karen Fiss, and Marcia Tucker, 17–43. Cambridge: Massachusetts Institute of Technology and New York: New Museum of Contemporary Art, 1990.

Gaines, Jane. "White Privilege and Looking Relations." In *Multiple Voices in Feminist Film Criticism,* edited by Diane Carson, Linda Dittmar, and Janice Welsch, 162–75. Minneapolis: University of Minnesota Press, 1994.

hooks, bell. *Black Looks: Race and Representation.* Boston: South End Press, 1992.

Hull, Gloria T., Patricia Bell Scott, and Barbara Smith, eds. *All the Women Are White, All the Blacks Are Men, But Some of Us Are Brave: Black Women's Studies.* Old Westbury, NY: Feminist Press, 1982.

Jackson, Lynne, and Jean Rasenberger. "An Interview with Martina Attile and Isaac Julien." *Cineaste* 14.4 (1988): 23–37.

Klotman, Phylliss Rauch, ed. *Screenplays of the African American Experience.* Bloomington: Indiana University Press, 1991.

Leab, Daniel. *From Sambo to Superspade: The Black Experience in Motion Pictures.* Boston: Houghton Mifflin, 1975.

Mercer, Kobena, ed. *Black Film/British Cinema, ICA Documents 7.* London: BFI, 1988.

Rich, B. Ruby. "In the Name of Feminist Film Criticism." In *Multiple Voices in Feminist Film Criticism,* edited by Diane Carson, Linda Dittmar, and Janice Welsch, 27–47. Minneapolis: University of Minnesota Press, 1994.

AUDRY, JACQUELINE (1908–77). France. France has had women working actively as directors since the dawn of the motion picture history, when Alice Guy directed one of the world's first narrative films at Gaumont in 1896. Women directors have flourished in France, both in commercial and avant-garde cinemas. In the early days of the French avant-garde, lesbian filmmaker Germaine Dulac helped forge a feminist version of artistic cinema. Silent French films were directed by Renée Carl, Rose Lacau-Pansini, and Marie-Louise Iribe. In the 1930s, Marie Epstein, Solange Bussi (*La Vagabonde,* 1931), and Marguerite Viel (*La Bauque Némo,* 1934) directed feature films.

In the postwar period, many women began directing shorts, documentaries, and experimental films, including Nicole Védrès (*Paris 1900,* 1942) and Yannick Bellon (*Góemons,* 1948). The student riots of May 1968 and the rise of the critical journal *Cahiers du Cinéma* spurred on a New Wave of "auteurist" cinema (cinema that represents the personal spirit of the director herself). Nelly Kaplan, Agnes Varda, Yannick Bellon, Nadine Tritignant, and other women directors were part of this New Wave of filmmakers. Agnes Varda is sometimes credited for one of the first New Wave films (*Cleo From 5 to 7,* 1961), but many women filmmakers, including Jacqueline Audry, have been largely omitted from the histories of French filmmaking.

Born in France, Audry worked as an assistant to Jean Delannoy, G. W. Pabst, and Max Ophuls. Perhaps one of the reasons for the critical neglect of her work is that her film work belongs to a more traditional style of filmmaking than that of the New Wave school. Audry's films, like those of Ophuls, are recognizable for their old-fashioned staginess, but, to some, this is a mark of quality. Audry was attracted to tasteful studio-backed period films, often literary adaptations, not unlike the films of Ophuls. New Wave critics could not see beyond Audry's glossy look, her emphasis on dialogue, and her production values. But in hindsight, we can now see that Audry infused her films with a distinctive feminist slant and often chose films that depicted central women characters. Several of her films are adaptations from Colette novels: *Gigi* (1948), *Minne* (1950), and *Mitsou* (1956). *Minne* was heavily censored because it depicted a young woman's sexual exploration outside wedlock.

In 1951, Audry directed her most famous film, *Olivia,* the story of a lesbian relationship. *Olivia* is based on an autobiographical novel by Dorothy Strachey Bussy and concerns life at an all-girl boarding school in which two girls compete for the love of the headmistress. It is interesting to note that *Olivia* is one of a small number of films that almost constitute a genre to themselves—the lesbian soft-core, girls'-school films, including *Mäedchen in Uniform* (Germany, 1931, director Leontine Sagan), *Club de Femmes* (France, 1936, director Jacques Deval), and *The Wild Party* (United States, 1929, director Dorothy Arzner).

Andrea Weiss places the subgenre of the all-girl boarding school film within the historical context of the warnings of the first "sex experts," Krafft-Ebing and Havelock Ellis. Ellis, for his part, direly pronounced that all-female environments "bred pathological attachments with women" (Weiss, 8). In all of her work, Audry displays a central preoccupation with the theme of female bonding. Audry returns to the girls'-school subgenre, in fact, with *L'École des cocottes* and deals with transgressive sexuality in *Le Secret du chevalier d'Éon,* a film about a famous transvestite.

Audry's cinema compares with that of Dorothy Arzner. Both worked within the studio system, both centered on strong female protagonists, and both were highly successful at the box office. It has taken years for feminists to recognize the work of Dorothy Arzner and to begin to unravel her complex feminist approach. Perhaps the films of Jacqueline Audry will begin to be recontextualized by modern feminists. Audry leaves behind an impressive body of feature films with strong female heroines, which is a significant achievement, especially within the rather sexist milieu of France in the 1950s and 1960s.

SELECTED FILMOGRAPHY

Les Chevaux du Vercors (short) (1943)
Les Matheurs de Sophie (1944)
Gigi (1948)
Sombre dimanche (1948)
Minne ou l'ingénue libertine (Minne) (1950)
Olivia (Pit of Loneliness) (1951)
La Caraque blonde (1952)
Huis-clos (1954)
Mitsou (1956)
La Garçonne (1956)
L'École des cocottes (1957)
C'est la faute d' Adam (1958)
Le Secret du chevalier d'Éon (1959)
Les Petits Matins (1961)
Cadavres en vacances (1961)
Cours de bonheur conjugal (1964)
Fruits amers (1966)
Le Lys de mer (1969)
Un grand Amour de Balzac (1972)

SELECTED BIBLIOGRAPHY

Ford, Charles. *Femmes Cinéastes, ou Le triomphe de la volonté.* Paris: Denoël/ Gonthier, 1972.
Hayward, Susan, and Ginette Vincendeau, eds. *French Film: Texts and Contexts.* London: Routledge, 1989.
Sadoul, Georges. *Dictionnaire des cinéastes.* Paris: Microcosme/Editions du seuil, 1965.
Smith, Sharon. *Women Who Make Movies.* New York: Hopkinson and Blake, 1975.
Weiss, Andrea. *Vampires and Violets: Lesbians in Film.* New York: Penguin, 1993.

B

BETH B. (1955–   ). United States. Beth B. and Scott Billingsly worked together to make bleak underground films in the late 1970s and early 1980s. The work of Beth B. and Scott B. belongs to the "no-wave" movement in experimental cinema. Artists such as Lydia Lunch, Vivienne Dick, John Ahearn, and others forged a new anticinema aesthetic, which catered neither to art houses nor to commercial venues. The films of the no-wave are directly connected to the punk movement. Films of this type are short, grainy, sloppy, loud, usually shot on Super 8mm film, and often contain violent, sordid images of sadomasochism. *G-Man* (1978), *Black Box* (1978), and *Letters to Dad* (1979) are some of Beth and Scott B.'s most innovative films.

G-Man is an assault on the power that society gives its authority figures. It depicts a policeman who hires a dominitrix to brutalize him. *Letters to Dad* is a postmodern film that cuts across the norms of spectator pleasures as nineteen people look and talk directly to the viewer, who, in effect, becomes "Dad." At the end of the film, the filmmakers reveal that the actors have been reading actual portions of letters to Jim Jones that were written just before the mass suicide at Jonestown. The film is truly disturbing in its cruel manipulation of the unsuspecting viewer into the "role" of Jim Jones.

Black Box is a terrifying allegory of societal restriction of the individual. The black box refers to an actual man-made torture chamber that was used in Iran and Latin America and designed in America. A young man is confined by some brutal men who put him into the black box, which tortures the man with the use of painful noise. As in *Letters to Dad,* the audience experiences the same torture as the man in the black box. *Vortex* (1983) was the last film on which Beth B. and Scott B. collaborated. Shot in 16mm, rather than Super 8, *Vortex* is a noir film, loosely based on the last years of Howard Hughes. Performance artist and punk rock star Lydia Lunch stars as the female detective. *Vortex* is not as effective as the first films of Beth and Scott B. Their early films exemplify protopunk nihilism.

Beth B. directed a number of films and videos since she ended her collaboration with Scott B. Her most recent film, *Two Small Bodies* (1994), appears to mark a crossover into Hollywood filmmaking. The film stars Suzy Amis as a morbid waitress who is searching for her lost children. Fred Ward plays a cop who is seemingly more interested in sadistically grilling the waitress than actually finding her lost children. Beth B. directed the film with considerable style and energy. Her directorial authority in this area is not surprising, given the noirish underground films she helped to create in the early 1980s.

Asked why they called themselves the B.'s, Scott and Beth replied that it was an homage to "B" filmmakers such as Sam Fuller, who often made interesting, if grim, films. Like the "B" filmmakers of 1940s and 1950s Hollywood, Beth and Scott B. claimed that their low budgets gave them more control over their material. The couple appear to have worked well together in their Super 8 films, but when they moved up to 16mm, they realized that codirection was nearly impossible (because a crew looks to one person for direction). The moderate success of *Two Small Bodies* (on the art house circuit, especially in New York City), coupled with the cult status of the early films with Scott B., assures Beth B. a singular place in the history of experimental cinema.

SELECTED FILMOGRAPHY

Codirected with Scott B.

G-Man (1978)
Black Box (1978)
Letters to Dad (1979)
The Offenders (1979)
The Trap Door (1980)
Vortex (1983)

Directed by Beth B. alone

Dominitrix (music video) (1984)
Joan Jett: I Need Someone (music video) (1984)
Taka Boom (music video) (1985)
Salvation (1986)
Belladonna (1990)
Two Small Bodies (1994)

SELECTED BIBLIOGRAPHY

American Federation of Arts. *A History of American Avant-Garde Cinema*. New York: AFA, 1976.
Ehrenstein, David. *Film: The Front Line/1984*. Denver: Arden, 1984.
Gidal, Peter, ed. *Structural Film Anthology*. London: BFI, 1976.

Grenier, Vincent, Kathy Dieckmann, and John Pruitt, eds. *10 Years of Living Cinema*. New York: Collective for Living Cinema, 1982.

Hoberman, J. *Home-Made Movies: 20 Years of American 8mm and Super-8 Films*. New York: Anthology Film Archives, 1981.

MacDonald, Scott. *A Critical Cinema Interview with Independent Filmmakers*. Berkeley: University of California Press, 1988.

Marchetti, Gina, and Keith Tishken. "An Interview with Beth and Scott B." *Millennium Film Journal* 10–11 (fall–winter, 1981–82): 158–67.

Turim, Maureen. *Abstraction in Avant-Garde Film*. Ann Arbor: UMI Research Press, 1985.

BANI ETEMAAD, RAKHSHAN (1953–   ). Iran. Before the Censorship Act of 1981, women had made some inroads into Iranian cinema, especially in the 1960s and 1970s. Though women directors were careful not to call themselves feminists, they explored feminist themes and occasionally criticized patriarchal Iranian society in this period. For example, Tahmineh Mir Mirany made a film about a lesbian relationship in 1975 (*Ghaire aze Khoudo Hitch Kass Naboud*), and Goly Tarragy directed *Bita* (1971), a film that criticized men who exploited women by taking advantage of social changes. In the 1980s, many of these films, as well as women directors, were banned in Iran. Later, the government relaxed some sanctions, leading to the success of a few women directors who were careful to comply with the law of the veil and who also avoided any feminist themes. Rakhshan Bani Etemaad's *Khareje Aze Mahdoudeh* (*Off the Limits*) (1987) was one of the few successful directorial efforts by a woman in modern Iran.

Bani Etemaad studied directing at the Teheran University of Dramatic Arts. She worked her way up the production ladder as a production manager and assistant director. Several of her first films are television documentaries. In 1987, Bani Etemaad began her career as a commercial director with the box-office success *Khareje Aze Mahdoudeh*. Next, Bani Etemaad directed *Zarede Ghaneri* (*The Yellow Car*) (1989). Both films are prerevolutionary period films, and both are traditional, nonconfrontational comedies. Nevertheless, Bani Etemaad infused her films, as Behjat Razaei notes, with an edge of feminism.

SELECTED FILMOGRAPHY

Eshteghal-e-Mohojereen Roustai (1981)
Sazemonhayi Moli Yahoud (1981)
Ta'dabir Eghtessadi-y-Janghi (1982)
Farahang-e-Massraffi (1983)
Tamarkoze (1984)
Rooze Jahoni Koreghar (1985)
Khareje Aze Mahdoudeh (*Off the Limits*) (1987)
Zarede Ghaneri (*The Yellow Car*) (1989)

SELECTED BIBLIOGRAPHY

Maghsoudlou, Bahman. *Iranian Cinema.* New York: New York University Press, 1987.
Razaei, Behjat. "Bani Etemaad, Rakhshan." In *The Women's Companion to International Film,* edited by Annette Kuhn, with Susannah Radstone, 35. Berkeley: University of California Press, 1994.

BARRIE, DIANA (1952–   ). United States. Diana Barrie is a well-known underground New York filmmaker whose films are rarely screened, probably because she has less interest in distribution than in filmmaking itself. Barrie is prolific, with a lengthy filmography of Super 8mm and 16mm films to her credit. Barrie's films consistently emphasize her interest in Goddess imagery. She is a playful, yet difficult artist who often hand-paints, scratches, and in other ways manipulates film in the tradition of Stan Brakhage, Maya Deren, Jean Cocteau, Bruce Conner, and many underground 1970s filmmakers. Barrie studied with Stan Brakhage at the Art Institute in Chicago. After graduation, Barrie moved to Arizona, California, and Iowa (where she taught) and finally settled in New York.

In *The Annunciation* (1974), Barrie rejects patriarchal depictions of the traditional imagery of the Virgin Mary as a submissive, objectified female body and as recipient of the light of a male god. Instead, Barrie posits the character of the Mary in the role of filmmaker, in a witty regendering of power and identity-politics. Barrie also places the audience in the role of Virgin and, in a revelatory moment of brilliant feminist revisionism, announces the daughter of the filmmaker, conceived by a female (filmmaker) creator. Barrie's own image becomes light, in a complete repositioning of gender dynamics in traditional religious iconography. Taking this transgression even further, Barrie makes the camera/light become an extension of her body, specifically her vagina, thus grounding her rereading of the Annunciation in the female body, in eroticism, exposing the lie of the traditional myth and at the same time reinvigorating it as a possible source of female mythic power. Barrie explains that *The Annunciation* is not an attack on Catholic imagery but, rather, that she was motivated by her own devotion to the Great Mother Goddess who existed before organized patriarchal religions. As she told Scott MacDonald, Barrie designed *The Annunciation* as a comment on the fact that the Goddess in modern religion is portrayed in binaristic terms: "the spiritual, which is good, and the physical, which is evil. That's happened in the male image too to some extent, but not quite as drastically as it has with women" (322). Interestingly, Diana Barrie herself is named after the goddess Diana.

My Version of the Fall (1978) is a feminist retelling of the myth of the Fall, in which Barrie as woman/creator redeems her own "fall." The film is an homage to the primitive cinema of Georges Méliès, in that it includes tricks and effects such as hand tinting, hand scratching, reversed and upside-down footage. The film reverses the gender order of early trick films of Méliès. Barrie depicts the Fall as a female "wizard" whose "fall" is her smoking habit. She "creates" a male figure and subsequently "makes" him disappear. This is an incisive and innovative remaking of early cinematic efforts that often featured male wizard/filmmakers, such as Méliès's "creating" women, only to make them disappear. *My Version of the Fall* uses avant-garde experimental technique as a format of feminist address toward the traditions of both religion and cinema. Barrie reclaims the objectified female body from both male-centered traditions and reconfigures it in an active, subjective position. Barrie, unlike many male experimental directors (Anger, Brakhage, and so on), moves experimental cinema beyond phallocentrism.

Night Movie #1 (1974), misperceived by some critics as pornography, redefines the term "self-portrait." In the film, Barrie makes love with the camera itself, transgressing the boundary between the artist's body and the artist's work. Many of Barrie's "diary" films continue this redefinition of the boundaries of self and space in a metaphysical experience of spiritual union between filmmaker and camera, camera and audience, spectator and spectacle. In this way, *Night Movie #1* playfully denies the limitations of scientifically defined time, space, and objectivity.

In *Magic Explained* (1980), Barrie returns to her role as filmmaker/magician, picking up the thread from *The Annunciation* and *My Version of the Fall*. *Magic Explained* has the gorgeous, handmade feel of the earlier Barrie films. Barrie's work is a Goddess-inspired creation of hand and eye and camera, infused with the symbology of female creative power. Barrie nods to French filmmaker Jean Cocteau in an homage to a scene from Cocteau's *Orphée* (1950) in which surgical gloves "magically" appear on the hands of death's emissary. In *Magic Explained,* Barrie uses the same technique that Cocteau used to achieve this effect—reversing the footage. The film appears to supersede laws of gravity, thus embracing the magical side of female creative energy. Creativity is a preoccupation of Diana Barrie. As she told Scott MacDonald, "[D]istribution is not the primary gratification that I get from film. My interest is more in making film" (333). The films of Diana Barrie are feminist, enigmatic, beautiful, painstakingly handcrafted, and, unfortunately, not widely distributed. Should they receive wider screenings, Barrie will undoubtedly be admitted into the pantheon of (largely male) underground American filmmaking. Even so, P. Adams Sitney, the canon-defining historian, includes *The Annunciation* in his personal pantheon of great underground films. A woman visionary, Barrie is an important figure in the male-dominated underground experimental filmmaking scene.

SELECTED FILMOGRAPHY

Untitled (1970)
To Clearlight (1972)
Eyes through Snow (1973)
A Curious Story (1973)
The Annunciation (1974)
Night Movie #1 (Self-Portrait) (1974)
Dear Diary Volume 1 (1974)
Portrait of Pamela (1974)
For the Dead Angels (1974)
Auto-Graph (1974)
The Red House (1974)
Sarah's Room (1974)
Night Movie #2 (Flashlight) (1974)
Dear Diary Volume #II (1975)
Hand-Maid #2 (1975)
Circus Vignettes (1975)
Letters from China (1975)
Dear Diary Volume III (1976)
A Song for Solomon (1976)
Day Dreams (1977)
By Sea (1978)
W'loo (1978)
My Version of the Fall (1978)
The Living or Dead Test (1979)
Le Mois de Fevrier (1979)
Night Movie #3 (The Party) (1979)
Untitled (1980)
Magic Explained (1980)
Stay Awake Whenever You Can (1982)
The Garden (1987)

SELECTED BIBLIOGRAPHY

Barrie, Diana. "Point of View." *Spiral 1* (October 1984): 10–11.
Canyon Cinema Catalogue No. 5. San Francisco: Canyon Cinema, 1982.
Curtis, David. *Experimental Cinema.* New York: Delta, 1971.
Film-Makers' Cooperative Catalogue No. 6. New York: Film-Makers' Cooperative, 1975.
Gidal, Peter, ed. *Structural Film Anthology.* London: British Film Institute, 1976.
Kaplan, E. Ann. *Women and Film: Both Sides of the Camera.* New York: Methuen, 1983.
MacDonald, Scott. *A Critical Cinema: Interviews with Independent Filmmakers,* 317–33. Berkeley: University of California Press, 1988.
Modleski, Tania. "The Films of Diana Barrie." *Wide Angle* 7.1–2 (1985): 62–67.
Museum of Modern Art. *Circulating Film Library Catalogue.* New York: Museum of Modern Art, 1984.
Rabinovitz, Lauren. *Points of Resistance: Women, Power & Politics in the New*

York Avant-Garde Cinema 1943–71. Urbana: University of Illinois Press, 1991.

Russett, Robert, and Cecile Starr. Experimental Animation. New York: Van Nostrand, 1976.

Turim, Maureen. Abstraction in Avant-Garde Film. Ann Arbor, MI: UMI Press, 1985.

Ward, Melinda, and Bruce Jenkins. The American New Wave 1958–1967. Minneapolis: Walker Art Center, 1982.

Youngblood, Gene. Expanded Cinema. New York: Dutton, 1970.

BAT ADAM, MICHAL (1950?–) Israel. The work of director Michal Bat Adam grew out of a cinematic period of individualism in Israeli filmmaking in the 1970s through the early 1980s. Though the Israeli filmmakers of this period are diverse and heterogeneous, film historian Ella Shohat finds a commonality of themes and styles among the group. Michal Bat Adam's *Moments* (*Each Other*) (1979) is one of a number of personal films of an introspective, contemplative, philosophic nature that explore the nature of the politics of identity formation. Adam's films often focus on lone protagonists at the outer margins of society. Romance, the aging process, and the act of creation are at the center of these films. Themes such as fragmentation, redemption, exile, and nationalism are explored in the films of Bat Adam and other Israeli filmmakers. Though the introspective films of this time tend to privilege a male prospective, Bat Adam's films transcend this problem.

Michal Bat Adam began her film career as an actress, later moving into film direction. *Moments* was her first film as a director. A coproduction of Israel and France, the film was released as *Each Other* in the United States. In the film, two women meet. One is a photographer, and the other is a writer. The filmmaker develops a lesbian relationship between her actresses in an oblique, experimental manner. Bat Adam uses strategies such as memory flashbacks in order to construct and, in some ways, deconstruct the relationship between the two women. Diane Kurys uses a similar device in *Entre Nous* (*Coup de Foudre*) (1983). Bat Adam allows the audience to make their own conclusion about the relationship in this metaphysical exploration of time, space, and narrative. In so doing, she foregrounds an aura of mystery that gives the film a distinctly cerebral effect, in the tradition of French filmmaker Alain Resnais, who also experiments with the themes of space, time, and biography. Bat Adam's other feature films are stylistically similar to *Moments*.

Michal Bat Adam is joined recently by many more women directing in Israel, including Orna Ben-Dor Niv (*Because of That Waf*, 1988), Nitza Gonen (*Deadline*, 1980), Mira Recanati (*A Thousand Little Kisses*, 1981), Shuli Eshel (*To Be a Woman Soldier*, 1981), Lihi Hanoch (*The End of the Orange Season*, 1989), and Rachel Esterkin (*Jacky*, 1991). These filmmakers were recently honored in a festival of films, "Israeli Women Direct," at the Brooklyn Museum in April 1992. Hopefully, the films of these talented directors will be more widely distributed in the West. At the present, screenings outside Israel are confined to major metropolitan centers in the United States, marginalizing the accomplishments of the women at the forefront of this new wave of Israeli feminist cinema.

SELECTED FILMOGRAPHY

Moments (Each Other) (1979)
A Thin Line (1980)
Ahava Rishona (First Love) (1982)
Boy Takes Girl (1983)
Hane 'ahev (The Lover) (1986)
A Thousand Wives (1988)

SELECTED BIBLIOGRAPHY

Jacob-Arzooni, Ora Gloria. *The Israeli Film.* New York: Garland, 1983.
Klausner, Margot. *The Dream Industry.* Herzliya: HSP, 1974.
Shohat, Ella. *Israeli Cinema: East/West and the Politics of Representation.* Austin: University of Texas Press, 1989.
————, and Robert Stam. "The Cinema after Babel: Language, Difference, Power." *Screen* 26.3 (May–August 1985): 35–38.
Smith, Sharon. *Women Who Make Movies.* New York: Hopkinson and Blake, 1975.

BATCHELOR, JOY (1914–   ). United Kingdom. Born on May 12, 1914, in Watford, England, Joy Batchelor studied art and began a career as a commercial artist for commercial cartoons. She worked on British cartoons such as *Music Man* (1936). She met and married John Halas, and in 1940 the partners developed a production company (Halas-Batchelor Productions). Though Halas has received much credit for his work, film scholars have generally ignored the contributions of Joy Batchelor. Batchelor worked as a coproducer, codirector, and cowriter and shared in all technical and aesthetic processes in their filmmaking efforts, which include the first British full-length feature cartoon, *Animal Farm* (1954), adapted from the George Orwell novel.

Halas-Batchelor Productions was the largest postwar animation house in Britain. During the war, Batchelor and Halas made public information and propaganda cartoons for the government, such as *Dustbin Parade* (1941), which stressed the importance of wartime recycling. They produced hundreds of commercial cartoons and commercials for their clients in industry, science, and advertising.

Animal Farm took three years to make and is widely accepted as one of the finest examples of early animation in Britain. The film was screened at many film festivals and received many awards. Batchelor and Halas are considered the first directors to use computer animation in math and science films. Batchelor's hand in early animation has been somewhat obscured in film history; for some reason, many historians prefer to concentrate on John Halas, rather than Batchelor's work for the pioneering team. Nevertheless, Joy Batchelor is to be credited for developing and maintaining a career in a completely male-dominated period of animation and creating a lasting legacy in the history of the British cinema.

SELECTED FILMOGRAPHY

Films directed with John Halas

Train Trouble (1940)
Carnival in the Clothes Cupboard (1940)
Filling the Gap (1941)
Dustbin Parade (1941)
Digging for Victory (1942)
Jungle Warfare (1943)
Modern Guide to Health (1946)
Old Wives' Tales (1946)
Charley Series (1946–47)
First Line of Defence (1947)
This Is the Air Force (1947)
What's Cooking? (1947)
Dolly Put the Kettle On (1947)
Oxo Parade (1948)
Heave Away My Johnny (1948)
The Shoemaker and the Hatter (1949)
Fly about the House (1949)
The Figurehead (1953)
Animal Farm (1954)
The Candlemaker (1956)
The First 99 (1958)
Dam the Delta (1958)
All Lit Up (1959)
Piping Hot (1959)
For Better for Worse (1959)

Films directed by Batchelor

Ruddigore (1964)
Classic Fairy Tales (series) (1966)
Colombo Plan (1967)
The Commonwealth (1967)
Bolly (1968)
The Five (1970)
Wet Dot (1970)
Contact (1973)
The Ass and the Stick (1974)
Carry on Milkmaids (1974)

SELECTED BIBLIOGRAPHY

Aldgate, Anthony, and Jeffrey Richards. *Britain Can Take It: The British Cinema in the Second World War.* Oxford: Blackwell, 1986.

Armes, Roy. *A Critical History of British Cinema.* New York: Oxford University Press, 1978.

Balcon, Michael, Ernest Lindgren, Forsyth Hardy, and Roger Manvell. *Twenty Years of British Cinema, 1925–1945.* London: Falcon, 1947.

Barr, Charles, ed. *All Our Yesterdays: 90 Years of British Cinema.* London: BFI, 1986.

Gifford, Denis. *The British Film Catalogue: A Reference Guide.* New York: McGraw-Hill, 1973.

Kotlarz, Irene. "Working against the Grain: Women in Animation." In *Women in Film: A Sight and Sound Reader,* edited by Pam Cook and Phillip Dodd, 101–4. Philadelphia: Temple University Press, 1993.

Manvell, Roger. *Art and Animation.* London: Halas and Batchelor, 1980.

Noake, Roger. *Animation.* London: MacDonald, 1988.

BEMBERG, MARIA LUISA (1940–1995). Argentina. Maria Luisa Bemberg is best known for directing *Camila* (1984), an Argentinian-Spanish coproduction based on a true story of a nineteenth-century woman who eloped with a priest and was hunted down and executed with her lover. A lush period drama, the film is typical of many Latin American films that feature the plight of a free-spirited woman who disregards the social codes of patriarchal order and authority, especially the figures of the church and the family. Camila disregards the authority of both powers. She ignores the fact that her grandmother was literally locked up for inappropriately displaying female sexuality. Like her grandmother, she loses her life to love. Bemberg's placement of the illicit love affair within the church itself is a subversion of clerical authority. As Barbara Quart observes, the love affair itself is traditionally defined as a form of "captivity" by many Western women filmmakers (253).

Camila is, indeed, a captivity narrative that may not allow the female protagonist a way out, but it provides a metadiagetic framework within which the woman takes a great deal of authority out of her oppressor's hands and willfully displays her self-defined eroticism. *Camila* has been called a melodrama, placing it in the female literary tradition of the romance novel. Both the romance novel and the melodramatic film are deprivileged by most male-authored criticism and canonization. Recently, however, feminist film critics and literary scholars have reassessed this admittedly overwrought form as a site of feminist political subversion and dialogic expression. This sheds a completely new light on the previously ignored or discredited films of many women directors, including Lois Weber in the United States and many other international women filmmakers.

Bemberg's melodramatic woman stands both as a signifier of objectified male gaze and as something else: a reconstruction of feminine subjectivity, authority, and voice. The defiant face of Camila, lit and photographed to highlight her superficially masked anger, is unmistakably feminist in nature. In addition, Bemberg voices patriarchal views through her male figures. For example, Camila's grandfather states in the film that "a single woman is a chaos . . . either the convent or matrimony . . . matrimony is order . . . neither the people nor the country can live without order."

Female sexuality is at odds with the political state, with patriarchal "normalcy" itself. It must be suppressed or ended. In *Camila,* it is ended, and Bemberg's film is one of the most tragic films of Latin American cinema history. The film implies a double-voiced discourse, or duality of intent. On one hand, it appears to conform to the narrative conventions of patriarchal film (the transgressive woman suffers and dies). But the handling of this death by Bemberg openly defies convention in that the director clearly conveys to the audience the complete lack of reason inherent in the act of patriarchal oppression, which is seen in all its ugliness. According to the reasoning of *Camila,* a woman's sexuality cannot, and should not, be repressed or oppressed.

In order to direct films, Maria Luisa Bemberg divorced her husband after raising an upper-class family. In a sense, on the screen in *Camila* she plays out the escape she made from what was apparently a form of captivity in real life. Her films and screenplays always center around female struggles and feminist transformations. *Miss Mary* (1986), Bemberg's fifth feature, concerns a woman who is an exile, in a sense, a British governess brought to Argentina in the 1930s to educate the children of an upper-class family. Another glossy, melodramatic film, it stars Julie Christie and was financed through North American funding. Bemberg locates the exiled woman within a different type of captivity (labor) and brings out many themes common in *Camila.* The confining of the female body and female desire in the bourgeois family, orthodox religion, and male-defined workplace are once again central themes in *Miss Mary.* Miss Mary is torn by sexual repression and attitudes toward women.

The image of the masked woman is another manifestation of a form of captivity narrative that is thematically contextualized in *Miss Mary.* In many films and literary works, women are often forced to mask themselves in order to somehow "contain" their sexuality and individuality. In *Miss Mary,* the mother figure usually wears sunglasses, and the daughters are obsessed with makeup. Miss Mary herself, like Camila, wears a mask of inscrutable erasure or lack, never allowing pain or desire to show, lest she pay the price for reclaiming her subjectivity. The young Latin American female, Carolina, desires to escape her life of masquerade and objectification. The oppression of women is shared across boundaries of land and culture between Carolina and the British woman, yet the two are separated by language and other cultural differences. Bemberg superimposes the colonialist order (through the figure of Miss Mary) over the Latin American patriarchal order. The director effectively portrays them in a complex power structure of multiple captivity narratives.

Bemberg's *Miss Mary* juxtaposes melodrama with a shorthanded feminist undertone of irony, especially in the letters that Miss Mary writes to her colonialist English family. Here Bemberg excels in a dark humor that exposes colonialist expectations through the words of its exiled figure. Miss Mary's letters create a fictitious world that conforms less to reality than to colonialist expectations of the exotic other's land. Instead of describing the atmosphere of decay and family rancor, Miss Mary writes about a picturesque hacienda filled with happy "natives." *Miss Mary* is a film of complexity because of its multilayeredness and because of Bemberg's dialogic interplay of melodrama, humor, and suffering.

Bemberg continued to make complex, yet glossy period films, which are often discredited as melodramas. *Yo la más pobre de todas* (*I, the Worst of All*) (1990) centers on a seventeenth-century Mexican nun and poetess who joins the church to find a room of her own in order to pursue a life of contemplation and writing. Maria Luisa Bemberg was not only the first commercially successful Argentine woman director but one of the few Latin American directors whose work had been well distributed internationally.

SELECTED FILMOGRAPHY

El mundo de la mujer (*The World of Women*) (1972)
Juquetes (*Toys*) (1978)
Momentos (*Moments*) (1980)
Señora de nadie (*Nobody's Wife*) (1982)
Camila (1984)
Miss Mary (1986)
Yo la más pobre de todas (*I, the Worst of All*) (1990)
I Don't Want to Talk About It (1994)

SELECTED BIBLIOGRAPHY

Brunette, Peter. "Political Subtext in a Fairy Tale from a Feminist." *New York Times,* September 25, 1994, 14H, 16H.

Burton, Julianne, ed. *Cinema and Social Change in Latin America.* Pittsburgh: University of Pittsburgh Press, 1990.

Freydberg, Elizabeth Hadley. "Women of Color: No Joy in the Seduction of Images." In *Multiple Voices in Feminist Film Criticism*, edited by Diane Carson, Linda Dittmar, and Janice Welsch, 468–80. Minneapolis: University of Minnesota Press, 1994.

Fusco, Coco, ed. *Reviewing Histories: Selections from New Latin American Cinema.* New York: Hallwalls, 1987.

King, John, and Nissa Torrents, eds. *The Garden of Forking Paths: Argentine Cinema.* London: BFI, 1987.

Lesage, Julia. "Latin American and Caribbean Women in Film and Video." In *Multiple Voices in Feminist Film Criticism,* edited by Diane Carson, Linda Dittmar, and Janice Welsch, 492–502. Minneapolis: University of Minnesota Press, 1994.

Lopez, Ana. "Tears and Desire: Women and Melodrama in the 'Old' Mexican Cinema." In *Multiple Voices in Feminist Film Criticism*, edited by Diane Carson, Linda Dittmar, and Janice R. Welsch, 254–70. Minneapolis: University of Minnesota Press, 1994.

Pick, Zuzana M., ed. *Latin American Film Makers and the Third Cinema*. Ottawa: Carleton University Press, 1978.

Quart, Barbara. *Women Directors: The Emergence of a New Cinema*. New York: Praeger, 1988.

BIGELOW, KATHRYN (1953–   ). United States. Kathryn Bigelow is a celebrated director of Hollywood action films. Luck and determination have landed her jobs directing films such as *Point Break* and *Blue Steel*. Few women in Hollywood have been accepted by the old-boys' network as action directors. Bigelow grew up in northern California and attended the San Francisco Art Institute. Graduating in 1972, Bigelow continued studying film in New York at the Whitney Museum Independent Study Program and the Columbia Graduate Film School, where she studied with Milos Foreman. She directed a short film, *The Set-Up* (1978), at Columbia and received a degree in film in 1979. In 1982, Bigelow codirected *The Loveless* with Monty Montgomery, a claustrophobic biker movie starring a young Willem Dafoe. Inspired by dark and gritty "B" movies such as Joseph H. Lewis's *Gun Crazy* (1950) and Edgar G. Ulmer's *Detour* (1945), Bigelow's *The Loveless* is a psychological thriller, a cerebral, punk biker film. Bigelow has an attraction to action and violence, and she demonstrates an ability to bring out the kinetic quality and the psychological tension of both themes in her film work. As Bigelow told Pam Cook, "We're all motivated by violence or resistance to violence . . . it's positive when the filmmaker takes a few risks and shakes up your world a little" (1990, 316). Bigelow affectively underscores the power positions between individuals and across gender. *The Loveless* did well both in Britain and in the United States, but Bigelow was not interested in directing other people's material, so she set to work writing the noirish vampire Western *Near Dark*, which she cowrote with Eric Red.

As the start of shooting for *Near Dark* (1987) approached, Bigelow found that the producer was interested in the script but hesitated to let her direct it. Bigelow made it clear that unless she was allowed to direct the project, the script would be unavailable. Bigelow let the producer think about it for twenty-four hours and eventually forced him to agree to her terms. Bigelow's gamble paid off: *Near Dark* is a brilliant feminist vampire thriller that exposes the horror latent in rural American existence. Jenny Wright, a mysterious young woman (who is actually a vampire), is part of a gang of vampires who drive through the midwest landscape in search of victims. A virginal young man, played by Adrian Pasdar, is attracted to the young woman. Pasdar finally meets the girl's "family," a malicious, motley group of low-life types who are led by the truly frightening Lance Henricksen. One critic called the film "the most hard-edged, violent actioner ever directed by an American woman" (Elley): this writer obviously is not familiar with the work of Ida Lupino.

Near Dark is also successful at reversing the gender roles of the classic Hollywood horror film. Instead of a female victim, we are presented with a male victim, in a refreshing gender switch that caters to the female spectator. Not only is the victim male, but he is passive and is soon dependent on his girlfriend's blood for life, neatly reversing the routine situation of women who depend on men for money or social position. One never quite knows where this unique film will go, and it is a great pleasure to watch the twists and turns of the plot unfold.

Near Dark redefines the horror film family, which is, in turn, a metaphor for the dysfunctional American family. The motherless young man is attracted to a family that feeds on other people, in a way symbolizing the American dream of mobility. The film displays a collective anxiety and violence inherent in American family life, which is preoccupied with freedom, mobility, and the appearance of normalcy. At the end of the film the all-American boy is reunited with his father and sister, and the vampires ride into the sunset. But along the way, Bigelow makes us contemplate the ramifications of our audience expectations by consistently undermining them. The American home becomes redefined, as critic Yvonne Tasker notes, as "safe, but also monstrous, restrictive space" (156).

Kathryn Bigelow found a powerful producer, Oliver Stone, for her next film, *Blue Steel* (1990). It is clear that with *Blue Steel,* Bigelow set out to make a blockbuster woman's action film. Female audiences crave and look forward to identifying with a female heroine who throws her own punches, captures the bad guy, and, most important, plays the role of action hero. Bigelow was so successful in her transgendered construction of the female action hero that when *Blue Steel* was screened at the Berlin Film Festival, many men found themselves identifying with the female hero.

In *Blue Steel,* Jamie Lee Curtis stars as Megan Turner, a rookie cop who comes face-to-face with her own desire for power. Megan is suspended from the force after she kills a bank robber during her first night on the streets and then loses her gun at the scene of the shooting. A psychotic, played by Ron Silver, begins carving Megan's name on bullets and committing serial murders with her gun. Film critics admire *Blue Steel* for its gender-bending strategy and its stylized look. Steven Shaviro calls *Blue Steel* "a perverse and powerfully stylized exercise in visual excess" (1). Shaviro also notes Bigelow's fetishistic display of weaponry, which is so exaggerated as to almost become a parody of male action films. Shaviro sees the film as a "postmodern" film about the excess of violence in American culture. Yvonne Tasker, however, is cautious in her estimation of the film's end, and finds "disturbing implications of a fetishism surrounding women and guns . . . as we are invited to share in it" (159). All too often, Megan is the victim of violent attacks. In some ways, *Blue Steel* is a successful feminist venture, but ultimately I agree with Tasker, who concludes that "*Blue Steel* might be said to enact a conventional scenario which punishes the female character's transgressive desire to become a powerful figure" (160). The film should not be completely dismissed, however, because of its positive representation of an armed female heroine. Women action figures remain the minority in Hollywood fantasy films; Bigelow's film is a step in a new and interesting direction.

Bigelow's next film, *Point Break* (1991), is another study of power and relationships between men and women. The action sequences may be unparalleled, but the film is lengthy and plot-heavy. Patrick Swayze stars as a macho surf veteran and part-time bank robber who buddies up to an undercover twenty-five-year-old Federal Bureau of Investigation agent, played by Keanu Reeves. Lori Petty apears in the film as a young woman who teaches Keanu how to surf. Though the visuals are often stunning, particularly the in-air, high-diving stunts, the film offers little more than action to viewers, feminist or otherwise.

Kathryn Bigelow remains a role model for many aspiring women directors (indeed, many active women directors) who wish to make blockbuster commercial action films. She recently married Hollywood action director James Cameron, and her new film, *Strange Days,* opened in 1995.

SELECTED FILMOGRAPHY

The Set-Up (1978)
The Loveless (codirector) (1982)
Near Dark (1987)
Blue Steel (1990)
Point Break (1991)
Strange Days (1995)

SELECTED BIBLIOGRAPHY

Clover, Carol J. *Men, Women and Chainsaws: Gender in the Modern Horror Film.* Princeton: Princeton University Press, 1992.

Cook, Pam. "Walk on the Wild Side." *Monthly Film Bulletin* 57.682 (November 1990): 315–16.

———. "Border Crossings: Women and Film in Context." In *Women in Film: A Sight and Sound Reader,* edited by Pam Cook and Philip Dodd, 9–23. Philadelphia: Temple University Press, 1993.

Elley, Derek, ed. *"Near Dark."* In *Variety Movie Guide,* 532. London: Hamlyn, 1993.

Kaplan, Cora. "Dirty Harriet/*Blue Steel:* Feminist Theory Goes to Hollywood." *Discourse* 16.1 (fall 1993): 50–70.

Margolis, Harriet. "*Blue Steel:* Progressive Feminism in the 90's?" *Post Script* 13.1 (fall 1993): 67–76.

Mizejewski, Linda. "Picturing the Female Dick: *The Silence of the Lambs* and *Blue Steel.*" *Journal of Film and Video* 45. 2–3 (summer–fall 1993): 6–23.

Sanders, Richard, ed. "Kathryn Bigelow—Director." *People* (Special Issue: *Women, Sex and Power*), (spring 1991): 85.

Schwendenwien, Jude. *"Blue Steel." Cineaste* 18.1 (1990–91): 51.

Shaviro, Steven. *The Cinematic Body.* Minneapolis: University of Minnesota Press, 1993.

Tasker, Yvonne. *Spectacular Bodies: Gender, and the Action Cinema.* London: Routledge, 1993.

Williams, Linda. *Hardcore: Power, Pleasure and the Frenzy of the Visible.* Berkeley: University of California Press, 1989.

BLACHÉ, ALICE GUY. *See* GUY, ALICE

BLACKWOOD, MAUREEN (1960–   ). United Kingdom. Black British filmmaker Maureen Blackwood is a founding member of Sankofa, a London-based collective dedicated to promoting and producing black films by black directors. In 1983, Martina Attile, Maureen Blackwood, Robert Crusz, Isaac Julien, and Nadine Marsh-Edwards formed the group to explore diverse images of the black experience beyond the realms of the exotic, the victim, and the violent assailant. For too long, white filmmakers have either ignored or distorted diverse black cultural experience. The cultural production of images for too long has been mired in the colonialist enterprise of suppressing the voice, body, and vision of nonwhite people. Black activists and artists are seizing power of the cinema, which oppresses, misrepresents, or erases the black body.

In 1986, Maureen Blackwood and Isaac Julien directed *The Passion of Remembrance* for Sankofa. The film is available through Women Make Movies, New York. *Passion of Remembrance* is considered a unique representation of the diversity of the experience of black people. The multi-leveled narrative is an experiment in multiple points of view. In the film, a black couple talk about the subject of diversity in black experience in a self-referential act of cinematic framing and doubling. The reconfiguration of black identity is grounded within the context of a series of rapidly changing video images of British history. *The Passion of Remembrance* is a moving, elegant feast of images, recommended for all people interested in the diversity of human experience.

Perfect Image? (1988) is a complex exploration of the notion of self and identity, seen through the perspective of two actresses. The actresses reach across the screen and draw the viewer into an almost hyperreal experience through their disregard for the camera apparatus. In this way, Blackwood moves the discourse to an intimate level, guiding the viewer on a rediscovery of our notion of self. Stereotypes of black women are thrown into a fresh perspective in this film. As Barbara Kruger observes, the films of the

Sankofa collective "break down the conventions of what is 'appropriate' Black visual production" (144). Blackwood's films are a movement toward an openly defined countercinema of black expression.

In 1992, Blackwood directed a documentary film about the unsung contributions of black Britons in boxing and music halls at the turn of the century. *A Family Called Abrew* (1992) is a warm and poignant browse through archival footage, oral history, and other important documentation of this neglected cultural moment in black history. The film concentrates on one particularly extraordinary family, the Abrews. As cultural and historical documents of lost family and racial identity, films such as *A Family Called Abrew* mark the rebirth of black cinema.

Home Away from Home is a short film about a black woman named Miriam, who lives near Heathrow Airport. Blackwood uses the metaphor of the continual mobility of the planes in the air over Miriam's house to underscore Miriam's displacement from her African cultural roots. Miriam wishes to reconnect with her exiled home in order to share her earth/mother home-place with her daughter, Fumi. Finally, Miriam builds a mud hut in her garden and creates a mystical space in which she metaphorically escapes her exiled existence. The outside world crushes her attempt to metaphysically travel home to Africa, when her neighbors dislike the physical structure she has built. *Home Away from Home* is a meditation on exile and spiritual communion. It is a poignant film for black people who have been torn from their cultural identity. It is a moving film for all of the postcolonial peoples who live with no connection to their motherlands.

In addition to directing, Maureen Blackwood is constantly active in all phases of production on other Sankofa films. She is an assistant cameraperson for *Territories* (1984) (director Isaac Julien), another contemplative film that addresses the issues of black identity. Blackwood is an assistant director on *Looking for Langston* (director Isaac Julien, 1988). The film is a study of the life of Langston Hughes, the famous black gay artist who flourished in the heyday of the Harlem renaissance. Blackwood also teaches in workshops sponsored by Sankofa. She is a formidable figure in black filmmaking in Britain and an admired feminist and role model abroad.

SELECTED FILMOGRAPHY

Passion of Remembrance (1986)
Perfect Image? (1988)
A Family Called Abrew (1992)
Home Away from Home (1993)

SELECTED BIBLIOGRAPHY

Alexander, Karen. "Julie Dash: *Daughters of the Dust,* and a Black Aesthetic." In *Women and Film: A Sight and Sound Reader,* edited by Pam Cook and Philip Dodd, 224–31. Philadelphia: Temple University Press, 1993.
Attile, Martina, and Maureen Blackwood. "Black Women and Representation,

Notes from the Workshops Held in London, 1984." In *Films for Women,* edited by Charlotte Brunsdon, 202–8. London: BFI, 1987.

Bhabha, Homi K. "The Other Question—The Stereotype and Colonial Discourse." *Screen* 24.6 (November–December 1983): 18–36.

Campbell, Loretta. "Reinventing Our Image: Eleven Black Women Filmmakers." *Heresies* 16 (1983): 58–62.

Fusco, Coco. "Sankofa and Black Audio Film Collective." In *Discourses: Conversations in Post Modern Art and Culture,* edited by Russell Ferguson, William Olander, Karen Fiss, and Marcia Tucker, 17–43. Cambridge: Massachusetts Institute of Technology and New York: New Museum of Contemporary Art, 1990.

Gaines, Jane. "White Privilege and Looking Relations." In *Multiple Voices in Feminist Film Criticism,* edited by Diane Carson, Linda Dittmar, and Janice Welsch, 162–75. Minneapolis: University of Minnesota Press, 1994.

hooks, bell. *Black Looks: Race and Representation.* Boston: South End Press, 1992.

Jackson, Lynn, and Jean Rasenberger. "An Interview with Martina Attile and Isaac Julien." *Cineaste* 14.4 (1988): 23–37.

Klotman, Phylliss Rauch, ed. *Screenplays of the African American Experience.* Bloomington: Indiana University Press, 1991.

Kruger, Barbara. "Sankofa Film/Video Collective and Black Audio Film Collective [at] the Collective for Living Cinema." *Artforum* (September 1988): 143–44.

Larkin, Alile Sharon. "Black Women Filmmakers Defining Ourselves." In *Female Spectators: Looking at Film and Television,* edited by E. Deidre Pribram, 157–73. London: Verso, 1988.

BORDEN, LIZZIE (1950–   ). United States. Lizzie Borden's radically feminist dystopian vision of the future is the premise of her now-classic *Born in Flames* (1983). She went into film upon graduating from Wellesley College, where she studied painting. She wrote art criticism for *Artforum* but decided to teach herself filmmaking and editing after she decided not to pursue a career in art. *Regrouping* (1976) was Borden's first film. Next, she started her own production company, Alternate Current, and began planning the radical science fiction film *Born in Flames.* Borden encouraged collaboration in the scriptwriting process, and she allowed the final script to evolve from a combined vision of her own plans and the input of the actors. *Born in Flames,* deemed "one of the most important feminist films of the eighties" (Jackson, 4), is set ten years in the future after a social revolution.

Born in Flames addresses the issue of frequent invisibility of black women in white women's films and feminism in general. In addition, Borden's film criticizes the lack of feminist consciousness outside the heterotopic mind-set, in its address of lesbian issues. *Born in Flames* is consciously aware of the complexity of the politics of race, class, gender, and sexuality. It is part of a wider movement in feminism to begin to recognize differences among women, to get beyond a feminism that addresses the needs of only upper middle-class white women. Borden's film is highly critical of the commonly held simplistic view of a one-step sweeping social revolution that will permanently release the oppressed. *Born in Flames* has elicited controversy for its criticism of simplistic leftist politics. The postrevolutionary future world of *Born in Flames* is a social democracy that has reverted to old patterns of male dominance and racial oppression. *Born in Flames,* as Teresa de Lauretis accurately observes, "addresses a female audience" (137) and, in a sense, remakes the revolution.

Women from many backgrounds mobilize in the film. Lesbians, heterosexuals, single mothers, intellectuals, pop singers, underground performers, disc jockeys, African Americans, Latinas, and an army of women unite because of their common recognition of differences, rather than an erasure of difference. *Born in Flames* marks a pivotal moment in feminism as much as it remakes women's political cinema. As feminists began to rethink difference, feminist filmmakers began to rethink pleasure. The film is pleasurable to watch, unlike many political films. Borden uses visual effects, rapid editing, flickering images, and an approach toward the material that entertains as much as it educates. The music of the rock groups the Bloods and Red Crayola adds to the freshness of approach of the film's political material. A vision of female warriorhood, *Born in Flames* entertains even as it makes demands of its audience: the viewer is forced to confront his or her political position and disallowed a passive, spectatorial position. Probably the most outstanding line of the film, among many outstanding lines, comes from Pat, one of the central characters. "We have to take over the *language*. We have to describe ourselves," she states, which is a rallying cry not only for feminists but for women artists and filmmakers. The language of film is a language that is immersed in the male gaze and patriarchal politics; a new language must be formed from the bottom up. In some ways, *Born in Flames* defies description. Apparently, this is intentional. As Borden told Anne Friedberg:

Trying to discuss the film as a logical political treatise just doesn't work. The film deals with highly irrational responses to simple things: Why does rape exist? Why does rape continue to exist? Why is there such virulent anti-female feeling in this country? Why is there such virulent anti-homosexual feeling in this country? Taking any group (and it could have been blacks) and making them spontaneously combust arouses people's fears. The film takes us to the point where women were finally just sick of the things they always had to grin and bear. (39–40)

Born in Flames struck a responsive chord in the women's movement, particularly because it was released during a political move to the right in the United States. Borden's next film, *Working Girls* (1986), created an even wider audience response because it deals directly with the sexual politics of prostitution. The title of the film is an homage to pioneer feminist director Dorothy Arzner, who directed a film entitled *Working Girls* in 1930.

Many feminists were surprised that the director of *Born in Flames* could present prostitution as a viable means of employment for women, but, ahead of her time, perhaps, this is exactly Borden's message. Borden formed her views on the subject through her association with women of COYOTE, a feminist alliance of prostitutes and labor activists who are interested in the professionalization of prostitution. It is perhaps unsurprising that Borden would once again challenge the dogma of a narrowly defined feminism. Borden relocates prostitution in the domain of work, and she does this mainly by de-eroticizing the depiction of sex between client and "working girl." Borden's *Working Girls* is critical of the feminists who oppress other women because of their retrograde, patriarchally fashioned views of prostitutes and work. As Borden told Lynne Jackson:

Women in the sex industry have been so reviled on both sides that there must be a way in which we can establish a dialogue which is not against women who work in this way. (4)

Working Girls is stylistically very different from *Born in Flames*. It is shot in a style that is much like that of Chantal Akerman. The film is composed of long takes and has the flavor of documentary, though it is obviously fictional. Borden, in a sense, invites the viewer to stare in seemingly real time at the mundane events in a Manhattan brothel. The film follows the lives of ten prostitutes and their johns. It includes a foregrounded lesbian framing device. It is one of the first films to recognize that many prostitutes have meaningful lesbian relationships. Borden manages to avoid objectifying the female nude body by presenting it as flat, neither glamorous nor ugly. The surprising thing is that Borden completely reverses this achievement in her next film, *Love Crimes* (1992).

Love Crimes is an example of what sadly happens to independent filmmakers, both male and female, when they join Hollywood's machine and lose their personal vision along the way. Though Borden has defended the film in interviews, *Love Crimes* is as sexist as any other soft-core thriller. It revels in the objectification of Sean Young's body and is plotted around an exploitational story line. Sean Young plays a district attorney who is lured into sex games with a fashion photographer/murderer. It is not the depiction of a woman's sadomasochistic desires that is disturbing, so much as the fact that the woman is led to "understand" her desires by a father figure/murderer. But women directors, just like their male counterparts, certainly deserve to make mistakes in public. One hopes that Lizzie Borden will get the opportunity to make additional films that live up to the refreshing unconventionality of her earlier efforts.

SELECTED FILMOGRAPHY

Regrouping (1976)
Born in Flames (1983)

Working Girls (1986)
Love Crimes (1992)

SELECTED BIBLIOGRAPHY

Cole, Janis, and Holly Dale. *Calling the Shots: Profiles of Women Filmmakers.* Ontario: Quarry Press, 1993.

Cook, Pam. "Border Crossings, Women and Film in Context." In *Women and Film: A Sight and Sound Reader,* edited by Pam Cook and Philip Dodd, 9–23. Philadelphia: Temple University Press, 1993.

Creed, Barbara. *The Monstrous Feminine: Film, Feminism, Psychoanalysis.* London: Routledge, 1993.

de Lauretis, Teresa. *Technologies of Gender.* Bloomington: Indiana University Press, 1987.

Erens, Patricia, ed. *Issues in Feminist Film Criticism.* Bloomington: Indiana University Press, 1990.

Friedberg, Anne. "An Interview with Filmmaker Lizzie Borden." *Women and Performance* 1.2 (1984): 37–45.

Gibson, Pamela Church, and Roma Gibson, eds. *Dirty Looks: Women, Pornography and Power.* London: BFI, 1993.

Jackson, Lynne. "Labor Relations: An Interview with Lizzie Borden." *Cineaste* 15.3 (1987): 4–17.

Lucia, Cynthia. "Redefining Female Sexuality in the Cinema." *Cineaste* 19. 2–3 (1992): 6–19.

Mayne, Judith. *The Woman at the Keyhole: Feminism and Women's Cinema.* Bloomington: Indiana University Press, 1990.

Mellencamp, Patricia. *Avant-Garde Film, Video, & Feminism.* Bloomington: Indiana University Press, 1990.

Quart, Barbara. *Women Directors: The Emergence of a New Cinema.* New York: Praeger, 1988.

Todd, Janet. *Women and Film.* New York: Holmes and Meyer, 1988.

BOX, MURIEL (1905–91). United Kingdom. Few women directed films in Britain, up until the very recent past. ("They elbowed you out," Box explains [McFarlane, 42].) Muriel Box is one of a handful of women directors in British film history; she and Wendy Toye were the only women directing in the 1950s in England. Before them, such forgotten figures as Dinah Shurey and Ethyl Batley (who directed sixty-seven films in the years between 1912 and 1916) were lost in the annals of male-authored British cinema history. Surprisingly little feminist scholarship exists on these women, including Box and Toye. Often their films are dismissed for their supposed lack of feminism. But a reassessment of the career and films of Muriel Box exposes a clear feminist agenda in the career of a woman who elbowed her way into an utterly sexist industry.

Muriel Box (born Violet Baker at Tolworth, England, in 1905) worked her way into film through the ranks as a typist, continuity "girl," and, finally, screenwriter. Her autobiography, *Odd Woman Out,* articulates her ability to move up through the male hierarchy. She combined a seemingly inconquerable spirit with a clever wit and persevering nature. Muriel Box's mother taught school and provided Muriel with a role model of an independently spirited, even stubborn woman who survived despite an argumentative, irresponsible, gambling husband. Muriel left home and began supporting herself at the age of seventeen. She eventually found a job typing at British Instructional Films.

Muriel proved that she could write and moved out of the menial task of typing other people's scripts. She did not have her eye on a directing career but, instead, thought she would be an actress or a dancer. When she lost her typing job, she worked as a continuity "girl" for British International Pictures, under such well-known directors as Anthony Asquith. Next, she was hired by Michael Powell, again as a secretary. Muriel met her future husband, Sydney Box, when she was working in the continuity department of Gaumont-British Studios. The two fell in love, but Muriel had no intention of marrying. The Boxes had an interesting working partnership as scenarists, but they wished to make their own productions. They collaborated on screenplays for British classics such as *Alibi Inn* (1935). Muriel and Sydney Box, along with Betty Box (Sydney's sister), began the production company Verity Films and began producing screenplays written by Muriel and Sydney.

Muriel wished to direct, but strict societal gender codes prohibited a woman from having access to such a recognizably powerful and public position. Thus, Muriel served as the screenplay writer of the early Box films. Betty Box was the producer, and Sydney directed the films. Their films were well received by the public, and the Boxes were invited to work for Gainsborough Pictures. Finally, after a great deal of success as a screenwriter, Muriel directed *The Happy Family* in 1952. Released under the title *Mr. Lord Says No!* in the United States, *The Happy Family* is a mildly amusing comedy that derives its humor from the class conflicts inherent in British society. *Street Corner* (1953) is one of Box's best feminist efforts, a sort of forerunner of *Blue Steel*. *Street Corner* is a narrative about the lives of women in the police force. It was made as a response to *The Blue Lamp*, a popular British film that completely ignored the contributions of women police officers. Box notes that "it never mentioned women and how they cooperated in police work. It was about time women had a chance to show what they did" (McFarlane, 42).

Box told interviewers exactly how difficult it was for a woman to direct in the British film industry. Unlike many women directors, Box was very outspoken on this point. In one story she makes it clear how nearly impossible it was, as a woman, to secure a directorial position. Box told historian Brian McFarlane how her agent attempted to discourage her when she pushed for bigger directorial assignments.

He sighed deeply and said, "Muriel, I wish I could tell you different but, if I mention the name of a woman as a director, they just turn away and look out of the window." That was absolutely true . . . even with my last film [*Rattle of a Simple Man*, 1964] for which Sydney had got me the contract, they were still worried about the woman director aspect. This was three weeks after we had booked the studio space. One of the officials at ABC said they hadn't used a woman director before and were chary of it. They would have preferred not to go ahead with the film if Sydney insisted on my directing. (42)

Box persevered, however, even in the face of such obstinate, seemingly immovable sexism.

The Passionate Stranger (1957) is another film that is quite feminist for its time. The female-centered narrative revolves around a woman novelist. *The Passionate Stranger* uses a foolish chauffeur as a framing device: the chauffeur reads the work of the woman novelist and mistakenly assumes that she is in love with him. Box filmed one section in color (when the novel is read) and the rest of the film in black and white. Clearly, Box seems to be addressing the British fear of sexuality in romance novels, by filming the scene from the "bodice-ripper" in lush and flamboyant color. Contemporary male critics were restrained in their praise, but the film ages gracefully, and Box's dry feminist wit is readily apparent to modern audiences.

Box was consistently interested in women's issues and women's stories and was most inspired by the writings of Virginia Woolf, particularly *A Room of One's Own*. Box recalls her finest achievement, in her eyes, in her autobiography *Odd Woman Out*:

The film personally significant to me above all others was *The Truth About Women* since the original screenplay (again written by Sydney and myself) was a comedy with serious undertones concerning the status of women in various societies from the turn of the century until today. . . . Woolf's *A Room of One's Own* made such an impact on me in my twenties that I had been possessed ever since with a strong urge to support the cause of equality between the sexes. Thus my approach to this subject was perhaps more enthusiastic and dedicated than to any other theme previously attempted. (122)

The Truth About Women (1958) is a film that, according to Louise Heck-Rabi, "struck a blow for equal rights for women" (180). Told in flashback narratives of an older man, the manner in which Box presents the relationships between the sexes is remarkably sophisticated and includes many feminist observations. The producers were thinking of shelving the picture, but critics and audiences loved it. The film became a substantial hit, much to Box's delight.

Too Young to Love (1960), Box's most controversial film, was an adaptation of a play entitled *The Pick-Up Girl* (1950). Though it is meant as an early exploitation vehicle, it comes off as a decidedly feminist take on female juvenile delinquency. A young girl's ignorance, poverty, and need for sexual pleasure are seen through the eyes of a female storyteller. *Too Young to Love* dealt frankly with pregnancy, societal views toward women, venereal disease, prostitution, and abortion. The British state censors cut the film drastically before release, which came as a surprise to no one but which was a severe disappointment to Box. Interestingly enough, early American women directors such as Lois Weber and Dorothy Davenport Reid had also tackled these "controversial" themes. Women directors often find ways of using commercial film vehicles to make political statements. The ideal of cinema as pure escapism does not always appeal to women directors or women audiences, perhaps because escapism encourages complacency. In a way, Box's films are a form of the countercinema that women directors only consciously began developing in Britain in the 1970s. Box was able, at an early date, to infuse political statements into films that were billed as pure and simple entertainment. As Box told Sue Aspinall, "[W]e were not engaged to indulge our own political or socialist views, however much we should have found satisfaction in doing so" (65).

Recently, the career of Muriel Box has been reassessed by critics such as Caroline Merz, who notes that Box managed to make films that seemed simple but were nevertheless feminist. For example, *Rattle of a Simple Man* (1964) appears to be a straightforward narrative, even a sexist comedy. But, as Merz notes, *Rattle of a Simple Man* "pokes fun very successfully at the ideology of the male group and its crude sexism" ("Tension," 126). Unfortunately, the film failed at the box office, effectively ending Box's directorial career. Box was often harshly criticized by male critics, who would not have been able to recognize, much less approve of, an early feminist streak of countercinema. Critics did not like that the laughs in Muriel Box films were often at the expense of male characters, in an effective reversal of gender "norms." In fact, a more recent assessment of the criticism leveled against Box tells more about the sexism of the journalism of film than about the films of Muriel Box. Even as late as the 1970s, film historians depreciated Box's films as "women's pictures," a term meant to marginalize films that might appeal to an audience other than men.

Muriel Box's career as a director is an impressive achievement and deserves a reassessment. Her work as a screenwriter is equally impressive. In addition to her filmmaking activities, in 1964, Box wrote a novel, *The Big Switch*. She was active in the campaign for nuclear disarmament. Later in her career, Muriel Box established a publishing company, Femina Books, over which she served as managing director. Vera Brittain, Anona Winn, and Anne Edwards wrote and worked for Femina. Muriel herself wrote the first book published by Femina, a biography of Marie Stopes, a feminist activist. Muriel and Sydney Box were divorced in 1969. In August 1970, Muriel Box became "Lady Gardiner" when she married Lord Chancellor,

Sir Gerald Gardiner. After a lifetime of work, Muriel Box Gardiner died in 1991.

SELECTED FILMOGRAPHY

The Happy Family (*Mr. Lord Says No!*) (1952)
A Prince for Cynthia (1953)
Street Corner (*Both Sides of the Law*) (1953)
The Beachcomber (1955)
To Dorothy, a Son (*Cash on Delivery*) (1956)
Simon and Laura (1956)
Eyewitness (1956)
The Passionate Stranger (*A Novel Affair*) (1957)
The Truth About Women (1958)
This Other Eden (1959)
Subway in the Sky (1959)
Too Young to Love (1960)
The Piper's Tune (1960)
Rattle of a Simple Man (1964)

SELECTED BIBLIOGRAPHY

Aspinall, Sue. "Interview with Lady Gardiner." In *BFI Dossier Number 18: Gainsborough Melodrama*, edited by Sue Aspinall and Robert Murphy, 63–65. London: BFI, 1983.

Barr, Charles, ed. *All Our Yesterdays: Ninety Years of British Cinema*. London: BFI, 1986.

Box, Muriel. *Odd Woman Out*. London: Leslie Frewin, 1974.

Durgnat, Raymond. *A Mirror for England*. London: Faber and Faber, 1970.

Heck-Rabi, Louise. *Women Filmmakers: A Critical Reception*. Metuchen, NJ: Scarecrow Press, 1984.

McFarlane, Brian. Sixty Voices: *Celebrities Recall the Golden Age of British Cinema*. London: BFI, 1992.

Merz, Caroline. "Box, Muriel." In *The Women's Companion to International Film*, edited by Annette Kuhn, with Susannah Radstone, 49. Berkeley: University of California Press, 1994.

———. "The Tension of Genre: Wendy Toye and Muriel Box." In *Re-Viewing British Cinema, 1900–1992*, edited by Wheeler Winston Dixon, 121–32. Albany: SUNY Press, 1994.

BREIEN, ANJA (1940–   ). Norway. "A female director is automatically thought of as being dominating. . . . Dominance and power traditionally give the man sensuality, but they deprive woman of it," Anja Breien told an interviewer (Hoaas, 334). Breien's comment exposes the popular thinking that discourages women from taking power positions. This same "old myth" (as Breien puts it) is as pervasive in Hollywood as it is abroad, perhaps an attitude that defies borders, with the exception, perhaps, of the Soviet Union. Norwegian director Anja Breien's films are cerebral, even difficult. But Breien smarts at the idea of aiming at the lowest common denominator. Decidedly political, she recognizes that it is often "dangerous to mean anything" (Hoaas, 389) in the current political climate.

Anja Breien trained at a French film school (IDHEC) and began making short films in the late 1960s. *Jostedalsrypa* (1967) is a female-centered film based on the medieval legend about a young girl's experiences during a plague. In 1969, Breien directed *17. Mai-en film om ritualer,* a short film that won an award at the Oberhausen Film Festival. *17 Mai* satirizes the celebration of the national Norwegian holiday. *Voldtekt* (1971) concerns a rape suspect who is wrongly accused and held by the authorities. The film is artistically interesting in its depiction of the male point of view, and the film was successful at the Cannes Film Festival. *Muren rundt fengslet* (1972) is an indictment of the penal system in Norway.

Breien worked for television for a brief stint, directing a documentary film on alcoholism (*Herbergisterne* 1973) and a documentary on artist Arne Bendik Sjur (*Mine soskend Goddad,* 1972). Breien's personal films began with *Hustruer (Wives)* (1975), which was inspired by John Cassavetes's *Husbands* (1970). *Wives* was an international success and launched Breien's career as a feature filmmaker. *Wives* is cinematically avant-garde in that it disregards mainstream Hollywood representations of experience that are artificially constrained by the filmmaking process. In *Wives,* Breien uses the camera to look at the lives of three women as they escape their mundane existence as housewives and spend several days together exploring their true feelings. Breien's formal training in documentary is apparent in her remarkably fresh framing and cutting of the story. The women discuss themes such as ambivalence toward gender restrictions, sexuality, and femininity as the film unfolds into a feminist exploration of meaning in everyday life. Breien encouraged her actors to collaborate and improvise, which perhaps explains the quiet mixture of brilliantly underplayed humor, anger, and irony in *Wives.*

Forfolgelsen (The Witch Hunt) (1981) is perhaps one of Breien's best-known films. The film is a drama about a seventeenth-century woman who frightens people with her forthright self-assertiveness and is persecuted for her overt sexuality. It is a tale of exile, misunderstanding, and myths rooted in fear. The fear of the power of witches is not unlike the fear of the power of women directors, and Breien adroitly draws on this thematic parallel between life and art. Gorham Kindem characterizes *Witch Hunt* as "a relatively unambiguous indictment of a traditionally patriarchal structure of Norwegian society" (37). The central character, a strong, sensual woman, is a threat to order because she upsets the power hierarchy. Breien's film invites comparison with any number of films directed by women, including *Camila* by Maria Luisa Bemberg. Both films are grueling, even uncomfortable to watch, when the central female character is unfairly and brutally treated by a hypocritical, cruel group of community leaders.

Both *Camila* and *Witch Hunt* end in the brutal corporal punishment of the female body. Camila is shot by a firing squad. Eli Laupstad, in *Witch Hunt,* is placed on the rack and tortured, then finally beheaded. Neither film flinches in its representation of male oppression, which often acts under the guise of religious sanction. *Witch Hunt* is located in the past, as is *Camila,* but both films encourage the female viewer to note that sexism hardly ended with the violent past. In this way, *Witch Hunt* and *Camila* question the notion of a romanticized view of history that moves toward the empowerment of the individual. Both films prove that eternal vigilance is the price one pays for freedom.

Breien's use of expressionist film techniques is highlighted in *Witch Hunt.* In the tradition of Ingmar Bergman, Breien paints a harsh landscape as a psychological backdrop of anguish and depravity. The use of superimpositions, dream sequences, and an oblique sense of time and space is typical of Norway's distinctive cinema. Breien's ability to straddle objective and subjective viewpoints is distinctive. She creates a mixture of realism, first-person, omniscient point-of-view camera work and expressionism that simultaneously discourages and invites viewer identification. Because of her unusual approach to her materials, the cinema of Anja Breien does not fit into the modernist avant-garde canon easily. Like the work of Chantal Akerman, it is difficult and personal. Anja Breien, along with Vibeke Lokkeberg and Laila Mikkelsen, constitute Norway's New Wave of women directors. They are unafraid of criticism, and they are unafraid of exploring new avenues of feminist expression. Yet, given the resolute intransigence of the cinema of Ingmar Bergman, whose deeply personal films created an international sensation in the 1950s, the emergence of a group of outspoken, yet unmistakably activist women directors in Norway is not surprising. Breien's films should be distributed more widely in the West, and a complete retrospective of her work is certainly indicated.

SELECTED FILMOGRAPHY

Jostedalsrypa (1967)
17. Mai-en film om ritualer (1969)
Ansikter (1969)
Voldtekt (1971)
Mine soskend Goddad (1972)
Muren rundt fengslet (1972)
Arne Bendik Sjur (1973)
Herbergisterne (1973)
Gamle (1975)
Hustruer (*Wives*) (1975)
Den allvarsamma leken (*Games of Love and Loneliness*) (1977)
Arven (*Next of Kin*) (1979)
Forfolgelsen (*The Witch Hunt*) (1981)
Papirfuglen (*Paper Bird*) (1984)
Hustruer ti år etter (*Wives—Ten Years After*) (1985)

SELECTED BIBLIOGRAPHY

de Lauretis, Teresa. *Alice Doesn't: Feminism, Semiotics, Cinema.* Bloomington: Indiana University Press, 1984.

Doane, Mary Ann. *The Desire to Desire.* Bloomington: Indiana University Press, 1987.

Hoaas, Solrun. "Anja Breien." *Cinema Papers* 39 (1982): 320–91.

Kaplan, E. Ann. *Women and Film: Both Sides of the Camera.* New York: Methuen, 1983.

Kindem, Gorham A. "Norway's New Generation of Women Directors: Anja Breien, Vibeke Lokkeberg and Laila Mikkelson." *Journal of Film and Video* 39.4 (fall 1987): 28–42.

Lovell, Terry. *Pictures of Reality.* London: BFI, 1980.

Mellen, Joan. *Women and Their Sexuality in the New Film.* New York: Horizon, 1973.

BRÜCKNER, JUTTA (1941–). Germany. Jutta Brückner's training in political science, philosophy, and history is the basis of her transcendent films, which fall into the category of New German Cinema. English-speaking critics are most familiar with the work of men such as Fassbinder, Herzog, and Wenders, yet they remain placidly ignorant of the work of women in the New Wave, including Brückner, Helke Sander, and Helma Sanders-Brahms. Though these women can be grouped with their male colleagues, as Judith Mayne notes, "There is such a thing as a feminist aesthetic" (167) that cuts across the diverse cinema of women in the New German Cinema. The cinema of Jutta Brückner combines the themes and style of Fassbinder films with a distinctly feminist aesthetic.

Born in West Germany, Brückner taught herself filmmaking after working as a writer of screenplays. Brückner wrote the screenplay for Völker Schlöndorff's *Der Fangschuss* (*Coup de Grace*), with Margarethe von Trotta. With financial backing from ZDF, Brückner began filming a sixty-minute feature entitled *Tue recht und scheue niemand* (*Do Right and Fear No-one*) (1975). ZDF, a West German television network, has commissioned many films by German women directors. With limited technical skills, Brückner began making a filmic study of her mother's life. As she told Patricia Habord, she was almost physically compelled to make the film: "I had no choice" (50). *Do Right and Fear No-one* is not only a woman's life story but an experimental film that provokes the audience to work on the difficult material, with little narrative guidance. A combination of history and biography, Brückner's film is a sketch of a woman fighting against the framework of society, which attempts to define her. As Brückner's film was being shot, her mother began taking part in her self-definition, arguing with the technicians and redefining herself as the film develops. *Do Right and Fear No-one* is a meditation on the subjective identity of women. As Brückner told Marc Silberman, a woman "is not a person in her own right. Rather she lives under the collective term 'someone': one should do this or one should do that" (254).

Brückner's film is a reconfiguration of the identity of her mother, Gerda Siepenbrink, who becomes an individual as she takes control of her identity through her daughter's eyes. The film is done out of love for the subject; a woman is documented as she documents herself. Siepenbrink's voice-over narrative is combined with images from scrapbooks, history books, and the presence of Brückner herself, in a form of self-reflexive autobiography that bridges new technique with old. The film, in a sense, becomes a mirror of Brückner's mother, a doubly signified image of identity. When Brückner's film showed on television, her mother told her father, "You just watch this now. Because in it are all the things you don't know about me" (Habord, 51). Brückner connects identity to filmic and real senses of space, time, and image. Hers is an ontological and metaphysical New Wave cinema that addresses the articulation of the presence of women.

In *Hungerjahre-in einem reichen Land* (*Years of Hunger*) (1979), Jutta Brückner plays an adolescent growing up in the midst of plenty who nevertheless suffers from emotional starvation. In *Years of Hunger* Brückner uncovers the cultural deprivation of adolescent females, much in the same way she exposes the erasure of older women in *Do Right and Fear No-one*. *Years of Hunger* is confrontational. In the film, a young woman finds her identity through confrontation with her mother. The film depicts the violent struggle for identity and control that all young women face. As Brückner told Marc Silberman, "In my films I try to bewilder, disturb, irritate" (256). Brückner involved her mother in *Years of Hunger* as she had in her earlier work. The planning of the film seems to have been as painful as the imagery in the film. Brückner describes the writing as a painful and drawn-out process in which the filmmaker was frequently physically ill. Ironically, *Years of Hunger* exposes the hunger inside the compulsive overeater. Brückner deals head-on with taboo issues such as menstruation, pregnancy, and women's ambivalence toward their own bodies, their own children's bodies.

Years of Hunger was well received in most countries as an avant-garde film. However, some critics found the film vulgar because it includes a shot of a bloody sanitary napkin. Brückner excoriates such a patriarchally defined taboo: "You can have seven murders, you can show someone chopped to pieces, but just don't show a sanitary napkin" (Silberman, 256). Brückner's inclusion of an image that is a part of female experience, even an extension of her identity, typifies her activist/feminist style of filmmaking. In the conclusion of *Years of Hunger,* the bulimic young woman attempts suicide, the logical extension of cultural denial and erasure. The act of creating *Years of Hunger* thus ends a cycle of societal abnegation of the female and, in a metaphoric sense, saves the filmmaker's own life. As with other international filmmakers in this volume, Brückner is an exceptional artist whose work deserves better international distribution; she is also a respected film critic as well as an innovative and confrontational film director.

SELECTED FILMOGRAPHY

Tue recht und scheue niemand (*Do Right and Fear No-one*) (1975)
Ein ganz und gar verwahrlostes Mädchen (*A Thoroughly Demoralized Girl*) (1977)
Hungerjahre (*Years of Hunger*) (1979)
Laufen lernen (*Learning to Run*) (1980)
Die Erbtöchter (*The Daughters' Inheritance* (codirector) (1982)
Kolossale Liebe (*Colossal Love*) (1984)
Ein Blick—und die Liebe bricht aus (*One Glance, and Love Breaks Out*) (1986)

SELECTED BIBLIOGRAPHY

Brückner, Jutta. "Women behind the Camera." In *Feminist Aesthetics,* edited by Gisela Ecker; translated by Harriet Anderson, 120–24. Boston: Beacon, 1986.

Carson, Diane. "Women Filmmakers." In *Multiple Voices in Feminist Film Criticism,* edited by Diane Carson, Linda Dittmar, and Janice Welsch, 456–67. Minneapolis: University of Minnesota Press, 1994.

Habord, Patricia. "Interview with Jutta Brückner." *Screen Education* 40 (1981–82): 48–57.

Knight, Julia. *Women and the New German Cinema.* London: Verso, 1992.

Kosta, Barbara. "Representing Female Sexuality: Jutta Brückner's Film *Years of Hunger.*" In *Gender in German Cinema: Feminist Interventions, Vol. 2, German Film History/German History on Film,* edited by Sandra Frieden, Richard W. McCormick, Vibeke R. Petersen, and Laurie Melissa Vogelsang, 241–52. Oxford: Berg, 1993.

Mayne, Judith. "Female Narration, Women's Cinema." *New German Critique* 24–25 (Fall/Winter 1981–82): 155–171.

Mayne, Judith, Helen Fehervary, and Claudia Lensson. "From Hitler to Hepburn: A Discussion of Women's Film Production and Reception." *New German Critique* 24–25 (fall–winter 1981–82): 171–85.

Sandford, John. *The New German Cinema.* London: Oswald Wolff, 1980.

Silberman, Marc. "Interview with Jutta Brückner: Recognizing Collective Gestures." In *Gender and German Cinema: Feminist Interventions, Vol. 2, German Film History/German History on Film,* edited by Sandra Frieden, Richard W. McCormick, Vibeke R. Petersen, and Laurie Melissa Vogelsang, 253–58. Oxford: Berg, 1993.

BUTE, MARY ELLEN (1906–83). **United States.** Born in Houston, Texas, Mary Ellen Bute became known as one of the pioneers of abstract experimental filmmaking in the United States. Her poetic, abstract films are studies of light, rhythm, and the imagination. After studying art at the Sorbonne, she settled in New York and began thinking about how to best create animation to incorporate with musical pieces. Always interested in the possibilities of uniting music and film in an abstract form, Bute eventually made some of the most important early kinetic animation films. In the early 1930s, Bute collaborated with electronic musician Leon Theramin. Later she worked with filmmakers Lewis Jacob and Joseph Schillinger on an uncompleted film *Synchronization* (1932). Bute designed and drew the abstract drawings for the film. She also coined the term "abstronics," which signified a wedding of the abstract and electronic forms. Many of the recent developments in computer technology that allow for the electronic "painting" of images for film and media are theoretical outgrowths of Bute's ideas. Always exuberant and energetic in her descriptions of her projects, she explains in an article she wrote for *Films in Review*:

By turning knobs and switches on a control board I can "draw" with a beam of light with as much freedom as with a brush. As the figures and forms are produced by light on the oscilloscope screen, they are photographed on motion picture film. By careful conscious repetition and experiment, I have accumulated a "repertoire" of forms. The creative possibilities are limitless. (263)

Bute's films are spare experiments in light, often based on mathematical formulas. In many ways they seem quite modern, aside from the music, which is the only thing that dates them. Cerebral, yet down-to-earth, the film work of Mary Ellen Bute is impressive. She used mirrors, oscilloscopes, and choreographed patterns through multiple exposure in her films, to create a visual world at once bizarre and familiar. She always tried new ways of using materials and machines.

Rhythm in Light (1934) was fairly straightforward animation. But Bute gradually moved into oscillation-generated imagery, with her husband, Ted Nemeth. In 1965, Bute made a full-length feature film, *Passages from Finnegan's Wake*. Critical praise for Bute's films was quite generous, yet few histories of abstract, experimental films and animation include her work. Like Joy Batchelor, Bute tends to be overshadowed in film history by her husband's name. All too often this is the case of working partnerships in film. Fortunately, the films and writings of Mary Ellen Bute live on as an enduring testament to her artistic innovation.

SELECTED FILMOGRAPHY

Rhythm in Light (1934)
Synchrony No. 2 (1936)
Evening Star (1937)
Parabola (1938)
Escape, Spook Sport (1939)
Escape (1940)
Tarantella (1941)
Polka Graph (1952)
Mood Contrasts (1953)
Abstronics (1954)
The Boy Who Saw Through (1956)
Passages from Finnegan's Wake (1965)

SELECTED BIBLIOGRAPHY

Acker, Ally. *Reel Women: Pioneers of the Cinema, 1896 to the Present.* New York: Continuum, 1993.

Bute, Mary Ellen. "Abstronics." *Films in Review* 5.6 (June–July 1954): 263–66.

Knight, Arthur. *The Liveliest Art.* New York: Mentor, 1957.

Pilling, Jane, ed. *Women & Animation: A Compendium.* London: BFI, 1993.

Russett, Robert, and Cecille Starr. *Experimental Animation.* New York: Van Nostrand Reinhold, 1976.

C

CAMPION, JANE (1955–). New Zealand/Australia/United States. Jane Campion's Gothic imagination is rooted in an embrace of the extraordinary, the strange, the untold, the erotic. Born in Wellington, New Zealand, she shares a sense of dark humor with Gillian Armstrong and Jocelyn Moorhouse, Australian women directors who seem to be remapping the cinema in an emerging body of work that is at once cinematically fresh and shorn of conventional narrative technique. Campion's family life was not ordinary. Her parents were extraordinary, both involved in the theater and both immersed in a life dedicated to art. Campion studied anthropology and art at Victoria University. After graduation, she dabbled in performance art and spent time abroad. She entered the Australian Film, Television and Radio School, where she developed a taste for surrealist films. As she told Myra Forsberg, she was overwhelmed by the work of Luis Buñuel: "I just died when I saw his films. I thought this guy is so wicked" (15). That irreverence comes through in Campion's work, especially her early shorts, including *Peel* (1982), a short film that won the Palme D'or at the Cannes Film Festival.

Jane Campion knew that nothing would get her into the world of film other than a substantial body of work. Therefore, she made a series of short films while in film school, including *A Girl's Own Story* (1984), which displays Campion's visual flair and dark humor in a twisted coming-of-age story. *Peel* is a painful short film about the inherent mixture of sexuality, power, and abuse in the family hierarchy. It has one of the most memorable scenes of psychological child abuse, in which a young boy is forced by his father, for no apparent reason, to pick up all the pieces of an orange peel that were tossed out of a car window during a family picnic outing. Campion's early shorts refrain from telling the audience what to feel about the films. After film school, Campion joined the Women's Film Unit, a government-sponsored program designed to address the imbalance of the male-to-female ratio in film direction.

Jane Campion's first feature, *Sweetie* (1989), starring Genevieve Lemon in the title role, defies synopsizing because of its utterly unique approach to filmic storytelling. *Sweetie* is a study of madness that never flinches from depicting the dark side of its protagonist, yet never preaches to the audience. A bleak domestic tragicomedy, *Sweetie* was cowritten by Campion with her ex-boyfriend, Gerald Lee. *Sweetie* is a female-centered narrative, told from the point of view of a young woman, played by Karen Colston, who wishes to escape from her depressing family, which revolves around her schizophrenic sister, Sweetie. Sweetie is out of control, completely irresponsible, overweight, and grotesque, yet she is infused with such a sense of beauty and charm that she becomes a metaphor for universalized loss of innocence.

Sweetie stumbles through the fragmented narrative, inhaling food, shrieking, laughing, and destroying everyone around her. Campion uses the claustrophobic, dark confines of the dysfunctional home as a surrealistic set piece that bespeaks the horror and humor of a family that tries desperately to live with Sweetie's illness. The use of unconventional cutting, a wide-angle lens, and painfully long takes shape the material in a style reminiscent of the phantasmagoric cinema of Buñuel or Germaine Dulac. The viewer never knows where the story is going, which is itself a refreshing break from the overworked foreshadowing and basic plot designs of common Hollywood films. Campion revels in the grotesque, but never in a manner that panders to audience expectations. *Sweetie* caused quite a scandal, in fact, at Cannes. Some critics were disgusted by the family relationship, and some found the cinematic style too difficult. But the critics at the New York Film Festival adored the film, praising its deliberately disorienting camera work and bleak story line. *Sweetie* is an important text in women's cinema, and its feminine film language remakes the art of film storytelling.

An Angel at My Table (1990) was originally meant for television. Campion planned the film as a three-part miniseries on the life of writer Janet Frame. It is another difficult film, but in many ways it is much more traditional than *Sweetie* or *The Piano*. *An Angel at My Table* was written by Laura Jones. Like *Sweetie,* it deals with societal views toward mental illness, but *An Angel at My Table* is told from the point of view of a writer who is wrongly diagnosed as schizophrenic. The narrative is fairly straightforward, beginning with the tragic loss of Frame's older sister in a swimming accident. Campion's ability to evoke the pain of growing up as a completely shy, young, aspiring writer is admirable. Next, Janet Frame (played by Kerry Fox) attempts to be a teacher but is simply too self-absorbed, shy, and socially inept to succeed. After her best friend also drowns, Frame spends the next eight years undergoing a series of shock treatments. Frame publishes her first novel in the last section of the film and subsequently has an affair with a poet. The potentially harrowing story is made bearable only because of Campion's delicate sense of humor.

Jane Campion won the hearts of critics and audiences with her Academy Award-winning film *The Piano* (1993). Interestingly enough, one critic, William Grimes, noted a critical backlash against the film that represents an assault on the success of a woman filmmaker and a film that speaks in and about women's language. Grimes notes that the initial critical praise of the film suddenly came to a screeching halt during the competitive period preceding the Academy Awards, in an effort that seems to have been made to ensure that Steven Spielberg, not Jane Campion, would receive the award for best director, for his direction of *Schindler's List* (1993). As Grimes notes, an article entitled "Seven Reasons Not to Like *The Piano*" ran in *New York Magazine,* and a campaign to discredit the film ensued, in which rival producers joked that no one knew what the film was really about. While Campion ultimately did not get the nod as Best Director from the academy, she did win the award for Best Screenplay.

The Piano is inspired by the feminist literary classics of the Brontë sisters, with a fairly straightforward plotline. Ada, played by Holly Hunter, is a Scotswoman with an illegitimate child. She arrives in New Zealand to meet her husband, who has been chosen for her through an arranged marriage. (It is interesting to note that arranged marriages are often at the center of the films of women directors.) Ada depends on her piano and her daughter as her means of communication. Her husband refuses to let her keep her piano. George Baines, played by Harvey Keitel, a settler who has adopted many of the traditions of the Maori people, buys the piano and subsequently uses it to "buy" Ada. The two strike up a bargain: he will give Ada her treasured piano, her voice, if she will give him lessons. The lessons develop into some of the most erotically charged scenes to ever evolve in the cinema; they are directly out of a literary tradition of women's novels of Gothic romance. Predictably, Ada's husband finds out about the affair, and the film vaults into scenes of domestic violence that are overplayed in the tradition of the Gothic novel.

As Georgia Brown puts it, "What's shocking about *The Piano* is how it resists the standard ready-made narrative, and follows its own logic." Campion reworks the logic of the Gothic novel in *The Piano.* Just as Charlotte Brontë used the moors in *Wuthering Heights* to underscore suppressed violence inherent in the arranged marriage, Campion uses the landscape of colonial oppression as a backdrop for the dark narrative of *The Piano.* Like a heroine in the Gothic tradition, Ada is obsessed with having some control over her identity. As a piece of chattel, a mute silenced woman, she appears to be trapped in a horrid marriage. But in Campion's reworking of the Gothic tradition, the central heroine escapes with her lover. Ada's ability to articulate herself through her piano is a commentary on the experience of female language. It is rendered in a new female language of the cinema that emerges from the work of women directors such as Jane Campion, Sally Potter, and Gillian Armstrong. Campion's feature films are generally available on videocassette; her early short films are available from Women Make Movies, New York, and are well worth viewing.

SELECTED FILMOGRAPHY

Tissues (1981)
Peel (1982)
A Girl's Own Story (1984)
After Hours (short) (1985)
Two Friends (Episode 5) (1986)
Sweetie (1989)
An Angel at My Table (1990)
The Piano (1993)

SELECTED BIBLIOGRAPHY

Brown, Georgia. "Say Anything." *Village Voice* 38. 46 (November 16, 1993): 72.
Bruzzi, Stella. "Jane Campion: Costume Drama and Reclaiming Women's Past." In *Women in Film: A Sight and Sound Reader,* edited by Pam Cook and Philip Dodd, 232–42. Philadelphia: Temple University Press, 1993.
Campion, Jane. *The Piano.* New York: Miramax/Hyperion, 1993.
Cantwell, Mary. "Jane Campion's Lunatic Women." *New York Times Magazine,* September 19, 1993, 40–44, 51.
Forsberg, Myra. "*Sweetie* Isn't Sugary." *New York Times,* January 14, 1990, 14, 15.
Grimes, William. "After the First Wave of Raves, *The Piano* Slips into a Trough." *New York Times,* March 10, 1994, 49, 63.
James, Caryn. "A Distinctive Shade of Darkness." *New York Times,* November 28, 1993, H13, 22.
McDonagh, Maitland. "Jane Campion's *Angel* Is Another Quirky Soul." *New York Times,* May 17, 1991, 22.
Murray, Scott, ed. *Back of Beyond: Discovering Australian Film and Television.* Sydney: Australian Film Commission, 1988.
Quart, Barbara. "The Short Films of Jane Campion." *Cineaste* 19.1 (1992):72.
Stone, Laurie. "Four Films by Jane Campion at the Millennium." *Village Voice* 39. 18 (May 19, 1994): 58.
Taboulay, Camille. "*An Angel at My Table.*" *Cahiers du Cinema* 442 (April 1991): 63.

CANTRILL, CORINNE (1928–   ). Australia. Avant-garde filmmaker Corinne Cantrill is one of Australia's best-known experimental filmmakers. With her husband, Arthur Cantrill, Corinne Cantrill began in film as a television director. She and her husband made a series of films on art for children in 1963. The Cantrills were offered a fellowship at the Australian National University in 1969, where they supported the collection and documentation of experimental films for the National Library collection. In

1971, the Cantrills began publishing *Cantrills' Filmnotes,* a serious film journal devoted to avant-garde filmmaking.

The films of Corinne and Arthur Cantrill are purist, aesthetic poems about the human body and subjective experience. Their work is often a cross between film and performance, utilizing multiscreen projections, color separations, and experimentations in audience perception. *Interior/Exterior* (1978) is a two-screen film. Both screens record the same scene, with slight differences. The film runs in real time and is comparable to the formalist films of Michael Snow and Stan Brakhage. *Interior/Exterior* is a contemplation of the act of seeing itself; it reverts the viewer's gaze back on itself, so that the audience is suddenly aware of the act of gazing. Similarly, *Studies in Image De/Generation* (1975) is also a structuralist film that contemplates the act of the gaze. In the film, the Cantrills use archival footage of native Australian Arunta rituals. The appropriated images are abstracted by the use of excessive optical printing. *Two Women* (1980) is another minimalist avant-garde film in which the Cantrills dispense entirely with editing. The film is a purist's dream of the celluloid imagination in which we view Pitjantjatjara women performing song and ritual.

Less formalistic, *Corporeal* (1983) is an experiment designed to bridge the distance between the body and the camera. Another two-screen film, *Corporeal* is a meditational tone poem on the body of the filmmaker and the landscape. The camera breathes with the body in a way that defeats objectification. The landscape hums at a different pitch on the other screen. The naturalistic sound track is simply made up of the buzz of insects. The films of Arthur and Corinne Cantrill strip down filmic artifice in a deconstruction and revisioning of the cinema. Their films embrace the camera apparatus as an extension of the body. Problematizing traditional filmic treatments of the body, the avant-garde writings and formalist cinema of the Cantrills remake the relationship between the self and experience, and the screen and the viewer.

SELECTED FILMOGRAPHY

Films Codirected with Arthur Cantrill

Eikon (1969)
4000 Frames, An Eye-Opener Film (1970)
Harry Hooton (1970)
Skin of Your Eye (1973)
At Eltham (1974)
Reflections on Three Images by Baldwin Spencer, 1901 (1974)
Studies in Image De/Generation (1975)
Three Colour Separation Studies—Landscapes (1976)
At Uluru (1977)
Interior/Exterior (1978)
Grain of the Voice Series: Rock Wallaby and Blackbird (1980)

Two Women (1980)
The Second Journey (To Uluru) (1981)
Floterian-Hand Paintings from a Film History (1981)
Corporeal (1983)
Waterfall (1984)
In This Life's Body (1984)
Note on Berlin, the Divided City (1986)
Walking Track (1987)
The Berlin Apartment (1987)

SELECTED BIBLIOGRAPHY

Collins, Felicity. "Cantrill, Corinne and Arthur." In *The Women's Companion to International Film,* edited by Annette Kuhn, with Susannah Radstone, 64. Berkeley: University of California Press, 1994.

Doane, Mary Ann, Patricia Mellencamp, and Linda Williams, eds. *Re-Vision: Essays in Feminist Film Criticism.* Frederick, MD: University Publications, 1984.

Kaplan, E. Ann. *Women and Film: Both Sides of the Camera.* New York: Methuen.

Mellencamp, Patricia. *Indiscretions: Avant-Garde Film, Video, & Feminism.* Bloomington: Indiana University Press, 1990.

Mulvey, Laura. "Visual Pleasure and Narrative Cinema." *Screen* 16.3 (autumn 1975): 6–18.

Silverman, Kaja. *The Subject of Semiotics.* Oxford: Oxford University Press, 1983.

Turim, Maureen. *Abstraction in Avant-Garde Film.* Ann Arbor: UMI Research Press, 1985.

CARDONA, DOMINIQUE. *See* COLBERT, LAURIE.

CAROLINA, ANA (1943–). Brazil. "Ana Carolina is a filmmaker who playfully mixes audience surprise, political acuity, and formidable visual prowess," (129) writes Barbara Kruger. Ana Carolina Teixeira Soares planned to be a doctor. But after medical school, she became a documentary filmmaker, directing eleven documentary films between 1967 and 1974. *Mar de Rosas* (1977), her first feature film, is an absurd, dark, twisted allegory about political power, sexual politics, and the politics of the family. In the film, a woman cuts her husband's throat and runs away with her daughter. *Mar de Rosas* is difficult to define because of its uniqueness. It is tempting to call it a black comedy, but this flat categorization would be misleading. Even Carolina, in an interview with Simon Hartog, admitted that the film almost defies categorization:

How would I classify my films? That is difficult to say for me. But I could call them dramatic comedies or amusing dramas or something like that. Although perhaps within Brazilian cinema, things are a bit different, it is difficult to fix particular categories. But they're not slapstick: they have a different kind of humour. So, if I had to settle on a category, it would be that of dramatic comedy. (65)

Few dramatic comedies open with an image of a close-up of a woman urinating at the side of the road, as *Mar de Rosas* does, setting up a hysterical yet gruesome road movie that revels in such grotesque imagery. The woman we first see is the vicious teenage daughter of even more vicious parents. Inside the car, the couple, played by Hugo Carvana and Norma Benguel, hurl insults and abuse at one another. At a roadside motel, the daughter, played by Cristina Pereira, brutally murders her physically abusive father, but she is also hell-bent on destroying her mother and herself. The daughter is a force of destruction, representing the people of Brazil in their power struggle with successive authoritarian political regimes.

Mar de Rosas is reminiscent of Jean-Luc Godard's *Weekend,* in that the characters spew political slogans such as "Eternal vigilance is the price of freedom," as they tour the countryside and careen about recklessly in their car. *Mar de Rosas* becomes a paean to the theater of the absurd when the bizarre family ends up in a dentist's office, which is filled with sand, and yet they continue screaming slogans like "Work is effort; capital is investment." The father, who has somehow survived the daughter's murder attempt, returns. At the end of the film, the daughter finally kills both parents by throwing them off a speeding train. As the film ends, the daughter turns directly to the audience and gives the camera the finger.

Carolina's second feature film, *Das tripas Coração (With the Heart in the Hands)* (1979), is a distinct departure from mainstream narrative. It is a surrealistic film of the dreams of one character, a male detective. In the film, Carolina exposes corruption in school administration, in the church, and throughout society. The detective dreams that he gets a teacher pregnant and breaks up lesbian relationships. Then he dreams he is held hostage by the women. The film is an unflinching analysis of male chauvinism, sexism, and homophobia. Carolina's work is, in some ways, comparable to Pedro Almodovar's, but Carolina's use of camp horror is that of a distinctly feminist lens. It is remarkable how critics have embraced the sexuality in Almodovar's films, yet in the work of a woman director sexuality is perceived with suspicion by Western critics. Ana Carolina continues to make provocative feminist New Wave Brazilian films and will undoubtedly be heard from even more decisively in the future.

SELECTED FILMOGRAPHY

Industria (1969)
Getulio Vargas (1974)
Mar de Rosas (A Sea of Roses) (1977)
Nelson Pereira dos Santos (1979)
Das tripas Coração (With the Heart in the Hands) (1979)
Sohno de valsa (A Waltzlike Dream) (1987)

SELECTED BIBLIOGRAPHY

Burton, Julianne. *The Social Documentary in Latin America.* Pittsburgh, PA: University of Pittsburgh Press, 1970.

————. *The New Latin American Cinema: An Annotated Bibliography of English Language Sources, 1960–1976*. Cineaste Pamphlet University. New York: Cineaste, 1976.

————, ed. *Cinema and Social Change in Latin America*. Austin: University of Texas Press, 1986.

Hartog, Simon. "A Conversation with Ana Carolina." *Framework* 28 (1985): 64–69.

Johnson, Randal, and Robert Stam. *Brazilian Cinema*. East Brunswick, NJ: Associated University Press, 1982.

Kruger, Barbara. "Ana Carolina, *Mar de Rosas:* Museum of Contemporary Hispanic Art." *Artforum* 25 (April 1987): 129–30.

Lesage, Julia. "Latin American and Caribbean Women in Film." In *Multiple Voices in Feminist Film Criticism,* edited by Diane Carson, Linda Dittmar, and Janice Welsch, 492–502. Minneapolis: University of Minnesota Press, 1994.

Rich, B. Ruby. "After the Revolutions: The Second Coming of Latin American Cinema." *Village Voice* (March 26, 1985): 26.

Torrents, Nissa. "Carolina, Ana." In *The Women's Companion to International Film,* edited by Annette Kuhn, and Susannah Radstone, 67. Berkeley: University of California Press, 1994.

Vance, Carole S., ed. *Pleasure and Danger: Exploring Female Sexuality*. Boston: Routledge, 1984.

CAVANI, LILIANA (1936–   ). Italy. Liliana Cavani was born in Capri in 1936. She was educated at the University of Bologna and later, the Centro Sperimentale in Rome. In the 1960s, Cavani began making feature films after directing documentaries and dramas for Italian television. Though she is best known for *The Night Porter* (1974), Cavani also made a series of interesting films about historical and mythological figures that are highlighted by their fresh rereadings of politics and the making of "history." *Francesco d' Assisi* (1966), *Galileo* (1968), *I cannibali* (1969), and *Milarepa* (1973–74) fall into this loose category. All of Cavani's films deal with the sadomasochistic nature of power and politics. Although until recently not widely embraced by feminist critics, Cavani's films are implicitly feminist in that they are highly critical of the nature of politics and sexuality.

The Cannibals relocates the female mythic figure of Antigone in a demythologizing look at repressive contemporary politics in Italy. Most of Cavani's films foreground central male characters, however. *Affair in Berlin* (1986) centers on a lesbian relationship, and *The Women of the Resistance* (1965) marks the struggle of women who defied fascism. *The Night Porter* (1974) is essentially a study in sadomasochism. Dirk Bogarde stars in the film as an ex-Nazi officer, and Charlotte Rampling stars as a concentration camp victim who has a love affair with her torturer. Bogarde's character belongs to a group of Nazis who have been acquitted through the destruction of evidence and the murder of witnesses. The love affair between the two is a warped psychological game that bespeaks an allegory of the relationship between oppressor countries and oppressed countries, which are often trapped in a manipulative power game and mutually dependent.

Theorist Kaja Silverman notes that Cavani's film is a rereading of the world of fantasy at the center of sadomasochistic power relationships. Silverman postulates that women filmmakers usurp such male-defined power games in order to divest them of their cultural power. However, Cavani's presentation of eroticism in *The Night Porter* marks a culturally dangerous sexualization of fascism, according to Susan Sontag. However the film is perceived, *The Night Porter* is undeniably a difficult film to watch. Liliana Cavani, like her contemporary, Lina Wertmuller, represents a challenge to the feminist viewer. The feminism of Cavani and Wertmuller calls for a heterogeneity of feminist responses. Cavani has expressed criticism of the feminist movement in the United States, which she feels is elitist. In her view, general political struggle is inextricable from a feminist struggle.

SELECTED FILMOGRAPHY

Incontro notturno (1961)
L'evento (1962)
Storia del terzo Reich (*History of the Third Reich*) (1963)
L'eta' di Stalin (1963)
La casa in Italia (*The House in Italy*) (1964)
Philippe Pétain processo a Vichy (1965)
La donna nella Resistenza (*The Women of the Resistance*) (1965)
Gesu' mio fratello (1965)
Il giorno della pace (1965)
Francesco d'Assisi (1966)
Galileo (1968)
I cannibali (*The Cannibals*) (1969)
L'ospite (*The Guest*) (1971)
Milarepa (1973–74)
Il portiere di notte (*The Night Porter*) (1974)
Al di la' del bene e del male (*Beyond Good and Evil*) (1977)
La pelle (*The Skin*) (1981)
Oltre la Porta (*Beyond the Door*) (1983)
Interno berlinese (*Affair in Berlin*) (1986)

SELECTED BIBLIOGRAPHY

Acker, Ally. *Reel Women: Pioneers of the Cinema 1896 to the Present.* New York: Continuum, 1993.
Bruno, Giuliana, and Maria Nadotti, eds. *Offscreen: Women and Film in Italy.* London: Routledge, 1988.
de Lauretis, Teresa. *Technologies of Gender: Essays on Theory, Film, and Fiction.* Bloomington: Indiana University Press, 1987.
———. "Rethinking Women's Cinema." In *Multiple Voices in Feminist Film Criticism,* edited by Diane Carson, Linda Dittmar, and Janice Welsch, 140–61. Minneapolis: University of Minnesota Press, 1994.
Kotz, Liz. "Complicity: Women Artists Investigating Masculinity." In *Dirty*

Looks: Women, Pornography, Power, edited by Pamela Church Gibson, and Roma Gibson, 101–23. London: BFI, 1993.

Quart, Barbara. *Women Directors: The Emergence of a New Cinema.* New York: Praeger, 1988.

Silverman, Kaja. *The Acoustic Mirror.* Bloomington: Indiana University Press, 1988.

Smith, Sharon. *Women Who Make Movies.* New York: Hopkinson and Blake, 1975.

Sontag, Susan. "Fascinating Fascism." In *Women and the Cinema: A Critical Anthology,* edited by Karyn Kay and Gerald Peary, 352–76. New York: Dutton, 1977.

CHADHA, GURINDER (1960–   ). Kenya/India/United Kingdom. Border crossings and diaspora are at the center of Kenya-born, Punjabi-parented, black filmmaker Gurinder Chadha. Raised in London, Chadha became interested in film when she wrote a dissertation on Indian women in British cinema. Among her early projects is a video entitled *Pain, Passion and Profit* (1992). In this documentary, Chadha shows how several African women successfully develop small businesses and the impact that their success has on the community and the economic development of women. *Pain, Passion and Profit* evokes a spiritual connection between women in the "First" and "Third" Worlds. In 1989, Chadha made a documentary film entitled *I'm British but . . .*

Bhaji at the Beach (1994) is Gurinder Chadha's first feature film. Written by Meera Syal, *Bhaji at the Beach* is a metanarrative of difference, a complex, yet witty look at nine Asian women, spanning three generations. Like the third-generation Asian immigrants in *I'm British but . . .* , the women in *Bhaji* tell one another's secrets. As Chadha explained to Ann Hornaday, "*Bhaji* is also about subverting many expectations of women." Financed by Channel 4, *Bhaji at the Beach* is set at a seaside resort in Blackpool. Simi, played by Shaheen Khan, organizes the all-girl trip, announcing, "It's not often we women get away from the demands of patriarchy . . . struggling as we do between the double yoke of racism and sexism. . . . Have a female fun time!" As the day unfolds, the complexities of race and gender unfold. One woman finds out she is pregnant. Another woman has run away from her abusive husband. Tensions emerge across age differences, but Chadha provides no easy answers. She entertains us with her ear for women's speech and her eye for difference.

Bhaji cuts across lines of difference, yet it is not so conventional as to erase cultural differences. Chadha is most concerned with pleasing her own people. "The idea of making a film about Asian women that ordinary Asian women from where I grew up would be able to see and enjoy was important," Chadha told Lawrence Chua. *Bhaji* was produced by Nadine Marsh-Edwards, a founding member of the black, British filmmaking cooperative,

Sankofa Films. Chadha's film has received a great deal of critical praise and has packed houses abroad. Chadha is currently at work on her next film project, which centers on lives of Asians from Kenya who, like Chadha, have relocated in England. In all her works, Gurinder Chadha is creating a New British cinema of diaspora that deftly combines education with pure entertainment.

SELECTED FILMOGRAPHY

I'm British but . . . (1989)
Pain, Passion and Profit (1992)
Bhaji at the Beach (1994)

SELECTED BIBLIOGRAPHY

Brown, Georgia. "Ticket to Ride." *Village Voice* 39. 21 (May 24, 1994): 26.
Chua, Lawrence. "Beach Blanket Britain." *Village Voice* 39. 22 (May 31, 1994): 62.
Hornaday, Ann. "In *Bhaji on the Beach*, Feminism Meets the Diaspora." *New York Times*, May 22, 1994, 29.
Lindsey, Beverly, ed. *Comparative Perspectives on Third World Women: The Impact of Race, Sex, and Class.* New York: Praeger, 1980.
Mohanty, Chandra Talpade, Ann Russo, and Lourdes Torres, eds. *Third World Women and the Politics of Feminism.* Bloomington: Indiana University Press, 1991.
Women Make Movies. *Women Make Movies Catalogue.* New York: Women Make Movies, Inc., 1994.

CHENZIRA, AYOKA (1956–   ). United States. Ayoka Chenzira is an African-American filmmaker with a strong background in dance, still photography, and editing. She not only directs films that address African-American experiences but is actively involved in the promotion and distribution of hundreds of black films as the program director of the Black Filmmakers Foundation (1981–84) and is an outspoken activist and lecturer. Chenzira's films are internationally distributed and available through Women Make Movies, Inc. Chenzira was a resident fellow at the Robert Redford Sundance Film Institute. She is a multitalented individual who is an inspiration to others. Along with a number of other black women filmmakers, she is clearly forging an entirely new kind of cinema. She has said that she is more inspired by Toni Morrison than by any filmmakers. She is equally inspired by her daughter and her husband, Thomas Pinnock, a choreographer. Chenzira studied at New York University Film School.

Hair Piece: A Film for Nappy-Headed People (1982) is an animated film that explores the politics of African-American female identity through an analysis of hair and hairstyling. Chenzira's satire of black hair-care products and devices and attitudes toward hair in black culture is one of a new genre of black documentaries that study cultural history in a fresh manner.

Like black British filmmaker Maureen Blackwood's *Perfect Image?* (1988), Julie Dash's *Illusions* (1982), and Kathleen Collins's *Losing Ground* (1982), *Hair Piece* is one of a growing body of films whose images are situated within a contextual exploration of black women's multifaceted cultural identity.

In *Hair Piece*, Chenzira employs a voice-over narrative that states that nappy hair is "bad" and unattractive and interferes with black women's ability to find a job or attract men. The voice-over appears to be poking fun at the voice-overs heard in instructional films of the past. As the film progresses, the animation fades away into a photograph of an African woman in a natural hairstyle. Audiences are not passive when they see the film. They often burst into laughter and discussion when they see the photograph. In this way, *Hair Piece* redefines documentary filmmaking. It does not inform as much as it promotes re-looking and rethinking identity. As Chenzira explains to Afua Kafi-Akua, Chenzira made *Hair Piece* out of a commitment to rethinking black history:

> One of the things I talk about in *Hair Piece* is that I think how you present yourself says a lot about who you think you are and in my mind most of us are really presenting ourselves as though we think we are an inferior and deficient model. You're passing that on to your children and everybody's growing up with a real bad self-image. We don't have to have white slave masters anymore because we're doing a wonderful job ourselves. (71)

As Gloria Gibson-Hudson observes, the films of African-American women are not homogeneous. Chenzira, Dash, and Collins show major cultural themes, yet they cut across different experiences and cinematic approaches.

Ayoka Chenzira's *Secret Sounds Screaming: The Sexual Abuse of Children* (1982) is a video documentary on sexual abuse from an Afrocentric point of view. Chenzira's approach to the material is novel. In the film, Chenzira blends the voices of experiences of people of color, for the first time addressing the issue. Chenzira's film differs from the many other films that deal with this issue because of her direct political slant and her exposé of the societal support system that condones the sexual abuse of children. Chenzira couples these criticisms with an examination of the laws that allow these sex offenders to go free and the attitudes that promote a power relationship that encourages and promotes sexual child abuse. *Syvilla* (1979) is a celebration of dance in African-American history, as is *Zajota and the Boogie Spirit* (1989). Chenzira is currently working on a feature film.

SELECTED FILMOGRAPHY

Syvilla (1979)
Hair Piece: A Film for Nappy-Headed People (1982)
Secret Sounds Screaming: The Sexual Abuse of Children (1982)
Flamboyant Ladies Speak Out (1982)

5 Out of 5 (1986)
The Lure and the Lore (1988)
Zajota and the Boogie Spirit (1989)

SELECTED BIBLIOGRAPHY

Acker, Ally. *Reel Women: Pioneers of the Cinema, 1896 to the Present.* New York: Continuum, 1993.

Attile, Martina, and Maureen Blackwood. "Black Women and Representation." In *Films for Women,* edited by Charlotte Brunsdon, 202–7. London: BFI, 1987.

Boseman, Keith. "Ayoka Chenzira: Sharing the Empowerment of Women." *Black Film Review* (summer 1986): 18.

Gaines, Jane. "Women and Representation: Can We Enjoy Alternative Pleasure?" In *Issues in Feminist Film Criticism,* edited by Patricia Erens, 75–93. Bloomington: Indiana University Press, 1990.

hooks, bell. *Black Looks: Race and Representation.* Boston: South End Press, 1992.

Kafi-Akua, Afua. "Ayoka Chenzira: Filmmaker." *SAGE: A Scholarly Journal on Black Women* 4.1 (spring 1987): 69–72.

Larkin, Alile Sharon. "Black Women Filmmakers Defining Ourselves: Feminism in Our Own Voice." In *Female Spectators,* edited by E. Deidre Pribram, 157–73. London: Verso, 1988.

Smith, Valerie. "Reconstituting the Image: The Emergent Black Woman Director." *Callalloo* 11.4 (fall 1988): 709–19.

Stubbs, Frances, and Elizabeth Hadley Freydberg. "Black Women in American Films." In *Multiple Voices in Feminist Film Criticism,* edited by Diane Carson, Linda Dittmar, and Janice Welsch, 481–91. Minneapolis: University of Minnesota Press, 1994.

Taylor, Clyde. "Black Cinema in the Post-Aesthetic Era." In *Questions of Third Cinema,* edited by Jim Pines and Paul Willemen, 90–110. London, BFI, 1989.

White, Patricia. "Chenzira, Ayoka." In *The Women's Companion to International Film,* edited by Annette Kuhn, with Susannah Radstone, 73–74. Berkeley: University of California Press, 1994.

CHILD, ABIGAIL (1948–   ). United States. Abigail Child is a prominent member of the avant-garde and experimental filmmakers based in New York. Originally based in San Francisco, Child worked on documentary films and later began her career as a personal filmmaker. Child's remarkable early works are created from rapid-editing and pixilation techniques that are frequently used in avant-garde films. Child's work springs from a tradition of women directors of the avant-garde, including Mary Ellen Bute, Julie Dash, Corinne Cantrill, Marie Menken, Carolee Schneemann, Diana Barrie, Joyce Wieland, Barbara Hammer, and Storm de Hirsch. In her pieces, Child is concerned with film form, with the perception of the frame of the image, and with the subjectivity of film spectatorship. Child demythologizes film pleasure and scrutinizes the way we look at the body in pornography, documentary, dance films, film noir, and the home movie.

Many of Child's films are poetical reflections on gender, identity, and lesbian eroticism. Child often blends imagery with appropriated sound tracks, in a style more frequently associated with postmodern filmmakers.

In *Ornamentals* (1979), Abigail Child explores rhythm and the poetry of the repetitive image form. Critics note that the film is a return to the body and a completely different viewing experience with each screening. In the early 1980s, Child began working on a series of films that are now gathered under the title *Perils, Mayhem and Mercy* (released in 1993 by Women Make Movies, Inc.). Another collection of Child's films, *Is This What You Were Born For?* (1981–89), is available for rental from the Film-makers' Cooperative in New York and Canyon Cinema Cooperative in San Francisco. As Child explains: "[T]he project is conceived as a way to bracket my ongoing film investigations in the context of aggressions of the twentieth century" (Film-makers' Cooperative, 107).

One of the works in this series, *Mayhem (Part 6)* (1987), is a feminist deconstruction of women's images in film noir, soap opera, and other visual forms of popular culture. *Mayhem* focuses on female sexuality, gay and straight, and includes an infamous scene of lesbian sex, appropriated from a Japanese porn film of the 1920s. The scene of the women's lovemaking is interrupted by the entrance of a male robber, who masturbates while watching the women. Child forces the viewer to notice that the lesbian sexuality is co-opted for the gaze of the male viewer. *Mutiny (Part 3)* (1982–83) is a feminist look at difference and diaspora within the women's movement. *Covert Action (Part 4)* (1984) is a bizarre reconfiguration of looped home movies that has been called "curiously anti-narrative" (Film-makers' Cooperative, 109). The film, a study of dating rituals in America, centers around the home picnics of two brothers who "bring home" women to meet the family over the years, culminating in the final scene in which the men bring home twins. *Perils (Part Five)* (1985–86) is a revelatory homage to silent films. Child's films are a challenge to the viewer. They remind us that our identities and sexualities are wrapped up in cultural imagery.

In 1980, Abigail Child moved to New York, and she is actively involved in avant-garde film as a lecturer, poet, curator, and theorist. Liz Kotz compares the films of Abigail Child with the works of Cecilia Dougherty and Su Friedrich:

I'd like to propose that works such as those of Child, Dougherty, and Friedrich suggest the reopening of questions which have long been marginalized from media criticism and the world of professional film studies, centering around issues of aesthetics, formal strategies, and what works as "art." (100)

As Kotz suggests, a reconsideration of the lesbian imagery in the films of Abigail Child is important to a comprehensive analysis of feminist media, lesbian subjectivity, and women's avant-garde cinema practice.

SELECTED FILMOGRAPHY

Except the People (1970)
Game (1972)
Tar People (1975)
Some Exterior Presence (1977)
Peripeteia I (1977)
Daylight Test Section (1978)
Peripeteia II (1978)
Pacific Far East Line (1979)
Ornamentals (1979)

Collections

Is This What You Were Born For? (1981–89)
  Includes: *Prefaces (Part 1)* (1981)
    Mutiny (Part 3) (1982–83)
    Covert Action (Part 4) (1984)
    Perils (Part 5) (1985–86)
    Mayhem (Part 6) (1987)
    Both (Part 2) (1988)
    Mercy (Part 7) (1989)
Perils, Mayhem and Mercy (1985–89)
  Includes: *Perils (Part 5)* (1985–86)
    Mayhem (Part 6) (1987)
    Mercy (Part 7) (1989)

SELECTED BIBLIOGRAPHY

Butler, Judith. *Gender Trouble.* New York: Routledge, 1990.

Canyon Cinema. *Canyon Cinema Catalogue.* San Francisco: Canyon Cinema, 1982.

Child, Abigail. "Program Notes: *Is This What You Were Born For?*" San Francisco: San Francisco Cinemateque, 1990.

de Lauretis, Teresa. *Technologies of Gender.* Bloomington: Indiana University Press, 1987.

Film-Makers' Cooperative. *Film-Makers' Cooperative Catalogue No. 7.* New York: Film-Makers' Cooperative, 1989.

Fuss, Diana, ed. *Inside/Out: Lesbian Theories, Gay Theories.* New York: Routledge, 1991.

Kotz, Liz. "An Unrequited Love for the Sublime: Looking at Lesbian Representation across the Works of Abigail Child, Cecilia Dougherty, and Su Friedrich." In *Queer Looks: Perspectives on Lesbian and Gay Film and Video,* edited by Martha Gever, John Greyson, and Pratibha Parmar, 86–102. New York: Routledge, 1993.

Rabinovitz, Lauren. *Points of Resistance: Women, Power, & Politics in the New York Avant-Garde Cinema, 1943–71.* Urbana: University of Illinois Press, 1991.

CHOPRA, JOYCE (1938–   ). **United States.** Like so many women directors, Joyce Chopra got into filmmaking through an early career as a documentary filmmaker. Chopra also spent time running a coffeehouse in the

1960s. A graduate of Brandeis, Chopra is well known in feminist circles for her appearance in *Joyce at 34* (1972), which she codirected with Claudia Weill. *Joyce at 34* documents Chopra's pregnancy. The film was a breakthrough feminist film in that the filmmaker documented her own experience on camera, rather than being an objectified body in another's film. Chopra continued making documentary films until she had the opportunity to direct *Smooth Talk* (1986), an adaptation of Joyce Carol Oates's short story, "Where Are You Going, Where Have You Been?"

Smooth Talk stars Laura Dern as a young girl who is raped as a result of her sexual experimentations. Some feminists were critical of the film, pointing out that the film could be perceived as a message film that teaches young women to repress their sexuality. Barbara Quart sees the film in less strictly defined terms and reads *Smooth Talk* as a multilayered work that calls into question notions of female sexual independence. In the film, Chopra emphasizes the cultural environment of a young woman who wishes to break away from her mother's expectations, as she begins to develop a consciousness of sexuality. Chopra exposes the inherent male violence in patriarchal culture, as the young woman is attracted to a violent male. Although *Smooth Talk* is, in some ways, problematic, the film effectively deals with the familial tensions inherent in most mother-daughter relationships, and Dern's performance in the film is a marvel of constraint and self-assurance.

In 1989, Chopra directed *The Lemon Sisters,* a big-budget Hollywood picture that centers on the lives of three childhood friends played by Diane Keaton, Carol Kane, and Kathryn Grody, who hope to make a career out of singing. The female-centered plot is a refreshing change from the endless series of male-centered narratives Hollywood keeps recycling on a seasonal basis, and Chopra offers an interesting examination of female relationships in the film. Chopra is a technically sophisticated director whose works have been widely distributed, and she remains an important force within the highly commercial arena of television and feature filmmaking.

SELECTED FILMOGRAPHY

Joyce at 34 (1972)
Girls at 12 (1975)
Martha Clarke Light and Dark: A Dancer's Journal (1980)
Smooth Talk (1986)
The Lemon Sisters (1989)
Murder in New Hampshire (1992)

SELECTED BIBLIOGRAPHY

Acker, Ally. *Reel Women: Pioneers of the Cinema, 1896 to the Present.* New York: Continuum, 1993.
Quart, Barbara. *Women Directors: The Emergence of a New Cinema.* New York: Praeger, 1988.
Rapping, Elayne. "*Smooth Talk.*" *Cineaste* 15.1 (1986): 36–37.

CHOY, CHRISTINE (1952–). Korea/United States. Christine Choy, née Chai Ming Huei, was born in China to a Chinese mother and a Korean father. Her father left her family in 1953 to return to his home in Korea. Choy was raised by her mother, who became independent out of necessity. After the cultural revolution in China, Choy and her mother returned to Korea and were reunited with her father. Choy developed a taste for American films in Korea, but she could not help notice that Asian people were treated as second-class citizens in American films. Choy was able to secure a scholarship to Manhattanville College of the Sacred Heart in New York State, where she studied architecture. Choy fell in with a group of hippies in New York City who were associated with Newsreel, an organization dedicated to the making of agitprop documentary films. Choy worked as an editor and animator there and then directed *Teach Our Children* (1974), her first documentary. She later became an executive at Third World Newsreel. She was familiar with the struggles of exile and migration and suffused her autobiographical experiences into *From Spikes to Spindles* (1976). The film concerns Chinese migration. Choy was one of the first major figures in American film production to be an Asian woman. The labels of identity are a central preoccupation of Choy, who is herself classified as a "political filmmaker," an "immigrant," an "Asian," a "woman of color," and, as she says, "the list goes on and on and on . . . so many labels" (Hanson, 17).

Choy's *Who Killed Vincent Chin?* (1988) is, in its own way, an examination of racist labels and their lethal ramifications. Codirected with Renee Tajima, *Who Killed Vincent Chin?* was nominated for an Academy Award for best documentary. It is based on a true story of a murder in Detroit in 1982 of a Chinese man by white men who were subsequently fined $3,000 and punished with only three years' probation. Choy made the film despite difficulties securing funding from the Corporation for Public Broadcasting (CPB). Choy managed to see the project through, raising $175,000 from CPB and another $95,000 from other sources. Finally, the film was screened by PBS as part of the series "Point of View."

Who Killed Vincent Chin? was edited by Holly Fisher, a prominent New York woman filmmaker. Critic Ed Ball notes that the film manages to "entertain as it instructs," noting its innovative story structure. Choy situates the murder contextually within the anti-Asian sentiment brewing in America as a result of the economic growth of Japan and the economic fall of the United States. Intercut with the actual story of the murder are clips of closed American car factories, ads for Chryslers, and newsreel footage of Asian-American history. We learn that the murderers were an unemployed auto worker and his stepfather, a Chrysler foreman. Choy examines the complexities of attitudes that contributed to the murder, from the xenophobic attitude toward foreign cars to the racism against any nonwhite peoples. *Who Killed Vincent Chin?* is a strong multicultural American film that reconfigures ethnographic filmmaking.

Sa-I-gu (1993) was codirected by Christine Choy and Dai Sil Kim-Gibson. The film enunciates the point of view of women Korean-American shopkeepers in riot-torn Los Angeles after the Rodney King verdict. In *Sa-I-gu* the media are criticized for their sensationalist tendency to play up the racial animosity between Koreans and African Americans. *Sa-I-gu* also dramatizes the losses that Asian-American women have suffered as a result of the riots.

Taken as a whole, Choy has a remarkable body of film work. In addition to her work as a filmmaker, Christine Choy is a professor at the Tisch School of the Arts in New York City, and her films are distributed by Third World Newsreel, also located in New York.

SELECTED FILMOGRAPHY

Teach Our Children (1974)
Fresh Seeds in a Big Apple (1975)
Generation of the Railroad Builder (1975)
From Spikes to Spindles (1976)
History of the Chinese Patriot Movement in the U.S. (1977)
North Country Tour (1977)
Inside Women Inside (1978)
Loose Pages Bound (1978)
A Dream Is What You Wake Up From (1978)
To Love, Honor, and Obey (1980)
White Flower Passing (1981)
Bittersweet Survival (1982)
Go Between (1982)
Mississippi Triangle (1982–83)
Fei Teir, Goddess in Flight (1983)
Namibia, Independence Now (1984)
Monkey King Looks West (1985)
Permanent Wave (1986)
Shanhai Lil's (1988)
Who Killed Vincent Chin? (codirected with Renee Tajima) (1988)
Best Hotel on Skid Row (1989)
Fortune Cookie: The Myth of the Model Minority (1989)
Sa-I-gu (codirected with Dai Sil Kim-Gibson) (1993)

SELECTED BIBLIOGRAPHY

Acker, Ally. *Reel Women: Pioneers of the Cinema, 1896 to the Present.* New York: Continuum, 1993.
Ball, Ed. "*Who Killed Vincent Chin?*" *Afterimage* 16.3 (summer 1988): 5.
Choy, Christine. "Interview: Women in the Director's Chair." *Profile: Video Data Bank* 5.1 (1985); Chicago: Art Institute of Chicago, 1985. (Videotape).
Cohan, Charly. "*Who Killed Vincent Chin?*" *Cineaste* 17.1 (1989): 20.

Dittus, Erick. "Mississippi Triangle: An Interview with Christine Choy, Worth Long and Allan Siegel." *Cineaste* 14.2 (1985): 38–40.

Goldman, Debra. *"Who Killed Vincent Chin?" American Film* 13.8 (May 1988): 8.

Hanson, Peter. "NYU Professor's Journey into Film." *Washington Square News,* March 29, 1989, 5, 17.

Kaplan, David A. "Film about a Beating Examines a Community." *New York Times,* July 16, 1989, 27.

Reynaud, Berenice. "Chris Choy et Renee Tajma." *Cahiers du Cinéma* 433 (June 1990): 61.

Third World Newsreel. *Third World Newsreel Catalogue.* New York: Third World Newsreel, 1994.

CHYTILOVÁ, VĚRA (1929–   ). Czechoslovakia. New Wave Czech filmmaker Věra Chytilová was not allowed to direct a film for six years because of the Soviet clampdown on Czech cinema. She was one of the most important radical filmmakers of the 1960s and the only woman director working in Czechoslovakia. Chytilová studied philosophy and architecture. She worked as a model, script clerk, and draftsperson and at other jobs before she fought her way into the Prague Film School (FAMU). Working at Barrandov studios, Chytilová encountered problems distributing her difficult, feminist work. Her early films were shot in the style of underground films being made in the 1960s in America, France, and abroad. They were gritty cinema vérité films that featured nonactors in philosophical investigations into the nature of power over women in Czech culture. Chytilová's formalism met with approval from Western critics, but it caused her to be completely silenced for several years by the political machine in her native country.

Sedmikrásky (Daisies) (1966) is Chytilová's best-known work abroad, but it was banned for several years. *Daisies* is aptly described as a Brechtian comedy about two young women who loll around naked as they talk directly to the audience about philosophical and political questions. *Daisies* is a prototypical New Wave feminist film, with alienating political statements ("Everything is spoiled for us in this world"); jarring editing (the women are intercut with stock footage of buildings falling apart); and existential ponderings (the women state that if "you're not registered, [there is] no proof you exist"). The bleak humor of *Daisies* debunks stereotypical myths about women. The suppressed violence of bourgeois culture is suggested through a bizarre orgy sequence, in which the young women see a raw meat locker and a full orchestra. The letters of the titles are underscored by gunshots on the sound track, as the camera pans over the ruins of a city. B. Ruby Rich calls *Daisies* "one of the first films by a woman to move in the direction of anarchic sexuality" (39).

When Chytilová was able to make films, she continued to make feminist statements, though she certainly toned down the aggressiveness of her form of materialist cinema. *The Apple Game* (1976) is a send-up of doctor movies in which nurses are seduced by philandering doctors. *Prefab Story* (1979) is an unrelenting look at life in a housing project where theft, poverty, and human degradation are everyday occurrences. *A Tainted Horseplay* (1988) is the first film from Eastern Europe to deal with acquired immunodeficiency syndrome (AIDS). Věra Chytilová continues to make challenging formalist cinema, despite an unrelenting series of obstacles.

SELECTED FILMOGRAPHY

Strop (Ceiling) (1961)
Pytel bleck (A Bagful of Fleas) (short) (1962)
O necem jiném (About Something Else) (1963)
Automat "Svet" (Snack-Bar "World") (1965)
Sedmikrásky (Daisies) (1966)
Ovoce stromu rajskych jime (We Eat the Fruit of the Trees of Paradise) (1969)
Hra o jablko (The Apple Game) (1976)
Cas je neuprosny (Inexorable Time) (short) (1978)
Panelstory (Prefab Story) (1979)
Kalamitz (Calamity) (1980)
Faunovo Prilis pozdni odpoledne (The Very Late Afternoon of a Faun) (1983)
Praha, neklidne srdce Europy (Prague, the Restless Heart of Europe) (short) (1985)
Vici bouda (Wolf's Hole) (1986)
Sasek a kralovna (The Jester and the Queen) (1987)
Kopytem sem, kopytem tam (A Tainted Horseplay) (1988)
Happiness Is All Well (1992)

SELECTED BIBLIOGRAPHY

Goulding, Daniel J., ed. *Post New Wave Cinema in the Soviet Union and Eastern Europe.* Bloomington: Indiana University Press, 1989.
Grilikhes, Alexandra. "Films by Women: 1928–1971." *Film Library Quarterly* 6.1 (winter 1972–73): 8.
Hames, Peter. *The Czechoslovak New Wave.* Berkeley: University of California Press, 1985.
Liehm, Antonin. *Closely Watched Films.* White Plains, NY: International Arts and Sciences Press, 1974.
Portuges, Catherine. *Screen Memories: The Hungarian Cinema of Márta Mészáros.* Bloomington: Indiana University Press, 1993.
Quart, Barbara. *Women Directors: The Emergence of a New Cinema.* New York: Praeger, 1988.
———. "Three Central European Women Revisited." *Cineaste* 19.4 (1992): 58–61.
Rich, B. Ruby. "In the Name of Feminist Film Criticism." In *Multiple Voices in Feminist Film Criticism,* edited by Diane Carson, Linda Dittmar, and Janice Welsch, 24–47. Minneapolis: University of Minnesota Press, 1994.

CITRON, MICHELLE (1948–). United States. One of the best-known independent women filmmakers, Michelle Citron was also one of the first feminist directors to bridge the gap between narrative and documentary films with her mock cinema vérité film *Daughter Rite* (1978). Critic Lauren Rabinovitz notes that feminist filmmakers such as Citron were ahead of literary theorists with their "self-reflexive examinations into the authority of image and narrative" (114) in the mid-1970s. Citron was amazed to find that audiences are so fervently programmed to believe what appears to be cinematic truth that they often mistake the faux documentary scenes in *Daughter Rite* for the real thing. *Daughter Rite* subverts passive spectatorship models in its new feminist cinema language. It is a study of motherdaughter and sibling relationships and is made up of home movies, faux documentary, and a voice-over narrative of a woman reading from a journal. The film is not only a classic in women's studies but a stunning technical achievement.

Thematically, *Daughter Rite* is similar to a number of films directed by women that deal with the ambiguities between mothers and daughters, and, as E. Ann Kaplan notes, the film is clearly constructed for the female viewer: it caters to the female gaze. Like Jutta Brückner's *Years of Hunger* (1979), another study of the mother-daughter relationship, *Daughter Rite* is pervasively autobiographical material. *Daughter Rite,* writes Annette Kuhn, is "a complex and critical stance on the 'truthfulness' of autobiographical and documentary discourses" (172). Michelle Citron reconfigures cinematic pleasure in a woman's voice, through a woman's deconstruction of narrative, documentary, and autobiography.

Michelle Citron became concerned, however, that feminist film practice was becoming too difficult to access, because of its formalism and because of the reduced number of women's film festivals and circuits in which the filmmaker could be present to take questions about the work. She therefore began to move her films toward more recognizable genres and accessible film markets. *What You Take for Granted* (1983) is a documentary on women in untraditional jobs. Currently working on a film called *Pandora,* Citron is a professor at Northwestern University in Illinois.

SELECTED FILMOGRAPHY

Self-Defense (1973)
April 3, 1973 (1973)
Integration (1974)
Parthenogenesis (1975)
Daughter Rite (1978)
What You Take for Granted (1983)
Mother Right (1983)

SELECTED BIBLIOGRAPHY

Feuer, Jane. "*Daughter Rite:* Living with Our Pain and Love." In *Films for Women,* edited by Charlotte Brunsdon, 24–30. London: BFI, 1987.
Kaplan, E. Ann. *Women & Film: Both Sides of the Camera.* New York: Methuen, 1983.

Kuhn, Annette. *Women's Pictures: Feminism and Cinema.* London: Routledge, 1982.

Mayne, Judith. *Cinema and Spectatorship.* New York: Routledge, 1993.

Miller, Lynn Fieldman. *The Hand That Holds the Camera.* New York: Garland, 1988.

Rabinovitz, Lauren. *Points of Resistance: Women, Power & Politics in the New York Avant-Garde, 1943–71.* Urbana: University of Illinois Press, 1991.

Welsch, Janice R. "Feminist Film Theory/Criticism in the United States." In *Multiple Voices in Feminist Film Criticism,* edited by Diane Carson, Linda Dittmar, and Janice Welsch, 443–55. Minneapolis: University of Minnesota Press, 1994.

Women Make Movies. *Women Make Movies Catalogue.* New York: Women Make Movies, Inc., 1994.

CLARKE, SHIRLEY (1927–   ). United States. Shirley Clarke is a daring and provocative maker of experimental films and videos. Born Shirley Strimerg in New York City on October 2, 1927, she was the eldest of three girls and came from a very rich family. Clarke has been active in the New York underground filmmaking movement for longer than just about any other living director. One of the founding members of the Film-makers' Distribution Center and the Film-makers' Cooperative, Clarke has been an ardent, activist, independent filmmaker since 1953, when she directed *Dance in the Sun.* Clarke's most celebrated films are undoubtedly *Portrait of Jason* (1967), *The Connection* (1961), and *The Cool World* (1963). In some ways, Clarke's films are most comparable to the underground films of Andy Warhol. *Portrait of Jason* and *The Cool World,* for example, deliberately call attention to themselves as spectacles. As in Warhol's *Vinyl, Portrait of Jason* is a gruelingly long-take film, on which we can hear the directions of Clarke. In Warhol's *Vinyl,* we can see the script being read and occasionally hear off-camera directions. In *Portrait of Jason* viewers are stared at by a black gay hustler who is also a junkie. His monologue is interrupted by Clarke's comments, such as "Keep the sound running" and "Come on, Jason." These deliberate interruptions constitute a breakdown of the traditional relationship among the viewer, the camera apparatus, and the screen. It displays a Brechtian influence of self-referentiality that constantly makes the viewer aware of her or his voyeurism.

Clarke's *Portrait of Jason* was shot in a single sitting, in much the same way that Andy Warhol made his films, almost in real time, with the "mistakes" embraced rather than cut out. Like Warhol's films, *Portrait of Jason* is a spectacle that denies any illusion of realism. It foregrounds the objectification of the drugged and drunken "actor" who himself participates in the objectification, thus demonstrating the camera's ability to become a predator. Similarly, Clarke's film *The Connection* disrupts the "invisibility" of the camera in traditional documentary when one of the actors (playing a junkie) screams at the audience, "Stop looking at me!" Clarke's more recent video works are, in some ways, similar to *Portrait of Jason* in that they, too, rely on direct address to the camera. *Savage/Love* (1981) and *Tongues* (1982) (in which Clarke collaborated with Sam Shepard and Joseph Chaikin) both fit this scheme. The "actor" reciting the monologue in *Savage/Love* breaks down when he asks the audience, "Which presentation of myself will make you want to touch [me]?" In all her work, Clarke repeatedly questions the distance between viewer and the person viewed through the mechanism of the cinema/video apparatus.

Clarke is completely self-assured in her work and has never been tempted to make anything except personal films, and yet she clearly wants to be noticed. "I was uncomfortable, even slightly insulted, when I succeeded at being anonymous. I wondered where people had been, that they shouldn't know me through my work," she once said (Rice, 21). Like Warhol, Clarke was completely self-taught as a filmmaker. She had a background in dance, but like so many women filmmakers, Clarke never studied film. Nevertheless, an early work of Clarke's, her 1959 film *Skyscraper,* won a prize at the Venice Film Festival and was nominated for an Academy Award. Her feature film *The Connection,* based on the play by Jack Gelber, was a groundbreaking semidocumentary examination of the shadowy world of heroin pushers in New York City, as a group of musicians and drifters anxiously await the arrival of their "connection," or dealer.

Early on, Clarke was involved in the civil rights movement, and many of her films are about the African-American struggle. She has always worked on political films, never allowing her formalism to interfere with her humanism. Lauren Rabinovitz recently stated that Clarke's films "staked out a potentially radical cinematic politics toward representation that may only be fully reclaimed in the 1990's as critics move to thoroughly interrogate the intersections of race, gender, and representational politics" (142). Clarke was also one of the first independent filmmakers to recognize and utilize video as an art form.

SELECTED FILMOGRAPHY

Dance in the Sun (1953)
In Paris Parks (1954)
Bullfight (1955)
Moment in Love (1956)
Bruxelles 'Loops' (1957)
Bridges Go Round (1958)
Skyscraper (1959)
A Scary Time (1960)
The Connection (1961)
The Cool World (1963)
Robert Frost: A Lover's Quarrel with the World (1964)
Man in the Polar Regions (1966)
Portrait of Jason (1967)

Videotapes: Series no. 1 (1972)
Videotapes: Series no. 2 (1973)
Angels of Light (1972)
Wendy Clarke's Whitney Show (1976)
24 Frames per Second (1977)
Four Journeys into Mystic Time (1979)
A Visual Diary (1980)
Savage/Love (1981)
Tongues (1982)
Johanna Went 'Performance' (1982)
Johanna Went 'The Box' (1983)
Ornette Coleman—A Jazz Video Game (1984)
Ornette—Made in America (1985)

SELECTED BIBLIOGRAPHY

Acker, Ally. *Reel Women: Pioneers of the Cinema, 1896 to the Present.* New York: Continuum, 1993.
Clarke, Shirley. "*The Cool World.*" *Films and Filming* 10.3 (December 1963): 7–8.
———, and Storm de Hirsch. "A Conversation." In *Women and the Cinema: A Critical Anthology,* edited by Karyn Kay and Gerald Peary, 231–42. New York: Dutton, 1977.
Cooper, Karen. "Shirley Clarke's Videos." *Filmmakers Newsletter* 5.8 (June 1972): 35–38.
Film-Makers' Cooperative. *Film-Makers' Cooperative Catalogue No. 4.* New York: Film-Makers' Cooperative, 1967.
Grant, Barry Keith. "When Worlds Collide: *The Cool World.*" *Literature/Film Quarterly* 18.3 (1990): 179–87.
Heck-Rabi, Louise. *Women Filmmakers: A Critical Reception.* Metuchen, NJ: Scarecrow Press, 1984.
Rabinovitz, Lauren. *Points of Resistance: Women, Power & Politics in the New York Avant-Garde Cinema, 1943–71.* Urbana: University of Illinois Press, 1991.
Rice, Susan. "Shirley Clarke: Image and Images." *Take One* 3.2 (1972): 20–21.

COCHRAN, STACEY (1959–   ). United States. Stacey Cochran is one of a new group of talented women directors currently working in Hollywood feature production. Tamra Davis, Darnell Martin, Jodie Foster, Julie Dash, Nora Ephron, Maggie Greenwald, Leslie Harris, Amy Heckerling, Agnieszka Holland, Sally Potter, Jane Campion, Barbra Streisand, Penny Marshall, Mira Nair, Katt Shea, Kathryn Bigelow, Penelope Spheeris, and Rose Troche are some of the many other women currently directing mainstream commercial films. More often than not, these outlaw women infuse their material with a feminist edge, if not a feminist core. Though women are still far outnumbered in directorial positions, there are enough women working as directors in Hollywood to begin to see changes in Hollywood films—often pleasant surprises.

Stacey Cochran wrote for children's magazines at the Children's Television Workshop and attended Columbia University's film school. In 1990, she directed her feature thesis-film, *Another Damaging Day,* which was screened at the New York Film Festival. At thirty-three, Cochran found the financing ($2.1 million) to direct her screenplay *My New Gun,* a surreal farce that lambastes yuppie materialism, sexless heterosexual couplings, and the deceptively boring hum of suburban perfection. *My New Gun* (1992) is a pleasant surprise for the theatergoers who are tired of conventional narratives, stale comedy, and one-dimensional female roles. Cochran (who grew up in the suburbs of New Jersey) creates a cinematic work of understatement, a quirky mix of sordidness, absurdity, and tragedy, situated around a gun and unpredictable situations. In the film, Debbie Bender (played by Diane Lane) is given a pearl-handled gun by her husband, Gerald (played by Stephen Collins). Debbie insists that she does not need a gun to protect herself. Ironically, Gerald accidentally shoots himself in the foot later. Debbie does not need chivalrous protection from strangers; she needs to get out of her new, but already staid, marriage. Debbie becomes romantically involved with a handsome neighbor, Skippy (James Le Gros, in a brilliantly underplayed comedic performance). Skippy, as it turns out, has a mysterious woman living with him. She turns out to be a pill-popping mother who is on the run from an abusive husband. Tess Harper plays the mother, a former country music star whose life is a living death and who represents what may have become of Debbie Bender if she had not escaped suburbia. At the end of the film's convoluted narrative, Harper commits suicide, and Debbie escapes the suburbs with Skippy.

My New Gun explores the myths surrounding guns in popular culture. It is one of a number of women-directed films that recently redefine the phallic tool in feminist terms. For example, in Tamra Davis's *Guncrazy,* Drew Barrymore's character has more than a slight gun fetish. Kathryn Bigelow's *Blue Steel* is a study of the aura of power invested in the gun, as it is placed in the hands of a policewoman. Katt Shea's *Poison Ivy* is a brilliant film noir about a gun-toting teen punk (Drew Barrymore). Maggie Greenwald's *Ballad of Little Jo* features a memorable scene in which cross-dressing "cowboy" Suzy Amis teaches herself how to use a gun. Lilli Fini Zanuck's *Rush* is notable for the scene in which Jennifer Jason Leigh confidently wields a huge gun. In all these films, putting women behind guns is a divestiture of the phallic power traditionally implicit in weaponry. These new films, in fact, mark a return to the power women displayed in early films, such as those directed by Dorothy Davenport Reid (*The Red Kimona,* 1926) and the gun-toting, self-directed "serial-queens" of the teens and twenties such as Kathlyn Williams (*The Adventures of Kathlyn,* 1913) and Grace Cunard (*The Purple Mask,* 1916). As Stacey Cochran told Jeff Silverman:

The idea for me was that the gun brought into the house to prevent chaos can become a magnet of chaos on its own. It was fun to play with three very standard elements in movies—men, women, and guns—and do something unexpected with them. I certainly wasn't about to turn a woman into a target. (25)

Stacey Cochran's *My New Gun* is a playful study of power mechanics and gender roles and one of a number of new films that are subversively changing American cinema. Cochran is currently finishing a film entitled *Boys,* starring Winona Ryder and James Le Gros.

SELECTED FILMOGRAPHY

Another Damaging Day (1990)
My New Gun (1992)

SELECTED BIBLIOGRAPHY

Jackson, Devon. "Under the Gun." *Village Voice* 37. 46 (November 17, 1992): 104.
Kotz, Liz. "Complicity: Women Artists Investigating Masculinity." In *Dirty Looks: Women, Pornography, Power,* edited by Pamela Church Gibson and Roma Gibson, 101–23. London: BFI, 1993.
Silverman, Jeff. "Romancing the Gun." *New York Times,* June 20, 1993, sec. 2, 1, 24, 25.

COLBERT, LAURIE, AND DOMINIQUE CARDONA (Colbert: 1958– ; Cardona: 1955–   ). Canada.

Thank God I'm a Lesbian (1992), distributed by Women Make Movies, Inc., is one of a growing number of films of the burgeoning lesbian/feminist cinema. Canadian lesbians Laurie Colbert and Dominique Cardona directed this celebratory documentary, which reveals the diversity of lesbian life in the 1990s. *Thank God I'm a Lesbian* is a straightforward documentary that includes interviews of Christine Delphy, Chris Phibbs, Chris Bearchell, LaVerne Monette, Sara Schulman, Julia Creet, Becki Ross, Lee Pui Ming, Nicole Brossard, and Dionne Brand. The fast-paced editing directs the viewer through issues such as feminism, sadomasochism, bisexuality, coming out, racism, activism, outing, and the ideology of compulsory heterosexuality.

In the tradition of pioneering lesbian documentaries, such as *In the Best Interest of the Children* (directors Frances Reid, Elizabeth Stevens, and Cathy Zheutlin) (1977), a groundbreaking film about lesbian mothers, *Thank God I'm a Lesbian* proposes a lesbian vision of community that is positive without being overdetermined or unrealistically one-dimensional. Lesbian cinema spent many years in the closet, with directors such as Dorothy Arzner, Germaine Dulac, and perhaps other women directors unable to openly take up radically feminist positions.

Though lesbians could actively seek out the "hypothetical" lesbian in mainstream films, from Greta Garbo and Marlene Dietrich to the lesbian vampires popular in the 1960s and 1970s, it would take many years for a lesbian independent film movement to get off the ground. In the 1970s, Barbara Hammer and Jan Oxenberg were among a small group of lesbian filmmakers. In the 1980s, many lesbians began to make films; among them were Greta Schiller and Andrea Weiss, Jennie Livingston, Sheila Mc-Laughlin, Su Friedrich, Monika Treut, Ulrike Ottinger, Sadie Benning, and Pratibha Parmar. *Thank God I'm a Lesbian* is an important lesbian documentary because it celebrates the lives of lesbians from a number of different backgrounds and classes, and it does so through the eyes of a lesbian sensibility. It is one of the films that B. Ruby Rich has dubbed "the new queer cinema" (164).

Thank God I'm a Lesbian should be required viewing in high school classrooms, on public television. The film would make a great double bill paired with *Forbidden Love* (directors Aerlyn Weissman and Lynne Fernie, 1992), a documentary about lesbian survival and community in the repressive 1950s. *Forbidden Love* brings lesbian history out of the closet while *Thank God I'm a Lesbian* demonstrates that lesbians are not only out of the closet but reforming a community that cuts across international borders. It is important that lesbian directors' work receive the same attention that homosexual male directors receive, both in gay and mainstream cultures. *Thank God I'm a Lesbian* was screened to great acclaim at numerous film festivals.

SELECTED FILMOGRAPHY

Thank God I'm a Lesbian (1992)

SELECTED BIBLIOGRAPHY

de Lauretis, Teresa. *Alice Doesn't: Feminism, Semiotics, Cinema.* Bloomington: Indiana University Press, 1984.
Dyer, Richard. *Now You See It: Studies on Lesbian and Gay Film.* London: Routledge, 1990.
Harris, Hilary. "Toward a Lesbian Theory of Performance: Refunctioning Gender." In *Acting Out: Feminist Performances,* edited by Lynda Hart and Peggy Phelan, 257–76. Ann Arbor: University of Michigan Press, 1993.
Hart, Lynn. "Identity and Seduction: Lesbians in the Mainstream." In *Acting Out: Feminist Performances,* edited by Lynda Hart and Peggy Phelan, 119–40. Ann Arbor: University of Michigan Press, 1993.
Rich, B. Ruby. "Homo Pomo: The New Queer Cinema." In *Women in Film: A Sight and Sound Reader,* edited by Pam Cook and Phillip Dodd, 164–75. Philadelphia: Temple University Press, 1993.
Straayer, Chris. "The Hypothetical Lesbian Heroine in Narrative Feature Film." In *Multiple Voices in Feminist Film Criticism,* edited by Diane Carson, Linda Dittmar, and Janice Welsch, 343–57. Minneapolis: University of Minnesota Press, 1994.
Weiss, Andrea. *Vampires and Violets: Lesbians in Film.* New York: Penguin, 1993.
Women Make Movies. *Women Make Movies Catalogue.* New York: Women Make Movies, Inc., 1994.

COLE, JANIS AND HOLLY DALE (Cole: 1954–   ; Dale: 1953–   ). Canada.

As many feminists note, the devaluation of women's language and the suppression of women's history are being radically altered by a women's movement that seeks to reclaim language. The documentary film is a site in which women are seizing language, reshaping history, and developing new feminist languages. Janis Cole and Holly Dale are Canada's best-known documentarists. Their films spring from a tradition of feminist documentaries. Cole and Dale first worked together as students and later began making films in the style of direct cinema, or cinema verité. They have a reputation for documenting the marginalized; those who are exploited by class- and gender-based oppression. *Minimum Charge No Cover* (1976) is an unflinching record of the sex-trade industry in Toronto. *P4W Prison for Women* (1981) is a feminist take on women stuck in the penal system, where they develop survival instincts and a sense of community. *Calling the Shots* (1988) treats a more autobiographical subject: the problems that women filmmakers meet in the feature film industry. *Hookers on Davie* (1984) is a documentary on prostitution in Vancouver. The best-known work of Cole and Dale is *Thin Blue Line* (1977), about the treatment of the criminally insane inmates of a maximum security prison.

Canadian women directors seem to excel in documentary filmmaking. One of the reasons for this phenomenon is that women need to tell truths that are suppressed by hegemonic culture. Women's documentaries offer a place for a dialogue to develop among filmmaker, subject, and audience. As Janice Welsch notes, documentaries "provide a climate and a situation in which women can focus on their experiences and achievements without pressure to conform to the expectations or dictates of patriarchal authority" (165). Cole and Dale recently coauthored a collection of interviews entitled *Calling the Shots* (Quarry Press, 1993).

SELECTED FILMOGRAPHY

Directed by Cole and Dale

Cream Soda (1975)
Minimum Charge No Cover (1976)
Nowhere to Run (1977)
Thin Blue Line (1977)
P4W Prison for Women (1981)
Hookers on Davie (1984)
Calling the Shots (1988)

Directed by Dale

Blood (N) Donuts (1995)

SELECTED BIBLIOGRAPHY

Armitage, Kay. "Cole, Janis and Holly Dale." In *The Women's Companion to International Film*, edited by Annette Kuhn, with Susannah Radstone, 90–91. Berkeley: University of California Press, 1994.

Kaplan, E. Ann. *Women in Film: Both Sides of the Camera.* New York: Methuen, 1983.

Lesage, Julia. "Political Aesthetics of the Feminist Documentary Film." In *Films for Women,* edited by Charlotte Brunsdon, 1–14. London: BFI, 1987.

Tregebov, Rhea, ed. *Work in Progress: Building Feminist Culture.* Toronto: Women's Press, 1987.

Welsch, Janice. "Bakhtin, Language, and Women's Documentary Filmmaking." In *Multiple Voices in Feminist Film Criticism,* edited by Diane Carson, Linda Dittmar, and Janice Welsch, 162–75. Minneapolis: University of Minnesota Press, 1994.

COLLINS, KATHLEEN (1942–88). United States. Though white women have made remarkable headway into the film industry, and black men have recently been welcomed in Hollywood, black women continue to be silenced by an industry that offers few opportunities to African-American women directors. With the exception of Leslie Harris, Darnell Martin, and Julie Dash, African-American women directors are not embraced by Hollywood. Zeinabu irene Davis, Ayoka Chenzira, Alile Sharon Larkin, and other African Americans are finding a voice in independent film production.

African-American Kathleen Collins (full name Kathleen Conway Collins Prettyman) was born on March 18, 1942, and grew up in Jersey City, New Jersey. After graduating from Skidmore College, she did graduate work in Paris. Collins was a writer of plays, screenplays, and fiction. From 1967 to 1974, she worked as a film editor for NET and Williams Greaves Productions. She was active as a filmmaker and taught at City College of New York. In 1979, Collins released *The Cruz Brothers,* on a tiny budget of $5,000. *The Cruz Brothers* concerns three Puerto Rican brothers. Collins was discouraged when she was criticized for making a film about people from a different culture, but the film did well, and Collins was able to secure funds for *Losing Ground* (1982), her next film project. During the filming of *Losing Ground,* Collins was diagnosed with cancer. She died of cancer just after the completion of *Gouldtown* (1988), a film about a long-established settlement of African Americans.

Collins was outspoken on her feelings about the need for black women to tell their stories on film as part of a "redemptive process" necessary to achieve change. She also felt that race comes before gender in political struggles; "[T]o separate oneself from black men is to allow America the final triumph of division," she said in an interview with David Nicholson (12). Collins leaves behind a legacy of great importance to African-American cinema.

SELECTED FILMOGRAPHY

The Cruz Brothers (1979)
Losing Ground (1982)
Gouldtown: A Mulatto Settlement (1988)

SELECTED BIBLIOGRAPHY

Acker, Ally. *Reel Women: Pioneers of the Cinema, 1896 to the Present.* New York: Continuum, 1993.

Collins, Kathleen. "Losing Ground." In *Screenplays of African American Experience,* edited by Phyllis Rauch Klotman, 126–85. Bloomington: Indiana University Press, 1991.

Gibson-Hudson, Gloria. "Aspects of Feminist Cultural Ideology in Films by Black Women Independent Artists." In *Multiple Voices in Feminist Film Criticism,* edited by Diane Carson, Linda Dittmar, and Janice Welsch, 365–79. Minneapolis: University of Minnesota Press, 1994.

Nicholson, David. "Conflict and Complexity: Filmmaker Kathleen Collins." *Black Film Review* 2.3 (summer 1986): 11–17.

COOLIDGE, MARTHA (1946–   ). United States. Martha Coolidge began as an experimental, independent filmmaker but has become one of the most successful women directors to work in the mainstream Hollywood system. Born in New Haven, Connecticut, she made her first film in her first year at New York University (NYU). She also directed theatrical productions, took acting classes, and made four films by her sophomore year. Then she left school, stayed in New York, and worked in commercials and documentaries, mostly as an assistant editor, editor, and script clerk. Coolidge returned to night school in film at NYU, the School of Visual Arts, and Columbia Graduate School. A teacher at NYU saw one of Coolidge's early films and hired her to direct an hour-long documentary about a "free school" on Long Island, which later was aired as a special on PBS. Coolidge became active in the New York film community and won a grant to make her next film, *Old Fashioned Woman* (1974), a portrait of her grandmother, which was also screened on PBS.

Subsequently, Coolidge secured investors for *Not a Pretty Picture* (1975), a semiautobiographical film that deals with rape and is considered an important feminist film. After *Not a Pretty Picture,* Coolidge decided to move to Los Angeles and try to break into the industry. She became an AFI (American Film Institute) intern with Robert Wise on *Audrey Rose* and later joined Francis Coppola at Zoetrope. At Zoetrope, she worked on an unfinished film entitled *Photoplay,* a rock and roll love story, which was shelved after two and a half years' work. Disillusioned, Coolidge moved to Canada and was immediately hired to direct a miniseries for the Canadian Broadcasting Corporation. Coolidge finally got an opportunity to direct a feminist film when she directed *The City Girl* (1984). Coolidge is proud of the film: "It's so much a woman's picture I can't even tell you. And it's not what anybody expects from a woman. It's absolutely a woman's picture—not soft, not light, not silly, not easy, not without violence and not without an edge" (Singer, 8).

Coolidge even managed to work a feminist edge into her previous film,

Valley Girl (1983), a low-budget exploitation film. In *Joy of Sex* (1984), a picture Coolidge only agreed to take on after every other director in Hollywood turned the project down, Coolidge again managed to infuse the exploitation film with humor addressed to a female audience. *Joy of Sex* demonstrates how directors often work social commentary into films that are considered B quickies, sometimes more easily than in A films. Coolidge treats menstruation, pregnancy, and contraception in the film. With the successful comedy *Real Genius* (1985), Coolidge established herself as a more than competent director with a terrific sense of comedy; after years of struggle, she had finally arrived in the world of commercial Hollywood cinema.

Rambling Rose (1991) and *Angie* (1994) mark Coolidge's return to her feminist roots. Both films explore female sexuality and societal attitudes toward young women. *Rambling Rose* stars Laura Dern as a "promiscuous" young woman in a coming-of-age story set in the South. One memorable scene depicts Dern introducing a thirteen-year-old boy to his emerging sexuality. This scene is one of the most remarkable sex scenes ever filmed, because it denies the male viewer scopophiliac pleasure by putting the male in the role of that-which-is-acted-upon, rather than catering to the routine male fantasy of a conquering male. *Rambling Rose* is a sensitive melodrama that sees female sexuality as healthy and shows how society tries to harness women's sexuality, to the detriment of women.

Coolidge's most recent film, *Angie,* is her most feminist film to date. Geena Davis stars as a working-class woman who has a child out of "wedlock." Her friendship with her best girlfriend (played by Aida Turturro) is a study in female community. *Angie* remaps the romanticism of the melodrama of the past as a feminist romanticism of the future. Working out of a long tradition of cautionary melodramas in which unmarried women bring up children, *Angie* breaks the mold by not punishing the central character for her choice but, instead, celebrating that freedom. Along the way, Coolidge criticizes men who often just pick up and leave pregnant women, observing that often the female friends stick by women in such situations. A number of women filmmakers are tackling the issues around pregnancy in contemporary films. African-American Leslie Harris's *Just Another Girl on the IRT* (1993) is a brutally honest film about unwed motherhood and the lack of available information on contraception. Alison Anders's *Gas Food Lodging* (1991) deals with teen pregnancy, and Gillian Armstrong's *The Last Days of Chez Nous* (1993) presents the pain of choosing an abortion while it openly acknowledges it as a choice for women.

Martha Coolidge is one of the most commercial women directors, along with Penelope Spheeris, Nora Ephron, and Penny Marshall. She is outspoken in her feminist criticism of the industry. As she told Sharon Bernstein, "[T]he studios don't develop material for women" (82). One central problem is the small number of women in power positions at the executive level in Hollywood. As Pat Newman, an MGM executive, put it, "There is a whole audience of women who aren't going to the movies who I think would go if more female-driven movies were being made" (Bernstein, 9). It takes female executives to "greenlight" such projects. In the meantime, women directors such as Martha Coolidge attempt to remake the cinema from within.

SELECTED FILMOGRAPHY

David: Off and On (1972)
More than a School (1974)
Not a Pretty Picture (1975)
Bimbo (1978)
Photoplay (unfinished) (1978–80)
Employment Discriminations: The Trouble-Shooters (1979)
Strawberries and Gold (1980)
Valley Girl (1983)
The City Girl (1984)
Joy of Sex (1984)
Real Genius (1985)
Plainclothes (1988)
Plainclothes Roughhouse (1988)
That's Adequate (1989)
Trenchcoat Paradise (1989)
Rambling Rose (1991)
Lost in Yonkers (1993)
Angie (1994)

SELECTED BIBLIOGRAPHY

Acker, Ally. *Reel Women: Pioneers of the Cinema, 1896 to the Present.* New York: Continuum, 1993.

Bernstein, Sharon. "But Is There Hope for the Future?" *Los Angeles Times,* November 11, 1990, 9, 82–83.

Byars, Jackie. "Feminism, Psychoanalysis, and Female Oriented Melodrama of the 1950s." In *Multiple Voices in Feminist Film Criticism,* edited by Diane Carson, Linda Dittmar, and Janice Welsch, 93–108. Minneapolis: University of Minnesota Press, 1994.

Chira, Susan. "Unwed Mothers: *The Scarlet Letter* Returns in Pink." *New York Times,* January 23, 1994, sec. 2, 13, 22–23.

Citron, Michelle. "Women's Film Production: Going Mainstream." In *Female Spectators: Looking at Film and Television,* edited by E. Deidre Pribram, 45–63. London: Verso, 1988.

Cole, Janis, and Holly Dale. *Calling the Shots: Profiles of Women Filmmakers.* Ontario: Quarry Press, 1993.

Quart, Barbara. *Women Directors: The Emergence of a New Cinema.* New York: Praeger, 1988.

Singer, Michael. "Interview with Martha Coolidge." In *Film Directors: A Complete*

Guide, edited by Michael Singer, 6–9. Beverly Hills, CA: Lone Eagle Press, 1984.

CRAIGIE, JILL (1914–   ). United Kingdom. Few women were allowed the opportunity to direct films in Britain in the 1940s and 1950s because of Britain's strictly defined gender roles and because British film was a particularly sexist and insular industry. Jill Craigie was among a handful of women who did direct films in this period, despite continual sexism and harassment. Craigie, like Mary Field, worked primarily as a documentarist. Wendy Toye and Muriel Box directed features. Betty Box was a highly successful producer. Oddly enough, Craigie is now dismissive about the importance of her films and her career as a director.

At eighteen, Craigie worked as a journalist, and she worked as a scriptwriter of documentaries for the British Council during World War II. Later she moved on to Two Cities Films, where she was offered the chance to write and direct documentary films. Like so many other women directors, from Alice Guy-Blaché to Jodie Foster, Craigie was perceived as an oddity because of her gender. It is interesting to note this persistent phenomenon. Because the history of women directors is continually buried and suppressed, each successive generation of women directors is assumed to be unique. In this way, women are denied role models.

In 1948, Craigie formed her own production company, Outlook Productions, and began planning a feature film. *Blue Scar* (1949) is Craigie's only film that is not a documentary. *Blue Scar* is a highly critical narrative film about the life of a working-class Welsh mining family, set in the years of the nationalization of the coal industry. The film was perceived as highly controversial and was censored and initially denied exhibition. A nationwide groundswell of public opinion, however, called for the release of *Blue Scar,* and it was finally shown to excellent reviews and enthusiastic audience response.

Craigie returned to documentary film after *Blue Scar,* probably realizing that she could infuse social criticism into this form more blatantly than in dramatic films. Her most important film is the 1951 documentary, *To Be a Woman,* which argues for equal pay for equal work for women. The film was supported by women's organizations. *To Be a Woman* was Jill Craigie's last film. She married Michael Foot, a member of Parliament, but continued to write for the BBC and the *Evening Standard.*

SELECTED FILMOGRAPHY

Out of Chaos (1944)
The Way We Live (1947)
Blue Scar (1949)
To Be a Woman (1951)

SELECTED BIBLIOGRAPHY

Brunel, Adrian. *Nice Work: The Story of 30 Years in British Film Production.* London: Forbes Robertson, 1949.

Cavender, K. *British Feature Directors: An Index to Their Work.* London, BFI, 1958.

Merz, Caroline. "Craigie, Jill." In *Women in Film: A Sight and Sound Reader,* edited by Pam Cook and Phillip Dodd, 99. Philadelphia: Temple University Press, 1993.

———. "The Tension of Genre: Wendy Toye and Muriel Box." In *Re-Viewing British Cinema, 1900–1992,* edited by Wheeler Winston Dixon, 121–32. Albany: SUNY Press, 1994.

Oakley, C. A. *Where We Came In: 70 Years of the British Film Industry.* London: Allen and Unwin, 1964.

Sadoul, Georges. *British Creators of Film Technique.* London: BFI, 1948.

CUNARD, GRACE (1893–1967). United States. Except for the few recent movies that feature female action-heroines, such as *Alien, Thelma and Louise, Blue Steel,* and a handful of other films, women are generally excluded from the role of savior/defender in action films. With the notable exception of Kathryn Bigelow, women directors are almost completely denied the opportunity to direct action films. This cultural phenomenon was not always the case in Hollywood film production. In fact, in the teens and 1920s women such as Grace Cunard, Kathlyn Williams, Ruth Stonehouse, and other "serial-queens" often wrote, directed, produced, and acted in their own films as action heroines. Grace Cunard rose to direction by starring in scores of silent serials. She was a multitalented example of the American New Woman. She could just as easily perform her own stunts as she could work the publicity machine. She wrote and directed scores of serials, historical films, Westerns, and melodramas.

Born in Columbus, Ohio, in 1893, Harriet Mildred Jeffries took the professional name of Grace Cunard. At the age of thirteen, she joined a traveling theater group. Cunard's first appearance as an actress in films was in *The Duke's Plan* (1910). The free-spirited Cunard did not particularly like working with D. W. Griffith, the director of *The Duke's Plan.* (Griffith was also responsible for the unspeakably racist tract *The Birth of a Nation* [1915] and, through savvy self-promotion, styled himself as the father of the narrative cinema, thus ignoring the work of Alice Guy, Lois Weber, and other feminist cinema pioneers who were shooting narrative films before Griffith ever entered a film studio.) Cunard appeared in many films before she formed a partnership with Francis Ford, an actor and director who was the brother of director John Ford. Ford and Cunard's partnership was one of the most successful Hollywood partnerships in motion picture history. In the beginning, Cunard was credited as writer and actress, while Ford was credited as director/actor, though many oral histories note that the two shared almost all these tasks equally. But later, Grace Cunard began taking codirector and director credit. Cunard was among many women directors who worked at Universal Studios in the teens and 1920s, including Ida May Park, Lois Weber, Ruth Stonehouse, Cleo Madison, Elsie Jane Wilson, and Jeannie Macpherson.

Cunard and Ford are best known for their serial *The Broken Coin* (1915), a highly successful action "cliffhanger" serial, starring and written by Grace Cunard. Though Cunard is not credited as director, it is well known that she actually codirected the serial. Cunard and Ford were responsible for some of the strongest representations of female action heroines on the screen. Cunard's depiction of strong action heroines marks an important, almost completely lost cultural moment in which women were portrayed as active, clever, physically adroit warrior archetypes who were quite capable of saving themselves and others. It is important to note that phallocentric film historians have promulgated a false history of early cinema by privileging films directed by men such as D. W. Griffith (whose films feature women who are usually helpless, objectified victims). A feminist history of the cinema should actively reclaim the suppressed body of films directed by women in the silent and early sound period. Many of these films have yet to be restored, while film historians, even feminists, support the canonization and restoration efforts of the reductive films of Griffith.

The films of Grace Cunard are comparable to many of the recently unearthed literary efforts of women writers who created independent women of action. Grace Cunard's action heroines include *The She Wolf* (1913), *The Mysterious Leopard Lady* (1914), *Lucille Love, Girl of Mystery* (1914), and *Lady Raffles* (1914). Lady Raffles, a character Cunard created and played, seems to have recently reappeared in the Jodie Foster character in *Maverick* (1994). *Lady Raffles* is a sexy thief who always escapes the good guys through her brilliant wit and physical adroitness. In *The Purple Mask* (1916) Grace plays a female Robin Hood type who consistently outwits a detective on her trail. In the matriarchal sci-fi comedy, *Last Man on Earth* (1929), Cunard plays a gangster who kidnaps the last surviving male on earth and holds him for ransom from the all-woman government. The career of Grace Cunard is certainly significant. Though her films were meant to provide pleasure for the male gaze, they appealed to the female audience. These women were looking for role models of action heroines who represented the New Woman in her abilities, self-determination, independence, and desire for fast cars, men's clothes, and, more significantly, societal power.

While women's roles occasionally called for action, particularly in B pictures, as sidekicks of male heroes or evil antiheroes, for the most part, women were completely driven out of the role of action hero and, at the same time, elbowed out of the director's chair. Even today, women directors are consistently denied the opportunity to direct action vehicles, with only a few exceptions. Women actresses scarcely get the opportunity to play an action hero; when they do, they are usually allowed only to save their children or, occasionally, themselves.

As the contemporary action director Kristine Peterson told me, "In order for a woman to be a savior, she has to be raped, she can also save a child. But she can't save a man because men can't be portrayed as vulnerable. We are in a cultural era in which film fantasies are supposed to make men feel better about themselves. Supposedly, their fantasy is to be the savior" (Personal communication, 1992). Even when women act to save themselves, as in the case of *Thelma and Louise,* the material is handed to a male director, so that men still control women heroes' images. In a recent case, the film *Bad Girls* was pulled out of the hands of director Tamra Davis, when it appeared that the film was going to be "too feminist" in the eyes of the producers. A male director (Jonathan Kaplan) was handed the project, the production budget was more than doubled, the lesbian plotline was cut from the film, and a male hero, who would save the women, was written into the script.

The early films of Grace Cunard demonstrate that women's images have, in some areas, regressed in terms of feminism since the early days of Hollywood. She is an important figure in a feminist rewriting of film history. Cunard was married to Jack Shannon in 1925, and retired from Hollywood in the 1930s. She died in 1967, after an extended fight with cancer.

SELECTED FILMOGRAPHY

The She Wolf (1913)
The Madonna of the Slums (1913)
Bride of Mystery (1914)
Lady Raffles (1914)
Lucille Love, Girl of Mystery (serial) (1914)
The Mysterious Leopard Lady (1914)
The Mysterious Rose (1914)
The Broken Coin (serial) (1915)
The Campbells Are Coming (1915)
The Doorway of Destruction (1915)
The Hidden City (1915)
Nabbed (1915)
One Kind of a Friend (1915)
The Bandit's Wager (1916)
Behind the Mask (1916)
Brennon O'the Moor (1916)
Born of the People (1916)
The Elusive Enemy (1916)
Her Better Self (1916)
Her Sister's Sin (1916)
The Heroine of San Juan (1916)

His Majesty Dick Turpin (1916)
Lady Raffles Returns (1916)
The Madcap Queen of Crona (1916)
Phantom Island (1916)
Peg O'the Ring (serial) (1916)
The Powder Trail (1916)
The Princely Bandit (1916)
The Purple Mask (serial) (1916)
The Sham Reality (1916)
The Strong Arm Squad (1916)
Circus Sarah (1917)
Her Western Adventure (1917)
In Treason's Grasp (1917)
The Puzzle Woman (1917)
Society's Driftwood (1917)
True to Their Colors (1917)
Unmasked (1917)
The Spawn (1918)
A Daughter of the Law (1920)
The Man Hater (1920)
The Woman of Mystery (1920)
The Girl in the Taxi (1921)
Her Western Adventure (1921)
A Dangerous Adventure (serial) (1922)

SELECTED BIBLIOGRAPHY

Acker, Ally. *Reel Women: Pioneers of the Cinema, 1896 to the Present.* New York: Continuum, 1993.

Foster, Gwendolyn, and Wheeler Winston Dixon. *The Women Who Made the Movies.* Lincoln, NE: NETV, 1991.

Henry, William M. "Her Grace and Francis." *Photoplay* 9.5 (April 1916): 27–29.

Rainey, Buck. *Those Fabulous Serial Heroines.* Metuchen, NJ: Scarecrow Press, 1990.

D

DALE, HOLLY. *See* COLE, JANIS

DASH, JULIE (1952–   ). United States. African Americans have long been excluded from Hollywood filmmaking. Except for a period of early independent black filmmaking, in which black men and women such as Oscar Micheaux and Eloyce Gist had a chance to direct, black people have been almost completely denied access to direct their own films in Hollywood. With the number of recent African-American men who have managed to make it into the system, one could certainly expect to see Hollywood make room for black women directors. But only a few women of color, including Julie Dash, Euzhan Palcy, Leslie Harris, and Darnell Martin, have had their films distributed by major Hollywood production companies. This is an example of consistent, deplorable racism, which has plagued cinema since its earliest days. The recent "celebration" of the restoration of D. W. Griffith's racist Klan-celebrating "masterpiece," *Birth of a Nation* (1915), is a powerful reminder that Hollywood resists change despite a societal embrace of multiculturalism. Film imagery, as Mark A. Reid explains, "has its roots in slavery," (26) and it is this imagery which Julie Dash seeks to overhaul in her film *Daughters of the Dust* (1991).

Daughters of the Dust remakes African cultural heritage on the silver screen. Set at the turn of the century, on a Caribbean island off the South Carolina coast, the film follows the story of the Gullah family, a story of exile, migration, and rootedness. Dash envisioned the film as a study of African culture and its survival, despite colonialist intervention. She chose the setting of this island because it retained African traditions as a result of cultural isolation. Dash told Zeinabu irene Davis, another black woman director:

I wanted the look of the film to come from a rich African base. . . . Like the "doorag" on the hair and how it's tied and all that kind of stuff. The way we approached it was to do as your mother did—and as did her mother before her. So, it would be tied in a much different way than what popular American culture would allow us to see it. The manner in which African women tie their heads with scarves has different meanings. Everything means something; there's a source for everything. You just don't put a scarf up on someone's head. You just don't put jewelry on someone; you put it on in a certain way. People's motor habits—the way they stand and the way they walk, the way they laugh—I tried to maintain the integrity of West African motor habits. (111–14)

Daughters of the Dust is highly stylized and makes extensive use of natural light and "stretch printing" (optically reprinting the imagery to slow down the action). It is told in elliptic, narrative sequences and shot in richly textured colors. It is a cultural remythologization and revisionist history of African diasporic history. Its focus on a matriarchal clan has a distinctively black feminist aesthetic that has been celebrated by many reviewers. The finished work is compared with the writings of Toni Morrison, but Julie Dash initially had trouble finding a distributor of her masterwork. It was eventually picked up by Kino International, a foreign film distributor, demonstrating that Hollywood still considers African Americans as exotic/others.

Julie Dash was born in New York City. She studied film at the American Film Institute (AFI) and the University of California—Los Angeles. She worked as an independent filmmaker for many years before the success of *Daughters of the Dust*. Her short film, *Illusions* (1982), is well known among feminist critics. It is a trenchant analysis of the manner in which Hollywood treated African-American women in the 1940s. *Illusions* (available from Women Make Movies, Inc.) is a fictional narrative about two African-American women, Ester Jeeter, whose voice is dubbed over a white actress, and Mignon Dupreé, a light-skinned studio executive who appears to be white. *Illusions* is an indictment of racism in the Hollywood film industry and, at the same time, a complex study of "passing," and the cultural politics of image. *Phillis Wheatley* (1989) is a documentary celebration of the famous African-American eighteenth-century poet.

Julie Dash is currently working on a remake of *La Lectrice,* which will feature an African-American woman who is absorbed in African-American literature. The success of Julie Dash, Leslie Harris, Darnell Martin, and other young African-American women directors marks the rise of a new age in Hollywood, in which African-American women will no longer be so underrepresented as cinema auteurs.

SELECTED FILMOGRAPHY

Working Models of Success (1973)
Diary of an African Nun (1977)
Four Women (1978)
Illusions (1982)

We Are Mothers Too Early (1983)
Breaking the Silence (1988)
Preventing Cancer (1989)
Phillis Wheatley (1989)
Relatives (1990)
Prairie House (1991)
Daughters of the Dust (1991)

SELECTED BIBLIOGRAPHY

Alexander, Karen. "*Daughters of the Dust,* and a Black Aesthetic." In *Women in Film: A Sight and Sound Reader,* edited by Pam Cook and Phillip Dodd, 224–31. Philadelphia: Temple University Press, 1993.

Baker, Houston A. "Not without My Daughters." *Transition: An International Review* 57 (1992): 150–66.

bell hooks. *Black Looks: Race and Representation.* Boston: South End Press, 1992.

Cole, Janis, and Holly Dale. *Calling the Shots: Profiles of Women Filmmakers.* Ontario: Quarry Press, 1993.

Dash, Julie. *Daughters of the Dust: The Making of an African-American Woman's Film.* New York: New Press, 1992.

Davis, Zeinabu Irene. "An Interview with Julie Dash." *Wide Angle* 13.3–4 (Black Cinema Issue) (1991): 110–18.

Gibson-Hudson, Gloria. "Aspects of Black Feminist Cultural Ideology in Films by Black Women Independent Artists." In *Multiple Voices in Feminist Film Criticism,* edited by Diane Carson, Linda Dittmar, and Janice Welsch, 365–79. Minneapolis: University of Minnesota Press, 1994.

Jones, Jacquie. "The Black South in Contemporary Film." *African American Review* 27.1 (spring 1993): 19–24.

Reid, Mark A. "Rebirth of a Nation: Three Recent Films Resist Southern Stereotypes of D. W. Griffith, Depicting a Technicolor Region of Black, Brown and Gray." *Southern Exposure* 20.4 (winter 1992): 26–28.

Tate, Greg, and Arthur Jafa. "La Venus Negre." *Artforum* 30.1 (January 1992): 90–93.

DAVIS, TAMRA (1963–   ). United States. Feminist film critics were looking forward to Tamra Davis's feminist Western *Bad Girls* (1994), but Davis's vision was apparently too feminist for the producers of the film. In one of the most public acts of sexism in the recent days of Hollywood, Davis was removed from the picture and replaced by a male director, Jonathan Kaplan. The strong feminist elements were removed from the film. A lesbian subplot was cut out, and what was left was described as "a western less arty than tarty" (Beck, 62). When Davis was fired, the budget was suddenly increased to $20 million for Kaplan's revised version. The woman who was the director of photography, Lisa Rinzler, was also fired and replaced by a male director of photography. Tamra Davis spoke out publicly about the resultant debacle, telling *US* magazine that "she didn't want to be another woman who keeps quiet" (Grey and Hruska, 74). Among the demands that Davis could not abide were changes in the way the women were portrayed. According to writers Juliann Grey and Bronwen Hruska, the producers "favored a sexier aesthetic that would feature more cleavage" (74). Davis did not agree: "These actresses are respectable. You don't go into the dressing room and say 'show me more boobs' " (74). The script for *Bad Girls* was completely rewritten, and the feminist sections were deleted. In one planned scene, a prostitute was supposed to protect herself against a rapist by biting his penis. The scene was cut from the script. Instead of a feminist rape-revenge narrative, *Bad Girls* ended up another male fantasy of girls in bustiers, being brutalized by men.

Yet before Tamra Davis became known for the *Bad Girls* fiasco, she had already directed a brilliant rape-revenge narrative, *Guncrazy* (1992), starring Drew Barrymore and James LeGros, in a feminist revisioning of the film noir genre, crossed with a rape-revenge narrative. Ostensibly a remake of the Joseph H. Lewis 1950 classic film noir *Gun Crazy/Deadly Is the Female*, Davis's *Guncrazy* has been compared with *Bonnie and Clyde*-type films, but on a closer inspection, it is an interweaving of a young woman's revenge against rape and sexual assault and a young man's revenge against a brutally violent father. In *Guncrazy*, Anita (played by Barrymore) kills her mother's boyfriend (Joe Dallesandro), who has repeatedly raped Anita for years. (In a neat touch, Dallesandro first teaches Anita how to use a gun.) Anita hides the body and falls in love with her pen pal, Howard (LeGros), a prison inmate who is obsessed with guns and has a history of violence. Anita helps Howard get out of prison, and the two burn the body of her mother's boyfriend. "Here lies a fucking pig. May he roast in hell for all eternity," are the words Anita offers in "prayer," as the boyfriend's body is consumed by the flames. The couple are bound together by this sacrificial act.

In the next scene, two boys who have sexually assaulted Anita show up while Howard and Anita are attempting to dispose of the remains of the body, and Howard shoots them to protect Anita. Their "outlaw" status thus confirmed, Howard and Anita go on the run. We get a glimpse of Howard's past in a television interview with his father, who says directly to the camera, "Strap him to the electric chair and I'll pull the switch!" Davis uses a brilliant cinematic shorthand that suggests that Howard has also been raped and abused by his father, stitching together the rape-revenge narratives of the central characters. The mise-en-scène of an America of ruined buildings and run-down trailers, punctuated by intermittent scenes of violence on television, is comparable to the postmodern wasteland depicted in *Gas Food Lodging*, directed by Alison Anders. Women directors like Davis and Anders infuse their material with a social critique of sexism and poverty, but they do so by placing their narratives within the context of class, race, and gender.

Tamra Davis also directed *CB4* (1993), a clever satire on rap-music videos that includes an incisive deconstruction of Hollywood's appropriation of African-American culture and an absolutely hysterical send-up of sexism in rap music. Written by Chris Rock and Nelson George, *CB4* deals with a rapper group's struggle to make it in Hollywood. The group is unable to get anyone to pay attention to them until they act like murderers and sexist gangsters. The funniest scene is a completely over-the-top performance in which the group tries to think up the most vile, sexist lyrics they possibly can, including "sweat of my balls," in which the band wears gigantic balloon testicles. With *CB4*, Tamra Davis proved she could direct a low-budget comedy. With *Guncrazy*, she proved she could brilliantly remake a classic film noir. With the disaster of *Bad Girls*, Davis proved that feminist filmmakers cannot always be co-opted by Hollywood. Sometimes, they refuse to be silent.

SELECTED FILMOGRAPHY

Guncrazy (1992)
CB4 (1993)
Bad Girls (removed from production during shooting; footage scrapped) (1994)

SELECTED BIBLIOGRAPHY

Beck, Henry Cabot. *"Bad Girls." Interview* (April 1994): 62.
Clover, Carol J. "High and Low: The Transformation of the Rape Revenge Movie." In *Women and Film: A Sight and Sound Reader,* edited by Pam Cook and Philip Dodd, 76–85. Philadelphia: Temple University Press, 1993.
Grey, Juliann, and Bronwen Hruska. "They Shoot *Bad Girls,* Don't They?: How a Low-Budget 'Feminist Western' Turned into a Big-Budget *Wild Bunch* with Women." *US Magazine* (May 1994): 74, 90.
Rich, B. Ruby. "At Home on the Range." *Sight and Sound* 3.11 (November 1993): 18–22.
Silverman, Jeff. "Romancing the Gun." *New York Times,* June 20, 1993, sec. 2, 1, 24, 25.
Tompkins, Jane. *West of Everything: The Inner Life of Westerns.* New York: Oxford University Press, 1992.
Whitehead, Colson. *"CB4." Village Voice* (March 23, 1993): 61.

DAVIS, ZEINABU IRENE (1961–). United States. "Feminist theory rooted in an ahistorical psychoanalytic framework that privileges sexual difference actively suppresses recognition of race," writes bell hooks, "reenacting and mirroring the erasure of black womanhood that occurs in films" (123). If, as hooks states, some feminist theorists have been guilty of erasing black women as spectators, they have been equally guilty of ignoring black women filmmakers. More important, film critics in general ignore the independent films of black women, while they champion the films of Spike Lee, Robert Townsend, Matty Rich, and other black male figures. But black women feminists and filmmakers are actively seeking to change these disparities. Zeinabu irene Davis is one of a growing number of independent black women filmmakers who are actively constructing "an oppositional gaze," a term bell hooks uses to describe films that look through/at African-American female experiences through a black lens.

Davis studied law at Brown University and became involved in film while studying abroad in Kenya. She was disgusted by the fact that white documentarists ignored the cultural diversity of African peoples in favor of a "Mutual of Omaha presents *The Wild Kingdom* kind of thing" (Filemyr, 7). Davis began working with writer Ngugi wa Thiong 'o on the idea for a film, but the project was subsequently shelved when Ngugi exiled himself to the United States. Davis was inspired by independent filmmakers such as Kathleen Collins. She describes herself as "hardheaded," in an accurate portrayal of the stubbornness and vision one needs to become an independent filmmaker. "You have to be so many different kinds of personalities, part hustler, part collaborator, part compromiser, part real persistence," Davis told Ann Filemyr (8).

Zeinabu irene Davis has produced, written, and directed several films, including *A Period Piece* (1987), *Cycles* (1989), and *A Powerful Thang* (1991). She believes that black filmmakers are developing a new genre that constitutes a black aesthetic. She compares the black movement of women directors with black blues and jazz musicians who redeveloped a medium into a new art form. *Cycles* is a participatory celebration of black femaleness. Davis draws on Caribbean folklore in this performative narrative about a woman waiting for her menstruation cycle to begin. The contrapuntal sound track is woven against the grain of the images, in a diasporic mix of voices as diverse as Miriam Makeba, Clara Bryant, and a Haitian women's chorus. *Cycles* (like Ayoka Chenzira's *Hair Piece*) combines animation and live-action sequences.

A Powerful Thang (1991) is an experimental film that loosely revolves around an African-American couple's complex relationship. Davis uses an ethnographic approach to the material that slowly unravels the "extraordinariness" of an ordinary day in the life of African Americans in Ohio. Gloria Gibson-Hudson, of the Black Film Center Archive at Indiana University, describes *A Powerful Thang*:

[It] ingeniously pits desire for sexual intimacy against the need for love. A catalyst for in-depth discussions of intimate relationships. Dynamic and entertaining. (Women Make Movies, 54)

Davis avoids a logocentric voice through the use of a mixture of animation and live-action sequences in *A Powerful Thang*. She is a professor at Northwestern University. She has had her work screened at the Whitney Museum of American Art and is a recipient of the 1991 Rockefeller Inter-Arts Media Fellowship, as well as National Endowment Fellowships. Davis's films belong to the diverse, heterogeneous New Black Feminist wave in independent film. Her films are available through Women Make Movies, Inc., and Third

World Newsreel. Davis is completing a forthcoming film tentatively entitled *Compensation.*

SELECTED FILMOGRAPHY

Crocodile Conspiracy (1980)
A Period Piece (1987)
Recreating Black Women's Media (1987)
Cycles (1989)
A Powerful Thang (1991)
Mother of a River (1995)

SELECTED BIBLIOGRAPHY

Davis, Zeinabu irene. "An Interview with Julie Dash." *Wide Angle* 13.3–4 (Special Issue: Black Cinema) (1991): 110–19.

Diawara, Manthia. "Cinema Studies, the Strong Thought and Black Film: Guest Editor's Introduction." *Wide Angle* 13.3–4 (Special Issue: Black Cinema) (1991): 4–11.

Filemyr, Ann. "Zeinabu Irene Davis: Filmmaker, Teacher with a Powerful Mission." *Angles: Women Working in Film and Video* 1.2 (winter 1992): 6–9, 22.

Gibson-Hudson, Gloria T. "African American Literary Criticism as a Model for Analysis of Films by African American Women." *Wide Angle* 13.3–4 (Special Issue: Black Cinema) (1991): 44–55.

———. "Black Feminist Cultural Ideology in Films by Black Women Independent Artists." In *Multiple Voices in Feminist Film Criticism,* edited by Diane Carson, Linda Dittmar, and Janice Welsch, Minneapolis: University of Minnesota Press, 1994, 365–380.

hooks, bell. *Black Looks: Race and Representation.* Boston: South End Press, 1992.

Pribram, E. Deidre, ed. *Female Spectators: Looking at Film and Television.* London: Verso, 1988.

Taubin, Amy. "Exile and Cunning." *Village Voice* (January 13, 1987): 68.

Women Make Movies. *Women Make Movies Catalogue.* New York: Women Make Movies, 1994.

DE HIRSCH, STORM (1931–). United States. The pioneering avant-garde cinema of Storm de Hirsch is almost completely ignored in histories of the New York 1960s underground filmmaking scene. Though critics Constance Penley and Janet Bergstrom exposed the sexist politics of the exclusion of women from the narrowly defined canon of New York experimental filmmakers, very little attention has been paid to Storm de Hirsch, one of the most important artists of that period. Storm de Hirsch was one of the founding members of the Film-Makers' Cooperative (FMC) in New York. She is a visionary poet and filmmaker whose work is usually described as formalist, but de Hirsch's work is not purely formalist in the monolithic sense of that word. Like *The Tattooed Man* (1969) (for which de Hirsch won the American Film Institute's (AFI) first independent film grant), *Journey around a Zero* contains images of a naked man, in a reversal of the cinematic tradition in which male filmmakers objectify and fetishize the filmed female body. Storm de Hirsch and Yoko Ono turned female objectification into female spectatorship, challenging a taboo that remains in force today. De Hirsch was a pioneer of technical devices such as frame-by-frame etching and painting and metadiagetic editing techniques. Stan Vanderbeek called *The Tattooed Man* "a major work in terms of style, structure, graphic invention, image manipulation and symbolic ritual" (FMC, 1975, 67).

Goodbye in the Mirror (1964) is a discursive analysis of three women's subjectivity and a contemplation on the philosophy of identity. After seeing the film, Jonas Mekas said, "I couldn't believe what beauty struck my eyes, what sensuousness" (FMC, 1975, 65). De Hirsch's formalism allowed for the intervention of pleasure; in fact, she directly catered to the audience's desire for pleasure. *Goodbye in the Mirror* is a visual feast of experimentation, comparable, in some ways, to the visual effects of MTV, which mimic sixties underground filmmaking. De Hirsch uses aural masking effects that are counterpointed against the visuals, such as the amusing song, "I Wish I Was a Fascinating Bitch." *Goodbye in the Mirror* is a female-centered experimental film that is mesmerizing in its ability to capture the phenomenon of apparent movement within the frame.

De Hirsch later directed a trilogy entitled *The Color of Ritual, The Color of Thought* in 1964–65. (The fascination with ritual is a frequent motif in de Hirsch's work, as it is in many women experimentalists, such as Zeinabu irene Davis, Diana Barrie, Daina Krumins, Yoko Ono, Maya Deren, and Ayoka Chenzira.) *Divinations* (1964), one part of the trilogy, is a violation of all the laws of traditional animation, with its ritualistic dismemberment and rearticulation of the frame. To make this film, de Hirsch used surgical instruments to scratch the surface of the film stock itself. Her films are assaults on the viewer in their brilliant use of color, pure light, and sensory imaginations of memory and beauty. *Sing Lotus* (1966) is a phantasmagoric film in which de Hirsch uses eighteenth-century Indian miniatures to enact a wedding ceremony. *Trap Dance* (1968) is another study of the cinematic frame, which is scratch-etched, manipulated, and underscored with repetitious, rhythmic "found" music.

In sum, it seems to me truly amazing that the work of Storm de Hirsch is so completely ignored in the canon of experimental filmmaking. Her work explores a prelinguistic discourse of feminine language of the cinema in a reconfiguration of the primal scene enacted among filmmaker, film apparatus, and spectator. It is an eye-opening experience to read the critical praise that de Hirsch received for her work from her contemporaries, considering that today she rarely rates even a cursory entry in most film encyclopedias or textbooks. The films of Storm de Hirsch are available from the Film-makers' Cooperative in New York. De Hirsch is also the author of several books of poetry.

SELECTED FILMOGRAPHY

Journey around a Zero (1963)
Goodbye in the Mirror (1964)
The Color of Ritual, The Color of Thought (trilogy) (1964–66)
   Divinations (1964)
   Peyote Queen (1964)
   Shaman (1966)
Newsreel: Jonas in the Brig (1966)
Sing Lotus (1966)
Cayuga Run (1967)
Trap Dance (1968)
Third Eye Butterfly (1968)
The Tattooed Man (1969)
An Experiment in Meditation (1971)
Wintergarden (1973)
River-Ghost (1973)
Lace of Summer (1973)
September Express (1973)
Charlotte Moorman's Avant-Garde Festival #9 (1973)
Malevich at Guggenheim (1973)
Ive's House: Woodstock (1973)
Deep in the Mirror Embedded (1973)
Silently, Bearing the Totem of a Bird (1973)
A Reticule of Love (1973)
Aristotle (1973)
The Recurring Dream (1973)
Geometrics of the Kabbaheh (1975)

SELECTED BIBLIOGRAPHY

de Hirsch, Storm, and Shirley Clarke. "A Conversation." *Film Quarterly* 46 (autumn 1967): 44–54.

Delphy, Christine. *Close to Home: Materialist Analysis of Women's Oppression.* London: Hutchinson, 1984.

Film-Makers' Cooperative. *Film-Makers' Cooperative Catalogue No. 6.* New York: Film-Makers' Cooperative, 1975.

Film-Makers' Cooperative. *Film-Makers' Cooperative Catalogue No. 7.* New York: Film-Makers' Cooperative, 1989.

Mellencamp, Patricia. "Receivable Texts: U.S. Avant-Garde Cinema, 1960–1980." *Wide Angle* 7.1–2 (1985): 74–91.

Penley, Constance, and Janet Bergstrom. "The Avant-Garde: Histories and Theories." *Screen* 19.3 (autumn 1978): 113–27.

Polan, Dana. *The Political Language of the Avant-Garde.* Ann Arbor: UMI Research Press, 1985.

Rabinovitz, Lauren. *Points of Resistance: Women, Power & Politics in the New York Avant-Garde Cinema, 1943–71.* Urbana: University of Illinois Press, 1991.

Smith, Sharon. *Women Who Make Movies*. New York: Hopkinson and Blake, 1975.

DEITCH, DONNA (1945–). United States. Lesbian feminist Donna Deitch has been both criticized and praised for her lesbian love story, *Desert Hearts* (1985), an unprecedented, artistically successful, independent film that was a genuine box-office hit. Adapted from the Jane Rule novel, *Desert of the Heart* (1964), *Desert Hearts* was one of the first mainstream, lesbian narratives in which the central love story does not end in tragedy. As Kathi Maio noted: "The most amazing thing about the film *Desert Hearts* is that it was ever made at all. And it wouldn't have been made without the total dedication of the movie's producer and director, Donna Deitch" (102). Deitch used her experience as a documentarist to persuade investors to back her first feature film. She ultimately spent several years securing $1.5 million to produce *Desert Hearts,* before she even shot a frame of film.

Desert Hearts is set in the 1950s. Two women fall in love against the backdrop of the Wild West. B. Ruby Rich notes that the use of the American landscape in the film "embodies a wonderful sense of female adventure . . . Deitch takes the landscapes for the ride, degendering the pitch-perfect country-western music . . . that fills the soundtrack, creating an expansive world outside the domestic sphere for women to inhabit" (72). *Desert Hearts* resembles, in many ways, a Douglas Sirk melodrama, but it is shot by a woman, and it feels like it. "I think there's definitely a female gaze," Deitch told Ally Acker (43).

Desert Hearts has all the trappings of melodramatic iconography. An uptight, cerebral woman is liberated by a free-spirited, sensually open lesbian. The film may be considered too mainstream, too syrupy, even too predictable by some critics, but for a Hollywood-style movie it is a huge, transgressive step away from movies that traditionally depict lesbians as deviants who must be punished. Mandy Merck accurately criticizes *Desert Hearts*'s conventionality, demonstrating how the narrative loses its freshness in the adaptation from novel to film. But, as Merck notes, "on the other hand, the female viewer is invited into the place which feminist film theory assigns to the male viewer: that of the voyeur gazing at the erotic spectacle of the woman, actively desiring her seduction and identifying with her seducer" (382). Dietch's film is successful as a commercial product infused with lesbian feminist iconography.

Donna Deitch is also well known for her early feminist documentary *Woman to Woman* (1975). In 1989, Deitch directed the miniseries *The Women of Brewster Place,* an adaptation of Gloria Naylor's novel about seven African-American women, including a lesbian couple. Deitch is forthcoming about the problems inherent in joining the Hollywood machine:

"It is important to stick true to your own vision, and that's hard to do when a thousand other hands are on your work" (Acker, 43).

SELECTED FILMOGRAPHY

Berkeley 12 to 1 (1968)
Memorabilia PP1 (1969)
She Was a Visitor (1970)
Portrait (1972)
Woman to Woman (1975)
"For George, Love Donna" (1975)
The Great Wall of Los Angeles (1978)
Desert Hearts (1985)
The Women of Brewster Place (1989)

SELECTED BIBLIOGRAPHY

Acker, Ally. *Reel Women: Pioneers of the Cinema, 1896 to the Present*. New York: Continuum, 1993.

Aufderheide, Patricia. "Desert Hearts: An Interview with Donna Deitch." *Cineaste* 15.1 (1986): 18–19.

Holmlund, Christine. "When Is a Lesbian Not a Lesbian: The Lesbian Continuum and the Mainstream Feminine Film." *Camera Obscura* 25–26 (January–May 1991): 145–78.

Maio, Kathi. *Feminist in the Dark*. Freedom, CA: Crossing Press, 1988.

Mayne, Judith. *The Woman at the Keyhole: Feminism and Women's Cinema*. Bloomington: Indiana University Press, 1990.

Merck, Mandy. "Dessert Hearts." In *Queer Looks: Perspectives on Lesbian and Gay Film and Video,* edited by Martha Gever, John Greyson, and Pratibha Parmar, 377–82. New York: Routledge, 1993.

Quart, Barbara. *Women Directors: The Emergence of a New Cinema*. New York: Praeger, 1988.

Rich, B. Ruby. "Desert Heart." *Village Voice* (April 8, 1986): 72.

Weiss, Andrea. "From the Margins: New Images of Gays in the Cinema." *Cineaste* 15.1 (1986): 4–8.

DENIS, CLAIRE (1950–   ). **France.** "Let's be honest," Claire Denis, director of *Chocolat* (1988), told Paul Chutkow, "it's horrible to start a new film. You spend years looking for money. Doors slam in your face. You are humiliated by people who don't like your script." Claire Denis's *Chocolat* is an uncompromised achievement in its honest approach to postcolonial white guilt. In her first feature film Denis fictionalized her own experience of growing up a privileged French white female in colonialized West Africa. In fictionalizing her story, she was perhaps able to be more honest about her feelings of guilt than if she had made a documentary of the subject of colonialism.

"I believe that when you make a documentary you concentrate on the 'other,' but when you make fiction you talk about yourself," Denis said at a filmmakers' panel in 1991 (Petrie, 66). *Chocolat* is a study in autobio-graphical truth-telling and the ambiguity of postcolonial experience. Denis drew upon her experiences as a child in Africa and as an adult living in France who tries to sort out her decidedly mixed feelings surrounding her colonialist upbringing. Denis made *Chocolat* after almost giving up entirely on filmmaking. She had graduated in 1971 from the French School of Cinema in Paris. She then worked on short films and was a production assistant for Costa-Gavras and, later, Wim Wenders and Jim Jarmusch. Finally, after years seeking funding, Claire Denis convinced Wim Wenders to produce her screenplay for *Chocolat,* which she cowrote with Jean-Pol Fargeau.

Chocolat is a New Wave approach to the bildungsroman. The movie revolves around "France," an appropriately named Frenchwoman who returns to the remote region of Cameroon, where she was raised. The opening scene, in which the woman hitches a lift to the airport, has a minimalist feel to it. Initially, the film has the look of an Eric Rohmer film or a Chantal Akerman film. We learn very little about the woman through straightforward diagetic narration. Instead, we are "told" France's story through long sections of flashbacks that are intercut as the American black driver figuratively drives the viewer through the narrative. In contextualizing the narrative against the point of view of the African-American driver, Denis problematizes the issue of "native" identity by linking the two central figures as people who both have ties to the African land. At the end of the film, the driver asks France if she is disappointed that he is not a "real native." This moment evocatively links France's fractured colonialist-native identity and the African American's broken link with Africa.

Denis did not want to make the mistake of narrating the film through a false black identity. She maintained that it was important to tell her story through the point of view of a young white girl who observed firsthand the colonialism, racism, and oppression of women in her father's house. The relationship between the young France (played by Cecile Ducasse) and the African servant Protée (Isaach de Bankolé) is the center of the film. Protée initially teaches the young girl African cultural knowledge, but, surprisingly, their relationship takes an abrupt turn in the film when Protée realizes that he can no longer have any ties to his oppressor. Protée deliberately allows France to burn herself, in a memorable scene that both metaphorically breaks their closeness and ties them together in the burning of her white skin.

Denis was strongly advised to rewrite the screenplay of *Chocolat* to construct an affair between Protée and France's mother, Aimée (played by Giúlia Boschi). The producers insisted that an interracial sex scene would be good for the box office, but Denis resisted. "This would have totally destroyed what the film was about for me," she said (Petrie, 67). In the film, Aimée makes only an attempt to seduce Protée. Here the filmmaker tells the truth about white colonialist women's sexual harassment of men. Protée turns her down and is banished from the house. The film is equally critical of colonialist white men, especially in its depiction of a coffee farmer who forces his black mistress to sleep on the floor and sadistically mistreats her. *Chocolat* is a complex film that underscores colonialist inability to come to terms with a shared colonialist past. In terms of audience reception, Claire Denis finds that Frenchwomen identify with the film, while Frenchmen tend to be critical of it. Denis is thus highly critical of "colonialist amnesia," and she is insistent that the story of colonialism, no matter how painful, must be told. Denis has continued her examination of racism and the colonial apparatus most recently in *S'en fout, la Mort* (1990).

SELECTED FILMOGRAPHY

Chocolat (1988)
S'en fout, la Mort (*No Fear, No Die*) (1990)
I Can't Sleep (1995)
U.S. Go Home (1995)

SELECTED BIBLIOGRAPHY

Bates, Peter. "*Chocolat*." *Cineaste* 17.2 (1989): 52.
Chutkow, Paul. "This *Chocolat* Is Bittersweet." *New York Times*, March 5, 1989, 11.
Diawara, Manthia. *African Cinema: Politics and Culture*. Bloomington: Indiana University Press, 1992.
Murphy, Kathleen. "The Color of Home." *Film Comment* 28.5 (September–October 1992): 62–63.
Petrie, Duncan, ed. *Screening Europe: Image and Identity in Contemporary European Cinema*. London: BFI, 1992.
Strauss, Frederic. "S'en fout la mort." *Cahiers der Cinema* 435 (September 1990): 64–65.
Tomaselli, Keyan. *The Cinema of Apartheid: Race and Class in South African Films*. New York: Routledge, 1988.

DEREN, MAYA (1917–61). United States. Few film buffs cannot recall their first experience viewing a Maya Deren film. Deren is rightly known as the "mother" of avant-garde filmmaking. Her films treat the body, female experience, mystical experience, and the filmmaking process in an entirely unique and unprecedented manner. Deren was a dancer, choreographer, filmmaker, philosopher, and writer. She was deeply influenced by phenomenology, psychology, Russian formalism, African ritual, and dance theory. Deren's father was a Russian-Jewish psychiatrist from whom Deren learned a great deal of Freudian theory and an interest in ontological investigations. She was educated in Switzerland and went to college at Syracuse University and New York University. She earned a Master of Arts degree from Smith College, where she wrote on the French symbolists' influence on imagist poetry. Deren then moved to Greenwich Village, where she wrote poetry and began a book on modern dance theory in collaboration with choreographer Katherine Dunham. Dunham was a leader of the emerging African-American dance movement, and she introduced Deren to African ritual, dance, and music. New York artists were preoccupied with African culture because of the widespread influence of Jungian psychology, which emphasized the theory of "the collective unconscious." Artists like Deren felt that African art was a bridge to the unconscious where universal symbols could be evoked and used artistically. Deren went to Los Angeles in 1941, where she met Czechoslovakian documentarist Alexander Hammid, with whom she collaborated on various projects and whom she later married. Hammid codirected and photographed Deren's first film, *Meshes of the Afternoon* (1943).

In *Meshes of the Afternoon,* Deren altered notions of time and space, in a film that closes the gap signifying subjective experience and objective experience. She deliberately fragments the body and denies a sense of linear time. *Meshes of the Afternoon* draws upon theories of French imagist poetry in its use of surreal imagery and contrapuntal score. The film is also reminiscent of the surrealist films of Jean Cocteau, Man Ray, and Germaine Dulac, but Deren usually preferred to stress her literary influences. Deren was annoyed at viewers who "misread" her films as purely symbolic. She wrote a great deal about her work, carefully articulating her aesthetic. In 1946, she wrote *An Anagram of Ideas on Art, Form and Film*. Later, she wrote "Cinema as an Art Form" and "Cinematography: The Creative Use of Reality." She lectured at many public appearances and taught throughout the 1950s. Deren was ahead of her time in her recognition of the importance of what has become object relations theory. Critical of filmmakers who believed that they were depicting objective reality, Deren was one of the first film critics to understand that the artist/filmmaker always makes subjective, creative choices, even in documentary, whether in choosing camera angle, editing, shot length, or point-of-view perspective.

Deren was also critical of Hollywood filmmakers' reliance on literary narrative form, especially nineteenth-century notions of realism, which she saw as artificial illusion of realism. Deren's formalist training and philosophy led to her formalist approach to film. She predated the structuralist filmmakers of the 1960s who were mesmerized by the manipulation of the image, the frame, and the creative process itself. The lyrical poetry of Deren's films is remarkable. Deren died in 1961 at the age of forty-four of a cerebral hemorrhage. She is one of the most important women artists, filmmakers, and theorists of the twentieth century, and her work continues to inspire a whole new generation of women film and video artists up to the present day.

SELECTED FILMOGRAPHY

Meshes of the Afternoon (1943)
At Land (1944)
A Study in Choreography for Camera (1945)
Ritual in Transfigured Time (1946)
Meditation on Violence (1948)
Medusa (1949)
Divine Horsemen (1947–51)
Ensemble for Somnambulists (1951)
The Very Eye of Night (1958)
Haiku Film Project (1959–60)

SELECTED BIBLIOGRAPHY

Anthology Film Archives. *The Legend of Maya Deren.* New York: Anthology Film Archives, 1988.

Cartwright, Lisa, and Nina Fonoroff. "Narrative Is Narrative." In *Multiple Voices in Feminist Film Criticism,* edited by Diane Carson, Linda Dittmar, and Janice Welsch, 124–39. Minneapolis: University of Minnesota Press, 1994.

Deren, Maya. *An Anagram of Ideas on Art, Form and Film.* Yonkers, NY: Alicat Book Shop Press, 1946.

———. "Cinema as an Art Form." *New Directions* 9 (1946): 111–20.

———. "Cinematography: The Creative Use of Reality." *Daedalus* 89 (winter 1960): 150–67.

———. "On a Film in Progress and a Statement of Principle." *Film Culture* 22–23 (summer 1961): 160–63.

———. "Poetry and the Film: A Symposium." *Film Culture* 29 (summer 1963): 55–63.

———. "The Very Eye of Light and a Statement of Purpose." *Film Culture* 29 (summer 1963): 70–71.

———. "Notes, Essays, Letters." *Film Culture* 39 (winter 1965): 1–86.

Hoberman, J. "The Maya Mystique." *Village Voice* (May 15, 1978): 54.

Mayne, Judith. *The Woman at the Keyhole: Feminism and Women's Cinema.* Bloomington: Indiana University Press, 1990.

Millsapps, Jan L. "Maya Deren, Imagist." *Literature/Film Quarterly* 14.1 (1986): 22–31.

Rabinovitz, Lauren. *Points of Resistance: Women, Power and Politics in the New York Avant-Garde Cinema, 1943–71.* Urbana: University of Illinois Press, 1991.

Smetak, Jacqueline. "Continuum or Break." *New Orleans Review* 17.4 (winter 1990): 89–97.

"Women of the Month." *Today's Woman* 15.90 (April 1946): 94.

DJEBAR, ASSIA (1936–   ). Algeria. Though Algerian cinema blossomed after Algeria won the War of Liberation against France in 1962, few women have had an opportunity to work in Algerian cinema. Assia Djebar is the only woman filmmaker to make a feature film in Algeria, according to film critic Heiny Srour. Born in Algeria in 1936, Djebar is also a well-known Algerian woman writer. (She has published many novels and essays in French.) Assia Djebar used her credentials as a writer to convince RTZ (Algerian television) to back her first film, *Noubat Nissa Djebel Chenoua* (*The Nouba of the Women of Mount Chenoua*) (1978). Though the film received poor international distribution, *Noubat Nissa Djebel Chenoua* was very well received in Algeria and France. Djebar intercut documentary footage and staged documentary in one of the first films of Algeria to make use of the pseudodocumentary technique. *Noubat Nissa Djebel Chenoua* is a female-centered narrative about the lives of elderly and young women in independent Algeria. Djebar's poetic documentary style can be compared with that of Trinh T. Minh-ha in its equating of colonialist oppression with the silencing of women. *Al Zerdal* (*The Zerda*) (1980) is also a study of the complexities of subalternity of women in postcolonial Algeria. Djebar recuts archival footage of French colonial Africa. Djebar's approach in *Al Zerda* (a subversive recutting of colonialist film into a postcolonial deconstruction of documentary method) is a forerunner of the style of Trinh T. Minh-ha. Trinh T. Minh-ha recut colonialist documentary footage for *Surname Viet Given Name Nam* (1989), a subjective documentary that examines the colonialist footage as much as it deconstructs the making of documentary films. Djebar's early attempts at subjective documentary are remarkably feminist in scope. She connects the suppression of the voice of the colonized "other" with the silencing of women in Algerian history. Assia Djebar is an example of one French-speaking subaltern woman filmmaker who actively engages in a radical remaking of a political counter-cinema.

SELECTED FILMOGRAPHY

Noubat Nissa Djebal Chenoua (*The Nouba of the Women of Mount Chenoua*) (1978)
Al Zerdal (*The Zerda*) (1980)

SELECTED BIBLIOGRAPHY

Beck, Lois, and Nikki Keddie, eds. *Women in the Muslim World*. Cambridge: Harvard University Press, 1978.
Diawara, Manthia. *African Cinema: Politics and Culture*. Bloomington: Indiana University Press, 1992.
Donaldson, Laura E. *Decolonizing Feminisms: Race, Gender & Empire Building*. Chapel Hill: University of North Carolina Press, 1992.
Pines, Jim, and Paul Willemen, eds. *Questions of Third Cinema*. London: BFI, 1989.
Salmane, Hala. *Algerian Cinema*. London: BFI, 1976.
Smith, Sidonie, and Julie Watson, eds. *De/colonizing the Subject: The Politics of Gender in Women's Autobiography*. Minneapolis: University of Minnesota Press, 1992.
Srour, Heiny. "Djebar, Assia." In *The Women's Companion to International Film*,

edited by Annette Kuhn, with Susannah Radstone, 122–23. Berkeley: University of California Press, 1994.

Suleri, Sara. "Women Skin Deep: Feminism and the Postcolonial Condition." *Critical Inquiry* 18.4 (summer 1992): 756–69.

Teshome, Gabriel. *Third Cinema in the Third World.* Ann Arbor: UMI Research Press, 1982.

Trinh T. Minh-ha. *Woman, Native, Other: Writing Postcoloniality and Feminism.* Bloomington: Indiana University Press, 1989.

Woodhull, Winifred. "Unveiling Algeria." *Genders* 10 (spring 1991): 112–31.

DÖRRIE, DORIS (1955–   ). Germany. Director and screenwriter Doris Dörrie was born in Hanover, West Germany, in 1955. Dörrie was educated at the Hochschüle für Film and Fensehen in Munich, the University of the Pacific in Stockton, California, and the New School in New York. Though Dörrie is best known for her feminist comedy *Men* (1985), her earlier films, such as *In the Belly of the Whale* (1984), represented a strong feminist vision within a more serious context. *In the Belly of the Whale* opens with a violent beating of a young girl by her father. The abused daughter searches for her mother with the help of a boyfriend. The mother, unhappily, turns out to be a prostitute. The search for a mother who turns out to be no source of help is a common motif in women's films. In many of these films, family life is depicted as a war zone predominated by abusive father figures. *In the Belly of the Whale* ends horribly for the young woman, who is finally killed by her father. The violence between men and women, which became humorous in later Dörrie films, is lethal in her early work. Dörrie, like many German women filmmakers, is fascinated and simultaneously repelled by sadomasochistic family interrelationships.

An interesting aspect of Dörrie's feminist vision is that she is consistently interested in the psychology of men, who come under Dörrie's scrutinizing gaze. As Barbara Quart notes, these men "are deeply ailing, and though they are power figures, utterly impotent" (133). In *Straight through the Heart* (1983), a young woman and an older man have a twisted heterosexual affair. The heroine ends up murdering the repulsively conservative man by electrocuting him in the bathtub. Dörrie seems less and less interested in women characters as her career progresses. With *Men,* Dörrie brutally scrutinized men themselves, scoring a critical and financially successful film. As Dörrie told a critic for the *New York Times:* "Men are the unknown creatures and they are more interesting to me than women. 'Why did a woman make a film about men?' Men have always made films about women" (Markham, 11). Men are again the subject of *Paradise* (1986), *Me and Him* (1988), *Money* (1989), and *Happy Birthday* (1990). *Happy Birthday* is a feminist reworking of the private-eye film, but the real center of the narrative is racism in Germany against Turkish peoples.

In *Happy Birthday,* Dörrie proved to be "appallingly convincing at violence," wrote critic Carole Angier. For Carole Angier *Happy Birthday* is Dörrie's "best combination of social criticism and technical skill since *Men*" (209). Like Kathryn Bigelow, Dörrie is staking out territory in traditionally "male" genres and themes. Dörrie is prolific, subversive, and yet commercially successful. She does not please all feminists, but she certainly has a grasp of the personal politics of men.

SELECTED FILMOGRAPHY

Der erste Walzer (*The First Waltz*) (1978)
Hättest was Gscheits gelernt (*If Ya'd Only Learned Something Practical*) (1978)
Paula aus Portugal (*Paula from Portugal*) (1979)
Von Romantik keine Spur: Martina (19) wird Schäferin (*No Trace of Romance: Martina (19) Becomes a Shepherdess*) (1980–81)
Dazwischen (*In Between*) (1981)
Unter Schafen (*Among Noisy Sheep*) (1981)
Mitten ins Herz (*Straight through the Heart*) (1983)
Im Innern des Wals (*In the Belly of the Whale*) (1984)
Männer (*Men*) (1985)
Paradies (*Paradise*) (1986)
Ich und Er (*Me and Him*) (1988)
Geld (*Money*) (1989)
Happy Birthday, Türke! (*Happy Birthday*) (1990)

SELECTED BIBLIOGRAPHY

Angier, Carole. "Monitoring Conformity: The Career of Doris Dörrie." In *Women and Film: A Sight and Sound Reader,* edited by Pam Cook and Phillip Dodd, 204–9. Philadelphia: Temple University Press, 1993.
Jaehne, Karen. *"Men." Cineaste* 15.1 (1986): 42–43.
Knight, Julia. *Women and the New German Cinema.* London: Verso, 1992.
Markham, James. "Behind *Men* Stands a Woman with a Sense of Humor." *New York Times,* July 27, 1989, sec. 2, 11, 19.
Quart, Barbara. *Women Directors: The Emergence of a New Cinema.* New York: Praeger, 1988.
Taubin, Amy. "Recent Films from Germany." *Village Voice* 37.51 (December 22, 1992): 94, 96.

DULAC, GERMAINE (1882–1942). France. Lesbian avant-garde filmmaker and journalist Germaine Dulac is commonly referred to as the mother of surrealism. Born Charlotte Elizabeth Germaine Saisset Schneider in Amiens, France, on November 17, 1882, into an upper middle-class family, Dulac had sophisticated and educated parents. She moved to Paris when her parents died, and she began a career as a socialist feminist journalist, writing for *La Française,* one of France's first feminist publications. She also wrote for *La Fronde,* a radical lesbian feminist journal. Dulac was multitalented and multifaceted. She interviewed women artists and writers and studied photography, music, philosophy, and art. She was a promoter of the first ciné clubs, or film clubs dedicated to watching and discussing nonmainstream films. Dulac was actively involved with a group of intellectuals who were dedicated to redefining the art of cinema. This group included Louis Delluc, an early film theoretician, filmmakers such as Marcel L'Herbier and Abel Gance, and Marie Epstein, another important woman director.

Dulac's best-known films are *The Smiling Madame Beudet* (1923) and *The Seashell and the Clergyman* (1927), but Sandy Flitterman-Lewis has unearthed a remarkable amount of information on Dulac's other films. Dulac made a six-episode serial, *Ames de fous,* in 1917, which is unique because it combines the structural elements of the cliffhanger with the surrealistic and impressionistic techniques of experimental filmmaking. *Ames de fous* includes atmospheric effects that serve to express an interior psychological state of female duality. *Gossette* (1922–23) is another little-known serial directed by Germaine Dulac. It was a commercial success in its day, but today it seems to have been forgotten. Flitterman-Lewis describes *Gossette* as a six-episode serial that combines a "conventional adventure story" with "poetic evocation through technical means" (1990, 57). In the film, a young female heroine is kidnapped and drugged. Dulac used wide-angle lens distortions, repeated images, and distorting devices to render the subjective point of view of the central female heroine. Though critics have traditionally scorned the serial film, the genre is one at which women have excelled in portraying a female point of view.

Dulac's film career is diverse; she could work in the area of pure Impressionism, as in the case of *The Seashell and the Clergyman,* or in pure documentary, with the newsreels she produced at Gaumont, or in a sort of hybrid form between narrative and Impressionist filmmaking, as in *The Smiling Madame Beudet* and the serials Dulac directed. Dulac was dedicated to freeing the cinematic art form from links to literature, theater, and standard narrative expressions. Like Maya Deren, she lectured and wrote a personal manifesto of the cinema, a cinema based on dream, desire, and the language of form over content. *The Smiling Madame Beudet* (1923) is a manifestation of Dulac's theory and perspective. It depicts a housewife's psychological escape from a boorish husband. Dulac used technical devices of film that are the equivalent of poetic metonyms in language or experiments in texture and form in painting. Dulac's double exposures, superimpositions, masks, distorting lenses, and uses of gauzes in *Beudet* display a filmmaker playing with form itself, not content with patriarchally defined film practices, not content with film's subject-object relationship between viewer and screen. With *The Seashell and the Clergyman,* Dulac overhauls narrativity entirely and presents us with pure feminine desire, intercut against masculine desires of a priest. Above all, Dulac is responsible for "writing" a new cinematic language that expressed transgressive female desires. The knowledge of Dulac's lesbian sexuality allows for a new and more incisive reading of *The Smiling Madame Beudet*. No doubt additional research into the work of Dulac will reveal similarly startling discoveries in the future.

SELECTED FILMOGRAPHY

Géo le mystérieux (1916)
Dans l'ouragan de la vie (1916)
Les soeurs ennemies (1916)
Vénus victrix (1916)
Ames de fous (1917)
Le bonheur des autres (1918)
La Cigarette (1919)
La Fête espagnole (1919)
La Belle dame sans merci (1920)
Malencontre (1920)
La Mort du soleil (1921)
Werther (*unfinished*) (1922)
Gossette (1922–23)
La Souriante Mme Beudet (*The Smiling Madame Beudet*) (1923)
Le Diable dans la ville (1924)
Ame d'artiste (1925)
La Folie des vaillants (1925)
Antoinette Sabrier (1926)
Le Cinéma au service de l'histoire (1927)
La Coquille et la Clergyman (*The Seashell and the Clergyman*) (1927)
L'Invitation an Voyage (1927)
Germination d'un haricot (1928)
La Princesse Mandane (1928)
Etude cinégraphique sur une Arabesque (1929)
Disques 927 (1929)
Thèmes et variations (1929)

SELECTED BIBLIOGRAPHY

Buchsbaum, Jonathan. *Cinema Engagé: Film in the Popular Front*. Urbana: University of Illinois Press, 1988.
Flitterman-Lewis, Sandy. "Theorizing the 'Feminine,' Women as the Figure of Desire in *The Seashell and the Clergyman*." *Wide Angle* 6.3 (1984): 32–39.
Flitterman-Lewis, Sandy. *To Desire Differently: Feminism and the French Cinema*. Chicago: University of Illinois Press, 1990.
Foster, Gwendolyn, and Wheeler Winston Dixon. *The Women Who Made the Movies*. New York: Women Make Movies, 1991. Video.
Hayward, Susan, and Ginette Vincendeau, eds. *French Film: Texts and Contexts*. London: Routledge, 1990.
Heck-Rabi, Louise. *Women Filmmakers: A Critical Reception*. Metuchen, NJ: Scarecrow Press, 1984.
Mayne, Judith. *The Woman at the Keyhole: Feminism and Women's Cinema*. Bloomington: Indiana University Press, 1990.

Williams, Alan. *Republic of Images: A History of French Filmmaking.* Cambridge: Harvard University Press, 1992.

DURAS, MARGUERITE (1914–). France. Marguerite Duras is an internationally famous director, novelist, actress, and screenwriter. Born Marguerite Donnadieu on April 2, 1914, she was raised in Indochina, though her parents were French. Duras was educated at the Sorbonne in Paris, where she published her first novel in 1943. Before Duras began directing her own screenplays and adaptations, her works were brought to the screen by other directors. Alain Resnais directed Duras's *Hiroshima mon Amour* in 1959 and won the International Critics Prize at the Cannes Film Festival. *Hiroshima mon Amour* exemplifies Duras's consistently difficult material, which privileges stylized poetic meditations on memory, subjectivity, time, and the nature of feminine experience.

In 1969, Duras directed her first film, *Détruire, dit-elle* (*Destroy, She Said*). Duras, like Agnes Varda, is an important figure in the French New Wave movement, whose most famous male figures are François Truffaut, Jean-Luc Godard, and Alain Resnais. In *Destroy, She Said,* Duras was working out a theoretical investigation of female subjectivity, well before theorists such as Julia Kristeva and Hélène Cixous wrote about the silencing of women, women's language, and complex philosophical investigations of women's identity as void or "other." Duras is a distinctly modernist filmmaker and writer. Her work not only questions the conventions of traditional linear forms of narrative but investigates transgressive forms of female narrative. Duras experiments with the silences of women and the voice of the speaking woman who subverts and ruptures the patriarchal language of society. In *Nathalie Granger* (1973), Duras constructs the film as a poem. In the film, a family decides whether to send eight-year-old Nathalie to a different school. The decision is made completely through nonverbal language. Duras moves the narrative freely across time-space relations and interweaves a repetitive voice-over narrative of a female principal's discussing Nathalie's disruptive behavior in school. As critic E. Ann Kaplan notes, "Duras's camera emphasizes the separation of the female inner, and the male outer, worlds" (96). The world of Duras is the world of language, and Duras demonstrates that silence is a form of female language.

Le Camion (1977) is another Duras film that deconstructs dominant cinema's privileging of image over sound, disrupting the representational nature of film and replacing representational articulation by signifying female language. *Le Camion* is a study of the multivalence of identity. In the film a man and a woman filmmaker (played by Duras) sit at a table in silence. The sound track is the voice of Duras herself, intercut with other voices. This has the effect of displacing identification and overloading the viewer with a metanarrative consisting of the "same" story told over and over again in different versions. Duras consistently uses an unreliable narrator in a subversion of traditional modes of storytelling. *Le Camion* is a poem about female writing as well as a manifesto calling on women writers to speak and write. In 1987, Duras said of her films:

It's because my cinema scarcely exists as cinema that I can make these films. The type of perfection to which mainstream cinema aspires (in its use of clever technique with the sole aim of maintaining order) is accurately inscribed in its precise adherence to prevailing social codes. We show incest but we cut it into eighty-five splices so that everyone recognizes it but no one witnesses it. Porn cinema shows it. Mainstream cinema can be very clever, but it is rarely intelligent. (Duras, 120)

Many of Duras's films directly address racism, colonialism, and imperialism. An avowed political activist, Duras attacks the dominant cultural imperialism of colonialism in *India Song* (1975), *Son nom de Venise dans Calcutta désert* (1976), and many of her other films and novels. Duras's films are also an attack on the concept of realism in the cinema. Duras emphasizes ambivalence over received "knowledge," experience over perceived "truths," and fluid, expressive subjectivity over representational immutable identity. Critics are divided over whether Duras's avant-garde strategies actually work to change dominant ideology. Christine Ann Holmlund, for example, notes that Duras's difficult cinema speaks to a small audience, but Holmlund agrees that Duras's work "displaces the limits of difference" (17). Duras is quite often criticized; in fact, she seems to thrive on criticism. When questioned about the politics of *Le Camion*, for example, Duras replied: "[T]he belief in one political solution—that's the great regression today. All we can do to fight against that is to perform free acts. *Le Camion* is a free act, it's an act against all power" (Duras, 121). The cinema of Duras is an embrace of the power of agency, and at the same time it denies the privilege of static concepts of meaning and existence, in the tradition of modernism.

SELECTED FILMOGRAPHY

La Musica (codirector Paul Seban) (1966)
Détruire, dit-elle (*Destroy, She Said*) (1969)
Jaune le soleil (1971)
Nathalie Granger (1973)
La Femme du Ganges (1974)
India Song (1975)
Son nom de Venise dans Calcutta désert (1976)
Des journées entières dans les arbres (*Days in the Trees*) (1977)
Baxter, Vera Baxter (1977)
Le Camion (*The Lorry*) (1977)
Le Navire Night (1979)
Aurélia Steiner (1979)
Agatha et les Lectures limitées (1981)
Il Dialogo di Roma (1983)
Les Enfants (*The Children*) (1984)

SELECTED BIBLIOGRAPHY

Cottenet-Hage, Madeleine, and Robert P. Kolker. "The Cinema of Duras in Search of an Image." *French Review* 63.1 (October 1979): 88–98.

Duras, Marguerite. *Marguerite Duras*. San Francisco: City Lights Books, 1976.

Glassman, Deborah. "Marguerite Duras's 'Indian Cycle': The Fantasy Text." In *Ambiguities in Literature and Film*, edited by Hans P. Braendlin, 33–41. Tallahassee: Florida State University Press, 1988.

Holmlund, Christine Ann. "Displacing Limits of Difference: Gender, Race, and Colonialism in Edward Said and Homi Bhabha's Theoretical Models and Marguerite Duras's Experimental Films." *Quarterly Review of Film and Video* 13.1–3 (1991): 1–22.

Kaplan, E. Ann. *Women and Film: Both Sides of the Camera*. New York: Methuen, 1983.

Léger, Susan H. "Marguerite Duras's Cinematic Spaces." In *Women and Film*, edited by Janet Todd, 231–57. New York: Holmes and Meier, 1988.

E

ELEK, JUDIT (1937–   ). **Hungary.** Hungarian cinema, like German and Soviet cinema, has always had a remarkable number of women directors. Márta Mészáros, Judit Ember, Livia Gyarmathy, György Szalia, Ildiko Enyedi, and Judit Elek are among the many women directors of Hungarian cinema. Elek graduated from the Academy of Theater and Film Art in 1955. She is associated with proponents of "direct cinema," filmmaking that is shorn of glossy Hollywood technique and pared down to an almost neorealistic approach to narrative. Though Elek is not well known in the United States, she is very highly regarded in French-speaking countries. In 1987, she was awarded a Chevalier de l'Ordre des Arts et des Lettres in France.

Elek's *Maybe Tomorrow* (1979) concerns a family destroyed by jealousy, adultery, and intramarital violence. It is perhaps typical of Elek's thematic concern with women's place in the family and young women's struggles for independence in a strictly patriarchal culture. *Maria's Day* (1983), set in the 1870s and written and directed by Elek, is an unflinching analysis of privileged aristocratic figures in Hungarian history. Judit Elek is an extraordinary filmmaker whose films clearly voice feminism and social protest. Her films revolve around questions of identity and "otherness" of women, Jews, Austrians, and Hungarians. Judit Elek is preoccupied with history and the constitution of national identity, as are many Hungarian and Central European directors.

SELECTED FILMOGRAPHY

Találkozás (*Encounter*) (1963)
Kastélyók lakoi (*The Inhabitants of Manor Houses*) (1966)
Meddig él az ember (*How Long Does Man Matter?*) (1968)
Sziget a szárazföldön (*The Lady from Constantinople*) (1969)
Találkozunk 1972-ben (*We'll Meet in 1972*) (1971)
Istenmezején 1972–73 (*A Hungarian Village*) (1974)

Egyszerü történet (*A Commonplace Story*) (1975)
Martinovics (1981)
Mária-Nap (*Maria's Day*) (1983)

SELECTED BIBLIOGRAPHY

Goulding, Daniel J., ed. *Post New Wave Cinema in the Soviet Union and Eastern Europe.* Bloomington: Indiana University Press, 1989.

Nemeskürty, István. *Word and Image: History of the Hungarian Cinema.* Budapest: Corvina, 1985.

Petrie, Graham. *History Must Answer to Man: The Contemporary Hungarian Cinema.* Budapest: Corvino Kiadó, 1978.

Portuges, Catherine. *Screen Memories: The Hungarian Cinema of Márta Mészáros.* Bloomington: Indiana University Press, 1993.

Smith, Sharon. *Women Who Make Movies.* New York: Hopkinson and Blake, 1975.

ENGSTRÖM, INGEMO (1941–   ). Finland. Born in Finland, Ingemo Engström studied film at the Munich School for Film and Television in Germany. She is an important early director of New German Cinema. *Flight North* (1985) focuses on women's concerns in Nazi-era Germany. Engström's film is one of a group of autobiographical films directed by women that deal with Nazi Germany and the postwar period, including Jutta Brückner's *Years of Hunger* (1979), Helma Sanders-Brahms's *Germany, Pale Mother* (1979–80), Marianne Rosenbaum's *Peppermint Freedom* (1984), and Alexandra von Grote's *November Moon* (1984).

Flight North is based on the Klaus Mann novel *Journey into Freedom.* The film is set in 1933 and follows the journey of a woman who flees Germany after witnessing the spectacle of Nazi horrors. The young woman, Johanna, goes to Finland and has a brief lesbian affair. Next she has another affair, with a man named Ragmar. The two set off on a romantic journey across the beautiful landscape of Finland, where Johanna finally decides she must return to Germany and face her opposition to Nazism. However, Julia Knight criticizes *Flight North* for its heterocentrism, noting that the lesbian sex scenes are passionless and dull, while the heterosexual sex scenes are highly passionate. Engström also angered feminists in 1974–75, when she released *Fight for a Child.* As Knight notes, the film came under attack for showing the difficulties women have juggling a career and children. However, *Fight for a Child* was released at a time when German feminists were working to legalize abortion. Despite these criticisms, Engström's films have richness and vitality and address many of the issues facing modern women in Germany today.

SELECTED FILMOGRAPHY

Candy Man (1968)
Dark Spring (1970)

Zwei Liebende und die Mächtigsten dieser Erde (Two Lovers and the Powerful on Earth) (1973)
Kampf um ein Kind (Fight for a Child) (1974–75)
Erzählen (Telling Stories) (codirector) (1975)
Fluchtweg nach Marseille (Escape Route to Marseille) (codirector) (1977)
Letzte Liebe (Last Love) (1979)
Flucht in den Norden (Flight North) (1985)

SELECTED BIBLIOGRAPHY

Knight, Julia. *Women and the New German Cinema.* London: Verso, 1992.
Weinberger, Gabriele. *Nazi Germany and Its Aftermath in Women Directors' Autobiographical Films of the Late 1970s.* San Francisco: Mellen Research University Press, 1992.

EPHRON, NORA (1941–   ). United States. Nora Ephron not only is a popular novelist and screenplay writer but has recently begun directing, with *This Is My Life* (1992) and the blockbuster success *Sleepless in Seattle* (1993). Ephron was born in New York City on May 19, 1941. She earned a master's degree at Wellesley College. In 1975, she became famous when she published *Crazy Salad,* a collection of essays. In addition, Ephron's numerous screenplays have been both commercially and critically successful. In 1983, she was nominated for an Academy Award for Best Screenplay for *Silkwood,* a highly acclaimed film about an antinuclear activist. Ephron's scenarios often feature strong female figures. She wrote the screenplay for *Cookie* in 1989, which she also executive-produced. She was again nominated for the Academy Award for Best Screenplay for *When Harry Met Sally* (1989), another highly popular film that she wrote and produced.

Ephron's films appeal to a wide audience, especially women. *Sleepless in Seattle* (1993), which Ephron directed and cowrote, is a romantic comedy that stars Tom Hanks and Meg Ryan. Though critics dismiss romantic comedies and melodramas as "unserious" films, this reveals a thinly veiled sexist pattern that privileges "masculine" genres, such as action, crime, and Westerns over supposedly feminine genres, such as melodramas ("weepies") and romantic comedies. Feminist film critics, such as Mary Ann Doane, Virginia Wright Wexman, and Jackie Byars, are resuscitating melodramas and romantic comedies as a feminine form of cinematic address to a predominantly female audience. *Sleepless in Seattle* may be read as an attempt to re-create the classic American romance film. (In fact, the film is interwoven with references to the classic romance *An Affair to Remember* [1956].) The romantic comedy traditionally incorporates a lush mise-en-scène with sophisticated editing techniques in order to naturalize and flatten the complexity of heterosexual relationships, according to Jackie Byars. *Sleepless in Seattle* represents a return to classic romantic comedies that appeal to the woman spectator.

Ephron's moderately successful film *This Is My Life* (1992) belongs to a tradition of career-woman comedies, such as the classic *His Girl Friday* (1940) or *The Thrill of It All* (1963), in which women must make a life choice or sacrifice something for a career. In *This Is My Life,* a stand-up comedian, played by Julie Kavner, is a divorced, Jewish, single mother who must choose between an extremely successful career and her role as a mother. Though *This Is My Life* is rife with feminist humor, it clearly resounds with the message that family is more important than career. Nevertheless, *This Is My Life* is admirable for its criticism of patriarchally defined social attitudes toward career and family. Nora Ephron, like Penny Marshall (*A League of Their Own,* 1992), is directing films that address a female audience and female desire. These women directors are a powerful presence in Hollywood, a presence that manifests a demand for films that address a mainstream female audience. Nora Ephron and Penny Marshall create for women in the 1990s the same kind of films that Howard Hawks and Frank Capra created for men in the 1930s and 1940s. Their films revel in sentiment, "shameless" romanticism, and female desire, yet they also encode a specifically female narrative and employ subversive feminine humor. Nora Ephron's most recent project is the comedy *Mixed Nuts* (1994).

SELECTED FILMOGRAPHY

This Is My Life (1992)
Sleepless in Seattle (1993)
Mixed Nuts (1994)

SELECTED BIBLIOGRAPHY

Byars, Jackie. *All That Heaven Allows: Re-Reading Gender in 1950s Melodrama.* Chapel Hill: University of North Carolina Press, 1991.

Doane, Mary Ann. *The Desire to Desire: The Woman's Film of the 1940s.* Bloomington, Indiana University Press, 1987.

Fischer, Lucy. *Shot/Countershot: Film Tradition and Women's Cinema.* Princeton: Princeton University Press, 1989.

Gledhill, Christine, ed. *Home Is Where the Heart Is: Studies in Melodrama and the Women's Film.* London: BFI, 1987.

Kaplan, E. Ann, ed. *Psychoanalysis and Cinema.* New York: Routledge, 1990.

Kuhn, Annette. *Women's Pictures: Feminism and Cinema.* London: Routledge, 1982.

Wexman, Virginia Wright. *Creating the Couple: Love, Marriage, and Hollywood Performance.* Princeton: Princeton University Press, 1993.

EPSTEIN, MARIE (1899–1995). France. The feminist historian Sandy Flitterman-Lewis notes in her groundbreaking rediscovery of neglected French director Marie Epstein that the omission of Epstein from film histories "necessitates a kind of foregrounding of her activity to redress the balance and involves a work of reconstruction as well" (166). Epstein is often mentioned as an aside in the biographical encyclopedic entries of her brother, Jean Epstein, and her other collaborator, Jean Benoît-Levy. Marie Epstein was an active director in the French avant-garde, as well as a writer, actress, and, later, film archivist at the Cinémathèque Française. She first codirected with her brother, Jean, and later with Jean Benoît-Levy, though she was credited not as codirector but as writer.

Marie Epstein's scenarios and films combine social issues, particularly the plight of poor children and disadvantaged women, with poetic imagery and advanced cinematic techniques. The best-known collaboration between Epstein and Benoît-Levy is *La Maternelle* (1933), which, according to film historian Alan Williams, "anticipates both French realism and Italian Neo-realism" (196). Williams notes that *La Maternelle* includes extraordinary examples of "subjective editing" that depict the horrific point of view of a neglected child of the slums. Flitterman-Lewis is more impressed by a montage sequence in *La Maternelle*, a subjective point of view of a woman about to commit suicide. During the sequence, the woman looks directly at the spectator, "implicating the spectator directly" (209) in the action. This constitutes a radical rupture of established rules of cinematic space and predates a postmodern cinematic use of this "fourth look" (the direct gaze at the audience).

Several other Benoît-Levy-Epstein films are also worth noting for their avant-garde techniques, feminine modes of subjectivity, and feminist subject matter. *Altitude 3200* (1938) depicts a utopian community based on platonic friendship. *Hélène* (1936) is a film told from the perspective of a single mother. *La Mort du cygne* (1937) is told from the point of view of a young female ballet dancer who has such a desire to succeed that she causes her rival to have an accident. The film won the Grand Prix du Film Français at the 1937 Exposition. *Peau de pêche* (1928), *Le Coeur de Paris* (1931), and *Maternité* (1929) treat the subject of children with great sensitivity and frequently rely upon a child's subjective point of view. Epstein employs repetitive poetic motifs throughout these films.

It seems ironic that Marie Epstein was almost completely omitted from film history, especially since she worked as a film preservationist at the Cinémathèque Française until her retirement in 1977. But French film critics also ignored the achievements of Alice Guy-Blaché, who made one of the first narrative films and directed hundreds of early films in France and the United States. Only through the recent feminist excavations and reconstructions of film "history" are we beginning to see a glimpse of film "herstory," and a compelling example of early cinema "herstory" can be found in the work of cineaste Marie Epstein.

SELECTED FILMOGRAPHY

Codirected with Jean Benoît-Levy

Ames d'enfants (1928)
Peau de pêche (1928)
Maternité (1929)

Le Coeur de Paris (1931)
La Maternelle (1933)
Itto (1934)
Hélène (1936)
La Mort du cygne (1937)
Altitude 3200 (1938)
Le Feu de paille (1939)

As Sole Director
La Grande espérance (1953)

SELECTED BIBLIOGRAPHY

Abel, Richard. *French Cinema: The First Wave, 1915–1929.* Princeton: Princeton University Press, 1984.
Benoît-Levy, Jean. *The Art of the Motion Picture.* New York: Coward, McCann, 1946.
Flitterman-Lewis, Sandy. *To Desire Differently: Feminism and the French Cinema.* Urbana: University of Illinois Press, 1990.
Museum of Modern Art. *Museum of Modern Art Circulating Film Library Catalogue.* New York: MOMA, 1992.
Williams, Alan. *Republic of Images: A History of French Filmmaking.* Cambridge: Harvard University Press, 1992.

EXPORT, VALIE (1940–). Austria. "I always felt like a political artist and the female body is the means to feminist art and feminist politics," Valie Export said in an interview that took place in 1987 (Eifler and Frieden, 268). The discourse of the female body has been at the center of the work of Austrian-born Valie Export, a performance artist, photographer, professor, and filmmaker who has been working to change the conception of female sexuality since her early experimental performance art in the 1960s. In 1968, for example, Valie Export appeared in public with a box attached to her chest and asked audiences to touch the object that is fetishized so often on-screen, her naked breasts. In this performance piece, *Tapp und Tastkino,* Export redefined the cinematic experiences, making her body the screen, bringing the screen out from the dark, and desexualizing the female breast. Export called it "touch cinema," and she calls it the first real "women's film" and the first "mobile film." The innovative approach to feminist political action used in *Tapp und Tastkino* resurfaced in Export's later films, in that they are all, in some way, a challenge to sexual representations of the female body, and they continually seek to redefine the subject-object relationship between audience and performer.

Export presently resides in Vienna and holds an alternating yearlong professorship at the University of Wisconsin, along with a position at the Hochschule der Künste, in Berlin. Export (born Waltrout Lehner) studied textiles and art and worked as an actor, model, script person, and film editor. In the 1960s, she became internationally known in avant-garde circles for her performance art, filmmaking, video, and installation work. In the late 1960s, Export collaborated with artist Peter Weibel on a variety of performance pieces. She has since established herself as a successful, independent filmmaker in Germany and the United States. Export is also a film theorist with a considerable number of publications.

Invisible Adversaries (1977) is Export's first feature film. It is a brilliant experimental science-fiction film that has been loosely described as a feminist version of *Invasion of the Body Snatchers*. In the film, Anna, a photographer, learns that mysterious forces are controlling the minds of people on earth. Anna is involved in video art that deconstructs concepts of feminine beauty through the use of video superimpositions of an actual woman's body over depictions of women in the artwork of Botticelli, Titian, and Blake. These superimpositions clearly show that the female body has been misconfigured by male artists because the postures in the artwork are impossible to mimic. *Invisible Adversaries* thus deconstructs and reconstructs the female body by looking across discourses such as art history and medical practice. Export exposes the phallocentricity of medical discourse in a scene between Anna and a psychologist. Anna describes the "invisible adversaries," and the doctor diagnoses her as a schizophrenic, promptly prescribing drugs for her "hallucinations." As it turns out, Anna is right; people have been taken over, not by extraterrestrials but by human discourses that brainwash people into subjection. Part of this subjection is a negative view of the body, particularly women's bodies.

The same idea recurs in *The Practice of Love* (1984), in which a woman reporter videotapes naked women who work in peep shows. The presence of the woman with a camera deeroticizes the female body for the male voyeurs, who become the object of Export's female gaze. Later in the film, Export reeroticizes the female body in a sex scene in which bodies are superimposed upon one another in a manner reminiscent of the bodies in Maya Deren's *At Land*. In *Syntagma* (1983), Export uses avant-garde techniques to demythologize conventionally mediated images of the female body in a manner that makes viewers aware of their active position as spectators. Taken as a whole, Export's filmmaking and performance art pose a challenge to dominant film discourse.

SELECTED FILMOGRAPHY

Menstruationsfilm (1967)
Cutting (1967–68)
Abstract Film No. 1 (1968)
Instant Film (codirector) (1968)
Auf + zu + ab + an (1968)
Ping Pong (1968)
333 (1968)
Tapp und Tastkino (1968)
Splitscreen—Solipsismus (1968)

Vorspann (1968)
Ohne Titel xn/Ohne Titel No. 1 (codirector) (1968)
Ohne Titel Nr. 2 (codirector) (1968)
Das Eine (1968)
Der Kuss (1968)
Ein Familienfilm von Waltraut Lehner (codirector) (1968)
Ars lucis (1968)
Gesichtsgrimassen (1968)
A World Cinema (codirector) (1968–75)
Eine Reise ist eine Reise wert (codirector) (1969)
Das magische Auge (codirector) (1969)
Bewegte Bilder über sich bewegende Körper (1969–73)
Split Reality (1970)
Facing a Family (1971)
Die unterbrochene Linie (1971–72)
Schnitte (1972–75)
Remote . . . Remote (1973)
mann & frau & animal (1973)
Adjungierte Dislokationen (1973)
Zeit und Gegenzeit (1973)
Interrupted Movement (1973)
Autohypnose (1973)
Sehtest (1973)
Die süsse Nummer: Ein Konsumerlebnis (1973)
Asemie (1973)
Hyperbulie (1973)
Raumsehen und Raumhören (1974)
Body Politics (1974)
Bewegungsmaginationen (1975)
Implentation (1975)
Inversion (1975)
Unsichtbare Gegner (Invisible Adversaries) (1976)
Positiv Negative Transfinit (codirector) (1976)
Adjungierte Dislokationen II (1978)
I Beat It (1978)
Menschenfrauen (1979)
Syntagma (1983)
Das bewaffnette Auge (1984)
Die Praxis der Liebe (The Practice of Love) (1984)
Tischbemerkungen—November 1985 (1985)
Die Zweiheit der Natur (1986)
Sieben Frauen—Sieben Sünden (Seven Women—Seven Sins) (codirector) (1985)
Yukon Quest (codirector) (1986)
Mental images oder der Zugang zur Welt (codirector) (1987)
Maschinenkörper—Körpermaschinen—Körperraum (1988)
Dokumente zum Internationalen Aktionismus (1988)
Unica (1988)

SELECTED BIBLIOGRAPHY

Curry, Ramona. "The Female Image as Critique in the Films of Valie Export." In *Gender and German Cinema, Feminist Interventions, Vol. 1: Gender and Representation in New German Cinema,* edited by Sandra Frieden, Richard W. McCormick, Vibeke R. Petersen, and Laurie Melissa Vogelsang, 255–66. Oxford: Berg, 1993.

Curtis, David. *Experimental Cinema: A Fifty-Year Evolution.* New York: Delta, 1971.

Eifler, Margret. "Valie Export's *Invisible Adversaries:* Film as Text." In *Gender and German Cinema, Feminist Interventions, Vol. 1: Gender and Representation in New German Cinema,* edited by Sandra Frieden, Richard W. McCormick, Vibeke R. Petersen, and Laurie Melissa Vogelsang, 241–54. Oxford: Berg, 1993.

———, and Sandra Frieden. "Interview with Valie Export." In *Gender and German Cinema, Feminist Interventions, Vol 1: Gender and Representation in New German Cinema,* edited by Sandra Frieden, Richard W. McCormick, Vibeke R. Petersen, and Laurie Melissa Vogelsang, 267–78. Oxford: Berg, 1993.

Export, Valie. "The Real and Its Double: The Body." *Discourse* 11 (fall–winter, 1988–89): 3–27.

———. "Aspects of Feminist Actionism." *New German Critique* 47 (spring–summer, 1989): 69–82.

Mueller, Roswitha. *Valie Export/Fragments of the Imagination.* Bloomington: Indiana University Press, 1994.

F

FAYE, SAFI (1943–). Senegal. One of a scant number of independent, female, black, African-born directors, Safi Faye was born in Dakar and is of Serer origin. The Serer people live in Senegal and have a strong cultural heritage, which Safi Faye records in *Fad'jal* (1979). Fad'jal is the village where Safi Faye's parents were born. Faye received her teaching certificate in 1963 and began teaching in the Dakar school system. Though she has traveled and studied abroad, she maintains close ties with her family and cultural roots. Faye studied ethnology at the École Pratique des Hautes Études and the Louis Lumière Film School in the 1970s. She worked in film sound effects, as an actor, and as a model to support her studies. After gaining experience as a student filmmaker, Safi Faye began looking for financial backing to shoot a feature film.

Faye found support from the French Ministry of Cooperation and made *Kaddu Beykat* (*News from My Village*) in 1975. The film is a semiauto-biographical work, a fictionalized study of a village that suffers economically because its people refuse to go along with colonial demand for single-crop cultivation. *Kaddu Beykat* was shot on a shoestring budget with a crew of three, according to Françoise Pfaff. Safi Faye's approach to film-making departs from Eurocentric documentary techniques that regard African peoples as the "other" or the cultural object. Faye's film is meant for an African audience. As Faye told Angela Martin in an interview at Cannes, her films are not "the observations of a stranger—a Westerner . . . I give people a voice, and I take a position within that" (18). Faye explains that she acts as an observer/participant, and she sees film as a form of community expression. For example, for *Kaddu Beykat* she often took the advice of the villagers on what to film and what not to film.

Kaddu Beykat won many international prizes, including the Georges Sadoul Prize and the International Film Critics' Award at the Berlin Film Festival. It has also been screened at the Museum of Modern Art in New York and the Racines Noires festival in Paris. Faye's ability to reconceive notions of "fiction" and "reality" challenges documentary form. As she told Angela Martin, the distinctions among fiction, documentary, and ethnology "make no sense" (18). Safi Faye's films transcend the usual documentarist representations of filmic "reality" and reinscribe the authenticity of daily village life and oral history.

Safi Faye took a Ph.D. in ethnology at the University of Paris in 1979. She was a professor at the Free University of Berlin, and she has done extensive production for German television. Faye lives in Paris, where she divides her time between raising her daughter and filmmaking. Though she makes no distinction between male and female directors, many of her films touch on gender issues either directly or indirectly. In *La passante*, Faye plays an African woman living in France. A Frenchman and an African man become interested in the African woman. The film is a study of the different cultural expectations of women. *Kaddu Beykat* records the routine activities of women in fields, at home, in courtship, and in traditional healing rituals. *Les âmes du soleil* (1981) documents the difficult conditions that women face living in Africa in times of drought and poor health. Faye's *Selbé et tant d'autres* (*Selbe: One Among Many*) (1982) records the lives of women who are left behind in villages when men migrate to the city in search of employment opportunity. But Faye is as much interested in questions of ethnicity, identity, and emigration as she is in women's issues. Faye's ability to "document" as an observer/participant is important. Safi Faye is redefining African subjectivity through a Senegalese woman's point of view. Like Sarah Maldoror, Safi Faye is searching for, and finding, a film language that reflects African culture.

SELECTED FILMOGRAPHY

La passante (*The Passerby*) (1972)
Revanche (*Revenge*) (1973)
Kaddu Beykat (*News from My Village*) (1975)
Fad'jal (*Come and Work*) (1979)
Goob na ñu (*The Harvest Is In*) (1979)
Man sa yay (*I, Your Mother*) (1980)
Les âmes du soleil (*Souls of the Sun*) (1981)
Selbé et tant d'autres (*Selbe: One Among Many*) (1982)
Ambassadores Nourricières (*Culinary Embassies*) (1984)

SELECTED BIBLIOGRAPHY

Hoberman, J. "Inside Senegal." *Village Voice* (February 6, 1978): 42, 48.
Martin, Angela. "Four Filmmakers from West Africa." *Framework* 11 (1979): 16–21.
Pfaff, Françoise. *Twenty-Five Black African Filmmakers: A Critical Study with Filmography and Biobibliography.* New York: Greenwood Press, 1988.
Schissel, Howard. "Africa on Film: The First Feminist View." *Guardian* (July 9, 1980): 7.

Taylor, Clyde. "The Screen Scene." *The Black Collegian* 9.5 (May–June, 1979): 94–96.

FERNÁNDEZ VIOLANTE, MARCELA (1941–   ). Mexico. Marcela Fernández Violante has been called "one of Mexico's most gifted, underrated, and persistent filmmakers to have endured the unsettled political climate of a male-dominated film industry" (Huaco-Nuzum, 154). Marcella Fernández Violante graduated from the University Center for Cinematographic Studies in Mexico City. She subsequently became director of the same film school, where she is now a professor and an active filmmaker. In 1972, she won an Ariel Award for her first film, a documentary on the artist Frida Kahlo. Marcela Fernández Violante is dedicated to documenting women's history in the arts and filmmaking. In a more recent project, she made a film about three pioneer women directors in the Mexican film industry: Matilde Landeta, Carmen Toscano, and Adela Sequeyro. As the only woman member of the film directors' union, Marcela Fernández Violante is personally well aware of the problems that women directors face in the Mexican film industry. She is thus continually attracted to political themes.

Whatever You Do, You Lose (1974–75) is told through the point of view of a female protagonist, a general's daughter. Set in the period of the Cristero Revolution, Fernández Violante's film criticizes powerful institutions, such as the military and the church. As she told Julianne Burton, "The film asks what combinations of power lead an apparently idealistic person to betray his or her goals" (198). *Cananea* (1976–77) examines similar issues, though the film is more critical of Anglo imperialism. Marcela Fernández Violante returned to female-centered narratives with *Departed Love in the Evening* (1987), a film about a working-class woman's search for her companion. The film is notable for its portrayal of a strong female heroine who takes on the Establishment in her search for the truth. When asked about her political beliefs, Fernández Violante says she dislikes being categorized as a "feminist" or "leftist." "I like to conserve my complexity," she told Julianne Burton. "I don't want to have to follow anyone else's slogans" (207). Fernández Violante is interviewed in a documentary on Mexican filmmaker Matilde Landeta, entitled *My Filmmaking, My Life* (1990); the video is available from Women Make Movies, Inc.

SELECTED FILMOGRAPHY
Frida Kahlo (1971)
De todos modos Juan te Ilámas (*Whatever You Do, You Lose* (1974–75)
Cananea (1976–77)
Misterio (*Mystery*) (1979–80)
En el pais de los pied ligeros o el Niño Raramuri (*In the Land of Light Feet*) (1980)
Nocturno amor que te vas (*Departed Love in the Evening*) (1987)

SELECTED BIBLIOGRAPHY

Burton, Julianne, ed. *Cinema and Social Change in Latin America: Conversations with Filmmakers.* Austin: University of Texas Press, 1986.

Huaco-Nuzum, Carmen. "Fernandez Violante, Marcela." In *The Women's Companion to International Film,* edited by Annette Kuhn, with Susannah Radstone, 154–55. Berkeley: University of California Press, 1994.

Lesage, Julia. "Latin American and Caribbean Women in Film and Video." In *Multiple Voices in Feminist Film Criticism,* edited by Diane Carson, Linda Dittmar, and Janice Welsch, 492–502. Minneapolis: University of Minnesota Press, 1994.

Mayne, Judith. *The Woman at the Keyhole: Feminism and Women's Cinema.* Bloomington: Indiana University Press, 1990.

Mora, Carl J. *Mexican Cinema: Reflections of a Society, 1896–1980.* Berkeley: University of California Press, 1982.

Pick, Zuzana, ed. *Latin American Film Makers and the Third Cinema.* Ottawa: Carleton University, 1978.

Quart, Barbara. *Women Directors: The Emergence of a New Cinema.* New York: Praeger, 1988.

FIELD, MARY (1896–1969). United Kingdom. Mary Field specialized in documentary nature films and children's films. Born in Wimbledon, England, she was a high school history teacher before she went to work for British Instructional Films in 1926, for which she directed and produced the well-known series of short films *The Secrets of Nature.* In 1933, Field began working for Gaumont British Instructional Films, where she made educational films for eleven years. Mary Field not only pioneered innovative cinematic techniques of documenting nature but also single-handedly developed the British children's film industry, initiating the notion that children need films about and for children. In 1944, Field started up the Children's Entertainment Division of the Rank Organisation, over which she presided as executive producer until 1950. Field was a devoted activist for children's entertainment, and she argued for the establishment and development of the Children's Film Foundation. The foundation was ultimately set up by the British film industry to ensure the production of children's films, and Field served as the executive producer of the organization. She also directed propaganda films for the British government during World War II. From 1959 to 1963, when she retired at age sixty-seven, Field was the children's program consultant for ATV/ABC television.

Traditionally, film historians and scholars have dismissed or ignored Field's accomplishments as a documentarist. She is criticized for intercutting documentary footage with dubbed sound, but Field was more interested in entertaining children than pleasing adult critics. Field described her feelings about the difficulties she faced in distributing her short films in an article she wrote entitled "Making Nature Films":

The film trade will waste little time on it, describing it as just an interest picture. Educationists will be contemptuous, condemning it as having been edited for theatrical purposes, though Heaven knows how nature films could continue to be made, if they did not get back some money by theatrical bookings. It would be a pity if the producers of nature pictures used up all their patience in making the films—they need it most when the films have been made. (71)

Unquestionably, Mary Field's work provided a great deal of pleasure to many adults and children. She was a determined woman who valued the environment and respected the children on whose behalf she worked so tenaciously. She also wrote extensively on the educational and social aspects of film. Her legacy as a documentarist and pioneering nature cinematographer is one of the cinema's great secrets; a reappraisal and re-viewing of her work are certainly overdue.

SELECTED FILMOGRAPHY

Secrets of Nature (series) (1922–33)
Strictly Business (1931)
The King's English (1934)
Secrets of Life (series) (1933–43)
This Was England (1934)
The Changing Year (1934)
They Made the Land (1938)
Shadow of the Stream (1938)
Babes in the Wood (1938)
The Medieval Village (1940)
Winged Messengers (1941)
I Married a Stranger (1944)

SELECTED BIBLIOGRAPHY

Field, Mary. "Making Nature Films." *Sight and Sound* 1.3 (autumn 1932): 70–71.
———. *Secrets of Nature*. London: Faber and Faber, 1934.
———. *Good Company: The Story of the Children's Entertainment Film Movement in Great Britain, 1943–50*. London: Longmans, 1952.
———. *Children and Films: A Study of Boys and Girls in the Cinema: A Report to the Carnegie United Kingdom Trustees on an Enquiry into Children's Responses to Films*. Scotland: Carnegie United Kingdom Trust, 1954.
Paskin, Sylvia. "Field, Mary." In *The Women's Companion to International Film*, edited by Annette Kuhn, with Susannah Radstone, 156. Berkeley: University of California Press, 1994.

FISHER, HOLLY (1942–   ). United States. "I've always wanted to explore the idea of power," avant-garde filmmaker Holly Fisher recently told critic Peter Brunette (4). Fisher explores the nature and power of images in her metaphysical assemblages of experimental film. She is also a well-known editor who has worked on documentaries such as *Who Killed Vincent Chin?* On her own, she has been making documentary and experimental films since the 1970s. *Glass Shadows* (1976) is a kinetic study of the female body. Fisher appeared in the film and used a window pane to reflect images of her body into the camera. Maureen Turim described *Glass Shadows* as "a film that challenges feminist theory to expand its vocabulary and judgement to include not only a mode of critique, but also a more positive exploration of visual pleasure" (Canyon Cinema, 123). Fisher, like Valie Export, is centrally preoccupied with reclaiming female representation and sexual pleasure from phallocentric film discourse. *From the Ladies* (1978) continues in this vein. Shot in a multimirrored bathroom, Fisher again explores the tensions resulting from a dialectic between herself as object/actor and herself as subject/artist. *From the Ladies* is linked to a number of women's experimental films that reconfigure women's representations and women's subjectivity, from Gunvor Nelson and Dorothy Wiley's *Schmeerguntz* (1966) to Barbara Hammer's *Multiple Orgasm* (1977).

In *From the Ladies,* Fisher demonstrates a ludic playfulness toward image and narrative technique that she pushes further into abstraction in the *Wildwest Suite* series. She uses multiple images through the device of the optical printer for most of the effects in these films. The looping techniques of her films manipulate conceptions of time and space, memory and reception. *Bullets for Breakfast* (1992), Fisher's most recent film, is a tour de force of optical printing. *Bullets for Breakfast* is similar to Valie Export's *The Practice of Love* (1984) in that it deconstructs images of women in Western films and in Renaissance painting through the use of multiple superimpositions. Fisher describes *Bullets for Breakfast* as "a western filtered through a post-feminist sensibility" (Women Make Movies, 19). Footage from John Ford's *My Darling Clementine* (1946), a "classic" Western film, is sewn into a patchwork of images of women from art postcards, footage of women working in a fish-packing plant, and footage of feminist poet Nancy Nielson reading her poetry. The sound track is also multileveled, often running several voices at once. *Bullets for Breakfast* breaks apart the iconicity of the Western film and patriarchal representations of women. The film was screened at the Berlin Film Festival, the Whitney Biennial, and the Museum of Modern Art in New York, and it won the best experimental film category at the Ann Arbor Film Festival. *Bullets for Breakfast* is available from Women Make Movies, Inc.

SELECTED FILMOGRAPHY

Apple Summer (1974)
Glass Shadows (1976)
Chicken-Stew (1978)
From the Ladies (1978)
This Is Montage (1978)
The Wildwest Suite Parts I–IV (1978–87)
Bullets for Breakfast (1992)

SELECTED BIBLIOGRAPHY

Brunette, Peter. "Imagin(in)ing Pictures: An Interview with Holly Fisher." *Film Quarterly* 47.2 (winter 1993–94): 2–7.

Canyon Cinema. *Canyon Cinema Catalogue 7*. San Francisco: Canyon Cinema, 1992.

Women Make Movies. *Women Make Movies Catalogue*. New York: Women Make Movies, Inc., 1994.

FOSTER, JODIE (1962–   ). United States. Performer/director Jodie Foster was born Alicia Christian Foster in 1962 in Los Angeles, California. Foster began her acting career at age three. She played many child roles before becoming internationally recognized for her performance in *Taxi Driver* (director Martin Scorsese, 1976). Foster's portrayal of a drug-addicted prostitute in the film exhibited sophistication and maturity beyond the actor's years. Foster continued to appear in film and television productions while she studied in high school and graduated class valedictorian. She went on to earn a degree in literature at Yale University. She won Academy Awards for her performances in *The Accused* and *Silence of the Lambs.*

In 1991, Foster made her debut as the director of *Little Man Tate. Little Man Tate* concerns a little boy who is a genius; however, it unfolds as a study of working-class motherhood. Foster herself portrays the single, working mother who struggles to bring up her gifted child. Challenged by an upper middle-class child psychologist, played by Dianne Wiest, the working-class mother wins as the better "ideal" mother figure. More recently, Foster was nominated for an Academy Award for her performance in *Nell* (1994).

Foster is currently in preproduction for her second feature film as a director, *Home for the Holidays,* a comedy that will star Holly Hunter and Anne Bancroft. Recently, Foster formed her own production company, Egg Pictures, a subsidiary of Polygram Entertainment.

SELECTED FILMOGRAPHY

Little Man Tate (1991)

SELECTED BIBLIOGRAPHY

Acker, Ally. *Reel Women: Pioneers of the Cinema, 1896 to the Present*. New York: Continuum, 1993.

Cameron, Julie. "Burden of the Gift." *American Film* 16.10 (November–December 1991): 44–45.

Corliss, Richard. "A Screen Gem Turns Director." *Time* 138.15 (October 14, 1991): 68.

Horton, Robert. "Life Upside Down." *Film Comment* 27.1 (1991): 38.

Lacayo, Richard. "Women in Hollywood." *People* (spring 1991): 35–43.

Sischy, Ingrid. "Interview with Jodie Foster." *Interview* 21.10 (October 1991): 79–84.

FRIEDRICH, SU (1954–   ). United States. Su Friedrich is one of the best-known avant-garde filmmakers of the New York experimental film movement. Friedrich, born in 1954, attended Oberlin College. Her best-known works, *Damned If You Don't, The Ties That Bind,* and *Gently down the Stream,* have been screened at the Whitney Museum of Modern Art, the New Directors/New Films Series at the Museum of Modern Art, the Rotterdam International Film Festival, the New York, San Francisco, Chicago, London, Vancouver, Copenhagen, and Frankfurt lesbian and gay film festivals, numerous women's film festivals, and women's studies classes. Friedrich's early works are autobiographical and stylistically innovative, with frequent use of hand-scratched titles over female imagery. In preparation for *Gently down the Stream* (1981), she kept a journal of her dreams. She asked her ex-lover, a man, and her current lover, a woman, to cull through them and select the dreams they found attractive. Then Friedrich filmed poetic images, freeze-framed them on an optical printer, and scratched words onto the film. Her work is filmed poetry. It should come as no surprise that Friedrich says that her influences range from Sappho to the late "structural" filmmaker Hollis Frampton. Critics compared the stunning use of poetic imagery in *Gently down the Stream* with the techniques employed by such disparate filmmakers as Jonas Mekas, Stan Brakhage, and Maya Deren. *Sink or Swim* (1990) was also well received by audiences and critics alike. The autobiographical film is told through the point of view of a girl who recounts memories of her childhood. Friedrich juxtaposes images from family vacations with a voice-over of the young woman, who comes to the conclusion that her father cared more for his career than his family. *Sink or Swim,* like all of Friedrich's work, is emotionally complex, ambiguous, and technically sophisticated.

In *The Ties That Bind* (1984), Friedrich drew further from her personal experience. *The Ties That Bind* is about her mother, who lived in Nazi Germany during the war. The mother's voice provides the running voice-over narrative, which Friedrich punctuates with etched-lettered questions from the daughter. *The Ties That Bind* deals with the inherent complexities of mother-daughter relationships, which are inimitably intertwined with the shifting attributes of memory, the reliability of narration, the repression of family history, and the horrors of war. *The Ties That Bind* is told from the triple-bound point of view of mother, grown daughter, and child, in a reconfiguration of the documentary form. Friedrich evokes a child's innocent scrawl through the use of hand-scratched questions, which silently ask, for example, why the mother did not join the resistance group in Ulm, her mother's hometown. The grown female point of view is articulated by the image of someone's pasting together a model house, which is at one point crushed by a black jackboot, firmly binding the women across shared guilt, shared pain, and shared loss. In some ways, *The Ties That Bind* depicts a daughter/filmmaker putting her mother on trial through documentation.

Like Friedrich, German director Jutta Brückner uses the same tactic in *Years of Hunger* (1979). Both women directors break a taboo by breaking silences and making female autobiographical narratives public, and both reimagine the subject/object relationship between author and experience.

Damned If You Don't (1987) is an experimental, multilayered construction of lesbian desire. In the film, the central narrative is about a nun's losing battle with her own lesbian sexual desire. Friedrich uses hand-scratched intertitles and numerous avant-garde techniques that combine the central "story" with a deconstruction of the representation of women in the classic film *Black Narcissus*. The sound track is sometimes the testimony of the trial of a nun in the seventeenth century who was accused of lesbian relations. As Andrea Weiss notes, "*Damned If You Don't* avoids the two major traps of lesbian independent cinema . . . the essentialist trap . . . that imagines lesbianism to be completely outside of patriarchal definitions, and . . . the trap that situates lesbianism so strictly within patriarchal definitions that it can't imagine any way out of them" (157). In *Damned If You Don't*, Friedrich expands filmic narration to interpolate feminist lesbian desires, repressions, and a web of discourses that connect fantasy to sources of empowerment and discourses of oppression, the church, gender expectations, identity restrictions, and history itself. As in *The Ties That Bind,* Friedrich works in narratives of drama logic in *Damned If You Don't*. The dream logic allows for metanarratives of "truth" to wind around one another, from the distorted representation of sexuality in *Black Narcissus,* to the "testimony" of Sister Benedetta's accuser. Friedrich's greatest achievement is turning low-budget experimental techniques into aesthetic assets. Friedrich's scratched words and rapid-fire editing technique imbue her films with the body of the filmmaker, transgressing boundaries of traditional narrative form. *Damned If You Don't* articulates lesbian subjectivity at the center of a narrative web of film pleasure. It is an articulate poem of guilt, pleasure, shame, and voyeurism. Friedrich resignifies the female body and explores the filmic space of lesbian sexualities.

Friedrich feels that experimental films can be just as pleasurable to watch as commercial films. Though she claims her major influences are Maya Deren, Rainer Werner Fassbinder, Stan Brakhage, and Hollis Frampton, she has a unique personal vision that is hers alone. She lives in Greenwich Village in New York City, where she continues to make experimental films. Her most recent film, *First Comes Love* (1991), is called by B. Ruby Rich "an indictment of institutionalized heterosexuality" (168). The short film was critically acclaimed when it opened at the Toronto Film Festival. Friedrich's films are distributed by Women Make Movies, Inc., Canyon Cinema, and the Film-makers' Cooperative.

SELECTED FILMOGRAPHY

Hot Water (1978)
Cool Hands Warm Heart (1979)
Scar Tissue (1979)
I Suggest Mine (1980)
Gently down the Stream (1981)
But No One (1982)
The Ties That Bind (1984)
Damned If You Don't (1987)
Sink or Swim (1990)
First Comes Love (1991)

SELECTED BIBLIOGRAPHY

Canyon Cinema. *Canyon Cinema Catalogue 7.* San Francisco: Canyon Cinema, 1992.

Cartwright, Lisa, and Nina Fonoroff. "Narrative Is Narrative: So What Is New?" In *Multiple Voices in Feminist Film Criticism,* edited by Diane Carson, Linda Dittmar, and Janice Welsch, 124–39. Minneapolis: University of Minnesota Press, 1994.

de Lauretis, Teresa, ed. *Feminist Studies/Critical Studies.* Bloomington: Indiana University Press, 1986.

Film-makers' Cooperative. *Film-makers' Cooperative Catalogue No. 7.* New York: Film-makers' Cooperative, 1989.

Kotz, Liz. "An Unrequited Desire for the Sublime: Looking at Lesbian Representation across the Works of Abigail Child, Cecilia Dougherty, and Su Friedrich." In *Queer Looks: Perspectives on Lesbian and Gay Film and Video,* edited by Martha Gever, John Greyson, and Pratibha Parmar, 86–102. New York: Routledge, 1993.

MacDonald, Scott. "*Damned If You Don't:* An Interview with Su Friedrich." *Afterimage* 15 (May 1988): 6–10.

Mayne, Judith. *The Woman at the Keyhole: Feminism and Women's Cinema.* Bloomington: Indiana University Press, 1990.

Mellencamp, Patricia. *Indiscretions: Avant-Garde Film, Video, & Feminism.* Bloomington: Indiana University Press, 1990.

Rich, B. Ruby. "Homo Pomo: The New Queer Cinema." In *Women and Film: A Sight and Sound Reader,* edited by Pam Cook and Philip Dodd, 164–73. Philadelphia: Temple University Press, 1993.

Weinberger, Gabriele. *Nazi Germany and Its Aftermath in Women Directors' Autobiographical Films of the Late 1970s.* San Francisco: Mellen Research University Press, 1992.

Weiss, Andrea. *Vampires and Violets: Lesbians in Film.* New York: Penguin, 1993.

Women Make Movies. *Women Make Movies Catalogue.* New York: Women Make Movies, Inc., 1994.

G

GAUNTIER, GENE (1891–1966). United States. A pioneer of the early serial film, Gene Gauntier wrote hundreds of films in which she starred and performed daredevil stunts. Born in 1891, she began as an actress in the formative years of cinema in the United States, at the Kalem Film Company. She was a remarkably prolific scenario writer for Kalem. Sidney Olcott, a producer at Kalem, first asked Gauntier if she would be interested in writing a screenplay based on *Tom Sawyer*. Gauntier wrote the screenplay and then wrote an adaptation of *Ben Hur*, which was directed by Olcott and Frank Oakes in 1907. Gauntier's scenario was problematic, though, and the Kalem Company was brought to court in one of the first copyright infringement cases (which Kalem lost). From 1907 to 1912, Gauntier was the "leading lady" at Kalem, except for a few pictures she worked on at Biograph.

Gene Gauntier continued writing and became one of the industry's most powerful and well-paid writer/actresses. Though she did not receive directorial credit, Gauntier certainly presided over the productions of the serial films that she wrote and starred in, such as the 1908–9 production *Adventures of a Girl Spy*, one of the first serial films. In *The Adventures of a Girl Spy*, Gauntier played a cross-dressing woman spy in an adventure action scenario set in 1861. Gauntier's performance transgressed the normative figure of the submissive female perpetuated from Victorian discourse in many male-authored novels and films. Gauntier, like serial heroines Grace Cunard, Kathlyn Williams, and Ruth Stonehouse, embodied the self-determined, feminist aspirations of the American New Woman, who replaced the passive Victorian heroine. Action heroines were almost entirely erased from Hollywood films in the late 1920s. Only recently have women directors such as Kathryn Bigelow (*Blue Steel*, 1990) and women writers such as Callie Khouri (*Thelma and Louise*, 1991) reimagined the female action heroine.

Gene Gauntier's performance as a female spy dressed in men's clothing was incredibly popular. Gauntier appealed to audiences' desire for action and, more important perhaps, provided a self-defined role model with which female audiences could identify. Gauntier recalled her experiences as stuntperson:

My own work was not light, and only youth and a strong constitution could have stood up under it. I was playing in 2 pictures a week, working in almost every scene, and writing 2 or 3 scenarios a week, in the effort to keep up with our production. And my screen work was all strenuous, horseback riding for hours each day, water scenes in which I committed suicide or floated on spars in shark-infested waters, climbing trees, coming down on ropes from second-story windows, jumping from roofs or rolling down to be caught in blankets, overturning skiff, paddling canoes, a hundred and one "stunts" thought out to give the action Kalem films demanded. I was terrified at each daring thing I had to do, but for some inexplicable reason I continued to write them. They never seemed difficult when I was seated before the typewriter in the throes of creating them, but as the moment for performance drew near they assumed unwarranted aspects of terror. A "double" was never even thought of in those days! (Everett, 22)

In 1910, Gauntier finally received directorial credit for *Grandmother,* which she also wrote. The film displays a decidedly feminist point of view. In *Grandmother,* a woman who is a famous dancer is the love object of a rich, young, elitist man. The woman, who is middle-aged, shows little interest in the attentions of her would-be suitor. Though the film was successful, Gauntier declined Kalem's offer to direct more films. Apparently, Gauntier was more interested in producing, rather than directing, her own scenarios. In 1912, Gene Gauntier and Sidney Olcott left Kalem and formed their own production company, the Gene Gauntier Feature Players, located in Jacksonville, Florida. In 1915, the pair joined Universal, because the smaller film companies were being bought up by larger companies. Gauntier wrote and acted at Universal for three years until she became a war correspondent in 1918.

Gene Gauntier is an important pioneer of the American cinema whose work is all too often ignored by contemporary cinema historians. Many critics routinely credit only a small cadre of male directors with the creation of both the American narrative film and the iconic presence of the female heroine. Though Sidney Olcott is duly credited for his work at Kalem, Gauntier appears in few film histories. Feminist film critics exhibit surprisingly little interest in Gauntier and other women serial writer/directors. Film historian Eileen Bowser reassessed the feminist aspects of the "serial queen":

The serial with its brave heroine signaled the emergence of the New Woman. She wore less restrictive clothes, she was active, she went everywhere she wanted, and she was capable of resolving mysteries, solving problems, and escaping from danger. . . . she wrote a large proportion of film scripts, and found it easier to get into directing than she would in later periods of film history. (186)

The women's movement is reflected on the screen in the popular serial genre pioneered by Gene Gauntier. Gauntier's cross-dressing girl in *The Adventures of a Girl Spy* signaled a cultural rupture of strictly defined gender roles of the nineteenth century. A comprehensive reassessment of the film work of Gene Gauntier is long overdue.

SELECTED FILMOGRAPHY

Grandmother (1910)

SELECTED BIBLIOGRAPHY

Acker, Ally. *Reel Women: Pioneers of the Cinema, 1896 to the Present*. New York: Continuum, 1993.

Bowser, Eileen. *The History of the American Cinema 2: The Transformation of Cinema 1907–1915*. New York: Scribner's, 1990.

Everett, Eldon K. "The Great Grace Cunard—Frances Ford Mystery." *Classic Film Collector* (summer 1973): 22–25.

Gauntier, Gene. "Blazing the Trail." *Women's Home Companion* (October 1928): 6.

Horwitz, Rita, and Harriet Harrison. *The George Kleine Collection of Early Motion Pictures in the Library of Congress: A Catalogue*. Washington, DC: Library of Congress, 1980.

Magliozzi, Ronald S. *Treasures from the Film Archive: A Catalogue of Short Silent Fiction Films Held by FIAF Archives*. Metuchen, NJ: Scarecrow Press, 1988.

Rainey, Buck. *Those Fabulous Serial Heroines*. Metuchen, NJ: Scarecrow Press, 1990.

Slide, Anthony. *Early Women Directors*. New York: Da Capo, 1984.

Stempel, Tom. *Framework*. New York: Continuum, 1988.

GISH, LILLIAN (1896–1993). United States. Lillian Gish is well known as an early screen actress who worked closely in collaboration with D. W. Griffith. Born in Springfield, Ohio, Lillian Gish and her sister, Dorothy Gish, are perhaps the best-known screen actresses from the silent film period. Lillian Gish usually played the victimized heroine in early Griffith films, the embodiment of Victorian notions of feminine sexual purity and, as Richard Dyer notes, the essence of "whiteness." Gish starred in *The Mothering Heart* (1913), *Way Down East* (1920), *Orphans of the Storm* (1921), and many more films until 1987, when she acted in *The Whales of August*. Gish may have been passive in front of the camera in her early roles, but she was active behind the camera and behind the scenes on many of her films. She not only was active as a producer and collaborator but also directed one film, *Remodeling Her Husband* (1920).

D. W. Griffith was initially slated to direct *Remodeling Her Husband*, starring Dorothy Gish, but at the last moment, for reasons that are still obscure, Griffith turned the direction of the film over to Lillian Gish. Dorothy Gish herself chose the story for the film, which was based on a cartoon in a magazine depicting a husband's dissatisfaction with his wife's appearance. Dorothy Parker wrote the comic subtitles for the film, which was her first Hollywood writing job. Unfortunately, *Remodeling Her Husband* appears to be a lost film, but if the plotline of the cartoon upon which the film is based is any indication, *Remodeling Her Husband* is a feminist critique of patriarchal gender expectations. The idea of making such a film must have attracted the Gish sisters, who were well aware of their iconic status as the quintessentially objectified women of the silent cinema. *Remodeling Her Husband* is a clever comedic subversion of male and female codes of beauty, which includes a scene of the leading man's having his nails filed at a barbershop. Dorothy Parker's subtitle for the scene reads, "The divinity that shapes our ends," a typical Parkeresque jab at masculine pomposity.

Remodeling Her Husband depicts an unfaithful husband whose wife goes to work to punish him for his actions. It seems appropriate that the Gish sisters, the penultimate screen "beauties," irreverently mocked male attitudes so blatantly in *Remodeling Her Husband*. The film was a critical and box-office success. Budgeted at $50,000, the film made over $460,000 and was one of Gish's most successful comedies. Despite this acclaim, after *Remodeling Her Husband,* Gish said she "never wanted to direct another film" (Gish, 226).

Lillian Gish describes the making of the film in detail in *The Movies, Mr. Griffith, and Me.* Not only was Gish responsible for directing *Remodeling Her Husband* in the winter of 1919, but Griffith also left her in charge of building a studio in his absence, while he went on location to shoot another film in Florida. Perhaps if Gish had not been saddled with the excess responsibility of overseeing construction on top of directing her first film, she may not have turned completely against the idea of film directing. Instead, Gish returned to acting and had one of the most famous and long-running careers in Hollywood. In 1970, she earned the Academy Award for her Life Achievement in films. She was also awarded the American Film Institute's Lifetime Achievement Award in 1984. Gish pioneered "naturalistic" acting and leaves a formidable legacy in motion picture history. It seems odd that Gish's one feminist directorial effort is lost, given the fervor with which Griffith is obsessively archived by film historians.

SELECTED FILMOGRAPHY

Remodeling Her Husband (1920)

SELECTED BIBLIOGRAPHY

Acker, Ally. *Reel Women: Pioneers of the Cinema, 1896 to the Present.* New York: Continuum, 1993.

Bowser, Eileen. *History of the American Cinema 2: The Transformation of Cinema 1907–1915.* New York: Scribner's, 1990.

Dyer, Richard. "The Color of Virtue: Lillian Gish, Whiteness and Femininity." In

Women and Film: A Sight and Sound Reader, edited by Pam Cook and Philip Dodd, 1–9. Philadelphia: Temple University Press, 1993.

Gish, Lillian, with Ann Pinchot. *The Movies, Mr. Griffith, and Me.* Englewood Cliffs, NJ: Prentice-Hall, 1969.

Rosen, Marjorie. *Popcorn Venus.* New York: Avon, 1973.

Slide, Anthony. *Early Women Directors.* New York: Da Capo, 1984.

GLYN, ELINOR (1864–1943). United States. Perhaps no author or screenwriter represented the liberation of female sexuality in the 1920s more than Elinor Glyn, creator of the "It Girl." *It* (1927), based on Glyn's novel and directed by Clarence Badger, starred Clara Bow as the epitome of the free-spirited, sexually active female who single-handedly ushers in the jazz-age New Woman. In *It,* Bow displaced the repressed Victorian image of womanhood, embodied in stars such as Mary Pickford and the Gish sisters. Glyn, born in England, was perhaps so successful at changing the female image because she manages to appear simultaneously risqué and conservative. Glyn's heroines were beautiful and erotic, but, like Glyn, they were hardworking and charming. Glyn wrote *Three Weeks* in 1906, and it immediately became a best-seller when it was published in 1907. Unfortunately, Glyn trusted her husband to invest their fortune, and he lost it through a series of poor and/or nonexistent investments. In financial desperation, Glyn finished writing a terrible novel that was nevertheless a commercial success, *The Reason Why,* in eighteen days. After her husband died in 1915, she moved to Paris and wrote for popular magazines. In 1920, Glyn was invited to Hollywood, at the age of fifty-six, to become a screenwriter. Her early screenplays were made into very successful films, but her biggest success was in 1927, with the production of *It.*

In 1929, Glyn was given the opportunity to direct *Knowing Men.* Like Lillian Gish's *Remodeling Her Husband,* Glyn's *Knowing Men* turned the camera on men as object of the female creator and the woman's gaze in a romantic comedy vehicle. *Knowing Men* is a blatant critique of sexual harassment, about a man who molests every woman he meets. Glyn's film was critically attacked because of its clear feminist agenda. As Elinor Glyn recalls in her autobiography, *Romantic Adventure:*

I thought that the critics would be kind to anyone spending their own money on the production of British films, and would make allowances for some imperfections. However, I was wrong; the storm of criticism ran to centre-page headlines, and the most extraordinary allegations of immorality were made against the poor little comedy. I have never understood why, as it was certainly not that. To complete the disaster, through some misunderstanding on the part of Mr. Knoblock's lawyer, he injuncted the showing of the picture on the first night of its West End run at the Regal Cinema and it had to be taken off. He lost the case, but it was too late to overtake the harm which had been done. Except for the guaranteed advance, the film was a dead loss to my little company. (333)

After the disastrous critical reception of *Knowing Men,* Elinor Glyn directed *The Price of Things* in 1929, but the film lost a great deal of money at the box office. With the commercial failure of this film, Glyn retired from directing.

Elinor Glyn's name is synonymous with the jazz-age flapper. Glyn's female heroines provided an alternative to the scheming, housebound wives who were often the archetypical models in other films. Yet, Glyn was not the only feminist voice in the industry during this period. Glyn was one of many women working in Hollywood in the 1920s, including Dorothy Arzner, Lois Weber, Jeannie MacPherson, and Grace Cunard. Ally Acker sums up the essence of Elinor Glyn as "Jackie Collins, Ann Landers, Emily Post, Jacqueline Susann and [producer] Dawn Steel all rolled into one" (166). If *Knowing Men* and *The Price of Things* are ever rediscovered and made available, perhaps modern audiences will be treated to another side of the prolific author Elinor Glyn.

SELECTED FILMOGRAPHY

Knowing Men (1929)
The Price of Things (1929)

SELECTED BIBLIOGRAPHY

Acker, Ally. *Reel Women: Pioneers of the Cinema, 1896 to the Present.* New York: Continuum, 1993.
Glyn, Elinor. *Romantic Adventure.* New York: E. P. Dutton, 1937.
Smith, Sharon. *Women Who Make Movies.* New York: Hopkinson and Blake, 1975.

GODMILOW, JILL (1950–   ). United States. Film and video artist Jill Godmilow came into prominence with her internationally recognized documentary *Antonia: A Portrait of a Woman* (1973). The straightforward documentary describes the life of Antonia Braco, an indomitable seventy-three-year-old conductor. Godmilow worked with Judy Collins on the film. *Antonia* opened at the New American Filmmakers Series at the Whitney Museum in New York and was subsequently nominated for an Academy Award. Godmilow's experimental documentary *Far from Poland* (1984) and her most recent narrative feature film, *Waiting for the Moon* (1987), a film about Gertrude Stein and Alice B. Toklas, have also been well received. When asked for her definition of a "feminist film," Godmilow called for a wider definition of the term that would be open enough to include political films such as *Far from Poland* and other socially conscious works. Godmilow told Wendy Patterson:

When I made *Antonia,* which was considered a feminist film, and which I think is a fair description, feminists would ask me what my next film was. And when it wasn't a "feminist" subject there was always some disappointment. . . . But I prefer not to say I'm a "feminist" filmmaker—exactly because it seems to say that I only care about certain issues. I think I do more for women, and for myself, if I just try to make good films and have the full range of subjects rather than just the subject of feminism. But it's so natural for me to think in feminist terms. (7)

Jill Godmilow got her start in films by making a film about Spanish Harlem, *La Nueva Vida* (1967). She worked on the film with her boyfriend, Joaquin Mercado, but ran out of money and ended up shelving the project. She then volunteered her services as an editor and gained a tremendous amount of experience cutting commercials and industrials. Later, Godmilow began to freelance as an editor and worked at KQED in San Francisco. In 1969, Godmilow made *Tales* with Cassandra Gerstein, another independent filmmaker, a film that documents varying attitudes toward human sexuality. Next, Godmilow directed *Where Have All The Mentally Ill Gone?*, an NBC television documentary about the New York State mental health system. In between, Godmilow continued to freelance and make traditional documentaries.

In 1981, Godmilow began to plan a cinéma vérité documentary about the political events surrounding the Polish Solidarity movement. She raised money for the film and planned to travel to Poland to document the Solidarity strike. But her plans were radically altered when she was denied entry into Poland, and the Polish government declared martial law. The Solidarity movement was crushed, and the filmmaker was left with only a little footage of the events as they unfolded.

Godmilow decided to make a film about making a film about Solidarity, entitled *Far from Poland* (a joking reference to the French antiwar film *Far from Vietnam,* 1967). Godmilow ended up creating a postdocumentary that questions the notions of vérité, of documentary "objectivity," and of the passivity of spectatorship. Well versed in the documentary tradition, Godmilow undermines the traditional documentary form, which mimics truth and experience. As she told Wendy Patterson, "I'm trying to say, you ain't experiencing nothing. You're sitting in a theatre experiencing a movie" (5). The first "rule" of the conventional documentary film that Godmilow breaks is that she makes herself a character in the film. She is, in turn, three voices; the voice of Godmilow in direct address, a soap opera version of Godmilow as filmmaker, and the presence of the offscreen filmmaker, who is obviously manipulating the images the audience sees.

This self-referentiality and self-reflexivity are reminiscent of the work of Jean-Luc Godard (one of the directors of *Far from Vietnam*), but Godmilow takes her construct a step further. She uses the distancing technique of shooting a fake video "documentary," running it on a monitor, and then, in turn, filming the monitor itself. Godmilow thus confronts the audience with a dazzling array of images that convey different levels of "truth." Godmilow reenacts Solidarity meetings and juxtaposes scenes of Anna Walentynowitcz, a shipyard worker involved in the Solidarity movement, with reenactments of Walentynowitcz's speeches, intercut with footage of a speech by Ronald Reagan. The viewer is constantly barraged with questions of verisimilitude that reimagine truth as multivalent. In manipulating filmic "truth," Godmilow makes it clear that there is not a binary formula for truth regarding Solidarity; it is either pro-Soviet or anti-American, as the dominant media would have it. There are, in fact, many tales of Solidarity, of which *Far from Poland* is only one. In an astounding and controversial move, Godmilow refuses to end *Far from Poland* with the downbeat return to Soviet domination and the crushing of the Solidarity movement. Instead, Godmilow imagines a utopic end in which Solidarity forces win. *Far from Poland* emerges as an audacious and agile deconstruction of truth and the documentary form.

After the success of *Far from Poland*, Jill Godmilow turned to narrative feature filmmaking with the art-house feature film *Waiting for the Moon* (1987), a coproduction with French television. Godmilow angered some lesbian feminists because she refused to show any sexuality between the main characters of the film, Gertrude Stein and Alice B. Toklas. Godmilow insists that if the couple was heterosexual, a sex scene would not be a necessity to portray a romantic relationship. But as Andrea Weiss notes, Godmilow's film completely erases the romantic relationship between Stein and Toklas. Traditionally, Hollywood appropriates lesbian subjects "while excluding lesbian spectators," notes Weiss (123). In view of this, it can be argued that Godmilow's poetic license is perhaps taken a bit too far in this film. Yet Jill Godmilow persists in making difficult, rule-breaking cinema, almost to the point that it seems as if she wishes to countermand audience expectations. Godmilow lives in New York City, where she continues to make films. Her next project was the completion of her film of Ron Vawter's one-person show, *Roy Cohn/Jack Smith*, shot just before the actor's untimely death from acquired immunodeficiency syndrome (AIDS) in 1994.

SELECTED FILMOGRAPHY

La Nueva Vida (codirector, unfinished) (1967)
Tales (codirector) (1969)
Antonia: A Portrait of a Woman (1973)
Where Have All the Mentally Ill Gone? (1974)
Nevelson in Process (1976)
The Popovich Brothers of South Chicago (1977)
With Grotoensky at Nienadowka (1980)
The Odyssey Tapes (1980)
The Vigil (1981)
Far from Poland (1984)
Waiting for the Moon (1987)
Roy Cohn/Jack Smith (1994)

SELECTED BIBLIOGRAPHY

Breitbart, Eric. "The Awful Truth: *Far from Poland*." *American Film* 10.2 (November 1984): 58–62.

Cole, Janis, and Holly Dale. *Calling the Shots: Profiles of Women Filmmakers.* Ontario: Quarry Press, 1993.

Erens, Patricia. "Interview with Jill Godmilow." *Women and Film* 2.7 (1975): 34.

Patterson, Wendy. "Far from Documentary: An Interview with Jill Godmilow." *Afterimage* 13 (February 1986): 4–7.

Smith, Sharon. *Women Who Make Movies.* New York: Hopkinson and Blake, 1975.

Weiss, Andrea. *Vampires and Violets: Lesbians in Film.* New York: Penguin, 1993.

GOGOBERIDZE, LANA (1928–   ). Soviet Union/Georgia. Lana Gogoberidze is one of the few Soviet women directors who prefer to be associated with feminist cinema. She was born in Tbilisi, Georgia, on October 13, 1928. She was not permitted to study film in Moscow because her parents were political exiles under the Stalinist regime. Her father was killed by the secret police, and her mother was sent to a labor camp for twelve years. Gogoberidze studied Georgian, American, and British literature at the University of Tbilisi, lecturing and writing on the American poet Walt Whitman. All the while she nurtured a secret desire to make films and bear witness to the plight of her mother and the destruction of her family by the Stalinist authorities.

In 1953, when Stalin died and Gogoberidze was able to travel for the first time with some degree of freedom, she finally pursued her dream of a career in film. She graduated from film school in Moscow in 1959 and has since directed many feature films. She is a professor of film at the Tbilisi Film Institute and has personally trained several Georgian women directors. Gogoberidze's *Some Interviews on Personal Questions* (1979) is distinctly autobiographical; as part of the narrative, the film's heroine is sent to a forced labor camp. In making *Some Interviews on Personal Questions,* Gogoberidze drew upon her real-life experience, when, at seventeen, she was reunited with her mother, who had just been freed from a labor camp. Tellingly, the most compelling scene in the film is the reuniting of a mother and her daughter after a long separation. One of the recurring themes of women's films is the difficulty of mother-daughter relationships. Gogoberidze remembers the strange feeling she had when she first "met" her mother, who was someone she felt she did not know. Gogoberidze works these emotions into *Some Interviews* in a uniquely feminine voice. "I always make films from a woman's point of view," Gogoberidze told Lynn Attwood (227–28).

Turnabout (1986) makes use of a multinarrative, female-centered plot. Gogoberidze weaves several seemingly disconnected women's lives through surprising twists of fate. The narratives are also connected by Gogoberidze's frequent intercutting of scenes from the women's lives with segments from a psychology class, discussing the representation of women in film.

Turnabout won the Director's Prize at the Tokyo Film Festival. Ironically, before Gogoberidze's mother was sent to a labor camp, she herself had been a filmmaker. Gogoberidze has recently located the negatives of her mother's films. All the prints had been destroyed, but Gogoberidze hopes to salvage the films and perpetuate her mother's legacy, including her mother's period of arrest and imprisonment. Gogoberidze's own film work is a testimonial legacy of her mother, a filmmaker who suffered for voicing her opinions. Currently, Gogoberidze is working with Saira Asenishrilli on a screenplay based on a story that her mother wrote during her internment. Gogoberidze is politically active, as a speaker, professor, and artist. She is concerned with the need to help Georgia remain independent and to move toward a more effective democracy. She is also active as the first president of Kino Women International (KIWI), an organization set up to further the position of women in the film industry. In 1987, Gogoberidze served as president of the International Association of Women Filmmakers.

SELECTED FILMOGRAPHY

Gelati (1957)
Tbilisi 1500 let (*Tbilisi, 1500 Years Old*) (1959)
Pod odnim nebom (*Under One Sky*) (1961)
Ia vizhu solntse (*I Can See the Sun*) (1965)
Rubezhi (*Borderlines*) (1970)
Kogda zatsvel mindal (*When Almond Trees Were in Blossom*) (1973)
Perepolokh (*Confusion*) (1976)
Neskolo interviu po lichnym voprosam (*Some Interviews on Personal Questions*)
    (1979)
Poslednoe pismo detiam (*The Last Letter to Children*) (1980)
Den dlinnee nochi (*Day Longer than Night*) (1984)
Krugovorot (*Turnabout*) (1986)

SELECTED BIBLIOGRAPHY

Attwood, Lynn, ed. *Red Women on the Silver Screen: Soviet Women and Cinema from the Beginning to the End of the Communist Era.* London: Pandora, 1993.
Goulding, Daniel J., ed. *Post New Wave Cinema in the Soviet Union and Eastern Europe.* Bloomington: Indiana University Press, 1989.
Kaplan, Ann. *Women and Film.* New York: Methuen, 1983.
Kuhn, Annette. *Women's Pictures: Feminism and Cinema.* London: Routledge, 1982.
Leyda, Jay. *A History of the Russian and Soviet Film.* New York: Collier, 1973.
Mayne, Judith. *Kino and the Woman Question: Feminism and Soviet Silent Film.* Columbus: Ohio State University, 1989.
Taylor, Richard, and Ian Christie, eds. *Inside the Film Factory.* London: Routledge Press, 1991.

GÓMEZ, SARA (1943–74). Cuba. Born in Havana, Sara Gómez grew up in a black, middle-class family. She studied ethnography and began a career in journalism before going into film. She joined the Cuban Film Institute in 1961, and she worked as an assistant director to Cuban film directors Tomás Gutiérrez Alea and Jorge Fraga and with French director Agnes Varda. For many years, Sara Gómez was the only woman director who belonged to the Cuban Film Institute and one of only two black directors in the institute. Gómez directed many documentary short films before she made her first and last feature film, *One Way or Another* (1975–77). Gómez died of an asthma attack when the film was in postproduction. Tomás Gutiérrez Alea completed the film.

One Way or Another is described by Julianne Burton as "a paradigmatic example of Third World cinefeminism" (178). In the film, Gómez interweaves documentary and narrative forms. The narrative thread is an analysis of machismo that destroys a love affair between Yolanda, a middle-class woman, and Mario, an underprivileged young man from the slums. The documentary footage includes views of buildings being torn down, archival material of Cuban life under colonialism, and capitalist propaganda film. As E. Ann Kaplan notes, "[T]he intercutting of the documentary and narrative forms gives the film its power, for the juxtaposition provides a commentary on the capabilities of each cinematic form" (190). *One Way or Another* examines the inexorable links among colonialism, gender expectations, racism, and classism. As Julia LeSage argues, *One Way or Another* "examines the Cuban revolutionary process from the vantage point of the neighborhood and the domestic sphere" (21).

In continually returning to the domestic sphere, Sara Gómez locates feminist and revolutionary struggle in the distinctly feminist voice of a black Cuban woman filmmaker. This is an important articulation of positionality, not only because of its representational integrity but also because it undermines the patriarchal notions of "realism" of Hollywood films. Cuban audiences are bombarded with Hollywood films and their vision of "realism." Gómez and other Cuban filmmakers provide a countercinema that rejects colonialist filmmaking and its ideologies. Sara Gómez leaves an important legacy in her films and life's work. Tomás Gutiérrez Alea pays homage to Gómez in his feature film *Up to a Point* (1984). Gutiérrez blends documentary and narrative footage in his film as Gómez had in *One Way or Another*. *One Way or Another* is available from New Yorker Films.

SELECTED FILMOGRAPHY

Iré a Santiago (*I Shall Go to Santiago*) (1964)
Excursion a Vueltabajo (*Outing to Vueltabajo*) (1965)
Y tenemos sabor (*And We've Got "Sabor"*) (1967)
En la otra isle (*On the Other Island*) (1968)
Isla del tesorel (*Treasure Island*) (1969)
Poder local, poder popular (*Local Power, People's Power*) (1970)
Un documental a propósito del transito (*A Documentary about Mass Transit*) (1971)

Atención pre-natal año uno (*Prenatal Care in the First Year*) (1972)
Sobre horas extras y trabajo voluntario (*About Overtime and Voluntary Labor*)
   (1973)
De cierta manera (codirector) (*One Way or Another*) (1975–77)

SELECTED BIBLIOGRAPHY

Burton, Julianne. "Gómez, Sara." In *The Women's Companion to International Film,* edited by Annette Kuhn, with Susannah Radstone, 178–79. Berkeley: University of California Press, 1994.

Chanan, Michael. *The Cuban Image: Cinema and Cultural Politics in Cuba.* Bloomington: Indiana University Press, 1985.

Kaplan, E. Ann. "The Woman Director in the Third World: Sara Gómez's *One Way or Another.*" In *Women in Film: Both Sides of the Camera,* edited by E. Ann Kaplan, 189–94. New York: Methuen, 1989.

Kuhn, Annette. *Women's Pictures: Feminism and Cinema.* London: Routledge, 1982.

LeSage, Julia. "*One Way or Another:* Dialectic, Revolutionary, Feminist." *Jump Cut* 20 (1979): 20–23.

Welsch, Janice R. "Feminist Film Theory/Criticism in the United States." In *Multiple Voices in Feminist Film Criticism,* edited by Diane Carson, Linda Dittmar, and Janice Welsch, 443–55. Minneapolis: University of Minnesota Press, 1994.

GORDON, BETTE (1950–   ). United States. Born in 1950, Bette Gordon is famous internationally for *Variety* (1983), a feature film about a woman who works as a ticket taker in the booth of a pornographic theater (*Variety Photoplays,* in New York City). For many years Bette Gordon worked as an avant-garde filmmaker with her then-husband, James Benning. Gordon attended graduate school at the University of Wisconsin at Madison and later became a professor at the University of Wisconsin in Milwaukee. Gordon's early experimental works, which she codirected with Benning, were formalist explorations of cinematic representation. *United States of America* (1975) is shot from a moving car on a cross-country trip. A radio announces the northern Vietnamese invasion of Saigon just as the viewer relaxes into viewing the panoramic imagery. *Michigan Avenue* (1973) is a poetic study of film grain and color composition. The film won critical praise and ran at several festivals. *Noyes* (1976) is a minimalist work that is influenced by the films of Hollis Frampton and Michael Snow.

   In 1979, Gordon moved to New York and became involved in underground, 8mm, punk filmmaking circles. Gordon's work took a decidedly feminist turn, combining ideas from feminist film theory with techniques of experimental filmmaking. In 1979, Gordon directed *Exchanges,* one of her first films to represent women as sexual subjects who are not objectified by a male gaze. In *Exchanges,* women exchange clothes with one another in a performance that displaces voyeuristic pleasure as it deconstructs the representation of the striptease. Gordon's film is directly linked to the theoretical writings of feminist film theory, particularly Laura Mulvey's "Visual Pleasure and Narrative Cinema." Mulvey's highly influential essay criticizes patriarchal cinema spectatorship as an objectification of the passive female by the active/voyeur male (gaze). Mulvey's theory did not allow for a feminine mode of spectatorship or a feminine gaze (though she later reformulated her theory). Both *Exchanges* and Gordon's next film, *Empty Suitcases* (1980), challenge the notion of passive spectatorship and criticize patriarchal imaging of women.

Suitcases reimagines female subjectivity through a deconstruction of cinematic discourse. Loosely described, *Empty Suitcases* concerns a multidimensional female subject—a professor, mistress, terrorist, and suffering artist. As Kaja Silverman notes, Gordon "negotiates these constant relocations through a multiplicity of female voices and discursive strategies, including not only the voice-over but the voice-off" (321). In one sequence, a woman lip-synchs the masochistic lyrics of "All of Me" sung by Billie Holiday. The lyrics are thus stripped of romanticism and held up to scrutiny. *Empty Suitcases* exposes the manner in which filmic representation encodes the female image as an eroticized object.

Gordon takes on the ultimate objectification of women, pornography, in *Variety* (1983), scripted by novelist Kathy Acker. In *Variety*, Gordon turned the gendered subject/object position around and constructed a woman voyeur of male voyeurs. The woman in the film becomes obsessed with pornography because she works selling tickets in a porno theater. As Bette Gordon told Karyn Kay, "If, as Laura Mulvey's first essay on visual pleasure implied, there was no place for the female spectator . . . then the idea of a female spectator of pornography was exciting to me. If she was a female voyeur, she would be a character seldom seen in cinema" (Gordon and Kay, 92–93). Gordon sought to release female representation from objectified status in *Empty Suitcases,* and she metaphorically inscribed the female as the bearer of the gaze in *Variety*. *Variety* was one of the first feminist films that challenged the doctrinaire antipornography stance of mainstream feminists. *Variety* is controversial because it deals with female sexual fantasy and because it does not take an antipornography stance. Gordon's films pose a number of challenges to feminist film structure. Critics Lisa Cartwright and Nina Fonoroff criticize Gordon's narrative disjunctive techniques, noting: "This process is intended to unfix meaning, opening up multiple readings and disengage the viewer. . . . But how long can a story continue before something takes place, before some specific meaning is produced?" (135). Gordon's interest in representation of women and women's sexuality is shared by many women filmmakers, including Valie Export, Barbara Hammer, Lizzie Borden, and many New Wave German women directors.

Bette Gordon not only challenges feminist film criticism with her films but also writes cinema criticism. She states her position clearly: "I am interested in interrupting the conventions of dominant culture by twisting them around . . . I am interested in investigating fantasy and pleasure, especially how they are constructed in culture and therefore cinema" (Gordon, 420). Gordon's most recent film is *Greed* (1986), a segment of the omnibus film *Seven Women/Seven Sins,* directed by seven women directors. Gordon is currently directing a horror genre television series. Bette Gordon's career to date, from feminist, independent filmmaker to television director, is typical of the grueling struggle most independents face in carving themselves a niche in the world of commercial cinema. But no matter what work Gordon takes on, it will undoubtedly be suffused with her own interests in gender constructs in the cinema.

SELECTED FILMOGRAPHY

Michigan Avenue (1973)
I-94 (1974)
United States of America (1975)
Central Times and Noyes (1976)
An Algorithm (1977)
Empty Suitcases (1980)
Variety (1983)
Greed (1986)

SELECTED BIBLIOGRAPHY

Canyon Cinema Cooperative. *Canyon Cinema Catalogue 7.* San Francisco: Canyon Cinema, 1992.

Carson, Diane. "Women Filmmakers." In *Multiple Voices in Feminist Film Criticism,* edited by Diane Carson, Linda Dittmar, and Janice Welsch, 456–67. Minneapolis: University of Minnesota Press, 1994.

Cartwright, Lisa, and Nina Fonoroff. "Narrative Is Narrative: So What Is New?" In *Multiple Voices in Feminist Film Criticism,* edited by Diane Carson, Linda Dittmar, and Janice Welsch, 124–39. Minneapolis: University of Minnesota Press, 1994.

Film-makers' Cooperative. *Film-makers' Cooperative Catalogue 7.* New York: Film-makers' Cooperative, 1989.

Gordon, Bette. "*Variety:* The Pleasure of Looking." In *Issues in Feminist Film Criticism,* edited by Patricia Erens, 418–22. Bloomington: Indiana University Press, 1990.

———, and Karyn Kay. "Look Back/Talk Back." In *Dirty Looks: Women, Pornography and Power,* edited by Pamela Church Gibson and Roma Gibson, 90–100. London: BFI, 1993.

Mayne, Judith. *Cinema and Spectatorship.* London: Routledge, 1993.

Mulvey, Laura. "Visual Pleasure and Narrative Cinema." *Screen* 16.3 (autumn 1975): 6–18.

Silverman, Kaja. "Dis-Embodying the Female Voice." In *Issues in Feminist Film Criticism,* edited by Patricia Erens, 309–27. Bloomington: Indiana University Press, 1990.

Williams, Linda. *Hard Core: Power, Pleasure and the Frenzy of the Visible.* Berkeley: University of California Press, 1989.

GORRIS, MARLEEN (1948–   ). Netherlands. Marleen Gorris is best known as the director of the radically feminist, uncompromisingly personal, commercially successful independent film *A Question of Silence* (1981). Gorris is one of a number of critically acclaimed, internationally recognized Dutch filmmakers to emerge from the government-subsidized Dutch film industry. *A Question of Silence* is a hybrid film that is both avant-garde and commercially viable. It is representative of that rare breed of film that emerges when a visionary director is fiscally supported by a government that is smart enough to recognize film as an art form and a good investment. Gorris began making films after studying theater. She had no background in film when she approached the government with her first screenplay *De Stille Rond Christine M (A Question of Silence)* (1981). Gorris initially showed the screenplay to Chantal Akerman, whom Gorris admired as a director. But Akerman urged Gorris to direct the film herself.

  A Question of Silence is a brilliant and deeply controversial film. Audiences and critics are stunned by its blatant violence toward men. In the film, three women spontaneously murder a shopkeeper. The three women do not know one another but are subsequently bound by their complete silence when questioned by the authorities. The murder seems to be completely unmotivated, yet, as the film proceeds, the audience (at least the female audience) sees a common thread in the women's lives. The thread of female oppression and submission is common to the women: a waitress, a housewife, and a secretary. The women are questioned by a female psychologist, who comes to represent them and ultimately deems them "sane." Gorris connects the silent women through the speaking female authority figure. The psychologist directly addresses the camera, saying, "I don't think these women are insane." The psychologist herself is increasingly attracted to one of the women killers. Her heterosexual relationship with her husband is violent and unsatisfying. Gorris uses traditional experimental film techniques to suggest a woman-identified perspective. This point of view is a reworking of the "rape-revenge film" identified by Carol Clover (137). In *A Question of Silence,* Gorris intercuts scenes of the woman psychologist being raped by her husband with shots of the three women standing over the body of the victim, thus inexorably linking one woman's rape with the three women's act of violence. Gorris's version of the rape-revenge film appeals to a female audience, rather than the male spectator. *A Question of Silence* does away with cinematic conventional narrative discourse. Linda Williams states that the film enters "the wild zone of female culture" (434). That we have entered the female "wild zone" is apparent when the women burst into laughter in the final courtroom sequence. The subversive laughter begins when the prosecutor asserts that the gender of the murderers, as well as that of the victim, is "irrelevant." The women's laughter erupts, as Nancy Reincke observes, "when women perceive the gap between what the men claim to know and what women do know" (31). The wild zone of *A Question of Silence* replaces women's silence with women's laughter and transgressive violence.

Violence is also the thematic center of Gorris's second film, *Broken Mirrors* (1984). *Broken Mirrors* depicts the lives of seven prostitutes and a psychopath who assaults women and holds them hostage until they die of hunger. *Broken Mirrors* shows little of the humor of *A Question of Silence*. In both films Gorris uses long takes and cinematic language reminiscent of Chantal Akerman films. But in *Broken Mirrors,* Gorris exposes what is unsaid in *A Question of Silence*. As Chris Straayer notes, "*Broken Mirrors* employs a feminist perspective to firmly establish sadism within male sexuality and the realm of the real" (505). *Broken Mirrors* did not achieve the critical or commercial success of *A Question of Silence,* perhaps because it is a realistic and serious feminist rape-revenge film or perhaps, as Jane Root suggests, because it was not distributed by a feminist distribution company. Both of Gorris's films exhibit a feminist separatist answer to male violence and patriarchal oppression of women.

SELECTED FILMOGRAPHY

De Stille Rond Christine M (A Question of Silence) (1981)
Gebrokene Spiegels (Broken Mirrors) (1984)

SELECTED BIBLIOGRAPHY

Clover, Carol. *Men, Women and Chain Saws.* Princeton: Princeton University Press, 1992.

Dittmar, Linda. "Beyond Gender and within It: The Social Construction of Female Desire." *Wide Angle* 8.3–4 (September 1986): 79–90.

Johnston, Sheila. "*De Stille Rond Christine M (A Question of Silence).*" *Monthly Film Bulletin* 50.589 (February 1983): 48.

Kuhn, Annette. *Women's Pictures: Feminism and Cinema.* London: Routledge, 1987.

Murphy, Jeanette. "A Question of Silence." In *Films for Women,* edited by Charlotte Brunsdon, 99–108. London: BFI, 1987.

Quart, Barbara. *Women Directors: The Emergence of a New Cinema.* New York: Praeger, 1988.

Ramanathan, Geetha. "Murder as Speech: Narrative Subjectivity in Marleen Gorris' *A Question of Silence.*" *Genders* 15 (winter 1992): 58–71.

Reincke, Nancy. "Antidote to Dominance: Women's Laughter as Counteraction." *Journal of Popular Culture* 24.4 (spring 1991): 27–38.

Rickey, Carrie. "Three Women Kill a Man—'For No Reason.' " *San Francisco Sunday Examiner and Chronicle,* November 11, 1983, 32.

Root, Jane. "Distributing *A Question of Silence*—A Cautionary Tale." In *Films for Women,* edited by Charlotte Brunsdon, 213–24. London: BFI, 1987.

Stack, Peter. "Three Women Who Murder a Man on the Spot." *San Francisco Chronicle,* Friday, October 21, 1983, 71.

Straayer, Chris. "Sexual Representation in Film and Video." In *Multiple Voices in Feminist Film Criticism,* edited by Diane Carson, Linda Dittmar, and Janice Welsch, 503–12. Minneapolis: University of Minnesota Press, 1994.

Williams, Linda. "A Jury of Their Peers: Marleen Gorris' *A Question of Silence.*" In *Multiple Voices in Feminist Film Criticism,* edited by Diane Carson, Linda Dittmar, and Janice Welsch, 432–42. Minneapolis: University of Minnesota Press, 1994.

GREENWALD, MAGGIE (1955–   ). United States. Maggie Greenwald is one of many women directors who are currently staking out their territory in Hollywood cinema. Tamra Davis, Stacey Cochran, Kathryn Bigelow, Sally Potter, Jane Campion, Julie Dash, and Jodie Foster are just a few of the other women directors who are securing a foothold in mainstream film production. Hopefully, Pam Cook is right, that "the days of male cultural ownership can now be numbered" (x), and books about marginalized women directors will no longer be necessary in the near future. But if the number of women in the Directors Guild is to increase substantially, each woman director needs to build up a body of work in genres that have traditionally been male-defined. One director who is making inroads into male-defined genres is Maggie Greenwald. She has made a screwball comedy (*Home Remedy,* 1988), a hard-boiled film noir (*The Kill-Off,* 1989), and a Western (*The Ballad of Little Jo,* 1993). She recognizes the fact that feminist struggles are in no way completed, especially in terms of employment opportunity. "It's difficult to really pursue a full career at equal pay with men, whether it's playing jazz or directing films or flying planes," she told Linda Lee.

Greenwald's most recent film, *The Ballad of Little Jo,* exhibits the lengths to which women have had to go to pursue equal employment opportunities. The film concerns a woman who is forced to cross-dress in men's clothing in order to survive in the Old West. Suzy Amis plays Little Jo, a character based on an actual woman (Josephine Monaghan) who lived as a man in the nineteenth century and worked as a cowboy and sheep tender. The screenplay of *The Ballad of Little Jo,* written by Maggie Greenwald, is designed to counterbalance years of sexist portrayals (or omissions) of women in the American West. Little Jo is abandoned by her family after she gets pregnant (out of "wedlock"). She survives an attempted rape and decides that the only way to live free is to live as a man. Greenwald deconstructs male gender identity through the vehicle of Little Jo's cross-dressing.

In one of the most memorable and transgressive scenes, Little Jo is almost shot for standing up to some homophobic cowboys who brag about murdering "dudes" (homosexual men). Violence seems ever-present in Greenwald's mise-en-scène. Jo is always in danger of being found out. She is unafraid, however, and even intercedes on behalf of a Chinese man whom the white men nearly torture to death. Little Jo falls in love with this man, who calls himself Tinman (played by David Chung). Their relationship is consolidated by their status as outsiders. Tinman works as a cook for Jo and one day tells her of the horrors of working on the railroad for slave wages for fifteen years. In scenes like this, Greenwald ties a number of traditional historical omissions into her revisionist Western. Violence is constructed as an everyday threat to peaceful existence, rather than a thrilling, escapist trope. Traditionally, the Western genre "exists in order to provide a justification for violence," writes Jane Tompkins (227). *The Ballad of Little Jo* demythologizes violence as much as it demythologizes the idea of a "good old" American West. Though Claire Monk dubs *The Ballad of Little Jo* as "the straightest cross-dressing film ever made," she admits that the film is "successful at reinstating female experience into a genre which has by definition sidelined it" (37). *The Ballad of Little Jo* is a downbeat, almost noirish vision of the West, though it does show a sense of humor. The women have the last laugh, literally and figuratively, in the final unveiling of Jo on her deathbed. A woman roars with laughter when the mortician announces that Jo was a woman.

Greenwald's sense of macabre humor is even more apparent in *The Kill-Off* (1989). This well-acted adaptation of a hard-boiled novel written by Jim Thompson concerns a bedridden, evil gossip, played by Loretta Gross. Greenwald's stylization of an unrelentingly grim mid-American town is particularly nihilistic but somehow retains a sense of sordid humor. Particularly memorable are the scenes of the telephone lines in a montage that suggests the evil of the gossip monger, who is hated and feared by the entire town. Greenwald is particularly adept at portraying the boredom and insularity of suburban America in *The Kill-Off,* as well as in *Home Remedy* (1988). Thus far, Maggie Greenwald's films have shown modest commercial success. *The Kill-Off* and *The Ballad of Little Jo* are already highly valued cult classics. Greenwald is successfully challenging the boundaries of genre filmmaking, and she is a versatile and adept writer/director with a distinctive stylistic tone.

SELECTED FILMOGRAPHY

Home Remedy (1988)
The Kill-Off (1989)
The Ballad of Little Jo (1993)

SELECTED BIBLIOGRAPHY

Cook, Pam. "Border Crossings: Women and Film in Context." In *Women and Film: A Sight and Sound Reader,* edited by Pam Cook and Philip Dodd, ix–x, 9–23. Philadelphia: Temple University Press, 1993.
Lee, Linda. "When Men Were Men (and So Were Women)." *New York Times,* August 15, 1993, 24.
Monk, Claire. "*The Ballad of Little Jo.*" *Sight and Sound* 4.4 (April 1994): 36–37.

Rich, B. Ruby. "At Home on the Range." *Sight and Sound* 3.11 (November 1993): 18–22.

Tompkins, Jane. *West of Everything: The Inner Life of Westerns.* New York: Oxford University Press, 1992.

GRIERSON, MARION (1900–   ). Scotland. Marion Grierson, sister of John Grierson, was one of a handful of women directors who made a contribution to the pioneering British documentary film movement. John Grierson is identified as the "father" of British documentary, but, as Sylvia Paskin and Annette Kuhn observe, Grierson's two sisters, Ruby and Marion, played "key roles" in the development of the British documentary (55). Ruby Grierson, according to Kuhn and Paskin, "was in fact responsible for directing the to-camera interviews" of John Grierson's *Housing Problems* (1935). Ruby also codirected *To-day We Live* (1937), a documentary about unemployment.

Marion Grierson worked for the Empire Marketing Board Film Unit, a pioneering documentary production group of the 1930s. In 1933, Marion Grierson directed *So This Is London. So This Is London* achieved international fame because of Marion Grierson's unflinchingly realistic approach to documentary journalism, yet she is almost completely forgotten in most histories of the British documentary movement. In 1935, she presided over the Associated Realist Film Producers, an independent production company formed by the British government. She directed many documentaries, including *London on Parade* (1938) and *Around the Village Green* (1937), which she codirected with Evelyn Spice, another forgotten woman director.

Marion and Ruby Grierson deserve to be reintegrated into a revisionist version of British film history. Their participation has been obscured by their brother's brilliant career. Perhaps the three Griersons should share credit as the founders of the British documentary movement. It is not surprising to uncover women filmmakers' contributions in this area. The movement's ideological support of social reform certainly shares common goals with the feminist movement.

SELECTED FILMOGRAPHY

So This Is London (1933)
To-day We Live (codirector) (1937)
Around the Village Green (codirector Evelyn Spice) (1937)
London on Parade (1938)

SELECTED BIBLIOGRAPHY

Forsyth, Hardy, ed. *Grierson on Documentary.* New York: Praeger, 1977.

Gifford, Denis. *British Film Catalogue, 1895–1970: A Reference Guide.* New York: McGraw-Hill, 1973.

Low, Rachel. *The History of British Film: 1929–1939, Filmmaking in 1930s Britain.* London: Allen and Unwin, 1985.

MacPherson, Dan, ed. *British Cinema: Tradition of Independence.* London: BFI, 1980.

Paskin, Sylvia, and Annette Kuhn. "British Documentary Movement." In *The Women's Companion to International Film,* edited by Annette Kuhn, with Susannah Radstone, 55. Berkeley: University of California Press, 1994.

GUSNER, IRIS (1941–   ). Germany. One of the very few women directors to work in East Germany before reunification, Iris Gusner was born in Trantenau in the (then) Soviet Union. She studied film in Moscow in the 1960s and worked for GDR television in the early 1970s. In 1972, she began directing feature films for DEFA Films, where she continued to work for many years. It is difficult to assess the career of Iris Gusner, because her films have not been distributed outside Germany, and little has been written about her work. According to Barbara Einhorn, Gusner's *All My Girls* (1979) and *If the Earth Wasn't Round* (1980–81) exude a "feminist perspective" (183–84).

All My Girls is a fictionalized, documentary-like film about the lives of five young women factory workers. *All My Girls* is based on the nonfictional lives of women workers at a NARVA factory. The women's lives are idealized in Gusner's film. Sigrun D. Leonhard characterizes Gusner's work as "unsuccessful" (65). Gusner's films perhaps suffered from a glossed-over inauthenticity found in many East German government-sponsored films of the period. Many of Gusner's films are love stories. Perhaps Gusner's aspirations as a filmmaker do not meet with critical approval because of her interest in escapist romanticism.

Women writers and filmmakers have been traditionally dismissed for their seemingly apolitical, romantic plots. Recently, feminist critics are revising the canonical exclusion of women romance novels and films. Romance films often display a dialogic voice that, on one hand, supports the status quo but, on the other hand, finds ways to subvert gender codes. Perhaps a full reconsideration of the films of Iris Gusner is overdue. The critical dismissal of Iris Gusner and Ingemo Engström, another German woman director of romance films, seems harsh and perhaps unwarranted.

SELECTED FILMOGRAPHY

Die Taube auf dem Dach (The Dove on the Roof) (1972–73)

Was halten Sie von Leuten, die malen? (What Do You Think of People Who Paint?) (1974)

Das blaue Licht (The Blue Light) (1975–76)

Man nennt mich jetzt Mimi . . . (They Call Me Mimi Now . . .) (1976)

Einer muss die Leiche sein (Someone Has to Be the Corpse) (1977)

Alle meine Maedchen (All My Girls) (1979)

Waere die Erde nicht rund . . . (If the Earth Wasn't Round) (1980–81)

Kaskade rueckwaerts (Backwards Somersault) (1985–86)
Ich liebe dich April, April (April, April, I Love You) (1987–88)

SELECTED BIBLIOGRAPHY

Einhorn, Barbara. "Gusner, Iris." In *The Women's Companion to International Film,* edited by Annette Kuhn, with Susannah Radstone, 183–84. Berkeley: University of California Press, 1994.

Kuhn, Annette, ed., *The Sexual Subject: A Screen Reader in Sexuality.* London: Routledge, 1992.

Leonhard, Sigrun D. "Testing the Borders: East German Film between Individualism and Social Commitment." In *Post New Wave Cinema in the Soviet Union and Eastern Europe,* 51–101. Bloomington: Indiana University Press, 1989.

Mellor, Ann K. *Romanticism and Gender.* New York: Routledge, 1993.

Radway, Janice. *Reading the Romance: Women, Patriarchy and Popular Literature.* Chapel Hill: University of North Carolina Press, 1984.

GUY, ALICE (Alice Guy-Blaché) (1873–1968). France/United States. The most inexcusable erasure from film history is that of Alice Guy, one of the inventors of the narrative film. Her astounding body of work went unnoticed until feminist historians began to reintegrate her life work into film history and scholarship, but Alice Guy is still omitted from classroom texts and most film histories. Though many of her films have been screened at retrospectives and women's film festivals, some critics continue to relegate her to the status of "house stylist" of Gaumont studios, which she built with Leon Gaumont. Guy is a truly exceptional pioneer of early French and American cinema. She contributed to the aesthetics and technical achievements of early cinema in many areas. She is also credited with the introduction of the feature film in America.

Guy appears to have had a feminist attitude toward work. In an interview with Harvey Gates in 1912, she spoke out against sexist treatment of women:

Women are commonly in a state of dependence . . . art is practically the only field open to them . . . so long as a woman remains in what they term "her place" she suffers little vexation. Yet let her assume the prerogatives usually accorded to her brothers and she is frowned upon. . . . I have a right to be where I am. It is a constant conflict when a woman in a French studio attempts to handle and superintend men in their work. Alice Guy was nevertheless very successful in working with men, despite sexism in the film industry.

Alice Guy was born in Paris in 1873. She was raised by a middle-class family, the youngest of four daughters of a bookseller. Educated at a convent in Switzerland, she was hired as a secretary by Leon Gaumont. Not very long afterward, she began to take on more duties at the studio. In fact, she later helped her employer build the first Gaumont studio in France. Gaumont experimented with moving cameras and projectors, eventually

building a 35mm (standard theatrical gauge) camera combined with a pro-
jector. Then Leon Gaumont designed and built an inexpensive machine for
projection only, which was to be aimed at other distributors in the industry.
Alice Guy worked closely with him on these projects. Her first stabs at
direction were instructional films, newsreels, and other short subjects,
meant for advertising, promotion, and demonstrational purposes. Gaumont
was interested only in technique. Guy was the artistic side of the partnership.

In 1896, Alice Guy directed *La Fée aux Choux,* probably the world's
first film with a plot. Described as a picture postcard that springs to life,
the film tells the story of a woman who grows children in a cabbage patch.
Alice Guy shot the film with the help of her friend Yvonne Mugnier-Serand,
in the garden of Gaumont's house, with a few back-drops for sets and the
help of some friends as actors. The film displayed the French style of light
humor and an appreciation for magic and the fantastic, similar to that of
Méliès and other early French film directors.

After her first narrative film, Guy began to make films with well-known
French opera singers and clowns. She tackled many different genres: fairy
tales, fantasy films, horror films, comedies, and trick films, making dozens
of films for Gaumont. For example, in her 1904 film *The First Cigarette,*
or *La Première Cigarette,* she was already using close-ups to heighten dramatic effects. She also included "reaction" shots, that is, shots showing
actors reacting to one another. In another short film, *Pierrot's Christmas,*
she used novel cinematic devices such as "masking" and "double exposure."

One of the most famous works that Alice Guy directed during her early
years was *La vie du Christ* (1905), an ambitious production that utilized
a lavish budget, large crew, and hundreds of extras, in settings designed
and executed by Henry Menessier. *La vie du Christ* was made specifically
to compete with the Pathe release of the same name. Alice Guy managed
to skillfully incorporate the use of extras to give added depth to her work,
the same way that the American director D. W. Griffith did many years
later in *Birth of a Nation* (1915) and *Intolerance* (1916). Under Gaumont's
supervision, Alice Guy also went on to direct many of the earliest sound
films. Gaumont invented a device that recorded sound on wax cylinders,
called the Chronophone. It worked by recording sound synchronously with
the camera's recording of the visuals. During 1906 and 1907, Guy directed
at least a hundred of these new "talking pictures."

Around this time Alice Guy started to hire more directors to keep up
with the output at Gaumont studios. She hired Ferdinand Zecca, who later
became a well-known French director, as her assistant. Guy could no longer
handle the whole production end of Gaumont single-handedly. She also
signed on Henry Menessier as permanent set designer, Victorin Jasset as
production manager, and, later, Louis Feuillade as a scriptwriter. It is ironic

that no more than a century later, film historians forgot the contribution of Alice Guy but remembered everyone she hired and even misattributed her films to them.

On an expedition to film a bullfight sequence in Nîmes, France, Alice Guy met her future husband, Herbert Blaché, an English cameraman. They were married in 1906, on Christmas. The newlyweds moved to New York to run Gaumont's American production office. Alice Guy took two years off to have children, but by 1910 she was eager to return to work. She formed her own company, Solax, which was registered in the United States in 1910, with Alice Guy as president. Solax was to turn out over 300 releases between 1910 and 1914, all of them supervised by Alice Guy. Located first in Flushing, Long Island, in New York, the company then moved to Fort Lee, New Jersey, where the beginnings of the studio system were forming their roots.

With Herbert Blaché in charge of Gaumont's New York office, Alice Guy had access to the technical facilities Gaumont had to offer, and she made full use of them. She also had access to Gaumont's American clients, who distributed her Solax films. The first Solax production, *A Child's Sacrifice* (1910), starred Magda Foy. It was a touching feminist melodrama. Perhaps one of the reasons Guy's films have been lost to history is her distinct style of direction. Guy's films are highly theatrical, and film critics have traditionally despised theatricality. Guy's use of deep-focus photography, lush, expensive sets, and theatrical subjects may have been ahead of its time. Those same qualities were later revered in the work of Max Ophuls and Ernst Lubitch. Alice Guy was fond of literary classics, which she adapted to the screen, including Victor Hugo's *Notre-Dame de Paris,* which Guy adapted for the screen as *La Esmeralda* (1905). Guy's notable literary tastes may have had some influence on her historical reception. Though popular in their time, literary adaptations have never been particularly appealing to cinema critics.

Many of Alice Guy's films are lost, but a few survive. Several Solax films directed by her are held in the Museum of Modern Art Film Library and the National Archives in Washington, D.C. *A House Divided* (1913) is the best-known surviving film of Guy's Solax productions. She uses intercutting to tell this comic narrative about a couple who refuse to communicate with one another, except through notes. The plot hinges on a number of coincidences that lead the couple to suspect one another of infidelity. *A House Divided* is a forerunner of the television situation comedy. Lis Rhodes and Felicity Sparrow note that *A House Divided* "plays upon the woman's independence within dependency, and the husband's apparent independence" (424).

The Girl in the Armchair (1912) is technically visceral, with color tinting and cinematic "tricks." It contains a dream sequence in which a young man sees swirling playing cards superimposed around his bed. *Officer Hen-*

derson (1912) is a gender-bending crime thriller in which two police officers cross-dress in order to arrest would-be sexual harassers. Most of the surviving Solax films directed by Guy are lighthearted feminist critiques of the institution of marriage; however, it would be unfair to characterize Guy as a "woman's film" director, because she made films in all genres. Many of the titles of Guy's "lost" films suggest that they may have been female-centered narratives. *A Daughter of the Navajos* (1911), *The Girl and the Bronco Busters* (1911), *The Woman of Mystery* (1914), and *The Heart of a Painted Woman* (1915) appear to have had central women subjects. Guy's horror films, such as *The Pit and the Pendulum* (1913), *The Vampire* (1915), and *The Monster and the Girl* (1914), may have been extraordinary, both from a cinematic perspective and from a feminist perspective.

The long list of directors who had an important impact on the development of the silent film is quite extensive, with each director's adding to the literature of the cinema his or her own particular, personal stylistic signature. Certainly, among those names should be the name of Alice Guy. She received the French Legion of Honor in 1953 in Paris, her native city. This televised clip was broadcast in the ceremony of the Society of Authors and Composers. Finally, at age seventy-eight, Guy was duly credited for her contributions to film history. Henri Langlois of the Cinematheque Française and a handful of interested film historians and journalists made this possible. Guy herself fiercely tried to correct historians with regard to the importance of her career. She died in Mahwah, New Jersey, in 1968.

Alice Guy was, above all, an innovator, a person whose work figured decisively in the history of the motion picture. Even though her name has entered the canon of film history, she still has not been given the critical or historical attention that is due a figure of her unquestioned stature. She was recently included in a traveling exhibit of the history of French cinema sponsored by Gaumont. The exhibit included a handful of Guy's early films. She was also honored by the Creiteile Women's Film Festival in France in 1994. *The Making of an American Citizen* (1912) is included in a recent video history of early cinema. There are a few documentaries in progress on the life and work of Alice Guy. Her films are also included in a video I wrote, directed, and produced with Wheeler Winston Dixon, called *The Women Who Made the Movies*. Alice Guy's own memoirs are insightful. The only book-length study on Guy, *Alice Guy-Blaché,* by Victor Bachy, is in French. Alice Guy's films are held in international archives such as the Gaumont Archive, the Cinémathèque Française, and the Museum of Modern Art Film Library. *The Pit and the Pendulum* is held in the National Archives of Film in Ottawa, and *Beasts of the Jungle* remains in the George Eastman House in Rochester, New York. It will no doubt take decades to restore and retrieve the films of Alice Guy, but her legacy as the first feminist of the cinema is unsurpassable. As interest in film "herstory" grows, no doubt more Alice Guy films will be rediscovered. Guy is survived by a daughter, Simone Blaché.

SELECTED FILMOGRAPHY

French releases

La Fée aux Choux (1896)
Au bal de flore (1896)
La Danse des Saisons (1900)
Hussards et grisettes (1901)
Sage-fenne de première class (1902)
Le Voleur Sacrilège (1903)
Les Petits Coupeurs de bois vert (1904)
La Courrier de Lyon (1904)
Paris la nuit (1904)
Le Crime de la rue du Temple (1904)
Une noce au lac Saint-Fargeau (1905)
Trist fin d'un vieux savant (1905)
La Vie du Christ (1905)
La Esmeralda (1905)

U.S. releases

A Child's Sacrifice (1910)
The Violin Maker of Nuremberg (1910)
Rose of the Frontier (1911)
Across the Mexican Line (1911)
A Daughter of the Navajos (1911)
The Silent Signal (1911)
The Girl and the Bronco Busters (1911)
The Mascot of Troop "C" (1911)
The Enlisted Man's Honor (1911)
The Stampede (1911)
The Holdup (1911)
The Alerted Message (1911)
His Sister's Sweetheart (1911)
A Revolutionary Romance (1911)
Greater Love Hath No Man (1911)
A Detective's Dog (1912)
Canned Harmony (1912)
The Girl in the Armchair (1912)
The Making of an American Citizen (1912)
The Call of the Rose (1912)
Winsome But Wise (1912)
His Lordship's White Father (1912)
Falling Leaves (1912)
The Sewer (1912)
In the Year 2000 (1912)
A Terrible Night (1912)
Mickey's Pal (1912)
Fra Diavolo (1912)
Hotel Honeymoon (1912)
The Equine Spy (1912)
Two Little Rangers (1912)

The Bloodstain (1912)
At the Phone (1912)
Flesh and Blood (1912)
The Paralytic (1912)
The Face at the Window (1912)
The Mysteries of Paris (or *The Child of Fate*) (1913)
A House Divided (1913)
Matrimony's Speed Limit (1913)
Beasts of the Jungle (1913)
The Rogues of Paris (1913)
Dick Whittington and His Cat (1913)
Kelly from the Emerald Isle (1913)
The Pit and the Pendulum (1913)
Western Love (1913)
Blood and Water (1913)
Ben Bolt (1913)
The Prisoner in the Harem (1913)
The Fortune Hunters (1913)
The Eyes That Could Not Close (1913)
The Tigriss (1913)
The Shadows of the Moulin Rouge (1914)
The Woman of Mystery (1914)
The Monster and the Girl (1914)
The Dream Woman (1914)
Beneath the Czar (1914)
The Million Dollar Robbery (1914)
Hood and Hand (1914)
The Yellow Traffic (1914)
The Lure (1914)
The Heart of a Painted Woman (1915)
My Madonna (1915)
The Vampire (1915)
Barbara Frietschie (1915)
What Will People Say? (1916)
The Girl with the Green Eyes (1916)
The Ocean Waif (1916)
The Empress (1917)
The Adventurer (1917)
A Man and the Woman (1917)
When You and I Were Young (1917)
The House of Cards (1917)
A Soul Adrift (1918)
The Great Adventure (1918)
Tarnished Reputations (1920)

SELECTED BIBLIOGRAPHY

Abel, Richard. *The Ciné Goes to Town: French Cinema 1896–1914*. Berkeley: University of California Press, 1994.
Acker, Ally. *Reel Women: Pioneers of the Cinema*. New York: Continuum, 1991.

Bachy, Victor. *Alice Guy-Blaché (1873–1968), La Première Femme Cinéaste du Monde.* Perpignan: Institut Jean Vigo, 1993.

Bowser, Eileen. *History of the American Cinema 2: The Transformation of Cinema.* New York: Scribner's, 1990.

Dixon, Wheeler Winston. "Alice Guy: Forgotten Pioneer of the Narrative Cinema." *New Orleans Review* 19.3–4 (fall–winter 1992): 7–15.

Flitterman-Lewis, Sandy. *To Desire Differently: Feminism and the French Cinema.* Urbana: University of Illinois Press, 1990.

Foster, Gwendolyn, and Wheeler Winston Dixon. *The Women Who Made the Movies.* New York: Women Make Movies, Inc., 1991. Video.

Gates, Harvey. "Alice Blaché: A Dominant Figure in Pictures." *New York Dramatic Mirror* (November 6, 1912): 28.

———. *The Memoirs of Alice Guy-Blaché.* Edited by Anthony Slide. Translated by Roberta and Simone Blaché. Metuchen, NJ: Scarecrow Press, 1986.

Hayward, Susan. "A History of French Cinema: 1895–1991: Pioneering Film-Makers (Guy, Dulac, Varda) and Their Heritage." *Paragraph* 15.1 (March 1992): 19–37.

Heck-Rabi, Louise. *Women Filmmakers: A Critical Reception.* Metuchen, NJ: Scarecrow Press, 1984.

Lacassin, Francis. "Out of Oblivion: Alice Guy-Blaché, *Sight and Sound* 40.3 (summer 1971): 151–54.

Maggliozzi, Ronald. *Treasures from the Film Archives.* Metuchen, NJ.: Scarecrow Press, 1988.

Rhodes, Lis, and Felicity Sparrow. "Her Image Fades As Her Voice Rises." In *Multiple Voices in Feminist Film Criticism,* edited by Diane Carson, Linda Dittmar, and Janice Welsch, 421–31. Minneapolis: University of Minnesota Press, 1994.

Slide, Anthony. *Early Women Directors.* New York: Da Capo, 1984.

Vincendeau, Ginette. "Feminism and French Cinema." *Screen* 31.4 (winter 1990): 454–57.

Williams, Alan. *Republic of Images: A History of French Filmmaking.* Cambridge: Harvard University Press, 1992.

H

HAENSEL, MARION (1952–   ). **France.** French filmmaker Marion Haensel was a successful actress before she became a film director. She studied at the Lee Strasberg Actor's Studio in New York but returned to Europe, settling in Belgium. Her film *Le Lit* (1982) centers on a wife's deathbed vigil for her husband and is a deeply felt study of the ties that have bound the couple together, using expressionist lighting and sparing mise-en-scène to create a compelling vision of a shared existence.

Dust (1984) is a brutal and efficient thriller that stars Trevor Howard and Jane Birkin. In *Dust,* Birkin's character murders her father for seducing one of the black servants on their South African ranch. The film is shot in a dry, near-documentary style. Birkin, who at one time had been a European pop star, emerges as a forceful screen presence, able to hold her own opposite veteran actor Howard. There is nothing sentimental about *Dust,* and the film moves forward with the inexorable assurance of a Greek tragedy. *Dust* is based on the novel by J. M. Coetzee. It is compared with *Chocolat,* Clair Denis's study of postcolonialism. In her final film to date, *Les noches barbares* (*The Cruel Embrace*) (1987), Haensel explores the flip side of the same familial obsession. A mother is murdered by her son because she is unable to care for him anymore after he has been raped. Haensel's world is usually brutal and cruel. Whether discussing apartheid in South Africa or dealing with rape and the dialectic of barbarism within the home, Haensel's cinematography is stark, unsentimental, and arched. The horrible events that overtake the destinies of her protagonists are seen as being beyond any mortal control. She seems to accept the brutality enforced upon women and men through the discourse of the human condition, but this acceptance is tempered with bitterness, feminism, and postcolonial aesthetics. In her view of human social discourse, Haensel is not unlike Rainer Werner Fassbinder, whose characters are trapped by codes of behavior that they neither shape nor comprehend.

Before directing the features upon which her principal reputation rests,

Haensel directed several short films in the late 1970s before breaking into feature production with *Le Lit*. Reflecting her work as an actress, Haensel is unusually sympathetic to the demands placed upon her actors by the difficult characters they portray and uses her training from the Strasberg school to bring out naturalistic performances from her actors. Her voice is an original, independent, and vibrant counterpart to the incessant, artificial optimism encoded in the dominant commercial French cinema.

SELECTED FILMOGRAPHY

Equilibre (1977)
Sannu Bature (1979)
Gongola (1979)
Hydraulip II (1979)
Bakh (1979)
Le Lit (*The Bed*) (1982)
Dust (1984)
Les noces barbares (*The Cruel Embrace*) (1987)

SELECTED BIBLIOGRAPHY

Kaplan, E. Ann. *Women & Film: Both Sides of the Camera*. New York: Methuen, 1983.
Kino International. *Kino International Nontheatrical Catalogue*. New York: Kino International, 1994.
Mayne, Judith. *The Woman at the Keyhole: Feminism and Women's Cinema*. Bloomington: Indiana University Press, 1990.
Quart, Barbara. *Women Directors: The Emergence of a New Cinema*. New York: Praeger, 1988.

HAMMER, BARBARA (1939–   ). United States. Experimental, independent, lesbian filmmaker Barbara Hammer is responsible for the most substantial oeuvre of lesbian feminist films. Surprisingly, Hammer did not start directing film until the age of twenty-eight. Her background is in psychology, art, and English literature. In 1961, she graduated from the University of California—Los Angeles with a B.A. in psychology. She immediately began painting and teaching at Marin County Juvenile Hall. She earned her first master's degree in English literature at San Francisco State. In 1967, she began shooting her first film, *Schizy,* an autobiographical diary film about her coming out and leaving a heterosexual lifestyle. She left her husband and toured Africa by motorcycle with her new partner. She taught in Germany and then decided to return to graduate school to study film at San Francisco State University, where she earned her second master's degree in 1975.

At San Francisco State, Hammer made her first 16mm film, *I Was/I Am* (1973). The film reenacts Hammer's coming out, showing her in a "feminine" gown wearing a crown and then as a "motorcycle dyke." In these early films, Hammer was directly influenced by the dream imagery of pioneering feminist filmmaker Maya Deren. Hammer was bowled over when first she saw Deren's films. "I knew there was a cinema for me to make . . . because I thought that the content that we have to express, as women, hasn't fully been explored," Hammer told Yann Beauvais (34). Hammer immersed herself in film and feminist film theory. She made thirteen films while studying for her master's degree. Her thesis, "The Phenomenology of Feminist Films," is an analysis of lesbian representation in the cinema. Her films are not only films of lesbian representation but philosophical studies of representation of the body. She was connected to women filmmakers like Jan Oxenberg, Gunvor Nelson, and Barbara Linkletter, who were also making films about the female body and representation. The act of "women filming women" raised a number of philosophical questions and concerns. How could women directors avoid the objectifying male gaze that they saw in the work of male underground filmmakers? Hammer worked out transgressive representational techniques that sought to answer this question, theoretically and formally. In many of her films she uses images of herself, often shooting her own naked image into a mirror, which is a successful gesture that displaces the objectifying eye. Hammer's films avoid pornographic representation through their dreamlike incorporation of superimpositions of nature imagery, goddess imagery, and montage editing.

As Richard Dyer explains, Hammer's work explores four main theoretical concerns: "autobiography, sexuality, lesbian collectivity and spirituality/nature" (194). I would add that these four themes are always manifested in a larger thematic context, the phenomenology of the body in cinematic representation. *Dyketactics* (1974), *X* (1974), *Women I Love* (1976), and *Double Strength* (1978) loosely fall into the category of diary films of lesbian sexualities. Hammer's erotic films were some of the first images of lesbian lovemaking made by and for lesbian spectators. Films such as *Dyketactics* and Jan Oxenberg's *Home Movie* (1972) were some of the first "conscious attempts to address a specifically lesbian audience" (Weiss, 139). Members of the radical feminist lesbian community wished to protect these images from male "appropriation"; thus, the films were frequently screened in women-only spaces. As a cultural feminist, Hammer began to move beyond radical separatism, however, as she explored ancient goddess religions and alternative forms of female power.

In films such as *Women's Rites* (1974), *Moon Goddess* (1976), *The Great Goddess* (1977), *Sappho* (1978), and *Stone Circles* (1983), Hammer exudes a dedication to ecofeminism and goddess imagery, myth, and ritual. *Women's Rites* is a ritual film which includes chanting and regenerative autumn rituals. *Moon Goddess,* made with Gloria Churchwoman, is a celebration of Native American goddess imagery. In the film, two women are guided by moon power in a spiritually desolate desert area. *The Great Goddess* (1977) was filmed in Mendocino, California, where the water snake, a female symbol, appeared every day during shooting. In this spiritual healing film, three crones spin spirals in a ritual that symbolizes birth, death, and rebirth. Hammer traveled on a pilgrimage to film Druid ruins in England for *Stone Circles* (1983). In the film, she used pixilation, rephotography emphasizing the stopped freeze frame, and rhythmic editing of images of 5,000 stone circle formations from the days of early goddess worship. The mesmerizing sound track evokes Neolithic voices through percussion and Celtic melody. *Sappho* is a reclamation of the sixth-century lesbian poet.

One of Hammer's best-known works in *Multiple Orgasm* (1977). The film shows a woman during masturbation. Hammer appears as the filmmaker subject/object of her own gazing camera, using a hand-held camera. As E. Ann Kaplan notes, *Multiple Orgasm* conveys "female ecstasy through diffusive sound and landscape images superimposed on the clitoris" (89). As Hammer said about her conception of the film, "[T]he reason why I made the film was I had never seen myself have an orgasm and I wanted to put what women hadn't shown before on the screen. I made the film for myself and not to be ashamed or to cover my part of the body" (Beauvais, 36). Hammer's films grew out of a need for lesbian representation and naming. Her more recent works are more formal in nature. As she wrote recently in *Queer Looks,* "[O]nce named, and identities established as artist and lesbian, I wanted to get on with other areas of expression that I had left unexplored" (73). *Optic Nerve* (1985) was Hammer's first film made entirely in an optical printer. The film is a meditation on footage she shot when she visited her grandmother in a nursing home. John Hanhardt, film curator of the Whitney Museum of American Art, commented on *Optic Nerve:*

The sense of sight becomes a constantly evolving process of reseeing images retrieved from the past and fused into the eternal present of the projected image. Hammer has lent a new voice to the long tradition of personal meditation in the avant-garde of the American independent cinema. (Canyon Cinema, 154)

Barbara Hammer's work has been screened at the Whitney Museum, the Festival des Films des Femmes, Creteil France, the Ann Arbor Film Festival, many women's International Film Festivals, and numerous lesbian and gay film festivals. Recently, she has begun to work in video with *Snow Job: The Media Hysteria of AIDS* (1989). *Snow Job* is a performance art piece that uses multiple video monitors and film projection. In 1985, Hammer accepted her first full-time teaching position at Columbia College in Chicago. She also taught at Evergreen State College in Olympia, Washington. However, she has now returned to New York to pursue her film/video career. Her most recent films include *Hot Flash* (1989), a study of menopause, *The History of the World according to a Lesbian* (1988), a lesbian feminist vision of history that culminates in the music of the Seattle-based band Sluts from Hell. *Still Point* (1989), which won the Women in Film Award at the 1990 Atlanta Film/Video Festival, is a study of homelessness. *Sanctus* (1990) and *Vital Signs* (1991) are experimental, manipulated images from found footage. In *Vital Signs,* winner of the Grand Prize at the Black Maria Film Festival, Hammer used archival X-ray footage in *Sanctus* and clips from Alain Resnais's *Hiroshima Mon Amour* intertwined with Michel Foucault's text *The Birth of a Clinic.* Hammer is one of the dominant voices in American experimental filmmaking.

Barbara Hammer continues to have a visionary spirit. She told Ellen Meyers and Toni Armstrong, Jr. of her utopic dream: "If I had a mega-budget, I think I would set up a film school for women of difference; lesbian women, women of color, physically challenged women, old women, children . . . we need to be strong in accepting difference, different voices, different work" (44). Appropriately enough, Barbara Hammer's *Nitrite Kisses* (1993) concerns female knowledge and the history of lesbian representation. Hammer is a highly visible and outspoken radical lesbian feminist artist. Her early work is currently the subject of several retrospectives of international film festivals and showcases.

SELECTED FILMOGRAPHY

Schizy (1967)
A Gay Day (1973)
Sisters! (1973)
Jane Brakhage (1974)
Menses (1974)
Women's Rites or Truth Is the Daughter of Time (1974)
X (1974)
Dyketactics (1974)
Women's Rites (1974)
Psychosynthesis (1975)
Superdyke (1975)
Moon Goddess (1976)
Women I Love (1976)
The Great Goddess (1977)
Multiple Orgasm (1977)
Double Strength (1978)
Haircut (1978)
The Great Goddess (1978)
Sappho (1978)
Eggs (1978)
Home (1978)
Available Space (1979)
Dream Age (1979)
Our Trip (1980)
Arequipa (1981)
The Lesbos Film (1981)

Machu Picchu (1981)
Pictures for Barbara (1981)
Pools (1981)
Synch Touch (1981)
Audience (1982)
Pond and Waterfall (1982)
Bent Time (1983)
New York Loft (1983)
Stone Circles (1983)
Doll House (1984)
Parisian Blinds (1984)
Pearl Diver (1984)
Tourist (1984–85)
Optic Nerve (1985)
Place Mattes (1987)
No No Nooky T.V. (1987)
Two Bad Daughters (1988)
Endangered (1988)
The History of the World according to a Lesbian (1988)
Still Point (1989)
Snow Job (1989)
Hot Flash (1989)
Sanctus (1990)
Vital Signs (1991)
Nitrite Kisses (1993)

SELECTED BIBLIOGRAPHY

Beauvais, Yann. "Interview with Barbara Hammer." *Spiral* 6 (January 1986): 33–
    38.
Canyon Cinema. *Canyon Cinema Catalogue 7*. San Francisco: Canyon Cinema
    Collective, 1992.
Dargis, Manohla. "Trying to Mix It Up." *Village Voice* (March 16, 1993): 37.
de Lauretis, Teresa. *Alice Doesn't: Feminism, Semiotics, Cinema*. Bloomington: In-
    diana University Press, 1984.
Dyer, Richard. *Now You See It: Studies on Lesbian and Gay Film*. London: Rout-
    ledge, 1990.
Film-Makers' Cooperative. *Film-Makers' Cooperative Catalogue 7*. New York:
    Film-Makers' Cooperative, 1989.
Hammer, Barbara. "The Politics of Abstraction." In *Queer Looks: Perspectives on
    Lesbian and Gay Film and Video,* edited by Pratibha Parmar, Martha Gever,
    and John Greyson, 70–75. New York: Routledge, 1993.
Kaplan, E. Ann. *Women & Film: Both Sides of the Camera*. New York: Methuen,
    1983.
Meyers, Ellen, and Toni Armstrong, Jr. "A Visionary Woman Creating Visions:
    Barbara Hammer." *Hot Wire* 7.2 (May 1991): 42–44.
Rich, B. Ruby. "Reflections of a Queer Screen." *Journal of Lesbian and Gay Studies*
    1.1 (1993): 83–91.

Springer, Gregory. "Barbara Hammer: The Leading Lesbian behind the Lens." *Advocate* (February 7, 1980): 29, 35.

Weiss, Andrea. *Vampires and Violets: Lesbians in Film*. New York: Penguin, 1993.

Women Make Movies. *Women Make Movies Catalogue*. New York: Women Make Movies, Inc., 1994.

Zita, Jacqueline. "Counter Currencies of a Lesbian Iconography: The Films of Barbara Hammer." *Jump Cut* 24 (1981): 26–30.

HARRIS, LESLIE (1959–   ). United States. Leslie Harris is an important new African-American woman filmmaker. Born and raised in Ohio, she has a background in art and cinema studies. She earned an M.F.A. in painting and moved to New York to break into the advertising business. Harris was unfulfilled in her job and began to write a screenplay for *Just Another Girl on the IRT* (1993). Motivated by her anger at the media's predominantly negative images of black youth, Harris wished to make a new kind of hip-hop film, a female-centered, positive film. Many people discouraged Harris, saying that a feature film was too ambitious, but she found support from Women Make Movies, Inc., which provided her with an emerging-artist's grant. *Just Another Girl* was shot on a shoestring budget in eleven days. She ran out of money and had no food, only film, in her refrigerator. Finally, she found finishing funds through Miramax Films, NEA, and the Jerome Foundation.

Just Another Girl is a refreshing look at female hip-hop culture. Karen Alexander calls Harris's film "the first hip-hop film where black women are not mere sexual sideshows or threats to black manhood" (224). Chantal, the film's protagonist, played by Ariyan Johnson, is a determined seventeen-year-old, who narrates her own story. *Just Another Girl* manages to teach by example and remain entertaining by allowing Chantal to matter-of-factly tell her story. "I wanted to give people a different insight, to make a film from the perspective of a seventeen-year-old-girl," Harris told Amy Taubin. Harris is a gifted storyteller, with a flair for narrative technique. When Chantal speaks directly to the camera/audience, Harris draws upon a postmodern denial of the theatrical convention of the fourth wall. (Sally Potter uses the same technique in *Orlando*.) Chantal is brutally honest with the viewer, and it makes you feel as if you know her. The ending of the film is gloriously unrealistic, but just as plausible as the events in *Sleepless in Seattle*. Chantal returns to college, her boyfriend becomes an active father, and Chantal is obviously going to make her dreams come true. *Just Another Girl on the IRT* is a revision of black female experience. It is equal parts realism (a gruesome birth scene) and fantasy (a happy ending). As bell hooks notes, filmmakers such as Julie Dash and Leslie Harris "act to intervene and transform conventional filmic practices, changing notions of spectatorship . . . opening up a space for black female spectatorship. They imagine new transgressive possibilities for the formulation of identity" (130). Like her African-American male counterparts, such as Spike Lee, John Singleton, and Matty Rich, Leslie Harris promises to become a major force in commercial cinema. Harris has a new screenplay, *Royalties, Rhythm and Blues,* a film about a woman hip-hop producer, which she hopes to begin shooting in the near future.

SELECTED FILMOGRAPHY

Just Another Girl on the IRT (1993)

SELECTED BIBLIOGRAPHY

Alexander, Karen. "Julie Dash: 'Daughters of the Dust' and a Black Aesthetic." In *Women in Film: A Sight and Sound Reader,* edited by Pam Cook and Philip Dodd, 224–31. Philadelphia: Temple University Press, 1993.
Coleman, Beth. "She's Gotta Do It." *Village Voice* 38. 12 (March 23, 1993): 58–60.
hooks, bell. *Black Looks: Race and Representation.* Boston: South End Press, 1992.
Larkin, Alile Sharon. "Black Women Filmmakers Refining Ourselves: Feminism in Our Own Voice." In *Female Spectators: Looking at Film and Video,* edited by E. Deidre Pribram, 157–73. London: Verso, 1988.
Phillips, Julie. "Growing Up Black and Female: Leslie Harris's *Just Another Girl on the IRT.*" *Cineaste* 19.4 (1992): 86–87.
Stubbs, Frances, and Elizabeth Hadley Freydberg. "Black Women in American Films." In *Multiple Voices in Feminist Film Criticism,* edited by Diane Carson, Linda Dittmar, and Janice Welsch, 481–91. Minneapolis: University of Minnesota Press, 1994.
Tate, Greg. "Just Another Girl: Flygirl on Film." *Village Voice* 38.12 (March 23, 1993): 58.
Taubin, Amy. "Working Girls." *Village Voice* 47.68 (November 24, 1992): 68.

HECKERLING, AMY (1954–   ). United States. Amy Heckerling is a highly successful Hollywood director/writer who specializes in comedy. Born in New York City, she studied at New York University Film School and the American Film Institute. Heckerling then worked as a television editor, where she learned the required sense of timing needed for successful mainstream comedy formula films. Her first film, *Fast Times at Ridgemont High* (1982), is a parody of high school comedy films. *Fast Times* was remarkably well received and introduced talented young actors Sean Penn, Judge Reinhold, and Jennifer Jason Leigh to general audiences.

Amy Heckerling was almost killed in a car crash early in her career, which perhaps accounts for her incredible ability to endure the Hollywood system, which makes and breaks people's careers at will. Her screenplay *My Kind of Guy* was stuck for years in "turnaround" (preproduction) and was bounced from Warner Brothers to Universal to MGM, only to be ultimately dropped by all three studios. But her persistence is admirable. Rather than giving up on writing, she began working on the screenplay for

Look Who's Talking (1989), which eventually became a major commercial hit. While working on this script, Heckerling directed a rather clever gangster comedy, *Johnny Dangerously* (1984).

Johnny Dangerously stars Michael Keaton, Dom DeLouise, and Maureen Stapleton. In the film, an honest man turns into a criminal to pay for his mother's operations. The film is a clever homage to 1930s gangster films, but it was apparently too clever for a mainstream audience. Heckerling was offered the chance to direct *National Lampoon's European Vacation* (1985), a comedy starring Chevy Chase, but although she tried her best with a rather weak script, the film was not a box-office success. Heckerling finally directed *Look Who's Talking* in 1989, and the film became one of the biggest hits of the year and her most successful film since *Fast Times at Ridgemont High*. American audiences apparently have a soft spot for comedies that involve babies, as the success of *Three Men and a Baby* (director Leonard Nimoy, 1987) had amply proven. *Look Who's Talking* spawned a sequel film, *Look Who's Talking, Too* (1990), which Heckerling again directed.

Heckerling is most comfortable as a comedy director, comparable in some respects to Penelope Spheeris (*Wayne's World*, 1992; *The Little Rascals*, 1994). Married to writer/director Neal Israel, Heckerling is currently directing for television and directed several episodes of the television version of *Fast Times at Ridgemont High*. She is also a talented comedy writer, and her screenplays are highlighted by fast-paced, witty repartee and droll humor. Underneath the laughs, she often uses the comedy form to expose sexism, hypocrisy, and the absurdities of our American consumer-oriented lifestyle. Her freewheeling sense of comedy is in the tradition of Jerry Lewis and Frank Tashlin. She is able to find humor in the most mundane of events.

The success of the *Look Who's Talking* films is largely grounded in Heckerling's ability to incorporate subversive feminine humor in a mainstream project. While these films would seem to be no threat to suburban heterosexual values, they are actually quite successful in criticizing contemporary America's rather vapid suburban lifestyle. The use of a child/man's voice-over narrative (Bruce Willis supplied the baby's voice) is a clever manipulation of the audience's reaction to the baby's persona. No matter what the "child" says, it will be considered cute and clever. By using this narrative formula, Heckerling constructs a vehicle through which she can criticize middle-American values. Heckerling's newest film, *Clueless*, was released in the summer of 1995. Though her films superficially present themselves as "no brainers," they contain a number of sophisticated subtexts that multiple viewings render readily accessible.

SELECTED FILMOGRAPHY

Fast Times at Ridgemont High (1982)
Johnny Dangerously (1984)

National Lampoon's European Vacation (1985)
Look Who's Talking (1989)
Look Who's Talking, Too (1990)
Clueless (1995)

SELECTED BIBLIOGRAPHY

Cole, Janis, and Holly Dale. *Calling the Shots: Profiles of Women Filmmakers.*
     Ontario: Quarry Press, 1993.
Francke, Lizzie. "Men, Women, Children and the Baby Boom Movies." In *Women
     and Film: A Sight and Sound Reader,* edited by Pam Cook and Philip Dodd,
     148–54. Philadelphia: Temple University Press, 1993.
Jackson, Lynne, and Karen Jaehne. "Eavesdropping on Female Voices: A Who's
     Who of Contemporary Women Filmmakers." *Cineaste* 16.1–2 (1988): 38–
     43.
Mayne, Judith. *The Woman at the Keyhole: Feminism and Women's Cinema.* Bloo-
     mington: Indiana University Press, 1990.
Quart, Barbara. *Women Directors: The Emergence of a New Cinema.* New York:
     Praeger, 1988.
Singer, Michael. "From the Directors' Chair: An Interview with Amy Heckerling."
     In *Film Directors: A Complete Guide,* edited by Michael Singer, 23–33. Bev-
     erly Hills: Lone Eagle, 1987.

HEIN, BIRGIT (1942–   ). Germany. Birgit Hein and her husband, Wilhelm Hein, are radical experimental filmmakers who are known in international avant-garde circles. Their early work is strictly formalist in nature,
but their later work explores radical female sexuality. Birgit Hein was born
in West Germany in 1942. She studied art history and began collaborating
with Wilhelm Hein in the late 1960s. Though the couple insisted on fully
crediting one another's participation, the Heins noticed that critics tended
to attribute the couple's films to Wilhelm alone. This is a dominant trend
seen across the whole spectrum of heterosexual filmmaking teams; it is an
international problem and a historical problem that leads to the loss of
women directors' contributions in histories of film. Though Birgit continued to make films with her husband, she established an independent identity as an art historian and critic of experimental and avant-garde art and
film.

   In the 1960s, Birgit and Wilhelm Hein's films were screened with films
of the underground New York film movement. Like many other formalist
abstract artists, the Heins' approach to the cinema was an assault on form.
Techniques such as scratching, punching holes, and manipulating the camera shutter to produce expansion of the time frame were common underground filmmaking practices. *Rohfilm* (1968) and *S & W* (1967) are
assaults on the language of traditional cinema. *S & W* is compared with
the work of Bruce Conner, Taylor Mead, and Jonas Mekas. The Heins,
however, made no "conscious attempts to include recognizable emotional
or associative references in their work" (Curtis, 181). Birgit and Wilhelm

Hein make intentionally brutal collage films in which they employ hand scratching, sprocket holes, and other techniques that are inherently self-referential and purposefully difficult. *Grün* (1968) and *Rohfilm* (1968) are filmmakers' films that revel in abstraction. *Rohfilm* is best described as an overwhelming visual attack.

Over time, the films of Wilhelm and Birgit Hein became increasingly structural and theoretically based. In *625* (1969), the Heins experimented by shooting a television screen in multiple sequences at different gauges of frames per second. The film uses an optical illusion in which the eye misperceives the bar line repeatedly. *Work in Progress Teil A* (1969) is a six-part formalist experimental film. In the late 1970s, the Heins decided to turn the camera on themselves and their relationship. Their films are difficult, but they are profound in insights about female sexuality. Birgit Hein, whose work explores the dark nature of some forms of female sexuality, can be compared with Valie Export and Monika Treut. Hein, Export, and Treut subvert the definition of passive female sexuality. As Hein told Julia Knight, "[T]he fact that some feminists have argued that aggression is an emotion totally alien to women is an indication of how successful patriarchy has been in this repression" (162). Monika Treut portrays violent lesbian, aggressive female sexuality in *Seduction: The Cruel Woman* (1984–85). Birgit Hein portrays violent heterosexual, aggressive female sexuality in several of the Hein films, especially *The Kali Films* (1987–88).

Birgit Hein might be best described as a radical feminist heterosexual. Her work challenges feminist models of the past and demonstrates that women and men can explore female sexuality together as they disrupt dominant patriarchal notions of voyeurism. *Love Stinks* (1982) is one of the best-known Hein films that display this explosion of old narratives about women's sexuality. Hein, like Treut, is on the cutting edge of a new wave of films that reconstruct and deconstruct female sexuality. As Birgit Hein told Julia Knight:

The worst form of oppression which women have to suffer is their sexuality. The repression goes so deep that many women even willingly relinquish their sexuality. To win back desire, to show it in its total diversity and to break existing taboos is for me the most important task for contemporary women artists. (161)

Birgit and Wilhelm Hein first staked out a territory in experimental film form. Then they graduated from cold minimalist formalism to transgressive eroticism. Like the work of many performance artists, the Heins' grim and difficult films shock us into a state far from the time when the mind-body split placed the blame and guilt on men for lust and honored the woman for passivity and virginity. As Linda Williams notes, "[T]oday sexual pleasure is far too important a commodity for women not to seek it in their own desire and agency" (189). In their work, Birgit and Wilhelm Hein offer women a different identificatory model of sexual representation, particularly in the Kali films. These films transgress taboos of dominant culture, especially in heterosexuality. In the Kali films, women use guns and knives and attack and kill men, intercut with clips from horror movies and women's prison films. The filmmakers found the images attractive because they depicted violent, aggressive, sexually confident women in action. To some audiences, this is a completely offensive turnoff, but other women find the image of the sexually dominant female attractive. Birgit Hein's work with her husband will continue to provoke controversy, particularly in the current lively debate over issues such as pornography, female desire, and sadomasochism. As radical filmmakers of the most uncompromising sort, Birgit and Wilhelm Hein's work is at the forefront of a radically new approach to the cinema.

SELECTED FILMOGRAPHY

All films codirected with Wilhelm Hein

S & W (1967)
Ole (1967)
Und Sie? (1967)
Grün (1968)
Werbefilm Nr. 1: Bamberg (1968)
Rohfilm (1968)
Reproductions (1969)
625 (1969)
Square Dance (1969)
Work in Progress Teil A (1969)
Sichtbarmachung der Wirkungsweise optischer Gesetze am einfachen Beispiel (1969)
Work in Progress Teil B (1970)
Porträts (1970)
Auszüge aus einer Biographie (1970)
Madison/Wis (1970)
Replay (1970)
Foto-Film (1970)
Reproduktionsimmanente Ästhetik (1970)
Porträts. 4. Nina I-III (1971)
Autobahn. 2 Teile (1971)
Work in Progress Teil C (1971)
Work in Progress Teil D (1971)
Doppelprojektion I (1971)
I Want You to Be Rich (1971)
Altes Material (1971)
Zoom—lange Fassung (1971)
Zoom—kurze Fassung (1971)
Videotape I (1971)
Liebesgrüsse (1971)
Yes to Europe (1971)

Porträts. Kurt Schwitters I, II, III (1972)
Porträts (1972)
Doppelprojektionen II–V (1972)
Aufblenden (Abblenden) (1972)
Dokumentation (1972)
Fussball (1972)
Ausdatiertes Material (1973)
God Bless America (1973)
Stills (1973)
London (1973)
Zu Lucifer Rising von Kenneth Anger (1973)
Strukturelle Studien (1974)
Jack Smith (1974)
Künstlerfilme I (1974)
Künstlerfilme II (1974)
Porträts II (1975)
Materialfilme I (1976)
Materialfilme II (1976)
Porträts III (1977)
Kurt Kren. Porträat eines experimentellen Fulmmachers (1978)
Verdammt in alle Ewigkeit (1978–79)
Superman und Superwoman (1980)
Die Medien und das Bild. Andy Warhol's Kunst (1981)
Love Stinks—Bilder des täglichen Wahnsinns (1982)
American Graffiti (1982)
Verbotene Bilder (1984–85)
Die Kali-Filme (The Kali Films) (1987–88)

SELECTED BIBLIOGRAPHY

Curtis, David. *Experimental Cinema: A Fifty-Year Evolution*. New York: Delta, 1971.
Frieden, Sandra, and Richard McCormick, Vibeke R. Petersen, and Laurie Melissa Vogelsang, eds. *Gender and German Cinema, Feminist Interventions Vols. 1 and 2*. Oxford: Berg, 1993.
Hansen, Miriam. "Visual Pleasure, Fetishism and the Problem of Feminine/Feminist Discourse." *New German Critique* (winter 1984): 95–108.
Knight, Julia. *Women and the New German Cinema*. London: Verso, 1992.
Kuhn, Annette. *Women's Pictures: Feminism and Cinema*. London: Routledge, 1982.
Silverman, Kaja. *Male Subjectivity at the Margins*. New York: Routledge, 1992.
Williams, Linda. "A Provoking Agent: The Pornography and Performance Art of Annie Sprinkle." In *Dirty Looks: Women, Pornography, Power*, edited by Pamela Church Gibson and Roma Gibson, 179–201. London: BFI, 1993.

HENNING, HANNA (1884–1925). Germany. Very little information is available on the life and career of Hanna Henning, a pioneer of German cinema. She is one of a handful of women directors who are recorded in the history of German filmmaking. Other German feminist cinema pioneers include Olga Wohlbrück, who is cited as the first German woman filmmaker (Knight, 2). Wohlbrück made only one film, *Ein Mädchen zu verschenken (A Girl for Giving Away)* (1913). American-born Fern Andra, a tightrope performer, moved to Germany in 1915 and shortly thereafter set up her own film company. She directed five films, but little is known about her work. Marie Louise Droop, according to Julia Knight, moved into film production from a career as a screenwriter during the silent era (3).

Of all of these artists, however, Hanna Henning appears to be the most prolific woman film director of the silent German period. Her first major film is *Die Siebzehnjähgen (The Seventeen-Year-Olds)* (1919), after which Henning made over forty films before her death in 1925 (Knight, 3). She worked with some of the most accomplished camerapersons of the era. *Der dämon von Kolno* (1920) was photographed by Charles Paulus, *Das Gross Licht* (1920) was shot by Otto Tober, and *Am Roten Kliff* (1921) was photographed by Günther Krampf. These films are held in a number of collections, associated with International Federation of Film Archives, and in view of the scarcity of information on Henning, they should be screened in international cinema retrospectives to give us a greater understanding of this important yet neglected film pioneer.

Clearly, despite her present obscurity, Hanna Henning was an important and influential figure in early German cinema. She is as important to German film as Lois Weber is to American film. That producer/director Hanna Henning is reduced to being a mere footnote in German film history is another example of sexism in the history-making process. Today, Henning is best remembered for her early films, a series of shorts about a young, rascal-like child. These films are referred to as the "Bubi" films. Henning appears to have moved into more serious Germanic themes, however, such as man against nature in *Das Gross Licht*. The list of cinematographers who worked for Hanna Henning is a testament to her highly professional status in the early German film industry. Yet, because of her death during the formative years of the medium and no doubt because of her sex, those films that still exist of Henning's are seldom screened today.

The process of historical canonization in cinema has been, as this book demonstrates, a decidedly haphazard affair, with the efforts of only a few women filmmakers valorized at the expense of many more of their sister artists. Henning's films deserve to be shown in a retrospective, at the very least, so that modern audiences might have a chance to see her long-forgotten visions.

SELECTED FILMOGRAPHY

Unverstanden (1915)
Im Banne Des Schweigens (1916)
Mutter (1917)

Bubi, Der Tansensassa (1918)
Unter Der Peitsche des Geschicks (1918)
Wenn Die Rote Heide Bluht (1918)
Die Siebzehnjährigen (*The Seventeen-Year-Olds*) (1919)
Der dämon von Kolno (1920)
Das Gross Licht (1920)
Die Mitternachtsgottin (1920)
Die Furcht vor Dem Weibe (1921)
Am Roten Kliff (1921)

SELECTED BIBLIOGRAPHY

Knight, Julia. *Women and the New German Cinema*. London: Verso, 1992.
Krautz, Alfred. *FIAF International Directory of Cinematographers Vol. 4*. Augsburg: K. G. Saur Verlag, 1984.
Silberman, Marc. "Women Filmmakers in West Germany." *Camera Obscura* 6 (fall 1980): 123–52.

HENNING-JENSEN, ASTRID (1914–). Denmark. Astrid Henning-Jensen, born Astrid Smahl in Copenhagen, was a stage actress before she teamed up with Bjarne Henning-Jensen. The couple soon became established as leading figures in the Danish cinema. Astrid Henning-Jensen co-directed, wrote, or directed many of the couple's collaborative films. Many of the Henning-Jensen films are documentaries, notable for their technical sophistication, cinema vérité cinematography, brilliant editing, and grim neorealism. *Dansk politi i Sverige* (*The Danish Brigade in Sweden*) (1945) exemplifies the trademark neorealistic style of the Henning-Jensens. The film reenacts the training of 200 Danish officers who fled the German occupation.

In addition to their extensive work in documentary form, the Henning-Jensens also directed many feature films. The best-known Henning-Jensen feature is probably *Ditte Menneskebarn* (*Ditte, Child of Man*) (1946). *Ditte, Child of Man* is an adaptation of Martin Anderson-Nexö's novel about an illegitimate young woman who becomes an unwed mother. The film is decidedly feminist in theme, exposing the double-bind system of gender-defined social codes. Children and young adults are often featured prominently in the work of the Henning-Jensens. Their son, Lars Henning-Jensen, often appears in their films.

Astrid Henning-Jensen wrote many of the films directed by her husband. Bjarne, in turn, assisted Astrid on her films. Astrid Henning-Jensen made her first solo effort in 1945. She is credited as the director of *Denmark Grows Up* (1947), *Palle, Alone in the World* (1949), *Unknown Man* (1952), *Ballet Girl* (1954), *Love on Credit* (1955), *Paw, Boy of Two Worlds* (1960), *Unfaithful* (1968), and *Vinterboern* (1978). *Vinterboern* touches on feminist themes such as childbirth, pregnancy, and birth control options. Astrid Henning-Jensen worked in Denmark, Norway, and Geneva.

Anu Koiven notes that Astrid Henning-Jensen's films are now being "rediscovered" (196) by feminist historians. Her films explore the private sphere of marriage, children, and adolescence. Along with her husband, Bjarne, Astrid Henning-Jensen created films that combined the brutality associated with social realism with the fantasy associated with children's films. *Palle, Alone in the World* (1949) is a fine example of this notably Danish combination. *Palle* concerns a poor young boy who dreams he has a streetcar to move around freely in the sleeping city in a magical fantasy montage sequence. *Palle* is one of the few Henning-Jensen films stored in many international film archives.

SELECTED FILMOGRAPHY

Films as codirector or director

SOS Kindtand (1943)
Når man kun er ung (1943)
De danske sydhavsoer (1944)
Flyktningar finnar en hamn (1944)
Dansk politi i Sverige (The Danish Brigade in Sweden) (1945)
Skibet er ladet med (1945)
Ditte Menneskebarn (Ditte, Child of Man) (1946)
Stemning i April (Impressions of April) (1947)
De pokkers unger (Those Blasted Kids) (1947)
Denmark Grows Up (1947)
Kristinus Bergman (1948)
Palle Allene i Verden (Palle, Alone in the World) (1949)
Vesterhavsdrenge (Boys from the West Coast) (1950)
Kranes konditori (1951)
Ukjent man (1952)
Better than Cure (1953)
Solstik (1953)
Tivoligarden spiller (1954)
Ballettens boern (Ballet Girl) (1954)
Kaerlighed pa kredit (1955)
Hest på sommerferie (Horse on Holiday) (1959)
Paw, Boy of Two Worlds (1960)
Et brev til en son (1961)
Forraederiet (1962)
Kvinden og soldaten (1962)
Een blandt mange (1962)
Den jagede (1963)
Der er noget i luften (1964)
Et minde om to mandage (1964)
Vend dig ikke om (1964)
De blå undulater (1965)
Min bedstefar er en stok (1967)
Nille (1968)

Utro (*Unfaithful*) (1968)
Mej och dej (*Me and You*) (1969)
Vinterboern (*Winterborn*) (1978)
Ojeblikket (1980)
Hodja fra Pjort (1985)
Barndommens gade (*Street of My Childhood*) (1986)

SELECTED BIBLIOGRAPHY

Johnston, Claire. *Notes on Women's Cinema.* London: SEFT, 1973.

Katz, Ephraim. *The Film Encyclopedia.* New York: HarperCollins, 1994.

Koivunen, Anu. "Henning-Jensen, Astrid." In *The Women's Companion to International Film,* edited by Annette Kuhn and Susannah Radstone, 195–96. Berkeley: University of California Press, 1994.

Mayne, Judith. *The Woman at the Keyhole: Feminism and Women's Cinema.* Bloomington: Indiana University Press, 1990.

Quart, Barbara. *Women Directors: The Emergence of a New Cinema.* New York: Praeger, 1988.

Smith, John M., and Tim Cawkwell, eds. *The World Encyclopedia of Film.* New York: Times Mirror, 1972.

HIDARI, SACHIKO (1930–   ). **Japan.** Sachiko Hidari made her reputation as an actress. Before her career as an actress and director, Hidari taught high school. She then appeared in many films directed by her former husband, Susumu Hani. In *Kanojo to Kare* (*She and He*) (1963), Hidari played an independently minded Japanese woman in the film, which reads as a semiautobiographical work. Sachiko Hidari was interviewed by Joan Mellen in 1975. Several of Hidari's statements in this interview reflect her strong feminist leanings. Hidari told Mellen, for instance: "It will take a long time for you to understand the Japanese. Many Japanese men don't like to have independent wives; you must realize that Japanese men are not ready to admit that men and women are equal" (205). Feminism in Japan is difficult to define from a Western perspective, and it is risky to conflate different feminist ideals across international ideological perspectives. So Hidari's viewpoint on gender is not easy to locate. Speaking about Japanese economic development, for example, Hidari displays a more traditional perspective. "If the Japanese have done anything great," said Hidari, "this has been accomplished because of the quiet, suffering, yet diligent Japanese women" (Mellen, 201).

Sachiko Hidari's portrayal of the working-class Japanese woman in *The Far Road* (1977) is a blend of traditional and feminist interpretation. Hidari produced, directed, and starred in the film, which was commissioned by the Japan National Railway Union. *The Far Road* concerns the plight of lower-class to middle-class railroad workers. It has the grim realism of a *shomin-geki,* a film that glorifies the struggle of the working class and the poor. The plot of *The Far Road* centers on the struggles of a railroad worker who is passed over for a raise and forced into early retirement because of his union ties. When the husband retires, the wife takes on the bulk of the family responsibilities and takes a job doing work at home to support the family. *The Far Road* is part realism and part melodrama.

Hidari is sensitive to the woman's perspective as well as the man's perspective. On one hand, Hidari evokes the stress, pain, and loss of face that the retired railway man experiences. On the other hand, Hidari evokes audience identification with a woman who works herself to the brink of collapse. Barbara Quart finds that Hidari's cinematography "gives a grounded attention to the daily stuff of life" (249). *Toi Ippon no Michi* (*The Far Road*) is a blend of feminism and Goshoism that, with extraordinary realism, depicts the difficulties of marriage.

Few women in Japan have had an opportunity to direct or produce feature films. The most prolific woman director in Japan is Kinuyo Tanaka, another actress turned director. Tanaka began directing in 1953 and has been active since then. Western audiences know Tanaka from her performance in *Ugetsu*. An an actress, Hidari has worked in a broad range of female roles and excels in the movement toward a feminist Goshoism.

SELECTED FILMOGRAPHY

Toi Ippon no Michi (*The Far Road*) (1977)

SELECTED BIBLIOGRAPHY

Anderson, Joseph, and Donald Richie. *The Japanese Film: Art and Industry*. Princeton: Princeton University Press, 1982.

Barrett, Gregory. *Archetypes in Japanese Film*. Selingsgrove, PA: Susquehanna University Press, 1989.

Buruma, Ian. *Behind the Mask: On Sexual Demons, Sacred Mothers, Transvestites, Gangsters, Drifters and Other Japanese Cultural Heroes*. New York: Pantheon, 1984.

Desser, David. *Eros Plus Massacre: An Introduction to the Japanese New Wave Cinema*. Bloomington: Indiana University Press, 1988.

Lent, John A., ed. *The Asian Film Industry*. Austin: University of Texas Press, 1991.

Mellen, Joan. *Voices from the Japanese Cinema*. New York: Liveright, 1975.

Nolletti, Arthur. "Woman of the Mist and Gosho in the 1930s." In *Reframing Japanese Cinema*, edited by Arthur Nolletti, Jr., and David Desser, 3–32. Bloomington: Indiana University Press, 1992.

Quart, Barbara. *Women Directors: The Emergence of a New Cinema*. New York: Praeger, 1988.

Yamada, Joanne Y. "Hidari, Sachiko." In *The Women's Companion to International Film*, edited by Annette Kuhn, with Susannah Radstone, 199. Berkeley: University of California Press, 1994.

HOFMAN-UDDGREN, ANNA (1868–1947). **Sweden.** Sweden's first woman director, Anna Hofman-Uddgren, is a completely overlooked pioneer of the cinema. One of the first theater owners to begin screening films in 1899, she is listed as a name "of passing interest" in a standard history of Swedish cinema (McIlroy, 21). She does not rate an entry in Peter Cowie's otherwise comprehensive, two-volume history of Swedish film.

Anna Hofman-Uddgren is more than a fascinating footnote in film history. She was a theatrical actress in Stockholm in the late nineteenth century. She bought a music-hall theater and was one of the first businesspeople to recognize the early cinematic art as a viable, profitable investment. She incorporated some of the first films ever made into her music-hall program. Hofman-Uddgren was also one of the first directors of an advertisement. She directed an early promotional travelogue, *Stockholmsfrestelser* (*The Temptations of Stockholm*), in 1911.

Miss Julie (1912) and *The Father* (1912) are Anna Hofman-Uddgren's adaptations of the stage productions of August Strindberg. Though Hofman-Uddgren directed only a few films, they show an understanding of the ability to produce dramatic highlights visually, rather than verbally. As Swedish critic Maaret Koskinen notes, Hofman-Uddgren depicts a dramatic sequence of a moving stagecoach in *The Father*, which is "conveyed only verbally in the play" (201). Though most of Hofman-Uddgren's films appear to be lost, *Fadren* (1912) is held in the archives of the Swedish Film Institute Cinemateque.

Sweden's silent cinema period is characterized as an active, technically innovative, thriving business arena. Women were not excluded from directorial positions until the 1930s. In addition to Anna Hofman-Uddgren, another woman film director who was particularly active in the silent cinema was Pauline Brunius. Brunius is better known to historians as the first woman director of Sweden's National Theatre. However, Pauline Brunius also directed many short comedies and farces. Though a handful of women directed in the years between the 1930s and the 1960s, women were pushed out of production and direction in this period until the emergence of Mai Zetterling, who directed many films, beginning in the 1960s. The presence of Anna Hofman-Uddgren in the silent period needs to be recorded and reevaluated.

SELECTED FILMOGRAPHY

Blott en dröm (1911)
Stockholmsfrestelser (*The Temptations of Stockholm*) (1911)
Stockholmsdamernas älskling (1911)
Systrarna (1912)
Fröken Julie (1912)
Fadren (*The Father*) (1912)

SELECTED BIBLIOGRAPHY

Koskinen, Maaret. "Hofman-Uddgren, Anna." In *The Women's Companion to International Film*, edited by Annette Kuhn and Susannah Radstone, 200–201. Berkeley: University of California Press, 1994.

McIlroy, Brian. *World Cinema 2: Sweden.* London: Flicks Books, 1986.

Slide, Anthony. *Early Women Directors.* New York: Da Capo, 1984.

Smith, Sharon. *Women Who Make Movies.* New York: Hopkinson and Blake, 1975.

HOLLAND, AGNIESZKA (1948–). Poland/France/Germany/United States. The formidable career of Agnieszka Holland ranges from the children's fantasy film *The Secret Garden* (1993) to the long-banned political thriller *Fever* (1981). Holland is an auteur of the cinema whose trademark stamp of magical realism is distinctive and remarkable. Her approach to violence, whether political or familial, exudes, as critic Fredric Jameson notes, "a strange and poetic visual reality" (305). Born in Warsaw, Poland, on November 28, 1948, Agnieszka Holland is Jewish. Holland experienced firsthand the horrors of anti-Semitism when the entire family on her father's side was murdered under the Nazi regime in World War II. Holland was educated in Czechoslovakia. She graduated in 1971 from the Prague Film School. Her first films were television productions for Czechoslovakian programming. Holland codirected *Zdjecia* (*Screen Test*) with Andrzej Wajda, with whom she became closely associated, in 1977. Holland wrote the screenplays of many of Wajda's films, including *Without Anesthesia* (1978) and *Danton* (1982). In 1979, Holland directed *Provincial Actors,* which won the critics' prize at the Cannes Film Festival.

Provincial Actors displays an early use of Holland's poetic realism in a political tract loosely allegorized in the play-within-a-film form. The company of players in the film put on the Polish play *Liberation,* yet Holland shows the stifling atmosphere of conformity and yearning for freedom that the players experience. Abused by a tyrannical director who obviously represents a figurehead of the colonizing forces ruling over Poland, one actor experiences a breakdown. As a result, his relationship with his wife becomes unbearable. As Barbara Quart notes, the "rage and misery of the outer and personal world are inseparable" (232) in the film. Holland's film is clearly a call for an insurrection. As one critic notes, it is "a statement about lost confidence and moral paralysis and a call for boldness and integrity" (Turaj, 158). Holland's politics eventually caused her problems with the government.

Holland's next film, *Fever* (1981), was banned by the Polish government for many years. Based on the novel by Andrzej Strug, *The Story of One Bomb, Fever* is another political struggle film set at the turn of the century when Poland struggled for independence, and workers struggled for recognition in 1905. *Fever* won the Grand Prize at the Golansk Film Festival. Holland's handling of the material is a gloomy portrayal of the violence and personal costs of the failed revolution. Holland excels at realistically painting the disorganized and selfish anarchists and the police spies, quislings, and corrupt members of the bourgeoisie who work against the political uprising. Released right after the imposition of martial law in Poland, the film was almost immediately banned because of its brutally realistic portrayal of the occupying Soviet forces. *Fever* supersedes the unified, cohesive narrative of most nostalgic rerenderings of history. Holland breaks with monologic discourse and reveals the gaps of the history-making process. "We are no longer necessarily in reliable hands," notes Fredric Jameson. "Things may never cohere" (306).

Holland's next film, *A Woman Alone* (1981), was the last film she directed in Poland. *A Woman Alone* chronicles the plight of an unmarried mother employed as a letter carrier who embezzles the money of pensioners as an act of desperation. Holland's film explores the theme of moral absence and human depravity in the film. The central character, Irene, is beaten down by poverty and beaten to death by her lover. The one hopeful figure in the film is Irene's son, whom we view in a foster home, waiting for his mother.

After the imposition of martial law, Holland emigrated to Paris, where she began planning *Angry Harvest* (1985), which was produced in West Germany. Holland drew upon her experience as a Polish Jew for the screenplay, which is set in World War II. The film examines the problematic love affair between a Jewish woman (played by Elisabeth Trissenaar) hiding from the Nazis and a Christian German farmer (played by Armin Muller-Stahl) who hides her. Nominated for an Academy Award for Best Foreign Language Film, *Angry Harvest* is a powerful study of identity, sexual repression, gender, and political victimization. The moral ambiguity at the center of the film is powerfully conveyed through the narrative and through the visceral, poetic cinematography.

Holland directly equates sexual relationships with fascistic manipulation and victimization in *Angry Harvest*. Once again conflating the personal with the political, Holland brings together the couple in a twisted, romantic entanglement, ending with the liberating figure of the farmer becoming a jealous, dominating, and brutalizing lover. As Holland told Peter Brunette, "[T]he idea of possession, of possessing things and people, is an important theme in the film" (16). Violence and power are inexorably linked in the bitter struggle for political and sexual domination, as *Angry Harvest* confirms.

Holland's next two films, *Europa, Europa* (1990) and *Olivier, Olivier* (1992), return to the inevitable themes of moral ambiguity, violence, and power. *Europa, Europa* was produced in France and became an international success. The plot is based on a true story of a young German-Jewish teenage boy who passes as a Gentile in order to survive in Nazi Germany. *Europa, Europa* explores the complexities of alternative identities and national allegiances thrust upon Jews and Europeans in World War II in an almost existential treatment of moral choice.

Olivier, Olivier is a horrifying film about a mother (Brigitte Rowan) who loses her identity as she searches for her lost son. As Holland is never one to flinch from sordid acts of sexual violence, the lost boy in her film turns out to be a victim of a child molester and brutal murderer. However, in a typically bizarre plot twist, Holland creates a character who poses as the woman's lost son, in another exemplification of "passing" and the mutability of identity characteristic of Holland's screenplays. The impostor is a street hustler (played by Gregoire Colin) who charms the mother, who so desperately needs a son through whom to find an identity that she accepts him even when she finds out the truth. As J. Hoberman notes, *Olivier, Olivier* operates "in a supernatural world of inexplicable affinities, fulfilled wishes, unseen powers, bizarre coincidences, and enigmatic patterns."

Magic and the supernatural are beautifully evoked in Holland's most recent film, *The Secret Garden* (1993). From Frances Hodgson Burnett's haunting children's story, *The Secret Garden* is Holland's first major Hollywood production. The film stars Maggie Smith and Mary Lennox and is a refreshingly poetic rendering of a child's point of view. Holland combines lush cinematography, a well-crafted narrative, and a female-centered children's story with her trademark magical realism in *The Secret Garden*. In 1986, Agnieszka Holland was already showing signs that she wished to be able to direct commercial films, not just political ones, complaining to Peter Brunette, "For me the thing that is most annoying is that you are condemned to be political" (17). With *The Secret Garden,* Holland proved that she could move into commercial filmmaking; however, even her children's story can be read as a political allegory. The young girl in the film shows a sick little boy how to be independent in the face of a dominating and manipulating father who needs his son to remain crippled to satisfy his own psychological needs.

The political and allegorical implications of *The Secret Garden* are obvious. The success of the film is a tribute to Holland's auteurist signature style and the thirst for films that feature female children as central quest heroines. The cinema of Agnieszka Holland fits the definition of a feminist auteur, as defined by Teresa de Lauretis. Holland's is a cinema "engaged in the project of transforming vision by (re)inventing the forms and processes of representation" (158). In redefining political cinema and moving politics across private and public spaces, Agnieszka Holland excels as a poet of the international cinema.

SELECTED FILMOGRAPHY

Wieczór u Abdona (*Evening of Abdon's*) (1974)
Niedzielne dzieci (*Sunday Children*) (1976)
Cós za cós (*Something for Something*) (codirector Andrzej Wajda) (1977)
Aktorzy Prowinejonalni (*Provincial Actors*) (1979)
Goraczka (*Fever*) (1981)
Kobieta samotna (*A Woman Alone*) (1981)
Bittere Ernte (*Angry Harvest*) (1985)

To Kill a Priest (1988)
Europa, Europa (1990)
Olivier, Olivier (1992)
The Secret Garden (1993)

SELECTED BIBLIOGRAPHY

Brunette, Peter. "Lessons from the Past: An Interview with Agnieszka Holland."
    Cineaste 15.1 (1986): 15–17.
de Lauretis, Teresa. "Rethinking Women's Cinema." In *Multiple Voices in Feminist
    Film Criticism,* edited by Diane Carson, Linda Dittmar, and Janice Welsch,
    140–61. Minneapolis: University of Minnesota Press, 1994.
Hoberman, J. "The Eternal Return." *Village Voice* (March 2, 1993): 23.
Jameson, Fredric. "On Magic Realism in Film." *Critical Inquiry* 12.2 (winter 1986):
    301–25.
Quart, Barbara. *Women Directors: The Emergence of a New Cinema.* New York:
    Praeger, 1988.
Turaj, Frank. "Poland: The Cinema of Moral Concern." In *Post New Wave Cinema
    in the Soviet Union and Eastern Europe,* edited by Daniel J. Goulding, 143–
    71. Bloomington: Indiana University Press, 1989.

HUBLEY, FAITH (1915–). United Kingdom/United States. Animator
Faith Hubley is almost completely forgotten in film history due to the fact
that she always collaborated with her husband, John Hubley. No matter
how often the couple stressed that their work was the effort of an equal
partnership, film historians persist in routinely dismissing Faith Hubley's
work as a codirector of the Hubley cartoons. In their recent study of creative partnerships, Whitney Chadwick and Isabelle de Courtivron note that
such partnerships are viewed as problematic to traditional biographers who
see creativity as an "extraordinary (usually male) individual's solitary struggle for artistic self-expression" (7). Thus, one partner is usually singled out
as the individual artist in a falsely conflated view of the efforts of a partnership. In an interview with Sharon Smith in 1975, John Hubley explained
the couple's working relationship as a simple partnership: "[T]he fairest
credit is just 'a film by John and Faith Hubley' " (60). Nevertheless, film
encyclopedias record the accomplishments of the couple under the name of
John Hubley, thus reducing Faith Hubley's work to that of a helpmate.
This is a persistent pattern in film scholarship that needs to be addressed.

Faith Hubley and John Hubley were leaders in the field of animation.
John Hubley worked for Walt Disney, UPA films, and began working with
Faith Hubley in the early 1950s, for their co-owned company, Storyboard
Productions. The early work of the Hubley team represents a departure
from classical studio animation of the 1930s and 1940s. The minimalist
UPA style of the Hubley cartoons constitutes an artistic response to rising
production costs in the animation field. While the Hubleys used a pared-
down approach to animation, they are celebrated for their primitive, ro-

mantic signature style of narrative storytelling. *Windy Day* (1968) is characteristic of the work of the Hubley team. It is narrated by the Hubleys' two daughters and made in response to the lack of female heroines in animated cartoons. Faith Hubley told Sharon Smith her daughters complained to their parents, "You like boys better" (61), in response to the lack of female characters with whom to identify in their parents' work. *Windy Day* is the record of the interior life of two young girls and is partially drawn by the girls. On the voice-over track, Georgia and Emily Hubley discuss everything from marriage to death, in a rare observance of the work of a family creative partnership. The film won an Academy Award as Best Animated Cartoon.

The subject matter of Hubley cartoons and shorts was often serious. *Of Men and Demons* (1970) also won an Academy Award. In the film, a man and woman fight to ward off the forces of evil. *Eggs* (1970) is an allegorical study of life and death. All told, John and Faith Hubley won several Academy Awards, including Best Animated Short Film for *Moonbird* (1959). They continued to collaborate until John Hubley's death in 1977.

After John's death, Faith Hubley wrote, produced, and animated a substantial body of work independently, including several experimental films held in the collection of the Museum of Modern Art in New York. Hubley's independent work centers on childhood, creation myth, and ecofeminist themes. *Step by Step* (1979) is an ethnographic study of childhood from an intercultural perspective. Created in honor of the Year of the Child, *Step by Step* includes imagery of abuse, sacrifice, and abandonment of children and moves into images of admiration for the child (such as the iconography of the Madonna and child). Hubley uses found images from artists from around the globe, including Japanese and Flemish painters. The film concludes with a section that calls for the political rights of children.

Sky Dance (1980) and *The Big Bang and Other Creation Myths* (1981) are imaginative celebrations of ecofeminist creation rituals. *Sky Dance* reconfigures patriarchal philosophy and religion in light of primitive cave paintings and the international pursuit of the unknown. In *The Big Bang,* Hubley explores the creation myths of Africa, Finland, China, and Australia and Native American and Hindu cultures. The "big bang" is represented as the feminine symbol of an egg bursting forth with the masks of many international ethnic peoples. The film also includes a representation of the archetypical myth of a woman who gives birth to the earth through bleeding. Faith Hubley's independent filmmaking displays a filmmaker dedicated to remythologizing a feminist, humanist, multicultural perspective. Like experimental filmmaker Diana Barrie, Faith Hubley uses the experimental cinema to envision a female-centered, child-centered, creation-centered universe. As Judith Mayne suggests, women filmmakers such as Hubley and Barrie tend to reconfigure the primitive space of experimental films. Hubley's films explore Judith Mayne's definition of "a mode of traditional femininity . . . the scene primitive, the primal scene" (208) of creation myth. Far from being her husband's mere helpmate, Faith Hubley is a collaborative and individual artist in her own right.

SELECTED FILMOGRAPHY

Codirected with John Hubley

The Adventures of an Asterisk (1957)
Harlem Wednesday (1958)
The Tender Game (1958)
Moonbird (1959)
Children of the Sun (1960)
Of Stars and Men (1961)
The Hole (1962)
The Hat (1964)
Herb Alpert and the Tijuana Brass Double Feature (1966)
Windy Day (1968)
Eggs (1970)
Of Men and Demons (1970)
Voyage to Next (1974)
WOW Women of the World (1975)

Directed by Faith Hubley

Step by Step (1979)
Sky Dance (1980)
The Big Bang and Other Creation Myths (1981)

SELECTED BIBLIOGRAPHY

Chadwick, Whitney, and Isabelle de Courtivron, eds. *Significant Others: Creativity and Intimate Partnership*. London: Thames and Hudson, 1993.
Gifford, Denis. *The British Film Catalogue, 1895–1979: A Reference Guide*. New York: McGraw-Hill, 1973.
Mayne, Judith. *The Woman at the Keyhole: Feminism and Women's Cinema*. Bloomington: Indiana University Press, 1990.
Pilling, Jayne, ed. *Women and Animation: A Compendium*. London: BFI, 1993.
Quinlan, David. *British Sound Films: 1928–1959*. Totowa, NJ: Barnes and Noble, 1984.
Smith, Sharon. *Women Who Make Movies*. New York: Hopkinson and Blake, 1975.

HUI, ANN (1947–   ). China/Hong Kong. Born in Manchuria, China, Ann Hui is an important figure of the Hong Kong New Wave cinema. She became a director after earning a master's degree in English and comparative literature. She spent two years studying at the London Film School and returned to Hong Kong in 1975, where she immediately began directing television documentaries and narrative films. *The Boy from Vietnam* (1978), *The Story of Woo Viet* (1981), and *Boat People* (1983) form a trilogy of films centering on the problems of Vietnamese and Chinese refugees. Hui has a talent for using Western genres as set pieces for social commentary. *The Story of Woo Viet* borrows from the gangster film to tell the story of a Chinese man from Vietnam who escapes to Hong Kong. Hoping to escape to America, the man is forced by circumstances into exile at sea, a fate all too common for Vietnamese refugees.

Hui's *Boat People* was internationally recognized at the Cannes Film Festival and received international distribution. *Boat People* raised a great deal of controversy because of Hui's handling of the issue of Vietnamese refugees in the film and because of its anti-Communist stance. Some viewers found the film excessively violent. Karen Jaehne asked Hui if the torture scenes were necessary, to which Hui responded: "No, the violence was in fact restrained. When I showed it to some of the refugees I knew, they asked me—why had I not shown some of the [more] dreadful violence?" (17). *Boat People* was banned in China. In Hong Kong, as Li-Cheuk-to notes, the film "touched a collective nerve among Hong Kong people who were by now increasingly worried over their future" (167).

Though Ann Hui is best known for *Boat People,* she has directed a considerable number of genre films, such as *The Secret* (1979), a murder mystery. *The Secret* is an interesting blend of Western cinematic tradition and Hong Kong cinematic flavor. Barbara Quart likens the film to a "female takeoff of *The Godfather*" (248), in which a woman acts as a detective investigating a female murderer. The narrative is interlaced with a ghost story more indicative of Chinese cinema, while the cinematography and genre are more Westernized. Hui playfully disregards Western conventions of objective reality, however, by interjecting ghosts into the narrative. Hui uses a similar strategy in *The Spooky Bunch* (1980), in which an opera company is haunted by the spirits of an army of soldiers who mean to avenge their wrongful death. The martial arts sequences are directed by Ching Siu-tung. The *Spooky Bunch* is a comedy/ghost/historical genre-blend.

Ann Hui is one of several Hong Kong New Wave directors who are forging a hybrid style of cinema that bridges cultural differences, their work falling somewhere between tradition and Westernization. Hui's most recent film, *Song of the Exile* (1990), is a semiautobiographical tale of a Hong Kong woman who returns from London to Hong Kong for her sister's wedding. The cultural differences among the mother, daughter, and sister cause conflict among the three women figures. *Song of the Exile* also shows the effects of racial discrimination. The protagonist is faced with job discrimination in England, cultural differences with her family in Hong Kong, and the cultural isolation of identity politics. *Song of the Exile* stars Maggie Cheung and Shwu-Fen Chang. Ann Hui is known for being an outspoken, politically active figure. She also tends to employ all-female crews and production members. *Song of the Exile, Boat People,* and many of Hui's works are elegant, prosaic, difficult, and personal works of personal and political struggle. Most of her films are available through Facets Video, Chicago.

SELECTED FILMOGRAPHY

The Boy from Vietnam (1978)
The Secret (1979)
The Spooky Bunch (1980)
The Story of Woo Viet (1981)
Boat People (1983)
Love in a Fallen City (1984)
The Romance of Book and Sword (1987)
Song of the Exile (1990)
My American Grandson (1991)

SELECTED BIBLIOGRAPHY

Cheuk-to, Li. "The Return of the Father: Hong Kong New Wave and Its Chinese Context in the 1980s." In *New Chinese Cinemas: Forms, Identities, Politics,* edited by Nick Brown, Paul G. Pickowicz, Vivian Sobchack, and Esther Yau, 159–189. Cambridge: Cambridge University Press, 1994.

Jaehne, Karen. "Boat People: In Interview with Ann Hui." *Cineaste* 13.2 (1984): 16–19.

Kaplan, E. Ann. "Problematizing Cross-Cultural Analysis: The Case of Women in the Recent Chinese Cinema." *Wide Angle* 11.2 (1989): 40–50.

Lent, John A. *The Asian Film Industry.* Austin: University of Texas Press, 1990.

Quart, Barbara. *Women Directors: The Emergence of a New Cinema.* New York: Praeger, 1988.

Rayns, Tony. "Chinese Changes." *Sight and Sound* 54.1 (winter 1984–85): 24–30.

HUILLET, DANIÈLE (1936–   ). France/Germany. Danièle Huillet and her partner, Jean-Marie Straub, together pioneered the stylistic approach to New German Cinema that is usually attributed to Rainer Werner Fassbinder, who acted in the Huillet/Straub films. Danièle Huillet was born in France in 1936. She studied film at universities in Nancy and Strasbourg. She met Jean-Marie Straub in Paris, where Straub was working as an assistant director on director Jacques Rivette's *Le Coup du Berger* (1956). Huillet and Straub moved to Munich and married in 1959. They began collaborating on films and quickly developed a reputation for their difficult, experimental, and challenging films. Though Huillet and Straub shared credit, critics typically tended to ignore Huillet's contribution to their working partnership until the 1980s. As Renate Möhrmann notes, Huillet "was tagged an appendage" (75) of Jean-Marie Straub. Huillet and Straub have said little to correct this lack of recognition of Huillet's side of the partnership, but, as Barton Byg suggests, perhaps "a feminist reception of Huillet/Straub might begin by cooperating with Huillet's concern for the films first, and the gendering of authorship afterwards" (210). Huillet sees women's issues as falling within the leftist political framework, rather than a separate issue.

The Huillet/Straub films are political agitprop, modernist in style, often shot in a minimalist, aesthetical approach to form. The team prefer static long takes, acting that is devoid of emotion, and the barest of mise-en-scène. Aesthetically, Huillet and Straub are influenced by Brecht, Kafka, and the Frankfurt school of critical theory. As Maureen Turim notes, Huillet/Straub films are "a critique of the intelligentsia . . . an artistic practice in which structural experimentation and the ideas formed by this reconstruction form an oblique angle on the vitality of cinematic possibility" (356). Huillet/Straub films thus interrogate the audience, cinematic representation, and the representation of history itself.

The Bridegroom, the Comedienne and the Pimp (1968) is an exploration of the representation of prostitution. The film includes a long opening tracking shot through an area in Munich where prostitutes work on a daily basis. Loosely adapted from the Ferdinand Bruckner play *Krankheit der Jugend* (*Sickness of Youth*), *The Bridegroom, the Comedienne and the Pimp* is a modernist reworking of the theatrical historicization of oppression. The Huillet/Straub version combines the murder of a pimp (played by Fassbinder), a condensed theatrical adaptation, Bruckner's play, and the lengthy tracking shot of the prostitutes on the boulevard at night. In its self-referentiality and insistence that the viewer work on the historical material, *The Bridegroom, the Comedienne and the Pimp* fits into the tradition of New German Cinema, founded on the rupture of classical Hollywood representational form.

Straub and Huillet interrupt standard cinematic practices by constantly reworking narrative space. Like Chantal Akerman, Huillet/Straub deconstruct and reconstruct visual pleasure by the use of the long take, which emphasizes subjective space, repetition, and the falseness of representation. *Class Relations* (1984) is based on Franz Kafka's novel *Amerika*. Shot in black and white, the usual structure of *Class Relations* is dominated by long, static camera takes. To further emphasize the theatricality of the film medium, Huillet/Straub hold the camera on the scene after the actors have left the screen. The cast is made up of a mixture of nonprofessional and professional actors who stand and recite their lines in purposefully singsong soliloquies, in much the same manner as that of Andy Warhol's "actors." Political rallies and beatings take place offscreen. Characters address one another outside the compositional field. The problems posed by *Class Relations* are endemic to both the politically radical theatre of Brecht, the agitprop of Kafka, and feminist film theory. As Barton Byg notes, *Class Relations* questions "how to envisage a realm of freedom for ourselves in this world when the language we have to describe it is one means of our enslavement" (213).

Other Huillet/Straub productions follow in this vein, including *Chronicle of Anna Magdalena Bach* (1967), a retelling of Johann Sebastian Bach's life through the perspective of his second wife's "journals"; *Not Reconciled*

(1965), a metaphysical meditation on Nazism and Communism from Heinrich Böll's novel, *Billiard um Halbzehn (Billiards at Half Past Nine);* and many other haunting and elliptic antinarrative films. Critics sometimes try to find easy metaphors for sequences in Huillet/Straub films, but these films defy reductionist critical approaches. Danièle Huillet and Jean-Marie Straub resist aesthetical categorization.

SELECTED FILMOGRAPHY

Codirected with Straub

Machorka Muff (1962)

Nicht versöhnt oder Es hilft nur Gewalt, wo Gewalt herrscht (Not Reconciled; or, Only Violence Helps Where Violence Rules) (1965)

Chronik der Anna Magdalena Bach (Chronicle of Anna Magdalena Bach) (1967)

Der Bräutigam, Die Komödianten und der Zuhälter (The Bridegroom, the Comedienne and the Pimp (1968)

Les yeux ne veulent pas en tout temps se fermer ou Peutetre qu'un jour Rome se permettra de choisir à son tour: Othon (The Eyes Do Not Always Want to Close or Perhaps One Day Rome Will Permit Itself to Choose in Its Turn: Othon) (1969)

Einleitung zu Arnold Schönbergs Begleitmusik zu einer Lichtspielscene (Introduction to Arnold Schönberg's "Accompaniment to a Cinematographic Scene") (1972)

Geschichtsunterricht (History Lessons) (1972)

Moses und Aaron (Moses and Aaron) (1974–75)

Fortini Cani (The Dogs of Sinai) (1976)

Toute Revolution est un Coup de Des (Every Revolution Is a Throw of the Dice) (1977)

Dalla nube alla resistenza (From the Cloud to the Resistance) (1978–79)

Zu früh, zu spät (Too Early, Too Late) (1980–81)

En Rachachant (1982)

Klassenverhältnisse (Class Relations) (1984)

Der Tod des Empedokles (The Death of Empedocles) (1986)

Schwarze Sünde (Black Sins) (1989)

SELECTED BIBLIOGRAPHY

Byg, Barton. "Straub/Huillet, Feminist Film Theory and *Class Relations.*" In *Gender and German Cinema, Feminist Interventions, Volume 1: Gender and Representation in New German Cinema,* edited by Sandra Frieden, Richard W. McCormick, Vibeke R. Petersen, and Laurie Melissa Vogelsang, 209–24. Oxford: Berg, 1993.

Hoberman, J. "Once upon a Time in Amerika: Straub/Muillet/Kafka." *Artforum* 23 (September 1984): 75–77.

Möhrmann, Renate. "The Second Awakening of Christa Klages." In *Gender and German Cinema, Feminist Interventions, Volume 1: Gender and Representation in New German Cinema,* edited by Sandra Frieden, Richard W. McCormick, Vibeke R. Petersen, and Laurie Melissa Vogelsang, 73–84. Oxford: Berg, 1993.

Perez, Gilbert. "Modernist Cinema: The *History Lessons* of Straub and Huillet."
    Artforum 17 (October 1978): 46–55.
Roud, Richard. *Straub*. New York: Viking, 1972.
Turim, Maureen. "Jean-Marie Straub and Danièle Huillet: Oblique Angles on Films
    as Ideological Intervention." In *New German Filmmakers from Oberhausen
    through the 1970s,* edited by Klaus Phillips, 335–58. New York: Ungar,
    1984.

**HUNT, CLAIRE, AND KIM LONGINOTTO (Hunt   –   ; Longi-
notto   –   ) United Kingdom/Japan.** Documentarists Claire Hunt and Kim
Longinotto seek to correct glaring silences in Japanese women's cultural
history in their documentaries *Eat the Kimono* (1989) and *The Good Wife
of Tokyo* (1992). Hunt and Longinotto dislodge preconceived notions of
the docile, sexually accommodating Japanese woman in these two films.
The British-based team crosses borders, both national and cultural, in its
provocative ethnographic films of marginalized peoples and strong women
figures whose struggles intersect at the margins of racism, classism, and
sexism.

Eat the Kimono is a biography of Hanayagi Genshu, a dancer and political activist who was arrested in 1980 for stabbing a dance teacher. After
serving eight months in prison, Genshu returns to her life as a performer.
Hunt and Longinotto skillfully intercut footage of Genshu's performances
with interviews with Genshu, brilliantly displaying a talent for leaving
moral judgments to the viewer. In the film, Hanayagi Genshu explains the
cultural significance of the kimono as an equivalent of the Victorian corset
in European society:

The kimono comes from Japan's feudal past. It traps women. My art is expressing
freedom, even though I'm restricted . . . you mustn't be eaten by the kimono . . .
you must eat the kimono, gobble it up.

Genshu performs in kimono while wearing a grotesque, oversize doll's
head, flaunting the conventions of her culture. Claire Hunt and Kim Longinotto speak to the practice of ethnographic cinema of documentary. They
never speak for the colonized figures of Genshu; instead, they allow her to
choose what she wishes to include and respect her subjectivity when she
does not wish to discuss something. Genshu's politically charged outbursts
are not stabilized to conform to a homogenized feminist purpose. Genshu
speaks about racism in the aftermath of the bombing of Hiroshima, claiming that injured Japanese people received medical treatment before Korean
people. Genshu is an extraordinary storyteller, as are documentarists Claire
Hunt and Kim Longinotto, who record the contrasts between the present
and the past, ritual and modern performance art, and privilege and mar-
ginality.

In *The Good Wife of Tokyo* (1992), Claire Hunt and Kim Longinotto document another performance artist, Kazuko Hohki, who is based in England and married to a British man. Hunt and Longinotto follow Hohki as she returns to Japan to get remarried in a proper traditional ceremony to please her mother. The documentary takes a narrative turn when Hohki's mother emerges as the center of the material. *The Good Wife of Tokyo* explores the gender hierarchy in Japan through the eyes of the daughter and mother in a simultaneous refraction of one another's point of view. Hohki, who has not been in Japan in fifteen years, seems genuinely surprised at what has become of her mother, who is a spiritual leader and a leader of a women's support group. The sequences of the women in the support group speaking out about their unhappiness with traditional gender roles in Japan are funny, surprising, and revelatory. The unspoken is spoken in *The Good Wife of Tokyo* in a documentary style that manages to convey insights into the less conventional side of Japanese culture. The filmmakers allow the subjects to tell their own stories, so that the viewer can see that Japanese women are not a monolithic type lacking in individuality. *The Good Wife of Tokyo* provides insight into the manners in which Japanese women find freedom within and outside traditions and ceremonies.

   Hidden Faces (1990) is an absorbing documentary about Egyptian women in Muslim society. Another study of postcolonial homecoming, *Hidden Faces* follows Safaa Fathay, a young Egyptian woman living in Paris, "home" to interview the internationally renowned feminist writer Nawal El Saadawi. Disillusioned by the writer/activist, Safaa Fathay journeys home to her family in Cairo. She is shocked by the contradictory feeling she has toward her family. Her mother has returned to the veil after twenty years, and her cousin has a clitoridectomy in the wake of the rise of fundamentalism. *Hidden Faces* challenges the viewer to imagine the problematics of defining feminism in a Muslim fundamentalist environment. *Hidden Faces* is invaluable for any study of feminism in the Middle East and North Africa. Claire Hunt and Kim Longinotto won Best Documentary Prize at the Melbourne Film Festival for *Hidden Faces*. The film also was awarded the Jury Special Mention at Films de Femines, Créteil, France. *Hidden Faces, Eat the Kimono,* and *The Good Wife of Tokyo* are available through Women Make Movies, Inc.

SELECTED FILMOGRAPHY

Eat the Kimono (1989)
Hidden Faces (1990)
The Good Wife of Tokyo (1992)
Dream Girls (Filles de rêve) (directors Longinotto and Jano Williams) (1993)

SELECTED BIBLIOGRAPHY

Hart, Lynda, and Peggy Pheland, eds. *Acting Out: Feminist Performances.* Ann Arbor: University of Michigan Press, 1993.

Watson, Julia and Sidonie Smith. "De/colonization and the Politics of Discourse in
    Women's Autobiographical Practices." In *De/Colonizing the Subject: The
    Politics of Gender in Women's Autobiography,* edited by Sidonie Smith and
    Julia Watson, 13–31. Minneapolis: University of Minnesota Press, 1992.
Women Make Movies. *Women Make Movies Catalogue.* New York: Women Make
    Movies, Inc., 1993.

I

IVERS, JULIA CRAWFORD (1871–1930). United States. Producer, writer, and director Julia Crawford Ivers's notable career is difficult to trace, due to the fact that she disliked publicity and was omitted from film scholarship. Ivers was a prolific screenwriter who adapted many literary works for the screen. She was under contract as a writer for Famous Players-Lasky Productions in the early 1920s, where she was responsible for many of the screenplays directed by William Desmond Taylor, including *Huckleberry Finn* (1919), *The Furnace* (1920), *Beyond* (1921), *Jenny Be Good* (1920), *Sacred and Profane Love* (1921), *Wealth* (1921), *The Witching Hour* (1921), and *The Green Temptation* (1922).

As a producer, Julia Crawford Ivers began working in the mid-teens, producing *Gentleman from Indiana* (1915), which was an adaptation of Booth Tarkington's famous novel. Ivers produced over twenty films in the years between 1915 and 1917, including *As Men Love* (1917), *Bond Between* (1917), *Her Own People* (1917), *The Intrigue* (1917), *Little Miss Optimist* (1917), *Molly Entangled* (1917), *Petticoat Pilot* (1917), *Spirit of Romance* (1917), and *Wax Model* (1917). Julie Crawford Ivers was an exemplification of the New Woman. She supervised all facets of the production of her films, as one of several women producer/directors working in Hollywood in the teens and 1920s. (Other women producer/directors working at this time include Lois Weber, Ida May Park, Alice Guy-Blaché, Lule Warrenton, and Alla Nazimova.) As the titles of Ivers's production credits demonstrate, Ivers often made sensational films centered around female heroines, though she certainly made many other types of films.

As a director, Julia Crawford Ivers is best remembered for *Call of the Cumberlands* (1916). The film starred Dustin Farnum and Myrtle Stedman. A critical success, *Call of the Cumberlands* is notable for its early use of natural outdoor lighting and setting. Prior to directing *Call of the Cumberlands*, Ivers directed at least three films in 1915, *The Majesty of the Law*, *Nearly a Lady*, and *The Rugmaker's Daughter*. Little is recorded about these films, but Ivers was apparently very fast and efficient as a director. In 1916, Ivers directed at least five films in addition to *Call of the Cumberlands*. *He Fell in Love with His Wife* appears to be a feminist-minded romantic comedy. *The Heart of Paula* was probably a romantic melodrama. Ivers gave up direction during the late teens and turned her attention to screenwriting. Her last screenplay was *Married Flirts,* produced by MGM in 1924. Ivers returned to direction in 1923 with *The White Flower*. Always in tune with public tastes, she traveled to Honolulu to film in its exotic locales. *The White Flower* centers on a female sorceress who casts spells on those around her.

Julia Crawford Ivers is an important figure in early American cinema. Her life and work are comparable to those of Ida May Park, a producer/director who made many films at Universal at approximately the same time as Ivers. Both women were remarkably versatile and prolific, yet both are almost completely forgotten to history. Ivers and Park wrote, directed, and produced explorational commercial films as well as literary adaptations. The careers of Ida May Park and Julia Crawford Ivers are historically significant because they represent a cultural moment in cinema history in which women were not excluded from managerial positions in Hollywood. Julia Crawford Ivers died in 1930 at the age of fifty-nine after a lengthy illness. Ivers's son, James Crawford Van Trees, became a cinematographer for Warner Brothers.

SELECTED FILMOGRAPHY

The Majesty of the Law (1915)
Nearly a Lady (1915)
The Rugmaker's Daughter (1915)
Call of the Cumberlands (1916)
The American Beauty (1916)
Ben Blair (1916)
The Heart of Paula (1916)
A Son of Erin (1916)
The White Flower (1923)

SELECTED BIBLIOGRAPHY

Acker, Ally. *Reel Women: Pioneers of the Cinema, 1896 to the Present.* New York: Continuum, 1993.
Carson, Diane. "Women Filmmakers." In *Multiple Voices in Feminist Film Criticism,* edited by Diane Carson, Linda Dittmar, and Janice Welsch, 456–67. Minneapolis: University of Minnesota Press, 1994.
Slide, Anthony. *Early Women Directors.* New York: Da Capo, 1984.

J

JAKUBOWSKA, WANDA (1907–   ). Poland. Born on November 10, 1907, in Warsaw, Wanda Jakubowska directed films in Poland for well over fifty years. She was educated at Warsaw University in art history. Though she is best known for *The Last Stop* (1948), a revealing account of the Nazi concentration camps, she was already involved in filmmaking as early as the 1920s. She was one of the founding members of the Society of Devotees of the Artistic Film (START), which later became the Cooperative of Film Authors. By 1930, Jakubowska was in the vanguard of the prewar Soviet documentary movement. The films of the Soviet documentary movement are typically shot with limited production values, but they espouse artistic and social commitment to cinema verité. The gritty exposés of *Report One* (1930) and *Report Two* (1931) exemplify the style and integrity of the period of Soviet documentary that predates the British movement toward documentary realism. Jakubowska collaborated with Eugeniusz Cekalski on *We Build* (1934), and she worked with Szolowski on *The Banks of the Niemnen* (1939). The spirit of early Soviet documentary was community-oriented, as Jakubowska's work with other directors demonstrates.

During World War II, Wanda Jakubowska was interned as a prisoner in the camps at Auschwitz and Ravensbruck. When Jakubowska survived, she was determined to record her firsthand experiences on film. *The Last Stop* was the first full-length film to bring international attention to the atrocities committed against the Jews in the concentration camps. Jakubowska used a cast and crew of women who had been in the camps. *The Last Stop* demonstrates how the Nazis pitted women against one another for small favors. The film includes a scene in which a woman who is giving birth is tortured by a woman guard. The heroines of the film are also women, one a doctor and one her interpreter. As Frank Bren notes, *The Last Stop* "is an affirmation of the courage of women known to the director and of their dignity compared to the captors' barbarity" (37). Bren recounts Jakubowska's ability to turn a lack of resources into an asset in the shooting of *The Last Stop*. Shot at Film Polski, where resources were extremely limited, Jakubowska used a group of rich tourists to make up for a lack of expensive costumes. She arranged that the tourists would be rerouted to the film set, and she photographed their horrified reactions as they looked upon a convincing reenactment of the death camp. *The Last Stop* was an international success, and Jakubowska won an International Peace Prize for the film. Jakubowska made two more films on the same subject as part of a trilogy, *The End of Our World* (1964) and *Invitation* (1985).

Wanda Jakubowska continued to direct for many years after the success of *The Last Stop*. Many of the films she directed return to political themes. Though critics tend to dismiss her work after *The Last Stop*, Jakubowska is one of the most important Polish filmmakers, leading the way in political documentary and drama. Among the themes she explores in her films are the corruption of political leaders, the conflict between East and West Germany, and life under Communism. *Encounters in the Shadows* (1960) represents a typical Jakubowska film in that it is a female-centered examination of moral complexities and identity. In the film, a pianist is faced with the opportunity of giving a concert in a village from which she was once deported. Jakubowska is at her best when she reveals the web of discourse of power as it affects, and is affected by, gender and ethnic identity. Her work compares with that of Agnieszka Holland and other New Wave Polish directors.

SELECTED FILMOGRAPHY

Reportaz nr 1 (Report One) (1930)
Reportaz nr 2 (Report Two) (1931)
Impressions (1932)
The Sea (1932)
Budujemy (We Build) (1934)
Nad Niemnem (The Banks of the Niemnem) (1939)
Budujemy nowe Wsie (We're Building New Villages) (1946)
Ostatni Etap (The Last Stop) (1948)
Zolnierz Zwyciestwa (Soldier of Victory) (1953)
Opowiese Atlantycka (Atlantic Story) (1955)
Pozegnanie z Diablem (Farewell to the Devil) (1957)
Krol Macius (King Matt) (1958)
Spotkania w mroke (Encounters in the Shadows) (1960)
Koniec Naszegoswiata (The End of Our World) (1964)
Goraca Linia (The Hot Line) (1965)
150 na Godzine (At One Hundred and Fifty Km an Hour) (1971)
Bialy Mazur (Dance in Chains) (1978)
Zaproszenie (Invitation) (1985)
Kolory Kochania (Colors of Love) (1987)

SELECTED BIBLIOGRAPHY

Attwood, Lynn, ed. *Red Women on the Silver Screen: Soviet Women and Cinema from the Beginning to the End of the Communist Era*. London: Pandora, 1993.

Bren, Frank. *World Cinema 1: Poland*. London: Flicks Books, 1986.

Goulding, Daniel J., ed. *Post New Wave Cinema in the Soviet Union and Eastern Europe*. Bloomington: Indiana University Press, 1989.

Kuhn, Annette. *Women's Pictures: Feminism and Cinema*. London: Routledge, 1982.

Quart, Barbara. *Women Directors: The Emergence of a New Cinema*. New York: Praeger, 1988.

K

KAPLAN, NELLY (1931–   ). **Argentina/France.** Writer and director Nelly Kaplan was born in 1931 in Buenos Aires, Argentina. Her Russian family had lived in Argentina for many generations. She studied economics at the University of Buenos Aires and entered film as an archivist for an Argentinean cinematheque. She went to Paris as a representative of Argentina for an international congress of film archivists and stayed on in France as a correspondent for Argentinean film periodicals. Kaplan met director Abel Gance in 1954 and became his colleague and collaborator. In the early 1960s, Nelly Kaplan directed her first short films. She won a Golden Lion Award in Venice for *Le Regard Picasso* (1966).

Kaplan has, since this time, become a commercially successful feature film director with a feminist edge. She has also published a number of books, including a collection of short stories and a book of erotica, published under the pseudonym Belen. Kaplan's approach to female sexuality is a celebration of female fantasy and female vision, rendered with beauty and a flavor of surrealism. Like Anaïs Nin, Nelly Kaplan's female eroticism causes debate in feminist circles. Kaplan also shares a thematic interest with Nin in her preoccupation with fantasy as a liberating force. Kaplan is clearly linked to the surrealist tradition of exploration of the link between desire and the imagination. Kaplan's films have been misperceived as pornographic commercial films, partly because the films have been retitled suggestively to ensure commercial success abroad.

La Fiancée du Pirate (*A Very Curious Girl*) was released in Italy under a title that translates as *Beautiful Serafina Liked to Make Love Morning and Evening. Nea* (1976) was released in Britain as *A Young Emmanuelle.* Audiences expecting male pornographic fantasies must have been surprised by Kaplan's female fantasy films. Christ Straayer describes *Nea* as a feminist "erotic art film" in which a "young female protagonist actively pursues sexual knowledge, trespasses filmic space in contrast to pornography's conventional use of woman as space to be entered" (511). According to Annette Kuhn, *Nea* was released in Britain with an "X" certificate and exhibited in soft-core porn houses (126). *Nea* was marketed as a sex film to please male audiences, but the film is directed by and for the female erotic gaze.

La Fiancée du Pirate (*A Very Curious Girl*) was also marketed as soft-core pornography. The plot centers around a young Gypsy girl who returns to the village to avenge herself on the people who used her sexually. The girl becomes a prostitute and takes revenge on her former abusers by flaunting her sexuality in order to enslave and destroy them. As Kaplan told Claire Johnston, *A Very Curious Girl* is intended as an allegorical fantasy of revenge of the archetypical witch/prostitute woman. Though Alan Williams claims that Kaplan's films and those of Diane Kurys are "stylistically polished and conventional, making essentially no effort to challenge the norms of mainstream cinema" (377), Nelly Kaplan is a radical feminist who infuses her work with a subversive reworking of pleasure as feminine. More recently, Kaplan's films have progressed toward less radical themes, yet her films, no matter how slick and commercial, are female-centered. Recently, Kaplan directed *Plaisir d'amour* (1994), a film about three generations of women. Nelly Kaplan continues to direct feminist commercial films in France. On the difficulties of being a woman director in a man's world, she told Claire Johnston that "a woman has to be better, to be at least the same as a man" (409). Nelly Kaplan's work is, in some ways, more transgressive and subversive than the countercinema of independent, underground filmmakers. Her work in the mainstream manages to compete in commercial venues and remain solidly feminist while reimagining feminine erotic pleasure.

SELECTED FILMOGRAPHY

Gustave Moreau (1961)
Abel Gance Hier et Demain (1963)
Le Regard Picasso (1966)
La Fiancée du Pirate (*A Very Curious Girl*) (1970)
Papa Les Petits Bateaux (1971)
Nea (1976)
Charles et Lucie (1980)
Abel Gance et Son Napoleon (1983)
Plaisir d'amour (1994)

SELECTED BIBLIOGRAPHY

Johnston, Claire. "Myths of Women in the Cinema." In *Women and the Cinema: A Critical Anthology,* edited by Karyn Kay and Gerald Peary, 407–11. New York: Dutton, 1977.
Kuhn, Annette. *Women's Pictures: Feminism and Cinema.* London: Routledge, 1982.
Martineau, Barbara Halpern. "Nelly Kaplan—Interviewed by Barbara Halpern

Martineau with an introduction by Claire Johnston." In *Notes on Women's Cinema*. Edited by Claire Johnston, 14–23. London: SEFT, 1974. Pamphlet.

Straayer, Chris. "Sexual Representation in Film and Video." In *Multiple Voices in Feminist Film Criticism,* edited by Diane Carson, Linda Dittmar, and Janice Welsch, 503–12. Minneapolis: University of Minnesota Press, 1991.

Vincendeau, Ginette. "Fathers and Daughters in French Cinema: From the 20s to 'La Bell Noiseuse.' " in *Women and Film: A Sight and Sound Reader,* edited by Pam Cook and Philip Dodd, 156–63. Philadelphia: Temple University Press, 1993.

Williams, Alan. *Republic of Images: A History of French Filmmaking*. Cambridge: Harvard University Press, 1992.

KARANTH, PREMA (1950–   ). **India.** In the 1980s, a New Wave of women directors emerged in India. Prema Karanth, Aparna Sen, Saj Paranipee, and Arunaraje Desai are just a few of the many women filmmakers active in Hindi cinema. Manjurath Pendakur notes that the Indian film industry has been recently significantly commercialized; thus, "there are significantly more opportunities to make one's first film in India now than 20 years ago" (248). Aesthetically, the new cinema in India is both commercial and socially responsible. Prema Karanth's *Phaniyamma* (1986) appears to fit the mold of Pendakur's description. It is both melodramatic and feminist and is shot through with an almost neorealist mise-en-scène, told from a female-centered perspective.

Phaniyamma is an adaptation from a book by M. K. Indira. The book is based on the true story of Phani, a young girl who is widowed at age ten, not even having yet consummated her arranged marriage. Phani is abruptly pulled out of school and forced into the life of a proper widow. The male leaders of the village decide that Phani must shave her head, wear only white, and live a sexless, austere life of devotion to others. *Phaniyamma* is told through flashbacks. The film opens with a birth scene. Karanth prefers to narrate the film visually, using close-ups of the faces of the woman giving birth, the midwife, and Phani. Phani is the center of the melodrama, a figure of strength against the backdrop of male cultural dominance.

Though Phani is forced into a role of the silent subaltern (the silent woman who must not desire but must help others), she gradually grows into a strong, independent figure who protests against the oppression of other women. As Phani grows older, she uses her position as a servile, deprivileged, desexualized figure to challenge traditions that oppress her people. As Barbara Quart observes, "In its quiet, unpolemic, unsensational, and very disturbing way, the film is made, one feels, not for the sake of pathos, but for protest" (252). Though critics such as Chandra Talpade Monhanty warn Western feminists to avoid the flattened, homogenized vision of international feminist sisterhood, it is obvious that Prema Karanth's film does share ideological underpinnings common to Western feminisms. But Karanth's feminism is culturally defined by decidedly different and unique sociocultural gender norms. *Phaniyamma* is both a film of pathos, in the tradition of Indian melodrama, and a film of social protest, in the tradition of Prema Karanth.

Prema Karanth works as one step of a chain of oral storytelling. Her story is autobiographically infused into the life story of Phani. Phani's story was told to Miki Indira, and Phani, the character in the film, retells the same story and breaks the chain of women as oppressed figures. In the film, Phani is successful in saving another young girl from a fate like hers by teaching the girl to stand up to her family. As an excluded figure, Phani is freed to make choices that go against the grain of tradition. Karanth herself is an outspoken and self-confident figure. Prema Karanth's *Phaniyamma* is a study of the pain and courage of an outsider figure, a nontraditional, single, child-free, strong woman, capable of both words and action.

SELECTED FILMOGRAPHY

Phaniyamma (1986)

SELECTED BIBLIOGRAPHY

Arora, Poonam. "The Production of Third World Subjects for First World Consumption." In *Multiple Voices in Feminist Film Critics,* edited by Diane Carson, Linda Dittmar, and Janice Welsch, 293–304. Minneapolis: University of Minnesota Press, 1994.

Lawrence, Amy. "Women's Voices in Third World Cinema." In *Multiple Voices in Feminist Film Criticism,* edited by Diane Carson, Linda Dittmar, and Janice Welsch, 406–20. Minneapolis: University of Minnesota Press, 1994.

Mohanty, Chandra Talpade, Ann Russo, and Lourdes Torres, eds. *Third World Women and the Politics of Feminism.* Bloomington: Indiana University Press, 1991.

Pendakur, Manjurath. "India." In *The Asian Film Industry,* 229–52. Austin: University of Texas Press, 1990.

Quart, Barbara. *Women Directors: The Emergence of a New Cinema.* New York: Praeger, 1988.

KIDRON, BEEBAN (1961–   ). United Kingdom/United States. Beeban Kidron, born and raised in London, became an award-winning photographer before she was a teenager. She later worked as an assistant to the world-famous photographer Eve Arnold, then enrolled in England's National Film School. Her intention was to become a cinematographer, but after working on several films as a camera operator, she decided to change to directing.

Her first film was the award-winning documentary *Carry Greenham Home* (1984), codirected with Amanda Richardson. It won the Golden Hugo Award at the Chicago Film Festival in 1983 and subsequently became a favorite at the Berlin Film Festival. Eventually, it was shown to an audience of 10,000 in a Japanese stadium. In 1986, Kidron directed *The Global Gamble,* a documentary about the deregulation of the city of London, for Channel Four Television. Next, she directed her first feature film, *Vroom,* for British Screen and Film 4 International. This film became the centerpiece of the 1988 London Film Festival.

Kidron came to the attention of international audiences with her next film, *Oranges Are Not the Only Fruit* (1989), based on Jeanette Winterson's novel of a young woman struggling to come of age in the midst of religious, parental, and sexual repression. The young girl finds freedom in a lesbian relationship and escapes the confines of her homophobic, heterosexist home culture and takes on the role of exile to find freedom. This comedy-drama won awards at film festivals around the world, was shown in the United States on cable television to great critical acclaim, and won a Cable ACE Award. *Oranges* received numerous other awards, including several BAFTA Awards and the award for Best British Television Series, as well as the Prix d'Argent at Cannes and the Prix Italia.

Kidron's next feature, *Antonia and Jane* (1991), was produced with the BBC and was released theatrically in the United States by Miramax. A comic vision of contemporary life as seen in the friendship of two women, the film was first seen at the 1990 Telluride Film Festival and was warmly received by the critics. *Antonia and Jane* is a delicate comedy about the complexities of female friendship. The low-budget film captured the international art circuit audience and bolstered Kidron's career. In 1992, Kidron was offered the opportunity to direct the big-budget film *Used People,* which featured Shirley MacLaine, Kathy Bates, Jessica Tandy, Marcello Mastroianni, and Sylvia Sidney. A warm, romantic melodrama, *Used People* is one of the very few films that explore love and sexuality in the context of aging. Kidron made her American feature film debut with this film, a comedy about how one man's search for love affected a New York Jewish family.

Great Moments in Aviation (1994), Kidron's next film, opened theatrically in 1994. It stars Rakie Ayola, Vanessa Redgrave, John Hurt, and Jonathan Pryce and tells the story of a West Indian woman who goes to England in the 1950s with dreams of flying.

Most recently, Kidron completed producing and directing *Hookers, Hustlers, Pimps and Their Johns* (1995), which she made for British television. The film explores the sex industry in New York City. Kidron is well known for her endearing representations of characters who are offbeat, exiled, or outcasts. Beeban Kidron's current project, *To Wong Foo, with Love, Julie Newmar* (1995), takes the director's offbeat sensibility on the road with a group of transvestites who tour the American Midwest. When their car breaks down in a small town, the group members (including stars Patrick Swayze and Wesley Snipes) fear the worst. However, the locals are tolerant of the travelers' alternative lifestyle and accept them into their community. Kidron's latest work is compassionate, caring, and well crafted, as are her other films. Combining commercial savvy with a strong authorial presence, Kidron will be a director to watch in the coming years.

SELECTED FILMOGRAPHY

Carry Greenham Home (1984)
Vroom (1988)
Oranges Are Not the Only Fruit (1989)
Antonia and Jane (1991)
Used People (1992)
Great Moments in Aviation (1994)
To Wong Foo, with Love, Julie Newmar (1995)

SELECTED BIBLIOGRAPHY

Cohn, Lawrence. "*Used People.*" *Variety* 349.8 (December 14, 1992): 43.
Denby, David. "*Antonia and Jane.*" *New York* 24.42 (October 28, 1991): 56.
Dwyer, Victor. "*Antonia and Jane.*" *Maclean's* 105.31 (August 3, 1992): 47.
James, Caryn. "*Antonia and Jane.*" *New York Times,* November 8, 1991, C3.
Maslin, Janet. "*Used People.*" *New York Times,* December 16, 1992, B3, C24.
O'Connor, John J. "*Oranges Are Not the Only Fruit.*" *New York Times,* November 28, 1990, B4, C22.
Salamon, Julie. "*Used People.*" *Wall Street Journal,* February 9, 1993, 12–14.
Travers, Peter. "*Used People.*" *Rolling Stone* 648 (January 21, 1993): 56.

KOPPLE, BARBARA (1946–   ). United States. Academy Award-winning documentarist Barbara Kopple was introduced to film as a student of Harvey College in Charleston, West Virginia. Kopple, who had no previous film training, was asked by a firm to make a film about people who had had lobotomies. She encouraged the patients to film one another and gained her first experiences as a documentary filmmaker. Before becoming a documentary filmmaker, Kopple worked as a gofer, sound recorder, and editor for various firms, gaining invaluable experience in all phases of film production. Finally, she was ready to strike out on her own. In 1972, she began planning *Harlan County U.S.A.,* a cinema vérité documentary of a coal miners' strike in Kentucky. It took Kopple several years to find the necessary financing, through foundations and church groups and her own Mastercard. Kopple became a spectator/participant of the July 1973 miners' strike in Harlan County. She moved to Harlan County with her cameraperson, Hart Perry, and her assistant director, Ann Lewis, and on a scanty budget of $200,000 managed to complete an exceptional film that features actual strike events, photographs of mining conditions, interviews with miners and company officials, and the everyday life of mining people. As Julia LeSage notes, Kopple's film "focuses on problems of identity in the private sphere" (15), in a feminist, documentarist, aesthetical approach. *Harlan County U.S.A.* shows how miners' wives reach solidarity in their kitchen spaces and how the women organizers interface with the striking men. E. Ann Kaplan praised Kopple's approach to realism in the film, as it "exposes the brutality of the management in the Kentucky mine" (137). Kopple won the Academy Award for Best Documentary Feature in 1976.

In 1979, Kopple codirected *No Nukes* with Haskell Wexler. The film is a concert documentary recording the No Nukes concerts in New York City, which were sponsored by Musicians for Safe Energy. In keeping with her interest in the American labor force, Kopple directed *Keeping On* (1983), about southern American textile workers, and *American Dream* (1992), about midwest American meat packers. *American Dream* follows a labor strike at a Hormel plant in Minnesota. The film won an Academy Award for Best Documentary Film in 1992.

Barbara Kopple is one of the few remaining politically active American documentarists who continue to make personally motivated political films despite the rise in film production costs, which has contributed to the decrease in documentary filmmaking. Though many filmmakers are using video due to its significantly lower cost, the art form of film documentary is becoming, to some degree, outmoded because of the rise in costs and aggressive distribution competition.

Though Barbara Kopple is well aware of sexism in the film industry, she never let prejudice dissuade her from documentary production. She told Jennifer Dunning, "I had thought being a woman would make things tougher, but actually people in the coal fields were less guarded with me." Kopple is a filmmaker of conscience who rises above sexism, funding problems, and production difficulties. She is an extraordinary woman in American film.

SELECTED FILMOGRAPHY

Winter Soldier (codirector) (1970)
Richard III (codirector) (1970)
Harlan County U.S.A. (1976)
No Nukes (1979)
Keeping On (1983)
American Dream (1992)

SELECTED BIBLIOGRAPHY

Dunning, Jennifer. "A Woman Film Maker in the Coal Mines." *New York Times*, October 15, 1976, 8.

Kaplan, E. Ann. *Women and Film: Both Sides of the Camera*. New York: Methuen, 1983.

LeSage, Julia. "The Political Aesthetics of the Feminist Documentary Film." In *Films for Women*, edited by Charlotte Brunsdon, 14–23. London: BFI, 1987.

Penley, Constance. "Documentary/Documentation." *Camera Obscura* 13–14 (spring–summer 1985): 85–161.

Porton, Richard. "American Dreams." *Cineaste* 18.4 (1991): 42.

Shulevitz, Judith. "Kopple, Barbara." In *The Women's Companion to International*

Film, edited by Annette Kuhn and Susannah Radstone, 229–30. Berkeley: University of California Press, 1994.

Welsch, Janice R. "Bakhtin, Language, and Women's Documentary Filmmaking." In *Multiple Voices in Feminist Film Criticism,* edited by Diane Carson, Linda Dittmar, and Janice Welsch, 162–75. Minneapolis: University of Minnesota Press, 1994.

KURYS, DIANE (1948–   ). France. Diane Kurys became famous internationally in 1977 for her directing debut with *Peppermint Soda,* the first in a trilogy of semiautobiographical female bildungsromans that delighted audiences and critics alike. *Peppermint Soda* was France's highest-grossing film of the year and won the Prix Louis Delluc as Best Picture of the Year in 1977. Born in 1948, Diane Kurys was a member of the Jean-Louis Barrault theater group before she turned to film direction. Kurys drew on her own experiences as a young Jewish girl in writing the screenplay for *Peppermint Soda.* The film is the story of two young girls and their friendship. The themes of initiation, female community, sexuality, and the transience of adolescence are compellingly treated on the screen in one of the few coming-of-age tales to center on young women. In the tradition of François Truffaut's *The 400 Blows,* Kurys's vision of an adolescent's point of view, set against the backdrop of the cold and austere world of her teachers, captures the anarchic spirit of youth. Kurys shot the film in the same school that she herself attended, in a self-reflexive autobiographical gesture. The two sisters in *Peppermint Soda* share female stories of the average adolescent, menstruation, boys, flirting, and romance.

The relationship between the girls is ambiguous, yet tender, much like that between the girls in Alison Anders's *Gas Food Lodging.* The younger girl, Anne, is obsessed with her older sister, Frederique, who has more knowledge about romance. Kurys tells the story visually, often relying on simple eye matches in close-ups that narrate the film in an understated manner. An erotic look between Frederique and another girl prefigures the romantic love between women in Kurys's later film, *Entre Nous (Coup de Foudre)* (1983).

Cocktail Molotov (1979) is another charming, humorous study of adolescence, this time centered around a girl who runs away with two boys and misses the 1968 student uprisings. Kurys is exceptional at capturing the ambiguity of mother-daughter relationships. In *Cocktail Molotov,* Anne runs away after a vicious fight with her mother. She leaves with a boy of whom her mother disapproves because he is of the working class. On the road, Anne experiences love, sex, abortion, and existential wandering. Anne's story is told much in the style of classic French New Wave cineasts. At the end of the film, Anne returns to find that she has missed the student revolution. "They said it was all over but we knew it was just the beginning," she says in voice-over, as the film ends with a bittersweet commentary of Kurys's feelings about the 1960s.

In *Entre Nous* (1983), Kurys drew upon her mother's experiences as a married woman who found herself attracted to another woman. In the film, the two women, played by Isabelle Hupert and Miou-Miou, become erotically attracted to one another. The women leave their husbands and move in together. Kurys injects her autobiographical persona in a title that reads: "My father left at dawn. He never saw my mother again. It's now been two years since Madeleine died. I dedicate this film to the three of them." *Entre Nous* is criticized by some lesbian feminists for its skirting of the issue of lesbian sexuality, while, at the same time, others praise the film for appealing to the lesbian spectator. Chris Straayer notes that *Entre Nous* adheres to a heterosexual structure but includes a "lesbian look of exchange and female bonding" (343) that is pleasurable for the lesbian viewer. Ultimately, however, the characters remain an example of what Straayer terms the "hypothetical" lesbian heroine. Andrea Weiss claims that *Entre Nous* "occupies more of a traditional art cinema space than a feminist one" (123), though I wonder if the two categories necessarily exclude one another. Judith Mayne notes that Kurys had interference from her financial backers, who were uncomfortable with the presence of two women and only one man within the film's narrative. Kurys told Marcia Pally that she was uncomfortable about selling *Entre Nous* as a lesbian film because she worried that "it would narrow or skew her audience and blind viewers to the nuances of the story." Regardless of the problematics of the homo-eroticism of *Entre Nous,* there is no doubt that the film is a woman's film and a pleasure to watch as a woman spectator. When asked about the concept of the woman director, Kurys told Ginette Vincendeau that she finds the idea "dangerous and reductive" (70), yet Kurys maintains: "I am a feminist because I am a woman, I can't help it. . . . Yes, my point of view is different, but I don't know whether it is because I'm called Diane, because I was born a Jew, or because I went to a particular kind of Parisian lycée" (70). Above all, Kurys maintains that she wishes to be considered "un metteur en scène" (70).

In *C'est la vie* (1990), Kurys returns to autobiographical material, again fictionalizing her parents' divorce. Told through the eyes of the children, the story is sensationalized somewhat and more sentimental than Kurys's earlier work. In the film, the father is physically abusive, but in Kurys's real life this did not happen. Surprisingly, Kurys worked on the period reconstructions as if they were for a documentary. As Jill Forbes wrote of *C'est la vie,* Kurys is "never better than when depicting the lower classes at play, treating them with an affection that derives from familiarity" (69). As in all of Kurys's films, *C'est la vie* continually mines the female imagination for insights about female sexuality, interpersonal relationships, and adolescent female point of view. Kurys's *Après L'Amour* (1992) is another examination of interpersonal relationships, this time a thirty-year-old woman novelist who is involved with two men at the same time. Diane

Kurys remains one of the most successful directors working in France to-day, and her work incorporates a feminist outlook. While her films purport to meet the requirements of dominant cinema, they are rendered with a distinctively female eye. Kurys is a director of well-crafted, intelligent studies of human relationships.

SELECTED FILMOGRAPHY

Diabolo Menthe (*Peppermint Soda*) (1977)
Cocktail Molotov (1979)
Coup de Foudre (*Entre Nous*) (1983)
Un Homme Amoureux (*A Man in Love*) (1987)
La Baule les Pins (*C'est la vie*) (1990)
Après L'Amour (1992)
Six Days, Six Nights (1994)

SELECTED BIBLIOGRAPHY

Doty, Alexander. *Making Things Perfectly Queer*. Minneapolis: University of Minnesota Press, 1993.

Forbes, Jill. "La Baule—les pins." *Monthly Film Bulletin* 58.686 (March 1991): 68–69.

Holmlund, Christine. "When Is a Lesbian Not a Lesbian: The Lesbian Continuum and the Mainstream Femme Film." *Camera Obscura* 25–26 (January–May 1991): 145–78.

Mayne, Judith. *The Woman at the Keyhole: Feminism and Women's Cinema*. Bloomington: Indiana University Press, 1990.

Pally, Marcia. "Come Hither—But Slowly: Dessert with Diane Kurys." *Village Voice* (January 31, 1984): 52.

Quart, Barbara. *Women Directors: The Emergence of a New Cinema*. New York: Praeger, 1988.

Straayer, Chris. "The Hypothetical Lesbian Heroine." In *Multiple Voices in Feminist Film Criticism*, edited by Diane Carson, Linda Dittmar, and Janice Welsch, 503–512. Minneapolis: University of Minnesota Press, 1994.

Vincendeau, Ginette. "Like Eating a Lot of Madeleines: An Interview with Diane Kurys." *Monthly Film Bulletin* 58.686 (March 1991): 69–70.

Weiss, Andrea. *Vampires and Violets: Lesbians in Film*. New York: Penguin, 1993.

L

LANCTÔT, MICHELINE (1947–   ). Canada. A true Renaissance woman, Micheline Lanctôt is an award-winning actress, animator, and film director based in Quebec. She trained as a musician at the Vincent d'Indy Conservatory in Montreal. She worked as an animator for the National Film Board in the late 1960s. In 1972, Lanctôt won the Canadian Film Award for Best Actress for her debut role in *La vraie nature de Bernadette* (director Gilles Carle). She also won acclaim for her role in *The Apprentice of Duddy Kravitz* (director Ted Kotcheff, 1974). Lanctôt starred in the Radio-Canada production of the series *Jamais deux Sans toi*. In the mid-1970s, Lanctôt spent three years in Hollywood but returned to Quebec to make personal films; her feminist vision completely clashed with the Hollywood milieu. As Lanctôt told Connie Tadros:

The notion of cinema as the American studios make it where all is gross, crass, commercial debilitating, was just *indigeste*—impossible for me to relate to . . . and plus the fact that being a woman, being somebody's wife in L.A., is just about the worst position you can imagine and it almost destroyed me . . . so it was flight, instant flight. (8)

Lanctôt returned to Quebec and became internationally recognized as a director of New Wave Canadian cinema. Her first film, an animation short made for the National Film Board, *A Token Gesture* (1975), is a satirical examination of gender codes and their effects on women. *L'homme à tout faire* (*The Handyman*) (1980), Lanctôt's first feature film, won an award at the San Sebastian film festival. In *The Handyman*, Lanctôt explored the theme of alienation and loss of identity, which would be fully developed in her brilliant film *Sonatine* (1983). *Sonatine*, which Lanctôt describes as a "film maudit," is a disturbing meditation on female adolescence. *Sonatine* is a bleak coming-of-age story of two adolescent girls that ends in their accidental death. The film stars Pascale Bussières (as Chantal) and Marcia Pilote (as Lonisette) as two alienated young girls who search for adult experiences. Both seek escape from the world by aimlessly roller-skating around the suburb with their Walkman tape players. The landscape of *Sonatine* is an alienating technological space, reminiscent of Antonioni's *Red Desert* (1964). Lanctôt's mise-en-scène is littered with machines and their deafening sounds, blaring radios, loud televisions, street noises, and the cold voices of intercoms. The young women search for meaning in a labyrinth of subways, highways, buses, ships, and computer terminals.

As Michael Dorland wrote, "*Sonatine* is a dark masterpiece of ellipsis, a film haunted by the impossibility of communication." Faced with the example of the ugly, empty lives of the adults around them, the young women decide to shock the public into awareness by announcing their suicides. *Sonatine* is a cinematic cry of rage, and its ending certainly circumvents the typical upbeat, happy ending of the Hollywood coming-of-age film. Lanctôt is uncompromising in her direction. As she told Connie Tadros:

I know that *Sonatine* is not a sellable film, and I think that I know exactly what has to be made to make a saleable film. But I don't want to. What I now have to find is a voice. . . . There are a very few filmmakers that I really admire nowadays and the ones that I find myself really relating to are . . . the most personal. (10)

Sonatine is thematically similar to Agnes Varda's masterpiece about female alienation, *Vagabond* (1985). Lanctôt's vision, in some ways like Varda's, is a meditation on despair, alienation, and social marginalization of young women. Though uncompromising, *Sonatine* won favor with both the public and the critics: Lanctôt won a Genie Award (the Canadian Academy Award) for *Sonatine*.

Refusing to be labeled, Lanctôt hates to be called a woman director: "I don't make feminist films. I don't believe in 'feminism' as such. I'm an anarchist. It's my voice and I speak it" (Tadros, 8). Her feelings are shared by many women filmmakers, such as Nelly Kaplan and Diane Kurys. Nevertheless, women as directors are culturally marginalized through omission from film history. Women directors do tend to render more compelling female coming-of-age stories. There are certainly exceptions, of course, such as Bill Forsyth's eloquent *Housekeeping* (1987), but consistently, women directors bring to life the female heroine quest story. Most recently, Lanctôt has created *The Pursuit of Happiness* (1987), a bitter film about the Americanization of Canadian culture, and *Deux Actrices* (1993).

SELECTED FILMOGRAPHY

A Token Gesture (1975)
Trailer (1976)
L'homme à tout faire (*The Handyman*) (1980)
Sonatine (1983)
The Pursuit of Happiness (1987)
Deux Actrices (1993)

SELECTED BIBLIOGRAPHY

Adler, Leonore Loeb, ed. *Women in Cross-Cultural Perspective.* New York: Praeger, 1991.
Cole, Janis, and Holly Dale. *Calling the Shots: Profiles of Women Filmmakers.* Ontario: Quarry Press, 1993.
Dorland, Michael. "Micheline Lanctôt's *Sonatine." Cinema Canada* 110 (1984): 11.
Evans, Gary, ed. *In the National Interest: A Chronicle of the National Film Board of Canada from 1949 to 1989.* Toronto: University of Toronto Press, 1991.
Tadros, Connie. "*Sonatine:* 'Film maudit,' A Conversation with Director Micheline Lanctôt." *Cinema Canada* 110 (1984): 7–11.

LANDETA, MATILDE (1913–). Mexico. In 1987, only 15 films out of the estimated 3,200 films produced in Mexico since the advent of sound films in 1931 were directed by women. Matilde Landeta is one of these few women; she worked her way into a directorial position after ten years as a scriptperson. Born in Mexico City in 1913 and orphaned at age three, Landeta was raised by her grandmother in San Luis Potosi. Landeta was introduced to the film industry by her brother, Eduardo, an actor. Landeta knew immediately that she wished to make a career as a film director, and she managed to secure a position as a scriptperson. After eleven years' experience, Landeta finally emerged as an assistant director, after much opposition from the Directors Association in the form of gender discrimination. In 1947, Landeta and her brother formed TACMA, an independent film company, in a move to escape the limitations of gender that were restricting her ability to become a director. Against her will, Landeta's first screenplay, *Tribunal para menores,* was assigned to a young male director, Alfonso Corona Blake. For six years "Landeta was ostracized for having violated the code of feminine behavior," according to Carmen Huaco-Nuzum (99).

In 1948, Matilde Landeta directed her first feature film, *Lola Casanova,* a film based on an ethnographic novel by Francisco Rojas Gonzales. Marcela Fernández-Violante, a prominent woman film director who made a film about pioneering women film directors in the Mexican film industry, calls Landeta's next film, *The Black Augustius* (1949), "a marvelous film, unique in Mexican film history because it shows a woman triumphant, a leader of men who maintains her superior position rather than surrendering it" (196). As Violante recounts to Julianne Burton, "I was startled by how modern the film seems, particularly since strong female figures appear so rarely in our cinematic mythology" (196). Landeta's construction of a strong, sexually irrepressible female figure in the cultural milieu of the late 1940s contradicted prevailing constructions of woman as passive victim, venerated mother, or evil vamp. Mexican women, it should be remembered, did not get the vote until 1953. *The Black Augustius* revisions the sexually liberated female who usually suffers and dies in films of classical Mexican cinema.

Matilde Landeta's final feature film, *Streetwalker* (1951), is an even more radical feminist attack on racism and sexism. In the film Landeta criticizes the exploitation of women and the representation of women as sex objects. She won an Ariel for her screenplay for *Tribunal para menores* (*Juvenile Courts*) in 1956. Landeta is now being rediscovered by feminists in Latin America and abroad and screened at international film festivals. In 1990, Patricia Diaz made a documentary on Landeta, *My Filmmaking, My Life,* which includes a lengthy on-camera interview with Landeta. The film is available from Women Make Movies, Inc. In addition to her feature films, Landeta directed over 100 short films. Matilde Landeta is one of the most significant pioneers of the Mexican cinema, along with Adela Sequeyro, Mimi Derba, and Marcela Fernández-Violante.

SELECTED FILMOGRAPHY

Lola Casanova (1948)
La Negra Augustius (*The Black Augustius*) (1949)
Trotacalles (*Streetwalker*) (1951)

SELECTED BIBLIOGRAPHY

Burton, Julianne, ed. *Cinema and Social Change in Latin America: Conversations with Filmmakers.* Austin: University of Texas Press, 1986.
Fernández-Violante, Marcela. "La Otra Cara de la Histoire del cine." Mexico City, November 27, 1986. Extract.
Gonzales, Francisco Rojas. *La Negra Augustius.* Mexico City: Edicion y Distribution Ibero Americana de Publicaciones, 1948.
Huaco-Nuzum, Carmen. "Matilde Landeta: An Introduction to the Work of a Pioneer Mexican Filmmaker." *Screen* 28.4 (1987): 96–106.
LeSage, Julia. "Latin American and Caribbean Women in Film and Video." In *Multiple Voices in Feminist Film Criticism,* edited by Diane Carson, Linda Dittmar, and Janice Welsch, 492–502. Minneapolis: University of Minnesota Press, 1994.
Mora, Carl J. *Mexican Cinema.* Berkeley: University of California Press, 1982.

LARKIN, ALILE SHARON (1953–   ). United States. Born May 6, 1953, Alile Sharon Larkin grew up in Pasadena, California. She studied creative writing as an undergraduate at the University of Southern California and earned an M.F.A. in film and television production from the University of California—Los Angeles. As cofounder of the Black Filmmakers Collective, Larkin is an outspoken filmmaker, educator, activist, and writer. She has been active as a filmmaker since 1979. In addition to her directorial achievements, she is an advocate of children's educational television. In 1984, she directed the cable production "My Dream Is to Marry an African Prince" (1984), which demonstrated how racist stereotyping affects children. In 1989, Larkin formed NAP Productions, which produces films and videos for African-American children.

Alile Sharon Larkin's best-known film is *A Different Image* (1982). In the film, a young woman named Alana, played by Margot Saxton-Federella, attempts to escape the stereotypical defining powers of race and gender. Larkin's portrayal of the everyday routines of Alana is beautifully underplayed in naturalistic cinematography. As Alana looks at images of African women, she wonders where she fits into her own culture. Her boyfriend, Vincent, misunderstands Alana's quest for self-representation and identity. Alana tells him: "You just have to see me differently. You have to learn to respect me." *A Different Image* won first prize from the Black American Cinema Society. It has been screened on WNET and also has been shown as part of a touring exhibition through Africa. *A Different Image* is also frequently screened in African studies and women's studies courses.

In her article "Black Women Filmmakers Defining Ourselves: Feminism in Our Own Voice," Larkin notes that *A Different Image* received mostly positive criticism, but "some negative criticism has come from 'radical' feminists and Marxists . . . it would be their demand that I condemn black men and align myself with white women against patriarchy" (171). Larkin points out that "feminism succumbs to racism when it segregates black women from black men and dismisses our history. The assumption that black women and white women share identical or similar histories and experiences presents an important problem. . . . Feminism must address these issues, otherwise its ahistorical approach towards black women can and does maintain institutional racism" (158–59). In *A Different Image*, Larkin explores multiple perspectives on the problems of racism and sexism in African-American culture. She gathered images from a variety of different sources, using both stock footage and original photography, finding the money for the film as she went along. She made the film for only $15,000. Her philosophy toward low-budget filmmaking is accurately described in these comments: "There seem to be two schools among independents. Wait until you have all the money, or shoot what you can when you can. I shoot what I can when I can" (Acker, 131). In contrast to most directors, who expect actors to follow the script faithfully within a given scene, Larkin is a collaborative director who approaches film as a mediation between actor and director. In *A Different Image*, Larkin encouraged the actors to ad-lib their monologues, so that the film would acquire a sense of realism.

This sense of realism is also prevalent in Larkin's first film, *Your Children Come Back to You* (1979), which is told from the perspective of an African-American girl who is interested in African culture. In a memorable scene, the young girl tells her favorite story, about orphans who return to their mother, Africa, represented by the sun. The Afrocentric perspective of the film is evocatively rendered through the child's narrative voice-over. *What*

Color Is God? (1986) is an examination of Christian imagery through an Afrocentric and feminist perspective. *Miss Fluci Moses* (1987) is another Larkin film that explores African-American storytelling. In the film, Larkin documents the life of a black poet named Louise Jane Moses, who wrote her first poem when she was a child but was not published until after she retired from a lengthy career as a teacher and librarian. Larkin combined five interviews, archival footage, and poetry readings into a celebration of the newly discovered African-American woman poet. *Miss Fluci Moses* and Larkin's other films are available from Women Make Movies.

SELECTED FILMOGRAPHY

Your Children Come Back to You (1979)
A Different Image (1982)
Miss Fluci Moses (1987)

SELECTED BIBLIOGRAPHY

Acker, Ally. *Reel Women: Pioneers of the Cinema, 1896 to the Present.* New York: Continuum, 1993.

Klotman, Phyllis Rauch, ed. *Screenplays of the African American Experience.* Bloomington: Indiana University Press, 1991.

Larkin, Alile Sharon. "Black Women Filmmakers Defining Ourselves: Feminism in Our Own Voice." In *Female Spectators: Looking at Film and Television,* edited by E. Deidre Pribram, 157–73. London: Verso, 1988.

Reid, Mark A. "Dialogic Modes of Representing Africa(s): Womanist Film." *Black American Literature Forum* 25 (summer 1991): 375–88.

Taylor, Clyde. "The L. A. Rebellion, New Spirit in American Film." *Black Film Review* 2.2 (1986): 29.

Wallace, Michele. *Invisibility Blues: From Pop to Theory.* New York: Verso, 1990.

LEAF, CAROLINE (1946–). Canada. Born in Seattle, Washington, Caroline Leaf studied art at Radcliffe. She invented the technique of sand animation and many other innovative techniques of animation. She worked for several years as a freelance animator and directed animated sequences for television films. In 1972, Leaf began to work for the animation department of the National Film Board of Canada. Rather than working in the male-defined techniques of Hollywood-type "cel" animation, Leaf experimented with new forms of animation in order to develop a personal style. As Leaf told Cecile Starr: "I believe every person's work is personal and therefore new. There are as many forms of expression as there are people" (15). Caroline Leaf conforms to a pattern recognized by Judith Mayne in women filmmakers: a return to primitive styles of narration that evoke "the realm of early filmmaking" (185).

In Leaf's first film, *Sand, or Peter and the Wolf* (1969), Leaf developed a technique of animation involving fine beach sand on backlit glass. She used her fingers and her hands to manipulate the sand into silhouettes, creating a chiaroscuro effect in black and white. In 1923, Lotte Reiniger had similarly created a silhouette animation technique, using a simple scissor-cutting technique. Leaf shares with Reiniger an "eye toward establishing a viable feminist tradition for an alternative cinematic practice," (25), which Sandy Flitterman-Lewis notes in women experimental filmmakers.

After pioneering with sand animation, Caroline Leaf developed the technique of painting directly on glass in *The Owl Who Married a Goose* (1974). Leaf continued to expand the possibilities of the animated film form with the use of soft color washes of watercolors and ink painted directly on the glass stage of the animation camera for *The Street* (1976). Thematically, Leaf's films are diverse, though her films are often re-visions of myths and legends. The *Owl Who Married a Goose,* for example, is based on Eskimo legend. Leaf collaborated with three Inuit storytellers to complete the dialogue for the sound track. *How Beaver Stole Fire* (1971) and *Orfeo* (1972) are also experimental reworkings of animal myths.

Leaf won an Academy Award nomination for *The Street* (1976), a serious animated film adapted from a book by Montreal author Mordecai Richler. In *The Street,* Leaf interprets the reaction of a middle-class Jewish boy who experiences his grandmother's death. *The Street* is a study in grief and aging. It is also a stunning achievement in the development of primitive animation technique. *Interview* (1979) is a hybrid mix of documentary (live action) film and animation. Leaf collaborated with Veronica Seul on *Interview,* a study of female friendship.

Recently, Caroline Leaf's work has been collected in *Wayward Girls and Wicked Women,* a collection of films by women animators (see Kotlarz). As Irene Kotlarz notes, "The presentation of woman as desiring subject is the uniting concern of all these films" (1993, 103). Caroline Leaf's *Two Sisters* (1990) captures the psychological complexity of female sibling relationships. Other films in the collection include Joanna Quinn's *Girl's Night Out* (1987), a humorous film that features a male stripper, and Suzan Pitt's *Asparagus* (1978), a classic hallucinatory experiment in animation form.

Caroline Leaf's experiments in primitive animation technique, along with her ability to interweave animation with live-action film, are a deliberate move away from standardized image-making techniques of dominant Hollywood animation in which the cinematic apparatus is "made to the measure of male desire" (Mayne, 160). Leaf's incorporation of animation in live-action films is similarly used by African-American pioneering directors Zeinabu irene Davis and Ayoka Chenzira—Davis's animation of Haitian dance rituals in *A Powerful Thang* (1991) and Chenzira's animation of the range of African-American hairstyles in *Hair Piece: A Film for Nappy-Headed People* (1982), which demonstrates that the use of animation allows women directors to express female subjectivity in ways that are limited in live-action filmmaking. Other women animators include Mary Ellen

Bute, pioneer of electronic "abstronic" animation; Sally Cruickshank, a brilliant and unique animator; Marie Menken, an abstract filmmaker associated with the New York experimental underground filmmakers of the 1960s; Faith Hubley, British pioneering animator; and her daughter Emily Hubley, who etches directly on film.

Caroline Leaf continues to be actively involved in animation and documentary filmmaking at the National Film Board. Her films are screened at international film festivals and held in the Museum of Modern Art Circulating Film Library. Films such as the impressionist *Le Mariage du Hibon* (1975) constitute a worldview of visionary warmth and depth typical of Leaf. She says she is influenced by literary figures such as Kafka, Genêt, Ionesco, and Beckett, but her work displays an affinity with French Impressionism and the primitivism of the early twentieth century. Her philosophy is deceptively simple: "I like to make things move. It is like making them alive" (Starr and Russett, 14). Caroline Leaf combines technical purity and primitiveness with a diversity of thematic concerns. It is fortunate that the Canadian government supports independent filmmakers and animators such as Caroline Leaf.

SELECTED FILMOGRAPHY

Sand, or Peter and the Wolf (1969)
Orfeo (1972)
The Owl Who Married a Goose (1974)
The Street (1976)
The Metamorphosis of Mr. Samsa (1977)
Interview (codirector Veronica Seul) (1979)
Kate and Anna McGarrigle (1981)
An Equal Opportunity (People at Work series) (1982)
The Owl and the Pussycat (1985)
Two Sisters (1990)

SELECTED BIBLIOGRAPHY

Carson, Diane. "Women Filmmakers." In *Multiple Voices in Feminist Film Criticism,* edited by Diane Carson, Linda Dittmar, and Janice Welsch, 456–67. Minneapolis: University of Minnesota Press, 1994.
Flitterman-Lewis, Sandy. *To Desire Differently.* Urbana: University of Illinois Press, 1990.
Kaplan, E. Ann. *Women and Film: Both Sides of the Camera.* New York: Methuen, 1983.
Kotlarz, Irene. "Working against the Grain: Women in Animation." In *Women and Film: A Sight and Sound Reader,* edited by Pam Cook and Philip Dodd, 101–4. Philadelphia: Temple University Press, 1993.
———. "Leaf, Caroline." In *The Women's Companion to International Film,* edited by Annette Kuhn and Susannah Radstone, 238–39. Berkeley: University of California Press, 1994.
Martineau, Barbara Halpern. "Women and Cartoon Animation, or Why Women

Don't Make Cartoons, or Do They?" In *The American Animated Cartoon: A Critical Anthology,* edited by Gerald and Danny Pearcy, New York: Dutton, 1980.

Mayne, Judith. *The Woman at the Keyhole: Feminism and Women's Cinema.* Bloomington: Indiana University Press, 1990.

Pilling, Jayne, ed. *Women & Animation: A Compendium.* London: BFI, 1993.

Starr, Cecile, and Robert Russett. *Experimental Animation.* New York: Van Nostrand Reinhold, 1976.

LIVINGSTON, JENNIE (1960–   ). United States. Jennie Livingston, who rose to international prominence in 1990 with *Paris Is Burning,* a documentary about Harlem's gay ball scene, is a lesbian of German Jewish extraction. *Paris Is Burning* opened at the New York New Festival of Gay and Lesbian Film in 1990 to overwhelmingly positive reviews. In *Paris Is Burning,* Livingston records the lives of African-American and Latino drag queens, who displace gender identities through cross-dressing, performative vogueing, and drag ball contests in which "every conceivable form of identity becomes subject to (re)interpretation" (Goldsby, 109). The gay men, transvestites, and transsexuals form communities known as houses, or families, headed by clan "mothers" such as Pepper Labeija, Angie Xtravaganza, and Willi Ninja, who are featured prominently in *Paris Is Burning.* Livingston's camera captures the everyday life of the individuals and records the performances in cinema verité style. Livingston spent two years filming and living with the film participants, who themselves actively took part in their self-rendering, often playing directly to the camera.

Many of the house members reveal during on-camera interviews that they have been disowned by their families because of their sexual orientation. The documentary footage is broken up with titles that visually punctuate the narrative. Livingston marks off sections with such titles as "Vogueing," "House," and "Realness." *Paris Is Burning* is a celebration of the drag ball world, scored with disco records such as "Got to Be Real" and playfully edited by Jonathan Oppenheim. The drag queens remake "home" as a site of the celebration of difference and an alternative to the homophobia of society. As Livingston told John Howell, "[A]t the ball, members of a despised subcult convert the hostility of the church, the homophobes, the middle-class, and their families into self-love" (11). The drag balls, as Ann Cvetkovich suggests, "allow for a utopian empowerment unavailable elsewhere" (162).

Though *Paris Is Burning* received glowing praise by most critics, bell hooks and Amy Taubin point out the problematic aspects of the film. Livingston is criticized by bell hooks for avoiding the issue of objectification of black men by a "white person in a white supremacist society creating a film about black life" (151). Taubin, bemoaning the lack of lesbian films about lesbian desire, notes that in *Paris Is Burning,* along with *Poison*

(Todd Haynes, 1991) and *Tongues Untied* (Marlon Riggs, 1991), women are marginalized figures. Taubin concludes that "queer cinema is figured in terms of sexual desire and the desire it constructs is exclusively male" (178). Since Taubin's comments, some films by lesbian directors, notably Rose Troche's *Go Fish* (1994), have received widespread distribution. Jennie Livingston's next project, *Not for Profit,* is a collaboration with lesbian videographer Sadie Benning. The filmmakers promise to include plenty of interracial lesbian romance.

SELECTED FILMOGRAPHY

Paris Is Burning (1990)

SELECTED BIBLIOGRAPHY

Cvetkovich, Ann. "The Powers of Seeing and Being Seen: *Truth or Dare* and *Paris Is Burning.*" In *Film Theory Goes to the Movies,* edited by Jim Collins, Hilary Radner, and Ava Preacher Collins, 153–69. New York: Routledge, 1993.

Goldsby, Jackie. "Queens of Language." In *Queer Looks: Perspectives on Lesbian and Gay Film and Video,* edited by Martha Gever, John Greyson, and Pratibha Parmar, 108–15. New York: Routledge, 1993.

hooks, bell. "Is Paris Burning." In *Black Looks: Race and Representation,* 145–56. Boston: South End Press, 1992.

Howell, John. "Exits and Entrances." *Artforum* 27 (February 1989): 9–11.

Livingston, Jennie. "The Fairer Sex." *Aperture* 121 (fall 1990): 6–14.

Rich, B. Ruby. "Reflections on a Queer Screen." *Gay Lesbian Quarterly* 1.1 (1993): 83–92.

Taubin, Amy. "Queer Male Cinema and Feminism." In *Women and Film: A Sight and Sound Reader,* edited by Pam Cook and Philip Dodd, 176–79. Philadelphia: Temple University Press, 1993.

LONGINOTTO, KIM. *See* HUNT, CLAIRE

LUPINO, IDA (1918–95). United States.

"I never wrote just straight women's roles. I liked the strong characters," (172) Ida Lupino told Debra Weiner in 1977. Lupino, the only woman director who managed to work in Hollywood in the repressive 1950s, is sometimes incorrectly characterized as an "anti-feminist" (Weiner, 170). Too often, feminist critics have taken Lupino's caustic remarks at face value. One of Lupino's most frequently quoted quips shows up regularly in articles about her:

Any woman who wishes to smash into the world of men isn't very feminine. Baby, we can't go smashing. I believe women should be struck regularly—like a gong. (Gardner)

Lupino's flippancy marked her as a transgressive figure of independence, a woman unwilling to abide by anyone else's rules. As the quote suggests, Lupino had a dark sense of humor and an irreverent, even volatile personality. If the things she said exhibited a duality between feminism and mockery toward feminists, Lupino's work showed an even more pronounced duality. As a broad generalization, Lupino's films tended to speak in a voice that adheres to heterosexist underpinnings of 1950s Hollywood melodrama but, at the same time, frequently disrupts notions of gender.

Ida Lupino was born into a British family of actors and theatrical people. Her father, Stanley Lupino, was a comedian, and her mother, Connie Emerald, was an actress. After appearing in several British feature films between 1932 and 1933, Lupino came to the United States and made a career for herself as a well-known actress. But she was multitalented. She wrote screenplays, plays, and musical compositions and worked as an independent film producer/director and later as a much-in-demand television director, until as late as 1982. Lupino spent fifty years working in Hollywood, making her the most prolific Hollywood woman director with the longest-running career.

Though Lupino often said she "never planned to become a director" (Lupino, 14; Fuller), at other times she stated that she always wanted to direct films: "Believe me, I've fought to produce and direct my own pictures" (Ellis, 48). Lupino was quite aware that it was important to appear as if she were not overly ambitious in order to fit into the gender constructions of 1950s Hollywood. Her working of the publicity machine of Hollywood is in itself fascinating, because she continually stressed her femininity and portrayed herself as a woman who accidentally fell into a directorial capacity. True enough, Lupino's first job as director for *Not Wanted* (1949) seemingly fell into her lap when veteran director Elmer Clifton became ill three days into shooting. But *Not Wanted* was cowritten by Lupino and released through Lupino's own production company, Emerald Productions (later known as The Filmakers), and some have argued persuasively that Lupino was angling for the director's chair from the start of preproduction.

Not Wanted is the story of a young woman who gives birth to an illegitimate child. An article on the making of *Not Wanted* published in *Negro Digest* suggests that Ida Lupino was already quite active in the preproduction planning stages of the film. Lupino told Robert Ellis that she was attempting to cast the picture with a multicultural group of young women but was having trouble getting her idea past "the man behind the man with the money for the picture" (47). Lupino was told she "couldn't have the heroine in the same room with a Negro girl and a Spanish girl and a Chinese girl" (47). Though shocked by the outright racism of the executive, Lupino gave in to his demands, but she told him that someday she would "be in a position where [she] shouldn't be beholden to men with such ideas as his" (47). True to form, Lupino "managed to sneak a Chinese girl" (47) into the scene.

In making her films, Lupino played the role of "one of the boys," while, at the same time, injecting her feminism and multicultural agenda into the film. She proudly announced the formation of her new company and its social agenda: "I've got a concern we call Filmakers. There'll be no stereotyped roles for any nationality group" (Ellis, 48). Far from being an accidentally successful film director, Lupino was more than ready for a career move into the capacity of producer/director, and she had a personal vision of the films she wished to make. As Lupino told Robert Ellis, she "always nursed a desire to direct pictures" (48), and she consistently chose female-centered themes for her projects.

While *Not Wanted* purports to be a melodramatic object lesson in which a young girl gets pregnant and is made to suffer, Lupino employs a female perspective quite common to the melodrama. This female perspective allows for a circumvention of the paradigm of punishment of the sexually active female. In the film, the young girl (played by Sally Forrest) gives up her baby for adoption, only to steal one, and ends up in the hands of the police. Simon Hartog of *Commonweal* faulted the film's "avoidance of any discussion of the immorality of the girl's behavior" (Hartung), yet this lack of punishment of the sexually active female is the key to understanding Lupino's feminism. While the film seems to adhere to the generic conventions of the melodrama, complete with a suffering female heroine, *Not Wanted* departs from the usual model of the genre, characterized by the "sin, suffer, and repent" model. Not only is *Not Wanted* an early feminist melodrama, in the tradition of Lois Weber and Dorothy Arzner, but it found a large, probably female, audience. The picture grossed over $1 million domestically.

Lupino's independently produced films of the 1950s do not fit the model of the slickly produced melodramas of the period. Though they nod to the conventions of repressive mainstream ideologies, they tend to question them. In choosing topics such as rape, bigamy, polio, unwed motherhood, and other controversial topics, Lupino questioned the construction of moral order in the slick melodramas of the 1950s, which created female consumers "all dreaming for Mr. Right to save them, only to discover painfully there's no Mr. Right" (Rickey). As Carrie Rickey notes, Lupino's grim melodrama displaced this type of narrative. "No other Hollywood movies of the time promoted such bitter wisdom" (43).

Most of Lupino's films center around struggling heroines. *Outrage* (1950) is one of the only movies of the period to directly represent rape and its aftermath. *Never Fear* (1950) is a study of a woman dancer fighting against polio. *Hard, Fast and Beautiful* (1951) is an acerbic study of a mother who tries to live her life through her daughter, a champion tennis player. The film attacks the model of motherhood championed in 1950s cultural ideology and is comparable to Dorothy Arzner's critique of passive sex roles in *Craig's Wife* (1936). *The Bigamist* (1953) and *The Hitch-Hiker* (1953) are film noir studies of masculinity and violence. Lupino's sometimes ambiguous feminism exemplifies the career of a woman director who refused to define herself as a feminist, yet clearly employed a feminist vision.

From the 1950s to the 1980s, Lupino directed many episodes of television programs such as "Thriller," "Have Gun Will Travel," "The Fugitive," "Alfred Hitchcock," "The Untouchables," "Dr. Kildare," and "The Virginian." As an actress, Lupino was memorable for her performances in *The Man I Love* (1946), *Road House* (1948), *On Dangerous Ground* (1951), *Private Hell 36* (1954), *The Big Knife* (1955), *High Sierra* (1941), and many other films. Lupino continued acting, writing, and directing until she retired in 1982. She always felt that she did her best work as a director, rather than as an actress, in the egalitarian atmosphere of The Filmakers. As she told Debra Weiner, "[F]or years, I never had a happier period in my life. I'm very sorry that my partners chose to go into film distribution. If they hadn't, I think we would still be going today" (176). When asked to pick out her favorite acting role, Lupino singled out her role as Emily Brontë in *Devotion* (1946) (Fuller), an apt choice for such a visionary film artist. Lupino was married to Louis Hayward from 1938 to 1945. She divorced Hayward and married Collier Young, whom she also later divorced. Lupino then married actor Howard Duff in 1951 and divorced him in 1973. Until her death she lived in Hollywood and worked on her memoirs.

SELECTED FILMOGRAPHY

Not Wanted (1949)
Never Fear (1950)
Outrage (1950)
Hard, Fast and Beautiful (1951)
The Bigamist (1953)
The Hitch-Hiker (1953)
The Trouble with Angels (1966)

SELECTED BIBLIOGRAPHY

Acker, Ally. *Reel Women: Pioneers of the Cinema, 1896 to the Present.* New York: Continuum, 1993.

Byars, Jackie. *All That Hollywood Allows: Re-Reading 1950s Melodrama.* Chapel Hill: University of North Carolina Press, 1991.

Dozoretz, Wendy. "The Mother's Lost Voice in *Hard, Fast and Beautiful.*" *Wide Angle* 6.3 (1984): 50–57.

Ellis, Robert. "Ida Lupino Brings New Hope to Hollywood." *Negro Digest* (August 1950): 47–49.

Fuller, Graham. "Ida Lupino." *Interview* (October 1991): 118.

Gardner, Paul. "Ida Lupino in Comeback after Fifteen Years." *New York Times,* October 10, 1972, C15.

Hartung, Philip T. "*Not Wanted.*" *Commonweal* (August 12, 1949): 438.

Heck-Rabi, Louise. *Women Filmmakers: A Critical Reception.* Metuchen, NJ: Scarecrow Press, 1984.

Johnston, Claire. "Women's Cinema as Counter-Cinema." In *Notes on Women's Cinema,* edited by Claire Johnston, 24–31. London: SEFT, 1974. Pamphlet.

Kuhn, Annette. ed. *Queen of the "B"'s: Ida Lupino Behind the Camera*. Wiltshire: Flicks Books, 1995.

Lupino, Ida. "Me, Mother Directress." *Action!* (May–June 1967): 14–15.

Rickey, Carrie. "Lupino Noir." *Village Voice* (November 4, 1980): 43.

Smyth, Cherry. "Lupino, Ida." In *The Women's Companion to International Film*, edited by Annette Kuhn and Susannah Radstone, 248–50. Berkeley: University of California Press, 1994.

Weiner, Debra. "Interview with Ida Lupino." In *Women and the Cinema: A Critical Anthology*, edited by Karyn Kay and Gerald Peary, 169–78. New York: Dutton, 1977.

LYELL, LOTTIE (1890–1925). Australia. Lottie Lyell, a pioneering figure in Australian cinema, directed twenty-eight films with Raymond Longford. Andree Wright pieced together the career of the forgotten pioneer in *Brilliant Careers*. Lyell had an impressive career as an actress, director, and writer of silent films. Born in Sydney on February 23, 1890, she grew up in Balmain, Australia. While Lyell pioneered the image of the bush girl, she also played melodramatic roles such as the unwed mother in *The Woman Suffers* (1918). Lyell was attracted to the image of the physically active New Woman, however, and she played such a role in several films. A champion horseback rider, Lyell played the strong-willed, outdoor girl in films such as *The Tide of Death* (1912), *'Neath Australian Skies* (1913), and *The Woman Suffers* (1918).

Curiously, the authorities banned bushranging films in 1912, because, as Wright notes, "[c]ritics had expressed a concern about the effects of such films on cinema audiences which consisted predominantly of women" (4). Nevertheless, an Australian generic tradition of female heroines (who saved men) continued to run through Australian films. This bushranger woman is comparable to the serial queens who reigned in the early days of Hollywood feature film production. Lottie Lyell was the quintessential bushranger woman who performed stunts and codirected all of her films, thus having more than a slight measure of control over her own image as a cultural production. The tradition of this Australian female type begins with Kate Kelly in *The Story of the Kelly Gang* (1906). As Andree Wright notes, the scenes in which Kate Kelly proves herself "as a skilled equestrian no longer survive" (4). Lyell would continue the tradition set out by the Kate Kelly type in *A Girl of the Bush* (1921). An unsigned article on the film in the magazine *Green Room* announced the presence of the strong, self-determined female figure without any apologies for a presumed lack of "femininity":

A real Australian girl in a real Australian picture! She can ride the "killer" to a standstill—brand a steer in ten seconds and rob a sheep of its wool while you're winking. ("*A Girl of the Bush*," 12)

Though Lottie Lyell excelled as an actress/director of naturalistic photography for outdoor adventures such as *A Girl of the Bush*, she was equally at home in creating the image of the urban working girl. *The Sentimental Bloke* (1919) was an international success for Lyell and Longford. In the film, Lyell plays Doreen, a young woman who works at a factory. The film is well known for its realistic mise-en-scène and "naturalistic" performances. In her time, Lottie Lyell was famous, well paid, and recognized as a leading actress of the early Australian cinema. However, Lyell did not receive screen credit for direction until *The Blue Mountains Mystery* (1921). A production photograph of the film shows Lottie dressed in men's clothing, a signature of her New Woman status as director.

In *The Woman Suffers* (1918), Lottie Lyell and Raymond Longford attacked the double standard that worked against women who were sexually seduced and abandoned. The poster for the film is a feminist statement in itself: "The woman suffers . . . while the man goes free . . . her good name gone, because she was a woman." In the film, two women become pregnant and are abandoned by their lovers. The first commits suicide; the second attempts to give herself an abortion but fails. She decides to have the baby with or without a husband, at which point her lover decides to marry her, and the film ends happily. The portrayal of the unmarried pregnant female runs through many films directed by women in the early cinema. Lois Weber's *Where Are My Children?* (1916) depicts an abortion, and many of Weber's other films attack the double standard that operated against sexually active women. Ida May Park and Dorothy Davenport Reid also tackled the same theme. Lottie Lyell's *The Woman Suffers* is one of the rare films in which the sexually transgressive female figure survives in a happy ending.

Lottie Lyell probably drew on autobiographical material for her portrayal and direction of the heroine of *The Woman Suffers*. Lyell was romantically involved with Raymond Longford, who was married and refused to divorce, despite his seventeen-year affair with Lyell. Longford finally divorced his wife and married Lyell when she was dying of tuberculosis. They were married for only a few weeks before Lottie Lyell's death on December 21, 1925. Many production associates insist that Lottie Lyell was the primary director of the Lyell-Longford productions, "yet she allowed him to take credit for everything—which he did" (Lacey Percival in Wright, 11). After Lyell's death, Longford was pushed out of the film business by the growing monopolization of the cinema trade in Australia.

The exclusion of the work of Lottie Lyell and Raymond Longford is, in some ways, characteristic of many films directed by both men and women that were not canonized and institutionalized texts in cinema's dominant, politically charged, canon-making process. The films of a handful of directors, most notably D. W. Griffith, are "handed down" as "the master and epitome of early cinema, subordinative and excluding others," as Janet Staiger notes (195). Reception studies, which include studies of female audiences and the films that appealed to them, are reviewing the authority of the dominant canon and demonstrating alternative models of film scholarship. The films of Lottie Lyell could profitably be read as constructions of the female for the female spectator of the period of the New Woman and the suffrage movement. They embody a cultural moment that has been all but erased from cinematic history. A rereading of these films is not necessarily a matter of a resurrection of neglected "masterpieces," but, more important, it represents "an attack on the politics of power of those representing canonized films as universal" (Staiger, 202).

SELECTED FILMOGRAPHY

The Fatal Wedding (1911)
The Romantic Story of Margaret Catchpole (1911)
The Tide of Death (1912)
'Neath Australian Skies (1913)
The Silence of Dean Maitland (1914)
The Mutiny on the Bounty (1916)
The Church and the Woman (1917)
The Woman Suffers (1918)
The Sentimental Bloke (1919)
Ginger Mick (1920)
Rudd's New Selection (1921)
The Blue Mountains Mystery (1921)
The Dinkum Bloke (1923)
Fisher's Ghost (1924)
The Bushwackers (1925)
The Pioneers (1926)

SELECTED BIBLIOGRAPHY

Collins, Felicity. "Lyell, Lottie." In *The Women's Companion to International Film,* edited by Annette Kuhn, with Susannah Radstone, 250. Berkeley: University of California Press, 1994.
Cooper, Ross. "*And the Villain Still Pursued Her.*" M.A. thesis, A.N.U., Canberra, 1971.
"*A Girl of the Bush.*" *Green Room* (March 1, 1921): 12.
Pike, Andrew, and Ross Cooper. *Australian Film: 1900–1977.* Melbourne: Oxford University Press, 1980.
Shirley, Graham, and Brian Adams. *Australian Cinema: The First Eighty Years.* Sydney: Currency Press, 1981.
Staiger, Janet. "The Politics of Film Canons." in *Multiple Voices in Feminist Film Criticism,* edited by Diane Carson, Linda Dittmar, and Janice Welsch, 191–209. Minneapolis: University of Minnesota Press, 1994.
Tulloch, John. *Legends of the Screen: The Narrative Film in Australia 1919–1929.* Sydney: Currency Press, 1981.
Wright, Andree. *Brilliant Careers.* Sydney: Pan Books, 1986.

M

MACLEAN, ALISON (1958–   ). Canada/New Zealand. Alison Maclean was born in Canada in 1958. She moved to New Zealand in the 1960s and studied as a sculptor and photographer at the School of Fine Arts in Auckland, New Zealand. As an aspiring filmmaker, Maclean was influenced by film criticism of avant-garde films by women directors. Maclean recounts the absurdity of being influenced by films she had not seen, such as Laura Mulvey's *Riddles of the Sphinx* (1977) and Maya Deren's *Meshes of the Afternoon* (1943). Maclean's attempt to "think back through our mothers" (Woolf, 79) was problematic because of the difficulty of viewing women's films in New Zealand. "It happens a lot out here since you just don't get to view them," she told Lizzie Francke (19). Maclean's isolation from a female cinematic tradition placed her in the position of becoming her own role model, though she cites Jane Campion as an influence, "not so much because of her films . . . but more because I see what she is doing and her courage as an example" (Francke, 19).

Maclean's first student film, *Taunt* (1979), is directly influenced by articles in *Screen* about Laura Mulvey's influential experimental film *Riddles of the Sphinx*. Mulvey's film and the film criticism she wrote in the 1970s defined women's place in the language of the cinema and women as spectators outside cinema. *Taunt* is an experiment in gender identification. In the film, a man chases a woman, but both roles are played by the same actor. Maclean's preoccupation with gender ambiguity is played out more rigorously in her first feature film, *Crush* (1992), which centers around the ambiguous gender identity of the central character, Lane (Marcia Gay Hardin), a postmodern femme fatale figure. In this Gothic film noir, Lane's friendship with Angela (Caitlin Bossley) is a highly charged sexual relationship that is interrupted by a male figure. *Crush* is controversial because Maclean refuses to spell out the sexual relationship between the women characters, but, as Chris Straayer observes, "efforts to subdue lesbian connotations can stimulate innovations" (350). *Crush* is an investigation of the darker side of same-sex relationships. Maclean admits that she wishes to explore the "feminist taboo born out of the 'sisterhood is powerful' idea" (Francke, 19), which, as Lizzie Francke notes, is evident in "positive imagism of recent women's cinema" (19). The manner in which Maclean explores the cruel, competitive, and dark sides of female friendship is comparable to other recent films by women that displace stereotypical, one-sided, positive images of female romantic friendship. Maclean places the femme fatale outside the realm of male spectatorship and male pleasure. Katt Shea's *Poison Ivy* (1992) explores similar territory, with equally compelling results. The presence of the femme fatale in women's cinema may "shock and repel," but it may also provide us with a means of understanding "the dark side of the patriarchal unconscious" (Creed, 166). Both Lane, in *Crush,* and Ivy, in *Poison Ivy,* exist to disrupt the heterogeneity of patriarchal, small-town values.

Alison Maclean had already explored sexual power relationships in her short film *Kitchen Sink* (1989). This memorable horror film includes an image of a woman pulling a fetus out of a kitchen sink. The woman falls in love with the fetus as he grows into an adult male. She fashions him to suit her, but he becomes a problem when her love invests him with power. *Talkback* (1987) is another early Maclean effort that rereads female power, this time through the media of talk radio. In the film, a woman is suddenly elevated into a powerful figure of talk-show host. An earlier film, *Rud's Wife* (1985), is less optimistic about the possibility of female power. *Rud's Wife* explores the hopelessness and alienation of a New Zealand housewife. Alison Maclean's career was possible only outside the confines of the Hollywood system, and she is fortunate to have the financial backing of the New Zealand Film Commission to support her work.

SELECTED FILMOGRAPHY

Taunt (1979)
Rud's Wife (1985)
Talkback (1987)
Kitchen Sink (1989)
Crush (1992)

SELECTED BIBLIOGRAPHY

Creed, Barbara. *The Monstrous-Feminine Film, Feminism and Psychoanalysis.* London: Routledge, 1993.
Dieckmann, Katherine. "*Crush.*" *Film Comment* (September–October 1993): 4–6.
Doane, Mary Ann. *Femmes Fatales: Feminism, Film Theory, Psychoanalysis.* New York: Routledge, 1991.
Francke, Lizzie. "Dark Side—*Crush.*" *Sight and Sound* 3.4 (April 1993): 18–19.
Glaessner, Verina. "*Crush.*" *Sight and Sound* 3.4 (April 1993): 44.
Hardy, Ann. "Maclean, Alison." In *The Women's Companion to International Film,* edited by Annette Kuhn and Susannah Radstone, 251. Berkeley: University of California Press, 1994.

James, Caryn. "A Distinctive Shade of Darkness." *New York Times,* November 28, 1993, H13, 22.

Straayer, Chris. "The Hypothetical Lesbian Heroine." In *Multiple Voices in Feminist Film Criticism,* edited by Diane Carson, Linda Dittmar, and Janice Welsch, 343–64. Minneapolis: University of Minnesota Press, 1994.

Woolf, Virginia. *A Room of One's Own.* San Diego: Harcourt Brace Jovanovich, 1929.

MADISON, CLEO (1883–1964). United States. Actress, producer, and director Cleo Madison's career is an important chapter in the development of American motion pictures. She worked with a female community of directors, actresses, producers, and writers who were the nexus of production of films at Universal in the teens and 1920s. She led a fascinating suffragette lifestyle that was simultaneously provocative and liberating for both herself and her work. Madison was born in Bloomington, Illinois. She moved to California and worked as an actress for the Santa Barbara Stock Company. Cleo traveled the vaudeville circuit and used her acting experience to secure a job at Universal Pictures, acting, writing, and eventually directing films.

Under Carl Laemmle, Universal's studio head, "Universal could boast the largest number of women directors on its payroll" (Slide, 52). Laemmle had no problem hiring women as directors: he was far more concerned with keeping up the output of films. As an actress, Cleo Madison worked with many women directors, scenarists, and other actresses. The Universal women's community became a power center for women in film that actively worked for women's rights. The Universal women set an example for other women, who read about their lives as working women and suffragettes. Madison worked for pioneering director Lois Weber in 1913 on *Shadows of Life.* Years later, Cleo Madison singled out Weber's work as a director, stating, "Lois Weber's productions are phenomenally successful" ("Chic," 24). During this period, Madison also acted in a number of films directed by Ida May Park, including *Alas and Alack, A Mother's Atonement,* and *The Dancer.*

After working with Ida May Park, Madison made the decisive move into the role of producer/director in 1915. As Joanna Russ notes, role models are important to all artists, but to women they are "doubly valuable . . . women need assurances that they can produce art without . . . [going] mad or doing without love" (87). The Universal women supported each other's careers and provided one another with role models. As Lois Weber had learned from Alice Guy on the set, Cleo Madison saw Lois Weber, Nell Shipman, Ruth Ann Baldwin, Grace Cunard, Lule Warrenton, Jeannie Macpherson, Ruth Stonehouse, and Elsie Jane Wilson busily directing films and also working on the set in a number of different capacities. Cleo Madison directed (or codirected) and produced about twenty films in which she also starred between 1915 and 1916. Though most of these films are "lost" through neglect and sexist archival practices (see Staiger), a few have survived.

Madison's films were noted for their cinematography. As one critic wrote, "[S]he accomplished results of staging and lighting which set something of a standard for future productions" ("Chic," 25). Cleo Madison's films fall into a number of different genres, from the Western to the melodrama. In attempting to reconstruct an overview of Madison's work, it is useful to look at her in her self-described position as an activist and suffragette. As Madison told William M. Henry in 1916, "One of these days, men are going to get over the fool idea that women have no brains [and will see that women] can do their work as well as they can" (108). Henry's description of Cleo Madison is typical of the masculine backlash against the women's movement. While Henry ostensibly admired Madison's politics, he tried to eroticize her as an object of beauty in order to soften her power as a feminist spokesperson:

With the lovely but militant Cleo at their head, the suffragettes could capture the vote for their sex and smash down the opposition as easily as shooting in a bucket. Cleo Madison is a womanly woman,—if she were otherwise she couldn't play sympathetic emotional roles.

Only seven months later, a writer for *The Moving Picture Weekly* (known only by the pseudonym "Mlle. Chic") implies that Cleo Madison is "too busy" to be a suffragette. In the same article, Cleo Madison announces that she is leaving her directorial role and that she will be appearing in the future under the direction of Rex Ingram. The repositioning of Cleo Madison in the female sphere is carefully staged in this publicity article, which contains a lengthy section about Madison's ability to cook and garden. Even in the age of the New Woman, the Hollywood patriarchal system was already beginning to push women out of the director's chair. The article dubs Madison a "dual" personality, a woman trying to fill a man's shoes. As Marjorie Rosen notes of the women's movement of the period, "[T]he more impetus the movement gained, the greater the masculine backlash" (29). It may not be far off the mark to suggest that Madison was removed as a director in response to the feminism of her films. Though the archival neglect of Madison's films has made it almost impossible to view a wide range of her work, surviving film synopses of Madison's films would tend to support this theory.

Madison's *Her Bitter Cup* (1916) is described as an "early suffragette classic" (Acker, 68). A synopsis of the film reveals it as a feminist melodrama that decries the oppression of poor women. Madison plays Rethna, a poor woman raised in a slum. She nurses the ill and works in a factory. The factory owner sexually harasses her and forces her to move into a "love nest." The film ends with the girl's crucifixion. Obviously, *Her Bitter*

Cup associated the oppression of women with Christian suffering, in a thematic trope typical of feminist suffragette films.

In *Her Defiance* (1916, codirected with Joe King), Madison plays an abandoned pregnant woman. Her brother tries to arrange a marriage for her, but Madison refuses to be ensnared in any form of captivity. Running away to the city, she bears an illegitimate child and finds a job as a cleaning lady to support herself and her child. In the final scene, in which the young woman confronts her lover, Madison's clever use of an insert, "matted" image telescopes time and distance to resolve the narrative. The father of the child explains his behavior on one side of the screen, as Madison "mattes" in a flashback from the couple's past. In this way, Madison represents the point of view of the female who is weighing the statements of the lover against her memories of the events.

Other titles directed by Cleo Madison can also be considered feminist melodramas, particularly *Alias Jane Jones* (1916), *A Soul Enslaved* (1916), and *A Heart's Crucible* (1916), the latter codirected with Kathleen Kerrigan. Cleo Madison's films were made around the same time that a number of suffragette films were produced, including *Eighty Million Women Want?* (1913, director Kate Corbally), *Your Girl or Mine* (1914), a film produced in cooperation with the National American Women Suffrage Association, and a lost film entitled *Daisies* (1910), which was shot at Vassar College by an unknown woman director (Bowser, 186). In *Daisies,* a young woman insists on an education but is opposed by her fiancé. The happy feminist ending includes a scene in which the fiancé admits that he was wrong and that women should seek higher education. In addition, serials such as *The Trey O'Hearts* (1914) and *The Master Key* (1914) (both starring Cleo Madison) were directly related to the feminist movement. Thus, Madison was only one of a number of women filmmakers actively using film as an artistic tool and/or a political medium during this period.

Cleo Madison envisioned herself as a pioneering, thrill-seeking, athletic New Woman. She lived at the center of a thriving female community, many of whose members were also successful women directors. Later in her life, she worked in a number of administrative positions outside the Hollywood milieu until she retired. She supported her mother and her physically challenged sister, with whom she lived, until her death at age eighty-one in 1964. Madison's obituaries recalled her accomplishments as an actress, citing her work with actors Wallace Reid, Herbert Rawlinson, and William Desmond in such classic silent films as *The Heart of the Cracksmen* (1913), *The Severed Hand* (1914), and *Damon and Pythias* (1914). But these obituaries failed to highlight her significant work as a pioneering feminist director, and for this work, Cleo Madison should be remembered today.

SELECTED FILMOGRAPHY

His Pal's Request (uncredited) (1913)
Liquid Dynamite (1915)

Ring of Destiny (1915)
The Power of Fascination (1915)
A Soul Enslaved (1916)
His Return (1916)
Her Defiance (codirector Joe King) (1916)
A Heart's Crucible (codirector Kathleen Kerrigan) (1916)
Her Bitter Cup (codirector Joe King) (1916)
Eleanor's Catch (1916)
Virginia (1916)
When the Wolf Howls (1916)
Alias Jane Jones (1916)
The Crimson Yoke (codirector William V. Mong) (1916)
Priscilla's Prisoners (1916)
The Girl in Lower 9 (1916)
The Guilty One (1916)
Tillie, the Little Swede (codirector William V. Mong) (1916)
Along the Malibu (codirector William V. Mong) (1916)
Triumph of Truth (1916)
To Another Woman (codirector William V. Mong) (1916)

SELECTED BIBLIOGRAPHY

Acker, Ally. *Reel Women: Pioneers of the Cinema, 1896 to the Present.* New York: Continuum, 1993.
Balshofer, Fred J., and Arthur C. Miller. *One Reel a Week.* Berkeley: University of California Press, 1967.
Bowser, Eileen. *History of the American Cinema 2: The Transformation of Cinema 1907–1915.* New York: Scribner's, 1990.
"Chic, Mlle." (pseud.) "The Dual Personality of Cleo Madison." *Moving Picture Weekly* (July 1, 1910): 24–25, 34.
Henry, William M. "Cleo, the Craftswoman." *Photoplay* (January 1916): 108.
"Obituary: Cleo Madison." *Hollywood Reporter* (March 12, 1964): 12.
Rainey, Buck. *Those Fabulous Serial Heroines.* Metuchen, NJ: Scarecrow Press, 1990.
Rosen, Marjorie. *Popcorn Venus: Women, Movies and the American Dream.* New York: Avon, 1973.
Russ, Joanna. *How to Suppress Women's Writing.* Austin: University of Texas Press, 1993.
Slide, Anthony. *Early Women Directors.* New York: Da Capo, 1984.
Staiger, Janet. "The Politics of Film Canons." In *Multiple Voices in Feminist Film Criticism,* edited by Diane Carson, Linda Dittmar, and Janice R. Welsch, 191–209. Minneapolis: University of Minnesota Press, 1994.

MALDOROR, SARAH (1929–). France/Guadeloupe/Africa. African filmmaker Sarah Maldoror, born Sarah Ducados, chose the name Maldoror after the nineteenth-century novel *Les Chants de Maldoror,* by Count de Lautréamont. Maldoror is of Afro-Caribbean ethnicity. Her parents were born in Guadeloupe and emigrated to the West Indies. Though Maldoror was born in France, she is considered a black African director and a Caribbean director. Maldoror told Sylvia Harvey that she dislikes categorization by nationality: "I'm against all forms of nationalism. Nationalities and borders between countries have to disappear. . . . I have to live where the money is to be raised, and then do my work in Africa" (75). Maldoror transcends the Eurocentric category of Third World woman director. As Chandra Mohanty notes, such categorization "is a mode of appropriation and codification" (337) that denies African women political consciousness and agency.

Sarah Maldoror is a political filmmaker whose perspective comes out of a commitment to political agency and postcolonial consciousness. Though she is best known to the Western world for *Sambizanga* (1972), a political call for action, Maldoror has had quite an extraordinary career as film director and political activist. She is married to Mario de Andrade, a noted Angolan political activist, writer, and leader of the Angolan liberation movement. Maldoror studied at the Moscow Film Academy and became politically active in the 1950s. She was involved in the African liberation movement in France, and she also founded the theater group Les Griotes, an agitprop collective, for which Maldoror adapted works by Jean-Paul Sartre and other political writers for the stage. Before she became a film director, Maldoror worked as Gillo Pontecorvo's collaborator on *The Battle of Algiers* (1966). The classic neorealist film records the bloodbath between Algerian freedom fighters and French militia in 1957 and 1958.

In 1970, Maldoror made her first film, *Monangambee,* which was shot in Algeria. The film is based on the life of political prisoner Luandino Vieira, who had been unjustly sentenced to a fourteen-year jail term by the Portuguese colonial rulers. Maldoror's next film, *Des Fusils pour Banta* (1971), was made by and with Algerian resistants, who acted as technicians for the film and portrayed themselves. Maldoror and the underground resistants spent three months recording life in the war zone. The mixture of authentic and staged material typifies Maldoror's approach to cinema, which draws upon the neorealist tradition.

Over many years, Maldoror has worked in African cinema as a political activist against colonialism and postcolonial rule. *Sambizanga* (1972) depicts a central female revolutionary in Angola. As Manthia Diawara notes, *Sambizanga* has been unfairly "criticized for being 'too beautiful' " (90). Critics of the film ignore Maldoror's intent, according to Diawara, "to create a positive role for women in the revolution" (90). *Sambizanga* exemplifies a third cinema "able to challenge official versions of history" (Gabriel, 57). The film reinscribes the role of women in revolutionary politics. As Maldoror told Sylvia Harvey, her feminist agenda went beyond representational imagery:

I'm only interested in women who struggle. These are the women I want to have in my films, not the others. I also offer work to as many women as possible during the time I'm shooting my films. You have to support those women who want to work with film. Up until now, we are still few in number, but if you support those women in film who are around, then slowly our numbers will grow. . . . Both in Africa and in Europe, woman remains the slave of man. That's why she has to liberate herself. (75)

Sambizanga won awards at many international film festivals. The film is screened regularly in African film festivals, women's film festivals, and African and women's studies courses. Sarah Maldoror is an activist for African cinema who sees the role of political marginalization of African film as part of a larger context of colonial imperialism. The greatest problem of African cinema is distribution, which is monopolized by the French. Maldoror notes that there was only one African country in the 1970s, Algeria, which had its own distribution company. Funding is also a problem for African filmmakers. Regardless, Maldoror insists, there is an African cinema, despite the prevailing view that denies its existence. Maldoror remains politically active both as a filmmaker and as a champion for the many voices of African cinema.

SELECTED FILMOGRAPHY

Monangambee (1970)
Des Fusils pour Banta (*Guns for Banta*) (1971)
Saint-Denis-sur-Avenir (*The Future of St. Denis*) (1971)
La Commun, Louise Michel et nous (1971)
Et les chiens se taisaient (*And the Dogs Fell Silent*) (1971)
Sambizanga (1972)
The Saint-Denis Basilica (1976)
Un Homme, une terre: Aimé Césaire (1977)
Paris, le cimetière du Pére Lachaise (1977)
Un Masque a' Paris: Louis Aragon (1978)
Miro (1979)
Fogo, l'île de fen (1979)
Un Carnival dans le Sahel (1979)
Un Dessert pour Constance (*A Dessert for Constance*) (1980)
Portrait de Madame Diop (1986)
The Tassili Passenger (1986)
Aimé Césaire, le masque des mots (1987)

SELECTED BIBLIOGRAPHY

Diawara, Manthia. *African Cinema: Politics & Culture.* Bloomington: Indiana University Press, 1992.
Gabriel, Teshorne H. "Third Cinema as Guardian of Popular Memory: Towards a Third Aesthetics." In *Questions of Third Cinema,* edited by Jim Pines and Paul Willemen, 53–64. London: BFI, 1989.
Harvey, Sylvia. "Third World Perspectives: Focus on Sarah Maldoror." *Women and Film* 1.5–6 (1974): 71–75, 110.
Kerbel, Michael. "Angola: Brutality and Betrayal." *Village Voice* (December 6, 1973): 85.
Martin, Angela. *African Films: The Context of Production.* London: BFI, 1982.
Mohanty, Chandra Talpade. "Under Western Eyes: Feminist Scholarship and Colonial Discourses." *Boundary* 2 (spring–fall 1984): 333–58.

Pearson, Lyle. "Four Years of African Film." *Film Quarterly* 26.3 (spring 1973): 42–47.

Pfaff, Françoise. *Twenty-Five Black African Filmmakers: A Critical Study with Filmography and Bibliography.* New York: Greenwood Press, 1988.

Quart, Barbara. *Women Directors: The Emergence of a New Cinema.* New York: Praeger, 1988.

Trinh T. Minh-ha. "Outside In Inside Out." In *Questions of Third Cinema,* edited by Jim Pines and Paul Willemen, 133–49. London: BFI, 1989.

MALLET, MARILU (1945–   ). Chile/Canada. Marilu Mallet is a Chilean writer/filmmaker based in Canada. She became a director after graduating from a program in architecture. She became active as a filmmaker in Chile during the popular unity period but left the country in 1973 after the political coup overthrew the socialist government. Mallet exiled herself to Quebec, where she directed many documentary films. Mallet's distinctive style is rendered through a juxtaposition of fictionalized, semirealist performances with improvisational acting techniques. Mallet's approach to documentary is a complex embrace of the "dialogue [which] can occur between filmmakers and participants or viewers, among the film participants or between them and viewers, among viewers, and within a viewer" (Welsch, 166). These multiple dialogic positions are highlighted by Mallet's creative use of documentary and narrative technique. Subjectivity and objectivity become difficult to define and are scrutinized as viable categories. Mallet circumvents the "female identity enclosure" (95) described by Trinh T. Minh-ha, and *Unfinished Diary* (1982) is an example of this dialogic circumvention. The film is best described as a "low drama" of autobiographical content and context. In the film, a Chilean exile and emigré film director (Mallet) struggles to make a film about her loss of subjective identity. Mallet's English-speaking husband, also a filmmaker, criticizes her anthropological approach to documentary. Mallet's son, who speaks only French, is also in the film. His presence problematizes the notion of language as it is used as a marking of identity. In setting the public struggle for subjectivity in the personal space of the domestic sphere and at the same time placing it in the traditionally public scene of the film itself, Mallet brilliantly uses space itself as a metaphor of identity. As Zuzana Pick notes, *Unfinished Diary* is a "clear departure from the conventions associated with Latin American and Chilean documentary" (53). *Unfinished Diary* uses flashbacks of a remembered past, an identity fused in a specific place, far different from the displaced, exiled, urban landscape of the filmmaker. Identity is removed from cultural enclosure and sutured across a poetic dialogic of the filmmaker herself.

Exile and identity, cultural displacement and subjectivity are central themes in the work of Marilu Mallet. Her experimental approach to these themes is not entirely unlike that of Marguerite Duras, Jill Godmilow, or

Chantal Akerman. The filmmakers share a simultaneous embrace and escape from the enclosures of exile that displace subjective identity. In *Les Borges* (1977), Mallet centers on the politics of displaced cultural ties common to immigrants in Canada from Portugal. The voices of a whole generation of Portuguese immigrant families bespeak a dialogic in the documentary. *Les Femmes de l'Amérique latine* (1980) is strategically similar in its voicing of the experiences of Latin American women across margins of age, color, class, and time. Mallet's work has been compared with the feminist films of Chilean film director Valeria Sarmiento. As Zuzana Pick notes, the work of "Chilean women filmmakers offers an interesting critical space for the objective implications of exile because it dislodges the political from the narrow boundaries of collective experience" (52). The fragmented, exiled self emerges from the daily experience of silence and stasis to a place of female identities. Marilu Mallet's *Unfinished Diary* is available from Women Make Movies, Inc. Mallet has also published several collections of short stories in French.

SELECTED FILMOGRAPHY

Amuhuelai-Mi (1971)
A.E.I. (1972)
Donde voy a encontrar otra Violeta (unfinished) (1973)
Lentement (*Slowly*) (1974)
Les Borges (1977)
L'évangile à Solentiname (1979)
Musique d'Amérique latine (1979)
Les femmes de l'Amérique latine (1980)
Journal inachevé (*Unfinished Diary*) (1982)
Mémoires d'un enfant des Andes (1985)

SELECTED BIBLIOGRAPHY

Chanan, Michael. *The Cuban Image*. London: BFI, 1985.
Freydburg, Elizabeth Hadley. "Women of Color." In *Multiple Voices in Feminist Film Criticism,* edited by Diane Carson, Linda Dittmar, and Janice Welsch, 468–80. Minneapolis: University of Minnesota Press, 1984.
Pick, Zuzana. "Chilean Cinema in Exile." *Framework* 34 (1987): 39–57.
Stam, Robert, and Louise Spence. "Colonialism, Racism, and Representation: An Introduction." *Screen* 24.2 (March–April 1983): 2–20.
Trinh T. Minh-ha. *Woman, Native, Other*. Bloomington: Indiana University Press, 1989.
Welsch, Janice. "Bakhtin, Language and Women's Documentary Filmmaking." In *Multiple Voices in Feminist Film Criticism,* edited by Diane Carson, Linda Dittmar, and Janice Welsch, 162–75. Minneapolis: University of Minnesota Press, 1994.

MANGOLTE, BABETTE (1941–   ). France/United States. Born in France, Babette Mangolte is an American independent filmmaker and also a renowned cinematographer. As a director of photography, Mangolte shot many classic feminist films, including Chantal Akerman's *Jeanne Dielman* (1974) and *News from Home* (1976), Yvonne Rainer's *Film about a Woman Who . . .* (1974), and Sally Potter's *The Gold Diggers* (1983). Mangolte has also directed four feature films: *What Maisie Knew* (1975), *The Camera: Je or La Camera: I* (1977), *The Cold Eye (My Darling, Be Careful)* (1980), and *The Sky on Location* (1982). Mangolte is a cinematographer's filmmaker. Her work challenges standard cinematic procedures. She often plays with formalist and minimalist strategies. This is not surprising, as Mangolte has worked with Michael Snow and Chantal Akerman, both formalists in style. Mangolte's *What Maisie Knew* has more in common with an Akerman film, however, than with a Michael Snow film. The structure of the film, a loose adaptation of the Henry James novel, utilizes the formalist long take; however, the mise-en-scène of *What Maisie Knew* is erotic and oddly humorous, more in keeping with Chantal Akerman's films. In *What Maisie Knew,* Babette Mangolte plays with the viewer by convincing us that the film is shot from the point of view of a young girl. The film captured the attention of the underground filmmaking scene and was screened at the Whitney Museum of American Art.

Mangolte's next film, *The Camera: Je or La Camera: I,* is an experimental feature film about the life of a still photographer. Much of the film is images of male models, redefining the look of the male gaze into the objectified male body gazed at by the female camera/eye. This shift is underscored by the continual emphasis on process, which grounds us in the realm of female subjectivity, the subjectivity of the woman director. As Lauren Rabinovitz notes, avant-garde women directors and artists such as Mangolte are problematic to male reporters' gazes because they locate positions of "refusal of the male gaze" (10). The reception of these films as films directed by women, according to Rabinovitz, is "always prefiguring the possibility for containment of their more radical film practices" (10). Mangolte's *The Camera: Je or La Camera: I* is a radical refiguring of cinema that cannot be disentangled from gender politics. To deny Mangolte is involved in the sexual politics of underground filmmaking would be to reduce *The Camera: Je or La Camera: I* to just another self-reflexive film about an artist. The fact that the film is by and about a woman artist is part of the aesthetic of a radical cinema that denies containment. *The Camera: Je or La Camera: I* is Mangolte's favorite film, as she told Scott MacDonald:

I think it's my most original film in terms of form. It's also about my deeply felt involvement with still photography. . . . Like everybody else, I went directly to my most immediate experience. One subject I felt had not been really treated in film, is the process of work. (287)

The Camera: Je or La Camera: I was screened at the Museum of Modern Art in New York and on French television.

Mangolte's subsequent feature, *The Cold Eye (My Darling, Be Careful)* (1980), is more of a conventional narrative film, though it is somewhat minimalist and difficult. *The Cold Eye (My Darling, Be Careful)* is told from the perspective of Cathy Digsby, a young painter, whom we hear offscreen but never see. *The Cold Eye (My Darling, Be Careful)* operates on a level of women's discourse in which woman is not "centered in character or psychic fetish, but on the 'woman's voice' heard intermittently among the social discourses drawn into the text of a film" (Gledhill, 118). Babette Mangolte reminds us with *The Cold Eye (My Darling, Be Careful)* that "identity, like the real, is a site of social and cultural negotiation," as Christine Gledhill observes (121). Being an independent artist takes continual renegotiating of identity. Mangolte expressed dissatisfaction with the film in an interview with Scott MacDonald: "[B]ecause I didn't have much money, I cut corners" (291). Despite financial problems, *The Cold Eye (My Darling, Be Careful)* addresses the most basic question of feminist radical cinema, how one can avoid objectifying the female image. Mangolte does this through a complex system of avoidance strategies, using a voice-over and relying on cutaways. While she was finishing *The Cold Eye (My Darling, Be Careful)*, Mangolte was funded by German television to direct *The Sky on Location*, an experimental travelogue. In *The Sky on Location*, the viewer is placed in the difficult position of reading visuals and texts that do not match in the sense of traditionally constructed narratives.

Mangolte came to New York from France to pursue a career in film, as she was always able to find work as a still photographer. Actually, she intended to stay in New York only a few months "to see Brakhage and Snow films" (MacDonald, 295), but she ended up staying several years. Mangolte has been involved in dance and theater in addition to photography and cinematography, but she now spends more time making films than working in photography. Babette Mangolte's independent films are extraordinarily difficult, yet they are some of the most radical departures from narrativity in independent cinema.

SELECTED FILMOGRAPHY

What Maisie Knew (1975)
Now (or *Maintenant entre parenthèses*) (1976)
The Camera: Je or La Camera: I (1977)
Water Motor (1978)
There? Where? (1979)
The Cold Eye (My Darling, Be Careful) (1980)
The Sky on Location (1982)

SELECTED BIBLIOGRAPHY

Camera Obscura Collective. "Interview with Babette Mangolte." *Camera Obscura* 3.4 (summer 1979): 198–210.
de Lauretis, Teresa. *Technologies of Gender.* Bloomington: Indiana University Press, 1987.

Film-Makers' Cooperative. *Film-Makers' Cooperative Catalogue 7.* New York: Film-Makers' Cooperative, 1989.

Gledhill, Christine. "Image and Voice: Approaches to Marxist-Feminist Film Criticism." In *Multiple Voices in Feminist Film Criticism,* edited by Diane Carson, Linda Dittmar, and Janice Welsch, 109–23. Minneapolis: University of Minnesota Press, 1994.

MacDonald, Scott. *A Critical Cinema: Interviews with Independent Filmmakers.* Berkeley: University of California Press, 1988.

Mayne, Judith. *The Woman at the Keyhole: Feminism and Women's Cinema.* Bloomington: Indiana University Press, 1990.

Quart, Barbara. *Women Directors: The Emergence of a New Cinema.* New York: Praeger, 1988.

Rabinovitz, Lauren. *Points of Resistance: Women, Power & Politics in the New York Avant-Garde Cinema, 1943–71.* Urbana: University of Illinois Press, 1991.

Turim, Maureen. *Abstraction in Avant-Garde Film.* Ann Arbor: UMI Research Press, 1985.

MARSHALL, PENNY (1942–   ). United States. "If you're lucky enough to have a hit movie, then you're allowed four failures," Penny Marshall told Carrie Fisher. "But I don't know if that applies to women. And I don't wish to find out" (96). Penny Marshall has been extremely lucky as a director. *Big* (1988) and *A League of Their Own* (1992) did very well at the box office. In an increasingly competitive Hollywood that is becoming more and more box-office-oriented, Penny Marshall has had one of the longest-running careers of any woman director in mainstream cinema. Most women directors do not get the opportunity to direct several major Hollywood productions. Though Penny Marshall has benefited from being the sister of Garry Marshall, a powerful producer/director, she still has had to prove herself twice-over to establish herself as a major director.

Born in the Bronx and educated in New Mexico, Penny Marshall went to Hollywood and became an actress/comedienne on television programs such as "The Odd Couple" and "Happy Days." Marshall was paired with Cindy Williams for a long-running situation comedy, "Laverne and Shirley" (1976–83). Penny Marshall directed several episodes of the series and three television movies for MTV. In 1986, she was set to direct *Peggy Sue Got Married,* but she was pulled off the project "on the excuse that she was too inexperienced" (Acker, 90). In the same year, Marshall was assigned to direct *Jumpin' Jack Flash* (1986), starring Whoopi Goldberg, after another director had been relieved from the film ten days into production. Though the film is considered a sleeper, Marshall considers the project a learning experience. "I thought it was okay, considering there was no script. . . . And it earned more than it cost to make" (Fisher, 96). Marshall's sardonic sense of humor is no doubt a cover for her sense of perfectionism. "I watch my movies, and I only see what's wrong with them," she told Carrie Fisher (96).

Penny Marshall's first major success came in 1988, when she directed *Big*, a fantasy film featuring Tom Hanks as a thirteen-year-old trapped in a thirty-five-year-old's body. *Big* is provocative as a study of male gender roles. The responsibilities thrust upon the thirteen-year-old boy and his reactions to them are, at the same time, comic and insightful. *Big* is as sentimental as a Frank Capra vehicle such as *It's a Wonderful Life* (1946), but Marshall works well with sentimental material. She understands Hollywood commercial film from an actor's perspective, and she understands timing from her years as a comic. Penny Marshall is a successful Hollywood director because she believes in the sentimental heart of the material she works with, and she never subverts it. She caters to the nostalgic longing for a supposedly better past, which mainstream American audiences desire. For example, *Awakenings* (1990) is almost dripping with sentimentality. In *Awakenings*, Marshall fulfills audience expectations and almost zealously underscores the upbeat theme of spiritual rebirth in a manner almost exactly like Frank Capra's *It's a Wonderful Life*.

If it were not for the strong theme of feminine community, the sentimentality of *A League of Their Own* would overwhelm the material. A comedy about the first season of the women's baseball league in 1943 (based on a story by Kim Wilson and Kelly Candaele), *A League of Their Own* is a "woman's film." The film's plot has been described as "hammy," "obvious," and "heart tugging," but Marshall weaves several feminist jabs into the otherwise banal material. Geena Davis's performance in a woman-centered film is unsurprising, given her success in *Thelma and Louise* (1991) and her more recent performance in *Angie* (1994). Davis has become emblematic of a feminist figure for the masses, a strong, working-class, heterosexual woman who wrestles with problems common to all women.

Penny Marshall's most recent film, *Renaissance Man* (1994), is a standard-issue comedy about a group of underprivileged army members who learn the value of education from a displaced ad executive (Danny DeVito) who is left in charge of the supposedly hopeless students. Predictably, De Vito triumphs as a teacher of Shakespeare, despite all odds. Though it has its heart in the right place, the film is marred by a slow pace and overly obvious, heart-tugging situations. *Renaissance Man* did not fare as well at the box office as Marshall's earlier commercial successes. It will be interesting to see what work Marshall attempts in the future; she is rumored to be recutting *Renaissance Man* in the hope of rereleasing the film to wider audiences.

SELECTED FILMOGRAPHY

Let's Switch (1975)
More than Friends (1979)
Love Thy Neighbor (1984)
Jumpin' Jack Flash (1986)
Big (1988)

Awakenings (1990)
A League of Their Own (1992)
Renaissance Man (1994)

SELECTED BIBLIOGRAPHY

Abramowitz, Rachel. "Shot by Shot." *Premiere* (January 1991): 21.

Acker, Ally. *Reel Women: Pioneers of the Cinema, 1896 to the Present*. New York: Continuum, 1993.

Baker, Rick. "Diamonds Are a Girl's Best Friend." *American Cinematographer* 73 (July 1992): 60–65.

Byars, Jackie. *All That Hollywood Allows: Rereading Gender in 1950s Melodrama*. Chapel Hill: University of North Carolina Press, 1991.

Fisher, Carrie, and Penny Marshall. "Rappin' with Penny and Carrie." *People* (Special Edition, *Inside Hollywood: Women, Sex & Power*) (spring 1991): 95–97.

MARTIN, DARNELL (1964–   ). United States. Darnell Martin's *I Like It Like That* (1994) is currently being hailed as an international critical hit film, one of the first major studio films by an African-American woman director (Columbia Pictures funded and distributed the project) to begin to break through into the international film scene. Darnell has recently received a blitz of publicity, which disguises the fact that she has been working in the film industry a long time to get where she is today. She was born on January 7, 1964, in the Bronx into a family life of extreme poverty, but she landed at Sarah Lawrence at the insistence of her mother, who believed that a proper education was the most important factor in determining one's later life. At Sarah Lawrence Martin first got a solid glimpse of the possibilities of expressing one's own personal vision through creative work.

After graduating from Sarah Lawrence, Martin applied at several film schools but was turned down and had to take a menial job checking out rental cameras to support herself. She also appeared as an actress in the low-budget 1987 thriller *Deadly Obsession* (director Jeno Hodl) to help pay the bills. While working at the camera rental facility, Martin made the acquaintance of Ernest Dickerson, who shot many of Spike Lee's early groundbreaking films. Impressed by Martin's spirit and tenacity, Dickerson got her a job as an assistant on Lee's *Do the Right Thing*. Finally, after a personal phone call from Spike Lee himself, Martin was accepted by the New York University Film School, but she left before graduating. She made a short film while there, *Suspect,* and this led to a stint at the directing workshop at Robert Redford's Sundance Film Institute.

By this time, Martin was beginning to attract some serious attention, and New Line Cinema offered her $2 million to film her script of *Blackout,* which later metamorphosed into *I Like It Like That*. However, the low budget meant that the film would have to be shot very quickly, and Martin was afraid that the rush would compromise the quality of the finished project. Accordingly, she held out until Columbia Pictures came up with a $5.5 million budget, which would allow for nine weeks of shooting. The film began in earnest in the late summer of 1993, shooting in the Bronx. When the film was completed and screened, the press response was ecstatic.

I Like It Like That is a coming-of-age story set in the mean streets of the Bronx but told from a woman's perspective. The early positive response to the film suggests that Martin has found a way to treat a woman's experience growing up in extreme poverty, while supporting herself and her children, in a way that is simultaneously gritty and commercial. It is still too early to tell where Darnell Martin will go in her career, with only one major feature under her belt. Nevertheless, she seems poised to be a breakthrough artist in African-American filmmaking. Unless she makes some very serious missteps, Darnell Martin will be a serious force in American contemporary commercial film throughout the 1990s and into the next century. More than anything else, her career proves that persistence and unwillingness to compromise will ultimately pay off if your vision is strong enough. Her next project, a psychological thriller, *Listening to the Dead*, is currently in preproduction.

SELECTED FILMOGRAPHY

I Like It Like That (1994)

SELECTED BIBLIOGRAPHY

Hoberman, Jim. "Making It." *Village Voice* 39.42 (October 18, 1994): 49.
Hoffman, Jan. "Mom Always Said, 'Don't Take the First $2 Million Offer.' " *New York Times,* October 9, 1994, 28.
Jackson, Devon. "As She Likes It." *Village Voice* 39.42 (October 18, 1994): 58.
Jones, Anderson. "Director's Debut Is Fresh, Touching." *Detroit Free Press,* October 14, 1994, 13E.

MAY, ELAINE (1932–   ). United States. Elaine May is a talented comic actress, director, and writer. She is the daughter of Jack Berlin, a Yiddish theater director, and Jeannie Berlin, an actress and comic talent. Born in Philadelphia, Elaine May began working as an actress when she was a child. She traveled quite a bit as a result of her family's theatrical lifestyle and had been in fifty different schools by the time she was age ten. She quit school at age fifteen, married, had a child, Jeannie, and struggled to support herself as a restaurant employee. May wanted to go to college, but without her high school diploma, she could only audit classes at the University of Chicago. Here May hooked up with Mike Nichols, and the team began performing improvisational theater. In 1957, Nichols and May moved to New York, where they opened their successful Broadway review, *An Evening with Mike Nichols and Elaine May.*

After this theatrical success, May worked primarily as a screenwriter until she began her career as a film director; she was also in demand as a

script doctor. She received an Academy Award nomination for Best Screenplay for *Heaven Can Wait* (1978). She also worked on the screenplays of
Reds (1981), *Such Good Friends* (1971), and *Tootsie* (1982). As an actress,
May worked in her own films and in comedies such as *Enter Laughing*
(1966), *California Suite* (1978), and, most recently, *In the Spirit* (1990). In
all her different working capacities, she is drawn to material that borders
on dry Yiddish humor. She works from the tradition of immigrant humor,
which provides "comic escapism," according to Sydney Stahl Weinberg in
her study of Jewish-American women. In the films directed by May, humor
exposes societal falseness, the bleakness of the relationships, and the humor
of day-to-day life struggles. May's sense of humor has not always been
successfully received at the box office. Nor has it been fairly received by
feminist critics. It is a humor that is best described by B. Ruby Rich as
"Medusan" (38). May's humor is a leveler and an anarchic weapon that
has more to do with the traditional Yiddish theater than traditional Hollywood cinema.

Elaine May's first film, *A New Leaf* (1971), which she also wrote and
starred in, is a sophisticated comedy in which a ne'er-do-well philanderer
(Walter Matthau) is in financial trouble and decides to marry a well-to-do
Jewish woman and then kill her off. Most of the film's dark comedy derives
from Matthau's incessant plotting to kill May and from May's performance
as the unglamorous wife. Barbara Quart unfairly dismisses the film because
of May's unflattering depiction of "intellectual Jewish women [as] basket
cases" (40). Quart also attacks May's second directorial effort, *The Heartbreak Kid* (1972), for presenting "one of the most negative images of a
Jewish woman on film" (42). Nevertheless, *The Heartbreak Kid* was
May's most successful comedy. It is a nihilistic spoof in which a Jewish
bridegroom (Charles Grodin) is revolted by his new wife (Jeannie Berlin).
Grodin's character falls for a WASPish blonde (Cybill Shepherd). *The
Heartbreak Kid* is a voice of protest against Jewish assimilation and commodification of women. May's daughter, Jeannie Berlin, won a nomination
for the Academy Award for Best Supporting Actress for her brilliant comic
performance. Elaine May disliked her next film, *Mikey and Nicky* (1976),
so much that she insisted on having her name removed from the film. She
is one of the few women directors to permit herself the luxury of being
"difficult" in a patriarchal Hollywood culture that expects women directors
to be docile and efficient, even as it celebrates the "difficult" male director
as a stock figure of idiosyncratic genius.

Ishtar (1987), May's best-known film, was attacked by the media even
during preproduction when it was announced that it was budgeted at over
$50 million. From the outset, it seemed as if everyone in the industry hoped
that the film would flop. As Ally Acker notes, May was "subjected to mi-
croscopic attention" (48), and the interest in the film "created a level of
expectation it couldn't satisfy" (48). It is hard not to wonder if gender

politics is not one of the main factors in the making of the film's reputation as one of the biggest flops in history, in light of the cool reception afforded John McTiernan's recent $80 million failure, *The Last Action Hero* (1993). To be fair, *Ishtar* is a plodding spoof of the Hope-Crosby road pictures, and May's style of humor here might have been more profitably suited to a theater piece; yet there are still moments of *shtick,* reminiscent of Mel Brooks, that are really quite funny. But the most important question about the failure of *Ishtar* was posed by Stephanie Rothman:

The real acid test is whether or not those women who have deals actually make the films; and, if the films are not commercial successes, will they go on working? (Honeycutt)

Elaine May has not directed any feature films after the highly publicized failure of *Ishtar*. She is still, however, highly regarded as a writer and actress.

SELECTED FILMOGRAPHY

A New Leaf (1971)
The Heartbreak Kid (1972)
Mikey and Nicky (1976)
Ishtar (1987)

SELECTED BIBLIOGRAPHY

Acker, Ally. *Reel Women: Pioneers of the Cinema, 1896 to the Present.* New York: Continuum, 1993.
Carson, L. M. "Hollywood Hot List: Women Who Should Be Running the Show." *Ms* 3.8 (February 1975): 58.
Dawson, Jan. "The Heartbreak Kid." *Sight and Sound* 42.3 (summer 1975): 176.
Haskell, Molly. "Are Women Directors Different?" In *Women and the Cinema: A Critical Anthology,* edited by Karyn Kay and Gerald Peary, 429–35. New York: E. P. Dutton, 1977.
Henshaw, Richard. "Women Directors: 150 Filmographies." *Film Comment* 8.4 (November–December 1972): 33–45.
Honeycutt, Kirk. "Women Film Directors: Will They, Too, Be Allowed to Bomb?" *New York Times,* August 6, 1978, 11.
Israel, Lee. "Women in Film: Saving an Endangered Species." *Ms* 3.8 (February 1975): 51.
Quart, Barbara. *Women Directors: The Emergence of a New Cinema.* New York: Praeger, 1988.
Rich, B. Ruby. "In the Name of Feminist Film Criticism." In *Multiple Voices in Feminist Film Criticism,* edited by Diane Carson, Linda Dittmar, and Janice Welsch, 27–47. Minneapolis: University of Minnesota Press, 1994.
Smith, Sharon. *Women Who Make Movies.* New York: Hopkinson and Blake, 1975.
Weinberg, Sydney Stahl. *The World of Our Mothers: The Lives of Jewish Immigrant Women.* New York: Schocken, 1988.

McCULLOUGH, BARBARA (1945–   ). United States. Los Angeles-based
filmmaker Barbara McCullough is an African-American director whose
films celebrate the African diaspora. McCullough's films go beyond resisting spectatorship and create "a space for the assertion of a critical black
female spectatorship, as . . . they imagine new transgressive possibilities for
the formulation of identity," as bell hooks describes the new Afrocentric
film tradition (130). McCullough became interested in filmmaking after an
artistic career in photography. She told Elizabeth Jackson she was inspired
by Zora Neale Hurston, and, stylistically, McCullough's films nod to Hurston's influence. McCullough directly confronts white critics' disparage-
ment of African womanist artists, especially in *Shopping Bag Spirits* (1980).
In the film, McCullough explores the place of ritual in African-American
life. Clyde Taylor notes that black women filmmakers tend to invoke African sources as "vehicles of symbol, icon, and ritual" (29). *Shopping Bag
Spirits* is a ritualistic display of repetitive catharsis that features the work
of the diasporic community. McCullough's earlier film *Water Ritual #1*
(1979) also evokes an Afrocentric cultural past through the use of ritual.
In the short film, an African woman refigures the deteriorating urban environment with a female fertility statue. In a purification ritual, the woman
reclaims her environment, her body, and her soul.

In an interview with Elizabeth Jackson, McCullough explains some of
the difficulties she finds as an independent African-American director:
"Whites are still doing the hiring. . . . In what I do [working with special
visual effects] there are only a very few black people out there. I have been
the only one whom I have come across in a management position in this
area" (96). McCullough observes that it is incredibly difficult to access
equipment, find funding, and obtain widespread distribution. Nevertheless,
she holds out hope for aspiring black independents: "Resilience is the key
to surviving in the midst of all of this" (Jackson, 97). McCullough's black
feminist cultural ideological perspective infuses her avant-garde films "as
participating art suggesting a paradigm for personal and collective introspection" (Gibson-Hudson, 377). McCullough is an admirer of the films
of Julie Dash. Both share a uniqueness and authenticity that suggest that
black women filmmakers find multiple approaches to similar, though in-
dividualized, themes.

Barbara McCullough's *World Saxophone Quartet* (1980) is an internationally well known short film that features the jazz quartet of the same
name. Though McCullough could not convince any PBS affiliates to run
her more formalist works, they did accept and feature *World Saxophone
Quartet* in 1988. McCullough's films have developed a reputation through
word of mouth, and they are shown at international film festivals, particularly during Black History Month. McCullough has worked extensively
in commercial production as a production manager, unit production manager, and visual effects artist at Cine Motion Pictures. She has worked on

an animated cartoon, as a music video director, and is currently working in digital animation.

SELECTED FILMOGRAPHY

Water Ritual #1: An Urban Rite of Purification (1979)
Shopping Bag Spirits and Freeway Fetishes: Reflections on Ritual Space (1980)
Fragments (1980)
World Saxophone Quartet (1980)

SELECTED BIBLIOGRAPHY

Gibson-Hudson, Gloria. "Aspects of Black Feminist Cultural Ideology in Films by Women Independent Artists." In *Multiple Voices in Feminist Film Criticism,* edited by Diane Carson, Linda Dittmar, and Janice Welsch, 365–79. Minneapolis: University of Minnesota Press, 1994.
hooks, bell. *Black Looks: Race and Representation.* Boston: South End Press, 1992.
Jackson, Elizabeth. "Barbara McCullough: Independent Filmmaker." *Jump Cut* 36 (1990): 94–97.
Larkin, Alile Sharon. "Black Women Film-Makers Defining Ourselves: Feminism in Our Own Voice." In *Female Spectators: Looking at Film and Television,* edited by E. Deidre Pribram, 157–73. London: Verso, 1988.
Reid, Mark A. "Dialogic Modes of Representing Africa(s): Womanist Film." *Black American Literature Forum* 25 (summer 1991): 375–88.
Taylor, Clyde. "The L.A. Rebellion: New Spirit in American Film." *Black Film Review* 2.2 (1986): 29.
Third World Newsreel. *Third World Newsreel 25th Anniversary Catalogue.* New York: Third World Newsreel, 1992.

McDONAGH, PAULETTE (1901–78). Australia. Paulette McDonagh is a recently rediscovered pioneering figure in Australian film history. McDonagh and her sisters Phyliss and Isobel were the only women to produce and direct a commercial motion picture before the release of Gillian Armstrong's *My Brilliant Career* in 1979. Paulette McDonagh taught herself film direction by going to the cinema and repeatedly watching the same film. Isobel aspired to an acting career and worked in a few silent films before the first McDonagh production. Phyliss became an art director and publicist and worked in various other capacities. Paulette wrote several versions of their first film, *Those Who Love* (1926). *Those Who Love* is a melodramatic film dedicated to, unsurprisingly, "those who love." It was primarily aimed at female audiences. Though only a few scenes survive, enough has been saved to study as a feminist historical relic. The original version of *Those Who Love* is a variation on the captivity narrative, which is the core of the romantic melodrama. A daughter avenges her mother, who dies after being metaphorically held captive by a faithless lover. One sequence included a particularly sentimental deathbed scene, in which the mother tells her daughter the truth about her life. *Those Who Love* was filmed in the McDonagh home, to add production value and a sense of realism. The film is notable for more naturalistic performances than the usual silent film. *The Far Paradise* (1928) is similar in style and plot to *Those Who Love*. *The Cheaters* (1930), however, depicts a woman safe-cracker in an odd departure from the melodramatic romance film. *The Cheaters* and *The Far Paradise* were rediscovered and restored in the 1970s.

In 1933, the McDonagh sisters made *Two Minutes' Silence*, an antiwar film based on Leslie Haylen's play about Armistice Day. Critics who had praised the earlier films of the McDonaghs were highly critical of the film's serious subject matter. As long as the sisters made melodramatic films, they did not threaten the patriarchal order, but with *Two Minutes' Silence*, the women were perceived as a threat. One critic wrote that the women should "concentrate on the beauties of Australia" (Wright, 41). Another found it to be "intelligently directed" (Wright, 41). *Two Minutes' Silence* failed at the box office. Years later, Paulette told Andree Wright:

We were fools to have made *Two Minutes' Silence*. The whole world would have eaten out of our hands if we'd made another romantic film. *Two Minutes' Silence* was too true. (42)

Though Phyllis McDonagh retired from filmmaking, Paulette continued to try to work in film as an unpaid, uncredited assistant to another director. She attempted to find backing for another feature film, but because of the depression and because she no longer guaranteed her sisters' involvement, she was denied another opportunity to direct a feature film. She did direct several short documentaries. Phyliss found a career as an editor and writer and wrote until her death in 1978. Isobel maintained her acting career until 1959. She lived in London until her death in 1982. Paulette did not live to see the rediscovery of her films. Phyllis McDonagh received an award on behalf of the sisters from the Australian Film Institute in 1978.

SELECTED FILMOGRAPHY

Those Who Love (1926)
The Far Paradise (1928)
The Cheaters (1930)
Two Minutes' Silence (1933)

SELECTED BIBLIOGRAPHY

Edmondson, Ray, and Andrew Pike. *Australia's Lost Films*. Canberra: National Library of Australia, 1982.
Long, Joan, and Martin Long. *The Pictures That Moved*. Melbourne: Hutchinson, 1982.
Matthews, Jill. *Good and Mad Women: The Historical Construction of Femininity in Twentieth Century Australia*. Sydney: Allen and Unwin, 1984.
Pike, Andrew, and Ross Cooper. *Australian Film: 1900–1977*. Melbourne: Oxford University Press, 1980.
Ryan, Penny, and Margaret Eliot. *Women in Australian Film Production*. Sydney: Women's Film Fund, 1983.

Tulloch, John. *Legends on the Screen in the Narrative Film in Australia, 1919–1929*. Sydney: Currency Press, 1981.

Weaver, John T. *Twenty Years of Silents, 1908–1928*. Metuchen: Scarecrow Press, 1971.

Wright, Andree. *Brilliant Careers*. Sydney: Pan Books, 1986.

McLAUGHLIN, SHEILA (1950–   ). United States. Sheila McLaughlin is a lesbian filmmaker whose work challenges the heterosexual biases of mainstream feminist theory. Like film and video artists such as Sadie Benning, Abigail Child, Cecilia Dougherty, Pratibha Parmar, Su Friedrich, Ulrike Ottinger, Rose Troche, and many other lesbian artists, Sheila McLaughlin explores erotic lesbian imagery. As McLaughlin told Alison Butler, her films work against a hegemonic "heterosexuality [which] is the dominant code of the society we live in" (370). As Butler notes, lesbian feminist filmmakers not only work against traditional heterocentric culture but "bear the additional burden of working against paralyzing paradigms of a feminist cultural theory" (368) that tends toward dogmatic pronouncements. *She Must Be Seeing Things* (1987) is at the center of theoretical debate, because the film explores butch-femme sexual role playing and fantasies of heterosexually defined sex acts. Reactions to the film range from delight to revulsion to political outrage.

She Must Be Seeing Things centers on the relationship between a white woman filmmaker and an African-American lawyer. The butch-femme couple explore fantasies of voyeurism, bondage, cross-dressing, heterosexual sex, and fetishism. McLaughlin wished to explore taboo areas in lesbian sexuality. As she told Alison Butler: "I wanted to undermine the idea of women as narcissistic extensions of each other. . . . Also women have been thought of as having sex that's very 'nice'. . . . It's so often thought of that way, I think, because of the absence of the phallus, since sex is thought of as a phallic thing" (371). Theoretically, McLaughlin is clear in her position: "What I wanted to do in the film was to make a voyeuristic female and constantly put her in the position of taking on the look" (Butler, 375).

Andrea Weiss finds *She Must Be Seeing Things* to be less transgressive than traditional; "[W]hile seemingly arguing the opposite, [it] ends up affirming the position that lesbians can find fulfillment in heterosexual sex" (153). Nevertheless, Alison Butler concludes that McLaughlin's use of masquerade "suggests that gender roles, like clothes, can be put on, and by implication, taken off, so that they aren't assumed as biologically determined, but as social constructs which are subject to variation and open to transformation" (371).

McLaughlin's earlier film, *Committed* (1984), was codirected with Lynn Tillman. It is an experimental, narrative film about the life of Frances Farmer. As McLaughlin told Pascale Lamche, "It was somehow more interesting to take her out of context and place her in daily life struggles with her mother, with her love affair, with trying to sort out her thinking about how she deals with her politics and what the repercussions of that are" (38). Although *Committed*'s extremely low budget (around $45,000) sometimes gives the film an exceedingly rough look in its execution, *Committed* is a deeply felt work that captures the spiritual essence of Frances Farmer's isolation.

Sheila McLaughlin's films exhibit a grasp of a developing new feminist language of cinema. *She Must Be Seeing Things* is a metanarrative construct that includes the device of a film within a film. In this interdiagetic narrative framework, McLaughlin adapts a Thomas De Quincy story of a seventeenth-century nun who rebels against the patriarchal convent. In this way, the level of fantasy in the main narrative is grounded to a level of realism and historicity. The film within the film recalls Su Friedrich's similar tale of repressed desire of a seventeenth-century nun in *Damned If You Don't* (1987). McLaughlin's intercontextual movement among the "real," the "representational," and history accounts for the tension that the viewer experiences in both *Committed* and *She Must Be Seeing Things*.

SELECTED FILMOGRAPHY

Committed (codirector Lynn Tillman) (1984)
She Must Be Seeing Things (1987)

SELECTED BIBLIOGRAPHY

Butler, Alison. "She Must Be Seeing Things: An Interview with Sheila McLaughlin." In *Queer Looks: Perspectives on Lesbian and Gay Film and Video,* edited by Martha Gever, Pratibha Parmar, and John Greyson, 368–76. New York: Routledge, 1993.
Butler, Judith. "Critically Queer." *GLQ: A Journal of Lesbian and Gay Studies* 1.1 (1993): 17–22.
de Lauretis, Teresa. *The Practice of Love: Lesbian Sexuality and Perverse Desire.* Bloomington: Indiana University Press, 1994.
———. "Rethinking Women's Cinema." In *Multiple Voices in Feminist Film Criticism,* edited by Diane Carson, Linda Dittmar, and Janice Welsch, 140–61. Minneapolis: University of Minnesota Press, 1994.
Dolan, Jill. *The Feminist Spectator as Critic.* Ann Arbor: University of Michigan Press, 1991.
Hart, Lynda. "Identity and Seduction: Lesbians in the Mainstream." In *Acting Out: Feminist Performance,* edited by Lynda Hart and Peggy Phelan, 119–37. Ann Arbor: University of Michigan Press, 1993.
Kotz, Liz. "Complicity: Women Artists Investigating Masculinity." In *Dirty Looks: Women, Pornography, Power,* 101–23. London: BFI, 1993.
Lamche, Pascale. "Committed Women." *Framework* 26–27 (1984): 36–43.
Weiss, Andrea. *Vampires and Violets: Lesbians in Film.* New York: Penguin, 1993.

McVEY DREW, LUCILLE (1890–1925). United States. Known in the industry as "Mrs. Sidney Drew," Lucille McVey was born in Sedalia, Mis-

souri, on April 18, 1890. She was a stage actress before she married actor
Sidney Drew, an uncle to the famous Barrymore acting family. Though she
was not usually credited, Lucille McVey Drew supervised all of the comedies in which she and Sidney Drew starred. The couple worked for Vita-
graph and Metro Pictures, where they made scores of domestic comedies.
Though many of the short films directed by the Drews are held in the
Archives of the Library of Congress and in other international archives,
their films have received little or no scholarly or popular attention. Perhaps
the popularity of the Drew comedies worked against their inclusion in the
canon of American silent film, or perhaps the themes of their films sub-
verted the American tradition of slapstick comedies, preferring a more high-
toned approach to farce. It is highly likely that the public knowledge of
Mrs. Sidney Drew's collaborative efforts undermined any possible categorization of Sidney Drew as an auteur, because, as a collaborative member
of a team, he could not have been perceived as a patriarchal unit of power
such as D. W. Griffith. For whatever reason, the films directed by Sidney
Drew and written and codirected by Lucille McVey Drew were omitted
from the canon even as Sidney Drew films. Janet Staiger notes that:

selective choices based on criteria supposedly for the good of society end up being
canons supportive of the interests of a hegemonic society, not necessarily in the
interests of all segments of that culture or other cultures. (196)

Lucille McVey Drew deserves to be rediscovered through a process designed by Giuliana Bruno in her groundbreaking book on Italian pioneer
filmmaker Elvira Notari. In Bruno's book, she scrutinizes film history and
"highlights a woman's tradition by underscoring the existence of a film
pioneer lost in a male-dominated culture" (40). A similar approach to the
films and writings of Lucille McVey Drew would open up a space for discussing women's role in the development of the domestic comedy. The films
directed by Sidney Drew and Lucille McVey Drew center around disrup-
tions of heterosexual romantic love. They display an anarchic sense of Medusan humor, often at the expense of a male dupe. They are often set in
the home, the private sphere, in which women sometimes had more power
over their romantic partnerships (or at least the mechanics of power could
be displayed through the farcical dimensions of the domestic comedy). Lucille McVey's domestic comedies might be profitably compared with Alice
Guy films of the same genre.

The humor in McVey-Drew films, as in the "Henry series," *Too Much
Henry* (1917), *Why Henry Left Home* (1918), and *Shadowing Henry*
(1917), is often based on the disruption of gender roles. Similarly, *Charming Mrs. Chase* (1920), *Emotional Mrs. Vaughan* (1920), and *Stimulating
Mrs. Barton* (1920) are grounded in a revision of the cultural notions of
femininity. The McVey-Drew team was highly successful in its own time.
As Eileen Bowser notes, Drew films were "the type of polite comedy based

on real life incidents that uplifters were calling for" (180). There is no question that the Drew films were comparable to the successful Mack Sennett films of the same period, yet film historians tend to ignore any comedies from this time that are not produced or directed by Mack Sennett at Keystone. Lucille McVey Drew and Sidney Drew continued to direct many comedies together until Sidney Drew's death in 1919. Lucille McVey Drew quit acting when her husband died, but she continued to direct. She died in 1925.

SELECTED FILMOGRAPHY

Codirected with Sidney Drew

Beauty Unadorned (1913)
Professional Scapegoat (1914)
Combination (1915)
Home Cure (1915)
Professional Diner (1915)
A Close Resemblance (1917)
Her Anniversaries (1917)
Her Lesson (1917)
His Curiosity (1917)
Lest We Forget (1917)
The Patriot (1917)
The Pest (1917)
Rubbing It In (1917)
Shadowing Henry (1917)
Safety First (1917)
Too Much Henry (1917)
Before and after Talking (1918)
Gas Logic (1918)
Help Wanted (1918)
His First Love (1918)
Special Today (1918)
Why Henry Left Home (1918)
Bunkered (1919)
Gay Old Time (1919)
Once a Man (1919)
Squawed (1919)
Romance and Ringo (1919)

Sole directorial credit

Charming Mrs. Chase (1920)
Emotional Mrs. Vaughan (1920)
Stimulating Mrs. Barton (1920)
Cousin Kate (1921)

SELECTED BIBLIOGRAPHY

Acker, Ally. *Reel Women: Pioneers of the Cinema, 1896 to the Present*. New York: Continuum, 1993.

Bowser, Eileen. *History of the American Cinema 2: Transformations of Cinema, 1907–1915.* New York: Scribner's, 1990.

Bruno, Giuliana. *Streetwalking on a Ruined Map: Cultural Theory and the City Films of Elvira Notari.* Princeton: Princeton University Press, 1993.

Kuhn, Annette. *Women's Pictures: Feminism and Cinema.* London: Routledge, 1982.

Library of Congress. *Catalogue of Copyright Entries: Motion Pictures: 1912–1939.* Washington, DC: Library of Congress, 1951.

Maggliozzi, Ronald S. *Treasures from the Film Archives: A Catalogue of Short Silent Films Held by FIAF Archives.* Metuchen, NJ: Scarecrow Press, 1988.

Museum of Modern Art. *Museum of Modern Art Circulating Film Library Catalogue.* Cedar Grove, NJ: Rae, 1984.

Slide, Anthony. *Early Women Directors.* New York: Da Capo, 1984.

Staiger, Janet. "The Politics of Film Canons." In *Multiple Voices in Feminist Film Criticism,* edited by Diane Carson, Linda Dittmar, and Janice Welsch, 191–209. Minneapolis: University of Minnesota Press, 1994.

MENKEN, MARIE (1910–71). United States. Almost entirely displaced in cinema history is the figure of Marie Menken, an underground, experimental filmmaker whose work has yet to receive full consideration by feminists or cultural critics. Stan Brakhage said of Menken, "She made me aware that I was freer than I knew" (46). Menken's hand-held camera technique and her playful and incisive manipulation of the film itself had a tremendous influence on the avant-garde filmmakers who are lionized and canonized as the leaders of American underground filmmaking. Marie Menken was at the center of the New York avant-garde film colony, which included figures such as her husband, Willard Maas, as well as Shirley Clarke, Storm de Hirsch, Maya Deren, and, later, Andy Warhol and the members of the Factory. A painter and an actress, Marie Menken made her first film, as legend has it, when she acquired a camera from a pawn ticket given to her by a friend. She used it to photograph Willard Maas's *Geography of the Body* (1943). Menken then directed *Visual Variations on Noguchi* (1945), an animated film that studies Noguchi's sculpture from a formalist perspective. Norman McLaren described the film with ebullient praise:

Never before have I seen such purely dynamic treatment of sculpture in film. Marie Menken transformed Noguchi's sculpture into her own medium. (Film-Makers' Cooperative, 181).

Menken continued to mine seemingly mundane source material that she sculpted with her own authorial stamp in films such as *Glimpse of the Garden* (1957), *Dwightiana* (1959), and *Arabesque for Kenneth Anger* (1961). In *Andy Warhol* (1965), Menken documents the elusive figure of Andy Warhol, the master of appropriation, in a film that displays Andy silk-screening various paintings and box sculptures at a manic pace, with the assistance of Gerard Malanga. Menken's use of stop-motion technique and her complete rupture from film time are a representational mastery of the artist as object. In addition to its technical and formal grace, *Andy Warhol* captures the frenetic pace with which the members of Warhol's Factory produced art. It is one of the few films, excepting Andy Warhol's own films, that render the cultural moment of creation with the frantically sculptured pace appropriate to the period. As an actress, Marie Menken appears in films of Willard Maas and Dov Lederberg and in Andy Warhol's *Life of Juanita Castro* and *The Chelsea Girls*. Menken supported her artistic activities with a job as a copy editor for *Time* and *Life* for much of the 1950s and 1960s. Her best films are experimental portraits, diaries, phantasmagoric fantasies, and studies in time-lapse photography.

Notebook (1962) is a semiformalist underground film, in that Menken uses commonplace objects in the private sphere as her source material. In *Notebook,* Menken sutures nine sketches or fragments in a work that, according to Paul S. Arthur, "bridges the options of both the 'informal' and 'metaphoric' approaches" (105). *Hurry! Hurry!* (1957) is a sardonic, feminist, experimental comedy about sperm cells seeking an egg, printed over footage of flames leaping out from the screen. Menken's irreverent humor cuts across her work as actress and filmmaker. In a recounting of the making of Andy Warhol's *Life of Juanita Castro,* Budd Myers recalls that "Marie's genius saved the whole proceeding . . . rather than fulfill the static requirements of the character of Juanita Castro, she . . . said her lines as she chose, happily, dully, belligerently" (39). Marie Menken's life was lived in irreverence and flagrant denial of male-defined precepts or filmic traditions. Menken is an extremely important artist of the postwar American experimental period. In view of her considerable output of work as an artist and actress, in addition to serving as an informal "den mother" for younger experimental filmmakers during the 1950s and 1960s, Menken and her Gryphon film group deserve a book-length monograph to adequately document her impact on experimental cinema. Her quiet lyricism and poetic sensibility informed the work of numerous, better-known female and male artists during this turbulent era.

SELECTED FILMOGRAPHY

Visual Variations on Noguchi (1945)
Hurry! Hurry! (1957)
Glimpse of the Garden (1957)
Dwightiana (1959)
Eye Music in Red Major (1961)
Arabesque for Kenneth Anger (1961)
Bagatelle for Willard Maas (1961)
Mood Mondrian (1961)
Notebook (1962)
Moonplay (1962)

Here and There with My Octoscope (1962)
Go! Go! Go! (1963)
Andy Warhol (1965)
Drips and Strips (1965)
Sidewalks (1966)
Lights (1966)
Watts with Eggs (1967)
Excursion (1968)

SELECTED BIBLIOGRAPHY

Acker, Ally. *Reel Women: Pioneers of the Cinema, 1896 to the Present.* New York: Continuum, 1993.

Arthur, Paul S. "1959–1963." In *A History of the American Avant-Garde Cinema,* edited by American Federation of the Arts, New York: American Federation of the Arts, 1976.

Brakhage, Stan. *Metaphors of Vision.* New York: Film-Makers' Cooperative, 1963.

Canyon Cinema. *Canyon Cinema Catalogue 7.* San Francisco: Canyon Cinema, 1992.

Cartwright, Lisa, and Nina Fonoroff. "Narrative Is Narrative: So What Is New?" In *Multiple Voices in Feminist Film Criticism,* edited by Diane Carson, Linda Dittmar, and Janice Welsch, 124–39. Minneapolis: University of Minnesota Press, 1994.

Film-Makers' Cooperative. *Film-Makers' Cooperative Catalogue 6.* New York: Film-Makers' Cooperative, 1987.

Myers, Louis Budd. "Marie Menken Herself." *Film Culture* 45 (summer 1967): 37–39.

Rabinovitz, Lauren. *Points of Resistance: Women, Power and Politics in the New York Avant-Garde Cinema, 1943–71.* Urbana: University of Illinois Press, 1991.

Sitney, P. Adams. *Visionary Film.* New York: Oxford University Press, 1974.

Smith, Sharon. *Women Who Make Movies.* New York: Hopkinson and Blake, 1975.

MÉSZÁROS, MÁRTA (1934–). Hungary. Born in Budapest and educated at the VGIK in Moscow, Márta Mészáros is the only Hungarian director who deals almost exclusively with women's issues. She is also one of the very few Eastern European women directors to have made a substantial body of work. Though she confidently states, "I've never made a 'feminist film' " (H26) in an interview with Annette Insdorf, Mészáros's oeuvre defines the term. Mészáros agrees that her films are "carried by this current" (H26) of feminism, noting that *Adoption* (1975) "wasn't necessarily a feminist film, but all you needed at the time was a tough independent female character for the movie to be categorized that way" (H26). Mészáros dislikes being labeled a feminist, because she does not wish to align herself with a movement she sees as being "against men" (H26); however, she does feel it is her duty to make films concerning women.

Mészáros is consistently interested in mining her autobiographical experiences. She dismantles identity and the politics of social, familial, and ideological structures that combine to form identity. She continually maps her films with a palimpsest of her own life experience, particularly issues of parenting, exile, and abandonment. In 1938, her father, a distinguished sculptor, was arrested and held by the Soviet authorities and executed. As Mészáros explains: "In all my films—not just *Diary*—it's my story that I'm telling. The problem of the child who is left alone in the world, searching for parents has been a dominant impression for me" (H21). Mészáros lost her mother, a talented artist, to a typhoid epidemic in 1942, when Mészáros was eleven years old. In 1960, Márta Mészáros married film director Miklós Janscó, with whom she raised three children. They divorced in 1973.

Though she has worked consistently as a director, she has only recently been properly recognized by Western feminist film critics, due to the unavailability of her films outside Hungary. Probably her best-known film is *Diary for My Children* (1982), though *The Girl* (1968), *Riddance* (1973), and *Nine Months* (1976) are available on video in the United States (Facets). *The Girl*, the first feature film directed by a woman in Hungary, is a stunning black-and-white New Wave film that follows a young woman's point of view as she searches for her mother. She finds her, and the mother is not interested in her, showing contempt and a desire for secrecy rather than affection. The sense of loss and deprivation is harshly rendered in a flat style of direction, which serves as a counterpoint to the painful material. Mészáros's direction calls for understated, even muted reaction. This is consistent throughout Mészáros's work, including *Diary,* in which she gives the central figure almost nothing to do. As she told Insdorf, "The conflicts are practically invisible—the emotion doesn't show. I prefer a kind of 'pseudo-realism' which is only superficially realistic: in fact I abstract a lot" (21). Mészáros prefers to observe, rather than comment. In her films such as *Riddance* and *Adoption,* Mészáros uses an almost clinically detached style of cinematography. Mészáros's films depict alienated, motherless women or women who have harsh, difficult mothers. Catherine Portuges, in her book on Márta Mészáros, notes that she is unlike Western women filmmakers in her treatment of mothers:

Mészáros negotiates female subjectivity in the context of the Oedipus complex. The maternal figure, as in the case of the Stalinist Magda, is often constructed as a "bad mother," a withholding or punitive presence that may appear harsh to the Western viewer accustomed to a more covert aggressivity. (9)

Portuges reminds us that this difference can be accounted for if we keep in mind cultural differences in gendered identity. Mészáros's conceptions of mother-daughter relationships are never easy to discern or are overdetermined. As always, "the effect Mészáros achieves is to complicate her subject matter, to give it multiple contexts" (Gentile, 103).

Thematically, Mészáros works through issues of identity, deviance, Stalinism, erotic intimacy, and female rebelliousness. *Diary for My Loves* (1987) is a reworking of autobiography around such themes. In the film, Mészáros incorporates documentary footage of people telling her not to become a director but to become an actress. *Diary for My Children* (1982) interweaves documentary newsreel footage from the 1950s with personal accounts of Mészáros's lost family and her search for a meaningful relationship that allows for space and autonomy, as well as affection and support. The film won a Special Jury Prize at the Cannes Film Festival in 1984. More recently, Mészáros has completed a diary film for her parents (*Diary for My Father and Mother*, 1990). She is currently in production for *The Seventh Dwelling*, a biography of the philosopher Edith Stein.

SELECTED FILMOGRAPHY

Eltávozott nap (*The Girl*) (1968)
A holdudvar (*Binding Sentiments*) (1969)
Szép lányok, ne sírjatok (*Don't Cry, Pretty Girls*) (1970)
Szabad lélegzet (*Riddance*) (1973)
Örökbefogadás (*Adoption*) (1975)
Kilene hónap (*Nine Months*) (1976)
Ök ketten (*The Two of Them [Women]*) (1977)
Olyan mint otthon (*Just Like at Home*) (1978)
Utközben (*On the Move*) (1979)
Örökség (*The Heiresses*) (1980)
Anna (*Mother and Daughter*) (1981)
Napló gyermekeimnek (*Diary for My Children*) (1982)
Délibábok országa (*The Land of Mirages*) (1983)
Napló szerelmeimnek (*Diary for My Loves*) (1987)
Little Red Riding Hood—Year 2000 (1989)
Diary for My Father and Mother (1990)
Looking for Romeo (1991)

SELECTED BIBLIOGRAPHY

Gentile, Mary C. *Film Feminisms*. Westport, CT: Greenwood Press, 1985.

Goulding, Daniel J., ed. *Post New Wave Cinema in the Soviet Union and Eastern Europe*. Bloomington: Indiana University Press, 1989.

Gyertyan, Ervin. "Look Back in Compassion: Mészáros: *Napló gyermekeimnek* (*Diary for My Children*); Janos Xantus: *Eszkimo Asszony fazik* (*Eskimo Woman Feels Cold*)." *New Hungarian Quarterly* 25.96 (winter 1984): 217–22.

Insdorf, Annette. "Childhood Loss Shapes a Director's Life and Art." *New York Times*, October 28, 1984, H21, H26.

Martineau, Barbara. "The Films of Márta Mészáros, The Importance of Being Banal." *Film Quarterly* 34.1 (1980): 21–27.

Petrie, Graham, and Ruth Dwyer, eds. *Before the Wall Came Down*. New York: University Press of America, 1990.

Portuges, Catherine. *Screen Memories: The Hungarian Cinema of Márta Mészáros*. Bloomington: Indiana University Press, 1993.

Quart, Barbara. *Women Directors: The Emergence of a New Cinema*. New York: Praeger, 1988.

MIKESCH, ELFI (1940–   ). Austria/Germany. Born in Austria in 1940, lesbian filmmaker Elfi Mikesch is best known for her filmmaking collaboration with Monika Treut on *Seduction: The Cruel Woman* (1984–85). Mikesch's thematic interest in sadomasochistic pleasure began in 1983, with *The Blue Distance,* a risky exploration of the taboo of women's masochistic erotic fantasies. *Seduction: The Cruel Woman* employs a feminist perspective to firmly establish sadomasochism as a form of lesbian and female pleasure. In the film, Wanda, a dominitrix, runs a pleasure house. The film encourages and welcomes voyeuristic spectatorship of Wanda's sensual encounters with men and women. Wanda's innocent lover, Justine, becomes a participant in these pleasures, by which she is at first disgusted, but very few graphic sex acts are shown in the film. *Seduction* is self-reflexively theatrical, in the tradition of Huillet/Straub, Fassbinder, and Warhol. Mikesch and Treut expose the theatricality inherent in scopophiliac pleasure fulfillment by self-consciously reminding us that film, like pleasure, is constructed. As Julia Knight observes, "By showing the theatrical nature of the practices indulged in at Wanda's pleasure palace, the film constructs the participants as consenting individuals" (165). Treut and Mikesch are among many German women directors interested in the politics of sexual pleasure. Cleo Übelmann explores the bondage from a feminist perspective in *Mano Destra* (1985). Birgit Hein confronts similar, highly controversial issues in the Kali films (1987–88), codirected with Wilhelm Hein.

Elfi Mikesch came to film with a background in photography. She used a pseudonym (Oh Vuvie) early in her career as a Super 8 filmmaker. In the 1970s, Mikesch worked as a designer for the radical feminist journal *Frauen und Film*. She has worked with many lesbian and gay filmmakers, particularly Rosa von Praunheim. In the 1970s, Mikesch began making her own films. Aesthetically, Mikesch is interested in the gap between documentary and experimental filmmaking, between constructions of "realness" and constructions of "reality." Mikesch, like many German women directors, enjoyed many years of German government subsidies that sustained her film career. In the 1980s, a political turnover caused changes in the policies of the film subsidy system that resulted in the withdrawal of funding from *Seduction: The Cruel Woman*. Julia Knight recounts the effects of the new conservatism on Germany's thriving feminist film culture. As support is withdrawn, women film directors such as Mikesch are increasingly forced to look for academic careers to support themselves. Elfi Mikesch enjoys an international reputation for her cinematographic skills, as well as her difficult and provocative films.

SELECTED FILMOGRAPHY

Family Sketch (1976)
Ich denke oft an Hawaii (*I Often Think of Hawaii*) (1978)
Execution—A Study of Mary (1979)
Was soll'n wir denn machen ohne den Tod (*What Would We Do without Death*) (1980)
Macumba (1982)
Die blaue Distanz (*The Blue Distance*) (1983)
Das Frühstück der Hyäne (*The Hyena's Breakfast*) (1983)
Verführung: die grausame Frau (*Seduction: The Cruel Woman*) (codirector Monika Treut) (1984–85)
Marocain (1989)

SELECTED BIBLIOGRAPHY

Cremen, Christine. "Female Fantasies That Celebrate Sexual Freedom." *Austrian* (May 17, 1984): 12.

Dyer, Richard. *Now You See It: Studies on Lesbian and Gay Film*. New York: Routledge, 1990.

Frieden, Sandra, Richard W. McCormick, Vibeke R. Petersen, and Laurie Melissa Vogelsang, eds. *Gender and German Cinema Vols. 1 and 2*. Oxford: Berg, 1993.

Knight, Julia. *Women and the New German Cinema*. London: Verso, 1992.

Kuhn, Annette. *Women's Pictures: Feminism and Cinema*. London: Routledge, 1982.

Straayer, Chris. "Sexual Representation in Film and Video." In *Multiple Voices in Feminist Film Criticism*, edited by Diane Carson, Linda Dittmar, and Janice Welsch, 503–12. Minneapolis: University of Minnesota Press, 1994.

Studlar, Gaylyn. "Visual Pleasure and the Masochistic Aesthetic." *Journal of Film and Video* 37.2 (1985): 5–26.

Vance, Carol S. *Pleasure and Danger: Exploring Female Sexuality*. Boston: Routledge and Kegan Paul, 1984.

Williams, Linda, ed. *Hard Core: Power, Pleasure and the Frenzy of the Visible*. Berkeley: University of California Press, 1989.

MIKKELSEN, LAILA (1940–   ). Norway. Laila Mikkelsen received her master's degree at the University of Oslo in the 1960s. Her films are directly involved in feminist issues and center on female adolescence. Mikkelsen's view of Norway exposes sexism, patriarchal abuse, and community indifference toward young women. Mikkelsen is active politically in both the socialist and feminist movements. *Growing Up* (1981) is plotted around a young girl whose mother is linked to a German officer during the occupation. The central character, Ida, is displaced from her abusive mother, whom she hears making love to a Nazi soldier. Ida herself suffers persecution from the townspeople because of her mother's behavior. *Growing Up* is obviously a feminist bildungsroman in which a lost young girl is taught how to live as a woman by a strong, older woman. When Ida is sent away to live with Mrs. Revosen, both women ritually enact the burial of Ida's two sisters. Ida displays her belief in Christian tradition when she insists on fixing the broken cross on her sister's grave site. Mrs. Revosen's reaction to her behavior makes Ida come to see the hypocrisy in organized patriarchal religion and its followers. Mrs. Revosen is a spiritual guide for Ida, who reclaims her self through the rejection of orthodox Christianity.

Growing Up proposes the location of "a community of women relating to and speaking to one another outside the constraints of language" (Williams, 145). The character of Ida is reduced to a purely biologically determined essence, an evil woman, because of societal codes, but she learns to speak, to be proud of her body, and to reject puritanical repression of women (including herself and her mother). As Gorham Kindem notes, Mikkelsen's use of "subjectivization through expressive use of sound" (40) evokes Ida's experience of abjection and melancholia. Mikkelsen constructs Ida's point of view with offscreen diagetic sounds such as deafening air sirens, radio news stories, and the disembodied voices of her mother and the German officer. *Growing Up* is less dependent on plot than on an absence of narrative. Ida experiences the world in a way that a young girl might: she is often terrified of her dreams and the sounds that she hears. She has little control of her body and her future until she meets Mrs. Revosen, who provides her first positive role model as a survivor of patriarchal oppression and wartime disillusionment. Mikkelsen's use of naturalistic photography and her preference for psychological depth is perhaps representative of the New Wave cinema of Norway.

Growing Up is specifically comparable to the films of other Norwegian women directors, particularly Anja Breien's *Witch Hunt* (1981). Both *Witch Hunt* and *Growing Up* center on a female outsider/exile adolescent, and both criticize the church and the patriarchal system it supports. It is also interesting to note that both *Growing Up* and *Witch Hunt* are Swedish-Norwegian coproductions. Without the support of both the Norwegian government and the Swedish cultural base, these independent films, which have little commercial value, would simply never be made. The women directors of the Norwegian Art Cinema find more support than American independents. Also, women such as Mikkelsen and Breien enjoy a political advantage of organization. As Gorham Kindem states, "Socialists and feminists in Norway are not as fragmented as they are in other Scandinavian societies" (33).

SELECTED FILMOGRAPHY

Snart 17 (Soon 17) (1980)
Liten Ida (Growing Up) (1981)
Sosken Po Guds Jord (Children of the Earth) (1983)

SELECTED BIBLIOGRAPHY

Fischer, Lucy. *Shot/Countershot: Film Tradition and Women's Cinema*. Princeton: Princeton University Press, 1989.

Kindem, Gorham. "Norway's New Generation of Women Directors: Anja Breien, Vibeke Lokkeberg, and Laila Mikkelsen." *Journal of Film and Video* 36.4 (fall 1987): 28–42.

McIlroy, Brian. *World Cinema: Sweden*. London: Flicks Books, 1986.

Mellencamp, Patricia. *Indiscretions: Avant-Garde Film, Video & Feminism*. Bloomington: Indiana University Press, 1990.

Quart, Barbara. *Women Directors: The Emergence of a New Cinema*. New York: Praeger, 1988.

Smith, Sharon. *Women Who Make Movies*. New York: Hopkinson and Blake, 1975.

Williams, Linda. "Something Else Besides a Mother." In *Issues in Feminist Film Criticism*, edited by Patricia Erens, 137–62. Bloomington: Indiana University Press, 1990.

MIRO, PILAR (1940–   ). Spain. Pilar Miro is one of the few women directors working in Spain today. In Spain, the number of films directed by women is still much below the average for other European countries. Rosario Pi is a pioneer woman director who worked in Spain in the 1930s. More recently, women directors such as Pilar Tavora, Ana Diez, Isabel Coixet, Cristina Andreu, and Pilar Miro are breaking down barriers that have traditionally excluded women's participation in the creation of the Spanish cinema. The annual Women's Film Festival (A teneo Feminista) in Madrid is a screening venue for "forgotten" films by Spanish women directors as well as current films directed by emerging women filmmakers.

Pilar Miro is not only a major director but an influential political figure in Spanish film production. In the 1980s, she worked as the director of the Film Department of the Ministry of Culture. She worked to liberalize national subsidies for film production during her tenure and is "responsible for the recent boom in Spanish cinema," according to Rosa Bosch. As a director, Miro is described as an enigmatic figure who displays both "an extremely sensitive feminism and a forceful masculinity in her films" (Schwartz, 133). Miro's work is often semiautobiographical. Her films tend to center around themes of power relations, freedom and individuality, and ethical questions.

Born in Madrid in 1940, Pilar Miro studied journalism and law and, later, screenwriting at the Official Film School (Escuela Oficial de cinema). In 1960, she began working for the publicity department of TVE (Spanish television). By 1966, she was directing television productions such as "Estudio 1," "Danza Macabra," and "El escarabajo de oro." In 1978, she directed her first feature film, *La Peticion* (*The Engagement Party*), an adaptation of a novel by Émile Zola. *The Engagement Party* was initially banned, but it was finally released after filmmakers and the media pressured the government to reconsider the film's artistic merit. The plot of the film centers around a wealthy young woman who is "simultaneously involved in sadistic and ultimately fatal sexual relationships with three men" (Schwartz, 126). The scandal surrounding *The Engagement Party* can be directly linked to the film's theme of irrepressible female sexuality as it is handled by a woman director. In the film, a woman pursues sexual knowledge and thus transgresses traditional filmic space. Woman is presented as the owner of sexual space, rather than the space to be entered and investigated by the male gaze. The portrayal of aggressive female sexuality is common in Spanish cinema, yet Miro's handling of the material is particularly realistic, harsh, and female-centered. *The Engagement Party* is an embrace of the dangerous femme fatale as a threat to societal codes of repression.

Pilar Miro's *El Crimen de Cuenca* (*The Crime of Cuenca*) (1979) is an assault on police brutality. As Ronald Schwartz notes, the film was censored by the military authorities, who also attempted to silence Miro with political criminal charges. *The Crime of Cuenca* "revealed illegal methods of interrogation by police under the Franco regime" (127), according to Schwartz. The ban on the film was lifted in 1981, and *The Crime of Cuenca* was an immediate critical and box-office success. The film concerns two men who are wrongly accused of a crime. The authorities fabricate evidence against them and torture them, almost to the point of death. Miro's use of graphic realism of the lengthy torture scenes typifies her disdain for films that gloss over, romanticize, or exclude scenes of graphic torture.

In *Gary Cooper, que estás en los cielos* (1980), Miro utilizes her grim realism in an autobiographical film about a television director who undergoes an abortion. Andrea is a television director in her thirties who suddenly finds that she must have an abortion because she has ovarian cancer. Pilar Miro allows the woman's story to unfold in three days of the life of Andrea, concentrating on her subjective position, her inner thoughts, and her alienation from society. Ronald Schwartz compares *Gary Cooper* with Agnes Varda's *Cleo from 5 to 7* (1961), finding Miro's film "vastly superior" (132). *Gary Cooper* ends with a scene of Andrea's being wheeled into the operating room. The audience never learns what happens to Andrea and is left with a feeling of alienation not unlike that of the central heroine.

Pilar Miro is a consistently controversial figure in Spain, both as a director and as an activist. Her films seem to swirl in controversy as much as her actions as director of the Film Department of the Ministry of Culture. In 1986, Miro left this position to direct *Werther,* based on Goethe's novel. She became director of Spanish television (TVE) but resigned amid political scandal that, according to Rosa Bosch, "exposed the misogynistic situation" that women face when they reach higher levels of power in the film industry.

SELECTED FILMOGRAPHY

La petición (*The Engagement Party*) (1978)
Sábado de Gloria (1979–80)
El Crimen de Cuenca (*The Crime of Cuenca*) (1979)
Gary Cooper, que estás en los cielos (1980)
Hablemos esta noche (*We'll Talk Tonight*) (1982)
Werther (1986)

SELECTED BIBLIOGRAPHY

Besa, Peter. "Review of *La petición*." *Variety* (August 25, 1976): 20.
———. "Review of *El Crimen de Cuenca*." *Variety* (January 23, 1980): 104.
———. "Review of *Gary Cooper, Who Art in Heaven*." *Variety* (February 4, 1981): 20.
Bosch, Rosa. "Miro, Pilar." In *The Women's Companion to International Film*, edited by Annette Kuhn, with Susannah Radstone, 267. Berkeley: University of California Press, 1994.
Hopewell, John. *Out of the Past: Spanish Cinema After Franco*. London: BFI, 1986.
Markham, James M. "Spanish Regime in First Film Ban." *New York Times*, January 6, 1980, C6.
Schwartz, Ronald. *Spanish Film Directors*. Metuchen, NJ: Scarecrow Press, 1986.

MITA, MERATA (1942–). New Zealand. Merata Mita is the first Maori woman to ever direct a feature film (*Mauri*, 1988). Born in 1942 in New Zealand, Mita is of the Ngati Pikiao tribe. She grew up in a traditional Maori household and remains tied to her cultural upbringing. Merata Mita found herself drawn into the film trade because of her ability to translate for European film crews that hired her to work as a cultural guide on their films about the Maori people. Mita decided that ethnographic films about her people should be directed by and about Maori people. Mita is well versed in the politics of objectification of the other, the cultural colonialization of indigenous peoples by nonindigenous filmmakers. Consequently, Mita's films are not simply documentaries on Maori issues but studies on the presumed objectivity of the ethnographic traditional cinema.

In *Patu!* (1984), Mita revisions documentary as an embrace of subjectivity. She dispenses with the notion of the "objective" filmmaker and foregrounds her own subjective position. *Patu!* is a postcolonial study about Maori and South African cultural suppression. Mita uses a polylogue of voices of indigenous peoples on the sound track of *Patu!,* along with music designed to underscore Mita's outrage about the treatment of Maori people. Her approach to documentary is, in some ways, comparable to the subjective documentary work of Vietnamese-born Trinh T. Minh-ha. Both filmmakers scrutinize the voyeuristic, objectifying gaze of the ethnographic filmmaker and call attention to themselves as active participants in the filmmaking process. The appropriation of the images of colonized peoples is directly bound up with the appropriation of the land and culture of indigenous people.

Maori people have been a traditional subject of colonist film directors who have misconstructed Maori identity as savage "Other." Maori directors such as Merata Mita are taking back ownership of their own images by producing Maori-language television programs, feature films, and documentaries. Their work has not always met with respect or approval from white audiences and legislators. *Patu!*, for example, was at the center of controversy when New Zealanders were outraged that the film was financed by government subsidies. The release of the film was delayed for several years because of the controversy.

Mauri caused considerably less controversy. The film centers around a strong grandmother figure who realizes the significance of spiritual loss in Maori women who are acculturated into the dominant Pakeha culture of New Zealand. Mita is concerned with the loss of oral culture, ritual meaning, and Maori identity. Tracey Moffatt is another woman director from Australia who is operating from a similar perspective. Moffatt's films demonstrate how Aboriginal women, like Native Americans, are stereotyped by dominant culture, dispossessed of their homeland and their culture, and removed from the process of creating their own images. Merata Mita's and Tracey Moffatt's films represent an active counternarrative cinema of self-construction.

SELECTED FILMOGRAPHY

Karanga Hokianga (1970)
Bastion Point: Day 507 (codirector) (1980)
The Hammer and the Anvil (codirector) (1980)
Keskidee-Aroha (codirector) (1981)
The Bridge: A Story of Men in Dispute (codirector) (1982)
Patu! (1984)
Mauri (1988)

SELECTED BIBLIOGRAPHY

Barclay, Barry. *The Control of One's Own Image.* Auckland: Longman Paul, 1992.
Gordon, Linda. "On Difference." *Genders* 10 (spring 1991): 91–111.
Hardy, Ann. "Mita, Merata." In *The Women's Companion to International Film,* edited by Annette Kuhn, with Susannah Radstone, 268. Berkeley: University of California Press, 1994.
Hass, Sandra K. "An Outward Sign of an Inward Struggle: The Fight for Human Rights of the Australian Aborigine." *Florida International Law Journal* 5 (fall 1989): 81.
Martin, Biddy, and Chandra Mohanty. "Feminist Politics: What's Home Got to Do with It?" In *Feminist Studies/Critical Studies,* edited by Teresa de Lauretis, 208–9. Bloomington: Indiana University Press, 1986.
Morgan, Robin. "Planetary Feminism: The Politics of the 21st Century." In *Sisterhood Is Global: The International Women's Movement Anthology,* 1–37. New York: Anchor P/Doubleday, 1984.
"Oral History No More." *Asiaweek* 16 (August 1990): 32, 49.

Spivak, Gayatri Chakravorty. "Acting Bits/Identity Talk." *Critical Inquiry* 18.4 (summer 1992): 770–803.

Suleri, Sara. "Woman Skin Deep: Feminism and the Postcolonial Condition." *Critical Inquiry* 18.4 (summer 1992): 756–69.

Trinh T. Minh-ha. *Framer Framed.* New York: Routledge, 1992.

Watson, Sophie, ed. *Playing the State: Australian Feminist Interventions.* New York: Verso, 1990.

MOFFATT, TRACEY (1960–   ). Australia. Australian independent filmmaker Tracey Moffatt makes films that challenge dominant myths about Aboriginal people. Aboriginal people are represented in mainstream films as either absent, "uncivilized," or happily colonized, while Australians are depicted as cultural heroes. While it is true that "the cultural image of Australia is not a monolithic mythic image" (Rattigan, 24), Aboriginal experiences are typically denarrated or viewed through a colonialist perspective. *A Change of Face* (1988) is a documentary about colonialist cultural image making. Moffatt interviews media professionals—actors, directors, and producers—and captures their racism and sexism in their on-camera responses. Moffatt's othering of the colonizer is a decolonizing technique, designed to demythologize the power of representatives of the media. Trinh T. Minh-ha characterizes such a displacing and decentering design as an instance of "she who steals language" (15). Moffatt steals the cinematic language of the oppressor and uses that same language to revision history and rearticulate the location of Aboriginal people.

Moffatt's *Nice Colored Girls* (1987) continues on the trajectory of demythologizing and revising Australian historicity. *Nice Colored Girls* exposes the history of exploitation of Aboriginal women by white men. Moffatt interweaves extradiagetic sounds, images, and printed texts to convey the multiple perspectives of Aboriginal women. *Nice Colored Girls,* however, is not an ahistorical reconstruction of Aboriginal women, as Moffatt acknowledges the role of oppression and enforced silence in the construction of colonized Aboriginal women. This identification of the subaltern is juxtaposed against a recognition of the acculturated, modern, urban Aboriginal woman in an unusual counternarrative. Thus, Moffatt escapes the tendency to represent the Aboriginal woman as a monolithic subject.

Night Cries (1990) exposes the problematic relationships between women across cultural margins. In the film, a middle-aged Aboriginal woman nurses her adopted white mother, and the psychology of racism between the two women involves both love and hostility. *Night Cries* is an exploration and indictment of assimilation policies that once forced Aboriginal children to be raised by white families, in which Moffatt utilizes expressionistic sets that serve to underscore the allegorical nature of the film as a fictive, staged construct. As a storyteller, Tracey Moffatt uses formalist strategies to revision history and incorporate Aboriginal histories into contemporary filmmaking. Like the recent storytelling by Australian Aboriginal women, Moffatt's work is equally formalist.

SELECTED FILMOGRAPHY

Nice Colored Girls (1987)
A Change of Face (1988)
Night Cries (1990)

SELECTED BIBLIOGRAPHY

Bell, Diane. "Aboriginal Women, Separate Spaces, and Feminism." In *A Reader in Feminist Knowledge,* edited by Sneja Gunew, 13–26. London: Routledge, 1991.
Brock, Peggy, ed. *Women, Rites and Sites: Aboriginal Women's Cultural Knowledge.* Sydney: Allen and Unwin, 1989.
Gale, Fay, ed. *We Are Bosses Ourselves.* Canberra: Australian Institute for Aboriginal Studies, 1983.
Longley, Kateryna Olijnyk. "Autobiographical Storytelling by Australian Aboriginal Women." In *De/Colonizing the Subject: The Politics of Gender in Women's Autobiography,* edited by Sidonie Smith and Julia Watson, 370–84. Minneapolis: University of Minnesota Press, 1992.
Narogin, Mudrooroo. *Writing from the Fringe: A Study of Modern Aboriginal Literature.* Victoria: Hyland House, 1990.
Rattigan, Neil. *Images of Australia.* Dallas: Southern Methodist University Press, 1991.
Trinh T. Minh-ha. *Woman, Native, Other: Writing Postcoloniality and Feminism.* Bloomington: Indiana University Press, 1989.
Women Make Movies. *Women Make Movies Catalogue.* New York: Women Make Movies, 1994.

MONTI, ADRIANA (1951–   ). Italy. Adriana Monti is an Italian filmmaker who also directed an independent filmmaking school (the Albedo Film School) in Milan in 1983–84. Monti has been a strong feminist voice in Italian independent cinema since the late 1970s. In 1979, Adriana Monti organized a group of "housewives" to shoot the film *Scuola senza fine (School without End),* which was released in 1983. As Monti explains, the women had taken a writing course, but "they were reluctant to go back to their afternoons ironing or playing cards. So first we devised new seminars on literature, the body, and the image" (80). The group eventually began working on the collaborative screenplay for *School without End.* Adriana Monti's cooperative approach to feminist filmmaking represents a challenge to traditional auterist cinema, which privileges a monologic perspective. *School without End* is a multiauthored, collaborative piece. Monti noted that the women's group that produced the film "is not dazzled by long words or theory; they used to play with theories or use them as magic formulas, but always to approach a question to which there was no answer" (81). Adriana Monti's films typically center around women's collaborative work and feminist issues. For example, *Filo a catena* (1986) is a documentary on women textile workers, depicting the harsh conditions under which these women labor on a daily basis for very little pay.

Adriana Monti's work is perhaps typical of the strong feminist movement in Italy that began making inroads into film criticism and production in the 1970s. During this period, many feminist film collectives, such as the Alice Guy Collective, the Neapolitan Collective (Nemesiache), and camerawomen in Turin, began supporting feminist film retrospectives and feminist filmmaking. RAI, Italian National Television, also supported the development of Italian feminist filmmaking. Governmental funding, mandated by Article 28, provides fiscal support for independent filmmakers, as well. In addition to Adriana Monti, women directors such as Gabriella Rosaleva, Fiorella Infascelli, Cinzia Torrini, Liliana Cavani, and Lina Wertmuller are actively producing and directing films and videos in Italy. Thanks to the film scholarship of Giuliana Bruno and Maria Nadotti, international circles of feminist film theorists are being informed about the activities of women directors both in current Italian film and in Italian film history.

SELECTED FILMOGRAPHY

Trame (1982)
Una scuola di cinema a Milano (1983)
Scuola senza fine (1983)
Tracce sulla pelle incantata (1984)
Spazi vocali (1984)
Filo a catena (1986)
Gentile Signora (1990)

SELECTED BIBLIOGRAPHY

Bordanella, Peter. *Italian Cinema: From Neorealism to the Present*. New York: Continuum, 1990.
Bruno, Giuliana. *Streetwalking on a Ruined Map: Cultural Theory and the City Films of Elvira Notari*. Princeton: Princeton University Press, 1993.
Conti, Bruna, ed. *La donna e il femminismo*. Rome: Riuniti, 1978.
Miscuglio, Annabella, and Rony Daopoulo, eds. *Kinomato: La donna nel cinema*. Bari: Dedalo Libri, 1980.
Monti, Adriana. "Introduction to the Script of the Film *Scuola senza fine*." Translated by Giovanna Ascelle. In *Off Screen: Women and Film in Italy*, edited by Giuliana Bruno and Maria Nadotti, 80–83. London: Routledge, 1988.

MOORHOUSE, JOCELYN (1965–   ). Australia. Jocelyn Moorhouse is a graduate of the Australian Film Television and Radio School. She worked extensively as a scriptwriter and film editor for television before she made her first short film, *The Siege of Barton's Bathroom*. This film was developed into a twelve-part television series. Moorhouse became an internationally recognized filmmaker in 1991, when she released *Proof,* a brilliant film directed on a budget of $1.1 million. Moorhouse wrote the screenplay for *Proof* as a response to a comment she remembered about a blind man who took photographs. As Moorhouse told Peter Brunette:

It was one of those things I couldn't get out of my mind. . . . I hit on the idea of using the photographs as a method of testing, of "proof" that you live in the same world as other people. (10)

Proof is a psychological drama of a blind photographer, his mother, and his housekeeper. Martin (played by Hugo Weaving) is a paranoid character who has been blind since birth. He takes photographs and asks people to describe them to test their ability to tell the truth. *Proof* decenters our notions of truth as a unitary, easily reducible form of representation. Martin's housekeeper Celia (played by Genevieve Picot) becomes infatuated with Martin, but he avoids her advances. Martin's friend Andy (played by Russell Crowe) is used by Celia as a means to capture Martin. Celia's character becomes the focal point of the narrative. As Moorhouse explains:

Most women can easily identify with her because she's what we fear we could all become if we were desperate enough for love. I think that being a woman allowed me to love her and yet also to show her destructive qualities. (Brunette, 10)

Proof exhibits a dark Gothic humor and a sexual tension common to recent Australian films such as Alison Maclean's *Crush,* Jane Campion's *The Piano,* and Gillian Armstrong's *The Last Days of Chez Nous.* Jocelyn Moorhouse is a subtle Gothicist who embraces ambiguity. *Proof* is compelling because of its tightly constructed screenplay and because Moorhouse never tells what she can show. Moorhouse is currently working on *How To Make An American Quilt,* which will feature Winona Ryder, Kate Capshaw, Alfre Woodard, Anne Bancroft, Ellen Burstyn, and Maya Angelou.

SELECTED FILMOGRAPHY

Proof (1991)

SELECTED BIBLIOGRAPHY

Brunette, Peter. "Just Looking: *Proof,* the Story of a Blind Photographer." *Sight and Sound* (November 1991): 10–11.
Durden, Mark. "*Proof.*" *Creative Camera* 317 (August–September 1992): 24–25.
James, Caryn. "A Distinctive Shade of Darkness." *New York Times,* November 28, 1993, H13.
McFarlane, Brian, and Geoff Mayer. *New Australian Cinema.* Cambridge: Cambridge University Press, 1992.
Rattigan, Neil. *Images of Australia.* Dallas: Southern Methodist University Press, 1991.
Romney, Jonathan. "*Proof.*" *Sight and Sound* (December 1991): 48–49.

MURATOVA, KIRA (1934–   ). Soviet Union. Kira Muratova's films were banned for two decades in the Soviet Union. According to Lynn Attwood,

Kira Muratova is one of the most controversial contemporary Soviet women directors (122). Even in the more liberal period of the Gorbachev era, Muratova's most recent film, *The Asthenic Syndrome* (1990), was denied general release and was screened only at cinema clubs. *The Asthenic Syndrome* inverts traditional gender roles "contrasting the passivity of the male hero with the aggression of a female protagonist . . . who swears ferociously, seduces a stranger and kicks him out of bed" (Attwood, 122).

Kira Muratova began directing in the 1960s, after graduating from the State Film School VGIK. *Brief Encounters* (1968) is a study of an independent urban woman. Muratova plays the role of Valya, a woman who is obsessionally dedicated to her job. With *Brief Encounters,* Muratova became known for her Bressonian approach to film drama. *Brief Encounters* is restrained and poetic. *Long Farewells* (1971) was Muratova's first major controversial film. It was banned for its negative view of a mother-son relationship. Muratova's films tend to explore the emotions of deeply unsatisfied women. In *Long Farewells,* Muratova develops a woman character whose "emotional equilibrium is based solely on her relationship with her son" (Attwood, 86). In addition to her exposure of the dissatisfaction of women, Muratova criticized inefficiency and corruption in *Brief Encounters* and *Long Farewells*. Both films were banned by the Soviet censors.

Getting to Know the Wide World (1979) is an exploration of alienated men and women. Muratova's characters lead exiled, deprivileged lives. *Among Grey Stones* (1983), which Muratova directed pseudonymously as Ivan Sidorov, features lost and hopelessly alienated outcast figures in harsh and disconcerting mise-en-scènes. Muratova's cinematography is distinguished by her long takes of depressing, depeopled, empty spaces. Her cinema of exile is only now beginning to be screened at international film festivals. She is featured in a documentary on Soviet women filmmakers directed by Sally Potter. The film is available from Women Make Movies.

SELECTED FILMOGRAPHY

Ukrutogo yara (*By the Steep Ravine*) (short) (1961)
Nash chestnyi khleb (*Our Honest Bread*) (1964)
Korotkie vstrechi (*Brief Encounters*) (1968)
Dolgiie proshchaniia (*Long Farewells*) (1971, released 1986)
Poznavaia belyi svet (*Getting to Know the Wide World*) (1979)
Sredi serikh kammey (*Among Grey Stones*) (directed pseudonymously as Ivan Sidorov) (1983)
Peremena uchasti (*Change of Fortune*) (1987)
The Asthenic Syndrome (1990)

SELECTED BIBLIOGRAPHY

Attwood, Lynn. *Red Women on the Silver Screen: Soviet Women and Cinema from the Beginning to the End of the Communist Era.* London: Pandora, 1993.
Kaplan, E. Ann. *Women and Film.* London: Methuen, 1983.

Kuhn, Annette. *Women's Pictures: Feminism and Cinema.* London: Pandora, 1982.

Lawton, Anna. "Toward a New Openness in Soviet Cinema." In *Post New Wave Cinema in the Soviet Union and Central Europe,* edited by Daniel J. Goulding, 1–50. Bloomington: Indiana University Press, 1989.

Mayne, Judith. *Kino and the Woman Question: Feminism and Soviet Silent Film.* Columbus: Ohio University Press, 1989.

Waters, Elizabeth. "Restructuring the 'Woman Question': Perestroika and Prostitution." *Feminist Review* 33 (autumn 1989): 3–19.

MURPHY, PAT (1951–   ). Ireland. Pat Murphy is an extraordinary independent filmmaker from Ireland whose work is internationally recognized as an exemplification of feminist cinema at its most challenging. Her first film, *Rituals of Memory* (1979), was made in England, where she studied art and cinema. Her films break from the language of dominant cinema. In *Rituals of Memory,* for instance, Murphy deconstructs narratives of personal memory, calling into question the reliability of memory and film narration. Murphy intercuts a recently filmed visit with her family with footage that seems to represent her subjective memories of her past. *Rituals of Memory* is a diary film that breaks with realism and documentary truth systems. It is as much a tale of the filmmaker's life as it is an abstract and intertextual study of formalist cinema. *Rituals of Memory* makes the notion of "text" problematic and decenters the monologic narrative of truth in tale-telling, exposing multivalent truths. The viewer is expected to actively participate in the making of narrative meaning throughout footage of the filmmaker's family moving from a Protestant housing project to a Catholic neighborhood in the midst of political turmoil. The filmmaker's relationship with, and subsequent estrangement from, a young republican is portrayed as unfinished material that informs the dialogic narrative.

After returning to Ireland, Murphy directed two of the most important films of modern Irish cinema: *Mauve* (1981) and *Anne Devlin* (1984). *Mauve,* like *Rituals of Memory,* is an experimental feminist narrative in which a young woman is silenced by a male republican tradition. *Mauve* is a reconstruction of identity as much as it is a deconstruction of received ideals of Irish history and women's history. As Claire Johnston notes, *Mauve* "describes men's relationship to women within nationalist culture as 'like England's relationship to Ireland. You're in possession of us. You occupy us like an army' " (92). Mauve, the main character, challenges women's silent position, yet she and her mother are continually interrupted by her father, a linear, narrative storyteller who seeks to control and order the grand master-narrative of the family. *Mauve* foregrounds the politics of narrative storytelling, exposing the power of speech and historicity. In one sequence, the family watches an important political event, the Orange March of July 12, on television, as it passes under their window. Murphy draws our attention to the spectatorial fascination with the mediated narratives presented by television rather than the value of the actual event. The deprivileged tales that are denarrated from history are the stories in which Pat Murphy is interested.

Anne Devlin is a historical drama, set at the 1803 rebellion, that renarrates the untold tales of women's roles in the history of Ireland. Kathleen Murphy writes, "*Anne Devlin* is a stubborn movie, refusing as it does every blandishment of romanticized history" (32). Anne Devlin (played by Brid Brennan) is a silenced narrator. During an interrogation, an English official tells her, "I will keep you in jail all the days of your life as a warning to women like you," but Devlin's silence becomes a narrative weapon. Murphy is brilliant in her exposure of silence as weapon. Both *Mauve* and *Anne Devlin* consistently mine the notions of female silence as a subversive method of transgressing patriarchal narrative form. Murphy's directorial approach undercuts the seductiveness of narrativity. According to critic Kathleen Murphy, Pat Murphy "questions the way storytelling colors everything, from love to landscape, for women abroad in male-dominated mise-en-scène" (32).

SELECTED FILMOGRAPHY

Rituals of Memory (1979)
Mauve (1981)
Anne Devlin (1984)

SELECTED BIBLIOGRAPHY

Johnston, Claire. "*Mauve*." in *Films for Women*, edited by Charlotte Brunsdon, 91–98. London: BFI, 1987.
McBride, Stephanie. "Murphy, Pat." In *The Women's Companion to International Film*, edited by Annette Kuhn, with Susannah Radstone, 274–75. Berkeley: University of California Press, 1994.
Murphy, Kathleen. "Herstory As Her Is Harped." *Film Comment* 30.3 (May–June 1994): 31–34.
Rockett, Kevin. "A Short History of Cinema in Ireland." *Film Comment* 30.3 (May–June 1994): 25–30.
———, Luke Gibbons, and John Hill. *Cinema and Ireland*. Syracuse, NY: Syracuse University Press, 1988.
Slide, Anthony. *The Cinema and Ireland*. Jefferson, NC: McFarland, 1988.

MUSIDORA (1889–1957). France. Few cinephiles are aware that Musidora, one of the most famous stars of the early French cinema, also produced and directed ten surrealist films. Musidora, born Jeanne Roques on February 23, 1889, in Paris, is credited with the creation of the first "vamp" of French films. She became an overnight sensation when she starred in Louis Feuillade's silent serial *Les Vampires* (1915–16). Musidora was adored by the surrealists, who viewed her as the essence of subversive erotic desire. Dressed in a sexy black leotard, Musidora signified both androgyny and unrepressed sexuality. Surrealists such as André Breton and Louis Arragon claimed Musidora as a figurehead of transgressive art. Poet Louis Arragon dubbed her "the tenth muse." Musidora was close friends with Marcel L'Herbier, Louis Delluc, Germaine Dulac, and Colette, the famous novelist/screenwriter with whom she collaborated and codirected.

Musidora was born into a family that nurtured artistic creativity. Her mother was an active feminist literary critic who founded the journal *Le Vengeur,* a periodical dedicated to feminism and the arts (Acker, 293). Her father was also a creative spirit, dedicated to music and philosophy. Musidora was drawn to the stage at an early age. At sixteen, she was already working in vaudeville. Musidora named herself after a character in a nineteenth-century novel, *Fortunio* (1870), written by Théophile Gautier. She acted in many films before her great success in *Les Vampires.* The success of the serial allowed her the chance to direct her first film, *Minne* (1915) (also known as *L'Ingénue Libertine*).

Minne appears to be a lost film, though some production photographs have survived. According to Ally Acker, *Minne* is based on the life story of Colette. Musidora's next film, *The Black Leotard* (1917), represents an attempt to reclaim the image that she created for another director in her own work, under her own name. Musidora consistently worked to claim ownership of her body and image, from her self-naming to her efforts as producer/director.

La Vagabonda (1918), adapted from Colette's novel, was a breakthrough success for Musidora as director. Musidora not only produced and directed the film but also starred in it. Colette worked on the film as an assistant. Later, in 1919, Colette and Musidora collaborated on *La Flamme Cachée,* from Colette's screenplay. Like most women directors, Musidora recognized that one way to sidestep the sexism of the industry is to form one's own production company, so for the release of *La Flamme Cachée,* Musidora formed her own production company, La Société des Films Musidora. Musidora wrote a feminist screenplay for *La Terre des Toros (Land of the Bulls)* (1924), which she shot in Spain. According to Sharon Smith, Musidora "tested her courage in the bullring to demonstrate that women were brave enough to 'deserve' the vote" (114).

Musidora was crowned the "queen of cinema" in 1926, but she did not direct any more films until 1951, when she made a compilation film, *La Magique Image,* which featured clips from her early films. She continued to write, and she also worked for the Cinémathèque Française. She also directed stage productions, such as *La vie sentimental de George Sand* (1946).

Musidora's legendary image in France is comparable to that of female sexual icons such as Marilyn Monroe. *Les Vampires* is repeatedly revived and screened at international film festivals. In the late 1970s, French feminist film critics began to recognize Musidora as a legendary filmmaker in her own right. Musidora was a multitalented woman artist who painted, wrote films, plays, novels, and songs, and produced, directed, and starred in early silent films. Her creation of the vamp as a masquerading figure is a significant feature of her biography as it "seemed to provide a feminine counter to the concept of fetishism which had [been] dominated [by] male spectatorship" (Doane, 39). Musidora's attempt to control and own her self-produced image is indicative of the feminist act of self-creation. She recognized that "women must write through their bodies, they must invent the impregnable language that will wreck partitions, classes, and rhetorics, regulations and codes" (Cixous, 229).

SELECTED FILMOGRAPHY

Minne (1915)
Le Maillot Noir (*The Black Leotard*) (1917)
La Vagabonda (*The Vagabond*) (Italy) (1918)
Vicenta (1918–19)
La Flamme Cachée (*The Hidden Flame*) (codirector) (1919)
Pour Don Carlos (codirector) (1921)
Une Aventure de Musidors en Espagne (1922)
Soleil et Ombre (*Sun and Shadow*) (1922)
La Terre des Toros (*Land of the Bulls*) (1924)
La Magique Image (1951)

SELECTED BIBLIOGRAPHY

Abel, Richard. *French Cinema: The First Wave, 1915–1929*. Princeton: Princeton University Press, 1984.
————. "Before *Fantômas*: Louis Feuillade and the Development of Early French Cinema." *Post Script* 7.1 (fall 1987): 4–26.
Acker, Ally. *Reel Women: Pioneers of the Cinema, 1896 to the Present*. New York: Continuum, 1993.
Armes, Roy. *French Cinema*. New York: Oxford University Press, 1985.
Cazals, Patrick. *Musidora: La Dixième Muse*. Paris: Editions Henry Veyrier, 1978.
Cixous, Hélène. "The Laugh of the Medusa." In *A Reader in Feminist Knowledge*, edited by Sneja Gunew, 224–30. London: Routledge, 1991.
Doane, Mary Ann. *Femmes Fatales: Feminism, Film Theory, Psychoanalysis*. New York: Routledge, 1991.
Flitterman-Lewis, Sandy. *To Desire Differently: Feminism and French Cinema*. Urbana: University of Illinois Press, 1990.
Hughes, Phillippe de, and Dominique Muller, eds. *Gaumont: 90 and de cinéma*. Paris: Ramsaye, 1986.
Smith, Sharon. *Women Who Make Movies*. New York: Hopkinson and Blake, 1975.
Vincendeau, Ginette. "Musidora." In *The Women's Companion to International*

Film, edited by Annette Kuhn and Susannah Radstone, 277. Berkeley: University of California Press, 1994.

Virmaux, Odette, and Alain Virmaux, eds. *Colette at the Movies.* New York: Ungar, 1980.

N

NAIR, MIRA (1957–   ). India/United States. Mira Nair was born in Bhu-
baneswar, India, in 1957. After three years as an actress in the theater
community in New Delhi, Nair came to the United States to study at Harvard University. *Jama Masjid Street Journal,* a documentary on cultural life
in India, is her student thesis film of 1979 and was screened at New York's
Film Forum in 1986. In 1983, Nair directed *So Far from India,* an hour-
long documentary about an Indian-American subway newsstand salesman
in New York and his wife, who waits for his return to India. *So Far from
India* was screened at the 1983 New York Film Festival, at the Cinema du
Réel in Paris, and on international television. Nair's third film, *India Cab-
aret* (1985), was selected as the Best Documentary at the Global Village
Film Festival in New York, and it won several international awards. *Salaam
Bombay!* (1988), a documentary on Bombay streetpeople, won the New
Director's Award at Cannes and an Oscar nomination in 1989.

Nair's 1991 film, *Mississippi Masala,* which she wrote, directed, and
produced, is a critical and commercial success. It is an interracial love story
that crosses lines of international diasporic communities. Mark A. Reid
states that filmmakers such as D. W. Griffith consolidated stereotyped images of the black community, while Reid notes that Mira Nair's film
"shows residents of different colors coexisting in peace" (27). The problem
emerges when Demetrius, an African American (played by Denzel Washington) falls in love with Mina (played by Sarita Choudhury), the daughter
of an East Indian motel owner. *Mississippi Masala* "shifts the spotlight to
debates and conflicts between 'minority' communities," according to Andrea Stuart. Stuart sees this shift as a formative period of hybrid cinema.
As Nair told Samuel G. Freedman, she is aware of the tensions among
generations of people of color. As a young woman, she herself felt tensions
within her family: "My parents always assumed that I would grow up and
earn a living and be independent. But as years go by, you change and have
new ideas, and they start to not recognize you anymore" (14). *Mississippi*

Masala draws upon Nair's own experience. As she told Andrea Stuart, Nair feels "strongly to be Masala, to be mixed, is the new world order" (212). As Stuart notes, "[M]igration is not necessarily a tragedy leading to irrecoverable loss. . . . In *Mississippi Masala,* Nair revels in the melange migration creates" (212).

Nair's films have not always met with sweeping approval. Poonam Arora criticizes *Salaam Bombay!* for "the film's utter failure to address the nuances of cultural specificity" (294). *Salaam Bombay!,* Arora warns, "renders voiceless its marginal subjects" (295) in its representation of Third World subjects as Other. Amit Shah defends Nair's work, which is sometimes described as objectifying. Shah states that "Nair's refusal to make a film that is a didactic treatise, a lecture on attitudes, ironing out the complexities of human personalities, is at the root of her problems with her critics" (23). *India Cabaret* (1985), which reveals the marginalized existence of strippers, is a unique presentation of "the unshakeable inviolability of double standards, of patriarchal values, of the strong conditioning of women never to question or challenge," Nair writes (Nair & Taraporevala, 62). Nair responds to objections that the film presents a "male gaze," by stating, "I think this idea . . . is basically lifted out of context from Western theorizing about film" (67). Nair insists that her films resist a male gaze and present an Indian woman's perspective that is new to Indian cinema. "In India, films don't exist which portray women and men as they are, the way they speak" (67). Nair would, however, probably agree that the criticism around her films shows a healthy dialogic between filmmaker and postcolonial critic. Nair's most recent film is *The Perez Family* (1995).

SELECTED FILMOGRAPHY

Jama Masjid Street Journal (1979)
So Far from India (1983)
India Cabaret (1985)
Children of Desired Sex (1987)
Salaam Bombay! (1988)
Mississippi Masala (1991)
The Perez Family (1995)

SELECTED BIBLIOGRAPHY

Anderson, Erika Surat. "*Mississippi Masala.*" *Film Quarterly* 46 (summer 1993): 23–26.
Arora, Poonam. "The Production of Third World Subjects for First World Consumption: *Salaam Bombay!* and *Parama.*" In *Multiple Voices in Feminist Film Criticism,* edited by Diane Carson, Linda Dittmar, and Janice Welsch, 293–304. Minneapolis: University of Minnesota Press, 1994.
Berry, Cecelie S. "*Mississippi Masala.*" *Cineaste* 19.2–3 (1992): 66–67.
Cole, Janis, and Holly Dale. *Calling the Shots: Profiles of Women Filmmakers.* Ontario: Quarry Press, 1993.

Freedman, Samuel G. "One People in Two Worlds: Mira Nair's *Mississippi Masala.*" *New York Times,* February 2, 1992, H13–14.

Guerin, Marie-Anne. "*Mississippi Masala.*" *Cahiers du Cinema* 448 (October 1991): 67–68.

Nair, Mira, and Sooni Taraporevala. "*India Cabaret:* Reflections and Reactions." *Discourse* 8 (fall–winter 1986–87): 58–72.

Reid, Mark A. "Rebirth of a Nation: Three Recent Films Resist the Southern Stereotypes of D. W. Griffith, Depicting a Technicolor Region of Black, Brown, and G(R)ay." *Southern Exposure* 20.4 (winter 1992): 26–28.

Shah, Amit. "A Dweller in Two Lands: Mira Nair, Filmmaker." *Cineaste* 15.3 (1987): 22–33.

Stuart, Andrea. "Mira Nair: A New Hybrid Cinema." In *Women and Film: A Sight and Sound Reader,* edited by Pam Cook and Philip Dodd, 210–16. Philadelphia: Temple University Press, 1993.

Willeman, Paul, and Behroze Gandy, eds. *Indian Cinema: BFI Dossier Number 5.* London: BFI, 1982.

NELSON, GUNVOR (1931–   ). United States. Born in Stockholm, Sweden, and married at one time to San Francisco filmmaker Robert Nelson, Gunvor Nelson has remained a vital force in American experimental film, while Robert Nelson's impact has faded from the scene. Starting out with the raucous feminist satire of her first film, *Schmeerguntz* (1966), which she codirected with Dorothy Wiley, Gunvor Nelson has created a vision that is uniquely her own. The fifteen-minute film was "slammed together" in the then-prevalent "funk" style of filmmaking dominant in San Francisco and consists of a series of brutal images that directly condemn American society's warped vision of the feminine. The film won numerous prizes at Ann Arbor, Kent State, and the Chicago Art Institute. *Fog Pumas* (1967), also comade with Dorothy Wiley, was described by critic Don Lloyd as "an updating of surrealism" (Canyon Cinema Cooperative, 253). *Kirsa Nicholina* (1969) is an erotic meditation on sexual desire that was praised as a masterpiece by many film critics.

My Name Is Oona (1969), Gunvor Nelson's most hypnotic film, takes us into the dream world of a young child (Nelson's daughter) as she repeats her name over and over as a sort of incantatory mantra. *Five Artists* (1971), again made with Dorothy Wiley, is a light and slight documentary of several Bay Area artists and not one of her major works. The same is true of *One and the Same* (1972), comade with Freude Solomon-Bartlett, a collage of several "famous" San Francisco couples who confront the camera in the nude. *Take Off* (1972), one of Nelson's most famous films, deconstructs the act of striptease as Ellion Ness, described by critic B. Ruby Rich as a "professional stripper" (Canyon Cinema Cooperative, 254), takes off her clothes for the camera and the audience, climaxing her routine by removing her arms, legs, and head for the spectators. *Moons Pool* (1973) is a mood piece contrasting the human nude figure with various natural landscapes.

Trollstenen (1973–76), Nelson's least seen but most deeply personal film, is a difficult and moving examination of Nelson's parents and family living in Sweden. At two hours' running time, it is her longest work. *Before Need* (1979) marks a return to working with Dorothy Wiley. The film is remarkable for its series of dream images that float mysteriously in front of the eyes of the viewer. *Frame Line* (1984) is a structuralist film collage using bits and pieces of sound and image, again concerning Nelson's life in Sweden. *Red Shift* (1984) is a meditation on Nelson's relationship with her mother and her own daughter, Oona, and is a highly personal and poetic work.

Gunvor Nelson terms her films "surreal childhood fantasies" (39), in an interview with Brenda Richardson. Nelson recalls being most influenced by Jean Cocteau's *Beauty and the Beast*. As independent, female creative artists, both Nelson and Wiley connect surrealism to freedom. While Bruce Bailley, Hollis Frampton, and a handful of other men who made experimental films in the 1960s have come to signify a loosely constructed canon of underground filmmaking, the canon has "functioned aggressively to intimidate and silence women" (Fischer, 9). As Janet Staiger notes, "[I]t is particularly in this situation that feminists have been concerned about canons" (194).

Gunvor Nelson and Dorothy Wiley's collaborative efforts displace the traditionally defined role of the unified visionary auteur as an aggressive, male individualist. Their films display an ability to cross-contextualize the public and private through the use of objects and experiences of daily life. Though Nelson's and Wiley's names have been marginalized in film history, their films received a great deal of attention in their initial releases. *Schmeerguntz* won the First Prize at the Ann Arbor Film Festival and also won prizes at the Kent State University Film Festival and the Chicago Art Institute Film Festival. *Fog Pumas* was screened at the Belgian and Oberhausen Film Festivals and is held in the collection of the Museum of Modern Art. *My Name Is Oona* is described as "revelatory" by Amos Vogel (Film-makers Cooperative, 196). The film has been screened internationally on French and British television. More recently, *Light Years* (1987), *Field Study* #2 (1988), *Natural Features* (1990), and *Time Being* (1991) continue to keep Gunvor Nelson in the eye of the public. Nelson continues to be interested in the ludic aspects of experimental filmmaking and in revisioning cinema as a poetic explorative space.

SELECTED FILMOGRAPHY

Schmeerguntz (with Dorothy Wiley) (1966)
Fog Pumas (with Dorothy Wiley) (1967)
Kirsa Nicholina (1969)
My Name Is Oona (1969)
Five Artists BillBobBillBillBob (with Dorothy Wiley) (1971)
One and the Same (with Freude Solomon-Bartlett) (1972)
Take Off (1972)

Moons Pool (1973)
Trollstenen (1973–76)
Before Need (with Dorothy Wiley) (1979)
Frame Line (1984)
Red Shift (1984)
Light Years (1987)
Light Years Expanding (1987)
Field Study #2 (1988)
Natural Features (1990)
Time Being (1991)

SELECTED BIBLIOGRAPHY

Canyon Cinema Cooperative. *Canyon Cinema Catalogue 7*. San Francisco: Canyon Cinema, 1992.
Fischer, Lucy. *Shot/Counter-Shot: Film Tradition and Women's Cinema*. Princeton: Princeton University Press, 1989.
Film-Makers' Cooperative. *Film-Makers' Cooperative Catalogue 7*. New York: Film-Makers' Cooperative, 1989.
Rabinovitz, Lauren. *Points of Resistance: Women, Power and Politics in the New York Avant-Garde Cinema, 1943–71*. Urbana: University of Illinois Press, 1991.
Richardson, Brenda. "An Interview with Gunvor Nelson and Dorothy Wiley." *Film Quarterly* 25.1 (fall 1971): 34–39.
Sitney, P. Adams. *Visionary Film: The American Avant-Garde, 1943–1978*. New York: Oxford University Press, 1979.
Smith, Sharon. *Women Who Make Movies*. New York: Hopkinson and Blake, 1975.
Staiger, Janet. "The Politics of Film Canons." In *Multiple Voices in Feminist Film Criticism*, edited by Diane Carson, Linda Dittmar, and Janice Welsch, 191–209. Minneapolis: University of Minnesota Press, 1994.

NISKANEN, TUIJA-MAIJA (1943–   ). Finland. Finland's Tuija-Maija Niskanen consistently foregrounds issues of sexuality and repressive codes of behavior. Many of her films criticize heterocentric societal conformity and place homosexuality in the mainstream cinema of Finland. *Avskedet* (1980) tells the story of a young woman's coming out as a lesbian and her subsequent success as a theater director. As she becomes more of a public figure, the young woman must face her homophobic father with the fact of her newly recognized lesbian sexuality. Niskanen sets this dual story in the repressive atmosphere of wartime Finland to demonstrate that policies of political repression are much like politics of personal oppression. Niskanen's ability to make *Avskedet* with Swedish funding represents a formidable accomplishment.

Niskanen studied theater at the Helsinki Institute. She graduated in 1968 and became a director for Finnish television, where she continues to direct. Often her television films are scripted by women. *Klyftan* (1972), for instance, centers around the events in the life of a ten-year-old girl in the

Finnish civil war. The film won the Finnish State Award in 1972. Niskanen turned to the life story of the Finnish-Swedish poet Edith Södergran for the film *Landet som icke är* (1977). The script was written by another woman director, Eija-Elina (Alitalo, 296), and the resultant film is definitively feminist, though it is sometimes narratively linear.

Few women from Finland have had the opportunity to direct feature films. In the 1950s, Mirjam Kuosmanen, a popular film actress, wrote and codirected many of her films. (Kuosmanen codirected *The White Reindeer,* according to Tuike Alitalo, without receiving any credit.) A handful of other women actresses-turned-directors have been able to occasionally direct a feature film in Finland. Tuija-Maija Niskanen herself works in Sweden, in order to receive funding, consistent work opportunities, creative support, and respect.

SELECTED FILMOGRAPHY

Nukkekoti (The Doll's House) (1968)
Ajolanto (Gotta Run!) (1969)
Malli (The Model) (1971)
Lokki (The Seagull) (1971)
Klyftan (The Chasm) (1972)
Valitsen rohkeuden (I Will Choose Courage) (1977)
Landet som icke är (Maa jota ei ole) (The Land That Does Not Exist) (1977)
Seth Mattsonin tarina (The Story of Seth Mattson) (1979)
Avskedet (Jäähyväiset) (The Farewell) (1980)
Yksinäinen nainen (The Donna) (1982)
Kolme sisarta (The Three Sisters) (1983)
Suuri Illuusio (The Grand Illusion) (1985)

SELECTED BIBLIOGRAPHY

Alitalo, Tuike. "Niskanen, Tuija-Maija." In *The Women's Companion to International Film,* edited by Annette Kuhn, with Susannah Radstone, 296–97. Berkeley: University of California Press, 1994.
Cowie, Peter. *The Finnish Cinema.* South Brunswick, NJ: A. S. Barnes, 1976.
Doty, Alexander. *Making Things Perfectly Queer: Interpreting Mass Culture.* Minneapolis: University of Minnesota Press, 1993.
Gever, Martha, Pratibha Parmar, and John Greyson, eds. *Queer Looks: Perspectives on Lesbian and Gay Film and Video.* New York: Routledge, 1993.
Mayne, Judith. *The Woman at the Keyhole: Feminism and Women's Cinema.* Bloomington: Indiana University Press, 1990.
Quart, Barbara Koenig. *Women Directors: The Emergence of a New Cinema.* New York: Praeger, 1988.

NOTARI, ELVIRA (1875–1946). Italy. Elvira Notari is the unheralded inventor of neorealist cinema. Between 1906 and 1930, she directed over sixty feature films and hundreds of documentaries and shorts for her own production company, Dora Film. Notari wrote, directed, and coproduced all Dora films. Her husband, Nicola, worked as cameraman, and her son, Edoardo, acted in their films. The rediscovery of the films of Notari, because of the work of Giuliana Bruno, throws into question a number of traditional notions of Italian cinema. Notari's films represent part of a thriving southern Italian film community that has been actively suppressed in favor of a falsely constructed, monolithic image of northern Italian film production. The historical notion that Italy excelled only at early super-spectacle productions in the primitive and early cinema is denarrated in Giuliana Bruno's excellent study of Notari and Neapolitan filmmaking. The early films of Notari were almost completely oppositional to the slick superperspectacles of the North. Dora films were shot on location, using the lower- to middle-class streets of the city of Naples, often with nonprofessional actors. Notari loved to show the crude living conditions of real people and the politics of the underclass in Italy.

Though a few Notari feature films survive, most are lost to history. Nevertheless, Giuliana Bruno found Notari's screenplays, press books, personal materials, reviews, photographs, and novelizations of Notari films to reconstruct some semblance of the life and work of Elvira Notari. Notari's work has been suppressed by a combination of factors. The rise of fascism in Italy effectively ended Notari's career and suppressed the films of southern Italy. The sexism of film criticism encouraged a monolithic view of male-dominated Italian cinema. Finally, the monopolization of the Italian film industry effectively suppressed southern Neapolitan filmmaking. The international demand for Italian superspectacles did not encourage neorealistic storytelling.

Notari's work seems to have been exceptionally erotic, visceral, and always interested in the plight of women and the underprivileged. *E' Piccarella* (1922), which was recently screened for a retrospective at the Museum of Modern Art in New York, is a violent melodrama, involving a woman who is courted by two men. Margaretella is attracted to the sinister figure Carluccio, instead of the "good" figure of Tore. The film ends tragically, with the death of Margaretella. *'A Santanotte* (1922) is a similarly downbeat, violent, and highly effective melodrama. Notari films often include women who are "mad," violent, and highly erotic. Many Notari films offer female viewpoints and women who refuse to conform to societal codes of behavior. Some were hand-colored in a rainbow of hues frame by frame or else colored in dye-tinting machines that gave a uniform color (deep blue, perhaps, for scenes of melancholy; red tints for anger) to the images and synchronized with live singing and music.

Elvira Notari's antinationalistic attitudes caused her to be the object of scrutiny of the Italian censors. Many of her films were denied entry into the United States, but they were smuggled into the Italian-American community of New York's Little Italy, nonetheless. Notari's films opposed fascist policies, exposed poverty, neglect, and abuse, and freely used dialect and "vulgar" language of the "common" people. Her films document an alternative cinematic history of personal filmmaking, community filmmaking, and an important cultural moment of Neopolitan filmic counterhistory. The omission of Elvira Notari from film history is equaled only by the injustice of the suppression of the knowledge of France's Alice Guy, who is a figure of equal importance.

SELECTED FILMOGRAPHY

Maria Rosa di Santa Flavia (1911)
Bufera d'anime (1911)
Carmela la pazza (1912)
Ritorna all'onda (1912)
La figlia del vesuvio (1912)
I nomadi (1912)
Guerra italo-turca tra scugnizzi napoletani (1912)
L'eroismo di un aviatore a Tripoli (1912)
Povera Tisa, povera madre (1912)
Tricolore (1913)
A Marechiaro ce sta 'na fenesta (1913)
Addio mia bella addio . . . l'armata se ne va . . . (1915)
Figlio del reggimento (1915)
Sempre avanti, Savoia (1915)
Ciccio, il pizzaioulo del Carmine (1916)
Gloria ai caduti (1916)
Carmela la sartina di Montesanto (1916)
Nano rosso (1917)
Mandolinata a mare (1917)
La maschera del vizio (1917)
Il barcaioulo d'Amalfi (1918)
Pusilleco Addiruso or Rimpianto (1918)
Gabriele il lampionaio del porto (1919)
Medea de Portamedina (1919)
A Piedigrotta (1920)
'A Legge (1920)
'A mala nova (1920)
Gennariello il figlio del galeotto (1921)
Gennariello polizziotto (1921)
Luciella (1921)
'O munaciello (1921)
Cielo celeste (1922)
Cielo 'e Napule (1922)
E' piccarella (1922)
Il miracolo della Madonna di Pompei (1922)
'A Santanotte (1922)
Scugnizza (1923)
Pupatella (1923)
Reginella (1923)

Core 'e frate (1923)
'O cuppe' d'a morte (1923)
Sotto il carcere di San Francisco or *Sotto San Francisco* or *'N Galera* (1923)
A Marechiaro ce sta 'na fenesta (remake) (1924)
La fata di borgo Loreto (remake of *Nano rosso*) (1924)
'Nfama or *Voglio a tte* (1924)
Piange Pierrot or *Cosi piange Pierrot* (1924)
8 e 90 (1924)
Mettete l'avvocato (1924)
Fenesta ca lucive (remake of *Addio mia bella addio*) (1925)
Fantasia 'e surdato (1927)
L'Italia s'é desta (1927)
La leggenda di Napoli (1928)
Napoli terra d'amore (1928)
La modonnina del prescatore (remake of *A Marechiaro ce sta 'na fenesta*) (1928)
Napoli sirena della canzone (1929)
Duie Paravise (1929)
Passa a bandiera (1930)
Trionfo cristiano (1930)

SELECTED BIBLIOGRAPHY

Bruno, Giuliana. *Streetwalking on a Ruined Map: Cultural Theory and the City Films of Elvira Notari*. Princeton: Princeton University Press, 1993.
———, and Maria Nadotti, eds. *Offscreen: Women and Film in Italy*. London: Routledge, 1988.
de Lauretis, Teresa. *Alice Doesn't: Feminism, Semiotics and the Cinema*. Bloomington: Indiana University Press, 1982.
Foster, Gwendolyn. "Giuliana Bruno: *Streetwalking on a Ruined Map*." *Post Script* 13.2 (winter–spring 1994): 54–56.
Hoberman, J. "Napoletana: Images of a City." *Village Voice* 38.46 (November 16, 1993): 59.
Museum of Modern Art. *Notes from the Napoletana Images of a City Series*. New York: Museum of Modern Art, November 12–January 27, 1994.

NOVARO, MARIA (1951–   ). Mexico. Maria Novaro graduated from the University Center for Cinematographic Studies in Mexico City (CUEC). She is the daughter of a prominent publisher and has two children. Novaro moved into film after years of experience as a political activist for the Mexican underclass and after working as a researcher for a documentary filmmaker. After graduating from CUEC, Novaro first made Super 8mm films but quickly moved on to 16mm film production. Perhaps Novaro's success can be attributed to her attitude toward her male colleagues. As she told Tim Golden, "[I]f these guys can make movies, so can I."

Novaro is viewed as one of the most "promising, politicized feminist filmmakers in Mexico" (Huaco-Nuzum), and she is proud of her feminist cinematic vision. In an interview following the release of her film *Danzón*

(1992), Novaro said, "I like it very much when people come away thinking 'only a woman could have made that film' " (Golden). *Danzón,* which stars Maria Rojo and Daniel Rergis, builds a feminist narrative from a plotline that seems at once to combine neorealism and melodrama. The film concerns the life of Julia (Maria Rojo), a dancer and a telephone operator, who goes in search of her missing dance partner. Stylistically, Julia's story unfolds in the tradition of neorealism, as Novaro's camera flatly records Mexico City dance-hall culture. Novaro frequented these dance halls and became fascinated by their cultural significance. The dances themselves signify a fairy-tale narrative of romantic perfection, yet the dancers' lives are marked by brutal hard work, uncompromising physical perfection, and competition. Julia's search for her missing dance partner, however, seems destined to conclude in a traditional Mexican melodramatic narrative ending. The viewer is carried along by a desire for the expected archetypical ending of the romantic melodrama: the reuniting of the heterosexual couple. Though Julia is one of the finest, best-recognized dancers, she loses her status when she loses her partner. Thus, as Gabriel García Marquez notes, Novaro "is trying to reveal something about the condition of women in Mexico" (Golden).

Danzón refigures female subjectivity through its hybridization of melodramatic expectation and neorealist mise-en-scène. Moreover, Julia does not conform to the traditional configuration of women in Mexican melodrama. She is neither the "archetypal good mother" nor the *mala mujer* (bad woman) identified by Ana M. López in her study of the Mexican melodrama (254). Julia's partner (Daniel Rergis) turns out to be an elegant older man, not the dashing, young romantic hero whom we expect to literally sweep Julia off her feet. Julia defines herself through her search, which ends with a recognition of self, rather than a usurpation of female as object.

Danzón was highly successful on an international level. It was the first Mexican film to be invited to the Directors' Fortnight at the Cannes Film Festival. Some critics compared the film unfavorably with Novaro's subsequent release, *Lola* (1988–89), which is a film of gritty social realism. A narrative of the plight of a single mother, *Lola* exposes urban decay and miserable living conditions of the areas at the outskirts of Mexico City. Both *Danzón* and *Lola* were cowritten by Novaro and her younger sister, Beatriz Novaro. Maria Novaro's films show a consistent interest in social issues and female fantasy, desire, and need. In 1982, Novaro directed *Conmigo las pasara muy bien,* a film in which a woman uses magic to make her nagging husband and child disappear, while in *Querida Carmen* (1983), a woman imagines herself as a liberated cowgirl. These early Novaro efforts display her ludic approach to female desire and subjectivity. Novaro's films challenge traditional notions of female identity in which "she can be either the wife or the sexual object" (López, 267).

SELECTED FILMOGRAPHY

Lavaderos (*Laundry Shed*) (1981)
Sobre la olas (*Over the Waves*) (1981)
De encaje y azucar (*Of Lace and Sugar*) (1981)
Es primera vez (*For the First Time*) (1981)
Conmigo las pasara muy bien (*With Me You Will Enjoy Yourself*) (1982)
7 AM (1982)
Querida Carmen (1983)
Una isla rodeada de agua (*An Island Surrounded by Water*) (1984)
Pervertida (*Depraved*) (1985)
La que quiere azul celest (*In Search of the Pale Blue Horizon*) (1988)
Lola (1988–89)
Danzón (1992)
El Jardin del Edén (*The Garden of Eden*) (1994)

SELECTED BIBLIOGRAPHY

Burton, Julianne, ed. *Cinema and Social Change in America: Conversations with Filmmakers.* Austin: University of Texas Press, 1986.
————. *The Social Documentary in Latin America.* Pittsburgh: University of Pittsburgh Press, 1990.
Golden, Tim. "*Danzón* Glides to a Soft Mexican Rhythm." *New York Times,* October 11, 1992, 24H.
Huaco-Nuzum, Carmen. "Novaro, Maria." In *The Women's Companion to International Film,* edited by Annette Kuhn, with Susannah Radstone, 300. Berkeley: University of California Press, 1994.
King, John. *Magical Reels: A History of Cinema in Latin America.* London: Verso, 1990.
López, Ana M. "Tears and Desire: Women and Melodrama in the 'Old' Mexican Cinema." In *Multiple Voices in Feminist Film Criticism,* 254–70. Minneapolis: University of Minnesota Press, 1994.
Mora, Carl J. *Mexican Cinema: Reflections of a Society 1896–1980.* Berkeley: University of California Press, 1982.
Moraga, Cherrie. "From a Long Line of Vendidas: Chicanas and Feminism." *Feminist Studies/Critical Studies,* edited by Teresa de Lauretis, 173–90. Bloomington: Indiana University Press, 1986.
Pick, Zuzana M., ed. *Latin American Film Makers and the Third Cinema.* Ottawa: Carleton University, 1978.

O

OBOMSAWIN, ALANIS (1932–). **Canada.** Alanis Obomsawin is a Canadian-based Native American filmmaker. She is one of a growing number of independent Native American filmmakers and video artists, including Sandra Sunrising Osawa, Susan Fanshel, Arlene Bowman, and Mona Smith. Obomsawin grew up on an Abenaki reserve near Montreal and later made a career for herself as a singer, becoming nationally famous. Obomsawin was subsequently asked to act as consultant on several film projects for the National Film Board of Canada. Eventually, Obomsawin began work on her own films. Her first projects were children's films, such as *Christmas at Moose Factory* (1971), in which she utilized children's artwork as source material.

Obomsawin's films demonstrate a consistent need to document the cultural traditions of Abenaki and other Native American peoples. *Mother of Many Children* (1977) documents the everyday lives and customs of Native American women from a cross-cultural perspective. Obomsawin traveled across Canada to document their lives on film. As Jacqueline Levitin notes, however, Alanis Obomsawin's films have not been broadcast on Canadian television. In general, women's rituals, both Native American and non-Native American, "have been largely ignored by folklorists, ethnographers, and literary [and film] critics," as Paula Gunn Allen concludes (268). The paucity of scholarship on Native American filmmaking, particularly, Native women's filmmaking, characterizes an acceptance of the myth that Native Americans have made no films. The continual devaluation and lack of distribution of Native American films help to support the myth.

Alanis Obomsawin continues to make films despite the suppression of Native American cultural voice. In 1986, Obomsawin directed *Richard Cardinal: Cry from a Diary of a Metis Child*. This film documents the life of a young, orphaned child who is shuffled from one foster home to another and finally commits suicide. Obomsawin continually tackles political issues, such as the governmental invasion of the Micmac reserve, in *Incident at*

Restigouche (1984). Her latest film, *Poundmaker's Lodge: A Healing Place* (1987), is about Native Americans and alcoholism. The film documents a program that works to cure alcoholism by returning to Native customs and rituals and observes the issues of insider-outsider status of assimilated Native Americans. *Poundmaker's Lodge* provides a glimpse into the complexities around the issues of Native identity and celebrates Native cosmology and ritual healing. The films of Alanis Obomsawin and other Native American directors are available at the Native American Broadcasting Consortium, located in Lincoln, Nebraska.

SELECTED FILMOGRAPHY

Christmas at Moose Factory (1971)
Mother of Many Children (1977)
Amisk (1977)
Old Crow and *Gabriel Goes to the City* (for the series of school telecasts *Sounds from Our People*) (1979)
Incident at Restigouche (1984)
Richard Cardinal: Cry from a Diary of a Metis Child (1986)
Poundmaker's Lodge: A Healing Place (1987)

SELECTED BIBLIOGRAPHY

Albrecht, Lisa, and Rose M. Brewer, eds. *Bridges of Power: Women's Multicultural Alliances.* Philadelphia: New Society, 1990.
Allen, Paula Gunn. *The Sacred Hoop: Recovering the Feminine in American Indian Traditions.* Boston: Beacon Press, 1986.
Bataille, Gretchen, and Charles L. P. Silet. *The Pretend Indians: Images of Native Americans in the Movies.* Ames: Iowa State University Press, 1980.
Dearborn, Mary. *Pocahontas's Daughters: Gender and Ethnicity in American Culture.* New York: Oxford University Press, 1986.
Levitin, Jacqueline. "Obomsawin, Alanis." In *The Women's Companion to International Film,* edited by Annette Kuhn, with Susannah Radstone, 302. Berkeley: University of California Press, 1994.
Miller, Randall M., ed. *The Kaleidoscopic Lens: How Hollywood Views Ethnic Groups.* Englewood, NJ: Jerome S. Ozer, 1980.
Trinh T. Minh-ha. *Woman, Native, Other: Writing Postcoloniality and Feminism.* Bloomington: Indiana University Press, 1989.
Weatherford, Elizabeth. *Native Americans on Film and Video.* New York: Museum of the American Indian, 1981.

ONO, YOKO (1933–   ). Japan/United States. Yoko Ono is well known as the wife of John Lennon, but few critics recognize the significance of her experimental films of the 1960s and 1970s. She is constructed as the partner of a significant artist, rather than an artist in her own right. She was already involved in the avant-garde well before she met John Lennon. In the early 1960s, Ono was involved with the Fluxus group, filmmakers and artists who were responsible for the creation, or at least the popularization, of the single-take structuralist film. According to David Curtis, the Fluxus group put together a collective reel of films that included Yoko Ono's *No. 4 (Bottoms, 1964)*. *Bottoms* is a collection of shots of naked buttocks shot on a simple Bolex camera. Reflecting on the experience of showing the film, Ono told Scott MacDonald in 1989 that the film was meant not only as a purely structural film, but also as a study of the beauty of the body: "After you see hundreds of bottoms you realize that during the whole time you watched the film, you never saw the 'correct,' marketable jean-ad bottom" (8). Ono made several films as sole creator before she began to collaborate with John Lennon.

No. 5 Smile (1968) is a single, extremely slow-motion shot of John Lennon's face. The single-shot film was popularized in underground American filmmaking by Andy Warhol. The meditative experience of the single-shot film contradicts the representational nature of traditional Hollywood filmmaking narrative technique. *Apotheosis* (1971) is another single-shot, sync-sound film of a camera's ascent from the ground level to the sky. John Lennon and Yoko Ono collaborated on the film, which David Curtis deems "a purely visual metaphor of the ascending spirit" (189). Lennon and Ono mounted a camera on a hot-air balloon and simply allowed it to rise and record a magnificent long take of clouds. The film is a stunning collaborative effort.

In 1989, the Whitney Museum of American Art featured a retrospective of Ono's films, including *Rape* (1969), a seventy-seven-minute study of a woman being stalked by a camera. *Fly* (1970) records a common housefly crawling on the body of a woman. At the end of the film, the camera moves out a window, to suggest that the fly has flown away. *Erection* (1970) documents the construction of a building in time-lapse photography. In 1971, Lennon and Ono made a video for John Lennon's single of *Imagine*. After Lennon's death, Ono continued to work as an artist, musician, and video director. Though she is recognized as an important conceptual artist and musician, Ono has yet to be embraced by film scholars as a pioneer of American underground filmmaking. In 1970, Ono wrote these cryptic but perhaps prophetic words about her films:

In 50 years or so, which is like ten centuries from now, people will look at the films of the 60s. They will probably comment on Ingmar Bergman as meaningfully meaningful, Jean-Luc Godard as the meaningfully meaningless, Antonioni as meaninglessly meaningful, etc., etc. Then they would come to *No. 4 [Bottoms]* . . . and I hope they would see that the 60s was not only the age of achievements, but of laughter. (32)

The laughter of Ono's discourse is dampened, however, by the manner in which she, like many women avant-garde filmmakers, has been systematically excluded from "the canon" because of "inherently sexist and elitist attitudes," as documented by Lauren Rabinovitz (24) and other

scholars. These attitudes distrust the notion of collaborative creative partnerships, often erasing the female partner in "historical" scholarship and
subsequent critical canonization.

SELECTED FILMOGRAPHY

No. 4 (Bottoms) (1964)
Wink (1966)
Match (1966)
Shout (1966)
Eyeblink (1966)
No. 5 (Smile) (codirector John Lennon) (1968)
Instant Karma (1968)
Two Virgins (codirector John Lennon) (1968)
Rape (1969)
Rape II (1969)
Cold Turkey (1969)
Up Your Legs Forever (1970)
Fly (codirector John Lennon) (1970)
Erection (codirector John Lennon) (1970)
Freedom (1970)
Imagine (codirector John Lennon) (1971)
Apotheosis (codirector John Lennon) (1971)
Walking on Thin Ice (video) (1981)
Woman (video) (1981)
Goodbye Sadness (video) (1982)

SELECTED BIBLIOGRAPHY

Chadwick, Whitney, and Isabelle de Courtivron, eds. *Significant Others: Creativity
& Intimate Partnership*. London: Thames and Hudson, 1993.
Chin, Daryl. "Walking on Thin Ice: The Films of Yoko Ono." *Independent* (April
1989): 19–23.
Curtis, David. *Experimental Cinema*. New York: Delta, 1971.
Hendricks, John. *Fluxus Codex*. New York: Abrams, 1988.
Hoberman, J. "Yoko Ono." *Village Voice* (March 14, 1989): 57.
Kay, Karyn, and Gerald Peary, eds. *Women and the Cinema: A Critical Anthology*.
New York: Dutton, 1977.
MacDonald, Scott. "Putting All Your Eggs in One Basket: The Single Shot Films
as Cinematic Meditation." *Afterimage* 16 (March 1989): 10–16.
———. "Yoko Ono: Ideas on Film (Interview/Scripts)." *Film Quarterly* 43.1 (fall
1989): 2–23.
Ono, Yoko. "On Yoko Ono." *Film Culture* 48–49 (winter–spring 1970): 32–33.
Rabinovitz, Lauren. *Points of Resistance: Women, Power, and Politics in the New
York Avant-Garde Cinema, 1943–1971*. Urbana: University of Illinois Press,
1991.
Whitney Museum of American Art. *Yoko Ono: Objects, Films*. New York: Whitney
Museum of American Art, 1989.

ONWURAH, NGOZI (1963–). United Kingdom. Ngozi Onwurah's first film, *Coffee Colored Children* (1988), is a disturbing study of the experience of children of mixed racial heritage. She draws from autobiographical experience as a black British woman. Her mother is white, and her father is Nigerian. In the short film, a woman and a man scrub their skin white with scouring powder. Onwurah is one of many emerging African women of the diaspora who are the "cultural storytellers . . . [who] promote exploration of self, attack racial polarity, instill racial and female pride, and encourage individual and collective activism" (Gibson-Hudson, 365). *Coffee Colored Children* problematizes the formulas of mainstream Hollywood's depictions of people of color and articulates the psychology of selfhood at the margins of the ideological world of racial identity. *Coffee Colored Children* is a difficult film, yet it provides a catalyst for speaking about the unspoken. *Coffee Colored Children* is used in many African studies and film studies courses. It has been screened at Films des Femmes in Creteil, France, and many other film festivals.

In 1991, Ngozi Onwurah directed *The Body Beautiful*, a study of women's body images. The plot centers around a young woman who becomes a model and her mother, who undergoes a radical mastectomy. Amy Taubin termed the film "as cathartic as it is transgressive" (Women Make Movies, 52). The exploration of the bond between mother and daughter reveals societal expectations and anxieties about beauty and sexuality. Ngozi Onwurah's approach to the body is completely raw and unnerving. Her camera gazes at the mother's mastectomy scar with a loving reverence and understanding, reimagining the scar as a mark of beauty and experience. Onwurah demythologizes shame and reconstructs it as power and a mark of experience in a new language of feminist cinema. Onwurah's dreamlike narrative moves across time and space, causing us to rethink the imagery of the female body as *The Body Beautiful*.

And Still I Rise (1993) is a documentary inspired by Maya Angelou. In the film, Ngozi Onwurah appropriates images of black people from popular culture sources but deconstructs the manner in which the media tend to represent black women's sexuality. Onwurah, like Alile Sharon Larkin, aggressively works to "create new definitions of ourselves within every genre, redefining damaging stereotypes" (Larkin, 172). Onwurah takes on issues of fear and fascination with the status of "Other" of black women. She incorporates interviews of anthropologists, sociologists, writers, and film critics who agree that black women's sexuality has been constructed to service colonialist theories designed to justify the idea that white people can rape African land and African people. Moreover, she shows how myths are enacted in historical and contemporary media images to distort the image of black women.

And Still I Rise moves toward an empowered, rearticulated black feminist perspective and is among a number of extraordinary films by black British women and about black British representation. Ngozi Onwurah, like Maureen Blackwood and other members of the Sankofa Film Collective, realizes the extent to which "media's racist representations of Black people maintain an oppressive society" (Larkin, 158). Films by women of the diasporic community are working to re/present the images of women of color through a process of negating false representations and reweaving a tapestry of the lives of actual women of color.

Ngozi Onwurah's most recent film, *Welcome II the Terrordome* (1994), is a political action movie. Onwurah promises that the film will overturn viewer expectations. In an interview with Trevor Ray Hart, Onwurah explains, "What they expect a black woman film-maker to be making is very definitely, definitely not the kind of movies I want to make." Onwurah wrote the film from true events, such as the Howard Beach incident and other, more personal stories. "What I did was put [in] lots of true stories— like a white friend of mine who was pregnant by a black guy, and her ex-boyfriend came and punched the baby out of her" (Hart, 19). *Welcome II the Terrordome* is meant to "address an audience that hasn't been catered to in the past; an audience more curious about how we live now than in the national heritage," according to Trevor Ray Hart (19).

SELECTED FILMOGRAPHY

Coffee Colored Children (1988)
The Body Beautiful (1991)
Monday's Girls (1993)
And Still I Rise (1993)
Welcome II the Terrordome (1994)
A Question of Numbers (1994)

SELECTED BIBLIOGRAPHY

Campbell, Loretta. "Reinventing Our Image: Eleven Black Women Filmmakers." *Heresies* 16 (1983): 58–62.

Gaines, Jane. "White Privilege and Looking Relations: Race and Gender in Feminist Film Theory." *Screen* 29 (autumn 1988): 12–26.

Gibson-Hudson, Gloria. "Aspects of Black Feminist Cultural Ideology in Films by Black Women Independent Artists." In *Multiple Voices in Feminist Film Criticism,* edited by Diane Carson, Linda Dittmar, and Janice Welsch, 365–79. Minneapolis: University of Minnesota Press, 1994.

Hart, Trevor Ray. "The Brit Pack." *Time Out* (March 23–30, 1994): 18–22.

Klotman, Phyllis Rauch, ed. *Screenplays of the African American Experience.* Bloomington: Indiana University Press, 1991.

Larkin, Alile Sharon. "Black Women Filmmakers Defining Ourselves: Feminism in Our Own Voice." In *Female Spectators: Looking at Film and Television,* 157–73. London: Verso, 1988.

Mercer, Kobena, ed. *Black Film/British Cinema.* London: BFI, 1988.

Reid, Mark A. "Dialogic Modes of Representing Africa(s): Womanist Film." *Black American Literature Forum* 25 (summer 1991): 375–88.

Women Make Movies. *Women Make Movies Catalogue.* New York: Women Make Movies, 1994.

OTTINGER, ULRIKE (1942–   ). Germany. Ulrike Ottinger is known as the queen of Berlin underground filmmaking. Her lesbian feminist film, *Madame X—An Absolute Ruler* (1977), is internationally celebrated as the embodiment of feminist surrealism and the best of queer cinema (White, Weiss). Ottinger's films envision feminist utopian allegories where women confront the politics of pleasure by banding together to question the history of art, ethnographic practice, and the notion of power. Ottinger was born Ulrike Weinbery in Constance, Germany, in 1942. She studied art and worked as an artist and photographer before she moved into filmmaking. She lived in Paris between 1962 and 1968, where she was involved in experimental theater and "happenings," as well as photography. Next, Ottinger returned to Germany after the Parisian authorities seized the screenplay for her film *Laocoon and Sons.* In 1969, she opened and ran a cine club until 1972. Around this time, she began experimenting with film. In 1974, she completed *Laocoon and Sons,* a film that questions the history of film and film genre. Already, Ottinger was forging her signature style of antinarrative filmmaking.

Ulrike Ottinger's films, like many other New Wave German films, bridge a gap between theater and film traditions. Her films not only question cinema practices but also reject and parody the conventions of art-house cinema. *Madame X,* for example, is a New Wave comedy and deconstruction of the women's movement. In the film, a pirate queen travels to an island in the China Seas, where she finds an island inhabited by women tourists. Ottinger describes the plotline as "a confrontation with the nature of the women's movement" (Grisham, 30). As Patricia White observes, Ottinger's women are neither "realistic" nor "allegorical." "They serve as so many figures in a mise-en-scène of female bodies which work through . . . scenarios of desire within the background fantasy of the pirate ship, the women's movement, [and] lesbian utopia" (277). *Madame X* does not, however, turn out to be another female utopic film. The women end up remaking power structures of the patriarchy that they set out to escape. They die and are resurrected. Ottinger told Marc Silberman that she finds it "unrealistic to make a film in which women revolt and triumph gloriously" (1993, 207). She explains how the film is situated within the context of a problematization of the women's movement:

I find the movement itself very important, but I still need to gently critique it. We have given too little thought to the power of traditional structures. (207)

Madame X not only criticizes the power structures of the women's movement but also presents female sexuality as inherently power-defined. As Andrea Weiss notes, however, Ottinger opens up new territory in lesbian sexuality "by rejecting the seriousness with which sexuality is so often laden" (130). The sex scenes between Madame X and her protegée, Noa-Noa, are marked by a sense of the theater of the absurd, as the figures role-play in theatrically exaggerated costumes. Some feminists criticized *Madame X* as a voyeuristic display of fetishism of the female body, but Ottinger dismisses this criticism as old-fashioned. She told Therese Grisham, "I think my work simply came too early" (30).

Ulrike Ottinger's films are often centered around societal outcasts or exiles. One of these, *Ticket of No Return* (1979), is a portrait of two women alcoholics who are pursued by the allegorical figures of "Reliable Statistics," "Common Sense," and "the Social Problem." The film was enthusiastically reviewed as "a celebration of lesbian punk antirealism" (McRobbie, 34). In *Ticket of No Return,* as in *Madame X,* Ottinger "radically subverts the terms in which patriarchal cinema has monopolized visual pleasure on behalf of the male gaze" (Hansen, 194). *Freak Orlando* (1981) works on similar poststructuralist territory, repositioning Virginia Woolf's character as a female wanderer who subverts patriarchal norms across epochs of time. *Dorian Gray in the Mirror of the Yellow Press* (1983) is a feminist reworking of Fritz Lang's evil Dr. Mabuse figure. Ottinger questions the basis of "objective truth" of newspaper reports that describe Mabuse, putting the press on trial as the evening of "truth."

Johanna d'Arc of Mongolia (1988) presents the female warrior figure in the form of a Mongolian warrior, a European girl, and an older woman named "Lady Windemere." In this film, modern women meet their counterparts from the ancient past and participate in a series of Mongolian female-centered rituals. The film brings up the question of "othering" and Orientalism in ethnography and historical practice. It is a demythologization of the "historical" film that subverts the norms of historical "reenactment" and history itself. The end of the film contains a section of scrolled texts containing the supposed events that take place in the future lives of the film's characters, effectively transgressing the borders of filmic "reality."

Ottinger's approach to filmmaking is, in some ways, comparable to that of Rainer Werner Fassbinder, in that she often uses both amateur and professional actors. Furthermore, she is unbound by cinematic formulas or genres, and she freely embraces theatricality and allegory. She is completely uncompromising in her artistic vision; thus, she consistently finds it difficult to secure financial backing. "80% of my energy and effort is devoted to getting funded," she told Therese Grisham (32). Thematically, Ottinger repositions the outsider as insider and "others" the normative figures. She dismantles power as an ideologically pervasive instrument of oppression. She rearticulates pleasure in a female form of the cinematic look and defines a countercinema of lesbian feminist spectatorship.

SELECTED FILMOGRAPHY

Laokoon und Söhne (Laocoon and Sons) (1972–74)
Vostell—Berlin-fieber (Vostell—Berlin Fever) (1973)

Die Betörung der blauen Matrosen (*The Bewitchment of the Drunken Sailors*) (co-director) (1975)
Madame X—eine absolute Herrscherin (*Madame X—An Absolute Ruler*) (1977)
Bildnis iener Trinkerin—Aller jamais retour (*Ticket of No Return*) (1979)
Freak Orlando (1981)
Dorian Gray in spiegel der Boulevardpresse (*Dorian Gray in the Mirror of the Yellow Press*) (1983)
Chine—die Künste—der Alltag (*China—The Arts—The People*) (1985)
Sieben Frauen—Sieben Sünden (*Seven Women—Seven Sins*) (codirector) (1986)
Usinimage (1987)
Johanna d'Arc of Mongolia (1988)
Countdown (1990)

SELECTED BIBLIOGRAPHY

Bergstrom, Janet. "The Theatre of Everyday Life: Ulrike Ottinger's China: The Arts, Everyday Life." *Camera Obscura* 18 (September 1988): 43–51.

Fischetti, Renate. "Ecriture Feminine in the New German Cinema." *Women in German Yearbook* 4 (1988): 47–67.

Grisham, Therese. "An Interview with Ulrike Ottinger." *Wide Angle* 14.2 (April 1992): 28–36.

Hansen, Miriam. "Visual Pleasure, Fetishism, and the Problem of Feminine/Feminist Discourse: Ulrike Ottinger's *Ticket of No Return*." In *Gender and German Cinema: Feminist Intervention Volume 1: Gender and Representation in New German Cinema,* edited by Sandra Frieden, Richard W. McCormick, Vibeke R. Petersen, and Laurie Melissa Vogelsang, 189–207. Oxford: Berg, 1993.

Knight, Julia. *Women and the New German Cinema.* London: Verso, 1992.

Kuhn, Annette. "Encounter between Two Cultures (a discussion with Ulrike Ottinger)." *Screen* 28 (autumn 1987): 74–79.

McRobbie, Angela. "Introduction to Interview with Ulrike Ottinger." *Screen* 4 (winter–spring 1982): 34.

Sabine, Hake. " 'Gold, Love, Adventure': The Postmodern Conspiracy of Madame X." *Discourse* 11.1 (fall–winter 1988–89): 88–110.

Silberman, Marc. "Women Filmmakers in West Germany: A Catalogue." *Camera Obscura* 6 (fall 1990): 123–52.

———. "Interview with Ulrike Ottinger: Surreal Images." In *Gender and German Cinema: Feminist Intervention Volume 1: Gender and Representation in New German Cinema,* edited by Sandra Frieden, Richard W. McCormick, Vibeke R. Petersen, and Laurie Melissa Vogelsang, 205–7. Oxford: Berg, 1993.

Treut, Monika. "Ein Nachtrag zu Ulrike Ottinger's film *Madame X*." *Frauen und Film* 28 (1981): 15–21.

Weiss, Andrea. *Vampires and Violets: Lesbians in Film.* New York: Penguin, 1993.

White, Patricia. "Madame X of the China Seas." In *Queer Looks: Perspectives on Lesbian and Gay Film and Video,* edited by Martha Gever, John Greyson, and Pratibha Parmar, 275–91. New York: Routledge, 1993.

Women Make Movies. *Women Make Movies Catalogue.* New York: Women Make Movies, 1994.

P

PALCY, EUZHAN (1957–   ). Martinique/United States. Euzhan Palcy is the first black woman to direct a Hollywood feature film, *A Dry White Season* (1989). Born on the island of Martinique, Palcy decided at the age of ten to become a director. She told Janis Cole and Holly Dale: "I made a kind of wish. I said I have to become a filmmaker. I have to talk about my people" (158). Palcy remembers being discouraged by many people, but her father supported her artistic and political ambitions. She decided to study in France at the Rue Lumière School and the Sorbonne. At the remarkable age of seventeen, Palcy directed *La messagère* (*The Messenger*) (1974) for French television. She also wrote and acted in the film. Palcy told Ally Acker that she initially met with resistance from the station manager: "[T]he boss of the station didn't want to do it. After all, it was the first West Indian drama" (119). Palcy shot *The Messenger* on location in Martinique. Though she had little experience as a filmmaker, she made up for experience with her exuberance. "People were so excited, they worked on it for free" (Acker, 119).

In Paris, Palcy continued to study and work as an assistant director for French and African films. She made another short film for French television, *The Devil's Workshop* (1981–82) and began writing and revising *Sugar Cane Alley,* based on a novel by Martinique author Josef Zobel. Palcy later met François Truffaut, who became interested in the project, and Truffaut and his assistant, Suzanne Shiffman, encouraged her and helped her to secure financial backing for the film. *Sugar Cane Alley* was finally produced in 1983 after three years of preproduction. The film is a semiautobiographical work, according to Palcy. Set in 1930, in Martinique's shantytowns, *Sugar Cane Alley* is the story of a ten-year-old boy's coming of age under slavery and colonial oppression. The boy meets Mr. M, a Caribbean storyteller who shows him the significance of oral tales and African rituals. Howard Rodman describes the film as "haunting and defiant, sentimental and astringent." The film was a substantial critical hit at the Venice Film

Festival. Suddenly, Palcy was being courted by Warner Brothers executives. She told them, "[I]f you give me a film, try to give me something that talks about black people, too, okay?" (Rodman).

Palcy's next film was *A Dry White Season,* financed by MGM. *A Dry White Season* is an antiapartheid drama that stars Donald Sutherland, Zakes Mokae, Marlon Brando, and Thoko Ntshinga and is based on a novel by André Brink. Colin Welland and Euzhan Palcy cowrote the screenplay, and Paula Weinstein produced the film. *A Dry White Season* is a brilliant study of the apartheid system, but it drew criticism because of its focus on a white man (Donald Sutherland) as an antiapartheid militant. Sutherland portrays a South African schoolteacher who is, at first, reluctant to believe that South African authorities beat and kill black children. He gradually becomes an antiapartheid activist when his gardener (Winston Ntshona) dies in police custody. Sutherland's life disintegrates as he becomes more and more involved in the antiapartheid movement. His wife leaves him, and his daughter plots against him to assist the police. Finally, Sutherland hires a lawyer (Marlon Brando) to help him and is further assisted in his fight for justice by an African driver (Zakes Mokae). Palcy fully recognized the political implications of being forced to have a white hero in order to find Hollywood support, but she dismisses her critics. "I want to scream to people who say this; they should write more, and they should join me and fight against those who have the money and the power to produce a movie" (Rodman).

bell hooks sees *A Dry White Season* as a call for militant resistance. hooks argues that Palcy's focus on a white man's political agitation and consciousness "is certainly a representation of whiteness that disturbs the status quo, one that challenges the white spectator to interrogate racism and liberalism in a far more progressive way than is normally seen in mainstream cinema" (360). It is not the triumph of the white hero that is the penultimate moment of the film; it is the unraveling of the real truth, which finally appears in a newspaper account of the police brutality surrounding the slaughter of an innocent boy and a gardener, which is more important than the actions of either Sutherland or Brando. Euzhan Palcy's attitude toward other women and blacks in the industry is characteristically supportive. She takes great pride that *A Dry White Season* paved the way for other Third World filmmakers. Palcy also finds it extremely encouraging that more and more women of color are making films.

SELECTED FILMOGRAPHY

La messagère (The Messenger) (1974)
L'Atelier du diable (The Devil's Workshop) (1981–82)
Rue cases nègres (Sugar Cane Alley) (1983)
A Dry White Season (1989)
Simeon (1992)

SELECTED BIBLIOGRAPHY

Acker, Ally. *Reel Women: Pioneers of the Cinema, 1896 to the Present.* New York: Continuum, 1993.

Burton, Julianne. "Marginal Cinema and Mainstream Critical Theory." *Screen* 26.3–4 (1985): 5, 20–21.

Canby, Vincent. *"Sugar Cane Alley." New York Times,* April 22, 1984, H15.

Cole, Janis, and Holly Dale. *Calling the Shots: Profiles of Women Filmmakers.* Ontario: Quarry Press, 1993.

Friedman, Lester, ed. *Unspeakable Images: Ethnicity and the American Cinema.* Urbana: University of Illinois Press, 1991.

Givanni, June. "Palcy, Euzhan." In *The Women's Companion to International Film,* edited by Annette Kuhn, with Susannah Radstone, 308. Berkeley: University of California Press, 1994.

hooks, bell. "A Call for Militant Resistance." In *Multiple Voices in Feminist Film Criticism,* edited by Diane Carson, Linda Dittmar, and Janice Welsch, 358–64. Minneapolis: University of Minnesota Press, 1994.

Mbye, Cham, and Claire Watkins, eds. *Black Frames: Critical Perspectives on Black Independent Cinema.* Cambridge: MIT Press, 1988.

Mercer, Kobena, ed. *Black Film/British Cinema.* London: BFI, 1988.

Reid, Mark A. *Redefining Black Film.* Berkeley: University of California Press, 1993.

Rodman, Howard A. "Between Black and White." *Elle* (October 1989): 132.

Wilmington, Mike. "Euzhan Palcy: For All the Black Shack Alleys." *Los Angeles Weekly,* May 11–17, 1984, 24.

Yearwood, Gladstone L., ed. *Black Cinema Aesthetics.* Athens, OH: Center for African Studies, 1982.

PARK, IDA MAY (1885–1954). United States. Ida May Park (also known as Mrs. Joseph De Grasse) was one of a number of women who directed at Universal in the somewhat liberated teens. Park was born in Los Angeles, where she became active in theater. She met Joseph De Grasse while working in the theater, and the couple later collaborated on scores of films. In the beginning of their collaboration, Park was credited as the scenario writer, but it is assumed that she codirected many of the films for which De Grasse is credited as sole director. It has long been accepted that all of Ida May Park's films are lost, but at least a handful of the films for which she received writing credit survive. *Alas and Alack* (1915), starring Lon Chaney, Sr., and Cleo Madison, is held in the British National Film Archive in London, as is *Dolly's Scoop* (1916). *The Fighting Grin* (1918) is part of the collection of the Department of Film at the Museum of Modern Art in New York. It may well be that many other films directed or written by Ida May Park lie undiscovered and neglected in international film repositories. Film historians seem to accept the "lost" and "neglected" status of Ida May Park, a curious phenomenon common to the films of early women directors. Janet Staiger's article on the canonization of only a handful of early filmmakers points at the ideological reasons for the exclusion of women from film history. Reclaiming the work of Ida May Park is further clouded by her status as codirector with her husband.

Like Lois Weber, Ida May Park seems to have been drawn to social melodrama. *Fires of Rebellion* (1917) concerns the working conditions of factory workers. *Bondage* (1917) is an early feminist film about the oppression of women. *The Model's Confession* (1918) and *Risky Road* (1918) expose the sexual harassment of women in the workplace. The significance of Park's films as a vehicle for the ideas of the New Woman is hard to overestimate. Ida May Park wrote over 500 scenarios and created Ida May Park Productions in 1920, where she was highly successful as a director and scenarist.

In 1924, Ida May Park contributed a chapter to a book entitled *Careers for Women*. The book is an interesting example of feminist intervention and community-mindedness. Park's chapter, "The Motion Picture Director," encourages women to join the film industry. Though she warns the reader that a career in film direction means a loss of personal time, she emphasizes women's "natural" affinity for the role of director, stating that "the superiority of [a woman's] emotional and imaginative faculties gives [her] a great advantage [in film production]" (337). In 1918, Park further defended her position as a woman director in an interview with Frances Denton: "A woman can bring to this work splendid enthusiasm and imagination, a natural love of detail and an intuitive knowledge of character" (49). Ida May Park's comments can be viewed as part of the suffragette rhetoric that defended women's "natural" abilities in the face of a system that used those same "natural" abilities to create the "cinematic woman" as a submissive, docile creature. Ida May Park's films offer a unique and lasting testament to one woman's ambition to create an alternative societal structure on the cinema screen.

SELECTED FILMOGRAPHY

Bobbie of the Ballet (1916)
Bondage (1917)
Fires of Rebellion (1917)
The Flashlight (1917)
Bread (1918)
Broadway Love (1918)
The Model's Confession (1918)
Risky Road (1918)
Vanity Pool (1918)
The Grand Passion/Boss of Powderville (1918)
Amazing Wife (1919)
The Butterfly Man (1920)
Bonnie May (1921)

The Midlanders (1921)
The Hidden Way (1926)

SELECTED BIBLIOGRAPHY

Acker, Ally. *Reel Women: Pioneers of the Cinema, 1896 to the Present*. New York: Continuum, 1993.

Bowser, Eileen. *The Transformation of Cinema 1907–1915*. New York: Scribner's, 1990.

Denton, Frances. "Lights! Camera! Quiet! Ready! Shoot!" *Photoplay* (February 1918): 48–50.

Kozarski, Richard. *Hollywood Directors 1914–1960,* 71. New York: Oxford University Press, 1976.

Library of Congress. *Catalogue of Copyright Entries, Motion Pictures 1912–1939*. Washington, DC: Library of Congress, 1951.

Magliozzi, Ronald S. *Treasures from the Film Archives: A Catalogue of Short Silent Fiction Films Held by FIAF Archives*. Metuchen, NJ: Scarecrow Press, 1988.

Park, Ida May. "The Motion Picture Director." In *Careers for Women,* edited by Catherine Filene, 335–37. Boston: Houghton Mifflin, 1924.

Slide, Anthony. *Early Women Directors*. New York: Da Capo, 1984.

Staiger, Janet. "The Politics of Film Canons." In *Multiple Voices in Feminist Film Criticism,* edited by Linda Dittmar, Diane Carson, and Janice Welsch, 191–209. Minneapolis: University of Minnesota Press, 1994.

PARMAR, PRATIBHA (1960–   ). Kenya/India/United Kingdom. The films and videos of Pratibha Parmar center around issues of representation, identity, cultural displacement, homosexuality, and racial identity. The Kenya-born British lesbian activist/writer/filmmaker began working in film and video in the 1980s. She moved to England in the late 1960s. She did not see herself as a marginalized "Other," but she could immediately sense the racism of colonialist England. In an article in *Queer Looks,* Parmar recalls the antiblack, anti-Paki feelings that she found at school:

It was in the school playground that I first encountered myself as an undesirable alien, objectified in the frame of "otherness." All those perceived as "marginal," "peripheral," and the "other" know what it is like to be defined by someone else's reality. (5)

Parmar describes herself as a resistant figure who refuses to be categorized by race. *Emergence* (1986), a short video directed by Parmar, reflects the director's interest in issues of racial identity, in the context of the experience of the diaspora. Parmar interviewed Audre Lorde, an African-American lesbian feminist, and Mona Hatoum, a Palestinian performance artist, for the video. Parmar's next video, *Sari Red* (1988), continued in the political activist vein of her early work. *Sari Red* is a call for action against the violence that Asian women face in postcolonial society. The film is made in memory of Kalbinder Kaur Hayre, an Indian woman who was killed in a racist attack in 1985.

Parmar is one of the founding members of Black Women Talk, a black women's publishing house in England. As a postgraduate student at the Centre for Contemporary Cultural Studies in Birmingham, Parmar was one of a group of students who published *The Empire Strikes Back,* a study of racism in Britain. Parmar and an activist Asian group published a poster called "Self-Defense: Not a Sport but a Necessity." In the poster an Asian woman states, "If anyone calls me Paki, I'll bash their heads in." Many of Parmar's political documentaries were produced by Britain's Channel 4. According to critic Meena Nanjii, she is "the only Indian woman to receive consistent funding" (28).

A Place of Rage (1991) features interviews with Angela Davis, June Jordan, and Alice Walker. Parmar intercuts a rarely screened 1970 prison interview of Angela Davis with June Jordan's poetry, exposing the relationship among racism, homophobia, imperialism, and the international oppression of all people of color. Alice Walker and Trinh T. Minh-ha are also interviewed in the film. *A Place of Rage* is regularly screened at numerous international lesbian and gay film festivals. The film won the award for Best Historical Documentary at the National Black Programming Consortium in 1992.

Pratibha Parmar's *Warrior Marks* (1993) is perhaps her most remarkable achievement to date. Alice Walker produced the film and appears in it; Walker's novel, *Possessing the Secret of Joy,* which deals with female genital mutilation, was an inspiration for *Warrior Marks.* Female genital mutilation affects over 100 million women in the world. For *Warrior Marks,* Parmar and Walker interviewed women from Senegal, the Gambia, Burkino Faso, and England who either actually experienced genital mutilation or are concerned about the implications of the practice. These interviews are intercut with Alice Walker's views on the subject and a poetic scene of an African woman dancing a liberating performance. The most astounding footage, however, is the interviews with women who actually perform the ritual act of female genital mutilation. Their inability and refusal to question such a thoroughly misogynist tradition anger Walker, Parmar, and the viewer. Parmar is careful to exhibit the cultural context of the practice, but, as Walker asks, if it were a cultural practice to murder women, would we sanction such an act as a cultural ritual? Parmar and Walker insist that all women rethink racist and misogynist "cultural practices" that brutalize women on a daily basis.

Pratibha Parmar is currently working on an Indian lesbian adventure-thriller. Her films and videos have been aired on the British gay/lesbian television series "Out on Tuesday." *Khush* (1991) is one of her best-known lesbian-centered films. In *Khush,* Parmar replaces the male scopophiliac gaze of an appropriated archival film with the gaze of two Asian women who watch as a dancer performs. In an article in *Queer Looks,* Parmar explains how she reedited the original film to remove the male gaze: "The gaze and the spectator become inverted. Clearly, postmodernist interest in reworking available material gives us an opportunity to use strategies of appropriation as an assault on racism, sexism, and homophobia" (10). The politics of homosexual pleasure are particularly significant to Asians because homosexuality is still illegal in India. Parmar's *Flesh and Paper* (1990) also celebrates lesbian sexuality; Suniti Namjoshi, the celebrated Indian lesbian poet, is featured in this documentary tapestry. Taken as a whole, Parmar's work effectively questions the rules of conventional filmic discourse and points the way to a new and broader perspective through which the viewer may appreciate the alternative vision posed by Parmar's groundbreaking films and essays.

SELECTED FILMOGRAPHY

Emergence (1986)
Sari Red (1988)
Flesh and Paper (1990)
A Place of Rage (1991)
Khush (1991)
Double the Trouble, Twice the Fun (1992)
Warrior Marks (1993)

SELECTED BIBLIOGRAPHY

Centre for Contemporary Cultural Studies. *The Empire Strikes Back: Race and Colonialism in 70s Britain.* London: Hutchinson, 1982.
Dargis, Manohla. "Worlds Apart." *Village Voice* 38.4 (November 16, 1993): 68.
Dyer, Richard. *Now You See It: Studies on Lesbian and Gay Film.* London: Routledge, 1990.
Mercer, Kobena, ed. *Black Film/British Cinema.* London: BFI, 1988.
Nanjii, Meena. "Pratibha Parmar." *High Performance* 15 (summer–fall 1992): 28–29.
Parmar, Pratibha. "Woman, Native, Other: Pratibha Parmar Interviews Trinh T. Minh-ha." *Feminist Review* 31 (spring 1989): 63.
———. "Black Feminism: The Politics of Articulation." In *Identity, Community, Culture, Difference,* edited by Jonathan Rutherford, 101–26. London: Lawrence and Wishart, 1990.
———. "That Moment of Emergence." In *Queer Looks: Perspectives on Lesbian and Gay Film and Video,* edited by Martha Gever, John Greyson, and Pratibha Parmar, 3–11. New York: Routledge, 1993.
Walker, Alice, and Pratibha Parmar. *Warrior Marks: Female Genital Mutilation and the Sexual Binding of Women.* New York: Harcourt and Brace, 1993.
Women Make Movies. *Women Make Movies Catalogue.* New York: Women Make Movies, 1994.

PASCAL, CHRISTINE (1953–). France. Christine Pascal is one of the many women directing films today in France; in the tradition of Agnes Varda, France has recently welcomed more feminist auteurs to the sphere of commercial film production. While Pascal has not yet had the international box-office success of directors such as Coline Serreau or Diane Kurys, she is a successful independent filmmaker whose work is highly praised and distributed throughout Europe. She is a multitalented actress/screenwriter/ director whose style is best described as commercial cinema with a New Wave flourish. *Le Petit Prince a dit* (1991), Pascal's most recent film, explores a father-daughter relationship. In the film, a father learns that his ten-year-old daughter has a fatal disease. He takes her on a journey from Lausane to Milan, Genoa, and Provence, hoping somehow to prevent her death. Instead, she helps him learn the meaning of life. *Le Petit Prince a dit* is an unabashedly tender, warm, and life-affirming film.

Perhaps one of the reasons Christine Pascal's films have not been released internationally is that her films tend toward the melodramatic. As Jackie Byars notes, melodramas traditionally "lacked cultural valorization because of their association with female audiences, and genres such as the Western or gangster film" (13).

Pascal's work, while aiming for a commercial audience, is, at the same time, a deeply personal testament of a woman working within the confines of genre. In her four films to date, Pascal is forging an original cinematic voice with links, oddly enough, to the work of the late Rainer Werner Fassbinder, who used the form of the melodrama to create morality tales of contemporary life. As the writer and director of her films, Pascal exerts the same sort of exclusive auteurist control that Fassbinder (or Fassbinder's predecessor, Douglas Sirk) did in his work. One hopes that Pascal's films will eventually reach a wider audience internationally and that the critics will "catch up" with her work—a cinema that is simultaneously conscious of the distribution/reception process and yet very much the product of Pascal's personal commitment to the tales she tells.

SELECTED FILMOGRAPHY

Felicité (1979)
La Garce (1984)
Zanzibar (1989)
Le Petit Prince a dit (1991)

SELECTED BIBLIOGRAPHY

Byars, Jackie. *All That Hollywood Allows*. Chapel Hill: University of North Carolina Press, 1991.
Darke, Chris. "*Le Petit Prince a dit*." *Sight and Sound* 4.5 (May 1994): 51.
Gledhill, Christine, ed. *Home Is Where the Heart Is: Studies in Melodrama and the Women's Film*. London: BFI, 1987.
Hayward, Susan, and Ginette Vincendeau, eds. *French Film: Texts and Contexts*. London: Routledge, 1989.

PERINCIOLI, CRISTINA (1946–   ). Germany. Born in Switzerland in 1946, Cristina Perincioli studied film at the Berlin Academy of Film and

Television in the late 1960s. Her early documentaries reflect her politically active position in the New German Cinema. One of her best-known films is a study of domestic violence against women, *Die Macht der Männer ist die Geduld der Frauen* (1978). Perincioli was one of the founding members of the first women's center for battered women in Germany. She and the women at the center made the film to bring the issue of domestic violence to the television-viewing audience. *Die Macht der Männer ist die Geduld der Frauen* is narrated by a voice-over commentary that flatly offers grim statistical information on the problem of violence toward women.

In the film, a woman reconstructs a dramatized story of her own experience as a battered woman. Having been hospitalized after one particular beating, the woman hears on television about the women's shelter and immediately finds help at the shelter. The film foregrounds the woman's subjective point of view in order to depict the woman as a survivor, rather than a victim. Perincioli is technically innovative. Stylistically, she uses long takes and simple camera angles, often wide shots. The "actors" are the women from the shelter, who freely improvised on the script. Perincioli used some professional actors in the film, but she found them to be more of a problem than an asset. As she told Gretchen Elsner-Sommer, "[T]he reason I wouldn't want to work again with actors is because they have so little to offer from inside" (53). To dramatize the brutality of her chosen material, Perincioli insisted on filming lengthy, uncut scenes of rape and battery, because she feels that "[r]ape is [usually] short in films and somehow elegant. We show it can be very long, as a man keeps on kicking, slapping, and punching a woman. This sense of on-goingness makes a difference and feels very ugly. Especially in a normal movie, you would never see a man kick a woman in the stomach for such a long time" (Elsner-Sommer, 53).

Other Perincioli film projects tackle social problems such as nuclear waste and labor issues. Her earliest pieces are influenced by Stan Brakhage's experimental films. After the student rebellions of 1968, Perincioli began to turn toward politically activist filmmaking and radio programming. In 1975, she was hired to make a film about lesbian relationships, *Anna and Edith* (1975), which suffered from interference from the producers, who rewrote her script. According to Julia Knight, the ZDF German television network replaced Perincioli with another director (95). Perincioli told Marc Silberman, "I was fired as director for my own script . . . because the TV network thought I was too partisan and that a man could deal better with a lesbian relationship (Silberman, 1984, 48).

Perincioli continues to be a feminist activist both in front of and behind the camera. In 1972, she directed *Women behind the Camera,* a documentary on German women film directors and technicians, and she is increasingly involved in computer animation, video, and theater. She is critical of other women directors who "produce films hardly distinguishable from typical male films except they use a woman as a main character. Their films may be beautiful, but they are not useful for public discussions. . . . These women filmmakers could be helping the movement" (Silberman, 1984, 51). Cristina Perincioli is an important figure in the tradition of Straub, Huillet, and Fassbinder whose claim on our attention is made all the more pressing by her marginalization from the canon of the New German Cinema.

SELECTED FILMOGRAPHY

Striking My Eyes (1966)
Nixonbesuch und Hochschulkampf (*Nixon's Visit and the University Struggle*) (co-director) (1968)
Besetzung und Selbstverwaltung eines Studentenwohnheims (*Occupation and Self-Administration of a Student Hall of Residence*) (codirector) (1969)
Gegeninformation in Italien (*Alternative Information in Italy*) (codirector) (1970)
Für Frauen—1 Kapitel (*For Women—Chapter 1*) (1971)
Kreuzberg gehört uns (*Kreuzberg Belongs to Us*) (codirector) (1972)
Frauen hinter der Kamera (*Women behind the Camera*) (1972)
Die Macht der Männer ist die Geduld der Frauen (1978)
Die Frauen von Harrisburg (*The Women of Harrisburg*) (1981)
Mit den Waffen einer Frau (*With the Weapons of a Woman*) (1986)

SELECTED BIBLIOGRAPHY

Acker, Robert. "The Major Directions of German Feminist Cinema." *Literature/ Film Quarterly* 13.4 (1985): 245–49.
Corrigan, Timothy. *New German Film: The Displaced Image.* Austin: University of Texas Press, 1983.
Dawson, Jan. "The Sacred Terror: Shadows of Terrorism in the New German Cinema." *Sight & Sound* 48.4 (1979): 243–63.
Elsner-Sommer, Gretchen. "Interview with Cristina Perincioli." *Jump Cut* 29 (1984): 51–53.
Hartnoll, Gillian, and Vincent Porter, eds. *Alternative Filmmaking in Television: ZDF—A Helping Hand.* London: BFI, 1982.
Johnston, Sheila, and John Ellis. "The Radical Film Funding of ZDF." *Screen* 23.1 (May–June 1982): 60–73.
Knight, Julia. *Women and the New German Cinema.* London: Verso, 1992.
Silberman, Marc. "Cine-Feminists in West Germany: A Catalogue." *Camera Obscura* 6 (fall 1980): 123–52.
———. "Film and Feminism in Germany Today." *Jump Cut* 27 (July 1982): 41–53.
———. "German Film Women." *Jump Cut* 29 (February 1984): 49–64.
———. "German Women's Film Culture." *Jump Cut* 30 (March 1985): 63–69.

POOL, LEA (1956–). Canada. French Canadian director Lea Pool was born in Geneva, Switzerland. She studied at the University of Quebec, where she graduated with a degree in communications. She worked for Radio Québec in the 1970s, for which she produced variety programs, dramas, and documentaries. After directing a number of student films, including *Laureut Lamerre Portier* (1978), Pool directed *Un Strass Café,* her first independent, low-budget, short film, in 1979. Shot in black and white, *Un Strass Café* is a poetic film about the loss of identity. Pool's first feature film, *La Femme de l'hôtel* (1984), was honored with the Critic's Prize and the International Critics Prize at the Montreal World Film Festival. *La Femme de l'hôtel* concerns three women characters: a filmmaker, an actress, and a mysterious, silent woman. *La Femme de l'hôtel* is a meditational poem on female identity as creator, author, and text. Pool's film is a working out of psychoanalytic feminist practices that seek to resituate female identity in the context of poststructuralist thought. As Constance Penley writes, "Each individual 'exists' only as a nexus of various and sometimes contradictory subjectivities which are legislated or assumed, either consciously or unconsciously" (179). Pool's style is comparable to that of her friend and colleague Chantal Akerman, as both rely on long, subjective camera takes and an antinarrative stream of consciousness created by the filmmaker. Akerman and Pool situate their protagonists against a backdrop of cold and lifeless streets and hotels, places of emptiness and exile. Akerman's *Hotel Monterey* (1972) and *Les rendezvous d'Anna* (1978) depict women as they loiter around hotels, train stations, and other urban scenes that suggest exile and the mutability of identity. Pool uses similar strategies in *La Femme de l'hôtel*. The film was received with great acclaim and allowed Pool to continue to make films that "speak of women, and are from the point of view of a woman" (Cole and Dale, 166).

Lea Pool's next project, *Anne Trister* (1986), was financed by the National Film Board of Canada. The themes of *La Femme de l'hôtel,* exile and identity, are reworked in *Anne Trister*. The central character, Anne Trister, embarks on a quest for self-understanding after her father's death. As Andrea Weiss notes, this "search is two-fold: a search for Jewish identity through her father, and a search for sexual identity through her mother" (125). Anne Trister falls in love with her woman friend, Alix, but Pool's direction of their sex scene is almost antierotic. Pool has been criticized for her handling of lesbian material in *Anne Trister*. The film appears to be "a reworking of the Oedipus myth" (Alemany-Galway) rather than a fully developed narrative of lesbian desire. As Andrea Weiss argues, the scene risks becoming a "rejection of lesbianism" (128). Pool explains that *Anne Trister* explores mother-daughter love, "because we lost this when we were young" (Cole and Dale, 170). Pool admires the lesbian love scene in Chantal Akerman's *Je, tu, il, elle* (1974), finding it "very beautiful, but very difficult" (Cole and Dale, 169). Akerman and Pool reject overdetermined notions of lesbian sexuality, preferring to articulate multiple perspectives of desire and lesbian subjectivity. Pool's next film, *A Corps Perdu* (1988), centers on the relationships of a bisexual (male) photographer. Jacqueline Levitin notes that Pool is "the only Quebec director/writer of popular film to sympathetically and openly treat the theme of homosexual relationships"

(318). In all of her films, Pool effectively questions supposedly normative values, offering a disturbing and distinctive vision of societal discourse.

SELECTED FILMOGRAPHY

Un Strass Café (1979)
La Femme de l'hôtel (1984)
Anne Trister (1986)
A Corps Perdu (1988)
La Demoiselle Sauvage (1989)
Hotel Chronicles (1990)
Montréal Vu Par (1991)
Mouvements du Désir (1994)

SELECTED BIBLIOGRAPHY

Alemany-Galway, Mary. "Lea Pool's *Anne Trister.*" *Cinema Canada* (April 1986): 22.
Cole, Janis, and Holly Dale. *Calling the Shots: Profiles of Women Filmmakers,* 163–71. Ontario: Quarry Press, 1993.
de Lauretis, Teresa. *Technologies of Gender.* Bloomington: Indiana University Press, 1987.
Gentile, Mary C. *Film Feminisms: Theory and Practice.* Westport, CT: Greenwood Press, 1985.
Levitin, Jacqueline. "Pool, Lea." In *The Women's Companion to International Film,* edited by Annette Kuhn and Susannah Radstone, 317–18. Berkeley: University of California Press, 1994.
Penley, Constance. *The Future of an Illusion: Film, Feminism, and Psychoanalysis.* Minneapolis: University of Minnesota Press, 1989.
Weiss, Andrea. *Vampires and Violets: Lesbians in Film.* New York: Penguin, 1993.

POTTER, SALLY (1949–   ). United Kingdom. Sally Potter began making Super 8mm films at the age of fourteen. In the 1970s, she became active as a political artist of the London avant-garde circuit. She is an accomplished performance artist, dancer, choreographer, musician, writer, producer, director, and actor. Though her films center on gender politics, she maintains that her "roots are not academic or theoretical; they are show-business roots, albeit avant-garde ones" (Dargis). Potter became a member of the London Filmmakers Coop after attending St. Martin's Art School for one year. She began to plan her first major independent production, *Thriller,* with a small Arts Council Grant. *Thriller* (1979) is best described as a feminist murder mystery, but it is also a deconstruction of dominant Hollywood cinema practice. It is an adaptation of Puccini's opera, *La Bohème,* in which a woman dies of consumption as a result of a doomed love affair. In Potter's version, the woman "investigates" her own death. As Annette Kuhn observes, "The female victim adds a twist to the reconstruction of her own death not only by telling the story herself, but also by considering causes for the unhappy romance and death of a young woman"

(169). Potter not only appropriates from opera and the film noir genre but also rescores the music from Alfred Hitchcock's *Psycho* (1960). *Thriller* is a self-reflexive film about feminist film theory as practice. The central character reads from radical feminists' theoretical texts and bursts into laughter. *Thriller* is a feminist classic that captured the attention of both academics and film production executives. Because of the success of the film, Sally Potter was able to secure financial backing for her next film, *The Gold Diggers* (1983), from the British Film Institute.

The Gold Diggers, starring Julie Christie, is an experimental feature film. Talking to Pam Cook, Potter describes the film as a "musical describing a female quest" (12). Potter made *The Gold Diggers* with an all-female production crew. The plot concerns two women quest-heroes in search of identity. Like *Thriller, The Gold Diggers* investigates archetypes of the cinema, particularly the femme fatale of film noir, the female detective, and the male pursuer. Though the film was ultimately "sunk under its own theoretical load" (Dargis), *The Gold Diggers* is still arresting visually and utilizes a number of intriguing imagistic strategies.

The multilayeredness of Sally Potter's most successful film to date, *Orlando* (1993), allows for a hyperreal quest-fantasy across the spectrum of time, space, gender, and the film frame. *Orlando* is adapted from the Virginia Woolf novel of 1928, in which the central character, Orlando, travels across 350 years. Potter updates Woolf's work to bring Orlando into the future. Though filmed literary adaptations tend to be flat slaves to the literary form, *Orlando* successfully evokes Woolf's modernist sensibility with her postmodern appropriation. Instead of copying Woolf's literary movement across time and gender, Potter uses film practices that remain true to Woolf's spirit. *Orlando* becomes liberated from the class and gender system by being disinherited in a plot twist that does not figure in the novel. As Potter explained to critic Gary Indiana, she wished to remain true to Woolf's intentions:

[t]o suggest that the human species happens to have been divided into two genders for the purpose of reproduction and not much else, and that it's perfectly possible and desirable for persons of the same sex (or opposite sex) to love and respect one another. (89)

At several points throughout *Orlando,* Tilda Swinton (who plays Orlando) smiles and talks directly to the viewer. This breakdown of traditional cinema practice, which enforces a gap between the film and the spectator, represents a postmodern sensibility, as well as a nod to Woolf's own self-reflexivity. When Orlando changes sex, looks directly at the audience, and says, "Same person, no difference at all, just a different sex," *Orlando* becomes a hyperreal, almost interactive text. As Amy Taubin observes, this postmodern practice is also used in Leslie Harris's *Just Another Girl on the IRT.* These women "refuse to be seen and not heard. They won't have their speech contained by a dumb 19th century theatrical convention of the fourth wall." Potter moves self-reflexivity one notch further by introducing Orlando's daughter as a budding young filmmaker herself in a clever adaptation of the traditional auteurist cameo appearance.

Potter hoped that the audience for *Orlando* would experience a sense of "hope and empowerment [from the film]. I want people to feel humanly recognized, that their inner landscape of hope and desire, and longing has found some kind of expression on the screen" (Donohue, 223). In addition to her feature filmmaking, Potter recently directed a television documentary on Soviet women filmmakers, *Women in Soviet Cinema: I Am an Ox, I Am a Horse, I Am a Man, I Am a Woman* (1988). This film, along with Potter's earlier efforts, is available from Women Make Movies.

SELECTED FILMOGRAPHY

Thriller (1979)
The Gold Diggers (1983)
The London Story (1987)
Tears, Laughter, Fear and Rage (1986)
Women in Soviet Cinema: I Am an Ox, I Am a Horse, I Am a Man, I Am a Woman (1988)
Orlando (1993)

SELECTED BIBLIOGRAPHY

Brown, Georgia. *"Orlando." Village Voice,* 38.24 (June 15, 1993): 51.
Cook, Pam. *"The Gold Diggers:* An Interview with Sally Potter." *Framework* 24 (spring 1984): 12–30.
Dargis, Manohla. "Sally Potter: A Director Not Afraid of Virginia Woolf." *Interview* 23.6 (June 1993): 42.
Donohue, Walter. "Against Crawling Realism: Sally Potter in *Orlando.*" In *Women and Film: A Sight and Sound Reader,* edited by Pam Cook and Philip Dodd, 217–23. Philadelphia: Temple University Press, 1993.
Dowell, Pat. "Demystifying Traditional Notions of Gender." *Cineaste* 20.1 (1993): 16–17.
———. "*Orlando,*" *Cineaste* 20.1 (1993): 36–37.
Ehrenstein, David. "Out of the Wilderness: An Interview with Sally Potter." *Film Quarterly* 47 (fall 1993): 2–7.
Indiana, Gary. "Spirits Either Sex Assume: Gary Indiana Talks with Sally Potter." *Artforum* 31 (summer 1993): 88–91.
Kruger, Barbara. *"Thriller." Artforum* 23 (April 1985): 94.
Kuhn, Annette. *Women's Pictures: Feminism and Cinema.* London: Routledge, 1982.
Muir, Anne Ross. *A Woman's Guide to Jobs in Film and Television.* London: Pandora, 1987.
Taubin, Amy. "Mirror, Mirror." *Village Voice* 38.29 (July 20, 1993): 57.
Women Make Movies. *Women Make Movies Catalogue.* New York: Women Make Movies, 1994.

PREOBRAZHENSKAYA, OL'GA (1881–1971). Soviet Union.

Ol'ga Preobrazhenskaya was a major Soviet director for over thirty-five years, but she was originally a stage actress before moving into film. She studied drama at the Moscow Arts Theatre and toured extensively in provincial Russian theater. Switching from the stage to the infant medium of the cinema, she became an overnight success as an actress in the film *Kliuchakh schastia* (*Keys to Happiness*) (1913). After building a career as a leading actress, she became a film director in 1916. According to Lynn Attwood, Ol'ga Preobrazhenskaya was one of the few Soviet women directors "to achieve any stature in the 1920s" (49), in addition to Esfir Shub. Nevertheless, in the 1920s, many Soviet women directors, such as Elizaveta Svilova, Iuliia Solntseva, and Vera Stroeva, were actively directing, but Denise J. Youngblood identifies Preobrazhenskaya as "Russia's first female director" (325). Preobrazhenskaya also taught at the first Soviet film school in the early 1920s.

Preobrazhenskaya's first directorial effort, *Baryshia-Krestianka* (*The Lady Peasant*) (1916), was codirected by Vladimir Gardin. *The Lady Peasant,* like many of Preobrazhenskaya's films, is centrally consumed with the question of woman's role in Russian society. One of Preobrazhenskaya's best-known works, *Baby riazanskie* (*Peasant Women of Riazan*) (1927), is considered to be the first "woman's film" of Russia (Attwood, 142). *Peasant Women* is a melodrama about the fate of two women. One is a traditional wife, Anna, who is raped by her father-in-law. The other woman, Vasilia, is an example of the Russian New Woman, a strong, sexually independent figure. Preobrazhenskaya's unabashedly feminist approach to melodramatic material reflected her own status as a New Woman in Soviet cinema. The inclusion of the rape of a daughter-in-law is an uncompromising critique of patriarchal power structures in Russian peasant culture. *Peasant Women of Riazan* is a highly schematic melodrama in its polarization of the suffering prerevolutionary female figure against the image of the free-willed New Woman. Many of the films directed by Ol'ga Preobrazhenskaya depict the realities of Russian peasant children. *Kashtanka* (1926), based on a Chekhov tale, and *Ania* (1927) redefined revolutionary politics through the eyes of young protagonists. Preobrazhenskaya often collaborated with director Ivan Pravov and continued directing through the 1930s and early 1940s.

SELECTED FILMOGRAPHY

Baryshia-Krestianka (*The Lady Peasant*) (1916)
Viktoriia (1917)
Kashtanka (1926)
Ania (1927)
Baby riazanskie (*Peasant Women of Riazan*) (1927)
Svetlii gorod (*Bright City*) (1928)
Poslednii attraktsion (*The Last Attraction*) (1929)

Tikhii Don (*The Quiet Don*) (1931)
Vrazhi tropi (*Enemy Paths*) (1935)
Stephan Razin (1939)
Paren iz taigi (*Boy from the Taiga*) (1941)

SELECTED BIBLIOGRAPHY

Attwood, Lynn. *Red Women on the Silver Screen: Soviet Women and Cinema from the Beginning to the End of the Communist Era.* London: Pandora, 1993.

Babitsky, Paul, and John Rimberg. *The Soviet Film Industry.* New York: Praeger, 1952.

Bonnell, Victoria E. "The Representation of Women in Early Soviet Political Art." *Russian Review* 50.3 (July 1991):267–88.

Buckley, Mary. *Women and Ideology in the Soviet Union.* Ann Arbor: University of Michigan Press, 1989.

Kaplan, E. Ann. *Women and Film.* New York: Methuen, 1983.

Kuhn, Annette. *Women's Pictures: Feminism and Cinema.* London: Routledge, 1982.

Lawton, Anna. "Toward a New Openness in Soviet Cinema, 1976–1987." In *Post New Wave Cinema in the Soviet Union and Eastern Europe,* edited by Daniel J. Goulding, Bloomington: Indiana University Press, 1989.

Usai, Paolo Cherchi, ed. *Silent Witnesses: Russian Films 1909–1919.* London: BFI, 1989.

Youngblood, Denise J. *Soviet Cinema in the Silent Era.* Ann Arbor: UMI Research Press, 1985.

R

RAINER, YVONNE (1934–   ). United States. Yvonne Rainer is a widely recognized, New York-based, experimental, lesbian filmmaker who has been actively dedicated to feminist counter cinema since the 1960s. Born in San Francisco in 1934, Rainer studied acting in New York City in the late 1950s. A dancer and choreographer, Rainer cofounded the Judson Dance Theater. She is often credited as one of the pioneers of the minimalist dance, a stylistic school that worked to move dance beyond artifice. In the late 1960s, Rainer began making minimalist/structuralist films in the tradition of formalist filmmakers such as Joyce Wieland. By the early 1970s, Yvonne Rainer rejected formalism in favor of a collage style informed by feminist postmodernism. For B. Ruby Rich, Rainer's work became the "clear product of a feminist cultural milieu" (32).

In *Lives of Performers* (1972) and *Film about a Woman Who . . .* (1974), Rainer plays with the language of dominant narrative cinema. *Lives of Performers* centers around a man and two women who play themselves as dancers working for experimental filmmaker Yvonne Rainer. As Annette Kuhn writes, the "lack of narrative closure [in *Lives of Performers*] sets up a radical heterogeneity in spectator-text relations, and finally refuses any space of unitary subjectivity of the spectator" (171). Rainer playfully subtitled the film "a melodrama," but *Lives of Performers* is really more an investigation of melodramatic form. Intertitles break up the narrative flow by self-reflectively calling into question our spectatorship position. The performers confront us with questions of identification, asking at one point, "Which woman is the director most sympathetic to?" Rainer's involvement in the criticism of spectatorship is directly linked to feminist critiques of traditional cinema's positioning of women as object and men as spectator. *Lives of Performers* and *Film about a Woman Who . . .* were criticized by some feminists as overly formal. However, as B. Ruby Rich concludes, the value of Yvonne Rainer's early work is "precisely her refusal to pander (visually and emotionally), her frustration of audience expectation of spectacle (physical or psychic), and her reworking of traditional forms of melodrama and elegy to include modern feminist culture" (33).

Rainer's more recent films, such as *The Man Who Envied Women* (1985) and *Privilege* (1990), move beyond purely cerebral investigation of spectatorship into a critique of pleasure in film viewing. *The Man Who Envied Women* makes reference to psychoanalytic and poststructural theorists such as Julia Kristeva, Michel Foucault, and Fredric Jameson within references to films such as François Truffaut's *The Man Who Loved Women* (1977) and Luis Buñuel's *Un Chien Andalou* (1928) in order to displace our pleasurable viewing of these films and move the audience into a critical stance. But viewing the film is not entirely without pleasure. Rainer's ability to invoke a parodic tone is matched by her ability to displace easily readable images. As Lucy Fischer observes, Rainer speaks in a "double-voiced discourse. Rather than present her views on sexual politics directly, she does so by quoting others, simultaneously displacing those discourses and refracting her own ideas" (316).

Privilege addresses film pleasure in the context of a discussion on menopause, lesbian sexuality, and women's community. In an interview with Scott MacDonald, Rainer talked about the initial reaction to *Privilege:*

In Australia, someone asked me—after screening *Privilege*—"Why are you so committed to depriving the audience of pleasure?" I was astounded, because I have never thought of myself as depriving anyone of pleasure . . . in the general course of things, *I* always thought I was introducing *new* pleasures—the pleasure of the text, of reading. (26)

Privilege is a political call to action and also a criticism of feminist politics. Subtitles in the film display Rainer's distinct philosophical sense of humor: "Utopia: the more impossible it seems, the more necessary it becomes." Among the many agendas in *Privilege* is a rereading of traditional representations of lesbian sexuality. In one scene, a woman reads from an erotic lesbian text to a seemingly disinterested audience, forcing the viewer to identify with either the reader or the audience members within the film. Andrea Weiss notes that the "incongruous, absolutely non-sexual visual presentation and its allusions to performance criticize the spectacle potential of most lesbian representation" (128). Rainer herself is outspoken on the politics of lesbian identity. In an article entitled "Working around the L-Word," Rainer observes the difference she is treated with, since she came out as a lesbian:

One thing I find unsettling is that in the gay and lesbian public sphere I am being paid attention to as a lesbian *before* doing any work that identifies me as one. . . . [A]s a former member of the dominant sexual category I can still see it as odd that the gender of the person one has sex with is a determining factor in public recognition. (14)

Yvonne Rainer consistently questions the boundaries of political and mainstream representation, often from autobiographically charged material. She is currently working on *MURDER and murder,* a film about a fifty-year-old lesbian who undergoes a mastectomy immediately after finding her first female lover. Rainer appears in the film and speaks directly to the audience, effectively breaking down the "fourth wall" between the camera apparatus and the viewer. She also defiantly exhibits her mastectomy scar. Rainer consistently speaks about the unsaid issues in women's lives: aging and menopause, female sexuality and subjectivity, and, now, mastectomy. It is no wonder, then, that she is known as the "dean of feminist filmmakers" (Taubin). Among her many awards are the American Film Institute's Maya Deren Award (1988) and, more recently, the MacArthur Foundation Genius Award (1990).

SELECTED FILMOGRAPHY

Volleyball (short) (1968)
Hand Movie (short) (1968)
Rhode Island Red (short) (1968)
Trio Film (short) (1969)
Line (short) (1969)
Lives of Performers (1972)
Film about a Woman Who . . . (1974)
Kristina Talking Pictures (1976)
Working Title: Journeys from Berlin/1971 (1980)
The Man Who Envied Women (1985)
Privilege (1990)
MURDER and murder (forthcoming)

SELECTED BIBLIOGRAPHY

Fischer, Lucy. *Shot/Countershot: Film Tradition and Women's Cinema.* Princeton: Princeton University Press, 1989.

Goldberg, Marianne. "The Body, Discourse, and *The Man Who Envied Women.*" *Women and Performance: A Journal of Feminist Theory* 3.2 (1987–88): 97–102.

Kuhn, Annette. *Women's Pictures: Feminism and Cinema.* London: Routledge, 1982.

MacDonald, Scott. "Demystifying the Female Body: Anne Severson–*Near the Big Chakra,* Yvonne Rainer–*Privilege.*" *Film Quarterly* 45.1 (fall 1991): 18–32.

Mellencamp, Patricia. *Indiscretions: Avant-Garde Film, Video & Feminism.* Bloomington: Indiana University Press, 1990.

Michelson, Annette. "Yvonne Rainer, Part One: The Dancer and the Dance." *Artforum* 12.5 (1974): 57–63.

Penley, Constance. *The Future of an Illusion: Film, Feminism, and Psychoanalysis.* Minneapolis: University of Minnesota Press, 1989.

Rainer, Yvonne. *The Films of Yvonne Rainer.* Bloomington: Indiana University Press, 1989.

———. "Working around the L-Word." In *Queer Looks: Perspectives on Lesbian*

and Gay Film and Video, edited by Martha Gever, John Greyson, and Pratibha Parmar, 12–20. New York: Routledge, 1993.

Reynaud, Berenice, Yvonne Rainer, and Coco Fusco. "Responses to Coco Fusco's
'Fantasies of Oppositionality.' " *Screen* 30.3 (summer 1989): 79–99.

Rich, B. Ruby. "In the Name of Feminist Film Criticism." In *Multiple Voices in
Feminist Film Criticism,* edited by Diana Carson, Linda Dittmar, and Janice
Welsch, 27–47. Minneapolis: University of Minnesota Press, 1994.

Russell, Katie. "Yvonne Rainer Eats Her Cake." *Cinema Studies* 2.3 (fall 1986): 2.

Taubin, Amy. "Art & Industry." *Village Voice* (July 26, 1994): 56.

Weiss, Andrea. *Vampires and Violets: Lesbians in Film.* New York: Penguin, 1993.

REID, DOROTHY DAVENPORT (1895–1977). United States. Like her
contemporary, Lois Weber, Dorothy Davenport Reid was an activist filmmaker, interested in social issues. Often dismissed as "moralists," both Lois
Weber and Dorothy Davenport Reid are largely unrecognized in film history. Reinscribing the work of Davenport Reid and Weber is problematic
because of the maintenance of a patriarchally defined film canon. As Janet
Staiger argues, film canonization is involved in a complex "politics of inclusion and exclusion" (194). Women such as Reid and Weber made films
to promote social change. They did this in a cultural moment in which
women were expected to be powerful social arbiters, and they made no
apologies for their moralism or sensationalism. Feminists in cultural studies, such as Christine Gledhill, argue that we ought not be "concerned with
the progressiveness or reactionariness of the text," but with "drawing the
text into a female or feminist orbit" (121–22). A reexamination of the
"melodramatic," "sensationalist," "moralist" cinema of Dorothy Davenport Reid and other women directors is long overdue.

Before she became a producer/director, Reid had been an actress in many
popular films at Universal. She was born in Boston in 1895 into a well-
known theatrical family. Dorothy Davenport married "handsome" Wallace
Reid in 1913. He became Paramount's most popular leading man but accidentally became addicted to morphine after a serious car accident. Wallace Reid died of an overdose in 1923. Almost immediately, Dorothy
Davenport Reid began a personal campaign against drug addiction. She
established a drug rehabilitation sanitarium in the name of Wallace Reid
and made *Human Wreckage* (1923) in the same year as her husband's
death. She also starred in the film. She found a network of support from
local authorities and industry executives for the project. This is not surprising, given the fact that early American motion picture producers found
that "[t]o uplift, ennoble, and purify was good business too" (Bowser, 38).
The "uplift movement" described by Eileen Bowser allowed women a voice
as social arbiters and also resulted in an increasing number of women ex-
hibitors (Bowser, 45).

Dorothy Davenport Reid continued to produce and direct social message films after the success of *Human Wreckage*. Many of her films exposed the double standards around sexuality that were imposed on women. *The Red Kimona* (1926; note the distinctive spelling of "Kimon*a*"), *The Road to Ruin* (1934), and *The Woman Condemned* (1934) are centered around this theme. *The Red Kimona*, from an original story by Adela Rogers St. Johns, is a feminist exposé of a woman who kills her ex-lover in a moment of passion. Dorothy Arzner, then a young, would-be director, wrote the film's scenario. Walter Lang is credited as director, but it is well known that Reid actually directed the film. *The Red Kimona* is a visually and emotionally compelling narrative. Reid builds sympathy for the central female figure by introducing the film with a plea for understanding of women in her situation. The scene in which the woman shoots her ex-lover is astonishing, in that Reid encourages audience identification with a transgressive female figure. *The Red Kimona* has a provocative feminist, ending. After the woman goes to jail, she meets a sympathetic prison warden and finds a community of support. In a feminist gesture, Reid suggests that the woman will be pardoned by the law and forgiven by the church for murdering out of passion.

Reid's films were always interested in the underprivileged and the powerless. *Broken Laws* (1924), for example, exposes child neglect. *Sucker Money* (1933) is an exposé of popular confidence-game schemes. Dorothy Davenport Reid was quite aware of limitations of gender roles, yet she was willing to use these limitations to her advantage on the set.

Reid continued to produce and direct until the mid-1930s. She wrote and produced several films directed by Arthur Lubin, with whom she was associated until the 1950s. Upon her retirement, Reid was decidedly critical of sexism in the motion picture industry. As she noted in an interview, "[M]en resent women in top executive positions in films, as in any field of endeavor" (Smith, 41). Reid retired in 1968 at the age of seventy-three. Along with Lois Weber, Alice Guy, Cleo Madison, and many other pioneering women filmmakers, Dorothy Davenport Reid is one of the most undervalued American women producer directors in American film history, while D. W. Griffith is still championed as "the master and epitome of early cinema, subordinating and excluding others" (Staiger, 195).

SELECTED FILMOGRAPHY

Human Wreckage (1923)
Quicksands (1923)
Broken Laws (1924)
The Earth Woman (uncredited) (1926)
The Red Kimona (1926)
Linda (1929)
Sucker Money (codirector) (1933)
The Road to Ruin (codirector) (1934)
The Woman Condemned (1934)

SELECTED BIBLIOGRAPHY

Acker, Ally. *Reel Women: Pioneers of the Cinema, 1896 to the Present.* New York: Continuum, 1993.

Bodeen, DeWitt. "Wallace Reid: Was an Idol in the Age of Innocence with Feet of Clay." *Films in Review* (April 1966): 205–30.

Bowser, Eileen. *The Transformation of Cinema 1907–1915.* New York: Scribner's, 1990.

Erens, Patricia, ed. *Sexual Stratagems: The World of Women in Film.* New York: Horizon Press, 1979.

Gledhill, Christine. "Image and Voice: Approaches to Marxist–Feminist Film criticism." In *Multiple Voices in Feminist Film Criticism,* edited by Diane Carson, Linda Dittmar, and Janice Welsch, 109–123. Minneapolis: University of Missouri Press, 1994.

Hansen, Miriam. *Babel & Babylon: Spectatorship in American Silent Film.* Cambridge: Harvard University Press, 1991.

Mayne, Judith. *Cinema and Spectatorship.* London: Routledge, 1993.

Peary, Gerald. "Sanka, Pink Ladies, and Virginia Slims." *Woman and Film* 1.5–6 (1974): 82–84.

Slide, Anthony. *Early Women Directors.* New York: Da Capo, 1984.

Smith, Sharon. *Women Who Make Movies.* New York: Hopkinson and Blake, 1975.

Staiger, Janet. "The Politics of Film Canons." In *Multiple Voices in Feminist Film Criticism,* edited by Diane Carson, Linda Dittmar, and Janice Welsch, 191–212. Minneapolis: University of Minnesota Press, 1994.

REINIGER, LOTTE (1899–1981). Germany/United Kingdom. Born in Berlin in 1899, Reiniger studied theater with Max Reinhardt. As a child, she had astonished her family with her ability to free-cut shadow pieces for family theatrical productions of Shakespearean plays. Lotte Reiniger invented a form of silhouette animation made from free-cut silhouettes that are hand-cut with a simple pair of scissors. While studying with Reinhardt, Reiniger met Paul Wegener, who hired her to design cutout titles for *The Pied Piper of Hamelyn* (1918). In 1919, Reiniger became involved in a group of Berlin artists who had set up a communal studio. Here she made *The Ornament of the Loving Heart* (1919), her first silhouette film. This started a career in animation that lasted until 1979.

In 1926, Reiniger directed the first full-length animation film, *The Adventures of Prince Achmed.* The film is an adaptation of *The Tales of Arabian Nights,* and it was intended for a young audience. Reiniger utilized many pioneering animation techniques for the film, including wax and sand animation. She designed a multiplane camera that predated later, similar technical innovations by the Disney animation studio. In 1935, Reiniger moved to England, where she worked during World War II, and she later became a British citizen. She worked at Crown International and the GPO film unit, turning out many children's films. After World War II, Reiniger and her husband, Carl Koch, directed a series of children's films for American television. After Koch's death, in 1963, Reiniger worked for the National Film Board of Canada, for which she directed *Aucassin et Nicolette* (1974). Lotte Reiniger had an incredibly successful film career, "unrivaled for its duration, originality, artistry and independence" (Starr, 19).

Reiniger borrowed techniques from Oriental shadow plays that were popular in Europe in the 1920s. *The Adventures of Prince Achmed* is a wedding of shadow-play technique, lighting, and characterization with Reiniger's inimitable silhouette animation. It is recognized as one of the most innovative early animation films in history. Reiniger also created the shadow-play sequence for Jean Renoir's *La Marseillaise* (1938). Renoir said of Reiniger, "[A]rtistically, I have to see her as a visual expression of Mozart's music" (Starr, 18). Diana Bryant, a silhouette artist, spoke about Reiniger's films at the 1980 American Film Festival:

She can reduce everything to its simplest terms, and the movement in her films is so superb that after the first few seconds you forget you are looking at flat paper. You see dancers whirling around as if they're three-dimensional. She can create an illusion even with the gesture of one finger. (Starr, 19)

In 1986, Lotte Reiniger was honored at the Museum of Modern Art in New York City with a retrospective program of her work. She remains a potent influence on many new animators. A television program on her work as an animator, *The Art of Lotte Reiniger,* was recently produced for German television by director John Isaacs.

SELECTED FILMOGRAPHY
Aschenputtel (*Cinderella*) (1922)
Die Abenteuer des Prinzen Achmed (*The Adventures of Prince Achmed*) (1926)
Harlequin (1931)
Carmen (1933)
Papagenus (1935)
Das Kleine Schornsteinfeger (1935)
Galathea (1936)
The King's Breakfast (1937)
The Tocher (1938)
Caliph Stork (1955)
Star of Bethlehem (1956)
La Belle Hélène (1957)
The Seraglio (1958)
Aucassin et Nicolette (1974)
The Rose and the Ring (1979)

SELECTED BIBLIOGRAPHY
Acker, Ally. *Reel Women: Pioneers of the Cinema, 1896 to the Present.* New York: Continuum, 1993.

Erens, Patricia, ed. *Sexual Stratagems: The World of Women in Film.* New York: Horizon Press, 1980.

Katz, Ephraim. *The Film Encyclopedia.* New York: HarperCollins, 1994.

Kotlarz, Irene. "Working against the Grain: Women in Animation." In *Women and Film: A Sight and Sound Reader,* edited by Pam Cook and Philip Dodd, 101–4. Philadelphia: Temple University Press, 1993.

Pilling, Jayne, ed. *Women & Animation: A Compendium.* London: BFI, 1993.

Reiniger, Lotte. "Scissors Make Films." *Sight & Sound* 5.7 (spring 1936): 13–15.

———. *Shadow Theatres and Shadow Films.* New York: Guptill, 1970.

Russett, Robert, and Cecile Starr. *Experimental Animation.* New York: Van Nostrand Reinhold, 1976.

Starr, Cecile. "Lotte Reiniger's Fabulous Film Career." *Sight Lines* (summer 1980): 17–19.

White, Eric Walter. *Walking Shadows.* London: Leonard and Virginia Woolf, 1931.

RIEFENSTAHL, LENI (1902–   ). Germany. Much has been written about Leni Riefenstahl, one of the most controversial and accomplished filmmakers in the history of the cinema. Best known for her infamous propaganda film, *Triumph of the Will* (1934–35), a record of the 1934 Nuremberg Party Convention held by Hitler and his followers, and her pioneering sports/reportage documentary *Olympia* (shot at the 1936 Olympics in Berlin but not released until 1938), Riefenstahl is still active as a still photographer and memoirist and maintains that she was never in sympathy with the Nazi cause, but rather a disinterested observer who became swept up in events. This claim is skeptically received by most observers.

Riefenstahl was born on August 22, 1902, in Berlin and entered the world of film acting in the "mountain films" of Dr. Arnold Fanck. She worked as an actress as late as 1933 in a variety of action films, including *Der grosse Sprung* (1927), *Die weisse Hölle vom piz Palü* (1929), and *SOS Eisberg* (1933), but in 1931 she also wrote, produced, directed, and starred in *Das blaue Licht,* an enormous box-office hit that made her a favorite with German audiences. In 1934–35 she directed *Triumph of the Will,* a cunningly constructed propaganda film that employed an army of cameramen and technicians to glorify Hitler and his associates. In 1936, Riefenstahl created *Olympia,* a highly stylized record of the 1936 Olympic Games. The film was not released until 1938, after two years of editing. *Triumph of the Will* and *Olympia* are still her two best-known films and form the nexus of her cinematic legacy.

By 1940, Riefenstahl was laboring on *Tiefland* (in which she also acted), a pastoral fantasy that occupied her attentions until 1944, by which time the collapse of the Nazi regime was imminent. *Tiefland* was released in 1954. Although Riefenstahl has since worked as a still photographer (notably on a lavish coffee-table book on the Nuba tribe of Africa) and essayist, Riefenstahl has never been able to escape the overwhelming impact of her past work with the Nazis. In 1993, Riefenstahl published *Leni Riefen-*

stahl: A Memoir, in which she set down her version of the events of her life. The subject of enormous controversy even today, Riefenstahl's body of work emerges as one of the most curious careers in the cinema. There is no denying that in her films, Leni Riefenstahl created images of great beauty, particularly in her use of slow-motion photography and plastic editing techniques in *Olympia* (such as the justly famed high-diving sequence). Nevertheless, her close ties to one of history's most infamous and irredeemable political regimes cannot be discounted, and Riefenstahl's continued protestations of political naiveté are impossible to accept.

SELECTED FILMOGRAPHY

Das blaue Licht (The Blue Light) (1931)
Sieg des Glaubens (Victory of Faith) (1933)
Triumph des Willens (Triumph of the Will) (1934–35)
Unsere Wehrmacht (1935)
Olympische Spiele/Olympia
  Pt. I: *Fest der Völker (Festival of the Nations)* (1936–38)
  Pt. II: *Fest der Schönheit (Festival of Beauty)* (1936–38)
Tiefland (Lowlands) (1954)
Die Nubas (The Nubas) (unfinished)

SELECTED BIBLIOGRAPHY

Acker, Ally. *Reel Women: Pioneers of the Cinema, 1896 to the Present.* New York: Continuum, 1993.

Elsaesser, Thomas. "Leni Riefenstahl: The Body Beautiful, Art Cinema, and Fascist Aesthetics." In *Women and Film: A Sight and Sound Reader,* edited by Pam Cook and Philip Dodd, 186–97. Philadelphia: Temple University Press, 1993.

Heck-Rabi, Louise. *Women Filmmakers: A Critical Reception.* Metuchen, NJ: Scarecrow Press, 1984.

Hinton, David B. *The Films of Leni Riefenstahl.* Metuchen, NJ: Scarecrow Press, 1978.

Katz, Ephraim. *The Film Encyclopedia.* New York: HarperCollins, 1994.

Quart, Barbara. *Women Directors: The Emergence of a New Cinema.* New York: Praeger, 1988.

Rentschler, Eric. "Fatal Attractions: Leni Riefenstahl's *The Blue Light*." *October* 48 (spring 1989): 46–68.

Rich, B. Ruby. "Leni Riefenstahl: The Deceptive Myth." In *Sexual Stratagems: The World of Women in Myth,* edited by Patricia Erens, New York: Horizon, 1979.

Riefenstahl, Leni. *Leni Riefenstahl: A Memoir.* New York: St. Martin's, 1993.

Sontag, Susan. "Fascinating Fascism." In *Women and the Cinema,* edited by Karyn Kay and Gerald Peary, 352–76. New York: Dutton, 1977.

S

SAGAN, LEONTINE (1899–1974). Austria/Germany. Born Leontine Schlesinger in Vienna, lesbian filmmaker Leontine Sagan became a film director after a career as a stage actress and director in Germany and Austria. In 1931, Sagan directed the international cult classic *Mädchen in Uniform*. Much critical writing is devoted to this film and the question of its representation of lesbian sexuality. In its own time, *Mädchen in Uniform* created a near scandal because of its handling of lesbian eroticism. Contemporary responses to the film range from praise to dismissal. Diane Carson lauds the film's "exploration of lesbianism in a girl's boarding school [which] startles with its deftly confrontational psychodrama" (461). B. Ruby Rich reads the film as "an exemplary work" (63), while Lisa Ohm asserts that the film displays negative attitudes toward homosexuality in its "clinical interpretation of lesbianism" (104).

Mädchen in Uniform is based on the Christa Winsloe novel *The Child Manuela* (*Das Kind Manuela*). The narrative takes place at a private girls' school, where one of the schoolgirls falls in love with a lesbian teacher. The film is a stylistic masterpiece. The all-woman atmosphere is beautifully rendered with women's fetishized bodies, clothing, and a female-defined space. Andrea Weiss places *Mädchen in Uniform* in the context of a subgenre of films set in women's schools, comparing it with *Club de Femmes* (Jacques Deval, 1936) and *The Wild Party* (Dorothy Arzner, 1929). Though all these films center on lesbian homoerotics, *Mädchen in Uniform* differs in its antifascist subtext. The film was censored for this subtext and for its embrace of lesbian desire. The uncensored print has been made available for quite some time, but the significance of the New York State censorship of the film should not go unnoticed. As B. Ruby Rich notes, *Mädchen in Uniform* is as much "a celebration of and warning for its most sympathetic audience: the lesbian population of Germany in 1931" (93). Rich further states that *Mädchen in Uniform* is "not only anti-fascist, but also anti-patriarchal" (64). The film is important politically and historically as one of the very few "coming out" narratives created in early cinema history.

Leontine Sagan moved to England in 1932, where she directed *Men of Tomorrow* (1932) for Alexander Korda. The film was a modest success. Some trade publications indicated that Sagan signed with MGM in the United States, but nothing seems to have come of the contract. The reasons for Sagan's defection from the world of film remain unclear, but in view of her uncompromising individuality with the production of *Mädchen in Uniform,* it seems probable that she met with resistance in developing other projects. Sagan returned to the theater as a director and actress in England and South Africa, and she was a cofounder of the National Theatre in Johannesburg. She died in 1974, leaving an important legacy of cinematic work.

SELECTED FILMOGRAPHY

Mädchen in Uniform (1931)
Men of Tomorrow (1932)

SELECTED BIBLIOGRAPHY

Carson, Diane. "Women Filmmakers." In *Multiple Voices in Feminist Film Criticism,* edited by Diane Carson, Linda Dittmar, and Janet Welsch, 456–67. Minneapolis: University of Minnesota Press, 1994.

Kuhn, Annette. *Women's Pictures: Feminism and Cinema.* London: Routledge, 1982.

Mayne, Judith. *The Woman at the Keyhole: Feminism and Women's Cinema.* Bloomington: Indiana University Press, 1990.

Ohm, Lisa. "The Filmic Adaptation of the Novel *The Child Manuela:* Christa Winsloe's Child Heroine Becomes a *Girl in Uniform.*" In *Gender and German Cinema: Feminist Interventions, Vol. 2,* edited by Sandra Frieden, Richard McCormick, Vibeke R. Petersen, and Laurie Melissa Vogelsang. 97–104. Oxford: Berg, 1993.

Pally, Marcia. "Women in Love." *Film Comment* 22.2 (March–April 1986): 35–39.

Rich, B. Ruby. "From Repressive Tolerance to Erotic Liberation: *Mädchen in Uniform.*" In *Gender and German Cinema: Feminist Interventions,* Vol. 2, edited by Sandra Frieden, Richard McCormick, Vibeke R. Petersen, and Laurie Melissa Vogelsang. 61–96. Oxford: Berg, 1993.

Russo, Vito. *The Celluloid Closet.* New York: Harper and Row, 1987.

Weiss, Andrea. *Vampires and Violets: Lesbians in Film.* New York: Penguin, 1993.

SANDER, HELKE (1937–   ). Germany. Helke Sander, cofounder of the feminist film journal *Frauen und Film,* is a feminist political activist and a major figure in New German Cinema. She studied acting and psychology before she became active in the theater in Finland. In the 1960s, she gained experience in film while working for Finnish television. She studied at the Berlin Academy of Film and Television and was one of the first graduates of the school in 1969. Sander is credited with spearheading a campaign to address women's issues within the student protest movement of the Socialist German Students Union. Though the group worked against authoritarianism and maintained Marxist political views, Sander noticed that they expected women to remain in traditional roles. In 1968, Sander gave a speech that drew attention to the oppression of women within the Marxist movement. According to Julia Knight, Sander's speech "is generally taken to mark the birth of the new women's movement in West Germany" (74). Sander and other women began the Action Council for Women's Liberation in 1968. In 1974, Helke Sander founded *Frauen und Film*. Miriam Hansen notes in her study of the rise of this journal that it was formed in order to "analyze the workings of patriarchal culture in cinema [and] recognize and name the feminist starting points in film" (295). Implicit in their agenda is a critique of the exclusionary canon that almost completely ignores women directors.

Helke Sander's films reflect her political activism, her involvement in the women's movement, and her awareness of feminist theoretical and aesthetic concerns. *Redupers,* also known as *The All-Round Reduced Personality* (1977), is a reflection on the representation of women through female voice-over narration and on-screen representation. Sander freely appropriates quotations from the works of Christa Wolf in the film. *Redupers* is semiautobiographical material situated in the context of a large number of autobiographical films by women in the New German Cinema. *Redupers* is a loosely woven narrative about Edda, a woman photographer (played by Sander) who is a member of a woman's photography group. Throughout the film, Edda questions her own ability to produce "objective" photographs. The women's group uses an oversized photograph of the Berlin Wall as a sort of traveling performance piece. They also set up a space in which a curtain is opened to "view" East Berlin. In another scene, Sanders superimposes footage from women's films over a newspaper, including scenes from Yvonne Rainer's *Film about a Woman Who* and Valie Export's *Invisible Adversaries*. Sander weaves together these appropriations with the voice of a female narrator who states that she is "obsessed by daily life as other women see it." The film emerges as an incisive commentary on the process of feminist film production.

As Judith Mayne observes, "[T]he female voice has several functions in *Redupers*. It personalizes the tracking shots of the city, describing the history of the women's group and the strategies the women have used to get their project funded" (165). The woman's voice, like the woman photographer's gaze, is relocated as an active participant and is a displacement of the objectified female as the object of the male gaze. Kaja Silverman notes that the use of female voice-over in *Redupers* also tends to "throw into doubt the notion of a fixed 'truth' representable on screen, thereby securing the viewer's complete engagement in the labor of producing meaning" (30). Sander explains her intentions to Marc Silberman:

[W]e articulate feelings, and what the consequences would be if we were to think like the women in the film. In other words, I ask the viewer to consider a given situation from an alternative perspective, namely a divided Berlin from a woman's perspective. (164)

Female subjectivity is foregrounded in Sander's *The Subjective Factor* (1981), which emphasizes that women are political subjects and objects in both the public and private spheres. *The Subjective Factor* restages the student uprisings of the late 1960s, and a commune serves as the backdrop for Sander's filmic criticism of the student movement, for the female members of the commune are denied both agency and voice. If *Redupers* used the Berlin Wall as a symbol of ideological boundaries, *The Subjective Factor* exposes silence as a wall of gendered suppression. *The Subjective Factor* is a poststructuralist feminist film that opens up the possibility for new avenues of communication across borders of identity, subjectivity, and gender. Helke Sander's approach to filmmaking is not always greeted with enthusiasm from film-financing authorities, but Sander holds to her convictions. As she told Marc Silberman, "I want to continue working in this direction, but find no money for such a form. We get money based on our scripts, which must be completely written to submit to the various funding commissions. That implies certain compromises if I do not want to accept the repressive nature of the script" (165).

SELECTED FILMOGRAPHY

Subjektitüde (*Subjectivity*) (1966)
Silvo (1967)
Brecht die Macht der Manipulateure (*Crush the Power of the Manipulators*) (1967–68)
Kindergärtnerin, was nun? (*What Now, Nursery School Teacher?*) (1969)
Kinder sind keine Rinder (*Children Aren't Cattle*) (1969)
Eine Prämie für Irene (*A Bonus for Irene*) (1971)
Macht die Pille frei? (*Does the Pill Liberate?*) (codirector) (1972)
Männerbünde (*Male Leagues*) (codirector) (1973)
(*Redupers*) (*Die allseitig reduzierte Persönlichkeit*) (*The All-Round Reduced Personality*) (1977)
Der subjektive Faktor (*The Subjective Factor*) (1981)
Der Beginn aller Schrecken ist Liebe (*The Trouble with Love*) (1983)
Nr. 1—Aus Berichten der Wach—und Patrouillendienste (*No. 1—From the Reports of Security Guards and Patrol Services*) (1984)
Nr. 8—Aus Berichten der Wach—und Patrouillendienste (*No. 8—From the Reports of Security Guards and Patrol Services*) (1986)
Nr. 5—Aus Berichten der Wach—und Patrouillendienste (*No. 5—From the Reports of Security Guards and Patrol Services*) (1986)
Sieben Frauen—Sieben Sünden (*Seven Women—Seven Sins*) (codirector) (1986)

Felix (codirector) (1987)
Die Deutschen und ihre Männer (*The Germans and Their Men*) (1990)

SELECTED BIBLIOGRAPHY

de Lauretis, Teresa. *Technologies of Gender.* Bloomington: Indiana University Press, 1987.

———. "Rethinking Women's Cinema: Aesthetics and Feminist Theory." In *Issues in Feminist Film Criticism,* edited by Patricia Erens, 288–308. Bloomington: Indiana University Press, 1990.

Elsaesser, Thomas. "It Started with These Images—Some Notes on Political Film-Making after Brecht in Germany: Helke Sander and Harun Farocki." *Discourse* 7 (fall 1985): 95–120.

Hansen, Miriam. "*Frauen und Film* and Feminist Film Culture." In *Gender and German Cinema, Feminist Interventions, Vol. 2,* edited by Sandra Frieden, Richard W. McCormick, Vibeke R. Petersen, and Laurie Melissa Vogelsang. 293–98. Oxford: Berg, 1993.

Knight, Julia. *Women and the New German Cinema.* London: Verso, 1992.

Mayne, Judith. "Female Narration, Women's Cinema: Helke Sander's *The All-Round Reduced Personality/Redupers.*" *New German Critique* 24–25 (fall–winter 1981–82): 155–71.

McCormick, Richard W. "Re-Representing the Student Movement: Helke Sander's *The Subjective Factor.*" In *Gender and German Cinema: Feminist Interventions, Vol. 2* edited by Sandra Frieden, Richard W. McCormick, Vibeke R. Petersen and Laurie Melissa Vogelsang. 273–92. Oxford: Berg, 1993.

Perlmutter, Ruth. "Two New Films by Helke Sander and Ulrike Ottinger." *Film Criticism* 9.2 (winter 1984–85): 67–73.

Quart, Barbara Koenig. *Women Directors: The Emergence of a New Cinema.* New York: Praeger, 1988.

Rich, B. Ruby. "She Says, He Says: The Power of the Narrator in Modernist Film Politics." *Discourse* 6 (fall 1983): 31–46.

Silberman, Marc. "An Interview with Helke Sander." In *Gender and German Cinema: Feminist Interventions, Vol. 1,* edited by Sandra Frieden, Richard W. McCormick, Vibeke R. Petersen, and Laurie Melissa Vogelsang. 163–65. Oxford: Berg, 1993.

Silverman, Kaja. "Helke Sander and the Will to Change." *Discourse* 6 (fall 1983): 10–30.

Women Make Movies. *Women Make Movies Catalogue.* New York: Women Make Movies, 1994.

SANDERS-BRAHMS, HELMA (1940–). Germany. Helma Sanders-Brahms was born on November 20, 1940, in Emden, Germany. She is best known to international audiences as the director of *Germany, Pale Mother* (1979–80). She is a descendant of Johannes Brahms, the composer. After studying theater, Sanders-Brahms enrolled at Cologne University. She worked in many capacities, including factory work, sales work, and teaching, before she found a job in German television as a voice-over narrator. In the late 1960s, she began making short films and documentaries, after working as an assistant director to Sergio Corbucci and Pier Paolo Pasolini.

Like Helke Sander, Helma Sanders-Brahms's films deal with issues of feminism, urban identity, and autobiography.

Angelika Urban, Sales Assistant, Engaged (1970) is Sanders-Brahms's first film. It draws upon the filmmaker's personal experience as a salesperson. *Angelika Urban* won two prizes at the 1970 Oberhausen Film Festival. Sanders-Brahms sold *Angelika Urban* to a German television station and was subsequently offered a number of directorial opportunities. *Shirin's Wedding* (1975) is an incisive study of a young Turkish woman who travels to Germany in search of the man she was betrothed to as a child. The woman's quest is a lost cause, and she ends up working as a prostitute to support herself. Julia Knight describes the style of the film:

Using a combination of low-key realism and conversational voice-over, the film not only offers a moving portrait of its central protagonist but also operates as an observation on the meeting of two alien cultures. (12)

Shirin's Wedding is a highly controversial film. It was successful commercially, but it was criticized by the Turkish community in Germany. In 1976–77, Helma Sanders-Brahms directed *Heinrich,* a film based on the writings and life of the nineteenth-century writer, Heinrich von Kleist. Julia Knight reports that the film is the first film by a woman director to win the top Federal film award. However, as Knight notes, *Heinrich* was criticized for having "little contemporary relevance" (13).

Germany, Pale Mother is also controversial among German film critics. It has been perceived as a trivialization of German history during World War II, but it has been praised as an autobiographical recounting of women's experience under the Nazi regime. *Germany, Pale Mother* is a daring investigation of Sanders-Brahms's mother's activities during World War II and has much in common with Su Friedrich's *The Ties That Bind* (1984), in which Friedrich directly questions her mother about her life under the Nazi regime. Women's experiences are often completely missing in patriarchal historical studies, and it is the unsaid that Sanders-Brahms negotiates. Her mother, like Su Friedrich's mother, was not supportive of the Nazi regime, yet both were forced to adopt an apolitical stance to survive. Questions of complicity, subjectivity, and memory are central to both films. Sanders-Brahms incorporates documentary and fictional footage in *Germany, Pale Mother,* in order to accurately place her film in the margins between biographical "truth" and subjectivity. Sanders-Brahms reenacts her mother's life, her courtship, marriage and the birth of her daughter, the loss of her home in the war, and her joining other women to rebuild Germany after the war. In doing so, Sanders-Brahms reenacts the experiences of many other German women whose voices are marginalized or silenced by exclusion. Sanders-Brahms speaks through her mother's experience, in a voice-over narrative. "From you I learned to speak," she says. Richard W. McCormick notes that Sanders-Brahms acts as "the 'enunciator' of the film, as the one who constructs it" (196). In one scene, Sanders-Brahms used the distancing technique of an extradiagetic voice-over narrative of the fairy tale "The Robber Bridegroom" in a scene in which the mother is raped by drunk American soldiers. Clearly, Sanders-Brahms is drawing a parallel between Nazi oppression and male violence. The tale's refrain, "Turn back, turn back, young bride, you are in the house of murderers," is used to full effect to underscore this connection. Though *Germany, Pale Mother* has been criticized by some as a slick art-house melodrama, Richard McCormick sees the film as a responsible political film that provides "the proof, as it were, that the horrors of war that shaped her mother's story were real, not a dream" (206).

SELECTED FILMOGRAPHY

Angelika Urban, Verkäuferin, Verlobt (Angelika Urban, Sales Assistant, Engaged) (1970)
Gewalt (Violence) (1970)
Die industrielle Reservearmee (The Industrial Reserve Army) (1970–71)
Der Angestellte (The Employee) (1971–72)
Die Maschine (The Machine) (1972–73)
Die letzten Tage von Gomorrha (The Last Days of Gomorrah) (1973–74)
Die Erdbeben in Chile (Earthquake in Chile) (1974)
Unter dem Pflaster ist der Strand (The Beach under the Sidewalk (1974)
Shirins Hochzeit (Shirin's Wedding) (1975)
Heinrich (1976–77)
Deutschland, bleiche Mutter (Germany, Pale Mother) (1979–80)
Vringsveedeler Tryptichon (The Vringsveedol Triptych) (1979)
Die Berührte (No Mercy No Future) (1981)
Die Erbtöchter (The Daughters' Inheritance) (codirector) (1982)
Flügel und Fesseln (The Future of Emily) (1984)
Alte Liebe (Old Love) (1985)
Laputa (1985–86)
Felix (codirector) (1987)
Manöver (Manoeuvres) (1988)

SELECTED BIBLIOGRAPHY

Kaes, Anton. *From "Hitler" to "Heimat": The Return of History as Film.* Cambridge: Harvard University Press, 1989.
Knight, Julia. *Women and the New German Cinema.* London: Verso, 1992.
Kuhn, Annette. *Women's Pictures: Feminism and Cinema.* London: Routledge, 1982.
Mayne, Judith. *The Woman at the Keyhole: Feminism and Women's Cinema.* Bloomington: Indiana University Press, 1990.
McCormick, Richard W. "Confronting German History: Melodrama, Distantiation, and Women's Discourse in *Germany, Pale Mother.*" In *Gender and German Cinema: Feminist Interventions, Vol. 2,* edited by Sandra Frieden, Richard W. McCormick, Vibeke R. Petersen, Laurie Melissa Vogelsang, 185–206. Oxford: Berg, 1993.

Quart, Barbara. *Women Directors: The Emergence of a New Cinema*. New York: Praeger, 1988.

Rentschler, Eric. *West German Film in the Course of Time*. Bedford Hills, NY: Redgrave, 1984.

Rentschler, Eric, ed. *German Film and Literature: Adaptations and Transformations*. New York: Methuen, 1986.

Silberman, Marc. "Women Filmmakers in West Germany." *Camera Obscura* 10 (fall 1980): 123–52.

SARMIENTO, VALERIA (1948–   ). Chile. Valeria Sarmiento is a leading Chilean film director who was exiled to France because of the political events of 1973, which forced many Chilean writers, poets, intellectuals, artists, and filmmakers out of the country. Sarmiento began making films during the 1970s in Chile under the Popular Unity government. Her first film, *Un sueño como de colores* (1972), concerns women striptease artists. Her feminist documentaries and melodramas are inspired by a strong interest in melodrama, romanticism, and feminism. As Sarmiento told Coco Fusco:

Sometimes I feel as though I am a Dr. Jekyll and Mr. Hyde. On the one hand I make melodramas which are to a certain extent distanced from reality. On the other hand, I love to immerse myself in reality and that is what the documentary allows me to do. (10)

Sarmiento's *A Man When He Is a Man* (1982) is a multilayered documentary on machismo that draws together Sarmiento's ability to combine cinema verité with romanticism and melodrama. *A Man When He Is a Man* is a quintessential example of dialogic, feminist, documentary technique, as identified by critic Janice Welsch. Sarmiento intercuts interviews with men and women on the subject of love and sexuality with footage from classic melodramatic films and scenes of a band of Costa Rican musicians singing popular romantic folk songs in a lush tropical forest. The effect of the juxtaposition is often compelling. The viewer is struck by the blatant duality and repressive double standards of patriarchal heterosexual culture. *A Man When He Is a Man* is a trenchant analysis of "innocent" romantic attitudes toward sexuality that ultimately lead toward violence against women. Sarmiento's humor and understatedness are remarkable. As viewers, we are lulled into the romantic songs and stories of young boys' and girls' first love. We hear one man tell us he has eight children with at least two wives. He tells us: "Women are like bread. They must be eaten hot, or you'll never get your teeth into them." As the film progresses, we are confronted with men who have been jilted. We feel ourselves identifying with them and feeling their pain when we suddenly realize that they are in prison for murdering their wives. Sarmiento intercuts a tableau of a group of men singing: "I grew tired of begging. Tired of telling her that without her I'd die." Through her skillful manipulation of these contradictory images, Sarmiento exposes the danger beneath the seemingly innocent, romantic lyrics. The lyrics are, in fact, a series of threats, implicit statements that romantic love is a commodified form of ownership. Any attempts at female self-determination will be met with violence. The documentary illuminates the climate that nurtures gender roles that lead to the domination of women. J. Hoberman said *A Man When He Is a Man* "offers the most outrageous psychosexual material with sardonic cool . . . [the film is] pointedly absurd and unexpectedly poignant" (Women Make Movies, 48).

   Nôtre Mariage (1984) is internationally Sarmiento's best-known film. Based on a romantic novel by Corín Tellado, *Nôtre Mariage* is full of deadpan humor. As Enrique Fernandez concludes, "This is a work that can be enjoyed on several levels—depending on whether the spectator glides along with the glitzy, absurdly bourgeois romance or pays attention to the Freudian subtext" (47). Sarmiento has long been interested in melodrama. As a child, she immersed herself in romantic, melodramatic films and radio programs. Later, she read romance novels "in secret because it was not looked well on" (Fusco, 10). In Europe she began reading the novels of the Brontës and watched many of Hollywood director Douglas Sirk's glossy melodramas of the 1950s. *Nôtre Mariage* is a witty feminist melodrama that uses a double-voiced narrative to provide both pleasure and criticism of women's romance novels and popular film melodramas. On the whole, Valeria Sarmiento claims that the feminist movement has helped her enormously. "I am sure that in France in the 60s it was much harder for women to make films. Now it is considered normal" (Fusco, 11). Sarmiento's films have been relatively well distributed. She continues to direct films for French television, both in France and on location in Latin America, and also edits many films by her husband, director Raul Ruiz.

SELECTED FILMOGRAPHY

Un sueño como de colores (1972)
La femme au foyer (1976)
La nostalgia/Le mal du pays (1979)
Gens de toutes parts, gens de nulle part (1980)
El Hombre cuando es hombre (*A Man When He Is a Man*) (1982)
Mi boda contigo (*Nôtre Mariage*) (1984)
Amelia Lopes O'Neill (1990)

SELECTED BIBLIOGRAPHY

Burton, Julianne. *The Social Documentary in Latin America*. Pittsburgh: University of Pittsburgh Press, 1990.
Fernandez, Enrique. "Miami's 'Autores.' " *Film Comment* 21.3 (May–June 1985): 46–48.
Fusco, Coco. "Dreaming Melodramas: An Interview with Valeria Sarmiento." *Afterimage* 19 (December 1991): 10–11.
Pick, Zuzana M. *Latin American Filmmakers and the Third Cinema*. Ottawa: Carleton University, 1978.

Stam, Robert, and Louise Spence. "Colonialism, Racism and Representation: An Introduction." *Screen* 24.2 (March–April 1983): 2–20.

Welsch, Janice. "Bakhtin, Language, and Women's Documentary Filmmaking." In *Multiple Voices in Feminist Film Criticism,* edited by Diane Carson, Linda Dittmar, and Janice Welsch, 162–75. Minneapolis: University of Minnesota Press, 1994.

Women Make Movies. *Women Make Movies Catalogue.* New York: Women Make Movies, 1994.

SAVOCA, NANCY (1960–   ). United States. Italian-American director Nancy Savoca was born in the Bronx in 1960. Her first feature film, *True Love* (1989), is a provocative examination and re-creation of Italian-American courtship and wedding rituals. It is also a tribute to the perseverance of Savoca, who spent several years raising funds to complete the film, which was cowritten in 1982 with Savoca's husband, Richard Guay, who is also the producer of Savoca's films. Though *True Love* was filmed on a limited budget of $750,000, it has the feel of ethnic authenticity common to all of Savoca's efforts. *True Love* stars Annabella Sciorra as a working-class Italian-American woman who is about to marry irresponsible, hard-drinking Michael (Ron Eldard). The film is told from a female-centered perspective, and much of the narrative centers around the relationship between Sciorra's character, Donna, and her best friend, Gracie (Aida Turturro). The two women make clinically detailed plans for the wedding while Michael spends all his time drinking in the local pub.

As Gloria Nardini notes, *True Love* exposes the nature of Italian-American female friendships that are based on nineteenth-century separate spheres of "emotional segregation" (14). Donna has a closeness with Gracie and with her own mother that supersedes her relationship with her fiancé. *True Love* questions gender roles and exposes the gap between the language of men and women. The ending of *True Love* is an ambiguous statement about the value of marriage and courtship rituals. The hand-held camera captures the details of the traditional wedding and exposes their absurdity. For instance, one of the family members offers his best wishes with a toast "to one hundred years and male children."

Gender roles are at the heart of Savoca's second feature film, *Dog Fight* (1991), which stars Lili Taylor and River Phoenix. Savoca sets up a misogynist scene in which young army buddies compete to find the "ugliest" woman. Eddie (River Phoenix) brings Rose (Lili Taylor) to the event. Savoca manages to turn the abhorrent ritual into an investigation of both male and female roles in American society. *Household Saints* (1993) marks a return to the almost neorealist display of Italian-American ethnicity in *True Love. Household Saints* is an intriguing blend of surrealist poeticism and neorealism that centers on a young woman's Catholic mysticism. Lili Taylor stars in the film as a devoutly Catholic adolescent who claims she has

had a mystical experience with St. Teresa. Her cynical parents are unable
to support her rituals of fasting and withdrawal from society. Savoca allows
the viewer to distinguish between the adolescent Teresa's subjective view
of reality and her parents' objective view of the world. Teresa's experience
is symbolized by female rituals around food, women's intuitive experience,
and a tradition of female piety in the Catholic Church, as well as Italian-
American custom. *Household Saints* is a deeply comedic and strangely
tragic enunciation of female fantasy and a rereading of the woman's film
from a female perspective. As Mary Ann Doane notes, in the woman's film
"there is an almost obsessive association of the female protagonist with a
deviation from some norm of mental stability or health" (36). *Household
Saints* rereads the female "deviant" in an "obsessive attempt to circum-
scribe a place for the female spectator" (Doane, 37). Nancy Savoca is dedicated to independent filmmaking. She is one of the few women-identified,
Italian-American-centered, personal filmmakers to successfully write and
direct feature films with her own unique visual signature.

SELECTED FILMOGRAPHY

True Love (1989)
Dog Fight (1991)
Household Saints (1993)

SELECTED BIBLIOGRAPHY

Doane, Mary Ann. *The Desire to Desire: The Woman's Film of the 1940s*. Bloo-
    mington: Indiana University Press, 1987.
Katz, Ephraim. *The Film Encyclopedia*. New York: HarperCollins, 1994.
Kutzera, Dale. "In *Dogfight*, Cruel Wager Leads to Love." *American Cinematog-
    rapher* 72 (September 1991): 26–28.
Nardini, Gloria. "Is It True Love? Or Not? Patterns of Ethnicity and Gender in
    Nancy Savoca." *VIA: Voices in Italian Americana* 2.1 (spring 1991): 9–17.

SCHNEEMANN, CAROLEE (1939–   ). United States. Carolee Schneemann's films are personal, feminist films. Her most celebrated film, *Fuses*
(1964–68), a poetic and evocative exploration of heterosexual lovemaking,
has been the subject of great controversy since its initial release. Schneemann herself calls the work "the first explicit feminist erotic film confronting traditional sexual taboos" (Film-Makers' Cooperative, 423). With
unabashed frankness and a visual style incorporating black-and-white and
color imagery, along with intentionally scratched footage and intermittently
repeated credit titles, *Fuses* is unquestionably a major work of the American
avant-garde cinema that influenced numerous films by both women and
men in the late 1960s and 1970s. *Fuses,* begun in 1964 and finished after
intense revision in 1968, is Schneemann's vision of her own identity as a
sexual human being and a woman in love. She considers the film Part One

of her "Autobiographical Trilogy"; the other two sections of the trilogy are *Plumb Line* (1971) and *Kitch's Last Meal* (1973–1978).

Schneemann has refused to bow to critical and/or aesthetic trends in experimental filmmaking, following her own vision no matter what the cost. Her early film, *Carl Ruggles' Christmas Breakfast* (1963), was shot on 8mm film and then blown up to 16mm. In black and white with hand-coloring, the film is available only with a separate tape sound track, rather than the traditional composite optical sound prints usually presented by filmmakers to the public. *Viet-Flakes* (1965) is Schneemann's indirect comment on the then-ongoing Vietnam War. She often works from "scrap diary footage shot in 8mm, hand printed as 16mm" (Film-Makers' Cooperative, 423), and she edits her films entirely to please herself, on her own schedule, with no one to hurry her or push her into artificial deadlines. By working in the experimental medium of Super 8mm film, she has, to a degree, confined herself to the margins of filmic discourse, but this self-imposed exile bothers her not at all. She works to please herself first; the audience can either accept or reject her works as it sees fit.

Fuses was once considered a highly controversial film. Now it can be viewed as an instance of radical heterosexual feminist ritualization, exhibiting "an interpretation of a healthy eroticism" (MacDonald, 135). In 1972, a group of lesbian separatists challenged Schneemann at a screening of *Fuses,* for some of the women in the group disliked the film for its lack of homosexual role models. Schneemann agrees that there do, indeed, need to be lesbian erotic films, but she was nonetheless surprised by their reaction, and she defended her position, saying, "All my life I've been pushed around by fascistic men telling me what to look at and what it means, and I'm not going to be pushed around by fascistic women telling me what to look at and what it means" (MacDonald, 141). Carolee Schneemann is perhaps one of the first filmmakers who can be described as a radical heterosexual feminist. Her uncompromisingly personal stamp has not always been embraced by the male or the female film community. As she told Scott MacDonald: "Whenever there's a show of personal, diary films, everybody's invited but me. I mean I'm not looking for confirmation, there are just places where it seems obvious that my work should be included, even if some people hate it" (151).

SELECTED FILMOGRAPHY

Carl Ruggles' Christmas Breakfast (1963)
Fuses (1964–68)
Viet-Flakes (1965)
Plumb Line (1971)
Reel Time (1971–72)
Acts of Perception (1973)
Kitch's Last Meal (1973–78)

SELECTED BIBLIOGRAPHY

Ballerini, Julia. Introduction to *Carolee Schneemann: Early and Recent Work.* Edited by Ted Castle and Julia Ballerini, N. pag. New Paltz, NY: Documentext, 1982.

Castle, Ted. "Carolee Schneemann: The Woman Who Uses Her Body as Her Art." *Artforum* 19. 3 (November 1980): 64–70.

Film-Makers' Cooperative. *Film-Makers' Cooperative Catalogue No. 7.* New York: Film-Makers' Cooperative, 1989.

Glassner, Verina. "Interviews with Three Filmmakers." *Time Out* 109 (March 17–23, 1972): 47.

Haller, Robert. "Rolling in the Maelstrom: A Conversation between Carolee and Robert Haller." *Idiolects* 14 (spring 1984): 50–55.

Le Grice, Malcolm. *Abstract Film and Beyond.* Cambridge: MIT Press, 1977.

MacDonald, Scott. *A Critical Cinema.* Berkeley: University of California Press, 1988.

McEvilley, Thomas. "Carolee Schneemann." *Artforum* (April 1985): 92.

Mekas, Jonas. *Movie Journal: The Rise of the New American Cinema. 1959–1971.* New York: Collier, 1972.

Museum of Modern Art. *Circulating Film Library Catalogue.* New York: Museum of Modern Art, 1984.

Ward, Melinda, and Bruce Jenkins. *The American New Wave 1958–1967.* Minneapolis: Walker Art Center, 1982.

Youngblood, Gene. *Expanded Cinema.* New York: Dutton, 1970.

SEIDELMAN, SUSAN (1952–   ). United States. Born in Pennsylvania, Susan Seidelman has had a remarkably successful career in commercial Hollywood filmmaking. Before attending New York University (NYU) Film School, she studied art and fashion design at Drexel University. A self-defined feminist, Seidelman directed three award-winning shorts as a student at NYU. She inherited a small sum of money and began planning to film her feature debut, *Smithereens* (1982). *Smithereens* is about a female punk-rock groupie who wishes to escape from the boring, confined environment of New Jersey. (The theme of female desire for escape runs through all of Seidelman's films.) *Smithereens* was critically acclaimed at the 1982 Cannes Film Festival. The success of this low-budget film launched Seidelman's career as an up-and-coming independent filmmaker.

Desperately Seeking Susan (1985), starring Rosanna Arquette and Madonna, is a female-centered quest narrative not unlike *Smithereens*. In *Desperately Seeking Susan,* a bored New Jersey housewife seeks escape from her yuppie existence through personal ads in the newspaper. In this film, however, the woman's quest for identity is infused into a send-up of the classic screwball comedy narrative of mistaken identity. The main character and Madonna are involved in an identity swap, highlighting the societal duality that codes women as "good" or "bad" girls. In her next film, *Making Mr. Right* (1987), Seidelman turned directly to the issue of female desire and power issues of sexuality. *Making Mr. Right* is a feminist revision of the male-centered Pygmalion narrative in which men literally design and build their fantasy woman as robot or submissive slave. In Seidelman's version, Ann Magnuson is put in charge of "socializing" an android (robot) version of the "perfect" male. *Making Mr. Right* is a wonderful example of female inversion of a sexist, mythmaking fantasy. In this film, the jokes are on men. Male critics, such as the anonymous critic in *Variety,* display a discomfort with Seidelman's feminist humor, terming the jokes "bad or vulgar (or both) in scenes that reek of contrivance" (Elley, 475).

Nevertheless, from a feminist point of view, *Making Mr. Right* is a fantasy of feminine creation with an offbeat feminist humor and a refreshing send-up of countless misogynist Pygmalion films directed by men, such as *My Fair Lady* (1964), *Vertigo* (1950), and *The Bride of Frankenstein* (1935). *Making Mr. Right* is less concerned with the role of women than the gender constructions of men. Seidelman displaces the male role as rational/scientist/creator with an empowered female who is emotive yet clever and who combines a healthy sex drive with an ability to "create" a fantasy male figure of desire. The ending of the film, in which the woman falls in love with the android, is the ultimate feminist statement against female compliance. Susan Seidelman emerges as an interesting combination of a commercial filmmaker who also has personal feminist stories to tell. Obviously driven by a very real need to reach out to her audience, Seidelman will undoubtedly continue to create audacious and original films in the future.

SELECTED FILMOGRAPHY

Smithereens (1982)
Desperately Seeking Susan (1985)
Making Mr. Right (1987)
Cookie (1989)
She-Devil (1990)

SELECTED BIBLIOGRAPHY

Acker, Ally. *Reel Women: Pioneers of the Cinema, 1896 to the Present.* New York: Continuum, 1993.
Citron, Michelle. "Women's Film Production: Going Mainstream." In *Female Spectators: Looking at Film and Television,* 45–63. London: Verso, 1988.
Elley, Derek, ed. *Variety Movie Guide 1994.* London: Hamlyn, 1993, 475.

SEN, APARNA (1945–). India. Born October 25, 1945, Aparna Sen entered the Indian cinema as a leading Bengali actress and appeared in many films directed by Satyajit Ray, including *Two Women* (1961). Sen was born into a household tied to the film industry. Her father, Chidananda Das Gupta, a film critic, was one of the founding members of one of the first cinema clubs in Calcutta. Since 1968, Aparna Sen acted in over fifty films until she found the opportunity to move into the role of director.

36 Chowringee Lane (1981) is Aparna Sen's first feature film. It is a study of identity politics in postcolonial society with an emphasis on the issues of age, gender, and multiracial subjectivity. Set in postcolonial Calcutta, *36 Chowringee Lane* presents an Anglo-Indian English teacher who lives an alienated, gloomy existence as a culturally marginalized woman. As an Anglo-Indian of mixed parentage, Miss Stoneham is rejected by both Indian and British sectors. An aging English teacher, she represents a remnant of the colonializing oppressive forces that once dominated India. Her students have no interest in learning Shakespeare, and she is replaced by a younger schoolteacher. She is a figure of exiled identity who ultimately acts as a bridge among modern India, independent India, and colonialized India, finding an identity in living through the characters around her. For instance, she befriends a young couple who use her apartment as a romantic meeting place. As Barbara Quart writes, "[Sen's] film can be seen as quite daring in an Indian context, for taking on the plight of an Anglo-Indian as its central subject . . . for the extra-marital status of the sexuality; and for the callousness the film ascribes to the attractive, upper-class, highly educated young Indian couple" (250). The ending of the film, in which the couple abandon Miss Stoneham, may be read as a commentary against colonialism, coupled with a degree of melodramatic pathos for the colonizer.

Parama (1985) also examines female subjectivity in the context of postcolonial Indian culture. *Parama* as a reconfiguration of the ethnographic film tradition in which Indian women were primarily subjects in white male-produced ethnographic films. As Poonam Arora notes, *Parama* "inverts the traditional paradigm wherein the ethnographer is male and speaks within a stronghold of patriarchal authority" (294). *Parama* has an anti-colonial narrative structure: it is the story of an Indian subject, told by an Indian man. In *Parama,* an Indian photographer is writing about an Indian housewife for *Life* magazine. The photographer objectifies the housewife, sees her as hopelessly traditional, and tries to get her to change her lifestyle. The photographer, interested only in career opportunities, uses Parama as an object and leaves her to be ostracized from her people. Poonam Arora sees Sen's film as an exposé of "the process whereby the Third World subjects are constructed by other Third World subjects for consumption by audiences elsewhere" (299).

SELECTED FILMOGRAPHY

36 Chowringee Lane (1981)
The Ultimate Woman (1984)
Parama (1985)
Sati (1987)
Picnic (1989)

SELECTED BIBLIOGRAPHY

Alloula, Malek. *The Colonial Harem*. Minneapolis: University of Minnesota Press, 1986.

Arora, Poonam. "The Production of Third World Subjects for First World Consumption: Salaam Bombay and Parama." In *Multiple Voices in Feminist Film Criticism*, edited by Diane Carson, Linda Dittmar, and Janice Welsch, 293–304. Minneapolis: University of Minnesota Press, 1994.

Burra, Rani, ed. *Indian Cinema: 1980–1985*. Bombay: Directorate of Film Festivals, 1985.

Mohanty, Chandra Talpade, Ann Russo, and Lourdes Torres, eds. *Third World Women and the Politics of Feminism*. Bloomington: Indiana University Press, 1991.

Quart, Barbara. *Women Directors: The Emergence of a New Cinema*. New York: Praeger, 1988.

Wimal, Dissanayake. "Questions of Female Subjectivity and Patriarchy: A Reading of Three Indian Women Film Directors." *East-West Film Journal* 3.2 (June 1989): 74–90.

SERREAU, COLINE (1947–   ). France. Coline Serreau is a highly successful French director who manages to make commercial yet feminist films working within the mainstream film industry. Born in 1947, she became an actress in both stage and screen productions before she moved into film direction. In 1977, she directed a short film for television, *Le Rendezvous*, before finding a career as a feature film director. *What Do These Women Want?* (1977) explores women's issues, and so do many of Coline Serreau's films, both as scenarist and director. Ginette Vincendeau maintains that Serreau has a "clearly feminine agenda" (26), regardless of her rejection of the label "woman director." Vincendeau goes so far as stating that Serreau "has contributed importantly to the 'feminization' of French comedy" (26). *What Do These Women Want?* is a feminist documentary that explores the range of female desires through interviews with a disparate group of Frenchwomen. *Why Not?* (1979) is a "utopian sexual comedy" (Vincendeau, 27) that privileges female desire in a feminist revision of the romantic love triangle. In *Why Not?*, the triangle is made up of a woman and two men who fulfill the woman's desires, rather the usual male-centered "triangular" structure of two women fighting over a single man.

Three Men and a Cradle (1986) was Serreau's first major success. *Three Men and a Cradle* has a gentle, quiet, understated air to it, yet it manages to combine breakneck farce with a story that could easily have veered into uncontrolled sentimentality. Three men are left in charge of an infant placed on their doorstep. In time, they grow to appreciate their domesticity and the role of the nurturing parent. When the child's mother returns to retrieve the infant, the men are visibly saddened. They have grown accustomed to taking care of her and are newly aware of the enforced emptiness of their carefree bachelor existence. When, at length, the mother finds that the demands of raising the child alone and dealing with her career are insurmountable, she surrenders the child again to the men, who welcome her gratefully back into their lives. Sharply observed, deftly edited, and sumptuously photographed, *Three Men and a Cradle* was an enormous hit in France and served as the basis of an American remake, *Three Men and a Baby* (1987), directed by Leonard Nimoy. In *La Crise* (1992), Serreau concentrates on the complex effects of economic recession on the upper middle class. Serreau continues her successful career as film director, but she is often critically "erased" (Vincendeau, 26) because of her critical success; in some circles, her commercial popularity seems to be held against her.

SELECTED FILMOGRAPHY

Mais Quest'ce Qu'elles Veulent? (What Do These Women Want?) (1977)
Pourquoi Pas? (Why Not?) (1979)
Qu'est-ce Qu'on Attend Pour Etre Heureux? (1982)
Trois Hommes et un Couffin (Three Men and a Cradle) (1986)
Romuald et Juliette (1989)
La Crise (1992)

SELECTED BIBLIOGRAPHY

Francke, Lizzie. "Men, Women, Children and Baby Boom Movies." In *Women and Film: A Sight and Sound Reader,* edited by Pam Cook and Philip Dodd, 148–55. Philadelphia: Temple University Press, 1993.
Katz, Ephraim. *The Film Encyclopedia.* New York: HarperCollins, 1994.
Quart, Barbara. *Women Directors: The Emergence of a New Cinema.* New York: Praeger, 1988.
Vincendeau, Ginette. "Coline Serreau: A High Wire Act." *Sight and Sound* 4.3 (March 1994): 26–28.
Wagner, Martha. "*La Crise*." *Sight and Sound* 4.3 (March 1994): 37–38.

SHEPITKO, LARISSA (1939–79). Soviet Union. Larissa Shepitko's career is a case of a great talent whose work was cut short by a tragic death. A car crash outside Moscow in July 1979 abruptly terminated the life of a filmmaker on the verge of an international breakthrough as a mature and sophisticated film artist. Born in Armtervosk in the Eastern Ukraine, Shepitko began her studies at the age of sixteen at the VGIK Film School, where the great Soviet filmmaker Alexander Dovzhenko was one of her instructors. By 1962, Shepitko had completed two short films, *The Blind Cook* (1961) and *Living Water* (1962), and she caused a great sensation with her first feature film, *Heat* (1963), which she completed when she was only twenty-two years old.

Heat documents the daily struggle for existence on a state-run communal farm, located in Kirghizan. The shooting location was unbearably hot, and Shepitko drove herself and her crew unmercifully. Intense heat caused the film stock to melt in the camera (Quart, 7). Conditions were so brutal that the director came down with jaundice and had to be carried onto the set on a stretcher to shoot some sequences, but she refused to shut down production and continued shooting at a terrific pace. The intensity of her commitment to the material is readily discernible on the screen, as the struggles of the farm community become real and immediate to the audience.

Shepitko consolidated her burgeoning reputation with the feature films *Wings* (1966) and *You and I* (1972), both of which questioned aspects of Soviet society. *Wings* deals with the life of a woman who had been a fighter pilot for the Soviet army during World War II and now finds herself having difficulty coming to terms with postwar social commerce. *You and I* explores the life of a young Soviet doctor of medicine who has a career crisis and abruptly departs for Siberia with his wife in search of deeper meaning in his life. By 1977, Shepitko had added a fourth feature to her résumé, *The Ascent*. Arguably her most mature work, the film centers on a group of soldiers during World War II who fight in the winter of 1942 under unimaginably brutal conditions. Photographed in stark black and white, the film won the Golden Bear at the Berlin Festival in 1978. By this time, although Shepitko's films were "unofficially suppressed" (Quart, 5) in the former Soviet Union, American studios were reaching out to her, and it looked for a time as if she might be able to make the jump to filming in Hollywood. But while looking for locations for her new film, *Farewell*, Shepitko and several of her key film crew members died in an auto accident. Shepitko's husband, Elem Klimov, shot the script for *Farewell* and released it in 1981.

SELECTED FILMOGRAPHY

Znoi (*Heat*) (1963)
Krylia (*Wings*) (1966)
V trinadtsatom chasu (*At One O'Clock*) (1968)
Ty i ia (*You and I*) (1972)
Voskhozdenie (*The Ascent*) (1977)

SELECTED BIBLIOGRAPHY

Attwood, Lynn. *Red Women on the Silver Screen: Soviet Women and Cinema from the Beginning to the End of the Communist Era*. London: Pandora, 1993.
Mayne, Judith. *Kino and the Woman Question: Feminism and Soviet Silent Film*. Columbus: Ohio State University Press, 1989.
Quart, Barbara. "Between Materialism and Mysticism: The Films of Larissa Shepitko." *Cineaste* 16.3 (1988): 4–11.
Vronskaya, Jeanne. *Young Soviet Film Makers*. London: Allen and Unwin, 1972.
Youngblood, Denise J. "Shepitko, Larissa." In *The Women's Companion to International Film*, edited by Annette Kuhn, with Susannah Radstone, 364. Berkeley: University of California Press, 1994.

SHIPMAN, NELL (1892–1970). Canada/United States. Nell Shipman was born in Vancouver in 1892. She worked as an actress in theatrical stock companies before she entered the film industry. At the age of eighteen, she sold the rights to her book, *Under the Crescent,* to Universal to be made into a serial. She quickly developed a reputation as a talented writer, actress, and director. In 1916, she became an overnight success for her production of *God's Country and the Woman.* The film is based on a James Oliver Curwood story. Shipman produced, directed, and acted in the film. She is credited as one of the first directors to shoot her films almost entirely on location, and the outdoor cinematography of *God's Country and the Woman,* for example, directly contributed to the film's popularity.

In 1989, film historian William K. Everson noted that many of Nell Shipman's "lost" films were being rediscovered and restored. Because she shot many of her films on location in Idaho, Boise State University began collecting her work and issued her autobiography, *The Silent Screen and My Talking Heart.* Shipman's book describes her location shoots in detail. An excerpt from her book conveys Shipman's style and approach toward filmmaking:

I wanted the wilderness inhabitants to blend in and out: here a wolf, there a bear, over in a tree a cougar, a raccoon washing his dinner in a stream, squirrels popping in and out, bobcats peering, porcupines bristling, all of them dissolving in montage against the dark background while I, at the bottom of the frame, dreamed it. It was the most difficult double-exposure ever attempted. (78)

Shipman continued with a string of successes with *Back to God's Country* (1919) and many other outdoor "wild animal pictures." Audiences were drawn to the seemingly exotic locations and "wild" animals in her films. She artfully created a persona of herself as a rugged and exotic "New Woman" of outdoor adventure. She often adapted the material of "masculine" authors such as Zane Grey, Edgar Rice Burroughs, and James Oliver Curwood. She was remarkably adept at perceiving and manipulating audience expectations. For example, she frequently cast herself against type as a strong woman "having to protect a weak and ailing husband" (Everson, 229). As Peter Morris notes, *God's Country and the Woman* "more than hints that male authority figures may not have a right to that authority" (204). Nell Shipman was not only an outspoken feminist and director but also innovative and daring in her technical approach to film. She frequently asked her cameramen to set up unusual or dangerous scenes. Though Everson labels her films as "often derivative in their technique" (230), they bear a recognizable authorial stamp.

By the 1920s, Shipman's films decreased in popularity, so she closed down her production company in Idaho and sold her animals to the San Diego Zoo, but she remained active as a screenwriter and novelist. Her novel *Get the Woman* was serialized in *McCall's* magazine. In the 1960s, she wrote her autobiography. She is remembered as an author, actress, and an important pioneering director of outdoor cinematography. She is one of the free-spirited women of the period who headed her own production company as producer, writer, director, and star.

SELECTED FILMOGRAPHY

God's Country and the Woman (1916)
Baree, Son of Kazan (codirector) (1917)
Back to God's Country (1919)
Something New (codirector) (1920)
The Girl from God's Country (codirector) (1921)
The Grub Stake (codirector) (1923)
The Golden Yukon (codirector) (1927)

SELECTED BIBLIOGRAPHY

Acker, Ally. *Reel Women: Pioneers of the Cinema, 1896 to the Present.* New York: Continuum, 1993.

Everson, William K. "Rediscovery: The Films of Nell Shipman." *Films in Review* 40.4 (April 1989): 228–30.

Fulbright, Tom. "Queen of the Dog Sleds." *Classic Film Collector* (fall 1969): 31.

Morris, Peter. "The Taming of the Few: Nell Shipman in the Context of Her Times." In *The Silent Screen and My Talking Heart,* 195–205. Boise, ID: Boise State University Press, 1987.

Shipman, Nell. *The Silent Screen and My Talking Heart: An Autobiography.* Boise, ID: Hemingway Western Studies Series, Boise State University Press, 1987.

Slide, Anthony. *Early Women Directors.* New York: Da Capo, 1984.

Walker, Joseph, and Juanita Walker. "Danger in 'God's Country.'" *American Cinematographer* 66.5 (May 1985): 34–43.

SHUB, ESFIR (ESTHER) (1894–1959). Soviet Union. Ukrainian-born Esfir Shub is one of the most important pioneers of Soviet cinema. A gifted editor, she studied and emulated the techniques pioneered by Dziga Vertov and his wife and collaborator, Elizaveta Svilova. Vertov and Svilova formulated the constructivist style of montage, essentially a form of editing disparate shots into a seemingly whole idea. Shub's flair for montage was so startling that she was hired in 1922 by the government to recut and retitle American films to render them "suitable" for Russian audiences. Shub is credited with the creation of the "compilation film" (Petric, 22), a method of appropriational filmmaking that depends entirely on the use of preexisting footage. Shub recut newsreel footage very successfully and "discovered some crucial principles of editing and intertitling, which were further developed by Einstein, Vertov, Pudovkin, and Kuleshov" (Petric, 22).

The Fall of the Romanov Dynasty (1927) is one of Shub's most famous surviving films. She made the film because there was no visual record of the Russian Revolution. *The Fall of the Romanov Dynasty* is made up of stock footage and film that Shub shot herself to make up for the lack of documentation. According to Ephraim Katz, Shub's films "remain among the finest examples of creative editing" (1248). Shub also pioneered the Soviet realist documentary, along with her colleagues, such as Sergei Eisenstein. Eisenstein learned from Esfir Shub by observing her editing techniques. In Shub's memoirs, she recalls working with Eisenstein on a reedit of Fritz Lang's *Dr. Mabuse* (1922). Shub and Eisenstein influenced one another and shared an interest in documentary and formalist editing technique. She visited the set of Eisenstein's *October* (1928), where they spent much time discussing possible editing strategies for the film. Her relationship with Eisenstein was that of a collaborative friendship.

Shub considered Vertov a teacher, but she disagreed with his disdain for films based on scripts. Vertov himself considered Shub to be "one of the most significant figures in Soviet documentary film of the silent era" (Petric, 29). Both shared an equal preoccupation with authenticity, yet Shub felt that a documentary could include a mixture of staged events and authentic events. Shub's naturalist theories prefigured those of the school of Italian neorealism, pioneered by such directors as Elvira Notari and, many years later, Vittorio DeSica and Roberto Rossellini. All told, Esfir Shub worked for over twenty years in the Soviet cinema. She helped to pioneer the sound documentary with *The Komsomol—Sponsor of Electrification* (1932). She worked exclusively as an editor in the late 1940s and early 1950s and wrote extensively on filmmaking technique in her memoirs. She also wrote a script entitled *Women* (1933–34), which traced women's roles in cultural and historical context. Unfortunately, the project was never realized, but the script survives as a testament to Shub's feminism.

SELECTED FILMOGRAPHY

Padenie dinastii romanovykh (*The Fall of the Romanov Dynasty*) (1927)
Velikii put (*The Great Path*) (1927)
Rossiia Nikolaia II i Lev Tolstoi (*The Russia of Nicholas II and Lev Tolstoi*) (1928)
Segodnik (*Today*) (1930)
KShE (*Komsomol—Shef elektrifikatsii*) (*The Komsomol—Sponsor of Electrification*) (1932)
Moskva stroit metro (*Moscow Builds the Metro*) (1934)
Strano Sovetov (*The Country of the Soviets*) (1937)
Turtsiia na podeme (*Turkey at the Turning Point*) (1937)
Ispaniia (*Spain*) (1930)
20 let sovetskogo kino (*Twenty Years of Soviet Cinema*) (1940)
Fashizm budet razbit (*Fascism Will Be Defeated*) (1941)
Strana rodnaia (*Native Land*) (1942)
Sud v Smolenske (*Court in Smolensk*) (1946)

SELECTED BIBLIOGRAPHY

Attwood, Lynn. *Red Women on the Silver Screen: Soviet Women and Cinema from the Beginning to the End of the Communist Era*. London: Pandora, 1993.
Katz, Ephraim. *The Film Encyclopedia*. New York: HarperCollins, 1994.

Kuhn, Annette. *Women's Pictures: Feminism and Cinema*. London: Routledge, 1982.

Mayne, Judith. *Kino and the Woman Question: Feminism and Soviet Silent Film*. Columbus: Ohio State University Press, 1989.

Petric, Vlada. "Esther Shub: Film as a Historical Discourse." In *"Show Us Life": Toward A History of Aesthetics of the Committed Documentary,* edited by Thomas Waugh, 21–46. Metuchen, NJ: Scarecrow Press, 1984.

Shub, Esfir (Esther). *Zhizn moya—Kinematogra [My Life—Cinema]*. Moscow: Iskusstvo, 1972.

SILVER, JOAN MICKLIN (1935–   ). United States. Director and screenwriter Joan Micklin Silver was born in Omaha, Nebraska, in 1935. After studying at Sarah Lawrence College, she lived in Cleveland and worked as a teacher and theater director. In the 1960s, she and her husband and three daughters moved to New York City, where Silver wrote for the *Village Voice* and began her filmmaking career as a scriptwriter. In 1975, Silver directed her first feature film, *Hester Street*. As she told Letitia Kent, "Frankly what distinguished me from other independent filmmakers—men and women . . . was that I had a husband, who was able—and willing—to help me." Her husband, Raphael Silver, raised the money for their low-budget independent feature. *Hester Street* draws upon Joan Micklin Silver's experience as the daughter of Russian-Jewish immigrants, and the film concerns the assimilation of such immigrants in New York City at the turn of the century. Silver made the film for a modest sum of $370,000, but it grossed over $5 million in domestic theatrical receipts. Though the Silvers had to fight for wide distribution, *Hester Street* was launched as a critical success at the Cannes Film Festival in 1973. The success of *Hester Street* is all the more remarkable because it not only is filmed in black and white but is partly in Yiddish. It has a strong ethnic center and highlights the lives of several generations of Jewish immigrant women.

Crossing Delancey (1988) returns to material about the Jewish-American experience. The film centers on a young, acculturated Jewish professional woman and her grandmother, who plans to marry her off through a marriage broker. Silver's ability to render the characterizations of Jewish Americans and her gentle, yet knowing sense of ethnic humor are similar to Nancy Savoca's approach to her own Italian-American experience in *True Love* (1989). Joan Micklin Silver's success is probably attributable to her ability to infuse a sense of documentary into her commercially oriented narratives. Her daughter, Marisa Silver, is also a director. Marisa Silver's films include *Permanent Record* (1988) and *He Said She Said* (codirector Ken Kwapis, 1991).

SELECTED FILMOGRAPHY

Hester Street (1975)
Between the Lines (1977)

Chilly Scenes of Winter (1979)
Crossing Delancey (1988)
Lover Boy (1989)
Big Girls Don't Cry: They Get Even (1992)

SELECTED BIBLIOGRAPHY

Acker, Ally. *Reel Women: Pioneers of the Cinema, 1896 to the Present*. New York: Continuum, 1993.
Kent, Letitia. "They Were behind the Scenes of *Between the Lines*." *New York Times*, June 12, 1977, H15.
Lichtenstein, Grace. "For Woman Director, *Hester Street* is Victory." *New York Times*, October 15, 1975, 34.
Quart, Barbara. *Women Directors: The Emergence of a New Cinema*. New York: Praeger, 1988.
Silver, Joan Micklin. "Independent Charts Her Success." *American Film* 14 (May 1989): 22–27.

SOLNTSEVA, IULIIA (1901–   ). Soviet Union. Iuliia Solntseva is probably best known to film scholars for her work as an actress in Yakov Protazanov's *Aelita* (1924). Few writers acknowledge, however, her lifelong collaborative partnership with Aleksandr Dovzhenko. Solntseva met and married Dovzhenko in 1929 and soon became "co-director of all Dovzhenko's films" (Enzenberger, 373). Her last acting role was in his famous film *Earth* (1930). She is also credited as assistant director of the film. Iuliia Solntseva has been relegated to the role of enabler of male genius. Like many female partners of creative, collaborative couples, Solntseva seems to have been comfortable with this role. Even after Dovzhenko's death, Solntseva completed his *Poem of an Inland Sea* (1958) and later directed *Chronicle of Flaming Years* (1961) and *The Enchanted Desna* (1964), both based on Dovzhenko's writings.

Iuliia Solntseva's immersion in Dovzhenko's identity is hard to understand from a modern feminist perspective. After his death, Solntseva said, "I must complete [*Poem of an Inland Sea*] in accordance with Dovzhenko's artistic conception, putting aside every trace of my own individual vision" (Enzenberger, 374). In addition to the two films previously mentioned made in 1961 and 1964, based on Dovzhenko's work, she directed *The Unforgettable* (1968), another film based on Dovzhenko's writings, and also created a film about her relationship with the director, *Zolotie vorota* (1971), also known as *The Golden Gate*. Tellingly, her 1974 film, *Takiie vysokiie gory* (*Such High Mountains*), gives us a glimpse of what Solntseva might have created had she not so thoroughly subsumed her identity within Dovzhenko's name. At the very least, one must consider her the cocreator of Dovzhenko's films and a woman who never received the credit due her for her considerable contribution to the art of Soviet cinema. There is no question that Solntseva's love, admiration, and respect for Dovzhenko were real and sincere, but it is unfortunate that she apparently felt that she had to live her life in the cinema so thoroughly through his works.

SELECTED FILMOGRAPHY

Bukovina—zemlia ukrainskaia (*Bukovina—Ukrainian Land*) (1940)
Bitva na nashu Sovietskaiu Ukrainu (*The Fight for Our Soviet Ukraine*) (1943)
Yegor Bulichov and Others (1953)
Revizori ponevole (*Unwilling Inspectors*) (1955)
Poema o morie (*Poem of an Inland Sea*) (1958)
Povest plamennikh let (*Chronicle of Flaming Years*) (1961)
Zacharovannaia Desna (*The Enchanted Desna*) (1964)
Nazabivaiemoie (*The Unforgettable*) (1968)
Zolotie vorota (*The Golden Gate*) (1971)
Takiie vysokiie gory (*Such High Mountains*) (1974)
Mir v triokh izmereniiakh (*The World in Three Dimensions*) (1980)

SELECTED BIBLIOGRAPHY

Attwood, Lynn. *Red Women on the Silver Screen: Soviet Women and Cinema from the Beginning to the End of the Communist Era*. London: Pandora, 1993.
Chadwick, Whitney, and Isabelle de Courtivron, eds. *Significant Others: Creativity and Intimate Partnership*. London: Thames and Hudson, 1993.
Dovzhenko, Alexander. *The Poet as Filmmaker: Selected Writings*. Edited and translated by Marco Carynnyk. Cambridge: MIT Press, 1973.
Enzenberger, Maria. "Solntseva, Iuliia." In *The Women's Companion to International Film,* edited by Annette Kuhn, with Susannah Radstone, 373–74. Berkeley: University of California Press, 1994.
Mayne, Judith. *Kino and the Woman Question: Feminism and Soviet Silent Film*. Columbus: Ohio State University Press, 1989.
Quart, Barbara. *Women Directors: The Emergence of a New Cinema*. New York: Praeger, 1988.
Usai, Paolo Cherchi, Lorenzo Codelli, Carlo Montanaro, and David Robinson, eds. *Silent Witnesses: Russian Films, 1908–1919*. London: BFI, 1989.

SPHEERIS, PENELOPE (1946–   ). United States. Penelope Spheeris is something of an anomaly; she began her career as an independent film-maker specializing in documentaries about rock and roll, then directed a film for exploitation producer Roger Corman (*Suburbia*, 1984), and, after directing the violent thriller *Hollywood Vice Squad* (1986), moved on to comedy in *Wayne's World* (1992), *The Beverly Hillbillies* (1993), and *The Little Rascals* (1994).

Spheeris is candid about her upbringing and her introduction to the world of cinema:

Here is the trailer for the movie of my life: I was born at this carnival that my father owned called Magic Empire Shows. He was a Greek immigrant, my brothers and sisters were born in different states, he got murdered over a racial incident in Alabama when I was seven, my mother sold the carnival, we travelled around living in trailer courts. You're talking to some poor white trash right here. And then we kind of settled in Orange County. I started working as a waitress when I was 14 and then I went to UCLA. (Jarrell, 24).

From then on, Spheeris's intense determination to make films got her through the early stages of her career, and her apprenticeship to Corman helped her learn to bring her films in on time and on budget. Before her association with Corman, Spheeris directed a number of short, satirical films for the television program "Saturday Night Live" and produced Albert Brooks's first film as a director, *Real Life* (1978).

But *The Decline of Western Civilization* (1981), a documentary on the Los Angeles punk rock scene, put Spheeris firmly in the public eye. Shot on a shoestring budget, the film vibrantly captured the energy and desperation of the punk movement. Her 1988 sequel, *The Decline of Western Civilization II: The Metal Years,* was also cheerfully incisive. The sequel covers the club scene with vigor and wit, featuring such bands as Faster Pussycat, Kill, Kill, and a scene in which a surprisingly domesticated Ozzy Osborne fries some eggs at home and ruminates on the ups and downs of his career with Black Sabbath and later as a solo artist. Both films were modest commercial hits, but her dramatic features did less well at the box office.

In 1992, however, Lorne Michaels of "Saturday Night Live" proposed Spheeris to direct *Wayne's World* (1992), and Spheeris shot the film on a modest budget of $14 million. The film went on to gross more than $100 million in the United States alone and spawned a sequel, *Wayne's World II,* which Spheeris did not direct. *The Beverly Hillbillies* is a rather bland adaptation of the hit 1960s television series, and *The Little Rascals,* which did surprisingly well at the box office, is a somewhat subdued homage to the long-running series of two-reel comedies from the 1930s. As she gets bigger and bigger projects, Spheeris's style becomes more and more utilitarian; her camera work becomes almost documentary, and she delights in printing lengthy sections of outtakes at the ends of her recent films over the credits. Spheeris's true passion seems to lie with the disfranchised and marginalized youth of contemporary American society, and her two documentaries on rock music remain her finest work. As a commercial feature director, in contrast, Penelope Spheeris sometimes seems uninvolved in her most recent projects. *Wayne's World* had plenty of inspired lunacy, but her two most recent films merely fulfill the requirements of the genre. Nevertheless, Spheeris's understanding of the commercial aspects of filmmaking would seem to ensure that she will be around for a long time as a director.

SELECTED FILMOGRAPHY

The Decline of Western Civilization (1981)
Suburbia (1984)
The Boys Next Door (1985)

Hollywood Vice Squad (1986)
Dudes (1987)
The Decline of Western Civilization II: The Metal Years (1988)
Wayne's World (1992)
The Beverly Hillbillies (1993)
The Little Rascals (1994)

SELECTED BIBLIOGRAPHY

Acker, Ally. *Reel Women: Pioneers of the Cinema, 1896 to the Present.* New York:
    Continuum, 1993.
Cole, Janis, and Holly Dale. *Calling the Shots: Profiles of Women Filmmakers.*
    Ontario: Quarry Press, 1993.
Diamond, Jamie. "Penelope Spheeris: From Carny Life to *Wayne's World.*" *New
    York Times,* April 12, 1992, 11H, 20H.
Elfman, Danny. "Penelope Spheeris and Danny Elfman." *American Film* 16.2 (Feb-
    ruary 1991): 42–45.
Jarrell, Joe. "Talkin' to Poor White Trash: Penelope Spheeris Speaks Her Mind."
    High Performance 14 (September 1991): 24–25.
Katz, Ephraim. *The Film Encyclopedia.* New York: HarperCollins, 1994.
Smith, Sharon. *Women Who Make Movies.* New York: Hopkinson and Blake,
    1975.

STONEHOUSE, RUTH (1893–1941). United States. Ruth Stonehouse was
born in 1893. She was a dancer in vaudeville at the age of eight and later
became an actress and a partner in the Essanay Studios of Chicago, with
Bronco Billy Anderson. She was one of Essanay's leading stars as early as
1911. In 1916, Stonehouse joined many women who wrote, directed, and
starred in their own films at Universal Pictures. Carl Laemmle, head of
Universal, hired many women directors, including Lois Weber, Ida May
Park, Cleo Madison, Grace Cunard, Elsie Jane Wilson, and Ruth Ann Baldwin.

Ruth Stonehouse was a dancer, aerialist, writer, actress, and producer/
director. Because the films she directed are unavailable or lost, it is hard to
summarize her directorial career. She told interviewers that she was proud
to direct her own "stuff" and that her ambition was to become a good
director. Ally Acker notes that Stonehouse was perceived as a submissive
"little girl" actress (65), which she seems to have overcome by producing,
directing, and writing. In the 1920s, Stonehouse returned to acting in character roles. She is remembered primarily as an actress who played alongside
Harry Houdini, Norma Shearer, and many other silent film stars. She felt
that she was typecast as too good-natured and not aggressive enough, and
she sought to overcome her image through active participation behind the
camera.

SELECTED FILMOGRAPHY

Dorothy Dares (1916)
The Heart of Mary Ann (1916)

Mary Ann in Society (1916)
Tacky Sue's Romance (1917)
The Stolen Actress (1917)
Daredevil Dan (1917)
A Limb of Satan (1917)
A Walloping Time (1917)

SELECTED BIBLIOGRAPHY

Acker, Ally. *Reel Women: Pioneers of the Cinema, 1896 to the Present.* New York: Continuum, 1993.
Heck-Rabi, Louise. *Women Filmmakers: A Critical Reception.* Metuchen, NJ: Scarecrow Press, 1984.
Katz, Ephraim. *The Film Encyclopedia.* New York: HarperCollins, 1994.
Rainey, Buck. *Those Fabulous Serial Heroines: Their Lives and Films.* Metuchen, NJ: Scarecrow Press, 1990.
Slide, Anthony. *Early Women Directors.* New York: Da Capo, 1984.

STREISAND, BARBRA (1942–   ). United States. Barbra Streisand was born Joan Streisand in Brooklyn, New York, in 1942. Her superstar status as a singer allowed her the opportunity to direct feature films. *Yentl* (1983) is an adaptation of Isaac Bashevis Singer's story. Streisand stars in the film as a young Jewish woman who wishes to study the Talmud and cross-dresses in order to appear as a man. *Yentl* is an interesting study of patriarchal definitions of religious devotion, though it was a critical failure. Streisand presents a female figure who is interested in studying sacred texts rather than conforming to a life of preconfigured, gender-coded behavior. In the next several years, Streisand concentrated on other aspects of her career but found the time to star in Martin Ritt's *Nuts* (1987), in which she turned in a remarkable performance as a prostitute charged with murder.

Streisand's next feature film as director, *Prince of Tides* (1991), is an investigation of gender identity, specifically, constructions of male identity. Nick Nolte stars in the film as a failed husband who is desperate to remake his identity with the help of a psychiatrist, played by Barbra Streisand. Streisand documents the outdated, stereotypically defined southern marriage as it unravels and exposes itself as a patriarchally defined nuclear family hopelessly mired in patterns of verbal and emotional abuse. Unfortunately, Streisand constructs the female psychiatrist as a muse who helps Nolte's character reconstruct his marriage, conforming to a pattern common to melodramatic Hollywood formula. However, Streisand is successful in her treatment of men's issues. The plot of the movie turns on Nolte's memory of being brutally raped as a child. The strictly defined social decorum of the South necessitated the complete silencing and repression of the event. As Streisand heals the vulnerable male, he comes to grips with the consequences of silenced events such as rape and battery. As Stuart

Poyntz notes, however, the rhetoric of the vulnerable male is used as a backdrop to reinforce notions of the supremacy of the nuclear family. "The only way this new man can sustain his new relationship with his body is by establishing a security and stability built on the control of . . . female authority" (Poyntz, 36). *Prince of Tides* is a step in the direction of issues around the construction of male identity, but it is painfully mired in the reconstruction of the patriarchal family. Barbra Streisand is at the preproduction stage with several films including *The Mirror Has Two Faces,* and an adaptation of Larry Kramer's *The Normal Heart,* a play about survival and AIDS.

SELECTED FILMOGRAPHY

Yentl (1983)
The Prince of Tides (1991)

SELECTED BIBLIOGRAPHY

Acker, Ally. *Reel Women: Pioneers of the Cinema, 1896 to the Present.* New York: Continuum, 1993.
Gross, Barry. "No Victim, She: Barbra Streisand and the Movie Jew." *Journal of Ethnic Studies* 3.1 (spring 1975): 28–40.
Jackson, Lynne, and Karen Jaehne. "Eavesdropping on Female Voices." *Cineaste* 16. 1–2 (1988): 38–43.
Poyntz, Stuart. "Hurt, Vulnerable and Sweaty: Looking in *Prince of Tides* and the Weight Room." *Reverse Shot* 1.1 (January 1994): 32–37.
Quart, Barbara. *Women Directors: The Emergence of a New Cinema.* New York: Praeger, 1988.

SVILOVA, ELIZAVETA (1900–75). Soviet Union. Few film historians recognize the important contribution of Soviet filmmaker Elizaveta Svilova. She is the uncredited collaborator and wife of the famous documentarist Dziga Vertov, who is considered the "father" of Soviet documentary. Svilova was a brilliant editor who contributed to the Kino-eye group, of which Vertov and Svilova were members. The Kino-eye group was dedicated to the theory and practice of Soviet montage, a formalist technique of film editing. Montage theorists were fascinated by the effects of film cutting that could reconstruct reality through the diagetic frame. The relationship between shots created new meaning through the interrelationship of close-ups, angles, movement within the frame, light and shade, and film speed. As Masha Enzenberger explains, "Vertov's experimental work in editing overlapped with the previous and simultaneous discoveries of acted cinema like Kuleshov, Eisenstein [and] Pudovkin" (101).

Elizaveta Svilova, like Esfir Shub, recognized the value of reediting documentary footage. Svilova noted the paucity of previous attention to the documentary form, stating that "it has never entered the head of a single director that documentary material can be edited into montage, that documentary material is life" (Enzenberger, 101). Svilova was not interested in narrative fictional film but, rather, in montage documentary form. She is variously credited as Vertov's editor, assistant, and codirector. Svilova and Vertov's collaborative partnership resulted in classic documentaries such as *Man with a Movie Camera* (1929). Using a wide array of optical effects, coupled with a dazzling display of virtuoso editing, *Man with a Movie Camera* chronicles one day in the life of a movie cameraman as he photographs life in the city. At once kinetic and formalist, the film is a landmark in experimental cinema. Other famous and important films, directed by Elizaveta Svilova and Dziga Vertov, include *Enthusiasm* (1930) and *Three Songs of Lenin* (1934).

In the 1930s, when Vertov was not employed, Svilova supported him by securing a career as a film editor. In addition, she continued to direct her own work. In the 1940s, the couple were able to find work together as documentarists. Svilova won the Stalin Prize for her work as editor in 1946 on her film *Fascist Atrocities,* which was actually used as evidence in the Nuremberg trials. Svilova shot another film, *Peoples' Trial* (1946), on the proceedings of the Nuremberg trials. After her husband's death in 1954, Svilova was largely responsible for the publication and dissemination of Vertov's theoretical work. She also diligently maintained archival prints of her husband's (and her uncredited) work. The legacy of Elizaveta Svilova, like that of many women directors whose lives were obscured by their famous husbands, remains to be rediscovered and contextualized. Recently, feminist theorists and historians, such as Masha Enzenberger and Lynne Atwood, have "rediscovered" women directors such as Elizaveta Svilova and Iiullia Solntseva.

SELECTED FILMOGRAPHY

O transporte (About Transport) (1939)
V kolkhozakh uchatsia (They Learn at the Collective Farms) (1939)
Krisha mira (The Roof of the World) (1940)
Reka Chusovaia (The Chusovaia River) (1940)
Piatiletie metro (Five Years of the Metro) (1940)
V predgoriakh Alatau (Near the Alatau Mountains) (1943)
Kliatva molodikh (The Oath of the Young) (1943)
Osventsim Auschwitz, Burei rozhdionnie (Born by the Storm) (1945)
Parad molodosti (The Parade of the Youth) (1946)
Zverstva fashistov (Fascist Atrocities) (1946)
Sud narodov (Peoples' Trial) (1946)
Slavianski kongress v Belgrade (The Slavonic Congress in Belgrade (1947)

SELECTED BIBLIOGRAPHY

Attwood, Lynn. *Red Women on the Silver Screen: Soviet Women and Cinema from the Beginning to the End of the Communist Era.* London: Pandora, 1993.
Enzenberger, Masha. "Dziga Vertov." *Screen* 13.4 (1972–73): 90–107.

Mayne, Judith. *Kino and the Woman Question: Feminism and Soviet Silent Film.* Columbus: Ohio State University Press, 1989.

Quart, Barbara. *Women Directors: The Emergence of a New Cinema.* New York: Praeger, 1988.

Vertov, Dziga. *Statii, Dnevniki, Zamysly.* Moscow: Iskusstvo, 1966.

T

TANAKA, KINUYO (1909–77). Japan. Kinuyo Tanaka is considered Japan's first woman director. Very few women have had the opportunity to direct in the Japanese film industry. She is also well known for her work as an actress in many films directed by Yasujiro Ozu and Kenji Mizoguchi, in which she excelled at roles that are defined by a limited patriarchal perspective. As a director, however, Kinuyo Tanaka instinctively displayed a "feminist awareness" (Yamuda, 399). Unfortunately, she was able to direct only two films due to the pressure to remove women from all leadership positions in the Japanese film industry. As Joanne Yamuda notes, director Kenji Mizoguchi (once head of the directors' union) "decreed that women should not make films" (399). Within this sort of a misogynist milieu, it is amazing that Tanaka was able to direct even a few films.

Love Letter (1953) is Tanaka's first film. It is a slightly feminist melodrama in the *shemin-geki* genre, which traditionally exposes the lives of everyday Japanese people. Tanaka's next film, *The Moon Has Risen* (1955), is a distinctly feminist melodrama. Based on a story written by Yasujiro Ozu, *The Moon Has Risen* concerns the plight of three sisters. The youngest sister is incapable of abiding by the strictly enforced codes of behavior expected of Japanese women.

Kinuyo Tanaka is one of the few women directors of the Japanese cinema. Hopefully, more women will be afforded the opportunity to direct in the future in Japan; their alternative vision is certainly needed.

SELECTED FILMOGRAPHY

Koibumi (*Love Letter*) (1953)
Tsuki ga Agarinu (*The Moon Has Risen*) (1955)

SELECTED BIBLIOGRAPHY

Anderson, Joseph L., and Donald Richie. *The Japanese Film*. Princeton: Princeton University Press, 1982.

Noletti, Arthur Jr., and David Desser, eds. *Reframing Japanese Cinema: Authorship, Genre, History.* Bloomington: Indiana University Press, 1992.

Yamuda, Joanne Y. "Tanaka, Kinuyo." In *The Women's Companion to International Film,* edited by Annette Kuhn and Susannah Radstone, 398–99. Berkeley: University of California Press, 1994.

TODD, LORETTA (1961–   ). Canada/Native American. Based in Vancouver, British Columbia, Native American director Loretta Todd is an intellectual and an activist. "My work is about empowerment," she told Sally Berger, adding, "It is not about power but hoping to influence the way people look at power, look at the world." *The Learning Path* (1991) is a documentary on the education of Native children. Todd interviewed several teachers for the film, who speak about the harsh effects of acculturation on young children schooled in white, church-owned, residential school systems. Todd feels that Native children desperately need images of their own lives and their own stories to empower and enrich their existence.

As a feminist, Todd notes that feminist filmic practice has brought change for all the members of the human family. She sees "the male and female [as] being the wings of the eagle. If one wing is harmed, we can't live" (Berger). Thus, her work seeks to create a new cultural, visual identity for Native Americans outside the narrow constraints of dominant Hollywood cinema. Now working in Vancouver, Todd realizes that her work is only beginning and that in the "process [of making films] I may have to reveal painful things" (Berger). But she is aware that to cling to outdated stereotypes is even more painful, and so she has chosen to create and record new images that will give Native American viewers a world to which they can relate and that they can inhabit. Beyond that, Todd's work is for all persons who would seek to transcend the artificial and delimiting boundaries of race, class, color, creed, and enforced societal sexual "identity."

SELECTED FILMOGRAPHY

The Learning Path (1991)
Forgotten Warriors (1995)

SELECTED BIBLIOGRAPHY

Bataille, Gretchen, and Charles L. P. Silet, eds. *The Pretend Indians.* Ames: Iowa State University Press, 1980.

Berger, Sally. "American Indians: The Films of a Native Daughter." *Interview* 23.4 (April 1993): 113.

Gunn Allen, Paula. *The Sacred Hoop.* Boston: Beacon Press, 1992.

Weatherford, Elizabeth, ed. *Native Americans on Film and Video.* New York: Museum of the American Indian, 1981.

TOYE, WENDY (1917–   ). United Kingdom. Wendy Toye began her career as a dancer and made her professional debut at the age of three at the

Albert Hall in London. By the age of nine, she was choreographing a dance extravaganza entitled *Japanese Legend of the Rainbow* to the music of Scarlatti at the London Palladium. In her teens, she danced at the Café de Paris in London with the Markova-Dollin Ballet Company and watched Sergei Diaghilev's famed Ballet Russe rehearse when the company was working with Jean Cocteau. By 1931, she appeared in a bit part as a dancer in Anthony Asquith's *Dance Pretty Lady,* which led to other film work as a dancer. In 1935, she worked as a choreographer on Paul Herzbach's *Invitation to the Waltz,* picking up valuable technical information along the way. Her break as film director came when producer George Arthur asked her to direct the short film *The Stranger Left No Card* (1952). Toye had originally been slated to do the choreography only but agreed to direct the film at the last minute when David Lean backed out of the project. Working with a budget of £3,000 and shooting without sync sound (using gramophone records to cue the actors), Toye finished the film on time and under budget. Cocteau, who was by this time chairman of the jury at the Cannes Film Festival, saw the finished film and enthusiastically endorsed it. He awarded *The Stranger Left No Card* the prize for Best Short Film of the 1953 Cannes Festival, and Toye's career was truly launched.

Put under contract to Alexander Korda's London Films Company, Toye was next assigned to direct *The Teckman Mystery* (1954), a suspense film for which she has no particular affection. Then, with *Raising a Riot* (1955), she shifted to broad British comedy and found herself with a substantial commercial hit on her hands. Comic Kenneth More, then a huge British star, agreed to appear in the film as a man forced to deal with being a "house-husband" at a time when the term did not even exist. As Toye put it in a 1992 interview with Wheeler Winston Dixon, "[T]here's a subtext in *Raising a Riot* in a very jokey way, isn't there? It's simply that in domestic matters, a man doesn't cope with it all quite as well as a woman" (141). *All for Mary* (1955) and *True as a Turtle* (1956) followed, and Toye was typed in the light comedy vein much against her will. By her own admission, Toye was interested more in fantasy material, but up to and including her last feature film, *The King's Breakfast* (1963), she was unable to break the stereotypical image that both the public and producers had of her as a comedy director.

In 1981, she directed a videotape version of *The Stranger Left No Card* for Anglia Television, starring Derek Jacobi. Until a recent illness curtailed her activities, she continued as a theater director, with productions of *See How They Run* at the Watermill Theatre in London and road tours of *The Sound of Music.* Summing up her career, Toye told Dixon, "[P]eople say, 'you've never been a feminist, and you never fight for women' . . . but I think an example of doing something and getting on with it . . . is probably better than getting on a platform . . . by being didactic, you alienate a large part of your audience" (142). In all her work, Wendy Toye has carried forward a coded feminist message that simultaneously empowers both men and women. Wendy Toye may feel her career did not turn out precisely as she expected, but in such films as *Raising a Riot* and *A Life to Be Lived* (1961), she has left a legacy of considerable substance and value. As Caroline Merz observes, "[I]t is the double personal input—of fantasy and the women's point of view—that makes her comedies so distinctive" (129).

SELECTED FILMOGRAPHY

The Stranger Left No Card (1952)
Three Cases of Murder (Toye directed one section, *In the Picture*) (1953)
The Teckman Mystery (1954)
On the Twelfth Day (1955)
Raising a Riot (1955)
All for Mary (1955)
True as a Turtle (1956)
A Life to Be Lived (1961)
We Joined the Navy (1962)
The King's Breakfast (1963)

SELECTED BIBLIOGRAPHY

Barr, Charles, ed. *All Our Yesterdays: 90 Years of British Cinema.* London: BFI, 1986.
Betts, Ernest. *The Film Business: A History of British Cinema: 1896–1972.* London: Allen and Unwin, 1973.
Dixon, Wheeler Winston. "An Interview with Wendy Toye." In *Re-Viewing British Cinema, 1900–1992: Essays and Interviews,* edited by Wheeler Winston Dixon, 133–42. Albany: SUNY Press, 1994.
Gifford, Denis. *The British Film Catalogue, 1895–1970: A Reference Guide.* New York: McGraw-Hill, 1973.
Merz, Caroline. "The Tension of Genre: Wendy Toye and Muriel Box." In *Re-Viewing British Cinema, 1900–1992: Essays and Interviews,* edited by Wheeler Winston Dixon, 121–31. Albany, SUNY Press, 1994.

TREUT, MONIKA (1954–   ). Germany. Monika Treut is one of the most controversial and influential directors of the New German Lesbian Cinema. Treut studied German and politics before she became involved in women's guerrilla filmmaking. As cofounder of the Women's Media Centre at Bildwechsel, Treut first worked as a video artist and later moved into filmmaking. *Seduction: The Cruel Woman* (codirected with Elfi Mikesch) (1984–85) elicited a wave of criticism and controversy, for the film is a study of sadomasochism that presents it as a means of control over the body. Set in a brothel, *Seduction: The Cruel Woman* is a postmodern experimental film that threatens preconfigured notions of female sexuality.

The Virgin Machine (1988) is a comic lesbian coming-out narrative. In the film, a journalist searches for love. She ends up leaving Germany and going to San Francisco, where she meets performance artist Susie Sexpert.

Susie takes the journalist on a whirlwind tour of San Francisco gay sub-culture, a world where women indulge in sadomasochistic sexual practices, strip shows, call-girl services, and a host of sexual practices. *The Virgin Machine* helped revolutionize the manner in which lesbian sexuality has been traditionally represented on the screen.

As a documentarist, Treut has also opened new areas of sexual transgression in lesbian cinema. *Female Misbehavior* (1992) is a collection of Treut's short documentaries, including *Bondage* (1983), *Annie* (1989), and *Max* (1992), a film about a female-to-male transsexual. *Female Misbehavior* also includes a short film that parodies the famous academic Camille Paglia. Treut's feature film, *My Father Is Coming* (1991), is also about transgressive sexuality. The film features the work of performance artists Annie Sprinkle and Susie Bright. As Julia Knight notes, "Treut has angered some lesbians by her failure to deliver the goods in terms of lesbian erotica" (185). Nevertheless, Treut reenvisions a transgressive cinema of sexual representation that challenges heterocentric presumptions and expectations.

SELECTED FILMOGRAPHY

Berlinale 80 (codirector) (1980)
Space Chaser (codirector) (1980)
Ich brauche unbedingt Kommunikation (*I Really Need Communication*) (1981)
Kotz-Bitchband (1981)
Die Frau von Übermorgen (*The Woman from the Day after Tomorrow*) (codirector) (1981)
Bondage (1983)
Verführung: die grausame Frau (*Seduction: The Cruel Woman*) (codirector Elfi Mikesch) (1984–85)
Die Jungfrauen Maschine (*The Virgin Machine*) (1988)
My Father Is Coming (1991)
Female Misbehavior (1992)
Erotique (1993)

SELECTED BIBLIOGRAPHY

de Lauretis, Teresa. *The Practice of Love: Lesbian Sexuality and Perverse Desire.* Bloomington: Indiana University Press, 1994.
Gibson, Pamela Church, and Roma Gibson, eds. *Dirty Looks: Women, Pornography, Power.* Bloomington: Indiana University Press, 1993.
Hart, Lynda, and Peggy Phelan, eds. *Acting Out: Feminist Performances.* Ann Arbor: University of Michigan Press, 1993.
Knight, Julia. "Female Misbehaviour: The Cinema of Monika Treut." In *Women and Film: A Sight and Sound Reader,* edited by Pam Cook and Philip Dodd, 180–85. Philadelphia: Temple University Press, 1993.

TRINH T. MINH-HA (1953–   ). Vietnam/United States. Trinh T. Minh-ha revolutionized documentary filmmaking with her poststructuralist documentaries that displace the voyeuristic gaze of the ethnographic documentary filmmaker. Theorist, filmmaker, and composer, she is one of the most respected postcolonial artists of the late twentieth century. Born in Vietnam, she came to the United States in 1970. After graduate school, she studied in Senegal and Dakar. Her work as an ethnographer led her to question the notions of ethnography. She argues that ethnographic filmmaking did not objectively represent the Third World subject, and she questioned the validity of "objective truth." In her first film, *Reassemblage* (1982), she redefined the documentary form by exposing its limited designs. *Reassemblage,* ostensibly "about" women in Senegal, is, instead, a film that challenges the role of the colonialized "other" (Third World women) as subjects of the filmmaker's gaze. *Reassemblage* was hailed as a critical success. Trinh writes extensively on her own work, and she is frequently part of interviews among prominent filmmakers and theorists.

Surname Viet, Given Name Nam (1989) looks not only at the role of Vietnamese women but at Trinh T. Minh-ha herself. The film is a metanarrative of interviews of Vietnamese women in Vietnam and the United States. Also included are archival footage, poetry, art, printed text, and footage of refugee camps in the United States. *Surname Viet, Given Name Nam* is a poetic investigation and celebration of Vietnamese women's rejection of their subjecthood. It is an avant-garde documentary that redefines the genre of the ethnographic film, as it redefines the positionality of the filmmaker. She is a revolutionary thinker whose work extends beyond filmmaking and critical film discourse. Her postcolonial feminist criticism, particularly her book *Woman, Native, Other,* has been extremely significant to cross-cultural studies and literary criticism. She, in turn, is inspired by writers such as Assia Djebar, Clarice Lispector, and Zora Neale Hurston, as well as critics such as Gilles Deleuze, Hélène Cixous, and Roland Barthes and filmmakers such as Chantal Akerman, Valeria Sarmiento, and Yvonne Rainer. Trinh T. Minh-ha is a well-recognized and active member of the academic community. She is a professor of cinema at San Francisco State University.

SELECTED FILMOGRAPHY

Reassemblage (1982)
Naked Spaces: Living Is Round (1985)
Surname Viet, Given Name Nam (1989)
Shoot for the Contents (1991)

SELECTED BIBLIOGRAPHY

Hill, Michael. "Abandoned to Difference: Identity, Opposition and Trinh T. Minh-ha's *Reassemblage.*" *Surfaces* 3.2 (1993): 1–29.
Jayamanne, Laleen, Leslie Thornton, and Trinh T. Minh-ha. "If upon Leaving What We Have to Say We Speak: A Conversation Piece." In *Discourses: Conversations in Postmodern Art and Culture,* edited by Russell Ferguson, William Olander, Marcia Tucker, and Karen Fiss, 44–66. Cambridge: MIT Press, 1990.

Mayne, Judith. *The Woman at the Keyhole: Feminism and Women's Cinema*. Bloomington: Indiana University Press, 1990.

Penley, Constance, and Andrew Ross. "Interview with Trinh T. Minh-ha." *Camera Obscura* 13–14 (spring–summer 1985): 86–111.

Trinh T. Minh-ha. "Outside in Inside Out." In *Questions of Third Cinema*, edited by Jim Pines and Paul Willemen, 133–49. London: BFI, 1989.

———. *Woman, Native, Other: Writing Postcoloniality and Feminism*. Bloomington: Indiana University Press, 1989.

———. *Framer Framed*. New York: Routledge, 1992.

Women Make Movies. *Women Make Movies Catalogue*. New York: Women Make Movies, 1994.

TROCHE, ROSE (1965–   ). United States. Rose Troche burst on the international film scene with the seemingly "overnight" success of her lesbian comedy/drama *Go Fish* (1994). Actually, the film was first conceived as a short entitled *Max and Ely* in 1991, written by Troche and Guinevere Turner, then both in their twenties (Rich, 14). When money ran out on the project, Troche and Turner asked producer Christine Vachon to assist, and the film was completed in 1993. Screened at Sundance, the film was an immediate hit, leading to a distribution deal with the Samuel Goldwyn Company before the festival even ended.

Troche crafted *Go Fish* as a series of deeply textured, carefully sculpted black-and-white images, and the narrative structure of the film pushes far beyond anything that had previously been done in the commercial cinema, for *Go Fish* became the first big breakthrough lesbian feature film. Critic J. Hoberman called *Go Fish* "extremely well shot and imaginatively edited . . . managing to be at once romantic and matter-of-fact sexy" (36). Martha Baer calls the film "brazen, muscular, tossing out all the apologies rife in the queer canon" and yet notes "a kind of shyness the entire film has about it" (Baer, 70).

As the first widely distributed film about "what a bunch of dykes do when no straight people are looking, where they live, what they like, how they fuck (or don't), and what they wear when dating" (Baer, 69), *Go Fish* is a landmark eruption of the lesbian consciousness transcribed and reinscribed across the screen of the dominant patriarchal cinema. It will be interesting to see how Troche and Turner cope with the media attention that is now being focused on them; one hopes that *despite* all the attention they are now receiving, they will be able to create equally daring and original work in the future.

SELECTED FILMOGRAPHY

Go Fish (1994)

SELECTED BIBLIOGRAPHY

Baer, Martha. "Go Figure." *Village Voice* 39.26 (June 28, 1994): 69–70.
Franke, Lizzie. *"Go Fish." Sight and Sound* 4.7 (July 1994): 42.
Hoberman, J. "Picking Up the Slack." *Premiere* 7.10 (June 1994): 35–36.
Rich, B. Ruby. "Goings and Comings." *Sight and Sound* 4.7 (July 1994): 14–16.

V

VARDA, AGNES (1928–). France. Agnes Varda was born in Brussels in 1928 to parents of Greek-French origin. She studied at the Sorbonne and the Ecole du Louvre. Before she became a film director, she spent several years working as a still photographer at the Théâtre National Populaire. Varda's background in still photography is evident in her filmmaking, which reveals an analytic eye for detail. Critics who discuss the New Wave in French film, which ostensibly began in 1959 with the first films of Jean-Luc Godard (*Breathless*) and François Truffaut (*The 400 Blows*), often forget that Agnes Varda was, in the words of Ginette Vincendeau, "the mother of the New Wave" (411), with the creation of her landmark 1954 film *La Pointe-Courte*. The film was rapidly and inexpensively made, and its production values and artistic concerns were quickly adopted by Truffaut, Godard, and other New Wave filmmakers. Varda consolidated her international reputation with the release of her second feature, *Cléo de 5 à 7* (*Cleo from 5 to 7*), made in 1961.

Cleo from 5 to 7 reveals the everyday details of the life of a female pop singer who, believing she has a terminal illness, spends her hours in a state of philosophical hyperawareness. *Cleo from 5 to 7* is a meditation on the state of femininity in France in the cultural movement of the 1960s. Varda told Barbara Confino that the film "was made at a time when psychosis of cancer was very strong in France as well as the idea that a woman should be blonde and busty." In the film, Varda displaces this notion of femininity, as typified by the stereotypes of the "nun and the whore, the mama and the bitch. . . . [W]e have put up with that [image] for years, and it has to be changed" (Confino). Though Agnes Varda has not always been welcomed into the feminist canon, recent reevaluations, such as that of Sandy Flitterman-Lewis and Susan Hayward, allow for a reclaiming of Varda's oeuvre as feminist texts. In fact, Susan Hayward observes with curiosity that "Varda's work is often passed over in silence in anthologies on women's film—and yet she herself claims to be an avowed feminist" (285).

In addition to the feminist aesthetics at work in *Vagabond* (1985), Varda explores a host of philosophical issues in the film. *Vagabond* stars Sandrine Bonnaire as a young woman who hitches rides aimlessly on the backroads of rural France, drifting from house to house and person to person without any real direction or ambition. The film tells the young woman's story from a number of perspectives and is framed within a flashback. At the beginning of the film, the body of the woman is found frozen to death in a ditch. Varda thereafter records different "recollections" of the characters in the life of the female vagabond. Each has a startlingly different perspective and recollection. Varda moves in and out of the discourses of narrative, documentary, and testimonial and fictional construct to create an ontological investigation of the woman's life, in which identity is viewed as a multivalent construct set against a backdrop of depressing realism. *Vagabond* challenges traditional and nontraditional filmmaking forms in Varda's masterpiece of postmodern, poststructuralist film artistry. In *Vagabond,* as in all her films, Varda mixes reality and fiction in a manner that is almost completely unprecedented and uses actors along with nonprofessionals to undermine the viewer's sense of conventional narrative construction. As Varda explained in an interview with Rob Edelman:

As the filming [of *Vagabond*] went on, the character and her story developed as we encountered various situations. Some of the witnesses are not actors but real people. Their reactions to her became a very important part of the film: in this way, the film mixes a certain reality into the fictional story of Mona. These witnesses glimpse her, sometimes for the smallest bit of time. She passes through their lives and is then gone forever—just as she passes through our lives. It's as if she comes toward us, and as she does, we learn more about her. But she never reaches us. She never really touches us. (21)

Vagabond was an international critical and commercial success, earning the Golden Lion Award at the Venice Film Festival. Sandrine Bonnaire won a Cesar, the French Academy Award for her performance in *Vagabond.* Varda's most recent film, *Jacquot* (1991), is a re-creation and homage to the childhood of her husband, film director Jacques Demy, who died in 1990 during production of the film. Varda intercuts footage of Demy onscreen recalling his past with clips from his films and re-creations of scenes from his youth. *Jacquot* is, in some ways, comparable to *Vagabond* in its handling of identity issues; however, it shows a much lighter touch not evident in Varda's earlier works.

SELECTED FILMOGRAPHY

La Pointe-Courte (1954)
Cléo de 5 à 7 (*Cleo from 5 to 7*) (1961)
Le Bonheur (*Happiness*) (1965)
Les Créatures (*The Creatures*) (1966)
Lions Love (1969)

Nausicaa (1976)
Daguerréotypes (1975)
L'Une chante l'autre pas (*One Sings the Other Doesn't*) (1977)
Mur murs (1980)
Documenteur (1981)
Une minute pour une image (1983)
Sans toit ni loi (*Vagabond*) (1985)
Le Petit Amour (*Kung Fu Master!*) (1987)
Jane B par Agnès V. (1988)
Jacquot de nantes (*Jacquot*) (1991)

SELECTED BIBLIOGRAPHY

Acker, Ally. *Reel Women: Pioneers of the Cinema, 1896 to the Present.* New York: Continuum, 1993.

Brückner, Jutta. "Women behind the Camera." In *Feminist Aesthetics,* edited by Gisela Ecker, 120–24. London: Women's Press, 1985.

Confino, Barbara. "An Interview with Agnes Varda." *Saturday Review* (August 12, 1972): 35.

Crain, Mary Beth. "The Mother of New Wave." *Los Angeles Weekly,* August 1–7, 1986, 33.

Edelman, Rob. "Travelling a Different Route: An Interview with Agnes Varda." *Cineaste* 15.1 (1986): 20–21.

Flitterman-Lewis, Sandy. *To Desire Differently: Feminism and the French Cinema.* Urbana: University of Illinois Press, 1990.

Hayward, Susan. "Beyond the Gaze and into Femme-Film'ecriture: Agnes Varda's *Sans toit ni loi.*" In *French Film: Texts and Contexts,* edited by Susan Hayward and Ginette Vincendeau, 285–95. London: Routledge, 1990.

Heck-Rabi, Louise. *Women Filmmakers: A Critical Reception.* Metuchen, NJ: Scarecrow Press, 1984.

Kaplan, E. Ann. *Women and Film: Both Sides of the Camera.* New York: Methuen, 1983.

Kuhn, Annette. *Women's Pictures: Feminism and Cinema.* London: Routledge, 1982.

Mayne, Judith. *The Woman at the Keyhole: Feminism and Women's Cinema.* Bloomington: Indiana University Press, 1990.

Mellencamp, Patricia. *Indiscretions: Avant-Garde Film, Video and Feminism.* Bloomington: Indiana University Press, 1990.

Quart, Barbara. *Women Directors: The Emergence of a New Cinema.* New York: Praeger, 1988.

Vincendeau, Ginette. "Agnes Varda." In *The Women's Companion to International Film,* edited by Annette Kuhn, with Susannah Radstone, 411–12. Berkeley: University of California Press, 1994.

VON TROTTA, MARGARETHE (1942–   ). Germany.

VON TROTTA, MARGARETHE (1942–   ). Germany. Margarethe von Trotta is one of the best-known directors of the German cinema. Born in Berlin, she studied literature in Paris and Munich before becoming an actress. She acted both on stage and in film productions, including those of her husband, Völker Schlöndorff. Von Trotta's first filmmaking experience was as codirector and coscreenwriter of *The Lost Honor of Katerina Blum* (1975). After working with Schlondorff, von Trotta went on to direct her first full-length solo project, *The Second Awakening of Christa Klages* (1978). This film, like most von Trotta films, focuses on a central female protagonist. Based on a true story, *The Second Awakening of Christa Klages* is the story of a German kindergarten teacher who stole funds to maintain an alternative day-care center. Von Trotta envisions terrorism as a feminist form of community making. A critical success, *The Second Awakening of Christa Klages* is popular among both ideologically determined critics and general audiences. Von Trotta won the National German Film Award for the film at the Berlin Film Festival. Her next film, *Sisters, or the Balance of Happiness* (1979), met with great success. It is the tale of two sisters' struggle for identity, each polarized by her associations with home and career.

Von Trotta's more recent films, *Marianne and Juliane* (1981) and *Rosa Luxemburg* (1985) demonstrate her persistent and continued interest in issues of female identity and the philosophy of filmic "reality." *Marianne and Juliane* is a narrative of two sisters' lives that is foregrounded by the events of West German terrorism. *Rosa Luxemburg* re-creates (and, to a large extent, reinvents) the history of the revolutionary figure of Luxemburg, who was a leading activist of the German Social Democratic Party. Though both films have been at the center of a lively critical debate about the politics of historical renarration, many critics have noted that von Trotta's greatest achievement in her films is her feminization of the Western discourse of history making.

Von Trotta excels at moving the personal into the political, at investigating "the personal motivations behind political acts, as well as the political responses to private incidences" (Jaehne and Rubenstein, 24). For a long time, von Trotta was fascinated by the career of Rosa Luxemburg and other political activists. "Among these people, political principles had a priority over their personal lives, because they saw themselves in political terms," von Trotta told Karen Jaehne and Lenny Rubenstein (26).

Throughout her work, von Trotta consistently delves into the issues of political activism and gender expectations. *Marianne and Juliane* is probably her finest work in terms of its rendering of female subjectivity. Von Trotta is one of the most prominent figures in women's cinema. She is outspoken about the need to fund films by women directors. In 1982, von Trotta told Annette Insdorf, "We are still the housewives, doing good cooking with little money. The others have the big budgets!"

SELECTED FILMOGRAPHY

Die verlorene Ehre der Katharina Blum (*The Lost Honor of Katerina Blum*) (1975)
Das zweite Erwachen der Christa Klages (*The Second Awakening of Christa Klages*)
    (1978)
Schwestern, oder die Balance des Gluecks (*Sisters, or the Balance of Happiness*)
    (1979)

Die bleierne Zeit (*The German Sisters*) (*Marianne and Juliane*) (1981)
Heller Wahn (*Sheer Madness*) (1983)
Rosa Luxemburg (1985)
Felix (codirector) (1987)
Fuerchten und Liebe (*Love and Fear*) (1987)
Die Ruckkehr (*The Return*) (1990)
The Promise (1995)

SELECTED BIBLIOGRAPHY

Acker, Ally. *Reel Women: Pioneers of the Cinema, 1896 to the Present.* New York: Continuum, 1993.

Byg, Barton. "German History and Cinematic Convention Harmonized in Margarethe von Trotta's *Marianne and Juliane.*" In *Gender and German Cinema, Feminist Interventions, Vol. 2,* edited by Sandra Frieden, Richard W. McCormick, Vibeke R. Petersen, and Laurie Melissa Vogelsang, 259–71. Oxford: Berg, 1993.

Insdorf, Annette. "Von Trotta: By Sisters Obsessed." *New York Times,* January 31, 1982, H19, 22.

Jaehne, Karen, and Lenny Rubenstein. "A Great Woman Theory of History." *Cineaste* 15.4 (1987): 24–28.

Knight, Julia. *Women in the New German Cinema.* London: Verso, 1992.

Kuhn, Annette. *Women's Pictures: Feminism and Cinema.* London: Routledge, 1982.

Kuhn, Annette. "A Heroine for Our Time: Margarethe von Trotta's *Rosa Luxemburg.*" In *Gender and German Cinema, Feminist Interventions, Vol. 2,* edited by Sandra Frieden, Richard W. McCormick, Vibeke R. Petersen, and Laurie Melissa Vogelsang, 163–84. Oxford: Berg, 1993.

Lant, Antonia. "Incarcerated Spaces: The Repression of History." *Yale Journal of Criticism* 1.2 (spring 1988): 107–127.

Möhrmann, Renate. "*The Second Awakening of Christa Klages.*" In *Gender and German Cinema, Feminist Interventions, Vol. 1,* edited by Sandra Frieden, Richard W. McCormick, Vibeke R. Petersen, and Laurie Melissa Vogelsang, 73–83. Oxford: Berg, 1993.

Mueller, Roswitha. "Images in Balance." In *Gender and German Cinema, Feminist Interventions, Vol. 1,* edited by Sandra Frieden, Richard W. McCormick, Vibeke R. Petersen, and Laurie Melissa Vogelsang, 59–71. Oxford: Berg, 1993.

Quart, Barbara. *Women Directors: The Emergence of a New Cinema.* New York: Praeger, 1988.

Seiter, Ellen. "The Political Is Personal: Margarethe von Trotta's 'Marianne and Juliane.' " In *Films for Women,* edited by Charlotte Brunsdon, 109–16. London: BFI, 1987.

W

WEBER, LOIS (1881–1939). United States. The paucity of scholarship on Lois Weber is stunning. Amazingly, no one has yet written a book-length study of the work of one of the most important pioneers of American cinema. Feminists have also overlooked the contribution of Lois Weber to the formation of "women's cinema," melodrama, and social drama. Only recently is she beginning to be recognized as an important auteur of early American film. Her films tended toward moralizing, which perhaps explains why it has taken so long for feminists or modern scholars to bring her into the critical canon.

Born in Allegheny, Pennsylvania, Lois Weber was a child prodigy. She toured as a concert pianist until the age of seventeen. Before she became an actress and director, she worked as a social activist. She began writing for early motion pictures at Gaumont, where she was known as "Mrs. Phillips Smalley." After writing, Weber began acting with her husband, Phillips Smalley, at Gaumont, where the couple were directed by Herbert Blaché (husband of Alice Guy-Blaché). Weber was multitalented: she wrote, directed, and played in many films, including early sound-on-disc shorts produced at Gaumont. She rapidly became one of the highest-paid directors in the industry. She was associated with Edwin S. Porter, Carl Laemmle, and Hobart Bosworth in her business dealings. Weber was one of the first American women directors to head her own production unit, Lois Weber Productions, in 1917. In her own time, Weber was as well known as D. W. Griffith and Cecil B. DeMille; however, she was subsequently erased from film history as an insignificant footnote because of sexism in film scholarship.

Her many films as director include *The Troubadour's Triumph* (1912), *The Jew's Christmas* (1913), *Hypocrites* (1914), *The Hand That Rocks the Cradle* (1917), *The Blot* (1921), and *What Do Men Want?* (1921). Although the bulk of her work was done in the silent era, she continued as a director until 1934, directing the talkie *White Heat* (not to be confused with the Raoul Walsh/James Cagney film of 1949 for the small Pinnacle Production Company). In all her films, Weber dealt with social issues that she felt were of great importance—birth control in *Where Are My Children?* (1916) and the plight of the poor academic class in *The Blot.* Weber's camera work pays great attention to little details, like the worn sofa in an indigent professor's living room or a meager snack of weak tea and crackers served to "impress" a guest; her naturalism extended to her use of natural-source lighting for exterior sequences and the use of actual locations, rather than sets, for establishing shots. Weber's work is, in many ways, superior to that of many of her silent male contemporaries, in that her characters are fully developed personalities rather than stock, "instant read," iconic figures. She also experimented in her early films with color tinting, using expressive blue, green, red, or yellow tints to enhance pictorial values in her early Universal/Jewel productions.

In particular, Weber's portrayal of women in her motion pictures is precedent shattering and is, in many ways, more realistic and sympathetic than contemporary feminist visions offered to us by today's cinema. Weber's female protagonists feel that they can change things for the better, and they often do, sweeping away social injustice and righting wrongs. That she did not lose her directorial touch with the coming of sound is evidenced by the fact that *White Heat,* an extremely low-budget "drama set on a Hawaiian sugar plantation" (Slide, 50), received rave reviews from the motion picture trade papers. "Among independent productions, this rates way up near the top of the ladder," announced *The Film Daily* for June 15, 1934 (Slide, 50), but even the commercial and critical success of this modest programmer could not halt the unjust, downward commercial spiral of Lois Weber's late career. When she died on November 13, 1939, she was "penniless . . . [and] her funeral expenses were paid by [writer] Frances Marion, to whom Lois Weber had given her first job in the film industry in 1914" (Slide, 51).

Weber's career as an actress, scenarist, director, producer, and codirector (with Phillips Smalley) of some of the most important early feminist cinema has for far too long been buried in the patriarchal canon of conventional cinema history. Now that some of her early films have been restored and are readily available for rental in the classroom, one hopes that this early pioneer of the cinema—and, as noted, at one time one of the highest-paid directors in the motion picture business—will at last receive some measure of the respect and critical attention that she so clearly deserves. The best of Lois Weber's films (*The Blot, The Doctor and the Woman* [1918], *Where Are My Children?,* and *Hypocrites*) stand up today as fresh, vital, and original works of cinematic art, coupled with Weber's burning desire to communicate her humanist and feminist message to the widest possible audience. Unlike many silent-film makers, Weber's sense of the visual was so highly developed that her films remain as vibrant as the year in which they were created and do not need either sound tracks or excessive intertitling to gain the viewer's attention. One can only speculate on what she might have accomplished had not the vise of sexism in the film directorial profession in the early 1920s cut her career short. As it is, what Lois Weber accomplished is extraordinary and a unique testament to her artistry and vision.

SELECTED FILMOGRAPHY

Japanese Idyll (codirector) (1912)
The Troubadour's Triumph (codirector) (1912)
Suspense (codirector) (1913)
The Eyes of God (codirector) (1913)
The Jew's Christmas (codirector) (1913)
His Brand (1913)
The Female of the Species (1913)
The Merchant of Venice (codirector) (1914)
Traitor (1914)
Like Most Wives (1914)
Hypocrites (1914)
False Colors (codirector) (1914)
It's No Laughing Matter (1914)
A Fool and His Money (1914)
The Leper's Coat (1914)
The Career of Waterloo Peterson (1914)
Behind the Veil (codirector) (1914)
Jewel (1915)
Sunshine Molly (codirector) (1915)
Saving the Family Name (1915)
A Cigarette, That's All (codirector) (1915)
Scandal (codirector) (1915)
The Flirt (1916)
Discontent (1916)
Hop, the Devil's Brew (codirector) (1916)
Where Are My Children? (codirector) (1916)
The French Downstairs (1916)
Alone in the World (1916)
Shoes (1916)
The Dumb Girl of Portici (codirector) (1916)
Idle Wives (1916)
Wanted—a Home (1916)
The Hand That Rocks the Cradle (1917)
Even As You and I (1917)
The Mysterious Mrs. Musselwhite (1917)
The Price of a Good Time (1917)
The Man Who Dared God (1917)
There's No Place Like Home (1917)
For Husbands Only (1917)
The Doctor and the Woman (1918)
Borrowed Clothes (1918)
When a Girl Loves (1919)

Mary Regan (1919)
A Midnight Romance (1919)
Scandal Managers (1919)
Home (1919)
Forbidden (1919)
Too Wise Wives (1921)
What's Worth While? (1921)
To Please One Woman (1921)
The Blot (1921)
What Do Men Want? (1921)
A Chapter in Her Life (1923)
The Marriage Clause (1926)
Sensation Seekers (1927)
The Angel of Broadway (1927)
White Heat (1934)

SELECTED BIBLIOGRAPHY

Acker, Ally. *Reel Women: Pioneers of the Cinema, 1896 to the Present.* New York: Continuum, 1993.

Bowser, Eileen. *The Transformation of Cinema 1907–1915.* New York: Scribner's, 1990.

Denison, Arthur. "A Dream in Realization." *The Moving Picture World* (July 21, 1917): 417–18.

Foster, Gwendolyn, and Wheeler Winston Dixon. *The Women Who Made The Movies.* New York: Women Make Movies, Inc., 1991. Video.

Heck-Rabi, Louise. *Women Filmmakers: A Critical Reception.* Metuchen, NJ: Scarecrow Press, 1984.

Peary, Gerald. "Sanka, Pink Ladies, & Virginia Slims." *Women and Film* 1.5–6 (1974): 82–84.

Rosen, Marjorie. *Popcorn Venus.* New York: Coward McCann and Geoghegan, 1973.

Slide, Anthony. *Early Women Directors.* New York: Da Capo, 1984.

Weber, Lois. "How I Became a Motion Picture Director." *Static Flashes* 1.14 (April 24, 1915): 8.

WEILL, CLAUDIA (1947–). United States. Born in New York City, Claudia Weill began making films while she was a student at Radcliffe. Weill is also a still photographer. In the 1970s, she directed a series of experimental and documentary short films. She collaborated with Shirley MacLaine to make *The Other Half of the Sky* in 1974, a documentary on China. *Girlfriends* (1978), which was codirected by Joyce Chopra, is one of Weill's best-known feminist films. *Girlfriends* is a documentary on growing up as a Jewish New Yorker. The film is a semiautobiographical account of a woman photographer who becomes involved with a man and a woman. *Girlfriends* was filmed on a small-scale budget, but it was distributed by Warner Brothers. Because of the success of *Girlfriends,* Weill was afforded the opportunity to direct *It's My Turn* (1980), which featured Jill

Clayburgh and Michael Douglas. *It's My Turn* considers a female point of view with its emphasis on the career goals of a woman math professor. More recently, Weill directed episodes of the television program "Thirty-something." Weill continues to direct, mainly for television.

SELECTED FILMOGRAPHY

Joyce at 34 (1972)
The Other Half of the Sky: A China Memoir (1974)
Girlfriends (1978)
It's My Turn (1980)
Johnny Bull (1986)
Once a Hero (1987)

SELECTED BIBLIOGRAPHY

Fischer, Lucy. *Shot/Countershot: Film Tradition and Women's Cinema*. Princeton: Princeton University Press, 1989.
Honeycutt, Kirk. "Women Film Directors: Will They, Too, Be Allowed to Bomb?" *New York Times,* August 6, 1978, sec. 2, 1, 11.
Jackson, Lynne, and Karen Jaehne. "Eavesdropping on Female Voices." *Cineaste* 16.1–2 (1988): 38–43.
Kuhn, Annette. "Hollywood and New Women's Cinema." In *Films for Women,* edited by Charlotte Brunsdon, 125–30. London: BFI, 1987.
Starr, Cecile. "Claudia Weill: From Shoestring to Studio." *New York Times,* August 6, 1978, 11.

WERTMÜLLER, LINA (1928–   ). Italy. Lina Wertmüller was born Arcangela Felice Assunta Wertmüller von Elgg in Rome in 1928. Educated at the Stanislavskyan Academy of Theater in Italy, she became a leading figure in the international cinema in the 1970s as an actor, director, and screenwriter. Before working in cinema, she worked in many artistic disciplines in a number of different capacities. She produced a number of avant-garde plays and worked as a puppeteer, stage manager, set designer, and writer for radio and television. Her first major break into the film industry came in 1962, when she worked as an assistant on *8 1/2* (directed by Federico Fellini, 1962). Fellini financed Wertmüller's first film, *The Lizards,* in 1963. Both *The Lizards* and *Let's Talk about Men* (1965) (Wertmüller's second film) concerned and examined male gender codes.

Wertmüller teamed up with Giancarlo Giannini, who acted in many of her films. *The Seduction of Mimi* (1972) is probably their most famous collaboration; Wertmüller won Best Director at the 1972 Cannes Film Festival for the film. *Love and Anarchy* (1973) was a commercial and critical success for Wertmüller, who became a cult figure in the United States when the film was released here in 1974. Giancarlo Giannini won the Best Actor Award at Cannes for his work in *Love and Anarchy*. All of Wertmüller's films are comic sociocultural studies of Italian machismo and sexuality. Wertmüller is consistently interested in sadomasochistic sexuality and leftist politics. *Seven Beauties* (1976) is a bizarre comedy about sexuality and sadomasochism in a Nazi concentration camp. Wertmüller's attitude toward women has often been criticized as antifeminist. Her early films tend to reduce women to vile, stereotypically defined caricatures. *Sotto . . . Sotto* (1983) features an erotic relationship between two women. As Anie O'Healy notes of the film:

The major question that the film raises about feminine eroticism and its link with masochistic spectatorship is: can female desire be considered apart from the representational structures of patriarchal culture? (54)

Though Wertmüller's attitudes toward women are problematic, her Marxist ties are evident throughout her films. Most recently, Wertmüller wrote and directed *Ciao, Professore!* (1994). The film concerns the plight of poor schoolchildren in Naples. Wertmüller continues to make films of social commentary; however, *Ciao, Professore!* is considerably less compelling and challenging than Wertmüller's earlier work, as she reaches out for a wider and more commercial audience.

SELECTED FILMOGRAPHY

I basilischi (The Lizards) (1963)
Questa volta parliamo di uomini (Let's Talk about Men) (1965)
Mimi metallurgico ferito nell'onore (The Seduction of Mimi) (1972)
Film d'amore e d'anarchia, or Stamattina alle dieci in via dei fiori nella nota casa di tolleranza (Love and Anarchy) (1973)
Tutto a posto e niente in ordine (All Screwed Up) (1974)
Travolti da un insolito destino nell'azzurro mare d'agosto (Swept Away) (1974)
Pasqualino settebellezze (Seven Beauties) (1976)
The End of the World in Our Usual Bed in a Night Full of Rain (1977)
Fatto di sangue tra due uomini per cause di una vedova: si sospettano motivi politici (Blood Feud) (1978)
Una domenica sera di novembre (1981)
A Joke of Destiny Lying in Wait round the Corner like a Street Bandit (1983)
Sotto . . . Sotto (1983)
Complicato intrigo di donne vicoli e delitti (1985)
Summer Night with Greek Profiles Almond Eyes and Scent of Basil (1986)
Up to Date (1988)
In Una Nolte di Chiaro di Luna (In a Full Moon Night) (1990)
Ciao, Professore! (1994)
A Joke of Destiny (1995)

SELECTED BIBLIOGRAPHY

Bruno, Giuliana, and Maria Nadotti, eds. *Off Screen: Women & Film in Italy*. New York: Routledge, 1988.

de Lauretis, Teresa. *Alice Doesn't: Feminism, Semiotics, Cinema*. Bloomington: Indiana University Press, 1984.

Mayne, Judith. *The Woman at the Keyhole: Feminism and Women's Cinema*. Bloomington: Indiana University Press, 1990.

O'Healy, Anie. "Reframing Desire in Lina Wertmüller's *Sotto . . . Sotto*." *Spectator* 10.2 (spring 1990): 45–57.

Vitti, Antonio C. "The Critics 'Swept Away' by Wertmüller's Sexual Politics." *NEMLA Italian Studies* 13–14 (1989–90): 121–31.

Wertmüller, Lina. *The Screenplays of Lina Wertmüller*. Translated by Steven Wagner. New York: Quadrangle, 1977.

WHEELER, ANNE (1946–   ). Canada.

Anne Wheeler is one of the most celebrated Canadian filmmakers. Born and raised in Alberta, Canada, Wheeler came to direct after a number of varied experiences as a mathematician, teacher, actress, photographer, and activist. Wheeler's films usually center around women's issues and women's stories. Her first film, *Great Grandmothers* (1975), is a documentary on the lives of prairie women. *A War Story* (1980) is a narrative docudrama based on her father's internment in a Japanese prisoner of war camp.

Loyalties (1985), written by Sharon Riis, is a powerful drama concerning child sex abuse. In the film, two women, one English and one Native American, are forced to bond together across lines of race and class to protect a young woman from further sexual abuse. Wheeler's handling of the controversial subject matter is admirable, particularly in its emphasis on female friendship and community-mindedness. Despite the difficulties Wheeler has faced in funding situations, she maintains that perseverance pays off in the end. *Bye Bye Blues* (1989) was a critical and commercial success. Based on Wheeler's mother's experiences during World War II, the film combines a feminist screenplay with a commercial, yet personal flavor. In *Bye Bye Blues*, a woman loses her husband during the war. Unsure if he is dead or not, she joins a jazz band and manages to make a new life for herself. Wheeler continues to direct feature films that are both commercial and intellectually stimulating, consistently working against genre and narrative stereotypes.

SELECTED FILMOGRAPHY

Great Grandmothers (1975)
Augusta, Priority: The Only Home I've Got (1978)
A War Story (1980)
A Change of Heart (1983)
Loyalties (1985)
Cowboys Don't Cry (1986)
Bye Bye Blues (1989)
Angel Square (1990)
The Diviners (1993)

SELECTED BIBLIOGRAPHY

Cole, Janis, and Holly Dale. *Calling the Shots: Profiles of Women Filmmakers*. Ontario: Quarry Press, 1993.

Jenish, D'Arcy. "Turning Homespun Ideas into Truth on the Screen." *Maclean's*

102.52 (December 25, 1989): 24.

Johnson, Brian D. *Bye Bye Blues*. *Maclean's* 102.38 (September 11, 1989): 72.

Murray, Karen. *The Diviners*. *Variety* 349.11 (January 11, 1993): 68.

WIELAND, JOYCE (1931–   ). Canada. Joyce Wieland became a major figure in American avant-garde films of the 1960s, working in New York City, a rather odd fate for a loyal and patriotic Canadian. Nevertheless, after such early films as *Tea in the Garden* (1958), *Larry's Recent Behaviour* (1963), and *Peggy's Blue Skylight* (1964) and her 1956 marriage to Michael Snow, the couple found their way to a loft in Manhattan, where Wieland created her best-remembered and most influential works. Michael Snow was a leader in the "structuralist" film movement, creating such highly formalized films as *Wavelength* (1966–67), which took the public and critics of the era by storm.

Wieland's work during this period, particularly *1933* (1967) and *Sailboat* (1967), are also highly structural films, using small bits of footage in repetitive patterns, offset by a contrapuntal sound track. *Handtinting* (1967), *Catfood* (1967), *Rat Life and Diet in North America* (1968), and *Dripping Water* (codirected with Snow) (1969) followed in rapid succession, but Wieland seemed to continue to labor in Snow's ever-lengthening shadow. Although many male critics are eager to cite Snow's influence on Wieland's work, they are slow to recognize Wieland's considerable influence on Snow. When Wieland's feature film about changes in Canadian society, *Reason over Passion* (1969), a "non-formalist" work, was less than rapturously received by the New York critics, Wieland began to think about where her life and career were going. With the creation of Anthology Film Archives, however, a canonical film projection/"preservation" facility in New York, Wieland realized that her own accomplishments would be obscured as long as she remained in New York. In 1971, she moved back to Canada, stating that it was "the beginning of having [my] own life" (Rabinovitz, 178).

Wieland became politically active in the Toronto art world as a leader of the local chapter of the Canadian Artists' Union (CAR). In 1972, she shot an interview with the revolutionary figure Pierre Vallières, which has been aptly described as a structuralist documentary. Wieland shows only the mouth of the interview subject in close-up. *Solidarity* (1973) is another political documentary directed by Wieland in this period. *Solidarity* concerns a worker's strike in Kitchener, Ontario. Wieland's camera shows only the workers' feet, as a voice-over recites political speeches. Wieland's next film, *The Far Shore* (1976), is described by Lauren Rabinovitz as a "feminist melodrama" (204). Throughout her career as an artist, filmmaker, and activist, Joyce Wieland has continually remade herself as an experimental pioneer. Her work is recently being reevaluated in a feminist context. She is finally being recognized as an innovative force that "bridges the avant-garde model of post-war experimental cinema and the socialist tradition of

Canadian nationalist art" (Rabinovitz, 212). In 1987, the Art Gallery of Ontario sponsored a major retrospective of her work. Wieland continues to make films occasionally; however, her main artistic output currently consists of oversize paintings. Her artwork combines many of the themes and approaches of her earlier film work: self-reflectivity, abstractions, and female eroticism and experience.

SELECTED FILMOGRAPHY

Tea in the Garden (1958)
Larry's Recent Behaviour (1963)
Peggy's Blue Skylight (1964)
Patriotism, Part One (1964)
Patriotism, Part Two (1964)
Water Sark (1966)
Bill's Hat (1967)
Barbara's Blindness (codirector Betty Ferguson) (1967)
Sailboat (1967)
1933 (1967)
Handtinting (1967)
Catfood (1967)
Rat Life and Diet in North America (1968)
Dripping Water (codirector Michael Snow) (1969)
One Second in Montreal (codirector Michael Snow) (1969)
Reason over Passion (*La raison avant la passion*) (1969)
Pierre Vallières (1972)
Solidarity (1973)
The Far Shore (1976)
A & B in Ontario (codirector Hollis Frampton) (1972–83)
Birds at Sunrise (1985)
Peggy's Blue Skylight (remake) (1985)

SELECTED BIBLIOGRAPHY

Armitage, Kay. "The Feminine Body: Joyce Wieland's Water Sark." *Canadian Women's Studies* 8.1 (spring 1987): 84–88.

Film-Makers' Cooperative. *Film-Makers' Cooperative Catalogue No. 7*. New York: Film-Makers' Cooperative, 1989.

Freedman, Adele. "Joyce Wieland's Re-Emergence: The Arctic Light at the End of *The Far Shore*." *Toronto Life* (June 1980): 184–185.

Gronou, Anna. "Avant-garde Film by Women: To Conceive a New Language of Desire." In *The Event Horizon: Essays on Hope, Sexuality, Social Space and Media(tion) in Art*, edited by Lorne Falk and Barbara Fischer, 159–76. Toronto: Loach House Press, 1987.

Kay, Karyn, and Gerald Peary, eds. *Women and the Cinema*. New York: Dutton, 1977.

Martineau, Barbara Halpern. "*The Far Shore*." *Cinema Canada* 27 (April 1976): 20–23.

Penley, Constance. *The Future of an Illusion: Film, Feminism and Psychoanalysis*.

Minneapolis: University of Minnesota Press, 1989.

Rabinovitz, Lauren. *Points of Resistance: Women, Power & Politics in the New York Avant-Garde Cinema, 1943–71.* Urbana: University of Illinois Press, 1991.

Reid, Alison. *Canadian Women Film Makers.* Ottawa: Canadian Film Institute, 1972.

WILSON, MARGERY (1898–1986). United States. Margery Wilson Bushnell, born Sarah Barker Strayer in Grace, Kentucky, is best known for her work as an actress in D. W. Griffith's *Intolerance* (1916). In addition to her extensive work as an actress in silent films, Margery Wilson directed and produced a handful of feature films notable for their realism and naturalism.

In 1920, Wilson directed *That Something* and *Two of a Kind.* In her autobiography, *I Found My Way,* Wilson recalls the sexism that she experienced as a producer/director. In one instance, after showing the dailies to a Hollywood executive, Wilson recalls that he asked her, "Who directed it for you, Margery?" (184). The executive insisted that "no woman directed that picture [because] no woman had that much clarity of mind" (184). Margery was not the kind of woman who would tolerate such sexism; however, she did try to conceal her anger. "Such remarks used to infuriate me. Now they do not anger me, they amuse me. When a man's traditional contempt for women's thinking gear is disturbed, his only recourse is to say some particular woman has a masculine mind, or has borrowed a masculine mind" (185).

Margery Wilson continued to produce, direct, and act in her own films, despite the attitudes against women filmmakers. She was particularly fond of shooting outdoors on location. Critics hailed the realism of *Insinuation* (1922) and *The Offenders* (1924). Wilson was unable to find consistent, fair distribution arrangements, however, so she turned her attention to writing self-help books, which were commercially highly successful. Among her books are *The Woman You Want to Be, Double Your Energy and Live without Fatigue, Believe in Yourself,* and *The New Etiquette.* Margery Wilson remade a career as an author and public lecturer. She was active until her death in 1986, at the age of eighty-nine. In addition to her writing and lecturing work, Wilson taught speech to actors, worked in radio, and became a counselor. Taken as a whole, Margery Wilson's work is a significant part of our feminist cinema heritage.

SELECTED FILMOGRAPHY

That Something (1920)
Two of a Kind (1920)
Insinuation (1922)
The Offenders (1924)

SELECTED BIBLIOGRAPHY

Acker, Ally. *Reel Women: Pioneers of the Cinema, 1896 to the Present.* New York: Continuum, 1993.

Jordan, Orma. "Kentucky Babe." *Photoplay* (October 1916): 41.

Slide, Anthony. *Early Women Directors.* New York: Da Capo, 1984.

Wilson, Margery. *I Found My Way: An Autobiography.* Philadelphia: J. B. Lippincott, 1956.

Z

ZETTERLING, MAI (1925–94). Sweden. Actress and director Mai Zetterling was born on May 24, 1925, in Vasteras, Switzerland. She was educated at the Royal Dramatic Theatrical School in Stockholm, where she made her acting debut at the age of sixteen. After an extensive career as an actress, Zetterling decided to make the jump into the director's chair in the 1960s. Her first short film, *The War Game* (1963) (not to be confused with Peter Watkins's 1966 film of the same title), won a prize at the Venice Film Festival. Zetterling made a number of feature films that are characterized by her distinctive auteurial stamp and the themes of sexuality, the body, and gender roles. Zetterling also coauthored, with her husband, David Hughes, a number of novels, including *Night Games,* on which her film of the same name is based.

Night Games (1966) and *Loving Couples* (1964) brought international recognition to Zetterling as a practitioner of personal cinema. *Night Games* is a particularly unique series of sexual tableaux. It is a narrative of a young man with an oedipal fixation. In 1969, Zetterling directed *The Girls,* a feminist exploration of three actresses in a production of *Lysistrata* who became obsessed with the theme of women's oppression off the stage. *Loving Couples* is another examination of women's lives. In this film, three pregnant women give birth and narrate their lives through a series of flashbacks. All Zetterling films display an interest in the body and the Western view of the body.

Mai Zetterling's work as a director, like that of Ida Lupino, is second in the eyes of the general public to her work as an actress. Yet, as with Lupino, we can see that Zetterling longed to break free from the cinematic conventions that were forced upon her by the patriarchal narrative structure and create works cast in her own vision. Both *Night Games* and *Loving Couples* secured Zetterling's international reputation as an uncompromising feminist filmmaker of the first rank, long before the term "feminist" was used in general conversation. On both sides of the camera, Zetterling's work as a filmmaker and performer offers a unique testimony to the life of this talented and courageous artist.

SELECTED FILMOGRAPHY

The War Game (1963)
Alskande par (*Loving Couples*) (1964)
Natt lek (*Night Games*) (1966)
Doktor Glas (*Doctor Glas*) (1968)
Flickorna (*The Girls*) (1969)
Vincent the Dutchman (1972)
Visions of Eight (codirector) (1973)
We Have Many Faces (1975)
Of Seals and Man (1980)
Love (1981)
Scrubbers (1982)
Amarosa (*Amorosa*) (1986)

SELECTED BIBLIOGRAPHY

Acker, Ally. *Reel Women: Pioneers of the Cinema, 1896 to the Present.* New York: Continuum, 1993.
Cowie, Peter. *Sweden* 2. New York: A. S. Barnes, 1970.
Fischer, Lucy. *Shot/Countershot: Film Tradition and Women's Cinema.* Princeton: Princeton University Press, 1989.
Heck-Rabi, Louise. *Women Filmmakers: A Critical Reception.* Metuchen, NJ: Scarecrow Press, 1984.
Stang, Joanne. "In Sweden It's Easier to Play *Night Games.*" *New York Times,* October 9, 1966, sec. 2, 13.

ZHANG NUANXIN (1940–). China. Zhang Nuanxin is one of the many active women directors of China. Since the days of pioneer women directors such as Dong Kena and Wang Ping, who worked in the 1960s, Chinese women directors have had an active role in the cinema. Women active in film production include Huang Shuquian, Peng Xiaolian, Lu Xiaoya, and Ann Hui. As Zhang Nuanxin explains in an interview with Chris Berry, women in China are educated to believe that "women could do anything that men could do, including driving tractors and fighting at the front" (23). Like Soviet women filmmakers, Chinese women are encouraged to become active in the cinema.

Zhang Nuanxin was born in 1940. She graduated from the Beijing Film Academy in 1962 and became a teacher at the same academy. After studying at the Shanghai Film School, she directed her first feature film, *The Drive to Win* (1981). The film is notable for its realism and the use of a hand-held camera. It is centrally concerned with the life of a woman basketball player. As Zhang told Chris Berry, the realism of *The Drive to Win* is a response to the theatrical cinema of the cultural revolution period, which she found "all very stagy and false" (21). Zhang used nonprofessional actors to bolster the sense of realism in the film.

Sacrificed Youth (1985) is the second film of Zhang Nuanxin. It is notable for its realism in the depiction of the life of a seventeen-year-old girl who moves to a small village after living in the city. Zhang Nuanxin drew on her personal experience as an adolescent. She told Chris Berry, "I wanted to express that feeling, the tragedy of my youth, the tragedy of our whole generation" (21). In *Sacrificed Youth,* the camera follows the young woman's subjective experience as she gradually readjusts to village life. She changes her physical appearance by wearing informal clothing, and she changes her behavior by getting involved physically in her cultural environment as a tree-cutter.

Zhang Nuanxin voices a complicated attitude toward being categorized as a "woman director":

I hate people saying that because I'm a director, I'm a "superwoman." There's an image of women directors shouting and smoking cigarettes, and being like men in every way. People think that's a real woman director. (Berry, 23)

Zhang Nuanxin continues to be an active force in Chinese cinema. She also teaches at the Beijing Film Academy.

SELECTED FILMOGRAPHY
The Drive to Win (1981)
Quingchunji (*Sacrificed Youth*) (1985)

SELECTED BIBLIOGRAPHY
Berry, Chris. "Interview with Zhang Nuanxin." *Camera Obscura* 18 (September 1988): 20–25.
Kaplan, E. Ann. "Problematizing Cross-Cultural Analysis: The Case of Women in the Recent Chinese Cinema." *Wide Angle* 11.2 (1989): 40–50.
Rayns, Tony. "The Position of Women in New Chinese Cinema." *East-West Film Journal* 1.2 (June 1987): 32–34.
Semsel, George S. "China." In *The Asian Film Industry,* edited by John A. Lent, 11–33. Austin: University of Texas Press, 1990.
Yan, Esther C. M. "Is China the End of Hermeneutics? or, Political and Cultural Usage of Non-Han Women in Mainland Chinese Films." In *Multiple Voices in Feminist Film Criticism,* edited by Diane Carson, Linda Dittmar, and Janice Welsch, 280–92. Minneapolis: University of Minnesota Press, 1994.
Zhang, Nuanxin. "Director's Comments on *Sacrificed Youth*." *Contemporary Cinema* 5 (1985): 134–36.

Appendix 1:
International Women Film
Directors by Nationality

Algeria:	Djebar, Assia (1936–)
Argentina:	Bemberg, Maria Luisa (1940–95)
	Kaplan, Nelly (1931–)
Austria:	Export, Valie (1940–)
	Sagan, Leontine (1899–1974)
Australia:	Armstrong, Gillian (1950–)
	Campion, Jane (1955–)
	Cantrill, Corrine (1928–)
	Lyell, Lottie (1890–1925)
	McDonagh, Paulette (1901–78)
	Moffatt, Tracey (1960–)
	Moorhouse, Jocelyn (1965–)
Belgium:	Akerman, Chantal (1950–)
Brazil:	Abreu, Gilda de (1904–79)
	Amaral, Suzana (1933–)
	Carolina, Ana (1943–)
Canada:	Cardona, Dominique (1955–)
	Colbert, Laurie (1958–)
	Cole, Janis (1954–)
	Dale, Holly (1953–)
	Lanctôt, Micheline (1947–)
	Leaf, Caroline (1946–)
	Maclean, Alison (1958–)
	Obomsawin, Alanis (1932–)
	Pool, Lea (1956–)
	Todd, Loretta (1961–)

	Wheeler, Anne (1946–)
	Wieland, Joyce (1931–)
Chile:	Mallet, Marilu (1945–)
	Sarmiento, Valeria (1948–)
China:	Hui, Ann (Manchuria) (1947–)
	Zhang Nuanxin (1940–)
Cuba:	Gómez, Sara (1943–74)
Czechoslovakia:	Chytilová, Věra (1929–)
Denmark:	Henning-Jensen, Astrid (1914–)
Finland:	Engström, Ingemo (1941–)
	Niskanen, Tuija-Maija (1943–)
France:	Audry, Jacqueline (1908–77)
	Denis, Claire (1950–)
	Dulac, Germaine (1882–1942)
	Duras, Marguerite (1914–)
	Epstein, Marie (1899–1995)
	Guy, Alice (Alice Guy-Blaché) (1873–1968)
	Haensel, Marion (1952–)
	Huillet, Danièle (1936–)
	Kaplan, Nelly (1931–)
	Kurys, Diane (1948–)
	Maldoror, Sarah (1929–)
	Mangolte, Babette (1941–)
	Musidora (1889–1957)
	Pascal, Christine (1953–)
	Serreau, Coline (1947–)
	Varda, Agnes (1928–)
Germany:	Alemann, Claudia von (1943–)
	Brückner, Jutta (1941–)
	Dörrie, Doris (1955–)
	Gusner, Iris (1941–)
	Hein, Birgit (1942–)
	Henning, Hanna (1884–1925)
	Mikesch, Elfi (1940–)
	Ottinger, Ulrike (1942–)
	Perincioli, Cristina (1946–)
	Reiniger, Lotte (1899–1981)

Riefenstahl, Leni (1902–   )
Sagan, Leontine (1899–1974)
Sander, Helke (1937–   )
Sanders-Brahms, Helma (1940–   )
Treut, Monika (1954–   )
von Trotta, Margarethe (1942–   )

Hong Kong: Hui, Ann (1947–   )
Hungary: Elek, Judit (1937–   )
    Mészáros, Márta (1934–   )
India: Karanth, Prema (1950–   )
    Nair, Mira (1957–   )
    Parmar, Pratibha (1960–   )
    Sen, Aparna (1945–   )
Iran: Bani Etemaad, Rakhshan (1953–   )
Ireland: Murphy, Pat (1951–   )
Israel: Bat Adam, Michal (1950?–   )
Italy: Cavani, Liliana (1936–   )
    Monti, Adriana (1951–   )
    Notari, Elvira (1875–1946)
    Wertmüller, Lina (1928–   )
Japan: Hidari, Sachiko (1930–   )
    Longinotto, Kim (–   )
    Ono, Yoko (1933–   )
    Tanaka, Kinuyo (1909–77)
Korea: Choy, Christine (1952–   )
Martinique: Palcy, Euzhan (1957–   )
Mexico: Fernández Violante, Marcela (1941–   )
    Landeta, Matilde (1913–   )
    Novaro, Maria (1951–   )
Netherlands: Apon, Annette (1949–   )
    Gorris, Marleen (1948–   )
New Zealand: Campion, Jane (1955–   )
    Mita, Merata (1942–   )
Norway: Breien, Anja (1940–   )
    Mikkelsen, Laila (1940–   )
Poland: Holland, Agnieszka (1948–   )
    Jakubowska, Wanda (1907–   )

Senegal: Faye, Safi (1943–   )
Soviet Union: Asanova, Dinara (1942–85)
                              Gogoberidze, Lana (1928–   )
                              Muratova, Kira (1934–   )
                              Preobrazhenskaya, Ol'ga (1881–1971)
                              Shepitko, Larissa (1939–79)
                              Shub, Esfir (Esther) (1894–1959)
                              Solntseva, Iuliia (1901–   )
                              Svilova, Elizaveta (1900–75)
Spain: Miro, Pilar (1940–   )
Sweden: Ahrne, Marianne (1940–   )
                              Hofman-Uddgren, Anna (1868–1947)
                              Zetterling, Mai (1925–94)
United Kingdom: Attile, Martina (1959–   )
                              Batchelor, Joy (1914–   )
                              Blackwood, Maureen (1960–   )
                              Box, Muriel (1905–91)
                              Chadha, Gurinder (1960–   )
                              Craigie, Jill (1914–   )
                              Field, Mary (1896–1969)
                              Grierson, Marion (1900–   )
                              Hunt, Claire (–   )
                              Kidron, Beeban (1961–   )
                              Onwurah, Ngozi (1963–   )
                              Parmar, Pratibha (1960–   )
                              Potter, Sally (1949–   )
                              Toye, Wendy (1917–   )
United States: Anders, Alison (1955–   )
                              Arzner, Dorothy (1906–79)
                              B., Beth (1955–   )
                              Barrie, Diana (1952–   )
                              Bigelow, Kathryn (1953–   )
                              Borden, Lizzie (1950–   )
                              Bute, Mary Ellen (1906–83)
                              Chenzira, Ayoka (1956–   )
                              Child, Abigail (1948–   )
                              Chopra, Joyce (1938–   )

Citron, Michelle (1948–)
Clarke, Shirley (1927–)
Cochran, Stacey (1959–)
Collins, Kathleen (1942–88)
Coolidge, Martha (1946–)
Cunard, Grace (1893–1967)
Dash, Julie (1952–)
Davis, Tamra (1963–)
Davis, Zeinabu irene (1961–)
de Hirsch, Storm (1931–)
Deitch, Donna (1945–)
Deren, Maya (1917–61)
Ephron, Nora (1941–)
Fisher, Holly (1942–)
Foster, Jodie (1962–)
Friedrich, Su (1954–)
Gauntier, Gene (1891–1966)
Gish, Lillian (1896–1993)
Glyn, Elinor (1864–1943)
Godmilow, Jill (1950–)
Gordon, Bette (1950–)
Greenwald, Maggie (1955–)
Hammer, Barbara (1939–)
Harris, Leslie (1959–)
Heckerling, Amy (1954–)
Hubley, Faith (1915–)
Ivers, Julia Crawford (1871–1930)
Kopple, Barbara (1946–)
Larkin, Alile Sharon (1953–)
Livingston, Jennie (1960–)
Lupino, Ida (1918–1995)
Madison, Cleo (1883–1964)
Marshall, Penny (1942–)
Martin, Darnell (1964–)
May, Elaine (1932–)
McCullough, Barbara (1945–)
McLaughlin, Sheila (1950–)

McVey Drew, Lucille (1890–1925)

Menken, Marie (1910–71)

Nelson, Gunvor (1931–   )

Park, Ida May (1885–1954)

Rainer, Yvonne (1934–   )

Reid, Dorothy Davenport (1895–1977)

Savoca, Nancy (1960–   )

Schneemann, Carolee (1939–   )

Seidelman, Susan (1952–   )

Shipman, Nell (1892–1970)

Silver, Joan Micklin (1935–   )

Spheeris, Penelope (1946–   )

Stonehouse, Ruth (1893–1941)

Streisand, Barbra (1942–   )

Troche, Rose (1965–   )

Weber, Lois (1881–1939)

Weill, Claudia (1947–   )

Wilson, Margery (1898–1986)

Vietnam: Trinh T. Minh-ha (1953–   )

Appendix 2:
International Women Film Directors: A Chronology of Influential Directors by Decades

1896–1910:   Gauntier, Gene
                 Guy, Alice
1910–20:   Cunard, Grace
                 Dulac, Germaine
                 Gauntier, Gene
                 Guy, Alice (Alice
                    Guy-Blaché)
                 Henning, Hanna
                 Hofman-Uddgren, Anna
                 Ivers, Julia Crawford
                 Lyell, Lottie
                 Madison, Cleo
                 McVey Drew, Lucille
                 Musidora
                 Notari, Elvira
                 Park, Ida May
                 Preobrazhenskaya, Ol'ga
                 Shipman, Nell
                 Shub, Esfir (Esther)
                 Stonehouse, Ruth
                 Weber, Lois
1920–30:   Arzner, Dorothy
                 Cunard, Grace
                 Dulac, Germaine
                 Epstein, Marie
                 Field, Mary
                 Gish, Lillian

Glyn, Elinor
Henning, Hanna
Lyell, Lottie
McDonagh, Paulette
McVey Drew, Lucille
Musidora
Notari, Elvira
Park, Ida May
Preobrazhenskaya, Ol'ga
Reid, Dorothy Davenport
Reiniger, Lotte
Shipman, Nell
Shub, Esfir (Esther)
Weber, Lois
Wilson, Margery

1930–40: Arzner, Dorothy
Bute, Mary Ellen
Field, Mary
Grierson, Marion
Jakubowska, Wanda
McDonagh, Paulette
Preobrazhenskaya, Ol'ga
Riefenstahl, Leni
Sagan, Leontine

1940–50: Abreu, Gilda de
Arzner, Dorothy
Audry, Jacqueline
Batchelor, Joy
Bute, Mary Ellen
Craigie, Jill
Deren, Maya
Henning-Jensen, Astrid
Landeta, Matilde
Menken, Marie
Solntseva, Iuliia
Svilova, Elizaveta

1950–60: Audry, Jacqueline

Box, Muriel
Clarke, Shirley
Craigie, Jill
Deren, Maya
Gogoberidze, Lana
Hubley, Faith
Lupino, Ida
Menken, Marie
Toye, Wendy
Varda, Agnes

1950–60:   Akerman, Chantal
Box, Muriel
Chytilová, Věra
Clarke, Shirley
de Hirsch, Storm
Export, Valie
Hammer, Barbara
Kaplan, Nelly
Menken, Marie
Mészáros, Márta
Nelson, Gunvor
Ono, Yoko
Rainer, Yvonne
Shepitko, Larissa
Toye, Wendy
Varda, Agnes
Wieland, Joyce
Zetterling, Mai

1970–80:   Akerman, Chantal
Asanova, Dinara
Barrie, Diana
Bemberg, Maria Luisa
Brückner, Jutta
Carolina, Ana
Child, Abigail
Chopra, Joyce
Citron, Michelle

Clarke, Shirley
Collins, Kathleen
de Hirsch, Storm
Deitch, Donna
Export, Valie
Faye, Safi
Fernandez Violante, Marcela
Hammer, Barbara
Hein, Birgit
Hidari, Sachiko
Huillet, Danièle
Kaplan, Nelly
Lanctôt, Micheline
Leaf, Caroline
Maldoror, Sarah
Mangolte, Babette
May, Elaine
Mészáros, Márta
Nelson, Gunvor
Sanders-Brahms, Helma
Schneemann, Carolee
Weill, Claudia
Wertmüller, Lina
Wieland, Joyce

1980–90:   Akerman, Chantal
Apon, Annette
Armstrong, Gillian
Attile, Martina
B., Beth
Bigelow, Kathryn
Blackwood, Maureen
Campion, Jane
Chenzira, Ayoka
Choy, Christine
Cole, Janis
Coolidge, Martha
Dale, Holly

Dash, Julie
Denis, Claire
Dörrie, Doris
Friedrich, Su
Godmilow, Jill
Gordon, Bette
Gorris, Marleen
Hunt, Claire
Karanth, Prema
Kopple, Barbara
Kurys, Diane
Larkin, Alile Sharon
Longinotto, Kim
McLaughlin, Sheila
Mita, Merata
Murphy, Pat
Nair, Mira
Novaro, Maria
Obomsawin, Alanis
Ottinger, Ulrike
Palcy, Euzhan
Pascal, Christine
Rainer, Yvonne
Sander, Helke
Sarmiento, Valeria
Seidelman, Susan
Sen, Aparna
Serreau, Coline
Silver, Joan Micklin
Treut, Monika
Trinh T. Minh-ha
Varda, Agnes
Von Trotta, Margarethe
Wheeler, Anne
Zhang Nuanxin

1990–95:   Anders, Alison
Armstrong, Gillian

Bigelow, Kathryn
Blackwood, Maureen
Campion, Jane
Cardona, Dominique
Chadha, Gurinder
Cochran, Stacey
Colbert, Laurie
Dash, Julie
Davis, Tamra
Davis, Zeinabu Irene
Ephron, Nora
Fisher, Holly
Foster, Jodie
Greenwald, Maggie
Hammer, Barbara
Harris, Leslie
Heckerling, Amy
Holland, Agnieszka
Hui, Ann
Kidron, Beeban
Livingston, Jennie
Maclean, Alison
Marshall, Penny
Martin, Darnell
Moorehouse, Jocelyn
Nair, Mira
Onwurah, Ngozi
Parmar, Pratibha
Potter, Sally
Savoca, Nancy
Spheeris, Penelope
Streisand, Barbra
Todd, Loretta
Treut, Monika

Selected Bibliography

Attwood, Lynn. *Red Women on the Silver Screen: Soviet Women and Cinema from the Beginning to the End of the Communist Era.* London: Pandora, 1993.

Blaché, Alice Guy. *The Memoirs of Alice Guy-Blaché.* Translated by Roberta and Simone Blaché; edited by Anthony Slide. Metuchen, NJ: Scarecrow Press, 1986.

Bruno, Giuliana. *Streetwalking on a Ruined Map: Cultural Theory and the City Films of Elvira Notari.* Princeton: Princeton University Press, 1993.

Carson, Diane, Linda Dittmar, and Janice R. Welsch, eds. *Multiple Voices in Feminist Film Criticism.* Minneapolis: University of Minnesota Press, 1994.

Cole, Janis, and Holly Dale. *Calling the Shots: Profiles of Women Filmmakers.* Ontario: Quarry Press, 1993.

Cook, Pam, and Philip Dodd, eds. *Women and Film: A Sight and Sound Reader.* Philadelphia: Temple University Press, 1993.

de Lauretis, Teresa. *Alice Doesn't: Feminism, Semiotics, Cinema.* Bloomington: Indiana University Press, 1984.

———. *The Practice of Love: Lesbian Sexuality and Perverse Desire.* Bloomington: Indiana University Press, 1994.

Diawara, Manthia. *African Cinema.* Bloomington: Indiana University Press, 1992.

Doane, Mary Ann. *The Desire to Desire.* Bloomington: Indiana University Press, 1987.

Flitterman-Lewis, Sandy. *To Desire Differently: Feminism and the French Cinema.* Urbana: University of Illinois Press, 1990.

Heck-Rabi, Louise. *Women Filmmakers: A Critical Reception.* Metuchen, NJ: Scarecrow Press, 1984.

hooks, bell. *Black Looks: Race and Representation.* Boston: South End Press, 1992.

Johnston, Claire. "Women's Cinema as Counter-Cinema." *Notes on Women's Cinema; Screen Pamphlet 2* (1974): 24–31.

Kaplan, E. Ann, ed. *Psychoanalysis and Cinema.* New York: Routledge, 1990.

Katz, Ephraim. *The Film Encyclopedia.* New York: HarperCollins, 1994.

Knight, Julia. *Women and the New German Cinema.* London: Verso, 1992.

Kowalski, Rosemary Ribich. *Women and Film: A Bibliography.* Metuchen, NJ: Scarecrow Press, 1976.

Kuhn, Annette. *Women's Pictures: Feminism and Cinema*. London: Routledge, 1982.

————, and Susannah Radstone, eds. *The Women's Companion to International Film*. Berkeley: University of California Press, 1994.

Mayne, Judith. *Loving with a Vengeance: Mass-Produced Fantasies for Women*. New York: Methuen, 1982.

————. *The Woman at the Keyhole: Feminism and Women's Cinema*. Bloomington: Indiana University Press, 1990.

Mulvey, Laura. "Afterthoughts on 'Visual Pleasure and the Narrative Cinema' Inspired by *Duel in the Sun*." *Framework* 15–17 (1981): 12–15.

PietroPaolor, Laura, and Ada Testaferri, eds. *Feminism in the Cinema*. Bloomington: Indiana University Press, 1995.

Pribram, E. Deidre, ed. *Female Spectators: Looking at Film and Television*. London: Verso, 1988.

Quart, Barbara Koenig. *Women Directors: The Emergence of a New Cinema*. New York: Praeger, 1988.

Rabinovitz, Lauren. *Points of Resistance: Women of Power and Politics in the New York Avant-Garde Cinema*. Chicago: University of Illinois Press, 1991.

Slide, Anthony. *Early Women Directors*. New York: Da Capo, 1984.

Todd, Janet, ed. *Women and Film*. New York: Holmes and Meier, 1988.

Trinh T. Minh-ha. *The Framer Framed*. New York: Routledge, 1992.

Weiss, Andrea. *Vampires and Violets: Lesbians in Film*. New York: Penguin, 1993.

Title Index

General Index

About the Author

GWENDOLYN AUDREY FOSTER teaches in the Film Studies Program, Department of English, at the University of Nebraska, Lincoln. She is the writer/director of *Women Who Made the Movies* (1992), a one-hour documentary on early women filmmakers. She has two forthcoming books, *Women Filmmakers of the Diaspora* and *The Films of Chantal Akerman*.

ISBN 0-313-28972-7

90000>

EAN

9 780313 289729

HARDCOVER BAR CODE

DATE DUE

			PRINTED IN U.S.A.